Praise for

THE FREAKS CAME OUT TO WRITE

"Some writers give voice to the voiceless. Romano gives voice to the *Voice*. For more than six decades, the *Village Voice* not only had its finger on the pulse of New York but quickened that pulse with its cultural criticism, investigative reporting, columns, cartoons, and more. I love this book!"

—Questlove

"A brilliant oral history that chronicles not only the *Village Voice*, the most important alt-weekly of our time, but also the history of New York City during the latter half of the twentieth century. One of the best narrative oral histories I have ever read—seamlessly edited, with anarchy on almost every page."   —Gillian McCain, coauthor of *Please Kill Me*

"An uncensored look at the freewheeling, kaleidoscopic lives of the people who wrote for the *Voice*. This book is essential reading for anyone who cares about politics, culture, history, or democracy. Romano makes me wish I was twenty again, reading the *Voice* while trying to score a futon."

—Gary Shteyngart, author of *Our Country Friends*

"*Freaks* reads like a garrulous night at the bar with the most brilliant, quarrelsome, passionate, and funny writers and editors of the Golden Age of insurgent media. The gossip! The fistfights! The passion! The fury! These collective voices and tales remind us not only of what writers once did, but what they can and should do RIGHT NOW. Hallelujah."

—Joe Hagan, author of *Sticky Fingers*

THE FREAKS CAME OUT TO WRITE

The Definitive History of
THE VILLAGE VOICE,
the Radical Paper That
Changed American Culture

Tricia
Romano

PUBLICAFFAIRS
New York

PublicAffairs
Hachette Book Group
1290 Avenue of the Americas, New York, NY 10104
www.publicaffairsbooks.com
@Public_Affairs

Printed in the United States of America

First Edition: February 2024

Published by PublicAffairs, an imprint of Hachette Book Group, Inc. The PublicAffairs
name and logo is a registered trademark of the Hachette Book Group.

The Hachette Speakers Bureau provides a wide range of authors for speaking
events. To find out more, go to hachettespeakersbureau.com or email
HachetteSpeakers@hbgusa.com.

PublicAffairs books may be purchased in bulk for business, educational, or promotional
use. For more information, please contact your local bookseller or the Hachette Book
Group Special Markets Department at special.markets@hbgusa.com.

The publisher is not responsible for websites (or their content) that are not owned by the
publisher.

Print book interior design by Amy Quinn.

Library of Congress Cataloging-in-Publication Data

Names: Romano, Tricia, author.
Title: The freaks came out to write : the definitive history of the Village Voice,
    the radical paper that changed American culture / Tricia Romano.
Description: First edition. | New York : PublicAffairs, 2024. | Includes
    bibliographical references and index.
Identifiers: LCCN 2023024929 | ISBN 9781541736399 (hardcover) |
    ISBN 9781541736405 (ebook)
Subjects: LCSH: Village voice (Greenwich Village, New York, N.Y.)—History. |
    Newspapers—New York (State)—New York—History—20th century. |
    Newspapers—New York (State)—New York—History—21st century. |
    New York (N.Y.)—Social life and customs—20th century. | New York (N.Y.)—
    Social life and customs—21st century.
Classification: LCC PN4899.N42 V535 2024 | DDC 071/.471—dc23/eng/20230818
LC record available at https://lccn.loc.gov/2023024929

ISBNs: 9781541736399 (hardcover), 9781541736405 (ebook)

LSC-C

Printing 1, 2023

For Skyler

TRICIA ROMANO: What's the greatest era of the *Village Voice*?
JAMES HANNAHAM: Whichever one you were there for.

CONTENTS

1980–1990: "This is the dark secret that they never talk about"

1990–2000: "There was some sort of cultural shift that we didn't understand"

2000–2023: "Wish You Were Here"

AUTHOR'S NOTE

Over the course of four years, I conducted more than two hundred interviews for this book. Most of what is included here is original testimony. Several people died during those years whom I was lucky to speak to before they passed—including Ed Fancher, who died just before this book went to press, Jonas Mekas, Tim McDarrah, Gloria McDarrah, Michael Feingold, and the great, dearly departed cultural critic Greg Tate. I am grateful for their contributions and offer my condolences to their families.

A few people, such as Stanley Crouch and Pete Hamill, died before I was able to speak to them. In instances where people were not alive or capable of speaking for themselves, I turned to surrogates (friends, family, and coworkers), their own writings (such as those of Nat Hentoff, Jerry Tallmer, John Wilcock, Norman Mailer, and Jack Newfield), and archival interviews from news stories or old television interviews (such as those with Ellen Willis, Karen Durbin, and Wayne Barrett). I was lucky to find that Dan Wolf and Mary Perot Nichols had given oral history interviews archived at Columbia University, and Stanley Crouch had sat down for many hours with the HistoryMakers. I have made judicious use of secondary materials as noted in the bibliography.

Quotes have been edited for clarity and length. In some cases, different interviews from the same subject may be combined. I have fact-checked names, dates, and places where possible and have tried to confirm how events took place from multiple sources. But in an oral history, a person's story *is* the story.

There are some racial and sexual slurs that appear as they were spoken or written, which is an accurate reflection of the times. Much has changed in language since then and there are words that are used that are no longer acceptable, but I believe it's important to remain true to how people spoke, given that this is an oral history.

While I strived to recognize the well-known stalwarts of the paper (Nat Hentoff, Jack Newfield, Wayne Barrett), I've tried to turn a brighter light onto some of the writers and subjects that don't reflexively get mentioned whenever the *Voice* makes the news: women writers and editors like Vivian Gornick, Mary Perot Nichols, Jill Johnston, Karen Durbin, and Susan Brownmiller, as well as the dozens of groundbreaking Black writers who came through in the '80s, like Greg Tate, Barry Michael Cooper, Carol Cooper, Stanley Crouch, Lisa Jones, Lisa Kennedy, and Nelson George. My own biases as a former music writer tend to tip the content toward the back of the book's cultural coverage, particularly of music and nightlife. I recognize that some people will wish there would be more about theater or film, or more about news investigations, or more stories from recent years. Two other books about the *Voice* covered the Dan Wolf era in more depth, and more than forty years have passed since those volumes came out, leaving me with more ground to cover, so I had to make choices.

While good work has certainly been published at the *Voice* and impressive journalists employed there during the New Times, Barbey, and Calle years, I wanted to tell the story of how media overall has been hampered on several fronts: by the rise of the internet, by the loss of advertising revenue to sites like Craigslist, and by greedy, imperious, and/or incompetent and negligent management. These factors have shrunk the media landscape, whittling it down to the largest, most powerful publications, leaving a void, most largely felt in local and independent news.

This book has been a labor of love and a years-long, life-altering endeavor. I am truly grateful for everyone who participated.

CAST OF CHARACTERS

VINCE ALETTI, freelance, 1975; contributor (music/art), 1985–1987; associate editor, 1988; senior editor (visual art/photography), 1989–2005. Current contributor to the *New Yorker*.

MICHAEL ALIG (1966–2020) was a New York party promoter who was convicted of felony manslaughter in the 1996 death of Angel Melendez.

HARRY ALLEN, contributing writer (music), 1987–2008.

HILTON ALS, designer, 1988–1989; picture editor, 1990; staff writer, 1991–1994, is a staff critic at the *New Yorker*.

BILLY ALTMAN, contributor (music, sports), 1976–1987; contributor (sports), 1998–2004, is an official scorer for Major League Baseball.

FLORIAN BACHLEDA, designer, 1989–1990; associate art director, 1990–1991; senior art director, 1991–1994.

R.C. BAKER, proofreader, 1987–1994; ad traffic supervisor, 1994; current editor in chief.

SALLY BANES (1950–2020), contributing writer, 1976–1986, was a dance historian and author of six books.

LESTER BANGS (1948–1982), contributing writer (music), 1976–1982, wrote for *Creem* and *Rolling Stone* and was the author of two posthumous collections.

AMIRI BARAKA (1934–2014), contributor, 1960s–late 1980s, was a playwright, poet, novelist, journalist, and critic, as well as the architect of the Black Arts Movement. He is the father of *Voice* columnist Lisa Jones.

BRUCE BARCOTT, intern, 1986, is the author of several books, including *Weed the People*.

ALLEN BARRA, contributor (sports), 1984–1988, 2007–2017.

MAC BARRETT is the son of investigative reporter Wayne Barrett and a former speechwriter for New York State governor Andrew Cuomo.

WAYNE BARRETT (1945–2017), contributing writer, 1971–1979; staff writer (news), 1979–2011, was the author of four books, including biographies of Donald Trump and Rudy Giuliani.

WILLIAM BASTONE, news intern, 1984; contributor (news), 1984–1988; staff writer, 1988–2000, is cofounder and editor of the Smoking Gun.

ARTHUR BELL (1939–1984), contributor, columnist, 1969–1984.

PAUL BERMAN, contributor (*Voice Literary Supplement*, politics, arts), 1978–1992.

LISA BIRNBACH, editorial assistant (Scenes), 1979–1980, is the author of the 1980 best-selling humor guide *The Official Preppy Handbook*.

DAN BISCHOFF, freelance editor, 1985–1988; senior editor, 1989; national affairs editor, 1990–1993.

MIKE BLOOMBERG was the mayor of New York City from 2002 to 2013 and is the publisher of *Bloomberg Businessweek*.

DAVID BLUM, editor in chief, 2006–2007, is an adjunct professor at the Columbia University Graduate School of Journalism.

HOWARD BLUM, staff writer (news), 1971–1975, is currently a contributor to *Air Mail*.

MARY BREASTED, freelance writer (news features), 1969–1973; interim news editor, 1971, 1972, is a former *New York Times* reporter, and the author of two books.

SUSAN BROWNMILLER, staff writer (news), 1965–1975, authored the breakthrough feminist work *Against Our Will: Men, Women, and Rape* (1975).

CARTER BURDEN (1941–1996), along with publisher Bartle Bull, was the second owner of the *Village Voice*, buying it in 1969. He merged ownership with Clay Felker and *New York* magazine in 1975, and ultimately sold his shares to Rupert Murdoch in 1977. He was elected to NYC's city council in 1969 and served three terms.

CLEM BURKE is the longtime drummer of influential new-wave band Blondie.

NANCY CARDOZO, copy editor, senior editor, 1984–1987, is an editor and the wife of Mark Jacobson.

TERESA CARPENTER, staff writer (1981–1991), won the Pulitzer Prize for Feature Writing in 1981 for her article "Death of a Playmate."

C.CARR, assistant art director, 1982–1983; contributor (On Edge, chronicling NYC's downtown art scene), 1984–1987; staff writer (performance art), 1987–2003, is a 2007 Guggenheim Fellow and the author of three books.

MICHAEL CARUSO, senior editor (sports), 1986–1988; features editor, 1988–1989; executive editor, 1990, is the CEO and publisher of the *New Republic*.

ROBERT CHRISTGAU, rock critic/columnist, 1969–1972; music editor, 1974–1976; senior editor (music), 1976–2006; contributor, 2016–2017.

ALEXANDER COCKBURN (1941–2012), staff writer, 1974–1984, was a columnist at *The Nation* for twenty-eight years and former coeditor of the website CounterPunch.

JOE CONASON, staff writer (news, national correspondent), 1978–1990.

BARRY MICHAEL COOPER, freelance writer, 1980–1981, 1987–1988; staff writer, 1989–1990, wrote the screenplay for *New Jack City* based on his *Voice* cover story "Kids Killing Kids: New Jack City Eats Its Young."

CAROL COOPER, freelance writer, 1978–1985 (books, music); proofreader, 1979–1985; contributor (books, music), 1987–1990; freelance writer (books, music), 1994–1996, 2000–2019, is an adjunct instructor at New York University.

BOB COSTAS, NBC sportscaster, 1980–2019.

STANLEY CROUCH (1945–2020), contributing writer, 1979; staff writer (music and cultural critic), 1980–1988, was a recipient of the MacArthur Fellowship grant.

ANDREW CUOMO, the eldest son of three-term New York State governor Mario Cuomo, was the fifty-sixth governor of New York State from 2011 to 2021.

CHUCK D is the cofounder, producer, and rapper of Public Enemy, the influential Grammy-winning hip-hop group.

MICHAEL DALY, staff writer (news features), 1977–1978, is a special correspondent at the *Daily Beast*.

MANOHLA DARGIS, contributor (film), 1988–1994, is a five-time Pulitzer Prize finalist and the chief film critic at the *New York Times*.

ANIL DASH, web developer, Village Voice Media, 2001–2003, was an advisor to the Obama White House's Office of Digital Strategy.

GARY DAUPHIN, intern (minority writing fellow), 1990; contributor (film), 1995–2002, is the director of digital interpretation at the Lucas Museum of Narrative Art.

THULANI DAVIS, proofreader, writer, and senior editor, 1979–1990; senior editor, 2002–2004, is an author, poet, librettist, playwright, journalist, and critic.

JACK DEACY, contributing writer (news), 1969–1975.

JESUS DIAZ, administration staff, 1976–1987; designer, 1993–1994; associate art director, 1995–2017.

CAROLA DIBBELL, freelance writer (music, books), 1975–1984, 1996–2003. Her husband is Robert Christgau.

KAREN DURBIN, assistant editor, 1974–1975; senior editor, 1975–1978; staff writer, 1978–1979; senior editor (arts), 1979–1989; editor in chief, 1994–1996.

CHUCK EDDY, freelance writer and contributor (music), 1984–1998; senior editor (music), 1999–2006.

JANIE EISENBERG, widow of Jack Newfield (married 1971–2004); former aide to Mayor John Lindsay (1970).

ED FANCHER (1923–2023), cofounder and publisher, 1955–1974.

JULES FEIFFER, staff cartoonist, 1956–1997, won the Pulitzer Prize for Editorial Cartooning in 1996. He is also a playwright and screenwriter.

LESLIE FEINBERG, transgender activist and author of *Stone Butch Blues.*

MICHAEL FEINGOLD (1945–2022), freelance writer (theater), 1971–1974; chief theater critic, 1974–2013, was a Tony Award–nominated lyricist and playwright, and a Pulitzer Prize finalist in Criticism.

CLAY FELKER (1925–2008), editor in chief and chairman, Village Voice, Inc., 1974–1977; publisher, 1975–1977, cofounded *New York* magazine in 1968.

SARAH FERGUSON, freelance writer (news), 1988–2008, 2016.

KAREN FINLEY is a performance and conceptual artist and a poet; she was plaintiff in the landmark 1998 Supreme Court case *National Endowment for the Arts v. Finley.*

DIANE FISHER, receptionist, 1962–1963; editorial assistant, 1963–1965; associate editor (arts), 1965–1974.

LAURA FLANDERS is the host and executive producer of the *Laura Flanders Show* on PBS. Her uncle was *Village Voice* columnist Alexander Cockburn.

DON FORST (1932–2014), editor in chief, 1996–2005. He was the editor in chief of the *Boston Herald* and *New York Newsday*.

JIM FOURATT, gay rights activist; cofounder of Yippies and the Gay Liberation Front; contributor, 1972–1986.

BETTY FRIEDAN (1921–2006) was a second-wave feminist and author of the groundbreaking book *The Feminine Mystique*.

ROBERT I. FRIEDMAN, editor in chief, 1985–1986.

DONNA GAINES, freelance writer (features), 1988–1998.

HUGH GARVEY, editorial assistant, associate editor, *Voice Literary Supplement*, 1993–1997.

NELSON GEORGE, contributor (music), 1981–1994; columnist, Native Son, 1988–1992, is a TV and film writer, producer, and director.

GARY GIDDINS, contributor and staff writer (jazz), 1973–2003; winner of six ASCAP Foundation Deems Taylor Awards for Excellence in Music Criticism.

RICHARD GOLDSTEIN, rock critic/columnist, 1966–1969; senior editor (arts), 1974–1988; associate editor, 1988; arts editor, 1988–1991; executive editor, 1991–2004, is currently an adjunct professor at Hunter College.

VIVIAN GORNICK, staff writer (news features), 1969–1971; freelance writer (books), 1975; staff writer, 1976–1978.

MARTIN GOTTLIEB, editor, 1986–1987; editor in chief, 1988, was the editor of *The Record* in Bergen County, New Jersey.

AKASH GOYAL, editorial assistant, *Long Island Voice*, 1999–2000; new media associate editor, 2000–2001; webmaster, 2001–2004; web manager, 2004–2006, is currently a vice president at Comedy Central/MTV Networks.

MICHAEL GROSSMAN, design director, 1985–1989.

DENIS HAMILL, freelance contributor, 1975–1976; staff writer, 1977, is a former *New York Daily News* reporter.

PETE HAMILL (1935–2020), contributor, 1968–1996. He was the editor in chief of the *New York Post* and the *New York Daily News*.

JAMES HAMILTON, staff photographer, 1973–1993.

JAMES HANNAHAM, assistant art director, contributing writer (theater, film, music, books), 1992–2003.

DEBBIE HARRY is the cofounder and singer of Blondie.

ROB HARVILLA, music editor, 2006–2011, is a senior staff writer at *The Ringer.*

MOLLY HASKELL, contributor (theater), 1969; contributor (film), 1969–1976; staff writer (film), 1976–1977.

JESSICA HENTOFF is the daughter of Nat Hentoff.

NAT HENTOFF (1925–2017), columnist/contributor/staff writer (civil liberties, politics), 1958–2009, was an author, journalist, jazz critic, and civil libertarian.

NICK HENTOFF is a criminal defense and civil liberties trial attorney and the son of Nat Hentoff.

DAVE HERNDON, associate editor and senior editor (sports), 1983–1986; managing editor, 1986–1988.

J. HOBERMAN, contributing writer, 1977–1983; staff writer (film), 1983–2012.

ANDREW HSIAO, contributing writer and senior editor, 1990–2002.

ADAMMA INCE, editorial assistant (listings), 1997–1998; assistant editor (research), 1998–1999; associate editor (research), 1999–2000; chief of research, 2000–2003; deputy managing editor, 2003–2007, is the former editor in chief of *Philadelphia Weekly.*

GARY INDIANA, art critic, contributing writer (art), 1985–1988.

JANE JACOBS (1916–2006) was a journalist, urban studies activist, and author of *The Death and Life of Great American Cities.*

MARK JACOBSON, staff writer, 1977–1982. His 1975 *New York* magazine feature "Night-Shifting for the Hip Fleet" inspired the prime-time TV series *Taxi* (1978–1983).

BILL JENSEN, assistant listings editor, 1998–2000, *Long Island Voice*; director of new media, Village Voice Media, 2006–2011, is an investigative journalist and true-crime podcast producer.

JOSEPH JESSELLI, classifieds department, 1978–1988; IT support, 1989–2001, is a cofounding editor of the Smoking Gun.

JILL JOHNSTON (1929–2010), writer, 1959–1981, was the author of *Lesbian Nation: The Feminist Solution*, which spearheaded the lesbian separatist movement of the early 1970s.

LISA JONES, copy editor, 1985–1986; associate editor, senior editor, staff writer, 1990–1998, is the daughter of poets Hettie Jones and Amiri Baraka, and penned the column Skin Trade.

DEBORAH JOWITT, contributor and staff writer (dance), 1967–2011.

LENNY KAYE is a writer, author, and lead guitarist for the Patti Smith Group.

TED KELLER, deputy design director, 1994–1996; design director, 1996–2007, is the design director at *Variety*.

SALLY KEMPTON (1943–2023), freelance and staff writer (news and features), 1964–1969; former editor of the spiritual magazine *Darshan*.

LISA KENNEDY, copy editor, 1986; deputy copy chief, 1986–1988; supplement and TV editor, 1987–1990; senior editor (film), 1990–1992; arts editor, 1992–1993; features editor, 1992–1994, is a freelance writer.

JEFF Z. KLEIN, senior editor (sports), 1990–1995, is a former hockey reporter for the *New York Times*.

ED KOCH (1924–2013) was briefly the lawyer for the *Village Voice* and served as the 105th mayor of New York City.

VICTOR KOVNER, chief counsel for the *Village Voice*, 1966–1999, is a partner at Koch, Lankenau, Schwartz, and Kovner.

LARRY KRAMER (1935–2020) was a playwright and activist and a cofounder of ACT UP New York.

MICHAEL LACEY, cofounder, *Phoenix New Times*, 1970–1974; editor, *Phoenix New Times*, 1977–1983; executive editor, New Times, Inc., 1983–2005; executive editor, Village Voice Media, 2005–2012; cofounder, Backpage, 2004–2017.

RUDY LANGLAIS, senior editor, 1978–1981.

JAMES LARKIN (1949–2023), cofounder, *Phoenix New Times*, 1970; publisher, New Times, Inc., 1970–2005; publisher, Village Voice Media, 2005–2012; cofounder, Backpage, 2004–2015.

JONATHAN Z. LARSEN, editor in chief, 1989–1994; son of Roy Larsen, former chairman of Time Inc.

MARIA LAURINO, staff writer (news), 1985–1989.

LIZ LECOMPTE, cofounder and director of the experimental theater group Wooster Group.

SPIKE LEE is the director of *She's Gotta Have It* (1986) and *Do the Right Thing* (1989), and won the Academy Award for Best Adapted Screenplay for *BlacKkKlansman* (2018).

WILL LEITCH is the founding editor of the Gawker Media sports blog *Deadspin*, and a national correspondent for MLB.com.

JOHN LELAND, freelance music writer, 1987–1988, is a Metro reporter for the *New York Times*.

JOE LEVY, senior editor (music), 1990–1994; interim editor in chief, 2016; editor, 2017, is an editor at large at *Billboard*.

PAUL LUKAS, columnist (sports), 1999–2003.

SUSAN LYNE, managing editor, 1978–1981.

STAN MACK, documentary cartoonist (Stan Mack's Real Life Funnies), 1974–1995.

NORMAN MAILER (1923–2007), cofounder and investor; columnist from January 11, 1956, to May 2, 1956 (seventeen issues).

JOHN MANCINI, editor in chief, *Long Island Voice*, 1996–1999, is director of the Writing and Reporting Program for the Craig Newmark Graduate School of Journalism at City University of New York (CUNY).

GREIL MARCUS, contributor, 1974–1986; columnist (Real Life Rock), 1986–1990.

M MARK, founding editor of the *Voice Literary Supplement*, senior editor (arts), 1977–1993.

FRED W. MCDARRAH (1926–2007), the *Voice*'s flagship photojournalist; staff photographer, 1962–1971; picture editor, 1971–1989; consulting picture editor, 1994–2007.

GLORIA MCDARRAH (1932–2020) was the wife of Fred McDarrah.

TIM MCDARRAH (1962–2021) was a gossip columnist, gallery owner, and the son of Fred McDarrah, with whom he coauthored three books.

CATHERINE MCGANN, intern (photography), 1986; contributor (photography), 1987–2001, was chief photographer for Michael Musto's weekly nightlife column, La Dolce Musto, for sixteen years.

DON MCNEILL (1945–1968), staff writer (counterculture), 1966–1968.

JONAS MEKAS (1922–2019), columnist (Movie Journal), 1958–1975, was the *Village Voice*'s first film critic and the cofounder of *Film Culture*, the nonprofit distribution network Film-Makers' Cooperative in 1961, and the Anthology Film Archives in 1969.

DONNA MINKOWITZ, freelance writer, 1987–1988; contributor, 1989; columnist (Body Politic), 1990–1995, whose 1994 *Village Voice* feature on Brandon Teena, "Love Hurts," inspired the Oscar-winning 1999 film *Boys Don't Cry*.

JUDY MISZNER, vice president of sales and marketing, 1998–2000; publisher, 2000–2006.

CARMAN MOORE, freelance music critic, 1966–1975, is a Juilliard School–trained composer.

MICHAEL MOORE is the director of *Roger & Me* (1989) and twelve other films.

ERIKA MUNK, freelance writer, 1976–1977 (arts); senior editor (arts, theater), 1978–1990; freelance writer, 1990s, is a former professor at Yale University's School of Drama and an author.

RUPERT MURDOCH, owner, 1977–1985.

MICHAEL MUSTO, freelance writer, 1981–1984; contributor (nightlife and La Dolce Musto columnist), 1984–2008; staff writer, 2008–2013 (La Dolce Musto); contributor, 2015–2018, 2020–present.

JACK NEWFIELD (1938–2004), assistant editor, 1964–1974; senior editor (investigative news), 1974–1988, won the American Book Award for *The Full Rudy: The Man, the Myth, the Mania* (2002).

ROBERT NEWMAN, associate art director, 1986–1988; art director, 1990; design director, 1991–1994.

CRAIG NEWMARK is the founder of Craigslist.

ELIZA NICHOLS is the daughter of Mary Perot Nichols.

MARY PEROT NICHOLS (1926–1996), news editor, 1958–1962; assistant editor (news), 1962–1965; senior editor (news), 1969–1976, was Robert Moses's antagonist.

PETER NOEL, staff writer, 1989–1995.

TIMOTHY L. O'BRIEN was a research assistant for Wayne Barrett's 1992 book *Trump: The Greatest Show on Earth: The Deals, the Downfall, the Reinvention*. He is currently a Bloomberg Opinion executive editor.

FRANK OWEN, contributor (music, investigative nightlife), 1995–2003.

BRIAN PARKS, assistant editor, 1990; copy editor, deputy copy chief, copy chief, senior editor, 1990–1997; senior editor, 1998–2003; arts editor, 2007–2013, is a writer, editor, and playwright.

MARIANNE PARTRIDGE, managing editor, 1976; editor in chief, 1976–1979, is the cofounder and editor in chief of the *Santa Barbara Independent*.

KIMBERLY PEIRCE is the director of the Oscar-winning film *Boys Don't Cry* (1999), based on Donna Minkowitz's *Voice* feature story.

TOM PEYER, columnist (sports), 1990–1991, is coeditor of *O Holy Cow! The Selected Verse of Phil Rizzuto*, based on *Voice* columns with Hart Seely.

SYLVIA PLACHY, picture researcher, 1974–1976; staff photographer, 1976–2004, is a contributing photographer at the *New Yorker*.

BERT POGREBIN, lawyer for *Voice* management in union negotiations.

ANN POWERS, senior editor (feminism), 1993–1994; senior editor (music), 1994–1996, is an NPR staff music critic.

JOY PRESS, senior editor (film), 1996; literary editor, 1997–2001; contributor (senior TV and book critic), 2001–2006; arts and culture editor, 2006–2007, is a correspondent for *Vanity Fair*.

KIT RACHLIS, executive editor, 1984–1988, has been editor in chief of the *LA Weekly*, *Los Angeles* magazine, and the *American Prospect*. He is currently a senior editor at ProPublica.

VERNON REID, freelance music writer, 1986–1988, is a songwriter, composer, and founder/lead guitarist of the Grammy-winning rock band Living Colour. In 1985, Reid cofounded the Black Rock Coalition with writer Greg Tate and producer Konda Mason.

ROBIN REISIG, freelance news writer, 1970–1975, is a professor emeritus at Columbia University's Graduate School of Journalism.

SIMON REYNOLDS, contributing writer (music), 1989–2018, has written eight books on music and culture. He is the husband of Joy Press.

JAMES RIDGEWAY (1936–2021), staff writer (investigative news, Washington correspondent), 1976–2006.

SONIA JAFFE ROBBINS, assistant editor, 1976–1978; copy chief/deputy managing editor, 1979–1986, is a contributing editor at *Publishers Weekly*.

TOM ROBBINS, contributor (investigative news), 1985–1988; staff writer (news), 2000–2011, is an investigative journalist in residence at the Craig Newmark Graduate School of Journalism at CUNY.

GORDON ROGOFF, contributing writer (theater criticism), 1961–1971.

MAIDA ROSENSTEIN is the president of United Auto Workers, Local 2110, the *Voice*'s union.

JACKIE RUDIN, local account manager, 1972–1976; associate advertising manager, 1976–1978; advertising manager, 1979–1987.

FRANK (FRANKIE "BONES") RUSCITTI, assistant to the director of classifieds, 1981–1984; editorial administration staff, 1984–1999.

JEFF SALAMON, senior editor, 1986–1996.

JERRY SALTZ, contributor (senior art critic), 1998–2007, is a senior art critic for *New York* magazine and author of the *New York Times* best-selling *How to Be an Artist*. He won the Pulitzer Prize for Criticism in 2018.

ANDREW SARRIS (1928–2012), freelance film critic, 1960–1974; film editor, 1974–1976; senior editor (film), 1976–1989, was a two-time finalist for the Pulitzer Prize for Criticism (1987, 2000).

LESLIE SAVAN, proofreader, 1983–1984; associate editor, 1984–1987; contributor, 1988–1990; staff writer, 1991–2000, was a three-time Pulitzer Prize finalist for Criticism for her *Village Voice* advertising column, Op Ad.

PETER SCHJELDAHL (1942–2022), contributor (art), 1990–1998, was the *New Yorker*'s art critic. He was a finalist for the Pulitzer Prize for Criticism in 2022.

DAVID SCHNEIDERMAN, editor in chief, 1978–1985; publisher/editor in chief, 1985–1987; president, VV Publishing Corporation/Stern Publishing, 1988–2000; publisher, 1994–2000; CEO, Village Voice Media, 2000–2005; president of digital operations, Village Voice Media, 2005–2006.

MARK SCHOOFS, contributor, 1993–1996; staff writer, 1997–2000, won the Pulitzer Prize for International Reporting in 2000 for the *Voice*.

CHARLES SCHUMER is a US senator for New York and the Senate majority leader.

MARTIN SCORSESE is an Italian American film director who has won twenty Academy Awards for films such as *Taxi Driver*, *Goodfellas*, and *Raging Bull*.

HART SEELY, columnist (sports), 1990–1991, is the coeditor of *O Holy Cow: The Selected Verses of Phil Rizzuto*, based on his *Voice* column with Tom Peyer.

TONICE SGRIGNOLI, associate editor (books, *Voice Literary Supplement*), 1983–1986.

AUDREY SHACHNOW, design director, 1994–1996, is a sculptor and artist.

ROBERT SIETSEMA, contributor (restaurant critic), 1993–2013, is an author, a four-time James Beard Foundation Award nominee, and a senior critic at Eater New York.

SAM SIFTON, editorial staff, *New York Press*, 1992–1998, is an assistant managing editor of the *New York Times* and the founding editor of *New York Times* Cooking.

DOUG SIMMONS, senior editor (music), 1985–1989; senior editor (features), 1990–1994; managing editor, 1994–2006; acting editor in chief, 2006.

JONATHAN SLAFF, an actor and theatrical press agent, is the literary executor of Jerry Tallmer.

HOWARD SMITH (1936–2014), contributor, 1957–1959; assistant publisher and columnist, 1967–1974; staff writer (Scenes), 1974–1980, codirected and coproduced the Oscar-winning 1972 documentary *Marjoe*.

KEVIN SMITH is the director of *Clerks* (1994).

LEE SMITH, editor (*Voice Literary Supplement*), 1995–1996.

MICHAEL SMITH, contributor, 1958–1962; associate editor (arts), 1962–1965; Obie Awards producer, 1962–1968; contributor (theater), 1965–1968, 1971–1974, is a playwright and theater director.

RJ SMITH, staff writer (music), 1981–1990.

ROBERTA SMITH, contributor (visual art), 1981–1985, is the co-chief art critic of the *New York Times*.

ALISA SOLOMON, contributor (theater), 1983–1989; staff writer, 1990–2004, teaches at Columbia University's Graduate School of Journalism.

ELIZABETH SPIERS, founding editor of *Gawker* (2002–2003), is a former editor in chief of the *New York Observer* (2011–2012).

ALLEN ST. JOHN, contributor (sports), 1991–2004, is a *New York Times* best-selling author and a senior editor at *Consumer Reports.*

MARK ALAN STAMATY, cartoonist, 1976–1994.

CHRIS STEIN is the guitarist of Blondie.

LEONARD STERN, chairman and president, VV Publishing Corporation, 1985–1987; chairman, VV Publishing Corporation, 1988–2000.

LAURIE STONE, contributor (books, theater, arts), 1975–1999.

ROGER STONE is a conservative political consultant.

JOHN STRAUSBAUGH was an editor at the *New York Press* from 1988 to 2002.

JERRY TALLMER (1920–2014), associate editor (arts), 1955–1962; contributor, 1964, was the *Voice*'s founding theater critic and creator of the Obie Awards, the paper's annual Off-Broadway awards. In 1962, Tallmer won the George Jean Nathan Award for Dramatic Criticism and became an arts critic at the *New York Post*, where he remained until 1993.

GREG TATE (1957–2021), contributing writer (music), 1981–1987; staff writer (culture), 1987–2002, was the cofounder of the Black Rock Coalition and the guitarist and conductor of the ensemble Burnt Sugar.

AMY TAUBIN, contributor (film), 1987–2002, is a contributing editor at *Artforum.*

ELIZABETH THOMPSON, editorial intern, 2006–2007; senior associate editor (music), 2007–2008, cohosts the podcast *Tell Me About Your Father.*

MICHAEL TOMASKY, staff writer, 1990–1995, is editor of the *New Republic* and *Democracy: A Journal of Ideas.*

GUY TREBAY, senior editor and columnist (culture), 1979–1999.

DONALD TRUMP is a New York City real estate developer, former reality TV star, and the twice-impeached forty-fifth president of the United States, indicted in at least four separate cases.

LUCIAN K. TRUSCOTT IV, freelance writer, 1967–1969; staff writer, 1970–1975, is a journalist, screenwriter, and author of five *New York Times* bestsellers. Truscott is a columnist at Substack and *Salon.*

KATE VALK is an actress and founding member of the Wooster Group.

ANDY WARHOL (1928–1987) was an American pop artist.

MAX WEINBERG is the longtime drummer for Bruce Springsteen's E Street Band.

JEFF WEINSTEIN, senior editor (art, architecture), 1981–1995, was also the *Voice*'s restaurant critic for fifteen years. As a *Voice* editorial union steward, Weinstein proposed and helped to win the nation's first large-scale health coverage for same-sex couples in July 1982.

ERIC WEISBARD, freelance writer (music), 1993–1997; senior editor (music), 1997–1998; contributor (music), 1999–2002.

ALAN WEITZ, courier/mailroom clerk, 1965–1968; editorial assistant, 1969–1972; assistant editor (news), 1973–1974; associate editor, 1974–1975; managing editor, 1977–1979.

ERIK WEMPLE, appointed editor in chief (but didn't serve), May 30–June 15, 2006, is the *Washington Post*'s media critic.

ROSS WETZSTEON (1932–1998), proofreader, copy editor, 1964–1966; associate editor, 1967–1973; executive editor, 1973–1975; senior editor (theater), 1976–1998.

CLARK WHELTON, freelance writer, 1968–1971; staff writer, 1971–1975 and 1977–1978, is a former speechwriter for New York City mayors Ed Koch and Rudy Giuliani.

COLSON WHITEHEAD, assistant editor, *Voice Literary Supplement*, contributing writer (TV, books), 1991–1997, is one of four novelists to win the Pulitzer Prize twice.

RIKI WILCHINS is a transgender author and activist.

JOHN WILCOCK (1927–2018), founding news editor, 1955–1956; associate editor (news), 1956–1957; columnist (The Village Square), 1956–1966, went on to edit *Voice* rival paper *East Village Other*, cofound the Underground Press Syndicate, and start his own radical newspaper, *Other Scenes*. In 1969, he launched *Interview* magazine with Andy Warhol.

ELLEN WILLIS (1941–2006), senior editor, 1979–1990; contributor, 1994–1995, was the first rock critic for the *New Yorker* and the author of four books.

NONA WILLIS-ARONOWITZ, the daughter of Ellen Willis, is a writer, editor, and author.

LANFORD WILSON (1937–2011) was a Pulitzer Prize–winning playwright.

JAMES WOLCOTT, circulation department, assistant, and writer, 1972–1973; staff writer, 1975–1982, is a cultural critic whose work has appeared in the *New Yorker* and *Vanity Fair*. He is a columnist at *Air Mail*.

DAN WOLF (1915–1996), cofounder of the *Village Voice* and its first editor in chief, 1955–1974.

LYNN YAEGER, classifieds department, 1978–1990; senior editor (fashion), 1999–2008, is a contributing editor at *Vogue*.

TIMELINE

OCTOBER 26, 1955
Started by Dan Wolf, Ed Fancher, and Norman Mailer, with two key editors and writers, Jerry Tallmer and John Wilcock. Wolf is the editor in chief. Fancher is the publisher. Mailer, in addition to being an investor, briefly writes a column.

1956
Jerry Tallmer launches the Obie Awards, celebrating Off-Broadway theater.
Jules Feiffer, the famed cartoonist, joins the paper.

1963
The *Voice*'s circulation rises to twenty-five thousand during the three-month-long Typographical Union strike.

1968
The *Voice*'s countercultural writer, Don McNeill, dies.

1969
The *Voice* captures the beginning of the gay rights movement at the Stonewall riots.

1970
Dan Wolf and Ed Fancher sell controlling interest to Taurus Communications' Carter Burden, a city councilman, and Bartle Bull, who is vice president. Wolf and Fancher remain in their roles as editor in chief and publisher, respectively.
Ross Wetzsteon begins to take over many of the editor's duties, with Wolf as an overseer.

1974
Carter Burden and Bartle Bull sell their shares to Clay Felker, the founder and editor of *New York* magazine, for $3.5 million. The *Voice* merges with

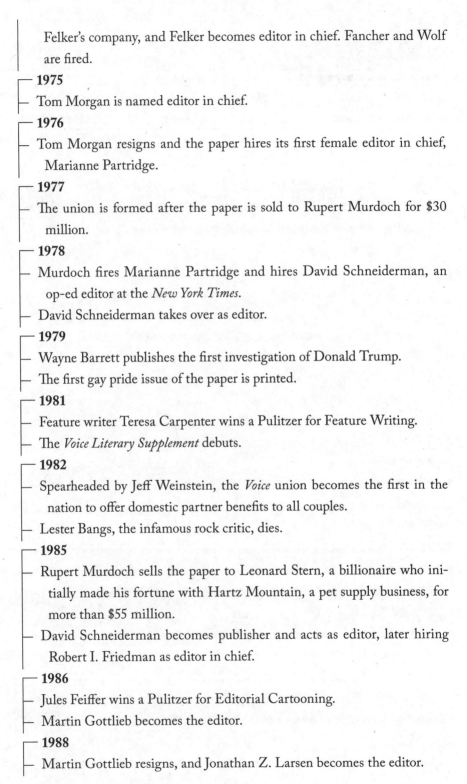

Felker's company, and Felker becomes editor in chief. Fancher and Wolf are fired.

1975

Tom Morgan is named editor in chief.

1976

Tom Morgan resigns and the paper hires its first female editor in chief, Marianne Partridge.

1977

The union is formed after the paper is sold to Rupert Murdoch for $30 million.

1978

Murdoch fires Marianne Partridge and hires David Schneiderman, an op-ed editor at the *New York Times*.

David Schneiderman takes over as editor.

1979

Wayne Barrett publishes the first investigation of Donald Trump.

The first gay pride issue of the paper is printed.

1981

Feature writer Teresa Carpenter wins a Pulitzer for Feature Writing.

The *Voice Literary Supplement* debuts.

1982

Spearheaded by Jeff Weinstein, the *Voice* union becomes the first in the nation to offer domestic partner benefits to all couples.

Lester Bangs, the infamous rock critic, dies.

1985

Rupert Murdoch sells the paper to Leonard Stern, a billionaire who initially made his fortune with Hartz Mountain, a pet supply business, for more than $55 million.

David Schneiderman becomes publisher and acts as editor, later hiring Robert I. Friedman as editor in chief.

1986

Jules Feiffer wins a Pulitzer for Editorial Cartooning.

Martin Gottlieb becomes the editor.

1988

Martin Gottlieb resigns, and Jonathan Z. Larsen becomes the editor.

1994

After Jonathan Z. Larsen resigns, Karen Durbin becomes the second female editor in the paper's history.

1995

The *Voice* launches its website.

1996

Karen Durbin resigns.

Don Forst is hired as editor. After Dan Wolf, he is the longest-serving editor in the paper's history.

The paper stops charging and goes free.

Craigslist launches.

2000

The paper wins its third Pulitzer (for International Reporting) for Mark Schoofs's eight-part series about AIDS in Africa.

Leonard Stern sells the *Voice* and the six other weeklies he owns, including the *LA Weekly*, to a financial management group, Weiss, Peck and Greer, for $170 million. The company is renamed Village Voice Media.

2001

The World Trade Center is attacked on September 11.

2004

Jack Newfield dies.

Richard Goldstein is among five editorial staffers who are laid off. Goldstein later sues for sexual harassment and settles out of court.

2005

The New Times newspaper chain merges with Village Voice Media, making it the biggest alt-weekly company, with seventeen papers.

Editor Don Forst resigns.

2006

Doug Simmons is interim editor in chief for four months.

Ward Harkavy is appointed as interim editor from April till July, when it is announced that Erik Wemple is to take over. He quits before starting.

David Blum is hired as editor in September 2006.

Robert Christgau is among eight editorial and art staffers who are fired.

2007

David Blum is fired after a year.

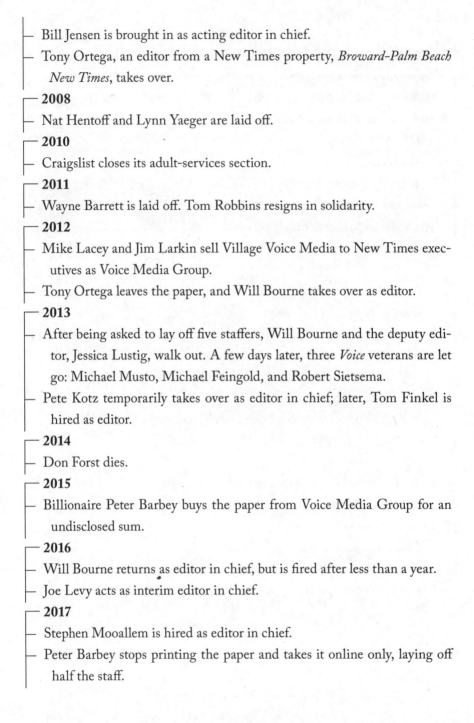

- Bill Jensen is brought in as acting editor in chief.
- Tony Ortega, an editor from a New Times property, *Broward–Palm Beach New Times*, takes over.

2008
- Nat Hentoff and Lynn Yaeger are laid off.

2010
- Craigslist closes its adult-services section.

2011
- Wayne Barrett is laid off. Tom Robbins resigns in solidarity.

2012
- Mike Lacey and Jim Larkin sell Village Voice Media to New Times executives as Voice Media Group.
- Tony Ortega leaves the paper, and Will Bourne takes over as editor.

2013
- After being asked to lay off five staffers, Will Bourne and the deputy editor, Jessica Lustig, walk out. A few days later, three *Voice* veterans are let go: Michael Musto, Michael Feingold, and Robert Sietsema.
- Pete Kotz temporarily takes over as editor in chief; later, Tom Finkel is hired as editor.

2014
- Don Forst dies.

2015
- Billionaire Peter Barbey buys the paper from Voice Media Group for an undisclosed sum.

2016
- Will Bourne returns as editor in chief, but is fired after less than a year.
- Joe Levy acts as interim editor in chief.

2017
- Stephen Mooallem is hired as editor in chief.
- Peter Barbey stops printing the paper and takes it online only, laying off half the staff.

2018

— Stephen Mooallem leaves as editor in chief.

— Peter Barbey closes all editorial operations of the *Voice*.

2020

— Street Media's Brian Calle buys the *Voice*. Calle had purchased the *LA Weekly* in 2017.

2021

— The *Village Voice* relaunches in print and online with R.C. Baker as its editor in chief. Since its reemergence, it has printed in irregular intervals but publishes regularly online.

INTRODUCTION

MICHAEL TOMASKY: There were always people like me, sitting hundreds of miles away in a small town in West Virginia, who identified with the *Village Voice* and said, "Wow. What a cool thing this paper is, and wouldn't it be amazing someday to be part of it?"

If you came to New York as a young journalist, and you just wanted a job, well, you could get a job at a TV station or the *Daily News* or something. But most of the people who worked at the *Voice* really wanted to work at the *Voice*. I can't think of anybody who was there just because it was a paycheck.

DAN WOLF: The *Village Voice* was originally conceived as a living, breathing attempt to demolish the notion that one needs to be a professional to accomplish something in a field as purportedly technical as journalism. It was a philosophical position. We wanted to jam the gears of creeping automatism.

RICHARD GOLDSTEIN: Our philosophy was you do not hire an expert; you hire someone who is living through the phenomenon worth covering. When midnight movies came along, I hired Jim Hoberman, not because he was already a critic, but because he was an underground filmmaker. A lot of the people I hired were effectively amateurs as writers but had amazingly interesting sensibilities and were totally attuned to the subjects they wrote about. The person who covered hippies was Don McNeill. He was a homeless guy. He had a bed on the top floor of the office. He knew the scene; he lived what he wrote about. That's the real ethos of the *Village Voice*. And that's why there was conflict—you were actually living what your byline was about.

ANDY WARHOL: The *Village Voice* was a community newspaper then, with a distinct community to cover—a certain number of square blocks in Greenwich Village plus the entire liberal-thinking world, from flower boxes on Mac-Dougal Street to pornography in Denmark. The combination of extremely

1

local news with international news worked well for the *Voice* because the Village intellectuals were as interested in what was happening in the world as in what was going on around the corner, and the liberals all over the world were interested in the Village as if it were a second home.

JONAS MEKAS: The first ten years or fifteen years of the *Village Voice*, there was no attempt and no wish, no desire to be objective. It was personal journalism. The writing came from the world itself. From that came a new kind of writing.

ED FANCHER: We didn't want to be seen as a left-wing newspaper particularly; we wanted to be seen as an independent newspaper. We published quite a few conservative articles. The idea of the *Voice* was independent journalism. And that idea is either lost or forgotten.

PAUL BERMAN: The *Voice* came out of a particular political tradition in New York, which was left-wing, anticommunist. The Socialist Party in New York was, in its mainstream, *vehemently* anticommunist, and not rivals, but enemies. And that's Norman Mailer.

DAN WOLF: If you're going to develop an ideology and cease to be an open paper, then you're going to have to question the political credentials of everyone who writes for you. The *Voice*, from the very beginning, attracted talented people who found no place in the regular media. Even though the paper was based in Greenwich Village and fought many local and political battles, it quickly took on the character—in a very modest way—of a national newspaper.

TOM ROBBINS: The *Voice* was like a free food fight between the people who work there. Fred McDarrah used to say in defense of the paper, "The *Voice* is many voices." And it was true. In the old days, Alex Cockburn—this amazingly brilliant, iconoclastic, British-born political columnist—would write letters attacking [journalist] Jack Newfield. And [columnist] Nat Hentoff would write letters attacking everybody.

HARRY ALLEN: The paper was called the *Voice*, and that's what it was. It was like a loud, open mouth.

HOWARD BLUM: It was a precursor to the internet. You could try to get your opinions in the *Voice*, no matter how weird or outlandish or interesting, and the *Voice* would print it.

RICHARD GOLDSTEIN: I don't think the culture could sustain anything like the *Voice* today because there is this great impatience for reading anything you disagree with. The people who wrote for the *Voice* would never be at the same party together.

ROBERT NEWMAN: The *Voice* is a microcosm of the cosmic history of New York.

LAURIE STONE: Jack Newfield would do this column every year called the 10 Worst Landlords. It was great, real investigative work. The other front-of-the-book investigative reporters did important investigative journalism that was about political corruption, not celebrating commerce and corporate gentrification, but the opposite.

R.C. BAKER: It is unique, utterly unique. We'd have a great article about what a deadbeat criminal Roy Cohn is in, like, 1976. This is before he even knows Trump. And it turns out now we're living in Roy Cohn's world, because Trump basically took his playbook and ran with it. The *Voice* was reporting about it because the *Voice* knows where all the New York bodies are buried.

KIT RACHLIS: There are a number of contributions the alternative press made to the culture. One of them was to elevate, and particularly force, newspapers to recognize that writing about culture was an extraordinarily important thing. For the longest time, arts writing, in the hierarchy of newspapers, was below the women's pages, which is to say it was at the bottom of the hierarchy. There was that old-fashioned view in newspapers for the longest time, which was, "Oh, anybody can be a film critic. It doesn't matter if we give it to the alcoholic copy editor." What the alternative press did was say loudly that culture was extraordinarily important to cover, write about, report on, think about, analyze.

ANN POWERS: The *Voice* style of criticism was the template for what everything is now—what has become the hot take and the deep dive on the web. The *Voice* was more about making those associative leaps, writing in a style that was informal but deep, and writing in the style that was personal but that was meant to make a mark, and wasn't just memoir.

JIM FOURATT: The *Voice* always wanted to be on the front line of culture. Who are the innovators? Who are the creative people?

JOY PRESS: I was a club kid, but gradually, I would be reading these theater pieces and these music pieces, and it opened up whole worlds. The *Voice* just became the ultimate in my mind. It was this combination of amazing writing and intellect. It was a place where it felt like these people knew the things that you needed to know to get into the corners and the crevices of New York.

COLSON WHITEHEAD: The *New York Times* was so stuffy. I was like, "Eh, that's The Man. I want to work for the *Voice*. It's swaggy, it's cool." I'm so into pop culture. You had these really educated people who would write about film one week and then music the next, and Basquiat and comic books and TV. No one else took hip-hop as seriously as the *Voice*, whether it was Run-DMC or De La Soul or Public Enemy.

LAURIE STONE: The whole idea of countercultural journalism was invented by the *Voice*, really. Then it spawned a whole industry of counterculture-type periodicals. It was the anti-*Times*. It was the investigation of everything that you wouldn't find on the regular grid, and it would clue you to where culture was going if it were not corporately produced and directed.

LENNY KAYE: When I was maybe fourteen, I had that moment where, you know, you read *On the Road*, and you read about Allen Ginsberg, and I was that kind of out-of-place animal in New Jersey. I always was attracted to that bohemian life. And the *Village Voice* was my window into it.

The Village Voice *was started by three people in 1955:*
novelist Norman Mailer,
journeyman editor Dan Wolf, and
psychologist Ed Fancher.
But like everything in Voice *lore, even this is bitterly contested. . . .*

1955–1970

"THE WRITING CAME FROM THE WORLD ITSELF"

CHAPTER 1

"WE WANTED A CERTAIN KIND OF NEWSPAPER"

ED FANCHER: Every time I went to a party in Greenwich Village somebody would say, "Why doesn't the Village have a good newspaper? You'd see Ginsberg, Kerouac, and Baldwin, and I knew all of these people. That's why we started the *Voice*. We said, "*The Villager** is a newspaper for little old ladies from Des Moines and doesn't reflect the intellectual and artistic firmament of this community."

DAN WOLF: When I first mentioned the *Voice* to Mailer, he was, "Yes, sure. I'll go in for it." I mentioned it first to Ed Fancher. It took him all of about twenty-four hours to say yes. He had a little money. I didn't. Norman was obviously the best off because he had this huge success, *The Naked and the Dead*. And so, we divided it up. It was my idea, their agreement. Norman had a secondary role because his world was much larger than just this newspaper. He was writing books.

ED FANCHER: Dan Wolf and I—we were simpatico. We were both just out of the army in 1946. He and I were both in line to register on the GI Bill to go to the New School for Social Research. We became friends in the line, talking.

DAN WOLF: Most of us lived in cold-water flats. I lived in one on First Avenue and Second Street. You had to take showers at the public facilities because there wasn't a tub in your room. The apartment cost thirty-two

---

* *The Villager* is a community newspaper focused on Greenwich Village and founded in 1933 by Walter and Isabel Bryan.

The first cover of the *Village Voice*.
Cover image © Village Voice/
Street Media.

dollars, but we lived there thinking we did pretty well. That's when the Village was the Village. It had these old families, mostly Irish and Italian and Polish, who lived over there.

LUCIAN K. TRUSCOTT IV: Wolf and Mailer were roommates on First Avenue after the war, and Mailer wrote *The Naked and the Dead* in the apartment he shared with Dan Wolf. Wolf told me that as Mailer wrote it, Wolf read the pages of the novel. In '55, Mailer dedicated *The Deer Park* to him. They were very close, and they talked all the time.

ED FANCHER: There were reasons why I was not friendly with Norman. I had broken up with my girlfriend, and Norman married her—the one he stabbed and almost killed. Adele.

NORMAN MAILER: Dan was the quarterback. We put the money in, the $5,000 on each side. That went very quickly.

ED FANCHER: Dan and I knew a lot of people who were writers and artists and theater people. So, we said, "OK, let's try it." We called up everybody we knew.

The first employee we got was Jerry Tallmer. We met him at a party. He said he was an unsuccessful freelance writer. He was also a veteran of World War II. Jerry was the only one of us who knew how to put out a newspaper. He had been the editor of the Dartmouth College daily newspaper. He knew the machinery of printing and distribution and so on. He was with us for the first five years.

JERRY TALLMER: The birthplace of the *Village Voice*, and its cradle for the next couple of years, was that little old floor-through one flight up at 22 Greenwich Avenue. There was a main space looking out on Greenwich Avenue and not much else; a tiny rear room containing a desk—Dan Wolf's desk—and an ancient daybed; a bathroom of sorts; two or three desks up front; a couple of battered Royal typewriters, an ink-splattering mimeograph machine, a broom, a wastebasket, and—not an odor exactly but a newspaper mustiness, even though there'd never before been a newspaper on the premises. I knew at once, as I stepped through the door, that this was it for me.

Even before I got there, there was somebody ensconced at a desk by the windows. This was John Wilcock, a chirpy little twenty-eight-year-old British refugee from Fleet Street and its *Daily Mail*, who—quite separately from Ed Fancher, Dan Wolf, or Norman Mailer—had wanted to start a newspaper more reflective of the onrushing beatnik counterculture.

JOHN WILCOCK: I came to New York with over a decade's experience in proper journalism. I loved New York from my first moment there, and by day two had moved into a Greenwich Village apartment for forty-six dollars a month. I could see the need for a new newspaper in the Village. Five days into my new life, I put up a handwritten card in a Sheridan Square bookshop, seeking anyone interested in such a publication. Two people who did meet with me were a pair of new friends named Ed Fancher and Dan Wolf.

Over the summer of 1955, we began on the first issue.

JERRY TALLMER: We had more than one meeting to decide on a name for the new newspaper. Norman later said the *Village Voice* was his name. I thought—still think—it was mine. The truth probably is that we both hit on it at the same time.

ED FANCHER: My former sergeant from war, Fred Fleck, had taken over a little trucking company, and he had gotten kicked out of Columbia

University. So that was the lead story.* We were just scrounging around to see what stories we could find.

There was a liquor store right across the street from the *Village Voice*, and they would cash any *Village Voice* postdated check. This is one of the ways that we survived.

DAN WOLF: Within a week or two weeks of the *Voice* starting, I got married. My wife was a social worker. So that meant that there was some income. We started off trying to give each other ten dollars a week. That didn't last long. We were down to nothing. Nothing was coming in.

ED FANCHER: I wasn't there every day. The psychology clinic I worked for agreed to give me work half-time so that I could spend half the time at the *Village Voice* trying to keep the damn paper going.

The people involved with the *Voice* were pacifists. We were against the Vietnam War. For a long time, people didn't appreciate that the *Village Voice* was really a product of World War II. Mailer wrote a novel about it, Dan Wolf was in the army under General MacArthur, I was in Italy fighting the Germans in the 10th Mountain Division.

JOHN WILCOCK: Dan, Ed, Norman, and Jerry were all World War II vets. And I was not one. The proudest vet of the four, Jerry Tallmer, seemed to dislike me instantly. So much so that in ensuing decades he became a vocal eliminator of my name from the *Voice*'s history. Out of the entire group—Norman, me, Dan, Ed—I'm the only one with any journalism experience.

JIM FOURATT: John was a handsome, maybe five-foot-seven British guy. John wasn't rich. He was a bon vivant.

ED FANCHER: John claims that he was one of the founders of the *Voice*. He certainly was there at the beginning, no question about it. He was not somebody who came before we first published. He came right afterward, like the first week. He wanted to write a column and we said, "Yes, go ahead." He always thought he was one of the founders, and that's OK. I don't care. Doesn't matter to me.

We felt we should make the world a better place. To have an open newspaper was a contribution. We started the *Voice*, and we had no experience in journalism, or in business, really. We just had an idea. We wanted a certain

---

* The leading story in the first issue was "Village Trucker Sues Columbia."

kind of newspaper. And we're going to hold on for dear life and try to steer it along so it could survive.

We thought we were out of our minds. We simply were determined. We were gonna put a goddamn paper out, and we didn't know how. It was a religious thing.

CHAPTER 2

"WE WERE AMAZED WITH HOW MANY WRITERS WALKED INTO THE *VOICE*"

ED FANCHER: We got a lot of writers just walking in the door. We were amazed with how many writers—some of whom were quite well known, and many of whom were completely unknown—walked into the *Voice*. They simply walked in, sat down, and started talking.

JULES FEIFFER: The newspaper comic strip was a big deal in those years. Before I got into the army, I thought I would be a much more traditional comic strip artist in newspapers. But my reaction to the army changed the kind of cartooning I wanted to do. I moved more into a social, radical political direction. The army made an activist cartoonist out of me.

I wrote my first cartoon—a social, political cartoon about a boy named Munro who was four years old and got drafted by mistake and tried to convince the military that he was only four. I did all of these pieces, which I was crazy about, and took them down to publishers. And all of them thought they were very promising, very exciting, but they didn't know how to market them. Essentially, the message I got was, "If you were only famous, we could publish this." So, I had to go out and get famous to be published. It occurred to me—I had only seen the *Voice* one or two times—that if I could get into the pages of this newspaper, I'd be famous, and they'd publish me.

14

ED FANCHER: Jules Feiffer walked in one day with a pile of cartoons under his arm, and he said, "I've been to every publisher in New York, and nobody wants what I have. If you want them, you can have them for nothing. As long as you agree to publish one every week." We loved them. "We said, 'Of course! They're great!'"

JULES FEIFFER: They all went crazy over it. I'd never gotten this kind of reaction. I joined the paper on its first anniversary, in October of 1956. I wasn't impressed. I couldn't tell the difference between it and *The Villager*. The *Voice* hadn't found its identity yet. Mailer had a column. However irritating he could be, he could be explosively interesting and put his finger on the pulse of the time in a way that nobody else did.

MICHAEL SMITH: I moved to New York in August 1956. I had dropped out of Yale. I had directed a couple of plays; I came to New York to be a director. I was already a writer in my own mind, but not really writing. I had a job at the *London Evening Standard* in Rockefeller Center as an office boy. And then a friend of my girlfriend's took me to meet Dan and Ed at the *Voice* in late 1957.

They started me off by having me write a car column. I never even had a sports car. I started writing this column called HubCaps.

Jerry Tallmer was a hard-boiled newspaperman. He was dry and straight to the point. He was a perfectionist. We were trying to put out an error-free paper. He had real standards of editing, copyediting, and accuracy. Dan worked with a lot of the writers directly, but Jerry really did all the back of the paper, the arts.

JULES FEIFFER: Jerry created the sensibility behind the paper; he had a free-ranging imagination, both literary and theatrical. He became its first theater critic and was one of the few people in New York—along with Kenneth Tynan, who had just come to the *New Yorker*, and Robert Brustein at the *New Republic*—who paid attention to Off-Broadway, and to what became known as the emerging Off-Broadway scene, which was in those years totally ignored by the *New York Times* and the *Herald Tribune*. He was a very open, curious guy. There wouldn't have been a paper without him. He put it all together because he was the only one with any professional experience.

JONAS MEKAS: He was the first person I met at the *Village Voice* in '58. I said, "How come you don't have a column on cinema?" He said, "OK, do you want to do it?"

MARY PEROT NICHOLS: I started to work at the *Voice* at the end of '58. My first article was about a state convention in Syracuse, where Carmine DeSapio took the nomination for the Senate away from Thomas K. Finletter.*

JULES FEIFFER: I started doing a weekly strip, which I called Sick, Sick, Sick, which was my way of introducing my outlook to the reader.

That was the beginning of my character Bernard and all of the relationship stuff that I later did. I started doing cartoons on what really happened in the conversations that I lived through. What led up to the sex or the failed sex, what they expected of each other, how they disappointed or let down each other. And this became basically a byword of what I was doing: over and over and over I discovered that my cartoon was not about pictures; it was about language and the misuse of language and how on every level, in relationships—between parents and children, between husbands and wives, between men and women, between the government and ourselves, between our politicians—language didn't mean what we said. That we spoke in code. What I was doing as a form of humor was a kind of outing of the code.

NAT HENTOFF: In 1958, Jerry Tallmer came to me one day and said, "The editor would like you to do a column." Most of the editors in town saw me only as a jazz person. So, I said, "I'll do it, but I don't have to write about jazz if I don't want to." They agreed to that. There was no money. I found out that having a byline can quickly make you an authority, at least to people who are not very intelligent about authorities. So, I began to write about education, civil rights, civil liberties.

TIM MCDARRAH: My parents came back from Europe. They had been on a four- or five- or six-month trip. When they came back to New York, they had spent every penny they had; they didn't have a pot to piss in. Neither one of them had a job. My mother was pregnant. They were living in

---

* Carmine DeSapio was the longtime notorious boss of Tammany Hall, the Manhattan Democratic Party machine. He was later convicted of petty bribery and went to prison.

what now is SoHo; it was a shit-hole neighborhood. So at that point, Fred reached out to the *Voice* and said, "I'm back, can I take some pictures? Can I sell some ads?" Because they had no money.

GLORIA McDARRAH: He did have a camera, he had a Rollei.

When Fred got out of the army, he lived in a railroad flat with different families on West 66th Street. And one of the families was Dan Wolf and his mother.

After the *Voice* started, Fred would occasionally be taking pictures of artists for his own entertainment. The picture of Bill Gambini was the first picture that Fred ever gave the *Voice*. Whether he got the full five dollars or not, he immediately saw this as a way to make some money.

JILL JOHNSTON: Around 1957, with no prior experience as a writer, having obtained a master's degree in dance and attended the famed Connecticut College summer school, and having then haunted the dance studios in New York City for several years and performed minimally on stage, I was seized with the inspiration to write dance criticism. Whatever my ambition's merit, it functioned as bravado in overcoming my humble beginnings as a dancer.

I was twentysomething just when a great sea change in the American modern dance tradition was underway. Summoned in 1959 by the upstart revolutionist paper the *Village Voice*, then only four years old, to write about dance, I had a forum obviously set up for covering or perpetrating all manner of outrage. The opportunity of learning to write on the job was not lost on me.

JULES FEIFFER: Dan Wolf was the benign philosopher behind it all. Wolf was quiet, reflective, charming, sweet—he was short and curious about everything that I was doing and would ask questions and let me talk and sat behind his desk as a therapist as I would shoot my mouth off. I was in my late twenties and had the maturity of a nineteen-year-old—if that.

JERRY TALLMER: I liked Dan Wolf the moment I laid eyes on him. He looked like me, slim, dark, average height. And he thought like me, full of political skepticism, not to say sarcasm.

GLORIA McDARRAH: Ed talked. Dan, in comparison, he spoke softly, and pretty soon you'd be telling him your life story.

ED FANCHER: Dan rarely used a red pencil on copy. Instead, he would sit down with the writer and say, "Well now, why didn't you say this? And did you think about that?" And he would talk it through. He was very good with young writers, beginning writers. He said he wouldn't hire anybody from journalism school. He wanted writers from English departments. He said journalism school spoils most of them.

MARY PEROT NICHOLS: I was a reporter and a civic activist. The *Voice* was not a conventional paper. They expected you to be involved.

NAT HENTOFF: At the beginning, there was no party line in the paper. Staffers criticized each other in print, and readers had—in addition to the fractious letters page—the Press of Freedom space in which to express their dissonant obsessions. The paper resonated with so many different views that once, when I was lecturing to the Nieman Fellows at Harvard, a professor of government sitting in told me how exasperated he was with the *Voice*. "I never know what the *Village Voice*—as the *Village Voice*—believes. I never know what it stands for." "That's the point," I said. "You can read all kinds of views in the *Voice*, and then make up your own mind. We don't tell you what to think."

CHAPTER 3

QUICKLY: A COLUMN FOR SLOW READERS

NORMAN MAILER: The spring and summer of 1955, Fancher and Wolf were alone in the labor of educating themselves to the thousand and more details which go into starting a weekly newspaper. Busy at first with the work of finishing *The Deer Park*, later dredged by the effort, I did not much more than contribute a few bits of amateur advice and the name: the *Village Voice*. When a first issue of the paper appeared in late September, I was able to read it with the detachment of someone who had paid a nickel at a newsstand. Two weeks later my novel came out.

The paper was losing a thousand dollars a week. I could give myself the excuse that I was needed. I began to work on the *Voice*, playing at one job and then another, too charged with impatience to plug at chores, too doubtful in stamina to see the end of a project through from its beginning.

I started writing my column. That drove Dan insane; he felt it was much too fast, much too ugly. I never found a tone for my column, and so I was not able to learn how much or how little was possible.

We were losing half the readers he wanted, but we were gaining the readers I wanted, and so forth.

NORMAN MAILER, QUICKLY, A COLUMN FOR SLOW READERS, *VILLAGE VOICE*, JANUARY 3, 1956

At any rate, dear reader, we begin a collaboration, which may go on for three weeks, three months, or, Lord forbid, for three-and-thirty years.

Village Voice cofounder and editor Daniel Wolf (1915–1996) (right) sits with author Norman Mailer (1923–2007) in the *Voice*'s offices in Sheridan Square, New York, April 14, 1964. Photograph © Fred W. McDarrah/MUUS Collection.

I have only one prayer—that I weary of you before you tire of me. And therefore, so soon as I learn to write columnese in a quarter of an hour instead of the unprofitable fifty-two minutes this has taken, we will all know better if our trifling business is going to continue.

ED FANCHER: He was going through a very bad state in those days. He had just published his third book, which was *The Deer Park*, and had gotten bad reviews. And then he had a play based upon it, and that got bad reviews.

JOHN WILCOCK: My cynical observation was that famous authors who were paid by the word had a tendency to be a bit windy. The column was basically an apologia for its own existence. This pretentious and condescending rubbish was not being sympathetically received by *Voice* readers, some resorting in response to parody, but most accusing the star columnist of pomposity, verbosity, half-baked opinions, being patronizing, and suffering from "illusions of grandeur."

Understandably, however, the publicity brought welcome attention to the paper, and this was magnified when Mailer chose to devote a half-page ad reprinting all the crappy reviews that had appeared deriding his third novel, *The Deer Park*.

JERRY TALLMER: He wrote the columns—an exploration of hipness inter-mingled with sneering put-downs of Village intelligentsia—by hand, with pen or pencil, in a sort of looping grade-school script, and brought or sent them in, always too late, much beyond deadline, and always, always far exceeding the allotted space. Our two secretaries, Susan Ryan and Flo Ettenberg, would de-cipher them, type them, and off we'd all (less Norman) go at six in the morn-ing, having had little or no sleep whatever the past seventy-two hours, all the way across New Jersey to the printers in Washington, Pennsylvania.

Somewhere along in there, the three words "nuances of growth" in Nor-man's column that issue had come out "nuisances of growth." Nobody had caught it.

I came into the office as the telephone was ringing.

I picked it up. A raging voice—Mailer's voice—said, "Tallmer, you schmuck, why don't you take your thumb out of your asshole? It's nuance . . . nuance, not 'nuisance'!"

And thus began the great *Village Voice* battle of the typo, an internal war that almost strangled that infant newspaper in its cradle.

ED FANCHER: Norman demanded that Jerry Tallmer be fired because of it, and I said, "Go fuck yourself." Really, the break with him over the *Voice* is he wanted Dan and me to make the *Voice* so radical that we go out of busi-ness. And we said no, we want to make it a success.

DAN WOLF: Norman saw the paper as an explosion. He always antici-pated the next move of society. He was fascinated by the idea that we're all becoming somewhat psychopathic, and approved of it in a way. He wanted a paper [where] you'd have your stories turned upside down, read sideways— real wild stuff. Ed Fancher and I wanted a paper that would survive. So that was a battle between Norman and me, over control of the paper. We brought in some other guy. He attempted to ally himself with Norman and take over the paper. We managed to beat that back with great effort. And the *Voice* then moved on and on, and on, not knowing from week to week how long we could keep the place going.

NORMAN MAILER: I would have wrecked it all over again in a few months because I was a wild man. I wanted the revolution to come; I wanted blood in the streets. There had been something there, the paper was exciting; it hadn't been before. Now they suddenly saw that there was a daring newspaper possible.

And then along came Feiffer and his cartoons, and Feiffer made the *Voice*. People would buy the *Voice* to see his cartoons. They were extraordinary. What I failed to do with the column Feiffer succeeded in doing each week with his panel. Then the articles got wilder, the insights got stronger, the attitude became bigger, and the *Voice* grew, and the *Voice* grew, and it grew, and I was out of it.

CHAPTER 4

"HE PRACTICALLY INVENTED OFF-BROADWAY THEATER"

JULES FEIFFER: The Village was full of ambitious young men and young women who were on the make. The energy was terrifying. The coffeehouse movement had started a few years before, and folksingers were abounding, and Washington Square was a hangout for singing, and there was a lot of action. And Off-Broadway and Off-Off-Broadway were exploding; a lot of talent which was then unrecognized was happening.

JIM FOURATT: There were all these things going on—LaMaMa, the Caffe Cino, the Old Reliable, which was a bar all the way over on the East Side on Third Street. The new playwrights—María Irene Fornés, Tom Eyen, Lanford Wilson—there was a whole category of playwrights that started at the Caffe Cino or the Café LaMaMa. Joe Cino invented a new kind of theater.

JULES FEIFFER: The *Voice*, through Jerry Tallmer as the theater critic, would visit these little holes in the wall and write about people you never heard of who later would become famous, like John Guare and Albee and others.

JIM FOURATT: One of his gifts was knowing what he could cover, and who could cover what, bringing in Michael Smith, who was part of the downtown scene. He lived with the guy who did all the lighting at the Caffe Cino.

DIANE FISHER: Jerry was straight Off-Broadway. Michael was Off-Off.

MICHAEL SMITH: I started working part-time at the *Voice* as Jerry Tallmer's assistant, copyediting and proofreading. And then he started sending me to review plays.

He coined the term "Off-Off-Broadway." He was very adventurous; he would go to all kinds of plays, and he started the Obie Awards. He started sending me to a lot of coffeehouse theater around 1960, when the Caffe Cino started doing plays every week.

Originally, they were existing plays by Tennessee Williams or Oscar Wilde—intellectual plays. And then gradually, original playwrights started turning up. At that point there was no place to do plays if you were not commercial in some way. There were only maybe half a dozen theaters Off-Broadway, and they mostly did classics. So, the Cino was really great that way because Joe Cino was completely open. He would not even read the script; he would just talk to whoever wanted to do it, and if he thought they were sincere, he would give them a date and then they would do their play. I directed a couple of plays there. But there was never any budget. It took a while before the uptown papers started noticing. It was a very, very small scale.

JERRY TALLMER, *VILLAGE VOICE*, 1959

What *The Connection* as a whole did for me as a layman was to flesh out, marvelously, my own layman's image of the world of heroin, its tired knowing endless deepfreeze of detumescence and utter hopelessness—and all such evocation of images I should consider well within the province of living theatre, if not necessarily of enduring drama. Yes, the Living Theatre's alive. . . .

ROBERT CHRISTGAU: When I was in college at Dartmouth, I started subscribing to the *Voice*. And by that time, I was hitchhiking in to see my girlfriend and spending a lot of time in Greenwich Village. We would go to see plays, and for all that stuff the *Voice* was invaluable. I can't really recall the plays except for *The Connection*, which was very important.* It was art. I went to see that at least twice, probably three times, because in the middle of it, Jackie McLean, who was then not allowed to play in New York as he lost his cabaret license because he was a junkie, would play a solo for about fifteen minutes after Warren Finnerty made his wonderful speech.** I mean, I can still remember this shit sixty years ago. Because it was really important. It just sort of burned into my consciousness.

DIANE FISHER: The *Times* always, always had to play catch-up.

ED FANCHER: Jerry Tallmer shamed them into beginning to cover Off-Broadway.

DIANE FISHER: And if the *Times* did it, then everybody had to do it.

---

* *The Connection* was produced by the Living Theatre, the oldest experimental theater troupe in the United States, cofounded by Judith Malina and Julian Beck. In 1960, it won three Obies, including Best Play, and was later made into a film, directed by Shirley Clarke.
** McLean was a jazz alto saxophonist who played with Sonny Rollins and was a member of Art Blakey's Jazz Messengers.

CHAPTER 5
"THE *VOICE* WAS HER WEAPON"

CLARK WHELTON: Do you know the story of Mary Nichols?

ELIZA NICHOLS: My mother was involved in the fight against Robert Moses, and in particular Washington Square Park, and to have it closed from traffic.* She kept going into the *Village Voice*: "You've got to write about this." Dan Wolf finally got sick of this mother coming to him and saying, "You got to write about this," and he said, "You write about it."

One of her good friends was the author of *The Death and Life of Great American Cities*, Jane Jacobs. My mother and Grace Paley and Jane Jacobs would take the kids to the park, and they became friends that way.

ED FANCHER: She was a housewife and a neighbor of mine. She had a great deal to do with destroying the career of Robert Moses because of the highway through the park, but the copy she would bring in to Dan, he said, was unreadable.

ELIZA NICHOLS: My mother had no formal training. She did have a college education in political science. That was a very important formation for her, to be on the ground and doing this reporting. That was definitely Wolf's brilliance. He hired people who cared about stuff.

Dan was warm and kind and funny and loving, and smart, and he was capable of thinking of how to not only hire a woman in those days and give her authority, but also retain her. She didn't have her own office. I had to come to her office after school, because there was no after-school program

---

* Robert Moses was a controversial urban planner who held various positions of power for four decades, serving as the New York City Parks Commissioner and New York state Secretary of State.

Photo of Mary Perot Nichols circa early '70s, adorned with a pin from the Lion's Head, the watering hole favored by *Voice* writers. Photo courtesy of Eliza Nichols.

in those days, and I was the youngest. I had nowhere to go, and she was working. So, he rented an apartment next door to the original *Village Voice* building, so that she would have an office where I could just sit and draw and play while she was working. My mother wrote a lot. She wrote under deadline, and she hated every minute of it. She loved her job. She was much more excited about the scent than the kill.

DIANE FISHER: Mary may be the only layman in the whole world who read the capital budget from the first item to the last.

ELIZA NICHOLS: The famous "follow the money"—that was something my mother did way early on. Her finally figuring out what the financial interests of the various constituencies were led her and Jane Jacobs to ask for a meeting with the Mafia boss, because they understood that he controlled all of the South Village and what is now SoHo and Tribeca.

He said something like, "Why should I care?" And my mother said, "If that freeway is built, your entire neighborhood's going to be destroyed. And all those small businessmen who pay tribute to you and who you control are no longer going to exist." I'm pretty sure it was the Gambino family that was in business then.

MARY PEROT NICHOLS: City planning issues like Moses—that was my bête noire until he got out of office.

ED FANCHER: Every week, she would be pounding away at Moses. He wanted to put a highway through Washington Square, and we stopped it by pounding away week after week. We made it clear that politically it would be suicide for Carmine DeSapio. Carmine DeSapio had to make the final decision because he was a very powerful figure, and if he didn't stand up to Moses and stop it, he would've been out of power. It's that's simple. And he finally did it after weeks and weeks of work.

JANE JACOBS: I saw Moses only once, at a hearing about the road through Washington Square; he stood up there gripping the railing, and he was furious at the effrontery of this, and I guess he could already see that his plan was in danger. Because he was saying, "There is nobody against this—NOBODY, NOBODY, NOBODY—but a bunch of, a bunch of MOTHERS!" And then he stomped out.

CLARK WHELTON: Then came "The Bath Mat Solution." Moses said, "All right, so I won't build a highway through the park, but we will just simply take the traffic around both sides of the park, turning the rectangle into an oval," and she beat him on that, too. Robert Caro gives her credit for being the first person to actually wrestle Moses to the ground and stop him.

ROBIN REISIG: There was going to be a cross-town, elevated highway—with exit and entrance ramps that would have destroyed SoHo and parts of Chinatown and everything else—crossing Lower Manhattan. There would have been no SoHo in the way we know SoHo. It would have been a disaster.

CLARK WHELTON: She stopped that, too!

ALAN WEITZ: Can you imagine an expressway across Canal Street? And they stopped him from building these tremendous West Village apartments and got the West Village declared a historical landmark.

CLARK WHELTON: She went through every line [of a document] to find out who was swindling who, and which landlords were getting away with murder. Through the *Village Voice*, she warned New York that landlords had in mind towers along the Hudson River. They want to block off our view of the Hudson. She said, "If we don't stop them, they're going to control through the Lower Manhattan Expressway and the various other techniques they have, they're going to end up wanting all that land."

ELIZA NICHOLS: Ed Fancher said my mother's writing saved the *Village Voice* from going under in about 1958.

CLARK WHELTON: The *Voice* was her weapon. The *Voice* saved the Village for years and years.

RICHARD GOLDSTEIN: The paper's forays into politics were about local Village politics. Its first crusade was overthrowing the boss of Greenwich Village, Carmine DeSapio, and replacing him with a young Reform upstart named Ed Koch. Ed became our lawyer.

ED FANCHER: He resigned as our lawyer when he went into politics.

DAN WOLF: Ed was always enormously impressed with the *Voice*. He felt that the *Voice* played a large role in his success. He would come in to give me the line on the Village Independent Democrats. The Village Independent Democrats were looking for publicity, explaining positions they attacked and all that. I suppose we were useful to him.

SUSAN BROWNMILLER: He was a simpleton in some regards. But he was a careful, good politician. He was often at those Friday afternoon soirees that Dan had in his office.

MARY PEROT NICHOLS: I thought he was kind of a silly person. I remember him being an orator on street corners in Sheridan Square. He was quite good at that, handling hecklers when he was campaigning for the VID. If he was ever gay at that time, it was certainly not apparent.

SUSAN BROWNMILLER: I went to visit Mr. DeSapio. He said, "I know that Ed Koch has been having a homosexual affair with"—and he mentioned the name of the guy, who was a VID judge. I thought, "Well, that's interesting." It was something to put in my story for sure. Dan saw that and took that paragraph out. That was the only major edit I ever had in the *Voice*.

Dan wasn't going to take any chances on besmirching Ed's always unclear sexuality. I had one date with him; it didn't go particularly well.

ELIZA NICHOLS: The *Voice* really helped Ed get elected his first few times. Ed was a better person in those days. He might have got corrupted by his own enormous ego.

EDITORIAL, *VILLAGE VOICE*, MARCH 24, 1966

Some of his friends believe he has an almost disastrous tendency—in politics—to say what he thinks and to make himself almost too clear. He is aware of this tendency—and he is even amused at it—but he never curbs it; he just hopes for the best.

ED KOCH: Well, I don't know the dictionary meaning of it, but the "hairshirt" to me has always meant someone who never is satisfied with the status quo, will not compromise, will be a constant irritant. And while I was extremely proud of the *Village Voice* editorial which was issued in 1962 when I lost my race—it was so lovely I had it on the wall of my office . . . it referred to the VID as a hairshirt, but I *was* the VID at that moment simply because I was the candidate.

MARY PEROT NICHOLS: I used to get him involved in my causes. I'd call Ed and I'd say, "Hey, Ed, do you want to be famous?" The highway commissioner wanted to slice up all the sidewalks on Bleecker Street, which would destroy the pushcart markets, and they want to put more traffic in. So, Ed held a press conference and called what they want to do "salami tactics."* He was always pretty good at quips that would get in the paper. But usually, they were my ideas.

---

* "Salami tactics" is a phrase coined by Hungarian Stalinist Mátyás Rákosi to describe a political maneuver to reduce or add reforms bit by bit.

CHAPTER 6

"JUST THE FACT THAT IT WAS THE '60s HELPED THE *VOICE*"

MICHAEL SMITH: The newspaper strike made the *Voice*'s success. It completely changed everything. There were seven dailies, and they went on strike for sixteen weeks, beginning in December 1962, into March of '63.

ED FANCHER: After the newspaper strike, our circulation went up twenty-eight thousand to about thirty-five thousand. From then on, we continued to get very good circulation increases. The newsstands up until then put us behind the other papers. But once we broke through, the newsstands could see people really liked the paper, bought the paper, paid for the paper. Then it kept going.

MICHAEL SMITH: The *Voice* was really the only place to advertise apartments. So it enormously expanded the paper. The page count went up week by week. We were putting out thirty-six pages and then forty-eight, then sixty and seventy-two, and it later got up to over a hundred. It must have been incredibly hard work, looking back on it. To fill up those pages, we had to generate a huge amount of copy because there were rules about what percentage of ads you can have in the paper.

SUSAN BROWNMILLER: Dan Wolf understood that the *Voice* had become the best showcase for young writers in New York.

ALAN WEITZ: The *Voice* played a major role in New Journalism, though it's usually not credited as doing so, because most of the New Journalists wanted to work for better money at *Esquire* and *New York* magazine.* Gay Talese and Tom Wolfe and Gail Sheehy, they had their own homes. Ron Rosenbaum and Jack Newfield were writing a different kind of New Journalism, a sort of advocacy journalism. There were a lot of pieces in the *Voice* about feminism and the women's movement. That was partly New Journalism.

HOWARD BLUM: There wasn't narrative journalism then. There wasn't first-person journalism back then. In the *Voice*, we were allowed to have a personality, then that was coupled with what was happening in nonfiction journalism: Mailer, *The Armies of the Night*; Truman Capote, *In Cold Blood*; Tom Wolfe, *The Electric Kool-Aid Acid Test*. The *Voice* was leading up to that. I remember reading people like Richard Goldstein, who was the first pop reporter when I was in high school. I wanted to be able to write like that.

RICHARD GOLDSTEIN: I had read the *Voice* since I was a teenager in the Bronx. I crossed the entire borough with two buses just to get to the one newsstand I knew that had the paper, and I became an addicted reader.

The *Voice* was this amalgam of literary bohemian culture and journalism, just perfect for me. I would write a story for the Columbia J School in the style of Tom Wolfe. I would get it back; it would say, "I don't know what this is, but you owe me a story." I baffled them with my shoulder-length hair, and I had this little sugar cube wrapped in aluminum on my desk, so they thought it might be acid. I just wanted to fuck with them. They would say, "What is that?" And I'd say, "Don't ask."

It was sugar.

There's a story I've told on a number of occasions about getting an appointment with Dan Wolf and Ed Fancher in the Sheridan Square office and going in there with my long hair and saying that I wanted to be a rock critic. And their response was, "What is that?" And my response to that was, "I don't know." "Well, try something." They let me go my own way. I was very glad to do that for very little money. I would have paid them to meet the Rolling Stones.

---

* New Journalism is a style of writing that first became prevalent in the 1960s and '70s, and which used novelistic writing techniques in reported journalistic pieces.

DIANE FISHER: It was an astonishing time in pop music. There came a point that there was so much going on that we started the Riffs column, and that was just to give five or six inches to a whole bunch of people.

CARMAN MOORE: I had my master's from Juilliard. I went to the *Voice* and offered the fact that I could write. They weren't going to pay very much. They had Leighton Kerner. But he only wrote about the big guys—the New York Philharmonic and the Metropolitan Opera. He didn't know anything about new music.

Some of us who were coming through the late '50s and much of the '60s found ourselves being the first Black person to do—fill in the blank. You just got used to it. Believe it or not, I didn't think about it that much. Jazz was the important music at the time, and what's called the "American popular music" came out of the African American musical experience. So, in a way, one didn't feel left out, because there was so much attention on things Black.

DIANE FISHER: A lot of these people Mary Nichols came up with. It was she who suggested Deborah Jowitt. She was a pro from the first word that she put on paper.

DEBORAH JOWITT: It was 1967. I had spent a whole summer touring with two star packages, *Oklahoma* and *On a Clear Day You Can See Forever.* I was dancing in both those shows for something like sixteen weeks. Leticia Kent said, "Why don't you try writing a review, and I'll put it on Diane Fisher's desk." I wrote something and nothing happened. And I said, "Do you think maybe it wasn't any good? Maybe I should write another one?" And she put that one on Diane Fisher's desk. And the next week, the *Voice* came out with both of them in the paper.

Jill Johnston was the chief dance critic, but she had not been writing about dance as much as about her life and what interested her. They didn't warn her that they were going to take me on, and I think that triggered a breakdown, one of the many breakdowns that she had.

DIANE FISHER: We always hired poets as art critics. Peter Schjeldahl was one of my favorites, who was the art critic for the *New Yorker* for years.

PETER SCHJELDAHL: I was a midwestern college dropout in the early '60s, worked my way east as a newspaper reporter and was always a poet, and settled on the Lower East Side poetry scene in the early '60s. And of course, the *Voice* was the weekly bible. But to my surprise, after barely starting to write art criticism, I was taken on in 1966 as the *Voice* art critic. God, my life was fantastic and chaotic. Meeting deadlines, you know, interfered with taking drugs. Anyway, I only lasted a few weeks. Maybe about three months. I was just too disorderly. I was just twenty-three, twenty-four, and out of the Midwest and out of my mind.

CLARK WHELTON: I'd come to New York to be a poet until I realized that poets are poor. I lived out in New Jersey and taught school out there, and I would listen to Jean Shepherd, and he would talk about the *Village Voice*. Around 1964, I began to send articles to the *Voice*, which weren't published. In 1966, my wife and I moved to the East Village, and I sent the *Voice* a poem which I had written, and they put it on the editorial page and paid me fifteen dollars. Which was about fifteen dollars more than I had made in my entire writing career, and it was a tremendous gift for me.

DIANE FISHER: No one called you. That is how Joe Flaherty came in.

JACK DEACY: Joe was a big Irishman. Big head, strong guy, and very, very funny. I was working at the community newspaper in my neighborhood, the *Bay Ridge Home Reporter*. Joe was a longshoreman, but he wanted to write in the worst way. In 1965, Mayor Lindsay was being booed by a huge mob, so Joe writes a piece called "Why the Fun Has Left Fun City." It's a good piece, but it's not the stuff that we handled. So, I drove over to the *Voice*, and I put the piece under the mail slot, not knowing what's gonna happen. I didn't tell Joe. The next Thursday, the piece is on the front page of the *Voice*. A friend of his calls him up at some gin mill he's at after work. "Joe, that was a great piece in the *Voice*." Joe goes, "What are you talking about? Don't kid around like that."

That's how I got connected to the *Voice*. And, of course, to the gin mill next to it, the Lion's Head. It's right next to the *Voice* office on Sheridan Square. You go down about three steps. As Flaherty says, it reminded him of his coffin. There were book jackets all over the place. It's a place *Voice* writers went because they were drinkers.

SALLY KEMPTON: It was very much a downtown male bar culture, what the *Voice* came out of, which was Norman's style as well. I always felt like it was an extension of the Lion's Head.

VIVIAN GORNICK: At the bar were all these guys hanging out, like Pete Hamill and Joe Flaherty and Ted Hoagland. I don't remember if Breslin hung out there. They were like the Irish Mafia in journalism, and I was terrified of them, and they were terrified of us, as it turned out. [*Laughs.*] Well, feminists scared the shit out of these guys. They were sexually incredibly immature, all of them.

JACK NEWFIELD: In September of 1964, Dan Wolf hired me to be a staff writer at a $100-a-week salary. When I came to ask Dan for the job, I had just "flunked" my summer tryout on the *New York Post* as a reporter and night rewrite-man. Before that I had been fired as the editor of the *West Side News*, a community weekly for Manhattan's Upper West Side. Before that I had worked for three months on *Women's Wear Daily*, covering the "fur market." Before that I had been fired as a copy boy on the *Daily Mirror* in April of 1961. Dan already knew most of my history as a loser and misfit, but he still decided to take a chance on me.

DIANE FISHER: I started on Halloween 1962. Dan pointed to me and said, "You can write fillers, can't you?" I tossed off a couple dozen fillers and handed them in to Dan. He looked at me and said, "You're a real pro, aren't you?" Little did I know that there was no worse insult in Dan's vocabulary, because he was a big believer in amateurism rather than careerism.

JACK NEWFIELD: Dan hired and inspired amateurs. He hired boxing writer Barbara Long, who had been working in a Linotype shop. He hired Marlene Nadle, a schoolteacher. And Paul Cowan, who had been a civil rights worker.

In the late 1950s, Dan gave the highly original literary critic Sy Krim his own column upon his release from a mental hospital, where he'd gone after suffering a nervous breakdown. Krim wrote some of the best pieces of the *Voice*'s early years, including a column describing what it had been like in the "looney bin." He eventually committed suicide.

ALAN WEITZ: I grew up in a middle-class, white, Jewish home in Queens. I went to a high school called Music and Art, which was very progressive, so I was very aware of the *Village Voice*.

Now, when I was in high school, I forget exactly which summer, my father was adamant about me getting a job—like a nine-to-five job. I knew my father would be mad if I didn't come home with a job. I started walking down Seventh Avenue, going into any place: "Can you use someone for the summer?" "No, no, no." I finally got down Seventh Avenue to Sheridan

Square, which is where the *Village Voice* was then located. I happened to meet the sister of an old girlfriend, and I told her about my trials during the day, and she said, "Why don't you go into the *Village Voice?*" It was the middle of the '60s, and there was this beautiful, hippie, young girl sitting behind the desk.

I walked into this office that, to me, is like, "Wow." It's filled with people with long hair and not your traditional office setting. They had an opening for a messenger and a mail clerk. I started working for the *Voice* in the summer of 1965.

SUSAN BROWNMILLER: When I came back from Mississippi working in the civil rights movement, I was really at a loss for what to do next with my life. And Jack Newfield proposed to Dan Wolf that he give me a shot, and it was just the best thing that could happen to me. I was almost homeless then. I was bunking with friends in Greenwich Village. The deal was if I wrote something that he liked, he'd give me seventy-five dollars. I wrote the first piece ever in a "white" paper on James Brown. It was bannered on the front page—"James Brown, Knocking 'Em Dead in Bed-Stuy." That was my first biggie, I think.

VIVIAN GORNICK: When I started to write, that was the place that seemed most natural to me to send my stuff to. There is a jazz club in the Village called the Village Vanguard. In the late '60s, early '70s, it used to run Monday night speakouts. So, one Monday night, there was LeRoi Jones, who was not yet Amiri Baraka, and the saxophonist Archie Shepp, and the painter Larry Rivers. And out in the audience was everybody like me— white, middle-class liberals and radicals.

LeRoi Jones got up there and he said, "Blood is soon going to run in the seats of the theater of revolution. And guess who's sitting in those seats?" So, the whole place went crazy. Everybody is yelling and screaming and defending themselves against this charge, because many were activists. I sat there terrified of him because he was really ferocious.

I thought, "He is mixing up class and race." He said, "You people have fucked the whole thing up."

I wrote up the whole evening and discovered my style, which was that of personal journalism. I sent it over the transom to Dan Wolf. A few days later he called me up. "Who the hell are you? Send me anything you're writing."

VIVIAN GORNICK, "THE PRESS OF FREEDOM: AN OFAY'S INDIRECT ADDRESS TO LEROI JONES," *VILLAGE VOICE*, MARCH 4, 1965

The audience was predominantly—predictably—white, liberal, middle-class. They had come to be entertained and instructed. They stayed to become serious or delighted. They left in a roar of confused frustration, feeling as though they had, with unexpected stunning, been dealt a kick in the stomach and a few swift blows to the side of the head. For LeRoi Jones and Archie Shepp, whose evening it was, had told them repeatedly, "Die baby. The only thing you can do for me is die."

SUSAN BROWNMILLER: It was a paper open to people who wanted to write, but it helped to have a connection. Dan Wolf liked the children of famous people. Sally Kempton—who was the daughter of Murray Kempton, the most famous journalist in New York—just graduated from college, and she was told, "The door is open for you with the *Village Voice*," and she was such a talented writer that she could do just fine. Paul Cowan had also been in the civil rights movement, but he was the son of Lou Cowan, who was the head of CBS. But maybe Dan and Ed Fancher thought that the fathers would give some money to them to help fund the *Voice* because it was such a shoestring operation for them.

SALLY KEMPTON: I got the job at the *Voice* through a friend who had worked there as an intern in high school. It's probably true that Dan hired me more or less immediately because of my father. My friend took me to meet him on the traditional *Voice* Friday, because Dan always held court on Friday afternoons. I gave him a bunch of my college newspaper things, and he hired me.

ED FANCHER: He liked to get a young writer who was not developed and build them up.

VIVIAN GORNICK: I was full of self-doubt. I was a terrible fuckup. I couldn't discipline myself. I hardly ever finished anything that I started writing. Like many of us. So, instead, I got married, and I left the city. And that was a disaster. Within two or three years, I was unmarried and back in the city, and I went to Dan Wolf, and I asked him for a job at the *Voice*. And he said to me, "You are a neurotic Jewish girl. You can only produce one piece a year. How can I give you a job?" [*Laughs.*]

So, I said, "Not anymore. I'll do anything you want." I pulled myself together. I wrote a piece on Dorothy Day at the *Catholic Worker*, and then Jack Kerouac died, and he sent me to cover the funeral, and one more piece and the job was mine. My natural bent towards personal journalism matched the *Voice* completely. I was utterly at home there.

ALAN WEITZ: Just the fact that it was the '60s helped the *Voice*.

SONIA JAFFE ROBBINS: Whoever was calling a demonstration or a march, they'd have a big ad in the *Voice*. That's how you knew what was happening.

CHRIS STEIN: There were papers that were further fringe than the *Voice*: the *East Village Other* and *The Realist*. It's odd when you think about it, that the *Village Voice* was more centrist. The *East Village Other* was fucking nuts.

JIM FOURATT: The *East Village Other* was trying to be the *Village Voice* of the emerging Lower East Side/East Village culture.

J. HOBERMAN: It was more overtly countercultural, but you couldn't get as good a handle on what was going on from *EVO* as from the *Voice*.

TIM MCDARRAH: Every single event of the 1960s that was pivotal, Fred McDarrah covered. He was at Stonewall. He was at Woodstock. He was at Martin Luther King's speeches. He was with Bobby Kennedy and Jack Newfield. There's a picture of Dylan, Joan Baez, and Peter Yarrow from Peter, Paul and Mary, alone backstage at the Lincoln Memorial, and my dad figures, "Everybody's gonna have pictures of Martin Luther King, but I'm gonna go and take pictures of these three unknowns." There's a picture from 1960 of Kate Millett. In 1960 she was a kindergarten teacher. This is before she wrote *Sexual Politics*. Every summer he went to the Fillmore East one or two nights a week because it was in the neighborhood. So, he has pictures that nobody else has of Hendrix and the Doors and Janis Joplin, pictures of Warhol with his Brillo boxes in 1964.

JACKIE RUDIN: I became enchanted with Greenwich Village, and the stories Howard Smith told and the portrait he painted about the Village.

I found myself on St. Mark's Place in the Summer of Love. You'd go for a walk, and half the Village would come home with you and stay for a couple hours, which would become a couple of months.

I left New York; I hitchhiked to Martha's Vineyard. I was picked up with a carpetbag full of marijuana and peyote and mushrooms and acid or whatever. Whatever, a million things happened. I wound up in a Meher Baba commune—Meher Baba was a spiritual being, a guru. His whole thing was a vow of silence. I mean, I'm the most talkative person on the planet, and I wound up in a commune where nobody's allowed to talk. So, it was an adventurous time, you know?

SALLY KEMPTON: In the first couple of years that I was there, the younger generation were very focused on civil rights and music and acid and the late '60s downtown party scene, and the whole style seemed to change. It was an anything-goes downtown climate. And everything that flourished in that climate appeared in the *Voice*.

I was very much a Lillian Ross–style reporter. I did a lot of interviews and features on downtown art-scene characters, like Taylor Mead and the Warhol girls. I got to be very involved in an observer's way in the downtown art scene in the mid- to late '60s and early '70s. I ran into Warhol often. In the later '60s I hung out at Max's. I would hang out at a table with them. I was at the Factory a couple of times. I was doing fairly straightforward New Journalism from the beginning. I wasn't, certainly, as talented as Tom Wolfe or Gay Talese, but it was basically the same style of using fictional tools on factual stories.

The *Voice* was a bridge between the old bohemian Village, the Village as a significant political entity, and the Lower East Side scene that really came into its own in the '70s.

The *New York Times* or the *Post* or the *Daily News*—they were much more about people with jobs, people with working-class backgrounds or professional people. The *Voice* was for the oddballs.

RICHARD GOLDSTEIN: Drugs, I have the "White Rabbit" attitude, which is anything your mother gives you don't do anything at all. But anything that was illegal was intriguing. I had a friend who discovered that if you took the dried pods that were used in the Flower District to decorate, they were basically opium. So, we made it in the coffeemaker at the paper.

We had to add a ton of sugar. It was really bitter. We drank a lot of it, a whole coffeepot of it, and got high.

JOHN WILCOCK: Ed Fancher called me one day, absolutely furious that I was writing for both the *EVO* and the *Voice*, and demanded I choose one.

ED FANCHER: We fired him since he was writing for a competing newspaper. He had no right to expect we wouldn't.

Jerry Tallmer came in one day, and he said, "One of the editors of the *Post* has told me if I left the *Voice* and came to the *Post*, he would get me the job of being the theater critic, and I wanted to be a theater critic of a major daily paper, so I'm giving my resignation."*

But the editor who promised him the job of being a drama critic had no authority, and he never became the drama critic at all. Had Jerry told us that he needed more money we would have squeezed money out to keep him, 'cause he was a very valuable person, and we were all so upset.

They would give him some art openings to review. Odds and ends. He never really was a success at the *Post*. When Murdoch bought the *Post*, he kept some writers, and other writers he dropped. Jerry Tallmer was one.

ALAN WEITZ: Dan always joked that Jerry left just before the *Voice* made it big.

---

* Tallmer resigned in 1962, the same year he won the prestigious George Jean Nathan Award for Dramatic Criticism.

CHAPTER 7

"JACK NEWFIELD REALLY WROTE ABOUT THE THINGS THAT HE BELIEVED IN"

SUSAN BROWNMILLER: Jack Newfield was my rabbi. I knew Jack from East Harlem Reform Democratic Party politics.

SALLY KEMPTON: He was a great brother to me, because he would accompany me into these worlds, which I would have been too shy to enter myself. When Bobby Kennedy was a senator from New York, Jack would take me to Washington to hang out in Bobby Kennedy's office with the young staffers. One of the things about Jack that was very striking was that he always got involved with the people he was writing about. Jack was very much a part of the world of the people he hero-worshipped, from Bobby to Tom Hayden, and the whole spectrum of the civil rights left, the SDS* Left, to the version of the Left that Bobby Kennedy represented.

JACK NEWFIELD: In 1964 Kennedy ran for the US Senate in New York against grandfatherly Republican incumbent Kenneth Keating. I wrote a supportive article about Kennedy for the *Village Voice*, which I had just started to work for, describing a night of his campaigning in Greenwich Village. I admit that his celebrity status excited me—enough to call him "the

---

* Students for a Democratic Society, a nationwide New Left student-activist organization formed in 1960.

The cover of the *Voice* the week Robert F. Kennedy died. Cover image © Village Voice/ Street Media.

fifth Beatle." His rally remarks did not make much of an impression for their content, and indeed I was still not a Kennedy enthusiast in the fall of 1964. What persuaded me to vote for him was an essay Norman Mailer wrote endorsing him in the *Village Voice*.

NORMAN MAILER, "A VOTE FOR BOBBY K.—POSSIBILITY OF A HERO," *VILLAGE VOICE*, OCTOBER 29, 1964

The appeal of the Right, since it is emotional, will attract demagogues. I think Bobby Kennedy may be the only liberal about, early or late, who could be a popular general in a defense against the future powers of the Right Wing. For there's no one else around. The Democratic Party is bankrupt, bankrupt of charisma; the Right Wing has just begun. Anyone who was at the Democratic Convention in Atlantic City must confess—if they can afford to—that the mood was equal to a yellow jaundice ward on the banks of a swamp.

JANIE EISENBERG: Jack grew up in Bed-Stuy as a minority white person in a majority Black community. He went to Boys High School, he was very identified with Black people, Black issues. Jackie Robinson was a lifelong hero of his.

Even though Robert Kennedy came from a wealthy family, there was something about him that he felt that he could talk to both working-class white workers and Black people.

JACK NEWFIELD: In January of 1966 I completed my first book. Shortly after that, my editor proposed a second book project to me—a biography of New York's newly elected liberal Republican mayor, John Lindsay. I went back to my editor and said I had a better idea: a biography of Robert Kennedy, then starting his second year as the junior senator from New York. By the spring I had a contract and a small advance to write that book.

For a few months I read everything I could about him and covered him occasionally for the *Voice*. Kennedy was in New York frequently during the summer and fall of 1966, trying to elect a Democrat against Governor Nelson Rockefeller.

I was able to have lunch with him. We clicked immediately. We made each other laugh. We talked about music, sports, movies, writers, the antiwar movement, pot-smoking, the *Village Voice*, and my growing up in Bed-Stuy, which fascinated Kennedy, who grew up an American prince of privilege.

Most days he spent in New York City, I was allowed to tag along. I was the fly on the wall who took notes under the table. Kennedy knew I was working on a book about him to be published in the distant future. But I also wrote sporadic *Village Voice* articles about him and would tell him what quotes I wanted to put on the record. He never quibbled or tried to improve what he had said.

TIM MCDARRAH: There's a memorable picture Fred took of Robert Kennedy walking in a tenement with a Jesus Christ painting hanging behind him. It was a poverty tour on the Lower East Side. They went to 112 Stanton

Street, which was a tenement building, where Jacob Javits had grown up. As soon as they got into the apartment, Fred recognized the layout of the apartment because he had grown up in similar tenement apartments. So, he made a beeline to the kitchen, knowing that Kennedy was going to pass on the other side of the wall, down the hallway. There was an air vent on the top. So, he puts his camera up there. "Click, click, click." It's the iconic Robert F. Kennedy Jr. picture. It ended up running across the entire front page of the *Voice*, along with Newfield's story about the day.

MARY BREASTED: One day Newfield brought Bobby Kennedy to the *Voice*, and he wanted to bring him upstairs to meet Dan Wolf. Dan hid in a closet and said, "Tell him I'm not here." Dan had such a soft heart that when he met people, if he liked them, he wanted to help them—he realized he would lose his objectivity. He didn't want to submit to the Kennedy charm.

JACK NEWFIELD: I could balance these rather obvious conflicts of interest only because I was working for a paper like the *Voice*, which specialized in personal advocacy reporting and made no pretense of objectivity. Dan said I should just keep him, and the readers, informed with full disclosure.

When he announced [for president], I wrote a piece in the *Voice* endorsing him. Mine was not a popular position with *Voice* readers or among liberal intellectuals, most of whom were for McCarthy.*

The primary season came down to California. Before the sun rose on June 4, I started to drive around Los Angeles with a couple of Kennedy campaign workers. By about 8:30 p.m. we were all gathered on the fifth floor of the Ambassador Hotel. Kennedy and his family and a few advisers were in room 511.

I wanted to avoid the crush of people. John Lewis, a close friend of mine—he and I stayed behind to watch the victory speech on TV. We watched it on television in the hotel. And then we ran downstairs when we realized that shots had been fired.

JANIE EISENBERG: Kennedy's death changed his whole way of thinking about the kind of journalism he wanted to do. He wanted to stay local,

---

* Presidential candidate Eugene McCarthy.

because that's where he felt that he would have the most influence in terms of changing things that he thought were wrong.

JACK NEWFIELD: In September of 1968, Dan gave me a nine-month leave of absence from the *Voice* to write my book on Robert Kennedy. When I came back, Nixon was president, the civil rights movement was a ruin, and the Vietnam War was still expanding. During my leave I had read, for the first time, *How the Other Half Lives,* by Jacob Riis, and Lincoln Steffens's autobiography, the two seminal works of urban American muckraking. I had already read, and been affected by, Mike Harrington's *The Other America.*

ALAN WEITZ: The first battle I remember him waging was over lead paint. From there, he moved on to the worst landlords. Jack was a muckraker.

JANIE EISENBERG: Paul Du Brul was a union organizer who went to Hunter around the same time that Jack was there. He had cystic fibrosis. He was a very radical activist, and got Jack interested in the lead-poisoning issue. Paul was from the Bronx.

JACK NEWFIELD: For a month I immersed myself in the science of lead poisoning. I became like a method actor, using sense memory—meeting the parents of victims of the disease, listening to bureaucrats tell me it was impossible to draw a blood sample from a one-year-old, attending a meeting of seventy-five doctors and nurses at Judson Church, and then going by subway with Paul up to the ill-named Tiffany Street in the South Bronx, to meet Brenda Scurry, whose twenty-three-month-old daughter, Janet, had died of lead poisoning that April.

My day with Brenda Scurry became the launching pad for five lead-poisoning articles I would write over the next four months. I took the subway back to the *Voice* office and that afternoon and evening wrote five thousand words in the white heat of fresh emotion. Dan read it and put it on the front page.*

---

* Newfield's series on lead poisoning prompted Mayor John Lindsay to start the first lead-prevention program in an urban area.

CHAPTER 8

"WHAT HE WAS DOING WAS VERY IMPORTANT FOR CINEMA AND FOR THE ARTS"

ANDY WARHOL: The Film-Makers' Coop was run by a young Lithuanian refugee by the name of Jonas Mekas. It was in a loft on the corner of Park Avenue South and 29th Street, across from the Belmore Cafeteria, where the cabbies hung out day and night. And day and night there were screenings going on at the Coop.

JONAS MEKAS: I landed in New York in the fall of 1949 when the new forms of cinema, arts, and styles began to emerge. Classical theater was ending, "happenings" were appearing. In music John Cage is appearing. In dance, there is Yvonne Rainer, also Erick Hawkins. That's the end of the old Balanchine–Martha Graham, and even the theater was in transition with Marlon Brando, Kazan, and the new styles of acting. The Actors Studio began having a real impact. And the same in cinema. Everything was changing. The Beat generation is coming in. Some new wind was blowing there. Not clear yet, not defined, but it's emerging.

ANDY WARHOL: You have to understand where Jonas came from, though, to understand his attitude toward movies. For him, they were like political art. I doubt that he ever once thought of a movie as entertainment. He was one of those people who are serious about everything, even when they laugh.

Anthology Film Archives opening, November 30, 1970: Michel Auder, Jonas Mekas (center), Andy Warhol. Photo © Gretchen Berg.

The farm he was born on in Lithuania got taken over by the Soviet Union when he was seventeen. Two years later the German army pushed the Soviets out, and the Nazis came along. All during the German occupation, he was involved in underground publishing. When he and his brother, Adolfas, were about to be arrested by the military police, somebody gave them fake papers so they could get into the University of Vienna.

Jonas didn't learn a word of English until after the war. Once, when I asked him how he got so interested in film, he said, "To write in a language, you have to be born to it, so I could never really communicate through writing. But in films you work with images, and I saw that I could use something other than written language to shout about what had happened to me and everyone else in the war."

JONAS MEKAS: I was very excited because when you come from a desert from wartime and five years of displaced person camps, suddenly you are in the middle of *everything*. I have to see everything, every new theater piece, every new music, every poetry reading—I was there! I saw Allen Ginsberg and Robert Frank, and, of course, Erick Hawkins and Carolee Schneemann.

I was working in a photo studio in Manhattan, and during lunch we used to hang around, go out and buy papers, and eat. There was between those six, seven, or eight daily papers—there suddenly appeared this little rag, eight pages or something, at the beginning.

I was working eight hours and ten hours in the photo shop for money. With my salary money I could publish *Film Culture* magazine. The first issue came out December '55. So, three years later I was ready to expand a little bit.

When I noticed that there was no column on cinema in the *Voice*, I went and I said, "How come you have no movie column?" And from there on every week, I turned in my column on time. I did that from '58. We were moving into a busy period for the independents, but also for commercial cinema. Nouvelle Vague was coming in and the New York school of filmmaking was coming in with Shirley Clarke, Morris Engel, a lot of people.

AMY TAUBIN: Jonas was one of the first film writers that really understood that this was a real, separate art form. And within it, there was the avant-garde.

ANDY WARHOL: As De [director Emile de Antonio] told me, "Jonas is very clever, particularly at promoting himself. He took over that movie column in the *Voice* at zero pay, which was what the *Voice* paid in those days, because he realized it was a good place to pull together a huge following." Which it was.

AMY TAUBIN: It's very hard to describe Jonas in any way. It would be easy to say he was a saint, and it would be just as easy to say he was a total control freak. Both are true. He was extremely poor. He had no source of income except whatever he was getting for the *Voice* column, fifty dollars, and so there were a bunch of people who were determined to keep Jonas eating. Richard* and I regularly had Jonas to dinner.

JONAS MEKAS: Until I began writing for the *Voice*, people did not know that the screenings were taking place in ten, fifteen different film societies in New York. About '58 there were at least ten showcases in New York for the independents, and nobody knew it except the filmmakers themselves. But I

---

* Foreman, her then husband and a playwright.

began writing, "You have to go and see that and that, there and there." Finally, those films gained more visibility, and the filmmakers were more excited.

ANDY WARHOL: When the independent filmmakers grouped together in '59 to form the New American Cinema Group, the organizing force behind it was Jonas Mekas. Out of what survived, Jonas created the Film-Makers' Cooperative.

JONAS MEKAS: The Film-Makers' Cooperative was created in January '62 so that the films were available. Between 1960 and '70, when the American Film Institute brought out their catalog of their universities with film courses, you had twelve hundred that were showing our films.

JIM FOURATT: Jonas documented so much of Andy from the beginning.

JONAS MEKAS: He used to come to my loft. He was not famous when I met him. And some of his early superstars he met there, like Jack Smith, or Taylor Mead, Mario Montez, all those people. It was a meeting ground for many artists and filmmakers. And then when he began making films, I was already running a filmmaker's cinematheque. I had rented a little theater and he needed space to show his films, so that was part of the friendship. I had the theater, he had films, and he needed the theater.

That was Andy's film school. Nobody took his work in cinema seriously except me in the press. Almost every column I was mentioning him. But he deserved it, because what he was doing, it was very important for cinema and for the arts.

JONAS MEKAS, MOVIE JOURNAL, *VILLAGE VOICE*, AUGUST 13, 1964

It is the work of Andy Warhol, however, that is the last word in the Direct Cinema. It is hard to imagine anything more pure, less staged, and less directed than Andy Warhol's *Eat, Empire, Sleep, Haircut* movies. I think that Andy Warhol is the most revolutionary of all film-makers working today. He is opening to film-makers a completely new and inexhaustible field of cinema reality.

AMY TAUBIN: Jonas lent him his 16-millimeter Bolex camera. Jonas had open screenings once a week; anyone could go and bring a roll of film and show it. There were no titles on Andy's films, and then the first thing he showed, in the context of avant-garde film, I remember seeing this—it was like a revelation—it was the *Kiss* series. They were 16-millimeter films, shown in slightly slow motion, of two people kissing for the length of a roll of film, which is two and two-thirds minutes, from end to end, and they were ravishingly beautiful.

No one wrote about the Warhol films, just Jonas, until Vincent Canby got to the *Times*.

ANDY WARHOL: David Bourdon started writing on art for the *Village Voice*. When I'd heard they were looking for an art person, I'd introduced him to the *Voice* theater critic, Michael Smith, who I knew from the San Remo/ Judson Church crowd.

Meanwhile, the phone at the Factory was ringing more than usual because we'd just put an ad in the *Voice* that read, "I'll endorse with my name any of the following: clothing, AC-DC, cigarettes, small tapes, sound equipment, rock 'n' roll records, anything, film, and film equipment, Food, Helium, Whips, money; love and kisses Andy Warhol. EL 5-9941."

TIM MCDARRAH: Warhol and my dad were quite friendly. Andy would call here at least once a week because he would want the publicity. My dad has more pictures of Warhol than of anybody else that he ever took.

LUCIAN K. TRUSCOTT IV: I knew all the Warhol transvestite super-stars. I was friends with them. They were fantastic people. Holly Woodlawn and Jackie Curtis.

The *Voice* ran a famous cover. Alice Neel, the artist, did portraits of War-hol and Anaïs Nin. She did these very strange Alice Neel cadaverous-looking portraits. They were pretty famous at that moment; they were in a show. So, the *Village Voice* put them side by side, and the typesetters switched the names. It was a misprint, but it was hilarious. The printer did it. And the way that Alice Neel had done the art, they looked like twins. And Warhol, Jackie Curtis told me, that was his favorite picture of himself—to be transposed with Anaïs Nin on the cover of the *Village Voice*.

AMY TAUBIN: When people think of the '60s as being so liberal, the first half of the '60s was really, really hard. Jonas wrote about this constantly, about censorship, and Jack Smith not being able to show *Flaming Creatures*, this great work of art. He must have ten columns.

JONAS MEKAS, MOVIE JOURNAL, *VILLAGE VOICE*, APRIL 18, 1963

Jack Smith just finished a great movie, *Flaming Creatures*, which is so beautiful that I feel ashamed even to sit through the current Hollywood and European movies. I saw it privately, and there is little hope that Smith's movie will ever reach the movie theatre screens. But I tell you, it is a most luxurious outpouring of imagination, of imagery, of poetry, of movie artistry, comparable only to the work of the greatest, like Von Sternberg.

Flaming Creatures will not be shown theatrically because our social-moral-etc. guides are sick. That's why Lenny Bruce cried at Idlewild Airport. This movie will be called pornographic, degenerate, homosexual, trite, disgusting, etc., home movie. It is all that, and it is so much more than that.

AMY TAUBIN: I was there at an early screening of *Flaming Creatures*. *Flaming Creatures* is a largely transvestite and transsexual orgy, although there were straight women there and straight men presumably. It's just a large orgy that's almost impossible to see because it's shot in high-contrast black and white set to various pieces of music by Tony Conrad, who was also involved with the avant-garde and was the great inspiration for Andy Warhol's films. It looks somewhat like art nouveau but in high-contrast black and white, and all the famous drag queens at the time are in it, and Jack is in it as well. And in the middle of it, there is a rape of a woman; it's a playacted rape. There was a while when I got extremely scorched-earth feminist and denounced *Flaming Creatures* because of the rape in the middle because it was kind of terrifying.

It's about thirty-five minutes. It's also extremely funny. It ends with "Be-Bop-A-Lula."

This went all the way to the Supreme Court, the *Flaming Creatures* case. It's the film which Susan Sontag defended by writing "Notes on 'Camp.'" It's a famous case; it's obsessed Jim Hoberman for his entire life.

J. HOBERMAN: I wrote a book about this. I know everything. The movie got into trouble because there's nudity in it; of course, it's the male nudity that is much more problematic for the authorities, even to this day. It could never have been licensed by the state.

There were all these prints of *Flaming Creatures* that have been confiscated at various places because SDS would use it, because it was guaranteed the administration would try and shut it down and call the police, and then there would be a riot, the students would get upset. SDS used it as a political tool.

It's shot on outdated film stock so it's very ethereal. It just doesn't look like anything else.

AMY TAUBIN: That was around the time of the censorship of people like Lenny Bruce.

JONAS MEKAS: Because the laws of censorship were still in existence in New York, every film shown publicly had to first be submitted to the Board of Licensing, and licensing permits had to be issued. Certain things that were not allowed to be seen on screen and certain parts of the human body were not permitted. Any sex activities could not be shown—cut it out, that's it. You cannot show gay film.

And I thought, "This is ridiculous."

My lawyer, who was a criminal lawyer, told me, "We are still in a period of censorship where you could get up to two, three years," so it was not a joke. The lawyer, whose name was Emile Zola Berman, was very well known. The judges that sentenced me had great respect for him, so I ended up with six months of suspended sentence.

It was normal to be arrested in those days. I was not the only one. There was Lenny Bruce, for performances. There was so much discussion provoked by the arrests that eventually, within the next two years, the licensing was abandoned. So, it was not for nothing.

AMY TAUBIN: The funniest story about *Flaming Creatures* is, as this case wound its way through the courts, Abe Fortas, who had been nominated for the Supreme Court, he had said, "This was not censorable." So, the people who were against Fortas in the Congress demanded that they see *Flaming Creatures*, and so *Flaming Creatures* was shown to the United States Senate. The ones that came and didn't fall asleep, they pronounced it disgusting because you saw penises, but they weren't erect.

J. HOBERMAN: They called it the Abe Fortas Film Festival. These senators went to see it at some, like, basement office in the Capitol or something, and one of them came out and says, "That movie was so sick, I couldn't even get aroused."

CHAPTER 9
"IS THIS OBSCENE?"

NAT HENTOFF, *VILLAGE VOICE*, SEPTEMBER 3, 1958

Some three weeks ago, a French-horn player, Negro, made arrangements by telephone to play four weeks in a small orchestra subsidized by the government of Ocean City, New Jersey. The horn player had been unemployed for some time; and had been bitter longer, since he has been trying to break through the racial barrier that exists for sidemen in classical music. . . . It was instantly clear by his arctic receptions that he'd be back in New York the same night. He even had to argue to get transportation money. The authorities preferred there be no French horn that night rather than have a Negro in the orchestra.

NAT HENTOFF: What could a jazz specialist know about education or civil liberties or politics? I broke through the stereotype occasionally, but not often enough to be able to stop scrambling to make the rent. At last, and unexpectedly, I was given a chance to break through.

STANLEY CROUCH: Of all the American arts, jazz is the only one that took a fierce public stand against racism and segregation in the 1930s, almost twenty years before the civil rights movement began, right? For a guy like Nat, all of those things would fit together.

JESSICA HENTOFF: I remember him coming to me when I was young and explaining that he was going down to Alabama to march with Dr. Martin Luther King, and explaining to me that it was really dangerous, but that he felt he had to go.

NAT HENTOFF: My own antiwar activities brought me, directly and indirectly, into contact with J. Edgar Hoover's Federal Bureau of Investigation.

NICK HENTOFF: I'm sure that every major person at the *Voice* had an FBI file.

JESSICA HENTOFF: Jazz led him to writing about civil rights, which led him to writing about civil liberties. And it was all one piece to him.

ED FANCHER: One of the things he started writing about was the press. Press criticism more or less. We liked that very much.

NAT HENTOFF: I got very interested then in the First Amendment. I heard about Lenny Bruce from Ralph Gleason, who was a jazz critic and also wrote a general entertainment column for the *San Francisco Chronicle*.

JULES FEIFFER: I was out in California supposedly talking to someone about writing a movie, and I knew Mort Sahl, slightly, and he invited me to hear Lenny Bruce do a show in Pasadena, and I went. I'd never seen his act; I thought he was just a dirty-mouthed comedian.

Lenny just brought down the house. I was screaming with laughter; I thought he was extraordinary and wonderfully inventive and funny. When he was in New York, I'd go to clubs all the time and hang out with him afterwards backstage. I liked him. I knew he was a force to be reckoned with. He was changing the nature of what was acceptable and not acceptable.

NAT HENTOFF: His many arrests around the country for alleged obscenity culminated in a trial in New York City. Before the trial started, Lenny told me, "If this bust holds, my working life is over, because if you're convicted in New York, club owners everywhere else are not going to take the chance of booking me."

JULES FEIFFER: Lenny was a friend. We didn't socialize a lot, but we liked each other. When he was put on trial for obscenity, Martin Garbus, one of his attorneys, asked me if I would testify. The defense wanted me to come on and defend Lenny as somebody who was a respected humorist. The prosecution decided they wanted to set me up as the *good* humorist and the *clean* humorist in the *Village Voice*, as opposed to the bad, dirty-mouthed humorist on the nightclub floor.

The prosecution's approach to all of the friendly witnesses, except me, was to attack them and be hostile to them, as they were to Nat. But when I got on, they started courting me with love. So, I went around to the best I could, feeling sandbagged by this approach. It wasn't going very well until the prosecutor started quoting lines from Lenny's act, and said, "Is this obscene? Is this obscene? Is this obscene?" And of course, they were obscene.

I said, "I can't judge them from what you say." And he said, "Well, did he say these things, or didn't he say them?" And I said, "Well, they were clearly tape recorded." And word for word they were accurate, but that doesn't mean anything. I said, "To see Lenny and to understand Lenny, you have to see him in person, you have to see his presence. He's a lot like Sinatra, you have to get a sense of the artist at work before you can understand the context in which he's working."

NAT HENTOFF: When he was busted in San Francisco for using "cock-sucker" in a skit, the arresting police sergeant said to him, "I can't see any way how you can say this word in public. Our society is not geared to it." Lenny looked at the sergeant and explained, "You break it down by talking about it."

I testified as somebody who knew something about the First Amendment. I'd gotten Lenny a very distinguished First Amendment lawyer, Ephraim London. He practiced before the Supreme Court. He wasn't quite used to what it was like in the trenches, in these lower courts. Lenny was convicted, and his career went down, down, and down. Great civil libertarian Governor Pataki gave him a posthumous pardon.

JULES FEIFFER: After Lenny's prosecutions, he stopped what made him so useful, which was his social and political and cultural commentary and his observations and became more like a jailhouse lawyer defending himself before the audiences.

Basically, they won. They shut him up from being this brilliant observer and unrivaled social and political and sexual satirist to just being a commentator on his own problems.

NAT HENTOFF: I wrote a three-piece series in the *Village Voice* about— not the Lenny Bruce trial, but how it was arranged, the people in the office, the assistant DAs who wouldn't take it.

I got a call from Robert Morgenthau. He had been the former US attorney [for the Southern District of New York]. And he said, "I've been reading those articles about Lenny Bruce. Is what you wrote about Dick Kuh, is that factual?"* And I said, "Look, I'll give you the backup."

He then said, "I never thought about running for district attorney, but now I'm interested." So, I gave him all the backup, and that's why Robert Morgenthau became the longest-serving district attorney in New York.

A midlevel New York state court reversed Lenny's obscenity conviction in February 1968, and the state's highest tribunal, the State Court of Appeals, confirmed that reversal in January 1970.

In the months before Lenny died on August 3, 1966, he had no jobs and spent his time writing about his case. On the day he died of an overdose on morphine, he had found out that he was going to lose his home. Lenny could not understand why he had become an international pariah as well as a criminal at home. "What I wanted people to dig," Lenny used to say, "is the lie. Certain words were suppressed to keep the lie going. But," Lenny insisted, "if you do them, you should be able to say the words."

---

* Richard Kuh served as the New York County district attorney from February to December 1974 and prosecuted Lenny Bruce for obscenity when he was assistant DA.

CHAPTER 10

"I CALL HIM THE FIRST ROCK CRITIC"

RICHARD GOLDSTEIN: I started reading the *Voice* in the late '50s, early '60s, before I got to college, even. I was a very alienated kid, sexually confused and all of that. I spent my time reading Dostoevsky and singing doo-wop; I had this dual identity where I loved rock 'n' roll and its sexuality, especially. It made me feel manly to sing with the Italian kids, and then the other part of me was the part that was alone by himself, reading literature, where I had my friends in the books.

I read "Howl" many times to myself, and would gravitate toward anything involving beatniks, and tried to dress like a beatnik. Although, I had to be careful in the Bronx because the kids thought it was some kind of treachery. I read James Joyce on Orchard Beach for a whole summer once and started to write stories of the Bronx in his style, which one cannot duplicate.

Along came the Beatles. In my book I said 1962, but Bob corrected me.

ROBERT CHRISTGAU: Goldstein's memory is absolutely the worst.

RICHARD GOLDSTEIN: It was '64. That's what made me want to be a rock critic. I wrote this article for the Hunter paper called "The Second Jazz Age," in which I predicted that the Beatles would usher in a new jazz age. I was on the staff of the college paper. It's now Lehman College, but then it was part of Hunter.

I got an interview at the *Voice* through Jack Newfield. At the end of the year, when you get your degree, they interview you and they say, "Well, where are you going?" "The *Village Voice*. I'm going to be a rock critic." And they said, "How much are they paying?" "Well, twenty dollars an article." They were apoplectic. They said I was bringing the whole earning curve of the class down. I was delighted.

I covered a concert at Yankee Stadium called Soundblast '66. The bill on this concert was Stevie Wonder, the Beach Boys, the Young Rascals, Ray Charles. I wrote the article, I gave it to the *Voice*, and when the paper came out on Wednesday, there it was on the front page, out of nowhere. No drug rush has ever affected me as intensely as that. From there I wrote another one and another one, and within a very short time I had a column, which I called Pop Eye.

ROBERT CHRISTGAU: Do I remember seeing a column called Pop Eye that was about rock 'n' roll? Yes, I sure do. Rock 'n' roll was considered teenage music and all that bullshit. Ellen Willis and I were delighted, completely delighted, that this was happening.

RICHARD GOLDSTEIN: I had no models. There were no rules. One day I got called into the office with Dan and Ed. "You're doing interesting work. Do you have to use so many four-letter words?"

My third article, I got to meet the Rolling Stones. There was a press event on this boat because no hotel would have them. They rented a yacht in the boat basin on 79th Street, in the Hudson. I spent an afternoon on that boat. It was about thirty, forty reporters and them. I was in awe of every performer that I met, without exception. And with the Rolling Stones, I barely could get any questions out. Charlie Watts came up to me and said, "Don't be nervous, ask your questions."

Charlie Watts took mercy on me, and I didn't look like a professional, I damn well did not. I looked like a guy from the Bronx with long hair. I was overweight, too. I was very cherubic-looking. My favorite letter was one saying, "How clever of you to hire a fourteen-year-old rock critic."

I was so shy that a lot of these performers felt that they could open up around me. I was able to get extraordinary quotes from people.

Once *Sgt. Pepper* appeared, rock 'n' roll had officially arrived in the haute monde, in the upper world. And suddenly every hip person, adult, had to know about it. Then my column really took off.

ROBERT CHRISTGAU: I grew up in Queens. I became aware of the *Village Voice* because I listened to this famous, notorious, late-night radio raconteur named Jean Shepherd. He's most famous for the film *A Christmas Story*. He believed in nonconformism, which in the '50s was a big deal. Jean Shepherd had a column in the *Village Voice*, and so I mailed off two bucks for a six-month subscription, and it began coming in the mail to my parents' dismay.

RICHARD GOLDSTEIN: Rock criticism began when working-class people with an education, the first of their family to be fully educated, discovered a cultural force that they had known as children that they loved, and elevated it into an art.

ROBERT CHRISTGAU: My girlfriend's father was a cop; I grew up among cops. An "antibohemian bohemian" is what I started calling myself a long time ago. I was never really a bohemian. I was a sloppy guy who liked cheap apartments and the arts, and who was very left-wing politically as the '60s progressed.

Commentary called me up and asked me to write a piece about the Free University. The Free University was this supposedly hippie organization that was, in fact, a secret, clandestine project of the Progressive Labor Party, the Maoist party. But it had a big open house, probably the first week of February. And I went, and Paul Krassner* was spieling—like the stand-up comedian he, among other things, was—and people were laughing, and somebody tapped me on the shoulder. And it was Ellen. I hadn't seen her since we graduated from junior high in 1955. She recognized me. And after Krassner was done, we talked, and we fucking hit it off. She had moved to New York, was working for Ralph Ginzburg's *Fact* magazine and it was basically at the Free University, to meet guys. Obviously, she was a leftist. I started talking to her about pop. It was a very, very deep mutual attraction. She was in journalism. I was in journalism. She didn't take it as seriously as I did. My spiel was journalism was a way to be an artist. This would have been in February of '66.

Marion Magid at *Commentary* had asked if I would write about Bob Dylan, and I wasn't a big Bob Dylan fan, but Willis was. They gave her the assignment, and then she worked on that piece for months. And it turned

---

* Countercultural author and satirist Krassner was a member of Ken Kesey's Merry Pranksters, a founding member of the Yippies, and founder and editor of *The Realist*.

out to be the first great seminal piece of rock criticism and was reprinted in *Cheetah*, where we both worked. William Shawn saw this piece and called her up and asked her to be the rock critic at the *New Yorker*.* Ellen saw more nuances than I did because she had this incredible concept-generating brain, like I've never encountered in anybody else.

RICHARD GOLDSTEIN: In 1966, it was a relatively small readership of people who liked this music.

There was a small group of people who loved rock and who were journalists, but serious, well-educated people. The ringmaster was this guy Danny Fields, and we hung out a lot together. This was a misbegotten crew that I hung out with. One of them was a photographer: Linda Eastman—i.e., Linda McCartney. Gradually, I realized that she had this legendary reputation among musicians, especially Brits, of being the greatest groupie in New York. They were very high status. They were like courtesans. If a British group came through, she would take me along on her shoots. While she was setting up she would say, "Talk to him." And the message was, if you want me to be with you, talk to him. I was amazed when she actually took up with Paul McCartney.

CARMAN MOORE: I felt a little above them because I was musically educated. And they were fans, you know. But I was happy to see that music taken seriously.

RICHARD GOLDSTEIN: I like to tell people the Velvet Underground played at my wedding. How did I get to meet the Velvet Underground? The answer was that Lou Reed knocked up a friend of mine, and we had to help her get rid of the fetus. He owed me, and so he got me entry into the Warhol discotheque. I saw Warhol sitting on the balcony, and I went up and introduced myself. I wrote about them just because I had access to them, and I certainly liked their music—although I did not like Nico. I once wrote that she sang like a moose in heat.

We were a little tight-knit circle of devotees who had been college-educated, and we're not going to ask these people, "What is your favorite color? What is your ideal date?" That's what they were used to. So, if

* Shawn was the *New Yorker* editor in chief from 1952 to 1987.

somebody came in and really wanted to talk about their ideas and their sense of the music, they would open up like a flower being watered.

RICHARD GOLDSTEIN, POP EYE, "CREAM: THEY PLAY BLUES, NOT SUPERSTAR," *VILLAGE VOICE*, OCTOBER 5, 1967

Backstage, the Cream wait in a barren dressing room with two broken chairs. There are eight of them, direct from England: Eric Clapton, Jack Bruce, Ginger Baker, and an entourage of wives, road managers, and friends. Clapton is England's most acclaimed blues guitarist. . . . "I can't get into a jazz musician's head," says Eric Clapton. "That music has a whole tradition we're not into. At the Fillmore, we were booked with Gary Burton, and that was very nice, because he complemented us."

He shrugs, tossing a mane of tumbleweed-hair. "You know, jazz is a very dirty word in England."

ROBERT CHRISTGAU: I call him the first rock critic. It's arguable, but I call him that. Jann Wenner was writing pretty close to when he was.* And then there was also Paul Williams at *Crawdaddy*, who predated both of them, but in a zine, not in a commercial publication.

RICHARD GOLDSTEIN: Whether that is or isn't the first rock criticism, I don't really care that much. I wasn't aware of *Crawdaddy*. I wasn't influenced by them in any way.

Some of these people don't like the idea that their profession was founded by a faggot. Not all of them, but some of them.

LENNY KAYE: Rock 'n' roll before *Crawdaddy* was mostly talked about in terms of teen magazines. And what happened with *Crawdaddy*—and then by extension the writers at the *Village Voice*—became a way to discuss music in a more adult fashion.

The best rock writers wrote about the music on the same level as the music. They wanted you to experience the music as music as opposed to

---

* Wenner is the founder of *Rolling Stone* magazine.

what it became, which would be more journalistic and record reviews and taking sides, stances, something as a rock writer I, of course, was guilty of myself.

There was a celebration of the music's potential as an art form. And the sense that this wasn't just teen fodder was really important, too. It happened at the same time as rock 'n' roll became progressive and more aware of itself as a cultural force.

ROBERT CHRISTGAU: Ellen and I would go to the Apollo every once in a while, and we found an Indian restaurant, which at that time there weren't any, right below where Richard lived in Morningside Heights. He and Judith, his wife, met us there. We hit it off. Well, he was into pop and so was I. Ellen and I were developing this theory in which we connected pop art to pop music and tried to politicize it.

My big journalistic coup was a piece called "Beth Ann and Microbioticism" at *New York*. That ended up in Tom Wolfe's journalism anthology.

ELLEN WILLIS: He got enough attention for that piece that he was able to quit his job and start freelancing. I was watching his trajectory, and this was at a time when there was an incredible amount of excitement and ferment, and journalism and magazines were very much open to experimenting.

RICHARD GOLDSTEIN: I couldn't do my column anymore at a certain point. Bob was a very worthy successor, because he was extremely adept as a critic, and genuinely progressive, and dedicated to the music in a much more systematic way than I was. He carried on the tradition and made it much richer than I did.

ROBERT CHRISTGAU: I took over his job, but as far as I'm concerned, he's Ellen's greatest living disciple. I had just been canned at *Esquire*. Goldstein told me he was sick of writing about rock 'n' roll, so I said, "Well, I guess I'm not doing this just for the money because I'll do it for the *Voice*."

Dan Wolf did hire me on the fucking spot. He had that gut thing. He found a lot of good writers. I met him in '69. My hair was long, and I'm sure I looked like a hippie out of water, which is what I was. I never was a hippie, but I did wear my hair long. And I'm pretty brash.

Richard Goldstein circa 1967. Photo courtesy of Richard Goldstein.

I was making five hundred bucks for a two-thousand-word column at *Esquire*, which in that time was pretty good. When I came to the *Voice*, what am I going to get—forty bucks?

I embarked upon the most significant career move of my life: a *Village Voice* column called Rock & Roll &.

CHAPTER 11
"WE WERE THE HIPPIE GENERATION"

JIM FOURATT: At its very peak—the '60s, '70s, '80s—the *Village Voice* was the go-to place to find out what was happening in music, film, local politics, national politics, books, what was happening in the art world. The *Voice* had the cultural elite.

LUCIAN K. TRUSCOTT IV: I was up there at West Point, and I had bought a copy of the *Village Voice* in '64, when I was seventeen. I rode my bicycle across the country with another guy who was also seventeen, and we started out by going to the World's Fair. So, we were staying in New York, and we went down to the Village, and I bought a copy of the *Village Voice*, and I just thought, "What an amazing fucking paper." They had all the listings of the clubs and cafés and theaters, so I subscribed to it so that when I went to New York I'd know what to do.

I read one of the very first articles about Abbie Hoffman, and Abbie Hoffman said a bunch of outrageous shit. So, I sat down at my desk at West Point and wrote a letter to the editor of the *Village Voice* that read the following: "Abbie Hoffman is an asshole." Signed, Lucian K. Truscott IV, West Point, New York. And they ran it—number one in the letters section! The next week I got attacked by Aryeh Neier, by Paul Goodman—fucking half the New York intelligentsia *laid* into me in the letters column. I thought, "These guys are full of shit." So, I wrote a letter the next week. They ran the letter. I didn't write weekly, but I wrote a lot.

On Christmas Day, there was an ad in the *Voice* for an event happening at the Electric Circus, and it was Wavy Gravy and the Hog Farm. I wandered over there and paid two dollars at the door and went in and watched

Before and after (1965 and 1972):
Lucian K. Truscott IV stars in a
Voice ad, 1972. Photo courtesy of
Lucian K. Truscott IV.

this—what I came to call "hippie fascism." You know, "You better have fun or else" attitude.

I went back to this place where I was staying with this girl, and she had a typewriter. I sat down and wrote a letter to the editor for the *Voice*, and I was describing the whole scene, and the letter got longer and longer, and then I thought, "Well, what the fuck." I was in New York; I didn't have to mail the fucking thing. I put it in an envelope and put "Letters to the Editor" on it and walked over to the *Voice* on a Sunday and nobody was there. So, I shoved it under the door, and then Wednesday the paper came out and they ran it on the front page.

SUSAN BROWNMILLER: Dan was really tickled that this was a person from West Point, from a family of generals.

RICHARD GOLDSTEIN: These letters would arrive signed by Lucian Truscott IV. There was no "fourth" anything at the *Village Voice*. Eventually, they invited him to the Christmas party. And he showed up in his dress uniform with sneakers. Suddenly there was this West Point cadet in the middle of the room at the Christmas party.

LUCIAN K. TRUSCOTT IV: I had my uniform on, I got on a bus, went down to New York, went down to West End Street, went over to Ed Fancher's apartment, hung up my fucking overcoat, hung up my hat, knocked on the door, and nobody answered. But I could hear this loud party going on inside. I opened the door and I hit Mayor Lindsay on the elbow, and he spilled his drink on Bob Dylan. There I was. I walked in there, and the next thing I knew somebody grabbed me and said, "You're that crazy fucker from West Point who's writing those letters." All these people were arguing with me.

I wanted to meet Wolf and Fancher because their names were on the invitation. It took me about an hour to fight my way through this fucking big crowd of people into the back room of that apartment. I walked up— somebody pointed them out to me—I had no idea what they looked like. I looked over and standing along this bookshelf was Wolf, Fancher, and Mailer. They were standing there greeting people and talking. I waited in line to talk to them. I introduced myself to one of them. He said, "I'm Dan Wolf. I'm the editor of the *Voice*, and it's very nice to meet you. I've really enjoyed your letters. By the way, I served in the Pacific as a rifleman in the infantry company." He introduces me to Ed Fancher standing next to him, and Fancher says, "I'm really glad to meet you. As for me, I served in the 10th Mountain Division under your grandfather in Italy in World War II." I said, "Holy shit!" I said, "That's why you guys are running my letters?" Wolf said, "No, that's not it at all. We're running your letters because it lights up the fucking letters column." Fancher told me the letters column was the most read page in the *Village Voice*.

I said to Fancher, "Jesus Christ. I've been Lucian Truscott IV for twenty fucking years now, and I've been trying to get away from that legacy and that general. Here I am, I'm going to the *Village Voice* party on West 10th Street. I'm as *far* as I can fucking get away from my family and my legacy and all this shit, and you were in the 10th fucking Mountain Division. I give up." They all laughed and Fancher introduced me to Mailer, and Mailer said, "I was in the infantry, too!"

ALAN WEITZ: I first met Lucian when he was still in the army. And then he started coming around the *Voice* more and more. He was discharged from the army, and his friend was John Kerry, Vietnam Vets Against the

War. Lucian was funny. He always wore cowboy boots. He would wear this suede-fringed western jacket. He would walk into the fourth floor of the *Voice*, where the writers were, like someone walking into a bar.

HOWARD BLUM: For some reason, Lucian carried a cane that was given to his grandfather, maybe by Eisenhower. His grandfather was General Truscott, and the cane turned into a sword. There was a blade, you pulled it out. He was picked up with it in the East Village. He was thrown into jail. I remember Dan helping to bail him out.

LUCIAN K. TRUSCOTT IV: I used to come down on Fridays, when I had time off from West Point. I get out of class at three o'clock, get a ride down to New York, get down to the *Village Voice* by about four, four-thirty, go up to Wolf's office, and get a chair and sit next to his desk and watch people come in and turn in their copy because Wolf would get out a bottle of scotch in these little paper cups. Michael Harrington would put his fucking copy down. Then Michael Smith was coming in. Then Leighton Kerner would come in and turn in his review of classical music. Then Feiffer would come in and hand in his cartoon. As they came in, they'd sit down and Wolf would pour scotch, and people would stand around and pull chairs in from other offices and sit around and talk.

All of that shit went on until about seven o'clock, and then Wolf would venture, "Boys, we're going out to the theater"—or going out to an opera, or going out to a play, or going out to see a movie, or going to dinner with somebody. I remember thinking to myself, "Man, look at the lives that they lead." Christ almighty. It was just heaven on earth.

RICHARD GOLDSTEIN: He ended up being a staff writer and he was wonderful. Absolutely wonderful. We formed this little phalanx because we were peers from the same generation, as opposed to most of the people who were older than us from a prior beatnik generation. We were the hippie generation, the counterculture generation.

There was a third person in our group called Don McNeill. He was my closest friend at the paper. He was the saint of the paper. He was from Alaska. His father was a journalist, so he was Don McNeill Jr. Don was a pacifist, and he had lanky black hair. I had a big crush on him, but nothing ever happened between us. We became very close friends. The three of us, I remember us being very close.

LUCIAN K. TRUSCOTT IV: Don was generous to a fault. There'd be so many people coming and crashing at his pad somewhere that he would move out and go in the Gramercy Park Hotel for a week at a time, just to get away from the scene he was in. His mother said he used to call her up from his hotel room and lament about his life because he couldn't control it.

JIM FOURATT: Don McNeill and I were good, good friends. He was like Dan Wolf's son, not in any patriarchal way. Dan saw in Don the future. Don was twenty-two years old, and he followed all the stuff that we did and wrote about it in the *Voice*, and he is one of the unsung heroes of that cultural moment.

I was a hippie trying to get people to drop back in and stop the war. Don McNeill did the big story about the Tompkins Square Park massacre. A bunch of hippies were in Tompkins Square, probably smoking weed, and the cops went in and beat the shit out of these kids. That became a big story. Don was in the neighborhood when it was happening. Don was generationally so right for reporting on the world of the hippies and politics that existed then. To Dan Wolf's credit, he gave this twenty-two- or twenty-three-year-old kid that beat.

Then there was the Groovy murder, the young woman from Connecticut and the hippie guy named Groovy. At the end of the park on 10th Street there was a building, and some hippies were crashing in the basement, and she got murdered. That was a big story. There was the "Death of the Hippie" march, both in San Francisco and in New York. The one in New York went across St. Mark's Place, and a casket was carried.

LUCIAN K. TRUSCOTT IV: He had a real sensitivity to the scene that he was covering and the people that he covered. And he also saw that it was headed for a big crash. He knew that the hippie thing was about an eighth of an inch deep and about half a mile wide, and it was headed for a cliff. He was quite skeptical about people like Wavy Gravy. He was skeptical of the hippie thing. He saw the people that were exploiting it already. It broke his heart a little bit because he wanted it to be what it said it was. And he was close enough to it that he saw it wasn't. He was right in the middle.

RICHARD GOLDSTEIN: Then along came Abbie Hoffman and the Yippies to try to politicize hippies and make them into revolutionaries. I said to Don, "You have to cover this growing politicization of hippies." He said,

"No, it's not going to be the revolution. The revolution is consciousness."
There was a whole faction that believed that it was only about consciousness,
not politics. Consciousness, as in acid-expanded consciousness. And the
more people who do acid, the more people are attuned to this expanded view
of being human. And eventually, as more and more people took acid, the
country would change and there would be no more wars and there would be
just gentleness and love, a lot of love, sex, which was something that hippies
took very seriously. This was genuinely utopian. Many people believed that
you couldn't have a revolution by having an uprising. You needed to expand
your consciousness and then get others to do the same.

I said, "Well, look, go to one demonstration and then cover that." This
was a demonstration at Grand Central Station. It was March '68. He got a
press card just for that story. And there was a riot in the middle of Grand
Central Station in the big hall. The police moved in, and they started beating people left and right. And they took Don, and they threw him head-
first through a plate-glass window. They split his head open. He came back
to the paper dripping with blood, and his picture ran on the front page
with him bleeding, and his bloody press card hung in the editor's office.
This event for Don was devastating. It just wiped him out. It wasn't that serious an injury. He needed stitches. But after that, he was so depressed. He
had completely lost his spirit. I said, "We'll both go and cover the Chicago
convention."

DON MCNEILL, "THE GRAND CENTRAL RIOT: YIPPIES MEET THE MAN," *VILLAGE VOICE*, MARCH 28, 1968

All the brass was watching, and the cops were having a ball. "It was the
most extraordinary display of unprovoked police brutality I've seen outside of Mississippi," Alan Levine, staff counsel for the New York Civil
Liberties Union, said at a press conference on Saturday. "The police re-
acted enthusiastically to the prospect of being unleashed." Levine reported
seeing several people forced to run a gauntlet of club-wielding cops while
trying to flee from what has been characterized as a "police riot." Spitting

invective through clenched teeth, cops hit women and kicked demonstrators who had fallen while trying to "escape the flailing nightsticks." It was like a fire in a theater.

RICHARD GOLDSTEIN: A couple of weeks before Chicago, Don went to visit somebody's country house, and they took acid. The guy who owned this house seduced him. And Don had never had that kind of an experience before, and he walked into a lake and drowned. The guy told me this story. I was so angry with him. You do not give someone acid and then give them their first gay experience and leave them. You don't do that. But he did.

JIM FOURATT: I don't know if you know about Paul Williams, but he wrote a number of books. His office was above the IFC Theater on Sixth Avenue. And *Sing Out!* magazine was in that office, which was the folk rag of record. Don and Paul Williams were very good friends. He and Paul had rented a place. They weren't gay, but I think they were lovers in some kind of way. They were just two smart white guys who loved rock 'n' roll and were journalists.

RICHARD GOLDSTEIN: He was fully clothed. He walked into the lake, and it was considered an accident. But I knew the real story, and I've always believed it was suicide. It is ambiguous because maybe he didn't intend to die. But he was still high and said, "You know what? I'll go into the lake."

But that sequence, the acid, the gay experience, the drowning—in my mind it was hard to believe that he didn't do it deliberately. And just out of the general despair he was feeling at the state of the counterculture in those days, which was becoming extremely violent as it got more political.

LUCIAN K. TRUSCOTT IV: Nobody saw that suicide coming. I still had a week or two before I went back to West Point, and his parents came to New York to get his things. I got to be fairly close with his parents because I was staying with him when he died. I helped gather up all of his things and all of his papers. He had all these notes and every story he'd ever written and scraps of novels that he was working on. It was really sad. I was really broken up. I really liked him. His mother told me that everybody liked him a lot.

Why did I think he was gay? I talked to his mother about that. I think his mother knew. It's a spectrum. I don't think that it was guilt. I think it was untenable, in some peculiar way. He couldn't figure how to live as himself and still do what he was doing.

They had a big memorial service for him. I went to it; it was at St. Mark's in-the-Bowery. Everybody came. Ed Sanders, the Fugs, Abbie—Christ almighty, everybody in downtown came.

RICHARD GOLDSTEIN: It was the only time I ever saw my colleagues cry. The whole church was full of people crying. He was a symbol of the paper, and he died. So, I went to Chicago alone.

CHAPTER 12
"I WAS SHOCKED BY WHAT I SAW THERE"

JACK NEWFIELD: Don's death hit Dan Wolf hard, but this reaction seemed out of proportion. Dan, as he grew more conservative, began to feel guilt over his own contributions to the excesses of the 1960s. I suspect he felt this guilt most sharply in the area of drugs. The paper had glamorized the counterculture of be-ins and Woodstock and making drug use seem cool and risk-free. It had made Timothy Leary into the guru-huckster of acid. Dan knew that too much drug abuse created casualties and zombies. I knew this, too, and though I smoked an occasional joint, I didn't make an issue out of all the pro-drug stories in the *Voice*.

Dan should never have lost his pride in the glory of this writing by young writers he had selected and nurtured.

RICHARD GOLDSTEIN: My column ceased being much about music at a certain point and really became about politics. I covered riots and rebellions and all of that. In 1966, I was in Chicago, and I heard that Martin Luther King was doing a housing march in Chicago, so I went to it, and I wrote about it in the *Voice*, and I watched Martin Luther King get hit by a rock and fall. We were in a bus. The crowd was so violent that the police said, "Go back in the bus and leave." The bus was leaving, and on the sidewalks there were piles of rocks that people were throwing at the bus. I saw nuns throwing stones, and every window in the bus was broken. We had to hide under the seats to get out.

LENNY KAYE: I had my own crossing of paths with it in '69. It was always my custom to go up to the Easter be-in at Sheep Meadow. There was a girl there who was obviously high on something. And she started dancing and taking off her clothes, and a crowd formed around her. And then they started kicking at her and attacking her. And it really disturbed me. I went home and I wrote an article. I put it under the door of the *Village Voice*, and they published it on the front page.

I was shocked by what I saw there. It chilled me to the bone that these people would take advantage of this poor girl who was obviously spaced out, and they moved in on her and soiled this vision that I had of the counterculture. This was a turning point for me, too. I think the first line was, "I saw . . . am seeing a girl murdered today." Perhaps that's what the editors at the *Voice* saw, that this was an honest expression of realization that the alternative culture was not going to have an easy time of it as the '70s began.

RICHARD GOLDSTEIN: I had covered the Columbia University student strike, and I had seen dozens and dozens of people with long hair clubbed. That was in my head, and then Don's suicide, and then Bobby Kennedy's assassination and the riots and all of that. I was completely destabilized, just completely. A nutcase.

I went out to Chicago. I decided I'm not wearing the press card anymore. I want to go just as a protester; I'm not going to be a professional in any way. I got a motel room. But I stayed in the park with the protesters.

The city had a curfew; they had twelve thousand cops on duty. There were only about twenty-five thousand demonstrators, but twelve thousand cops, plus the National Guard, plus Secret Service men, and FBI men in plainclothes. All of a sudden, we pass the curfew, this flood bank of orange lights from trucks come on, and hoses are pouring tear gas on the crowd. And when you get gassed, if it's not directly in your face, it's just in the air, it will get your adrenal glands pumping madly, so you go out into the streets ready to completely smash things.

I have a wet T-shirt around my face because I was told that it would mitigate the effects of tear gas. I had Vaseline because it wards off mace. I had a helmet that the *Voice* had issued to us, after Don McNeill got his head split open. I look just like a protester. I see people ahead of me getting clubbed. I see this in slow motion. Fortunately, if you're going to club somebody, you look for a big person, because they're easier to spot.

I went back to my motel, and I fell asleep. I woke up and turn on the set. It's night now. And the whole world is watching the police closing in on the demonstrators in front of the Hilton. I knew seeing it on TV that this was history-making. It was more dramatic than the real thing because it was on TV.

RICHARD GOLDSTEIN, "THEATRE OF FEAR: ONE ON THE AISLE," *VILLAGE VOICE*, SEPTEMBER 5, 1968

Watching these kids gather sticks and stones, I realized how far we have come from that mythical summer when everyone dropped acid, sat under a tree, and communed. If there were any flower children left in America, they had heeded the underground press, and stayed home. Those who came fully anticipated confrontation.

RICHARD GOLDSTEIN: I thought, "I'm becoming addicted to rioting." It replaced rock 'n' roll in my life. It's the same feeling of complete exhilaration. I thought, "I can't be like this." So that was the last time I ever did something like that.

I've always thought that the millions of people who participated in the movement in one way or another understood, on some level, that there was a danger of the country collapsing, and they stepped back from the brink.

CHAPTER 13

"I SURE HOPE THOSE PEOPLE GET THEIR RIGHTS"

TIM MCDARRAH: Stonewall was four doors down from the *Voice*.

RICHARD GOLDSTEIN: The Stonewall bar was known as the bar for people who couldn't function in other gay bars because they were "shabby," or they were too "femmey." Or they were drag queens, or they were Black.

SUSAN BROWNMILLER: This wasn't a regular gay bar. This had the drag queens from New Jersey. That was their bar.

LUCIAN K. TRUSCOTT IV: I stumbled into that Stonewall thing. I was going to the Lion's Head one night and just walked right into that riot because it was right next to the Lion's Head. The Lion's Head was where *Village Voice* writers and all kinds of writers went to drink.

When I was living there in that summer of '69, that's where I went in the evenings. I turned off of Waverly Place, turned left on Christopher. And right there in front of me was a large crowd of people and a couple of cop cars. They had just busted the place. They hadn't taken anybody out of there in cuffs yet, but the bust was ongoing; there were cop cars with lights going outside. So, a crowd was gathering. That was on Friday night.

JIM FOURATT: I was working at Columbia Records for Clive Davis. I was coming home; I'd worked late. It was about 10:30. I lived on Waverly Place, which was a block and a half away from Christopher Street. And I saw a police car in front of the Stonewall. I was a '60s radical; I knew the straight template of radicalism. And I go, "What's that cop car doing in front of that sleazy bar?" It was a really fucking sleazy bar. They romanticize it.

An unidentified group of young people celebrates outside the boarded-up Stonewall Inn (53 Christopher Street) after riots occurred over the weekend of June 27, 1969, leading to the formation of the modern gay rights movement in the United States. Photograph © Fred W. McDarrah/MUUS Collection.

RICHARD GOLDSTEIN: We knew that the bar was a Mafia bar and that payoffs were being made. But when the riot happened, they forgot to make the payoff, or they decided not to. That's why the police came and raided the place. They didn't pay off the cops.

JIM FOURATT: There wasn't a single gay bar that was not paying off the cops. It was institutionalized. The door policy, the price of the drinks, the watering down of the drinks, certainly with the Stonewall, they had no hot water to clean glasses with, they watered down the alcohol. This is standard practice.

RICHARD GOLDSTEIN: My gay roommate took me to Julius', which was a gay bar. It was mobbed up in those days like most of the bars. There's a sign, it says, "Gentlemen must face the bar." "Why is the sign here?" People are dancing, all of a sudden, a red light goes on and everybody separates. The police would let the bar know, because they paid them, that they were about to do a raid. So, then the bright light would come on, and everyone would be just guys in a bar. It was a crime to sell a drink to a homosexual in New York City—that's why the Mafia ran the bars.

HOWARD SMITH: That night I'm in my office. I looked down the street, and I could see the Stonewall sign, and I started to see some activity in front. So, I run down there, it's getting bigger by the minute. And the people coming out weren't going along with it so easily.

JIM FOURATT: The door opens and out comes a cop with this . . . well, the nice word would be called a "passing woman." It was the nice term for bull dyke, very masculine, very butch lesbian. She's short, and she's stout, and she's all dressed in men's clothing, and she looks Italian. I see them taking this butch passing woman, put her in the police car. I don't know what the fuck is going on. The cop goes back inside. She's rocking the car back and forth, and one of the doors was unlocked and it pops open, much to her surprise. She comes out and starts throwing her bulky body against the police car. And it starts to tip. And now we're maybe fifty people, and we're cheering.

LUCIAN K. TRUSCOTT IV: And before you know it, they pulled the paddy wagon up right there by the door of the Stonewall, they started bringing people out in cuffs, and they were manhandling them and being rough with them. And the crowd started yelling, "Fuck you, cops!"

JIM FOURATT: Something happened that fundamentally changed me forever. I got in touch with my internalized homophobia that I have layered over. I looked at the other people that were in the street and on the sidewalk, and most of them were young gay men.

There was so much cheering. I can only describe it if you're in the middle of a dance floor and you have a great DJ, who's building, building, building to a peak moment and then—whoosh—cuts the sound, and everyone is cheering. That's what was happening outside.

LUCIAN K. TRUSCOTT IV: I was standing there watching. Somebody threw a handful of pennies at the cops, and all of a sudden everybody reached in their pocket and started grabbing change and throwing pennies, and they were yelling at the cops, and saying, "You're not worth two cents!"

And then they brought out this drag queen, who it turned out was Marsha Johnson. And they brought her out in cuffs, and so she stopped on the street just short of the paddy wagon and struck a pose. And she was calling out to people, "Come down to the Tombs and bail me out."

And this cop pushed her, and she turned around to the cop and said, "Hey, give me a minute." And the guy took a nightstick and stuck it in her back and *really* shoved her right into the back of the paddy wagon. And that was it. That was the thing that set it off.

People started rushing the paddy wagon. The cops shoved her in and slammed the door, and the paddy wagon drove off, and the cops retreated back into the Stonewall. And then the next thing I knew somebody had picked up a paving stone, threw it through the window.

MICHAEL SMITH: By then the *Voice* had taken the floor of the building next door to that little triangular building on the corner of Sheridan Square. I had an office that looked right out on Sheridan Square, three doors down from the Stonewall, when that happened, and that whole scene happened right in front of my eyes.

RICHARD GOLDSTEIN: We were in the office working, and we all went to the windows to look at the spectacle that was going on. Mind you, there were riots every week in that neighborhood. This was just another riot as far as I could ascertain.

I turned to my colleagues and said, "I sure hope those people get their rights."

I wasn't hiding; I had no idea that these people had anything to do with me. I was married, I was going out with women; once in a while, it would be a guy. But I didn't want to be gay.

HOWARD SMITH: It really should have been called Stonewall uprising. They really were objecting to how they were being treated.

SUSAN BROWNMILLER: It was the first time that the gays had resisted.

LUCIAN K. TRUSCOTT IV: Me and Howard went up into the *Voice* office. The *Voice* had a couple police press passes. He went up into Wolf's office, and he got one police press pass for me and one for him.

JACKIE RUDIN: Howard Smith did the Scenes column. He was a crazy guy that just had his nose in absolutely everything. He would find out about things way ahead of everybody else. He was in Stonewall that night it happened, locked in with the police.

HOWARD SMITH: At a certain point, it felt pretty dangerous to me, but I noticed that the cop that seemed in charge, he said, "You know what, we have to go inside for safety. Your choice, you can come in with us or you can stay out here with the crowd and report your stuff from out here." I said, "I can go in with you?" He said, "OK, let's go." He pulls all his men inside. It's the first time I'm fully inside the Stonewall. It was getting worse and worse. People standing on cars, standing on garbage cans, screaming, yelling. The ones that came close, you could see their faces in rage.

LUCIAN K. TRUSCOTT IV: I was outside, he was inside. Somebody lit some newspapers and threw it in the front of the window. It had a glass window that said "Stonewall" on it, and there was plywood inside. And that was very typical of gay bars back then. People that went to gay bars didn't want to be seen, so they would block the windows.

HOWARD SMITH: There were little tiny pinholes in the plywood windows. We could look out from there, and every time I went over and looked out through one of those pinholes, we were shocked at how big the crowd had become. They were getting more ferocious. Things were being thrown against the plywood; we piled things up to try to buttress it.

TIM MCDARRAH: Lucian and Howard called the second night, and Fred went out. It was only a two-minute bike ride from the house; he goes over there, and he takes about nineteen pictures of the Stonewall riots. Fred was the only photographer at Stonewall.

LUCIAN K. TRUSCOTT IV: Fred walks up and says, "Lucian, where's the fucking riot?" And he looks at his watch and he says, "I got a dinner party to go to. Look, just get some of these guys together and put them on that stoop over there."

So, I went and gathered up those guys that are in that iconic picture. Fred stepped up about four or five feet, held up his little fucking camera, and shot like two frames and left. That's how that picture got taken. Fred was notorious for that. That famous photograph he took of Bob Dylan on a bench there in Sheridan Square when he was about nineteen or twenty years old? Somebody told me once that Fred showed up for that shoot right about the time Dylan's first album came out and took like two frames and just walked away. He was famous for being parsimonious with his film.

TIM MCDARRAH: People would come into the *Voice* literally every day trying to promote their book or music or whatever it was. He had a habit of taking one single solitary frame of the person, because his thinking was, you never know what's going to happen to them. One of the people was Valerie Solanas, who ended up shooting Andy Warhol. She came into the *Voice* one day. She was the basic nutty person coming in off the street, ranting and raving. The picture of Valerie Solanas was one of the few pictures of her that exists. That's how it was with Stonewall.

JEFF WEINSTEIN: Howard Smith wrote a ridiculously homophobic report about Stonewall. The *Village Voice* did not do a good job with Stonewall, except for Fred's photos, which are still important records. And he didn't do any interviewing. He's lazy.

HOWARD SMITH, "FULL MOON OVER STONEWALL," *VILLAGE VOICE*, JULY 2, 1969

The detectives locate a fire hose, the idea being to ward off the madding crowd until reinforcements arrive. They can't see where to aim it, wedging the hose in a crack in the door. It sends out a weak stream. . . .

By now the mind's eye has forgotten the character of the mob; the sound filtering in doesn't suggest dancing faggots anymore. It sounds like a powerful rage bent on vendetta.

RICHARD GOLDSTEIN: Did Lucian tell you that he referred to the "forces of faggotry"? He meant it as a witticism.

LUCIAN K. TRUSCOTT IV: The lede that I wrote was some lame attempt to be clever. There we were, the sophisticated *Village Voice* in 1969, and Wolf and Michael Smith and the rest of the people there thought it was clever. They ran it. No, nobody said, "Oh, we shouldn't do this." Enough of a consciousness had not been raised enough at that point. Gay people themselves were using the word "fag" all the time. I quoted Allen Ginsberg saying "fag" in the story.

I got the words "gay power" in there because they were shouting, "Gay power." It came right off of "Black power." I should've had a line in there saying, "This is the Rosa Parks moment for gay people," but we didn't know that.

I knew some gay guys in the Village, and I ran into a couple of them on Sunday night. They were watching from a distance, and they were amazed. In the story, Allen Ginsberg said he'd never seen anything like that before.

LUCIAN K. TRUSCOTT IV, "GAY POWER
COMES TO SHERIDAN SQUARE,"
VILLAGE VOICE, JULY 2, 1969

The forces of faggotry, spurred by a Friday night raid on one of the city's largest, most popular, and longest lived gay bars, the Stonewall Inn, rallied Saturday night in an unprecedented protest against the raid and continued Sunday night to assert presence, possibility, and pride until the early hours of Monday morning. "I'm a faggot, and I'm proud of it!" "Gay Power!" "I like boys!"—these and many other slogans were heard all three nights as the show of force by the city's finery met the force of the city's finest.

MICHAEL SMITH: I edited Lucian Truscott's story about the Stonewall riots, which he treated rather flippantly. There was not a sense that this was—to us anyway—a significant event at the time. It was kind of ridiculous. He used the phrase "the forces of faggotry" in that story, which I let him do, and the gays took violent exception to it and started protesting and marching back and forth outside of our windows. We had the glass windows right on the corner on the street. It was scary. We felt like we were under siege.

RICHARD GOLDSTEIN: But compared to the other coverage, the *Daily News* headline, "Queen Bees, Stinging Mad," or the *Times* referring to a "homosexual haunt"—now they're much more enlightened, don't you know? Because a lot of ads come with enlightenment.

A group formed in the wake of it called the Gay Liberation Front. They believed that gay liberation could only occur in the context of revolutionary socialism.

JIM FOURATT: I called Bob Christgau, who was teaching a course at Alternate U. on rock and revolution. Bob said, "I'm teaching tomorrow night, but if you can't find a space you can have my room. I'll tell the class that we're not meeting there." The Gay Liberation Front was founded in that room on the third night of the Stonewall rebellion.

RICHARD GOLDSTEIN: Within it, a large group decided, no, we need our own movement. This has nothing to do with world revolution. This is just homophobia, and we need another organization that focuses only on gay issues. They formed the Gay Activists Alliance.

The Gay Activists Alliance prevailed. There was a derelict firehouse in SoHo on Wooster Street. They took it over and held dances in the firehouse. There would be a political meeting early in the evening and then a dance, and this was the origin of disco. That organization became the dominant gay organization, and then they started to have zaps. "Zap" means an invasion of an oppressive institution. They zapped the *Times*; they zapped the *Voice* on more than one occasion.

JIM FOURATT: The *Voice* was precious to us; we didn't expect the *Voice* to be our enemy, quote-unquote. One of the first actions of the Gay Liberation Front—we wanted to put an ad in the classifieds advertising a gay and lesbian dance. And the advertising director said, "But we don't use the words 'gay and lesbian.'" The editorial side would use the words "gay and lesbian." It was only when the classified department refused to run an ad—that may have been our first demonstration: against the *Voice*.

LUCIAN K. TRUSCOTT IV: One of those two groups demonstrated outside the *Voice* that week against the use of the word "fag" in that story. They had a demonstration right out there on Christopher Street and Seventh Avenue. They had a few handwritten signs, and they were yelling, "Stop saying 'fag.'" And somebody came inside and demanded a meeting with Dan Wolf, and Dan Wolf was sitting up there, "Well, should I meet with them or not? If I don't meet with them, they're going to be out here for days." A couple of guys went in, and Dan met with them, and he said, "OK, we won't say 'fag' anymore." And once they got the *Voice* to say, "OK, we won't say 'fag' anymore," it went from there to the *New York Times*.

MICHAEL SMITH: Dan and Ed called me in to be at that meeting, and they complained about the *Voice*'s attitude and said that there were no gay people on the *Voice*. And I said, "I'm gay," which I was at that time. That slowed them down a little bit.

It was hard for the *Voice* to figure out how to deal with that. When Dan was the editor of the *Voice*, he skated a thin line; he really didn't want the paper to become "the voice" of any faction. But they realized that they needed to open up to the gay issue.

TIM MCDARRAH: A month afterwards, in July of 1969, they had the first gay rights march, which was pretty significant, because if you were gay in the late '60s, you didn't tell anybody.

Somebody said to Fred, "You were at the equivalent of the battle and the first shot over Lexington and Concord that started the American Revolution. Why did you only take nineteen pictures?" And my dad goes, "Who knew?!"

LUCIAN K. TRUSCOTT IV: I didn't realize what was happening. Nobody did.

CHAPTER 14
RUNNING SCARED

JERRY TALLMER: Mary had the kind of anger that made abolitionists.

CLARK WHELTON: Robert Caro was a reporter at the *New York Times* and wanted to get the goods on Robert Moses. But Moses wouldn't talk. And Caro had a little bit of this and a little bit of that. He could put together a small story, but he could never get the big story. Then in 1965, with *Village Voice* support, John Lindsay won the mayoralty in New York City, and because the *Voice* supported Lindsay, he made Mary Nichols an assistant parks commissioner.

ROBIN REISIG: The reason Central Park has the Park Drive that makes a circle within the park was two people—Mary and Ted Diamond, it was their idea. Nobody'd ever closed the park to traffic before then.

CLARK WHELTON: One of her jobs was to look around and get a feel for the whole place. The Arsenal up on Fifth Avenue in Central Park—she got into a storage area under Central Park itself. There was an iron door built into a stone wall, and she said, "What's behind there?" And they said, "Oh, it's just a bunch of old records and things." She said, "I want to see it."

She was very curious, very nosy person, great newswoman. So, they opened the iron door, and there is the cave-like, gigantic room, full of file cabinets with papers. She started opening the filing cabinets, and lo and behold, they're the files of Robert Moses—all the goods on Moses, all his correspondence—because he had been parks commissioner at one time.

She dials the phone and said, "Bob Caro, have I got a surprise for you. Meet me in Central Park."

MARY PEROT NICHOLS: I went back to the *Voice* after two years in the Lindsay administration. I was very interested in all these inner-city, or inter-urban expressway, fights around the country, and I wrote about them a lot.

DIANE FISHER: When she came back from Parks, she became city editor.

MARY PEROT NICHOLS: I got bored. I also got to dislike Lindsay. Shortly after Lindsay became mayor, he betrayed us on the Lower Manhattan Expressway. And two weeks after he became mayor, he switched, because David Rockefeller was his largest contributor.

ELIZA NICHOLS: She totally tore him apart in Running Scared.

LUCIAN K. TRUSCOTT IV: It was just little six-line, four-line things, you know—"Did you hear? Tony Scotto was in this restaurant in Brooklyn, and he had dinner with Carlo Gambino's third cousin." All this kind of shit, you know.

MARY PEROT NICHOLS: One good advantage of being in the city government is that you've met a lot of officials you wouldn't meet as a reporter that you could call in a friendly fashion. So, when I got to this top guy in the City Planning Commission, I said, "What does this report say?" They decided to suppress it.

He gave me just enough that I could run a little front-page story about it and say that the Lindsay administration was suppressing the rest of it. Then I called up Ed Koch. I said, "Ed, you want to be famous?" Again. Of course he wanted to be famous. Ed held a press conference with the report and released it. So, it was the lead blow, almost killed the Expressway. But Lindsay had lost the Republican primary and needed the Reform Democrats desperately at this point. All these Reform Dems had no idea what to ask for from Lindsay, so I wrote a long piece on what they should ask for in the *Village Voice*. Since they were hollow people, I figured, well, I'll give them a program. I included killing not only the Lower Manhattan Expressway, but the Cross-Brooklyn Expressway.

ROBIN REISIG: Mary and Arthur Bell lived the movie *Dog Day Afternoon*.* The guy in the bank, as he was robbing it, called up Arthur Bell, wanted him to get the mayor there.

ELIZA NICHOLS: Arthur Bell was one of the first openly gay reporters.

---

* Sidney Lumet's 1975 film, which starred Al Pacino and John Cazale, is based on Bell's story about an August 22, 1972, bank robbery. Bell knew one of the robbers from the Gay Activists Alliance. The film won an Academy Award for Best Original Screenplay.

ROBIN REISIG: Arthur and Mary went out to the scene of the bank heist. And Arthur was kind of a negotiator, somehow became an intermediary.

ELIZA NICHOLS: She was training people to do the work. Most of those people were very young and had not been journalists before.

LUCIAN K. TRUSCOTT IV: She had her door open all the time. I could hear her bellowing into the phone, cackling and laughing. She would call people up, one after the other. "He said that?!" She'd write it down, laughing. She was real brassy and fun to be around. But she could be a real pain in the ass. I don't think she ever gave me an assignment to cover something I really wanted to cover. But I was a staff writer. That's what you did.

ELIZA NICHOLS: She was very proud of the journalists that she mentored and hired and who went on to do well. Mary Breasted went off to the *New York Times*. Lucian Truscott became a well-known writer; Howard Blum went on to big things. Annette Kuhn became the arts and culture person for the mayor of New York.

MARY BREASTED: She had a little tiny office—this is when the *Voice* was over in Sheridan Square, in that corner building that came to a point. I sat on a chair by her desk. Everything was a mess, piled up high. And we just immediately hit it off. We shared a sense of humor. She had endless curiosity; she knew about everything. After this conversation, she said, "OK, Breasted, I have an assignment for you."

CLARK WHELTON: All the press releases arrive—thirty, forty a day— one after the other. I would go to Mary's office, and there she would be, with a stack of envelopes, reading every word in every press release. She would underline certain things and put it over on the to-do pile. She could make connections between seemingly unrelated events. That allowed her to write great stories.

HOWARD BLUM: She liked to drink a lot of beer and go to the movies. I had a girlfriend, Annette Kuhn, who wrote for the *Voice*, and she was very close to Mary. Mary would go to movies with the six-pack of beer and a salami and would sit there, finishing off the beer and the salami.

ALAN WEITZ: She wanted to establish a morgue at the *Voice*—an old newspaper term for going down to the basement where all the files are kept. So, Mary would wake up, have breakfast, read the papers, bring in the papers for me to clip. We started making a morgue about various political issues affecting New York City. As my editorial duties increased, and as I wrote more and more about politics, sometimes she actually had me write her Running Scared column, which was wonderful. Four years before, I was a mail sorter, and now I'm writing about the mayor and the commissioners and all that.

ROBIN REISIG: On Thursday nights three nights of the month, not the fourth, she would have parties. Mary's parties could sometimes be odd because you didn't know who'd show up. It might be all artists one week; it might be all Conservative Party members from the outer boroughs another; it might be the mayor and the district attorney another night. The fourth Thursday was the community planning board meeting.

ELIZA NICHOLS: There was one night where James Baldwin and Frank Serpico were there at the same time. And my mother told Frank that he had to leave. He was totally paranoid at the time because he thought he was going to be killed, and he had a knapsack full of guns, and she said, "You have to put them in the closet; there's no guns allowed in my house."

HOWARD BLUM: That's how I first met Serpico and David Durk—they were two cops involved in [exposing] police corruption. You were able to develop sources. You could be a kid of twenty and have better sources and know people on a social level than people at the *Times* who were reporters. It was very handy to me when I went to the *Times*.

ELIZA NICHOLS: My mother was a specialist at the connections between the Mafia and government and corruption. People feared being outed by her in that column. The reason Lucian knows the story about the Mafia's involvement in those bars is because my mother had been doing investigations into the Mafia.

LUCIAN K. TRUSCOTT IV: She put me on the Roy Cohn beat.

ELIZA NICHOLS: There was a guy she sent to prison, Anthony Scotto— racketeering conviction. She had a lot to do with him being convicted.

ROBIN REISIG: He was famous in New York, he was a labor leader, very respected, friend of the mayor. He showed up at the fancier parties that union leaders don't usually show up at, and she wrote a story saying he was a capo in this crime family. Three powerful male columnists wrote columns attacking her. At least, Jack Newfield, Murray Kempton, and either Pete

Hamill or Jimmy Breslin, probably Hamill. And years later, FBI wiretaps were released, and it was all true. She said the only one who ever apologized was Murray Kempton.

LUCIAN K. TRUSCOTT IV: Being gay was basically illegal. That's why the gay bars were owned by the mob. They wouldn't license a bar owned by homosexuals because the State Liquor Authority code had a so-called morals clause in it. The first gay-owned bar that got its own license happened because of the *Village Voice* and Mary Nichols.

The guys who ended up owning the Ballroom, a gay cabaret, originally opened on West Broadway. Mary Nichols knew one of the guys that was gay and wanted to get a liquor license, and he couldn't get it.

Mary knew an agent for the State Liquor Authority. This guy was straight, but he thought it was ridiculous that all the gay bars were mob owned. Mary said, "Look, why don't you do a story on how all of these Italian restaurants in the Village have got real gangsters hanging out in them?" I'd been telling her that I'd been seeing all these mob cars on Friday nights. I lived on Houston and Sullivan, and I saw them all over the neighborhood outside of these conventional Italian restaurants. She said, "You get the license numbers and I'll give them to this SLA guy, and we'll have him run the licenses." Then I wrote the story saying, "They won't give a license to the Ballroom, the mob owns all these gay bars, but these fucking straight Italian restaurants have got Carlo Gambino and we got the names of these guys."

Mary and the guy from the SLA went in to see the head of the SLA. Mary Nichols handed him the article and said, "Either you license the Ballroom or that article runs on fucking Wednesday."

They licensed the Ballroom, and we never ran the story.

ALAN WEITZ: As the *Voice* grew, our libel lawyer's work grew. Mary and Jack Newfield took up most of his time.

ELIZA NICHOLS: Vinny "the Chin"* was in our building. So, when he moved in, she said, "I can't write about him. Because there's a code of ethics that the Italians follow, and I can't break that code." When you live under the same roof, you can't betray somebody who lives under the same roof. So,

---

* Vincent Gigante was a Mafia boss of the Genovese crime family who was convicted of racketeering, extortion, and conspiring to murder another Mafioso, John Gotti.

she went to him, and she said, "You know who I am?" And he said, "Yes, I know who you are." She said, "I just want you to know, now that you moved into the building, you're my neighbor, and I will not write about you."

That was about protection, too. Everybody was connected, right? Not everyone was pro-Mafia. But they all had connections. We had that SWAT team across the street on the roof. The feds rented apartments across the way. They were listening in on everything in his apartment.

She would send me out in the morning to walk the dog, and I would follow the bookies so that she would know which establishments were actually bookmakers. For a while, once a week she would get a butcher's hook in the mail. There'd be somebody who we nicknamed Deep Throat because he had a gravelly voice and it was around the time of Watergate. This guy who would call me when she wasn't there and ask me where she was. And then he would proceed to remind me that he knew my name. He knew my dog's name. He knew where I went to school. And he would say, "Tell your mother."

His job was to scare her, and her job was not to be scared. But I was scared. I was a kid; I was fucking terrified. And she would say, "Don't worry, the Italians have a code, and my name is Mary, and they won't kill you. They might break a few bones." She was deadpan funny.

When she died in '96—and I had come back to take care of her because she had cancer and I was pregnant—I was riding up the elevator, and one of these Italian guys came in that was connected. He looked at me and he said, "Your mother?" I thought, "What the fuck is he going to say?"

He said, "She was all right. She was a real lady."

CHAPTER 15

"CARTER BUYING THE PAPER DIDN'T SEEM LIKE A BIG DEAL"

ED FANCHER: Dan was nine years older than me. He was fifty-four years old. His father had died at the age of fifty-four of a heart attack, and he needed to get some money. He'd worked for years without very much money, so we sold it to get some money. We agreed to sell controlling interest to Carter Burden, a wealthy, young man-about-town who seemed to be very liberal and sounded like the right kind of person. The agreement with Carter Burden—Dan Wolf and I would run the paper for five years. It was an unspoken understanding that he was not going to be selling it to somebody that we didn't like.

HOWARD BLUM: Dan was very charmed by Carter Burden. Carter Burden had great glamour, a certain charisma, and endless money. And Dan was going off with him to the Harvard Club.

MARY BREASTED: He was good-looking, blue-eyed, and he kept his blonde hair combed straight back. He was a Vanderbilt, and his wife, Amanda, was the daughter of Babe Paley and William Paley, who was head of CBS. They were a big couple. Amanda's mother was a big, big, big hostess, socialite beauty. She and Carter were very happy for a while. He was restless. He might have liked to have been a writer. He was maybe wanting to go into politics, but he was too blue-blood to make it big in politics. He was interested in what was hip and what was cool. He was searching around to try to find his way. But he loved writers and writing. He had an amazing collection of books, so he was pretty smart. And he loved Dan.

ED FANCHER: The last minute, Carter brought in Bartle Bull. He said he would like to learn to be a publisher. He became my assistant publisher for five years. And Bartle had an office in the building I was in. There was no agreement that Bartle would take my job, but he really wanted it. So, at the end of the five years, I was out, Dan was out, and Bartle Bull would become the publisher of the *Village Voice*.

HOWARD BLUM: Bartle Bull, who turned out to be an extremely smart and generous-of-spirit man, came in and antagonized the *Voice*. He pulled up in an Aston Martin with a bull as the hood ornament. Then he came in with the cowboy boots to show he was hip. But once you got to talk to him, he was absolutely lovely, fascinating, and kindhearted.

MARY BREASTED: I did a long profile of Carter Burden when he was running for the city council, and I handed the piece in to Dan. I didn't know anything about Carter approaching Dan to buy the *Voice* at the time. Carter was an interesting, conflicted candidate; he had worked for Bobby Kennedy and then started a political career of his own. But he always seemed like a Henry James character, reluctant to be too involved in the world.

I went out with Carter Burden. He came after me in the fall of 1971. He was separated from his wife. So, I put him off for a while because he was publisher of the *Voice* and because he was married. And then he just beat me down.

I didn't make it known. I was already in discussions with the *Times* about going to work there. I thought, "Gee, he's a city councilman, he's my publisher, I have to think about, do I want to be the wife of this man?" I decided I really couldn't marry him.

ROBIN REISIG: Carter buying it didn't seem like a big deal, because he left everything the same. Except there was a lot more money. We didn't get expenses, and then suddenly we did. The paper got bigger, more writers, more articles after Carter was involved.

HOWARD BLUM: Dan was poor, grew up poor. After he sold the *Voice*, he became rich. He considered it rich. But it took until he was fifty-some-odd to do it.

ALAN WEITZ: But the people who had been there a long time were resentful that Dan and Ed did not share their newfound wealth. I thought these writers and photographers had a good bargain. They could write anything they wanted. They could write it as long as they wanted. There was very little attempt to change things. That bargain for a writer was a pretty good one. And because I loved Dan, there may be some blindness in me.

VIVIAN GORNICK: I left for a year, I went to Egypt, and I wrote a book about my experience there. I came back and he was mean to me. Dan wouldn't give me the job. He resented the fact that I'd gone—like a baby, like an outraged father. He thought of us as his children. When we wanted money for what we wrote, he got insulted. He thought we should be doing it out of love. When I first started writing for the *Voice*, I got thirty dollars a piece, and he didn't want to pay that! So, it was complicated. He would actually say to us, "I published you when nobody would publish you." So, therefore, I'm a slave for the rest of my life here?

JOHN WILCOCK: When Dan died in 1996, there were endless eulogies about his editorial skills and encouragement of young writers, but to me he always seemed an amiable cipher, never attending any public function and rarely being seen outside the office. Certainly, he never offered me any encouragement, or indeed thanks, unless one counts the maximum twenty-five dollars that I was ever paid for a thousand-word column.

LUCIAN K. TRUSCOTT IV: Newfield and Paul Cowan came up with the idea of unionizing the *Voice*. One night, Cowan and Newfield organized what amounted to an organizing meeting.

JACK NEWFIELD: Dan attacked the group, again saying that the *Voice* "is not a parking place for life," and the *Voice* veterans were keeping fresh blood from entering the paper by staying around too long.

RICHARD GOLDSTEIN: Dan was antiunion. That's a beatnik thing, you know? They're individualists, and they don't see the value of this stuff. Do you know what he actually said? "I don't know about why you people need a union. The door is always open." That is the greatest cliché of managers. The family company had no problems. He would always listen to the workers if they would just come to him.

JACK NEWFIELD: A few weeks later Dan agreed to give us across-the-board pay raises and expanded Blue Cross Blue Shield benefits.

But there was no union, and Dan swore there would never be a union as long as he was in control. I got my raise—but I had lost my father figure.

So began an era of demoralizing factionalism at the *Voice*. After a while there were factions within factions. Writers began to forget the reasons for their feuds, only that they were enemies and wouldn't speak in the elevator. It felt like a combination of high school and Bosnia. "It's like Yeats's description of Ireland," said Richard Goldstein. "'Great hatred, little room.'"

1970–1980
"THERE WAS A PALACE REVOLUTION"

CHAPTER 16

"HOLY MOTHER IRELAND. IT'S THE WOMEN'S LIBERATION MOVEMENT"

LUCIAN K. TRUSCOTT IV: The *Village Voice* was the organ of the feminist movement long before *Ms.* magazine was even a gleam in anybody's eye. You couldn't turn around at the *Village Voice* without bumping into a feminist when I was there. I was friendly with all of them.

SUSAN BROWNMILLER: I was the first person to write about abortion, but the *Voice* was always proabortion. The newspapers weren't yet on to it as a big subject. Before *Roe v. Wade*, there were suits in thirty states against district attorneys, basically, to overturn the abortion bans. I never read that in the *New York Times*. But it was happening, and the cases were getting thrown back to lower courts.

This abortion doctor that I knew said, "Would you like to come with me? I'm going up to see Dr. Spencer." I said, "The legendary Dr. Spencer, who gave abortions to, like, half the women on the East Coast?!" I did my little piece called "Last Trip to Ashland." Dr. Spencer was incredibly sick and would be dying soon.

And Joe Flaherty started bad-mouthing me. He said, "I'm writing all this important stuff about the Brooklyn docks, and she goes and interviews an abortionist, and it gets on the front page!" Oh, it was not a happy little group of writers pooling together. Flaherty was one of the worst. He was part of this whole crew, and it influenced Jack Newfield, too. It was Pete Hamill, Jimmy Breslin—there were these guys who were reveling in their own machismo—and it'd got into the *Village Voice.* Jack Newfield was such a nice guy, and all of a sudden he's holding fight nights at his apartment. When the guys talk about the *Voice,* they always forget the women.

Unfortunately for me, Spencer was never working, he'd been shut down when I needed an abortion. I discussed my abortions earlier in our first group, New York Radical Women. Kathie Sarachild—well, she was Kathie Amatniek then—was sort of the leader, and she'd say, "Let's go around the room." My normal competitiveness kicked in, and I said, "I've had three illegal abortions, and I never told anybody except those who needed to know that I was going to go."

I realized at that moment that this women's movement was going to go places, that we were talking about stuff that was quite personal, that'd never been articulated out loud before.

Within a year or so, the Redstockings women had their abortion "speak-out." This was the first time women had gotten together to speak out [about abortion] in the public space. They asked me if I'd testify. I was already in the women's movement; because of what I thought journalism should be, you don't bring yourself into it, that's confessional. I said, "I'll do y'all a favor: I'll write about it for the *Village Voice.*"

SUSAN BROWNMILLER, "EVERYWOMAN'S ABORTION: THE OPPRESSOR IS MAN," *VILLAGE VOICE*, MARCH 27, 1969

Make no mistake, the oppressor was Man, who on Friday night played the passive role of auditor, or at most, respectful questioner. It was the women's night. Not a "Ladies' Night," or an evening for the "girls," but a night when Woman spoke and was listened to, seriously. . . .

The first time I got pregnant, I was a young little thing. The man didn't use any contraceptive. He told me something like, "Don't worry, when I come the second time, it washes away the sperm."

RICHARD GOLDSTEIN: Second-wave feminism begins on the left with Students for a Democratic Society. There was a group of women who left SDS—that's the leading student activist group in the '60s—because they found it sexist. This was a critique that emerged from the New Left, and it was a famous essay by Robin Morgan called "Goodbye to All That," about leaving the left to form your own movement.

SUSAN BROWNMILLER: They were outraged, outraged! And they'd come to all our meetings and say, "What do you people do? Don't you know, men are dying in Vietnam, men are dying in the ghettos in this country, and you're contemplating your navels in your living room!"

SALLY KEMPTON: Susan and I became good friends mostly through the women's movement. I got involved in the New York Radical Feminists in 1969. It was a classic consciousness-raising group. There would be small groups of ten or twelve women meeting in apartments. Susan and I were in a group together called the West Village Branch of the New York Radical Feminists. It met in her apartment most of the time. Many people in it were writers and in media in one way or another, so it naturally segued into articles, books—you know, Susan's career as a professional feminist.

Susan and Lucy Komisar and I helped organize this protest at the *Ladies' Home Journal.*

SUSAN BROWNMILLER: We had not had any big kinds of demos, which were the style of the day. I was in this group called Media Women, and Media Women started to talk one day: "We need an action." We did it. There were two hundred people there, women and reporters from all over the world. We stayed for eleven hours, and we got eight pages in the magazine for a future issue and $10,000 to produce it. It was the first big successful women's movement sit-in.

We wrote the demands: must be a woman as editor in chief, Black women must be hired in proportion to their place in society—which is a lot of nice demands. Sally wrote up twenty pages of article suggestions. I didn't write about it for the *Voice*—Minda Bickman did.

When the women's movement started, there was a feeling among the first organizers and thinkers that our movement should have no leaders. We were getting out from under men, and why would we suddenly want to have some of our own people plucked from obscurity and made into media stars? It affected Kate Millett* far more than it affected me, but it affected a lot of us who were trashed for, quote, "seeking to rise to fame on the back of the women's movement." They made it really hard for me. I was tremendously confused because I had to decide for myself: Am I an organizer? Or am I a writer?

ROBIN REISIG: It was the rule: if you went to a restaurant or bar and you were just women, no men included, all these places didn't serve you. It was an antiprostitution measure. They didn't want prostitutes hanging out in bars. It certainly wasn't the law.

I was covering an event where women, Susan included, were going to go from bar to bar that didn't serve unescorted women. It was a small group of women that was doing this. It wasn't as though we were overwhelming places, but it was fun. We sat outside at Café de la Paix, a restaurant on Central Park South, and ordered drinks, and they wouldn't serve us. We went to Gallaghers, where I'd had dinner with my father many times, and they wouldn't serve us. People felt they had drunk so much they should probably postpone Gallaghers. It's a theater district restaurant that had prime ribs and steak. Gallaghers was smart. They called the press.

I remember one of the first East Side bars we walked in, and the bartender said, "Holy Mother Ireland. It's the women's liberation movement."

ROBIN REISIG, "LIBERATING THE BARS," *VILLAGE VOICE*, JUNE 4, 1970

By 1964 Negros had the legal right to eat and drink at public restaurants in deepest Mississippi or Alabama. But in 1970 women in New York still don't have that right. So radical feminists were taking a spirited sit-in tour of midtown restaurants which refuse to serve unescorted women at their bars. . . .

---

* Second-wave feminist, author of *Sexual Politics*.

The Café de la Paix, our next target, refused an initial twosome, then panicked at the 20 who followed. "What do you think we are? A whorehouse on a field trip?"

LUCIAN K. TRUSCOTT IV: I had Frankie FitzGerald over for dinner one night. She wrote *Fire in the Lake*; she wrote all these great books. She had a few drinks, and she said, "Oh, you're so lucky. Because you can write about yourself, because you can make the things that you write personal. Do you know how many times I've tried to do that?"

I never understood two things. Number one: how much writers that were constrained from doing that at a place like the *New York Times* really wanted to do that. The other thing was they had this admiration for the fact that you were able to do it, and that's what made the stories readable.

You could read a *Village Voice* story, and not only were you learning what was going on in the world, whatever the person was writing about; you were also reading about the person that wrote it, so you were getting a sense of who this person is, and where he or she is coming from. When Susan Brownmiller, Claudia Dreifus, and Vivian Gornick and those women were writing about their lives as women in the early days of feminism, that was what feminism was. It was who they were, and why they were like that, and they were willing to tell you, out loud, in print, who they were, and why they felt the way they felt. And that was revolutionary. There was a real intimacy between *Village Voice* writers and *Village Voice* readers.

ROBIN REISIG: At the *Voice*, I wrote the way I felt like writing, and that was my writer's voice, whatever it was. I remember telling Ross Wetzsteon once that a friend of mine wanted to write for the paper, and he just said, "Tell her not to imitate our style." It would never have occurred to me to try to imitate what that person might perceive as the *Voice* style. They wanted people to write in their own voice.

Vivian's piece "The Next Great Moment in History Is Ours"*—did you ever read that? That's the one to read, of everything Vivian wrote. It came before the movement was very widespread.

---

* Actually, "The Next Great Moment in History Is Theirs."

VIVIAN GORNICK, "THE NEXT GREAT MOMENT IN HISTORY IS THEIRS," *VILLAGE VOICE*, NOVEMBER 27, 1969

It was only when Elizabeth Cady Stanton and Lucretia Mott were not allowed to be seated at a World Anti-Slavery Conference held in the 1840s that the intellectual abolitionist women suddenly perceived that their own political existence resembled that of the blacks. They raised the issue with their radical men and were denounced furiously for introducing an insignificant and divisive issue, one which was sure to weaken the movement. Let's win this war first, they said, and then we'll see about women's rights. But the women had seen; in one swift visionary moment, to the very center of the truth about their own lives, and they knew that first was now, that there would never be a time when men would willingly address themselves to the question of female rights, that to strike out now for women's rights could do nothing but strengthen the issue of black civil rights because it called attention to all instances or rights denied in a nation that prided itself on rights for all.

SUSAN BROWNMILLER: It should be "ours," but it was "theirs." That was a very important piece.

VIVIAN GORNICK: Those were days when I was on the barricades for radical feminism, and I saw sexism everywhere, just everywhere. If I go out to dinner, or I saw a movie, or read a book, I'd write a piece that would somehow point out the sexism of the situation. I became known as a feminist journalist, and that was me and the *Village Voice*. It was a great proponent of personal journalism. It picked up that ball and ran with it. It published a lot of garbage. It also published some really significant ways of looking anew at a subject. It taught some of us how to do that kind of work well.

The danger of personal journalism is that you end up talking about yourself. I learned early that "I" was an instrument of illumination. "I" was not what it was about. I was to *use* myself to open the subject and to interact with it. There were a lot of people at the *Voice* who were doing that one way or another. A lot of the work was marred by amateurism, but a lot of it really made its mark.

SUSAN BROWNMILLER: I once counted the *I*'s in someone's story. I couldn't believe it. I think the *Voice* overdid it. But now it's just a regular part of journalism.

ROBIN REISIG: Someone gave me *The Feminine Mystique* in college, and I just got bored.* I didn't take it seriously—this woman complaining because she's a housewife? I mean, give me a break. You don't want to be a house-wife? Don't be a housewife.

VIVIAN GORNICK: After the liberationist movements hit, then the *Voice* really came into its own—in terms of Blacks, gays, and women—and I came into my own. That's when I really began to move towards actual writing rather than reporting. They gave us the most astonishing amount of space and time, and it was amazing. You would think that they were the internet. They let us go on and on and on. [*Laughs.*]

ROBIN REISIG: It was the paper of record for the women's movement.

MARY BREASTED: It was where you could read about the Redstockings. Susan Brownmiller's pieces were being read by everybody.

VIVIAN GORNICK: Women, if you could demonstrate that you could do it at the *Voice*, you could do it. It's a big difference between us and the con-ventional world above 14th Street.

RICHARD GOLDSTEIN: There might have been more women than at most publications. They weren't really macho, but they were very spirited. They were traditional journo-women, but with a more bohemian edge. We had a female sportswriter, for instance. She was very aggressive.** Our fashion writer was Blair Sabol, and she was raunchy. Then Jill Johnston, of course. These were fairly funky, spirited women.

MARY BREASTED: Dan was very good about women. He did not treat them with less respect than the men.

VIVIAN GORNICK: He was very remote. He was hard to talk to, for me. I think he felt more at ease with men. I think he felt ill at ease with a lot of

---

* *The Feminine Mystique* (1963) was written by feminist Betty Friedan.
** Barbara Long, who became known for covering boxing.

what we did. Politically, he was savvy, and he knew that this was the way to go. When feminism hit and women started writing in the *Voice* like crazy, their sales went through the roof. It gave new life to the *Voice*.

SALLY KEMPTON: Several of the women who wrote for the *Voice* were people like Stephanie, who was married to Mike Harrington, and Margot Hentoff, who was married to Nat. Dan did tend to hire the articulate wives of well-known male writers and thinkers, partly because they didn't have to pay them so much. The *Voice* was very much a family enterprise in a certain way.

MOLLY HASKELL: I started writing about film from a feminist viewpoint. Certain "women's films"—now they call it "melodrama"—were a product of a repressed world where marriage was forever and any misstep had dire consequences. It was a genre I was trying to legitimize.

One of my first reviews was about *Butch Cassidy and the Sundance Kid*, and I talked about the "buddy film." Well, this year,* we have *The Two Popes*, we have *Ford v Ferrari*—it's two guys, I mean, two guys, two guys. We have *The Lighthouse* with Willem Dafoe, and *The Irishman* is all male. Men, men, men—I mean, unbelievable.

In '73, I published this book *From Reverence to Rape: The Treatment of Women in the Movies*, and that was a historical, chronological account. Nobody in Richmond** could even bring themselves to say the title.

SUSAN BROWNMILLER: After the women's movement started big-time, we really, I call it, "discovered" rape. Well, before us, all the talk about rape was that white women falsely accused Black men, or white women lie in general. That was the thinking on rape, until we started listening to women who'd been raped. And my god, they thought they were gonna die. Whatever they thought, it was not anything that I'd ever thought before. But that was our way in.

Alix Shulman testified at the rape speakout that Gail Sheehy wrote about for *New York* magazine, and she described this ritual called "depantsing,"

---

* 2019.
** Richmond, Virginia, where Haskell is from.

where on the way from school to home, you had to go through this gauntlet of guys who'd try to pull your pants off. I'd never heard that in my life. Women were saying the most extraordinary things.

Ellen Willis had gone to Europe for six months; when she came back there was all this new rape consciousness, and she admitted that she'd missed something, and she never recovered from it. When I'd seen her at the New York Radical Women meetings years before, she was already a star. She was a great theorist. But then her ideas and mine certainly diverged as I made pornography and prostitution enemies, and she didn't. She was quite on the other side.

ELLEN WILLIS: The paramount issue then was just getting into public consciousness, that there really was a problem called "male supremacy," or male domination of women, that women were oppressed, and our main project was analyzing and making public all the different ways in which women were considered as secondary human beings. A lot of things that are second nature now simply weren't. There was a reflexive, taken-for-granted sexism that doesn't really exist now. People thought you were crazy if you said, "Well, I don't like walking down the street and being hassled by men." "What do you mean? They're being appreciative. What are you talking about?"

SUSAN BROWNMILLER: I did one piece just before our rape conference. I and other women are handing out the leaflets. One of the people in New York Radical Feminists and I—we were leafleting on Eighth Street. While I was on the street, this guy goosed me. I was just standing there, blindly handing out leaflets, and this guy comes up behind me, gooses me. Up my ass. An experienced gooser.

I kicked him back, but I didn't know how to kick, and I had taken some ballet classes and modern dance. In a sweeping arc, I brought up my leg and kicked him in the ass. But when I brought my leg down, I sprained my ankle. I wrote a piece called "On Goosing." My lede was "I am sitting here with my foot in the air, as they told me to do at St. Vincent's Hospital," and then I explained the story of getting goosed on the street. Since we were all thinking about rape, and I said, this is one big continuum: from getting goosed on the street to being raped.

SUSAN BROWNMILLER, "ON GOOSING," *VILLAGE VOICE*, APRIL 15, 1971

Men take all they want at all levels. Where does one draw the line between the gooser and the seducer? Between the john who pays for it outright and the date who expects it free in return for the dinner check? Between the rapist and the husband who has bullied his wife into believing that sexual intercourse is his marital right?

SUSAN BROWNMILLER: Nora Ephron called and said, "You are funny. Do you know you can be funny?" which is a great compliment from Nora Ephron. I wasn't known for being funny. When that piece was published in the *Voice*, *Time* magazine said that "On Goosing" proves the women's movement has no sense of humor. James Wolcott wrote to the *Voice*'s letter page saying, "God help us if she's ever raped." Wolcott at that moment was languishing in the circulation department at the *Voice*, and that letter was his break into print. So, if you interview Wolcott, ask him if he remembers that, because he lies.*

JAMES WOLCOTT, LETTER TO THE EDITOR, *VILLAGE VOICE*, MAY 13, 1971

"On Goosing," by Susan Brownmiller is a fascinating, dreadful collection of inanities, hopefully unshared by her sister feminists. Goosing is certainly a repulsive activity, but for Susan Brownmiller it is a trespass of almost metaphysical dimensions. (God help us if she ever gets raped—we will be buried under an avalanche of rhetoric.) To fit her ideology, Miss

---

* In college, Wolcott sent Norman Mailer an article he had written for the student paper, and Mailer was so impressed he wrote a letter of introduction to Dan Wolf. "I think you have a career," he wrote to Wolcott. His letter of recommendation to Wolf read: "I have taken the liberty of telling a young college kid, 19, to go and look you up for a job. His name is James Wolcott and he sent me a piece of reporting he did about the Cavett show I did with Vidal which I must say impressed me . . . I think this fellow has talent which I don't feel too often about young writers . . . would appreciate it if you would let him have a little of your time and give a try out on a story or two."

Voice writers Susan Brownmiller and Sally Kempton debate feminism with *Playboy*'s Hugh Hefner on *The Dick Cavett Show* on March 26, 1970. Photo © ABC Photo Archives/Disney General Entertainment Content via Getty Images.

Brownmiller is not satisfied with labeling goosing as a small, ugly act, but instead must suffer a spasm of orgiastic indignities and aggrandize it into monstrous proportions.

SUSAN BROWNMILLER: It was a piece that won a lot of attention. I thought, "This is going to be mine. I'm going to write a book about rape." It took me four years, and it changed my life.

There was a woman in my own consciousness-raising group who said to me, "Why don't you be the first feminist who doesn't put her name on her book?" I knew—"Well, I think I will be saying goodbye to this part of my life."*

---

* Brownmiller's 1975 book, *Against Our Will: Men, Women and Rape*, is a groundbreaking feminist text.

CHAPTER 17

"SHE WAS A WOMAN TALKING FROM INSIDE HER MIND"

SALLY KEMPTON: You can't have a book about the *Voice* without Jill Johnston.

JAMES WOLCOTT: Originally, she covered dance, and also the art world, but then it became a running diary. And then as she became more and more a lesbian spokesperson, it became more and more about that. It was very Joycean, lots of puns, lots of run-on sentences, lots of in-jokes. But she had a following.

JILL JOHNSTON: I was schooling myself in a form of illiteracy. It was anecdotal, a travelogue. I was creating my own thing.

RICHARD GOLDSTEIN: She didn't use capital letters because she thought they were masculinist. She was, by the way, a wonderful person.

J. HOBERMAN: Jonas Mekas and Jill Johnston were the original bloggers. They were just writing whatever they felt like.

JILL JOHNSTON: Most outrageously, for a newspaper of the *Voice*'s increasingly broad-based circulation, it was seen fit to print a group of pieces, beginning with "About the Ash Tree," of January 23, 1969, patently in the word-salad mode, written from inside a crack-up, on the run from any authorities who might corral, detain, and arrest me. While I was not delusional exactly, the writing is protractedly oracular, megalocentric, and declamatory.

Jill Johnston in Cape Cod, 1975. Photo © Jan Roby, courtesy of Lesbian Herstory.

JILL JOHNSTON, "ABOUT THE ASH TREE," *VILLAGE VOICE*, JANUARY 23, 1969

I made an elaborate prison escape out of our great city, I never saw so many assassins in one day. And all so helpful. I even discovered the fundamental nature of employment.

. . . We create jobs for each other in a pathetically beautiful way. A computer, a single tiny computer, could run the world and possibly all the cosmic enterprises when it comes to that.

SONIA JAFFE ROBBINS: I'd sometimes try to read Jill Johnston. But it always felt like I was reading the middle of a letter to people I didn't know about things that I didn't know. I couldn't manage it. So, when I went to work at the *Voice*, the first article they gave me to copyedit was a Jill Johnston column, and so when I had to read it very closely, word for word, I thought, "Oh! Now I see what she's trying to get at."

SUSAN BROWNMILLER: She was a woman talking from inside her mind. Somebody has claimed recently that she was the first feminist at the *Voice*, but I don't see that. She may have been the first lesbian at the *Voice*.

We assumed we were all heterosexual, you know. It was hilarious.

JILL JOHNSTON: In 1969, a few women in the GLF,* finding me writing about my travels cross-country with a young woman, correctly divining that she was a lover, invited me to their meetings at a church on Ninth Avenue in Manhattan. Having been schooled in all the art forms, being very apolitical, I had a lot of resistance at first, especially to understanding the status of women in political terms. I had not a clue, in fact, that the genders were so seriously segregated, to the historical disadvantage of women. The fact that certain women, called lesbians, were outcasts was not hard to get. So, I started there.

JILL JOHNSTON, "ON A CLEAR DAY YOU CAN SEE YOUR MOTHER," *VILLAGE VOICE*, MAY 6, 1971

The title of this episode is new approach: All women are lesbians except those who don't know it naturally they are but don't know it yet I am a woman who is a lesbian because I am a woman and a woman who loves herself naturally who is other women is a lesbian a woman who loves some loves herself naturally this is the case that a woman is herself all woman is a naturally born lesbian so we don't mind using the name like any name it is quite meaningless it means naturely I am a woman

SONIA JAFFE ROBBINS: She was very much a lesbian separatist. When women's liberation started, there was a period where I was seriously wondering, like, "Should we all be separatists, should we all just leave men?" I really struggled with the question of female separatism. But then I thought that doing that might also ghettoize us.

* Gay Liberation Front.

JILL JOHNSTON: It depends how you're defining "lesbian." I have a political definition of lesbianism, and what it really means is self-commitment. And we know that we have a feminist movement because women have been denied self-commitment, and we're just updating feminism by calling it lesbianism because we feel that total commitment to ourselves would include every phase of our activities.

I remember walking into the *Village Voice* one day, and a woman there who worked in the office for years had heard that my book was coming out, published by a major publisher, and it was called *Lesbian Nation*. It was beyond her credulity to imagine that. She just thought the whole country would be seized perhaps with a lesbian mania if a major publisher put out a book like this.

The role that the *Voice* played in "those turbulent times" was that it continued to publish me. I became good copy. During the early '70s they received hundreds of letters to the editor about my column. I received hundreds of them myself. And I never wrote about sex per se, by the way. It was just the L-word that did it.

C.CARR: I met her when she was on her book tour for *Lesbian Nation*. I went to a big bookstore in downtown Chicago, and I walk up to the counter with this book that says, "*Lesbian Nation*," and the clerks are like, [*gasps*]. That's how it was—just a different time. It took a little courage for her to do what she did.

We met at a typical lesbian space—a church basement, very dingy and shabby. The room was packed. She came in and said that she didn't really want to read from the book—so she would just answer questions.

A woman in the front of the room got up and said, "What do you think happens to people after they die?" And Jill said, "Is that a big issue around here?" Jill was a little bit stoned. This was at the height of lesbian separatism—when there were certain people who wanted to maybe take over a state just for lesbians: "Just one state, we're only asking for one." And some earnest young woman in the back stood up and said, "After we get our state, how will we have kids?" At that point, another woman leaped to her feet and said, "We'll steal them!" [*Laughs.*]

JILL JOHNSTON: We were developing an identity that didn't exist. It was the first wave of lesbian feminism.

I had to get over the repercussions of that book and figure out a new life after that, and a new style. I was going around the country and being interviewed by lots of people who were very hostile. And I am somebody who liked being liked by people. I found this a stunning reverse of my life.

We were riding on a certain crest of popularity in New York. It was the big issue of the moment. The backlash was very quick.

On my own, one way or another, I was reliably unpredictable and reckless.

BETTY FRIEDAN: The benefit at Ethel Scull's on August 8 turned out to be a riot.* The press got quite a story, however. While I was giving a poolside speech on our demand for herstory, not just history, Jill Johnston slipped into the pool, stripped to the waist, and started swimming laps.

JILL JOHNSTON, "BASH IN THE SCULLS," *VILLAGE VOICE*, AUGUST 8, 1970

I sat down to organize the explosion. . . . I walk quickly to the center of the shallow end. Almost fall skidding on the slippery edge. Last Chance Balloon. Tarzana from the trees at cocktails. I didn't cross myself. I didn't yell geronimo. I dove in and did my lengths. I hoped my colleague reporters would be noting my 10 point Australian crawl. I did a little exhibition breast stroke as well.

JILL JOHNSTON: I was hot and drunk.

JAMES WOLCOTT: There was a famous documentary called *Town Bloody Hall*. It's taken from Germaine Greer; she says something at one point like, "I didn't come here to be insulted at town bloody hall." It's a classic moment in New York life because you've got Mailer, Diana Trilling, Germaine Greer, Jill Johnston, and in the audience you have Susan Sontag, Cynthia Ozick, Anatole Broyard, and a lot of *Village Voice* people. When I resaw the movie, I was struck by how many *Village Voice* people I recognized, including

* Ethel Scull was a prominent art collector. The benefit was a fundraiser for the Women's March.

Nat Hentoff. It was incredible. Everybody was yelling at each other. The thing begins with, there's some woman, she didn't get in, she's yelling at all these people—"Gloria Steinem harms the poor. Germaine Greer harms the poor!" It set the tone for this hectoring night.

RICHARD GOLDSTEIN: This was after Mailer's book *The Prisoner of Sex*, a notorious sexist work about the women's movement.*

NORMAN MAILER, *THE PRISONER OF SEX*

Some of the women were writing like very tough faggots. It was a good style. . . . Every point was made with a minimum of words, a mean style, no question of that. It used obscenity with the same comfort a whore would take with her towel.

SUSAN BROWNMILLER: That was when she famously rolled off the stage with another woman in the middle of the event.

At some point Mailer was railing against her. He said, "Jill, be a lady." I think Cynthia Ozick got up in the questionnaire time and said, "Mr. Mailer, when you dip your balls into the ink, what color do your balls become?" It was a wild event.

JILL JOHNSTON: Just to appear at town hall was to acknowledge Mailer. And to concur in the tacit premise of the occasion: that women's liberation is a debatable issue. In this sense, that the event occurred at all, it was a disaster for women. As a social event, it was the victory of the season.

My career as an impromptu clown is studded with glorious exploits. It's necessary in order to attract attention, to dazzle at all costs, to be disapproved of by serious people and quoted by the foolish. If anyone should think my exhibitionism is a symptom of my neglect as a writer, they're wrong because this behavior is an art form.

SUSAN BROWNMILLER: She was a world unto herself.

SALLY KEMPTON: She was exactly like her legend.

---

* A sexist article by Mailer denouncing both the women's liberation movement and Kate Millett's book *Sexual Politics* appeared first in *Harper's*, and it was later turned into a book.

CHAPTER 18

"CLAY FELKER WAS A CELEBRITY FUCKER"

ALAN WEITZ: Do you know that feeling when you love going to work? Or you love doing your work? Those of us who were lucky enough to feel that are very grateful, so I was very grateful to the *Voice*. One day, I walk in, and I'm told that Carter Burden and Bartle Bull have sold their controlling interest to Clay Felker and *New York* magazine.* And I thought, "Oh my god, what is this gonna mean?" People forgot about their criticisms of Dan and aimed everything at Clay Felker, because everyone was afraid Clay would turn the *Voice* into *New York* magazine, and the freedom some writers had would be eroded, and that Clay would sensationalize the *Voice*.

ED FANCHER: The agreement with Carter Burden was that Dan Wolf and I would run the paper for five years. We would have editorial control, and at the end of the five years we would sell him the rest of the paper, or at least controlling interest. He decided to sell controlling interest to Clay, and this is exactly what we did not want, because Felker was not the kind of journalist that represented the *Voice*. There was nothing we could do about it. And a lot of *Voice* writers didn't really like Clay Felker.

CLAY FELKER: Any lawyer can tell you that a minority interest—it's very weak. The majority can totally screw the minority if it wants to.

MARY BREASTED: The problem came when Carter needed the money for another one of his campaigns, or maybe he just needed to pay back the loan he had taken to buy the *Voice*. Felker started changing the *Voice* in dramatic ways.

---

* The merger was announced June 5, 1974.

SALLY KEMPTON: I had never felt that Dan was a particularly visionary person. Clay was much more of a visionary.

MARK JACOBSON: He's from Webster Groves, Missouri, right? He's a complete rube. He just loved New York City journalism. He came from Missouri, and then he lived this unbelievable life. He married a movie star. He became like this Citizen Kane. He was this dumpy guy, like a linebacker gone to seed. He didn't look like a dashing editor-type guy.

He knew what he was doing. He pumped a lot of air into *Esquire*, which was dead on the doorstep. And then he moved over to *New York* magazine. He started it in the *Herald Tribune*. He's the major figure in the history of magazine journalism of the second half of the twentieth century.

ALAN WEITZ: The staff all got together. Clay came down with Milton Glaser, the art director. He probably played down the changes he wanted to make. But afterwards, though, there were a number of questions to him about what he intended to do. I don't think Clay was even clear on what he wanted to do at that point. He just wanted this media property. He had it and he and Milton had to figure out what the hell they were gonna do with it. They certainly wanted a different look. That was the main thing. So, they hired new art directors.

RICHARD GOLDSTEIN: It was laid out like clothes on a line. Your story could jump forward, not just back, but forward. Then Milton Glaser redesigned it. It was geometric. Pictures were bigger. It was a very different paper when Clay came in.

STAN MACK: And one of the things they came up with was this idea they called A Page of Urban Comics. I knew them both. I walked in and said to them, "Guys, could I get an assignment where I would just walk around town and listen to people and talk to them and put it together into a story?" "Sure, but remember," Milton said, "comics are circulation-builders. If you're gonna do this, you have to think in terms of every week." And I thought, "Well, that's crazy, but I'll try." They said, "Well, let's call it Real Life Funnies."

I was a huge admirer of Jules's style, because my style was very dense, complicated, filled with cross-hatching. Jules had this wonderful way of drawing—this loose, easygoing way that he had evolved himself. Somebody described how Jules worked, and it was that there was a constant voice in his head, and all he had to do was turn up the volume and write it down. Well, I had to go out into the world and follow people and face up to them and hope for the best. I was always envious of the ease with which he could story-tell.

MARK ALAN STAMATY: In 1976, I started doing some illustrations for them. I lived on MacDougal Street, so I called it *MacDoodle St.* There's a lot of detail, a lot of little gags, flattened-out street scenes. There was, like, all these falafel places. There was Crazy Eddie's over by Eighth Street and Sixth Avenue, and then there was another hi-fi electronics place nearby. And Crazy Eddie had a sign he would beat anybody's price. I had guys running back and forth between the two stores, getting him to take the prices down, down, lower.

It was a big hit. Feiffer was my hero. And I got this strip right up front with Jules.

ALAN WEITZ: At six o'clock, I walked Dan home—Dan just lived a block away from the paper. He bought a gorgeous apartment on Fifth Avenue after he and Ed sold the paper. I said something like, "Are you OK?" And he said, "Alan, I feel like I've just been let out of a birdcage."

JONATHAN Z. LARSEN: Well, I did not like Clay Felker. So many people have tried to ruin the *Village Voice*, and many of them have succeeded, and Felker was really the first. Felker always wanted to do the same thing to everything—he wanted celebrities. He wanted high-society stories. He was a celebrity fucker. He wanted to move in society himself, and people were happy to have him. He was very colorful, very funny, bigger than life. What we might call a big swinging dick. And along the way, he hired some brilliant journalists and published some great stuff in *New York* magazine, no question about it.

But then he lost the mojo somewhere. He tried to do at the *Voice* what he'd done in *New York* magazine. The *Voice* was not interested. The *Voice* was downtown, didn't care about his socialites and didn't care about his celebrities. And it stopped doing really hard-hitting journalism, so it lost a lot of its gritty, Norman Mailer–esque feel from the old days. Then he said, "I'm gonna make it national. We're gonna have a national *Village Voice*. It's dogshit now—wait till you see what I'm going to do with it."

It's like Donald Trump taking over the United States.

JACK NEWFIELD: At first, nobody quit. One reason was that during his first month, Clay gave everyone raises. He raised the base weekly staff salary to $300 and the base freelance fee to $200.

CLAY FELKER: I didn't do it to buy them off. I really believe that people should get paid adequate money, and that's been our policy here at *New York* magazine.

ROBIN REISIG: We were called to a meeting with Felker when he bought the paper. And at one point in the meeting, he said to the *Voice* writers, "All people care about is money and power."

RICHARD GOLDSTEIN: He had these class aspirations, Clay.

ROBIN REISIG: A friend came to the *Voice* Christmas party and said that we were the worst-dressed group of people she'd ever seen. Partly it was we didn't care that much how we dressed, but partly it was because we didn't have money to buy clothes.

He was looking at a room full of people who cared so little about money that they were willing to work for very little in order to have the freedom to write about things that seemed important to them and to be free to write in their own voice, and to tell the whole truth and not censor it.

RICHARD GOLDSTEIN: We had at least three writers who wouldn't use punctuation, and Clay, you can just imagine, he said, "What? Three writers don't use punctuation?!" I said, "Well, they have their reasons."

ALAN WEITZ: Jill Johnston he didn't understand at all. To tell you the truth, half the time I didn't know what Jill was writing about either.

CLAY FELKER: My quarrel with Jill is not what she says, but the technique, the fact that she doesn't use capital letters, punctuation, paragraphing. I feel that that is selfish. It is noncommunicative, and it is contempt for the readers. It is elitist in the extreme. And nobody reads it.

ROBIN REISIG: I was in Ross's office being edited, and he got a phone call and he explained he had to leave to walk to the staircase in the back of the building and unlock it because Jill Johnston was dropping off her story and she had just developed a phobia about elevators.

ALAN WEITZ: We were going to put an article on the front page, Pete Hamill's call for socialism. Clay wanted these great graphics, but it was not a traditional front page for the *Voice*. The staff, again, saw this as Clay trying to sensationalize things. It was a difficult time.

CHAPTER 19

"I WAS A LITTLE BIT INTIMIDATED BY KAREN DURBIN"

RICHARD GOLDSTEIN: We didn't have editors, really, before Felker. He hired Karen Durbin after trying to get it on with her, and she wouldn't have it. He hired her anyway. That's how I got to know her.

VIVIAN GORNICK: Karen told me they were at some fundraising affair, and they took a taxi together, and she said she could see his hand was moving towards her knee. And she picked up his hand, put it back, and said, "Don't even think about it."

GUY TREBAY: She was very pretty, very super shapely in her youth, almost pinup-esque, right? She was Bardot-esque. That was part of her show in a way. She was obviously a committed feminist but enjoyed being a hottie. She had red hair and lots of it. She liked high boots and '70s lady clothes.

C.CARR: She was born in Cincinnati, grew up in Indianapolis, and then went to college at Bryn Mawr. Her family had a dry-cleaning business, although her father had started out as a jazz musician.

After she got out of school, she got a job at the *New Yorker*. That's where she met Ellen Willis. Ellen was a writer, but Karen was, like, a secretary or something. At that point, Ellen was a founder of second-wave feminism: She was a founder of Redstockings, she was friends with Shulamith Firestone. Talking with Ellen would have been a way to get interested in feminism.

NONA WILLIS-ARONOWITZ: They were best friends, and they were intellectual soulmates.

ELLEN WILLIS: In 1972, Karen Durbin showed some passages from her journal to a friend. After reading the material he told her, "This is great stuff! You should expand it into an article."

"But who would publish such a thing?" she said. Personal journalism was still an oddity then.

"The *Village Voice* might."

The journal entries became Durbin's first *Voice* essay, "Casualties of the Sex War." It was a cri de coeur against the devolution of the women's liberation movement into puritanical condemnations of heterosexuality ("We'd been living together for two years. As far as I know, only my parents and the movement disapproved") and the devolution of the sexual revolution into the glorification of loveless fucking.

KAREN DURBIN: My first encounter with the *Voice* was when I moved to New York. It wasn't like anything I'd seen. And it became the paper that I read most faithfully, because it was also the paper that was reflecting what was going on in a way that even the *New York Times* could not get a grip on. This was the fall of '66, and the antiwar movement was in full flail. I was thrilled by it. It was a mess. Articles would jump five and six times, and occasionally they would jump backward and then jump forward again. But it was just so full of life. I didn't agree with all of it, but later, when I started working at the *Voice*, I said that what it always made me think of was a great bar in the Village, a funky bar. And everybody's sitting at the bar, and having whatever they're having, and talking about everything under the sun. And sometimes an argument and sometimes a chorus. I thought the *Voice* was like that.

What the *Voice* did to a great extent, and especially politically, was advocacy journalism. And advocacy journalism is not biased. It's very frank in its own way. It's the most honest kind of journalism, because you know where the writer is coming from. And at the *Voice* we did, for the most part, hold advocacy journalism to a high standard. We didn't just do legal checks; we did really serious fact checks. The *Voice* had a crackerjack fact-checking department. It is more useful and there's nothing wrong with having many points of view. On the contrary, you want that conversation at that bar, or you're just a bunch of boring drunks.

JAMES WOLCOTT: I can remember M Mark, Karen Durbin, and Ellen Willis conferring, sometimes making party plans together.

M MARK: I wasn't quite their age; I was a little younger. My one claim to exoticism in New York is that I come from Waterloo, Iowa, which is—now just hold on, this is pretty impressive—home to the National Dairy Cattle Congress every year, and the world HQ of John Deere tractors. I came out of the '60s in a very conservative place in Iowa. I moved to New York; I knew I wanted to live downtown. And the only place that I could figure out that I wanted to really work with was the *Village Voice*.

I saw an ad for—I don't remember the title of the editor. I went through the previous issue and saw how badly it was edited. So many, not only typos, but grammatical errors and misstatements of fact. No fact-checking going on, as far as I can tell. I spent a couple of days of intense labor with a pencil. I did not have editorial experience except school publications, but I thought, "I'm going to pretend that I'm an editor and I know how to do it." They said, "Whoa, OK! You got the job." I came to the *Voice* in '76.

C. CARR: I joined this women's group that had Karen Durbin, Ellen Willis, Ann Snitow, Roz Baxandall, who had been part of WITCH—Women's International Terrorist Conspiracy from Hell. They would do these antic actions. They'd dress up and invade the stock market. That's where I originally met Karen, before I was at the *Voice*. Alix Kates Shulman was in the group, too.

It was like going to graduate school. Because there were so many smart women in this group who'd experienced more, read more—they were all older than me. This is the weird thing. I got invited in because they needed a lesbian. I think that's how I got my job at the *Voice*, too. They said the affirmative action committee decided that I could be hired because I was a lesbian! I had never had it work to my advantage before.

I was a little bit intimidated by Karen. She had this incredible essay-like way of talking that was daunting to hear.

GUY TREBAY: Karen was very deeply simpatico.

LESLIE SAVAN: Oh, Karen was a ball of energy. She and Richard shared an office on Broadway. They were really good buddies. And it was a real hub of the cultural writers. But at one point, they had a falling-out—she and Richard—and they were in the same office, and they didn't talk to each other.

RICHARD GOLDSTEIN: Karen smacked me once. Because I had written a piece called "Keep Dope Alive: What We Lose When We 'Just Say No.'" So, this must have been the Nancy Reagan era. She was sober, but I'm perfectly happy with my drug habits, such as they are.

JAMES HAMILTON: Karen and I very pretty quickly became romantically involved. She was funny. Fun to be with. Very pretty. I think she had numerous affairs within the *Voice*.

C.CARR: Her famous piece was called "On Being a Woman Alone," which was a cover story. She had broken up with a boyfriend and was trying to reorient herself as a woman alone. That's what the whole thing was about—about trying to see herself as someone who's not part of a couple.

KAREN DURBIN, "ON BEING A WOMAN ALONE," *VILLAGE VOICE*, AUGUST 30, 1976

There is still no ready way for a woman in her late middle age to be alone and still integrated into society. She's a social awkwardness; her peers are couples, and they have little use for a single woman. Is she supposed to go to bars? On cruises? Hang around museums? . . .

The woman alone is self-oriented, she stands at the center of her universe. The words worry me; they have double meanings. "Self-oriented." Self-respecting? Or just selfish? "Alone." On my own, taking responsibility for myself? Or disconnected, cut off from others?

C.CARR: She still has the cover of that framed out at the nursing home, actually. She really struggled with that and always talked about how she was a blocked writer. I think it had to do with stuff with her parents: "Do I have permission to really be doing this writing?" Which seems ironic because that would be a thing that comes up more for women than for men, and here she's a big feminist. But she couldn't overcome that feeling sometimes.

CHAPTER 20

"WE'RE AGAINST GENTRIFICATION, AND WE'RE FOR FIST-FUCKING"

RICHARD GOLDSTEIN: Clay brought in Judith Daniels as managing editor, a woman who descended from the Straus family, an important German Jewish family in New York—one of them died on the *Titanic*. Lovely person. She had a raven-like chic about her. There she was, sitting among these ragged maniacs that she had to put up with every day and corral. A big issue was that there was no ladies' room. There were just bathrooms, and the bathrooms were really stinky and filthy. She demanded a women's room and got it. I remember women in the Judy Daniels epoch throwing tampons around to freak out the men, because there were these cubicles. Everyone was in a cubicle, and you could just throw things over the top of it very easily. People did it all the time. Food, but also tampons. It was a very rowdy environment. And there was this very chic woman in the midst of it, doing her job.

JAMES WOLCOTT: Somehow I got promoted; they wanted me to be Mary Perot Nichols's assistant. But it was a weird arrangement because she was a political writer. I didn't know anything about politics. But Mary Perot Nichols never wanted me there. And then one day—it was like, five o'clock, closing time—and my desk was totally cleared off because I was ready to leave for the weekend. And she walked by, and she looked at my empty desk and me not doing anything. She said, "Don't you get bored sitting there doing nothing?" And I said, "I meditate."

She went into her office. She was in a fury, and I didn't realize it. When I came back to the office the next week—you know how you *know* you're gonna get fired? I thought, "Oh, I'm a goner."

She would tell people for decades, "Oh, you know, I fired him." Take your points of pride where you can.

It was Clay who hired me back. I was on unemployment, but I was still turning in pieces to the paper all the time. I started writing rock reviews for all kinds of different, weird little places that were publishing then, like *Circus* magazine. Clay liked some of the stuff I was doing. Clay brought in a lot of people, and the funny thing was they all said, "Oh, Clay is going to make the paper uptown and slick and mainstream." But Clay actually hired the people who pushed the paper further to the left. It was under Clay that Ellen Willis was brought back in, and certainly there was Karen Durbin, and M Mark.

CLAY FELKER: The *Voice* is a collection of voices. They speak for themselves. They don't speak for me.

SYLVIA PLACHY: I worked for Clay Felker at *New York* magazine when I was five months pregnant. So, I only had the job for three months, because my son came early. I periodically picked up the *Village Voice*, and it was very interesting, but it wasn't on my radar. So, when I got there, I, of course, fell in love with it.

ROBERT CHRISTGAU: There are two schools of thought: The first is that it was a great newspaper until Clay Felker came in and ruined it. And the second, which is my position, is that it was an excellent newspaper until Clay Felker came in and made it much better. He hired me, he hired Durbin, he hired Goldstein, three really talented people, in addition to letting Ross Wetzsteon run the show—that wasn't necessarily such a great idea.

ROBIN REISIG: An interesting quote from Bob Christgau—he said all of us would probably agree 50 percent of the *Voice* was excellent and 50 percent was awful. We just wouldn't agree on which 50 percent.

ROBERT CHRISTGAU: Felker, he was an incredibly tempestuous boss. He really never fucking knew what he was doing. The old people were Clark Whelton and Ron Rosenbaum and many other of the Wolf loyalists—they hated us. They hated Felker. So that was very tempestuous, but it was so exciting.

RICHARD GOLDSTEIN: Ron Rosenbaum had long, flaming, curly, Long Island red hair, and he had a wild look in his eyes at all times. He came in and took his paycheck, tore it up, and threw it in Felker's face. So, Clay turned to me and said, "Who the fuck is that?"

Clay hired Ross Wetzsteon as the editor. He ended up as a theater editor. Ross was an alcoholic. He brought a big bottle of liquor to work in an attaché case every day. He had a private office. He was kind of burly, bohemian. He presided over the Obies.

One day we were working on the fifth floor, and we hear this crash, like a window smashing. We thought it came from Ross's office. The door was closed. We thought, "He's jumped out of the window!" We looked down, there was no body on the street, and we said, "What could this be?" He opens the door; his whole hand is bloody. He had put it through the window because Clay refused to give him money to buy a birthday cake. We realized that he was really out of control, so essentially nobody ran the paper.

VIVIAN GORNICK: He was given the editorship, and he just couldn't do it. He also was a little bit of a predator.

MARY BREASTED: He wasn't vengeful when you turned him down. But it was still distasteful.

ALAN WEITZ: I started doing all the editing.* Editing the *Voice* was very difficult. Whoever was doing the editing was editing not just twelve different writers, but twelve different personalities. And the *Voice* was full of personalities. Clay wasn't that much of a problem. He just came down on Fridays, and especially on Mondays; he wanted to make sure the front page was OK.

JAMES WOLCOTT: He was perfectly nice, but he was very much a commander, the way he talked: HE. WAS. LIKE. A. COMMANDER.

CARTER BURDEN: Bartle used to use Churchill's old quote about the Germans to describe Felker: "He's either at your throat or at your feet."

---

* Though Ross Wetzsteon was the executive editor, Felker was editor in chief. What editorial duties Ross could not handle fell to Alan Weitz, until he left in April 1975.

RICHARD GOLDSTEIN: Have I told you about the time I punched him? There were all these Hamill brothers—the youngest of them was John Hamill, who was this pretty hard-core Marxist, and he had written a piece in praise of the Vietcong. Clay had come down to the office. He looked at the piece and took it out of the typewriter, and he said, "This piece gives aid to our enemies. We're not publishing it." So, I punched him.

It had happened the day a very close friend of mine killed himself, so I was, without realizing it, quite out of control. Judy Daniels explained this to him, so nothing happened. He invited me to breakfast. That's very Felker. He wasn't a vicious person in any way.

JAMES WOLCOTT: He had these bizarre ideas. He said, "I just saw a survey that Rich Little is, like, one of the most popular people on television, so I'd like you to do a piece on Rich Little." "Oh, OK." And I did. But that was the kind of thing that horrified *Village Voice* people. "Rich Little? What the hell are we doing?"

MARY BREASTED: The Village was becoming a community where male homosexuals were very predominant. It was always a community where gay people felt safe. But then it became a real scene. The scene moved down towards the river and became very decadent when these all-night places opened. Because Felker was very commercially minded and wanted to get advertising, he decided to turn the *Voice* into a gay-oriented paper. He ran a number of articles on the gay scene—and sensational ones. There was a cover story about fist-fucking. Everybody was appalled, because it was making being gay seem only decadent and only like that, not like something that was a slice of life. And he was exploiting it, making it sensational. We all thought it was quite distasteful. It was getting away from the contemplative, ruminative writing that had been in the *Voice*.

JACK NEWFIELD: There is one frequently retold anecdote from a staff meeting in the mid-1970s that is actually true. A square young intern sat listening to a typical debate about what to cover and what not to cover, about new trends in gay sexual practices. After the meeting, this young intern, scratching his head, approached a senior editor and asked for guidance.

"Now let me get this straight," he said. "We're against gentrification, and we're for fist-fucking. Do I have this right?"

JAMES WOLCOTT: The one in that era who really blew himself up was Lucian Truscott. I met Lucian somewhere, and I was having some problem with the *Voice*, and he said, "Well, here's what you ought to do: You want to go in there and turn the piece in as you wrote it originally, and just say, 'If you don't like it, you can just stick it up your fucking ass! I'm sick of all this!'" And I'm nodding and I'm thinking, "No, I am not gonna do that!" I was a popular writer at the paper then, but nobody is indispensable.

LUCIAN K. TRUSCOTT IV: Clay went to the fifth floor all the time. I had a desk on the fourth floor, and I can hear him screaming at people at the top of his lungs. I got on the subway one day and went to the *New York* magazine's office and went in and asked to see him. We went down the street for a cup of coffee. I ordered coffee. He didn't drink coffee, he drank Ovaltine. He said, "Well, what's on your mind?" I said, "Well, actually only one thing, and that is I've been hearing you scream at people on the fifth floor. I just wanted to let you know, you can go ahead and scream at as many of them as you want to, but you're not going to *fucking* scream at me." I had a rule that nobody yelled at me. That applied when I was in the army. The last time I was yelled at was when I was a plebe at West Point.

I let it drop and he looked at me in awe. I waited for him to say something, and he didn't say anything. I said, "Well, that's all I got." I just dropped a dollar on the fucking table and left. Three days later, Judy Daniels called me up and said, "Felker wants you to go to Israel. He said the Golan Heights peace accord's gonna be signed; everybody's convinced there's going to be a war." I was gone for fucking—I don't know, four months. I wrote a whole series of articles on terrorism. I got over there—there was no war, but there's lots of terrorism.

JAMES WOLCOTT: They only ran a couple of them. He was just furious about it. It was basically, "I'm risking my life over there. . . ." He threw a big tantrum in the office. He wasn't [yelling] at Felker. He was doing it at the managing editor, who was a woman, Judy Daniels.

LUCIAN K. TRUSCOTT IV: I wrote a story about Bob Dylan when he was putting the Rolling Thunder tour together. I was going over to the Bitter End every night, because a friend of mine was playing in the house band. I wrote a story about it, and I handed it in, and the *Voice* didn't want it.

Christgau came up with some phony fucking reason why he wouldn't run the story, and he didn't even tell me. Judy Daniels told me. I dropped it off at the *New Yorker*, because I knew William Shawn. When they told me they're going to run this story, I went back down to the *Voice* and got a piece of paper and wrote my resignation and quit.

ROBERT CHRISTGAU: If that happened, I don't remember it.

JAMES WOLCOTT: He was just browbeating Judy Daniels and stormed out. It probably worked for him at a time pre-Felker, maybe he did it with other people, but it was not going to work in this era.

MICHAEL FEINGOLD: After he had owned it a few weeks, I had brought in a piece. We did the edit and I said, "Is that Clay Felker over there?" And Ross said, "Yes." And I said, "I've never met him." So, we finished the edits, and he walked me over and he said, "Clay, I don't think you've met Michael Feingold, he's one of our drama critics." And Felker, without looking up, said, "Oh, tell him to write shorter."

VIVIAN GORNICK: When Clay Felker took over, he called us all together, and he delivered this address in which he said to us, "Here's the way it's going to go: the *Village Voice* is going to go on exactly as it did before only now we're going to have a naked lady on the cover."

And he said, "Inside, it will be just like it was before, but on the outside you'll have a naked lady and therefore will draw all the readers we would not have drawn otherwise." And we all went ballistic. We called a strike of all writers and editors to deal with this. We were going to take control, like, we were going to run it. But it didn't go anywhere. It was an alarming development.

MICHAEL FEINGOLD: That was when all the features became like *New York* magazine, and somebody said, "The basic *Village Voice* feature is something about how Jews talk to their gay plants."*

ALAN WEITZ: A woman named Judy Coburn had written an article about Vietnamese refugees. Clay objected to something in Judy's article. He thought it was much too leftist, and he started yelling. He was in the art

---

* Alexander Cockburn wrote this in his *Voice* column.

department. Karen Durbin was trying to defend the article because she was editing it, although it then would have to go through me.

This big fight broke out. People gathered around, and Clay was yelling. I went over there, and Judy Daniels was standing next to me. I don't know what possessed me, but Clay started shouting, "Why can't I get any cooperation!?" And I said in a very low voice, "Because you don't know how to be civil." I thought Judy was going to faint, because people didn't talk back to Clay, and I never had before.

MOLLY HASKELL: It was not loose at all anymore. They were trying to systematize something whose whole nature was to be free-flying. These were not some nine-to-five writers. Somehow, the *Voice*'s spirit survived all these things, still.

ALAN WEITZ: One night when Judy Daniels and I came back from the printer, I said to her, "I'm going to resign." She said, "You can't!" And she took me up to her house, her gorgeous apartment, and made tea. She had a silver tea set—I don't think I'd ever seen one. She tried to talk me out of it. I knew I was going to resign. It was a terrible career move, but I felt I had to be loyal to Dan.

VIVIAN GORNICK: We also thought the paper was finished. He was a slick. We thought he didn't understand downtown New York—and he didn't. He never was at home at the *Voice*, never. We were not his people. He was Midtown. He was Uptown. I don't know what he was.

ROBIN REISIG: I was there for one year of Felker when people slowly quit, and it was lucky I quit when I did, because I would have had to quit a few months later because they fired Mary Nichols. They hired Nelson Rockefeller's son-in-law to be editor of the paper. One of the things Mary regularly muckraked was Nelson Rockefeller, and he was vice president. So, when the Rockefeller connection guy came in, she chose to do a big new muckraking piece about Rockefeller, and she handed it in to him, and he said, "I just don't think it's going to work out between us."

HOWARD BLUM: Tom Morgan became the editor of the *Voice*, and Tom fired Mary. It was real belligerence. And then I was young enough to walk out in protest. I went off and did my first book at twenty-four or so.

MARY PEROT NICHOLS: One day I came in with this very strong piece on Rockefeller in the UDC.* He threw it back at me, and I said, "Well, can I publish it elsewhere?" He said, "Yes," then he told me to go collect my severance. I published the story in the *SoHo Weekly News*. I actually wanted to be out, so I was pushing things a little harder than I might have. I thought they'd give me a decent severance, which they didn't. They offered me, after seventeen years, eleven weeks' salary, and I thought that was an outrage.

I sued Hamill, Newfield, and Tom Morgan when I left the *Voice*. I sued Hamill and Newfield for defamation, because they went running to *The Villager* when I got fired from the *Voice* by Tom Morgan and said that I was crazy and a whole lot of other things. Would have made it impossible for me to ever get a job again.

Another one of my causes was the Mafia on the Brooklyn waterfront, which drove Lindsay absolutely wild, because I used to keep asking, "What's Mr. Clean doing with Mr. Dirty?" I was told years later by an Italian guy who used to work in Tom Morgan's office that that's the real reason that Tom Morgan fired me at the *Village Voice*—because they were so furious at what I did to Lindsay's image by reminding everybody that he'd gotten into a bed with a capo.

---

* Urban Development Corporation.

CHAPTER 21

"THE MUSIC SECTION WAS SUDDENLY IN FLOWER"

ROBERT CHRISTGAU: My takeover of Riffs was in itself a crucial moment. It changed, the pieces were longer, better. It turned the *Voice* into the most important music publication in the country except for *Rolling Stone* within six months.

At the same time, rock criticism via *Creem* was in this incredible efflorescence. There were these two poles: there was *Rolling Stone* and *Creem*, which conceived itself as the anti–*Rolling Stone*. While I preferred *Creem*, I certainly didn't think there was no good writing in *Rolling Stone*, where Greil Marcus is editing the review section for a while and changes everything by doing so.

And then there's Lester Bangs. He was dynamite and is kicked off of *Rolling Stone* because he pans somebody wrong, and then they pick him up at *Creem*, and he basically takes the magazine over on sheer energy.

LESTER BANGS: I got this letter from Dave Marsh at *Creem* that said, "Yeah, kid, I've been looking at your stuff for a while. It looks really good." And something to the effect that "you take way too much acid and don't drink half enough whiskey."

CAROLA DIBBELL: There were a lot of terrific *Creem* writers. It gave you permission to be wrong, to be a fan, to be amateurish, and to be experimental, maybe in even an arty way, while writing about this popular form. And that was really clear in *Creem*, and it wasn't just Lester. Meltzer was amazing.

ROBERT CHRISTGAU: Richard Meltzer was *Crawdaddy*, and Richard Meltzer was a law unto himself. And there's Vince Aletti, this gay guy who

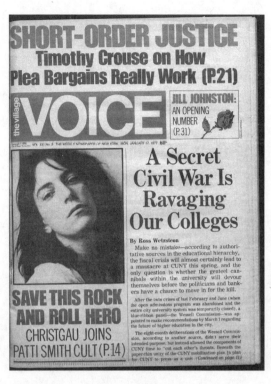

SHORT-ORDER JUSTICE
Timothy Crouse on How
Plea Bargains Really Work (P.21)

the village VOICE

JILL JOHNSTON:
AN OPENING
NUMBER
(P.31)

VOL XXI No. 3 THE WEEKLY NEWSPAPER OF NEW YORK. MON. JANUARY 17, 1977 60¢

A Secret
Civil War Is
Ravaging
Our Colleges

By Ross Wetzsteon

Make no mistake—according to authoritative sources in the educational hierarchy, the fiscal crisis will almost certainly lead to a massacre at CUNY this spring, and the only question is whether the genteel cannibals within the university will devour themselves before the politicians and bankers have a chance to move in for the kill.

After the twin crises of last February and June (when the open admissions program was abandoned and the entire city university system was temporarily closed), a blue-ribbon panel—the Wessell Commission—was appointed to make recommendations by March 1 regarding the future of higher education in the city.

The eight-month deliberations of the Wessell Commission, according to another source, didn't serve their intended purpose, but instead allowed the components of CUNY time to "cut each other's throats. Beneath the paper-thin unity of the CUNY mobilization plan [a plan for CUNY to press as a unit (Continued on page 11)

SAVE THIS ROCK
AND ROLL HERO
CHRISTGAU JOINS
PATTI SMITH CULT (P.14)

Patti Smith's star-making turn on the *Voice* cover, 1977. Cover image © Village Voice/ Street Media.

likes Black music and disco, and before there is disco, and *Creem* published him, too.

VINCE ALETTI: All of us were freelancing; we weren't making much money, but we all were dying to talk about the things that we were excited about. And eventually, I got a regular column in *Creem*, and I had some regular slots at different places. Bob was my first editor at the *Voice*. And for me, he and Richard were the most influential.

ROBERT CHRISTGAU: I was interested in pop albums right from the start. The first was Vince Aletti on the Jackson 5. That was the first lead, and the second lead was Richard Meltzer on Waylon Jennings, a country singer. Neither of those people were writing for the *Village Voice* or for *Rolling Stone*, and I wanted people like that to have a voice, a place to go.

VINCE ALETTI: I started going to The Loft in '71 or '72 with a group of friends. It became a weekly experience for me. Going at midnight, dancing for hours with friends, and realizing that this was one of a number of underground scenes that were generating music that I didn't hear in any other place. "Disco" was not a word.

I was one of the few people writing about what I was writing about. So, if Bob was looking for somebody to cover Aretha Franklin or the Jackson 5 or Mary Wells or something, I was the person. I became the go-to person for R&B and Black pop records.

BILLY ALTMAN: I wrote punk pieces at the *Voice*. Jon Pareles filled in for Bob when he went on vacation several times, and then, of course, got his job at the *Times*. I wrote a number of pieces for Jon that were some of the funniest pieces I ever wrote for the *Voice*. Jon asked me to write about Styx. I couldn't possibly take that seriously. I wrote what would now be a live Twitter feed. I did a minute-by-minute review. Just like: "9:32: They take the stage. 9:35: This happened." One of my favorite pieces for the *Voice*. Nobody from Styx has ever talked to me since.

ROBERT CHRISTGAU: There were many, many new, good writers work-ing for the *Voice*, starting with Greil Marcus, Lester Bangs, Stephen Holden, Janet Maslin. I published Richard Meltzer. I gave Gary Giddins his column and encouraged him to write longer and more ambitiously. I could see he was a fucking genius. The music section was suddenly in flower, and people were flocking to it. I remained on the lookout for new writers all the time. I can't tell you how exciting that was.

JACKIE RUDIN: I was enthralled with the *Voice*. That was like my bible. Sandy Fendrick, who was the director of advertising—we immediately charmed each other. She was a hard-ass bitch. She loved my gumption. She hired me on the spot. She walked me up to Bartle Bull, who was then the publisher of the *Village Voice*, and said, "We're hiring this young woman, and she's starting today." That must have been 1971 or '72. I had an apartment on Prince Street at the time. My rent was seventy-five dollars a month.

I knew everybody; everybody knew me. I found heaven. There was noth-ing in the world more exciting than going to work every day at the *Village Voice*—the people you'd meet, the fact that I was living in a place that was reflecting everything about my own lifestyle. I hung out with gay men. I went out every night. I would go to Max's, CBGB's, the Mudd Club, and the Limelight. And eventually got turned on to some lesbians and hadn't even thought that was something I was interested in and fell in love with someone and came out. I remember the first day that I slept with this woman, who lived down the block from the *Village Voice*, and I came to work the next morning, and I paraded myself on the advertising floor. And I said, "Guess what happened to me last night?" I got a standing ovation. That's how it was at the *Village Voice*.

I dealt with music and the clubs. I was there the day Hilly Kristal walked in to place the first ad for CBGB and helped design it.

LENNY KAYE: You would open up the *Voice* and see who's playing at CBGB's, so the listings were very important.

FRANK RUSCITTI: You couldn't buy ad space in the *Voice* it was so hot. Every single person in New York wanted to be on the *Village Voice* bulletin board on the back page. The classifieds themselves—the apartment ads, which are, historically, the thing from the *Voice*—pretty much kept that paper in the black, year after year after year. Tuesday nights, people standing on line at the different kiosks, waiting for the earliest copy of the *Voice* to come in. And every single one of them was there because of the apartment ads.

GUY TREBAY: The thing was so thick, it was like a doormat in the '70s and '80s.

JACKIE RUDIN: Nothing sold as much per line than a classified ad. We couldn't even handle the amount of classified advertising that came in. This is all apartment searching. People found their lives through the *Village Voice*, whether it was a partner, or a job, or an apartment.

CLEM BURKE: My two apartments I found in the *Voice* for sure; I found one on East Chelsea, and then my loft in Gramercy Park through the *Village Voice*.

CHRIS STEIN: Debbie and me, I wouldn't be surprised if we got our 17th Street apartment through the *Voice*—the one with the photograph of her in the kitchen with the flaming frying pan. The music ads were a whole thing. That's how we got Clem, our fucking drummer.

CLASSIFIEDS, MARCH 10, 1975

Freak energy Musical Experienced drummer needed female fronted estab. working NYC rock band. Excell optty. money. Fun. Call NOW 925-0531.

DEBBIE HARRY: Yeah, "freak energy drummer." There were sixty applicants. It was insane. Some of the craziest people in New York, or ever anywhere, and all different kinds, all different types. It shows what kind of reach the *Village Voice* had.

CLEM BURKE: It wasn't really a typical musical audition. Famously, they really liked my shoes.

MAX WEINBERG: I got my job with Bruce Springsteen and the E Street Band through the *Village Voice*. The best thing about the *Village Voice* was it had every listing of every live show, it had extensive album reviews, and it had the largest want ads. The *Village Voice* really took their public-notice music section very seriously.

I was going to college, and I fell in with this group of musicians from upstate New York, and the *Village Voice* was their bible. I'd heard the name Bruce Springsteen around, but I hadn't heard any of his music. Joe Delia, a well-known composer and pianist, said, "They're still looking for a drummer. Here's the ad they put in the *Voice*." It said, "Wanted drummer and keyboard player." For the drummer: "No Junior Ginger Bakers here." Ginger Baker was the incredible, flamboyant, recently deceased drummer for Cream. He was a soloist. And it said, "All must sing, and the piano player should be able to play Chuck Berry to classical." The wording of it was very specific, because

No Junior Ginger Bakers: The Bruce Springsteen classified ad that Max Weinberg answered. Photo © Village Voice/Street Media.

where they refer to the drummer as "not a junior Ginger Baker," that spoke to me; they wanted an accompanist.

Somewhere north of sixty drummers auditioned. I went there for an audition knowing nothing and having no preconceptions, and I thought I did terribly. But I saw immediately that him and the guys were unbelievable. He played standing five feet in front of me with the same intensity that he plays with in a stadium. It's pretty hard not to feel that energy.

Everybody got a half hour whether they were good or not. But we played three hours that first time, so I didn't know any different. Plus, I was from New Jersey. He asked me where I was from, and he said, "That's good." He was from South Jersey.

That's how I got the job. So, the *Village Voice* had a major role in the next forty-six years of my life.

ROBERT CHRISTGAU: I get there in August of '74. By April of '75, I'd gotten this handwritten invitation to go see the Ramones. I saw them in April of '75, and Patti Smith was beginning her first stay. She had a residency at CBGB.

LUCIAN K. TRUSCOTT IV: I got her one of her first paying gigs at Reno Sweeney. She and Lenny Kaye were just starting out.

She used to come by the *Voice*, and when I wasn't there she would get one of those pink memo slips for the telephone and write a little poem that basically said, "Hi, Lucian. It's Patti. Why weren't you here? I wanted a drink. I wanted to go to Bradley's with you." She wrote probably ten of them.

Reno Sweeney had just opened; they had an open mic night on Monday nights, and it was sucking. I said, "Well, I know somebody that can play for you." At that point, Lenny Kaye was playing his guitar and she was chanting poetry, basically. I went to the first Monday night she played. There weren't that many people there, but the word of mouth started spreading, and they got more people in there.

The thing that got me about her that was a little off-putting—but it's the thing that she made her career out of—she had this earnestness. She was able to take what I thought at the time was a really limited amount of musical talent and just wring every fucking drop of *oomph* out of it. She really felt it in her bones.

CHRIS STEIN: I saw her super early on. She would read poetry, and then Lenny would come out and accompany her, and it was almost like a parody. But she was amazing. I remember leaving one show and going, "Why doesn't she have a band?"

LENNY KAYE: Before CBGB's, all the places for New York bands to play were gone. All the other clubs were national acts. Max's had closed, which had a brief spell of booking local bands. It was as simple as, "Gee, there's a place for bands to play." When we started performing regularly, we found a lot of support and energy from the *Voice* because it was our target audience.

CAROLA DIBBELL: Bob endeared himself to Patti. She was singing, it was just her and Lenny, and there was some asshole who wouldn't exactly say, "Take it off," but he was that mentality. He started to go like this [*claps*], and Bob typed up, "What is the sound of one asshole clapping?" It was a good opening.

JAMES WOLCOTT: I got hired in the circulation department. I also manned the phones and listened to everybody's complaints.

LUCIAN K. TRUSCOTT IV: I was friendly with Wolcott. Wolcott was always complaining to me, saying, "God. How do you get to be a writer here? I don't want to sit here at this desk forever." I said to him, "Well, if you want to write for the *Voice*, fucking write. What did you do last night?" He said, "I went into this place called CBGB." I said, "Write about that." And he did.

ROBERT CHRISTGAU: The motherfucker was a dream of a writer.

JAMES WOLCOTT: Clay put me on a stipend, and then I had to turn in a certain number of pieces and keep writing. I was writing about television, and it became an actual column. I was assigned to write a performance review of Patti Smith, of whom I knew very little. I asked people about her, and I got totally disparate things. Some people said, "Oh, she's fantastic, she's really funny, she's great." And other people going, "Oh, she's a complete poser." It was fantastic, and I just loved CBGB. It was so cruddy and so informal and so loose.

JAMES WOLCOTT, "PATTI SMITH: MUSTANG RISING," *VILLAGE VOICE*, APRIL 14, 1975

Patti Smith moves through a room like a shark through the lower depths. Sharp features, oilblack hair, dark intense eyes. A lithe toughness.

So her smile catches you by surprise, not only because it's switchblade quick, but because it's not the smile of a killer. So many reports on Patti Smith have made her sound demonic, word-crazed—a cocaine Ophelia—that I was surprised to see her so poised a performer. Her flakiness is legendary but her smile carries the weight of professional confidence.

JAMES WOLCOTT: I kept going back, and she was one who was, "You gotta see this band, Television. They're really loud and often out of tune, but you gotta see them." I was there maybe four, five nights a week, depending on who was playing. I saw the whole thing unfold.

Christgau was very dubious at first about the whole thing. He had a real devotion to the New York Dolls, and in the beginning he didn't feel like any of these bands matched the New York Dolls. But Bob was nearby, so you would see him there, and he certainly wrote about it a lot.

ROBERT CHRISTGAU: I loved it myself. The things that were happening at CBGB were things I wanted to happen in music.

JAMES WOLCOTT: All of a sudden, it was one amazing band after another. I saw the very first performances Talking Heads did there. They would open for the Ramones, and they were coming out in their little Lacoste shirts.

ROBERT CHRISTGAU: We adored the Ramones the first time we saw them, and it was early. Short, fast, catchy songs with a good beat. Just simple as that. That was the Ramones more than anybody, but it was also true of Blondie.

DEBBIE HARRY: We started together in 1973. It wasn't really a scene when we started playing there. And then we'd drag our shit in there and we'd play, and a lot of the older guys would sit at the bar holding their ears. We would have ten friends sitting around in front closer to the stage. And that was it. It was like a private party in your basement or something.

LENNY KAYE: I remember standing outside CBGB's once, maybe '75, '76, and thinking, "This is a lot like the San Francisco scene."

It was Cheers for the Lower East Side. Everybody knows your name. What I loved about CBGB was that the early bands there sounded nothing like each other. Tom Verlaine once said that every band was like an idea. And there was very little similarity between us, Television, the Ramones, Talking Heads, Blondie, and the other twelve bands that played there early on.

DEBBIE HARRY: We started in '73. I don't think CBGB's started to be a scene until '76. It was like three years of farm work. Then all of a sudden, some people latched on to a couple of bands, and it became important very quickly.

CHRIS STEIN: The *Voice* and the *SoHo News* were instrumental, certainly.

ROBERT CHRISTGAU: We treated every one of those albums as being a major piece of work, and I thought hard about who should review them.

CAROLA DIBBELL: Talking Heads were really remarkable in that era. That's when Richard Goldstein said his famous thing, right? About his voice?

ROBERT CHRISTGAU: About David Byrne. In a good way. He turned in what I consider this fucking classic piece.

RICHARD GOLDSTEIN, "TALKING HEADS HYPERVENTILATE SOME CLICHÉS," *VILLAGE VOICE*, FEBRUARY 2, 1976

Talking Heads is organized around a remote and skinny guy named David Byrne, who sings in a high somber voice, somewhat like a seagull talking to its shrink. . . .

If Jonathan Richman plays the kid who ate his snot, David plays the kid who held his farts in. He doesn't move like any rock star ever. He wobbles and cranes his neck—not spastically but with tension—and his voice rises as though he is about to yell at his mother. One soon comes to accept this as yet another pose—the neurasthenic Roy Orbison.

ROBERT CHRISTGAU: We spent two nights a week at CB's, for about a year and a half. It was not unusual to have a double bill. Television and

Talking Heads, two of the greatest rock bands in fucking history and on the same bill! Just for that, it was amazing.

Hilly put on this big ten-day festival, which we* missed because we were on vacation upstate, and Goldstein, not me, assigned Wolcott to cover it, and that story was a major, major story in the increasing visibility and importance of the *Village Voice*.

JAMES WOLCOTT: I ran into people years later who said that that piece made them want to come to New York: "I wanna see this."

JAMES WOLCOTT, "A CONSERVATIVE IMPULSE IN THE NEW ROCK UNDERGROUND," *VILLAGE VOICE*, AUGUST 18, 1975

What CBGB is trying to do is nothing less than to restore that spirit as a force in rock and roll. One is left speculating about success: Will any of the bands who play there ever amount to anything more than a cheap evening of rock and roll?

I don't know, and in the deepest sense, don't care. These bands don't have to be the vanguard in order to satisfy. In a cheering Velvets song, Lou Reed sings: "A little wine in the morning, and some breakfast at night / Well, I'm beginning to see the light." And that's what rock gives: small unconventional pleasures which lead to moments of perception.

CHRIS STEIN: That was when everything really picked up a notch.

JAMES WOLCOTT: There were no real barriers at CBGB. There was a long bar. There was a little backstage area, but nobody wanted to hang around the backstage area because it was so cruddy.

And then you had people like Lester Bangs, who was writing, but also he had a band.

He came to New York from *Creem*. People loved Lester, and they loved reading him. You couldn't help but like him. He could be very funny, very self-deprecating. He was ready for anything. He was just another big fish among other big fish. He had to submit pieces, and he had a hard time initially.

GREIL MARCUS: I noticed his reviews in *Rolling Stone*—I think the first was of the MC5's *Kick Out the Jams*, which he hated, and compared to the Troggs, which he put down. Of course, he later wrote his heart out about both. When I became the records editor there in June of 1969, I found he was sending in five to fifteen reviews a week, most of which were ignored. I took two to make up the heart of my first section, a definitive hit piece on *It's a Beautiful Day* and a historic embrace of Captain Beefheart's *Trout Mask Replica*, not because I wanted to cover those records—I didn't care—but because I wanted to showcase and introduce a particular critic and a particular critical sensibility.

ROBERT CHRISTGAU: Lester was writing for the *Voice* while he was still in Detroit, and then he decided to move to New York. He was there, there, there, there, there. You couldn't miss him. Twice as large as life.

BILLY ALTMAN: How many people would you know who are writers who are the same off the page as on? It's why he was such a popular writer, because he was what he wrote. If you met him, you'd have the conversation with him as if it was a piece he'd written. That's how terrific he was at translating his thoughts into writing. That was him, on and off the page.

ROBERT CHRISTGAU: He lived a few blocks from the *Voice*, at a place that didn't have a phone, and more than once I went and knocked on his door. Kit Rachlis said I am the only editor who made house calls.

Fall of '76, he could cover stuff in New York, and he began hanging out at the *Voice*. And it changed him. The *Voice* changed him, as it changed other people. Stanley Crouch is another one. They'd come to understand that we weren't ideologues, that we were really people who cared about other people's happiness and were serious and nowhere as rigid as we were imagined to be, or as ideological—because we weren't. There were very few people like that at the *Voice*.

People think that the famous piece he wrote about racism and punk—that I wrote it for him or made him write it. He came in and started raving about it himself to me. He initiated that conversation.

LESTER BANGS, "THE WHITE NOISE SUPREMACISTS," *VILLAGE VOICE*, APRIL 30, 1979

The other day I was talking on the phone with a friend who hangs out on the CBGB scene a lot. She was regaling me with examples of the delights available to females in the New York subway system. "So the train came to a sudden halt and I fell on my ass in the middle of the car, and not only did nobody offer to help me up but all these boons just sat there laughing at me."

"Boons?" I said. "What's boons?"

"You know," she said. "Black guys."

"Why do you call them that?"

"I dunno. From 'baboons,' I guess."

I didn't say anything.

CAROLA DIBBELL: Lester remembers having had a conversation with Ivan Julian in which Lester had used the word "nigger." This is long after Lester says to him, "You probably don't remember that." And Ivan Julian said, "No, I do remember."

ROBERT CHRISTGAU: Ivan was a guitarist in Richard Hell's band. Hell of a good guitarist too. He was a Black guy.

CAROLA DIBBELL: Lester was talking about himself, too. People say that he regretted having written the article, and maybe he did, but it was definitely worth somebody saying it.

LESTER BANGS: If anything I'm too moralistic and pompous. I'm always preaching. I should knock that shit off. Don't you think so?

ROBERT CHRISTGAU: He still gets shit for it, and there's not a FUCK-ING thing wrong with it.

CHAPTER 22

"A SITTING STATE SUPREME COURT JUSTICE READ THE DECISION AND BROKE DOWN AND CRIED"

MARIANNE PARTRIDGE: I ran into Clay at a dinner party with Jann Wenner. I worked for *Rolling Stone*, which at that time was in San Francisco. I was a senior editor and organized the copy department. I came in as a copy chief; I was the first woman editor.

Clay was like, "I've been trying to meet you."

I was hired first as a managing editor, and within a very short time I became the editor of the *Voice*. I started bringing the paper back to some serious stuff.

LUCIAN K. TRUSCOTT IV: Jack Newfield's influence went up. They went back to doing the things that the *Voice* had always done the best. Like the 10 Worst Landlords, the 10 Worst Judges. Wayne Barrett came on board in those years. And the *Village Voice* went back to being what it had been.

MARIANNE PARTRIDGE: Richard Goldstein wrote something that was negative about the children's ballet. But it enraged Clay, and he wanted me to fire him. He yelled and screamed at me for a long time in his office. I kept saying, "If I'm not in charge of hiring and firing, then I'm not the editor, and you'll have to fire me first." I was calm, I was quiet. He kept saying, "This is good. You could really take my yelling. I like this. This is good."

MARIANNE PARTRIDGE: When I became the editor of the *Voice*, I was living uptown, and our building got sold. There were older people in the building that were telling me, "Did your heat come on?" I told Jack. He said, "This sounds very suspicious. I'm going to look into it." Well, by god, it turns out that these assholes were terrible landlords, and they were *deliberately* running the older people out of the building because they had rent control.

DENIS HAMILL: Newfield was a great muckraker. He's the one that started the 10 Worst Landlords, the 10 Worst Judges. They were compelling reads.

TOM ROBBINS: The first story we did together was one of the Worst Landlords. I lived in an apartment in Brooklyn with a roof leak, and I was sitting there with buckets all around me, typing up the Worst Landlords.

JACK NEWFIELD: The background to the 10 Worst Judges piece was a series of judge-raking exposés I had written for the *Voice* early in 1972, exposing one judge's lenient favoritism toward mobsters and drug dealers and another judge's racist attitude toward Blacks. Felker suggested that I do a piece naming New York's ten worst judges and printing all of their pictures with the text. I did two months of fresh reporting, finding cops, court officers, and court stenographers my best sources.

It caused a sensation when it came out. People went nuts. My lawyer, Martin Garbus, called me up one day and said, "I have good news and bad news for you. The good news is the bar association is starting an investigation because of your article. The bad news is they are investigating you, not the judges."

VICTOR KOVNER: In 1966, I joined a small firm that soon thereafter became known as Koch, Lankenau, Schwartz, and Kovner. Edward I. Koch was then a district leader in the Village with political ambitions, and among his clients were the *Village Voice*. I started to act as its outside counsel. I became involved in media law—libel, privacy, copyright, trademark.

You want the highlights? There are so many highlights. Among the highlights was the Rinaldi litigation, Justice Dominic Rinaldi. After describing an incident in the court where a judge released without bail an alleged drug dealer, Newfield concluded in the harshest language that the conduct was incompetent and probably corrupt.

JACK NEWFIELD, "THE POLITICS OF JUSTICE," *VILLAGE VOICE*, NOVEMBER 9, 1972

Brooklyn Supreme Court Justice Dominic Rinaldi is a typical machine judge. And as I have written in these pages before, Rinaldi has been simultaneously repressive toward blacks, and permissive with heroin dealers and members of the Mafia.

VICTOR KOVNER: I was comfortable not that we weren't going to be sued, but that we would win. It led to two lawsuits. It ultimately went, after a tangled history, to the highest court in the state and to the Supreme Court of the United States, which didn't take it.

We lost in the state supreme court and in the appellate division. And those decisions were reversed in the court of appeals, the highest court of our state.

The key thing was Newfield's statement that Rinaldi was incompetent and probably corrupt based in large part on letting a drug dealer free on bail and giving a hard time to the police officer who made the arrest. The court found that it was almost entirely a threat protected by opinion, based upon disclosed facts. It was a very challenging victory, but it's frequently cited today.*

TOM ROBBINS: There is an opinion and a perspective in the headline. "These are the worst! These are bad people!" Right? There is a perspective and a judgment that's included in that, which other papers clearly wouldn't do. And you wouldn't read that in the *New York Times*. For many years, you wouldn't read it in any other newspaper, too. Now you might.

---

* The case has been cited more than five hundred times in state and federal decisions.

VICTOR KOVNER: The *Voice* changed government ethics, practices, and rules in New York and elsewhere. It fought for and helped change the manner in which the criticisms of judges are handled. It helped establish these judicial conduct commissions which exist in almost every state. I worked for the *Voice* from the mid-'60s through roughly 2000; there was never a plaintiff's judgment against the *Voice*.

JACK NEWFIELD: The legal establishment's overreaction to the piece convinced me I should do it regularly, to accustom judges to journalistic scrutiny.

JANIE EISENBERG: Every time I would go for jury duty and they would interview me and I would mention that I was married to Jack Newfield, I was immediately dismissed.

VICTOR KOVNER: The chief judge of the court of appeals who wrote the decision, the late Lawrence Cooke, told me later that a sitting state supreme court justice not involved in the case read the decision and broke down and cried.

CHAPTER 23

"WE STARTED WRITING WHAT THEY CALL THE NEW JOURNALISM"

JAMES RIDGEWAY: I got into the *Voice*, literally, because of Jack Newfield. If you were on his side or he liked you, he'd never drop you. You could always, always depend upon him, even when he had some of the more boring ideas in the history of mankind.

I went to Princeton University. I was a pretty straight, middle-class person. I thought I had to work in these big papers. When I got fired from the *Wall Street Journal*, I thought the fucking world was caving in. I went to England and worked at *The Observer* and *The Economist*. Since I'd written for these British papers, advocacy journalism didn't mean much to me because that was what I did anyhow. I would always look at something like a brief, and I'd try to get to the bottom of it and figure out what was going on.

Yeah, I was the one that created Ralph Nader. See, Ralph Nader was the one who first revealed the problems with the Corvair car—it had a gas tank in the front part, and I guess it blew up every once in a while.

MICHAEL MOORE: Ralph wrote his first book, *Unsafe at Any Speed*, and boom! That was the end of that car. Ridgeway then, through his investigative reporting, discovered that General Motors had hired spies that followed Nader and violated his privacy, and wrote that story that resulted in General Motors having to apologize and pay Nader an out-of-court settlement.

I was at my office in Flint one day. A knock on the door. He introduces himself as Jim Ridgeway. And I read the *Village Voice*. The postmaster told me in town, "You know, there's only, like, two people here in Flint that get the *Village Voice* sent to them, and you're one of them."

He said—this is when the first big round of layoffs started taking place at General Motors—"I'm going to do a story on how the Klan and the neo-Nazis and these white supremacists are taking advantage of what was then the 29 percent unemployment rate in Flint." They were convincing a lot of white people to join their group. He and this other filmmaker were thinking of doing a documentary on it, and did I know anything about these groups? I said, "Yeah, I know a lot about them. I've interviewed them, I've gone to their places where they worship." So, they asked me if I would help them and come with them on the shoot. It's the first time I'd been on a movie shoot.

So, the first time I did anything like this on camera is 1985, '86. It's called *Blood in the Face.** It's how white people are identified, because if you touch the skin, pinch it, slap it, whatever, it turns red. People of color don't show blood as easily. It will look somewhat scary that I rattled the white supremacists in the way that I did, but it also gave me an idea that maybe I should think about making a movie.

JAMES RIDGEWAY: Moore came to Washington, and he didn't have much of anywhere to go, so Nader hired him, and kept him and his wife employed, and he made his first movie. And Kevin, my partner in the film, I think he shot it for free.

MICHAEL MOORE: That is the great gift of Jim Ridgeway and Kevin Rafferty, that they had me be part of their film, and a year later I was making *Roger and Me* for the next three years.

JAMES RIDGEWAY: I've always dealt with marginal scenes, so I'm pretty familiar with the neo-Nazi, Klan scene. I knew a lot of those people, I filmed them, and I used to talk to them quite a bit. They actually liked my book because it was pretty straight. A lot of lefties didn't like it because they thought, "They're bad, and why should you be writing about bad people?" I told them to go fuck themselves. I'm very much a regular journalist; I don't pay much attention to what I should do and what I shouldn't do.

---

* *Blood in the Face* is a 1991 documentary inspired by Jim Ridgeway's 1990 book of the same name.

Press Clips columnist Alexander
Cockburn (right) and his editor Ron
Plotkin at the *Voice*, circa 1980.
Photo © Allen Reuben.

MARK JACOBSON: Ridgeway and Cockburn, they had a similar relationship to Newfield and Wayne. They worked closely together, but Cockburn
was the star. His name was big.

JAMES RIDGEWAY: I joined with Cockburn, whom I'd become friends
with, and we started writing this stuff together that was what they call the
New Journalism, which is a lot of supposition. Smart-ass stuff.

He was also writing the Press Clips column.

LAURA FLANDERS: The type of media criticism that has become so popular these days was started by Alexander. His Press Clips column at the *Village Voice* in the '70s through the '80s was really the first to take a weekly
look at the drivel that came out of the corporate media, and to hold it up
against the light of reality and say, "What gives?"

MARK JACOBSON: You gotta look up his father, Claud Cockburn. He's a
famous British left-wing writer.

PAUL BERMAN: It's an aristocratic Anglo-Irish family. His remote an-
cestors are George Cockburn, the British admiral who—we've been hearing
about how the Capitol in Washington has only been attacked once before, in

1814 by the British? That was Alex's ancestor. He thought it was good that his ancestor was a pirate for British imperialism.

RICHARD GOLDSTEIN: He was a certified upper-class British communist. Like a hard-core commie. But he was a wonderful writer. A wonderful guy. Afghanistan was in revolt against the Soviet Union, and he wrote this column calling Afghanis "wogs," and we screamed at him.* He was very pro-Soviet.

MARK JACOBSON: He was upset when Mao died. The guy was a murderer, man!

RICHARD GOLDSTEIN: He liked to wear tangerine scarves. He was a little bit of a dandy, but British.

JAMES RIDGEWAY: He had these girlfriends who were very rich, and big deals. He went from one big-deal girlfriend to another. He had Lally Weymouth, the daughter of Katharine Graham of the *Washington Post*, and he was with a Rothschild, and then he was with the daughter of the owner of the *Wall Street Journal*. He always had girls, and he never had any money.

PAUL BERMAN: He was totally different from everyone else. The *Voice* was, in general, a very plebeian place. It was not a place of upper-class finesse. But he was a man of the genuine aristocracy. Charming, humorous, witty. Handsome, appealing to the ladies. Affable. A brilliant stylist in a certain limited way. His Press Clips column was very readable. It was a marvelous column if you ignore what he actually said in it.

LAURA FLANDERS: There are a lot of fights that Alexander picked.

RICHARD GOLDSTEIN: Alex was reporting on this British scandal involving a cabinet minister and his male lover. The male lover had not been named. He had obtained a picture of the guy and his male lover, one of the few that showed them together, and he wanted to run this picture with his column. He wrote a caption—"Which one bites the pillow?" [*Laughs.*] That's very Alex.

---

* "Wog" is a racial slur used in Britain for people of color from the Middle East, East Asia, and North Africa.

CHAPTER 24

"THE *VILLAGE VOICE* IS AN APOCALYPTIC PUBLICATION"

MARY BREASTED: I had a friend named Wayne Barrett, who was a classmate of mine at Columbia Journalism School. Mary Nichols made me city editor to substitute for her when she was away on vacation. Wayne came to me with some story idea. I knew that he was interested in the Black politicians in Brooklyn, some of which were good, some of whom were corrupt. Wayne knew the difference.

WAYNE BARRETT: I was teaching in Ocean Hill–Brownsville, which had a demonstration project* that was despised by the teachers' union and that they were looking to shut down, so I got involved in the politics of that and found myself forced out of the school system.

MARY BREASTED: He called me about something to do with Brooklyn politics or schools, and I knew he knew what he was talking about. I knew he was a really good reporter. He'd been a reporter at UPI, United Press International.

ROBIN REISIG: Mary Nichols said to me in the '90s that Wayne was the best investigative reporter New York had ever seen, and that was an especially high tribute because Mary hadn't hired him.

Wayne did something no one had ever done—in my lifetime, anyway: he covered African American politicians in the outer boroughs. He was a

---

* A small-scale, low-cost method of testing out new proposals by governments or organizations.

watchdog of people who've never had watchdogs that were read by people in Manhattan.

WAYNE BARRETT: Ed Koch and I were inaugurated on the same day in 1978. He became mayor, and I became his weekly tormentor. I had written a few pieces for the *Voice* before I took over the Running Scared column that January, going back as far as 1973.* But I was now inheriting a column that Mary Nichols had made famous, and that had been written by greats like Jack Newfield, Ken Auletta, and Joe Conason.

JACK NEWFIELD: During Marianne's two years as editor, the *Voice* enjoyed one of its most vital cycles. She hired an eclectic group of excellent writers—including Michael Daly, Denis Hamill, Mark Jacobson, and Wayne Barrett. Those two years were the most fun I would have at the *Voice*, except for my early apprenticeship under Dan Wolf.

DENIS HAMILL: I was a rock 'n' roll freak, and I was into city politics, and I loved Newfield and I loved Nat Hentoff. I was a hippie growing up, so the *Village Voice* was standard reading. My first piece was cowritten with my brother, Pete. I had been working for a little local paper in Brooklyn called *Flatbush Life*. I wrote a column called Under the Boardwalk, which was all about Brooklyn. Pete was a good friend of Jack Newfield's, and Newfield started reading my stuff from *Flatbush*. When he read about the awful decline of the neighborhood, he said, "That would be a good piece for the *Voice*—would you and Pete be interested in doing it?" It was a thrilling thing for a young kid to get a byline in a citywide paper. I was about twenty-two, twenty-three.

MICHAEL DALY: I started at these community newspapers on Flatbush Avenue: *Flatbush Life*, *Kings Courier*, *Bay News*, and *Canarsie Digest*. It was eighty hours a week for eighty dollars a week. The perfect thing to start at, like going to the gym with your brain. I took a particular interest in Coney Island, and I developed a—I guess "friendship's" an odd word, but it really was a friendship, with the gang called the Homicides. The leader was a guy they called Outlaw. His real name was George Rivera. When George was about to have his first kid, his girlfriend was pregnant, and I went with him,

---

* Barrett's earliest stories for the *Voice* were actually published in the summer of '71.

and he sold his gun to buy Pampers. I wrote a piece about them. I got a free-lance assignment from the *Voice*. Marianne Partridge offered me a job.

It was February '77. I just started writing pieces.

MICHAEL DALY, "A REPORT FROM THE BOWERY: THE BOYS IN THE BOTTLE," *VILLAGE VOICE*, APRIL 18, 1977

The stomach cramps hit at four in the morning, twisting Bubba out of his sleep. At age 27, Bubba needs a drink every two hours. It was his fourth Good Friday on the Bowery and as he lay in a cubicle at the Prince Hotel Bubba knew that he had slept too long. Unless he got a drink, convulsions would soon follow the cramps. Bubba rolled onto the floor and groped for the quart of wine he had bought the night before. He took one taste and flung the bottle against the door. The bartender had sold him water.

DENIS HAMILL: I had a desk next to Mark Jacobson and Michael Daly. We all sat together; we were buddies.

MICHAEL DALY: Mark Jacobson had written about this basketball team out in Bath Beach, and he said it was at the "ass end of Brooklyn." I wrote him a nasty letter saying that Manhattan is "at the ass end of Brooklyn." I was there like a month or two, and all of a sudden he said, "Wait a minute." We'd both forgotten it.

He's a genius, Mark. You'd call him, and the music would be so loud you'd have to hold the phone away from the ear. You'd hear him going [*sucks, making a deep, Cheech Marin–like inhale*] on a joint, and you'd go, "Whatta ya doing?" And he'd go, "Just working, man. Just working."

MARK JACOBSON: That TV show *Taxi* is based on a story I wrote in *New York* magazine. I was driving a cab, and it was a whole new world. This is 1973. You couldn't go above 96th Street. You couldn't really go below 14th Street. Nobody would *ever* take you to the outer boroughs. It was embattled, right? Late at night, really the only guys you could pick up that weren't going to kill you were gay guys. They had their whole little scene over there on 12th Avenue. Guys would come out of a place called the Mineshaft wearing these leather masks zipped up—people you just didn't see in 1973. This was all new! What the fuck is this, the creature from the Black Lagoon or something? Once they got into the cab, they would be really polite.

They always would invite me into these clubs at night. "Come on, man. You're cute." So, one very fortuitous time I said, "Sure. What the hell? I'm not making any money anyhow." I went in, and it was like this paradise! It was like gay people and straight people and white people and Black people. The beginning of disco, right? Nobody knew anything—it was like hip-hop back in the South Bronx or something. It was just this unmarked place. I'd never seen anything like this before. So, I wrote a story about it. Vince Aletti helped me out. That's when I first met Vince Aletti.

I happened to be taking a class at the City College of New York at 138th Street uptown, and the teacher was "the famous Richard Goldstein."* He was working for *New York* magazine. So, I said, "What do you think of this?" He says, "Wow, man, this is really interesting. I'm going to give it to my editor at *New York* magazine." About a week later, I get a phone call. They ran the story, and they offered me a job, because they didn't have anybody like me. I was twenty-four years old.

Clay was obsessed with keeping me at *New York* magazine, because he saw me as part of his empire: "Having this guy who wears shorts, who, like, has an earring working for me at *New York* magazine—that's good. At the *Village Voice*, they got a hundred guys like that! You're too valuable here. At the *Voice*, you'll just be another asshole. Going down to the *Village Voice* is like death."

He turned out to be right, too. It's only now that I really realize that being a *Voice* writer, even for the few years that I was—because I was only there for four or five years tops—I mean, it's the most treasured part of my career. I had a fantastic time. But people, they look at you funny, man, they think you're weird. If you're pitching even pretty relentlessly mainstream stuff—that kind of patina follows you around. They're like, "Oh, he's probably some stoner or something like that."

Which is true, but anyhow.

---

* After writing his column Pop Eye, Goldstein left the *Voice* and became a contributing editor at *New York* magazine. When Clay Felker bought the *Voice*, Goldstein returned and became arts editor.

JONATHAN Z. LARSEN: I did a cover story in *New Times*.* It was the decline and fall of Clay Felker. Lucian had gotten on the inside of what was going on, and at some point in the article he talks to Rupert Murdoch, who describes his conversation with Clay Felker in which Felker says, "I don't know what I'm doing at the *Voice*. We just published the worst issue of *Village Voice* in its entire history." Felker knew that he was screwing it up.

LUCIAN K. TRUSCOTT IV: It was a six-thousand-word article about how Clay Felker lost the *Village Voice* and *New York* magazine to Rupert Murdoch.

They were making money hand over fist, but Felker was spending it hand over fist. When he took over the *Voice* in '74, the *Voice* had a staff, including classified, of about thirty. Within a year he had eighty people working at the *Village Voice*. Their profit margin was really slim. He didn't feel like he was being successful unless he saw a lot of buzz in front of him. But his circulation didn't go up, so they couldn't raise their ad rates, so the profits went down. The board of *New York* magazine, which owned the *Village Voice*, started getting upset with him.

They had a board meeting, and Felker came and asked for a raise. They were angry with him because the profits were getting pissed away. Felker was looking at Alan Patricof, Bartle Bull, Carter Burden, and these other rich guys, and he started saying, "But you guys all have houses in the Hamptons, and you own them, and I rent!" and he started crying.

CARTER BURDEN: He was living a total expense-account life. At one point, we found out that his maid was on the company payroll. I don't know where his money was going.

CLAY FELKER: We found that a lot of people in New York simply did not like the *Voice*. I was doing everything I knew how to do, and nothing seemed to work. We were doing huge promotional campaigns, radio advertising, trade-off ads with other publications, every kind of promotion I could think of. But it seemed as if there was an ingrained hatred for the *Voice* among certain New Yorkers.

---

* *New Times* was a biweekly newsmagazine unrelated to the alt-weekly newspaper chain New Times. Before editing the *Voice*, Larsen edited *New Times* magazine.

JONATHAN Z. LARSEN: The national edition was a terrible disaster. It ran a couple of months. People outside the *Village Voice*, and inside it, really quickly couldn't *stand* what Felker was producing. It finally led to this phone call with Rupert Murdoch, where he confessed he didn't know what he was doing. And Murdoch buys him out and takes it over.

RUPERT MURDOCH: Felker rang me up—and he was incredibly abusive. He was in the bullpen, at his desk in the office. I could hear people around him over the phone. He wanted an audience, and he was really giving it to me. "I'll sue you, I'll finish you in this town!"—he was making all kinds of threats. Then suddenly, after two or three minutes of abuse, he quieted down and was completely rational. He began telling me about his problems with the *Voice*. He said he had "completely lost it," lost a sense of what the paper was. The most recent issues had been the worst in the paper's history, he said. Then suddenly he's screaming at me again, threatening lawsuits, and I said, "Look, Clay, we're serious, but we haven't made up our minds. I'll get back to you."

What Clay never realized was the simple fact that there are ways to deal with a board of directors. He could have had them to lunch twice a year at the offices of *New York* with the governor or Teddy Kennedy or somebody. He could have flown them all to the West Coast for the founding of *New West*, given them a dinner at the Beverly Wilshire, introduced them as "my colleagues and friends."* With a few simple moves, he could have kept them happy. Instead, he made enemies of them, one by one.

ROBIN REISIG: Felker and his people would talk about how unfair it was what happened to him. He did exactly the same thing to Don and Ed. He's got no right to complain. Murdoch and Felker were friends, and Felker told Murdoch he was having some financial problems in his little empire, and then, because he knew that, Murdoch chose to come in and swoop down.

SONIA JAFFE ROBBINS: In early December '76, there was some news story that said, "Felker categorically denies that the *New York* magazine and the *Voice* were for sale," in which we all thought, "Oh no, this means that definitely we're for sale." It was a very dark period.

---

* *New West* was a failed West Coast version of *New York* magazine.

The paper's first female editor in chief, Marianne Partridge. Photo © James Hamilton.

RUPERT MURDOCH: The *Village Voice*, the bane of my existence.

MARK JACOBSON: I read about it in a Mexican newspaper when I was in Melaque taking magic mushrooms, and I was like, "What?"

I came back, and Murdoch is now the owner of the *Village Voice* and *New York* magazine. In a period of chaos, that's when you want to make your move. I went down to the *Voice*. I said, "I'd rather work here, can you work it out?" Marianne Partridge had been appointed by Felker. She hired me in 1977.

ALAN WEITZ: At some point, the *Voice* was going through a unionization process, and I was working for a media magazine called *More*. So, I went down to the *Voice* to see what was going on because there was going to be a big meeting, maybe a picket line, and I saw Marianne. She said, "I need to talk to you."

MARIANNE PARTRIDGE: I got a call and from somebody who said, "Heads up, I think Murdoch is going to fire you." I said, "Really? He hasn't even met me." Murdoch said to come and meet him at the *Post*'s office. We had a bizarre conversation. He said right away, "You're fired." I said, "I think you're making a terrible mistake. You don't really know me. It's a difficult group to run." He named who he was thinking of. I said, "No, he'd be eaten alive."

This person called Jack Newfield, and said to Jack, "What would you say if I was to become the editor of the *Voice*?" And Jack said, "Pearl Harbor."

ALAN WEITZ: Rupert hatches a plot to get rid of Marianne and make Michael Kramer—who was now the editor of this magazine *More*—the editor. Michael wants to bring me with him as his managing editor. I knew that the *Voice* was going to go crazy when they heard this. I'm alone at *More*, and the phones start lighting up. All of a sudden Jack's calling me. He says, "What are you doing coming down here as managing editor?" I said, "Wait, wait, wait, slow down, slow down. I'm not part of this coup d'état."

MARIANNE PARTRIDGE: Alex Cockburn happened to have a girlfriend who went to the same private school where Mr. Rupert Murdoch's daughter went, so he had the home address of Murdoch. Alex and Jack Newfield—it could have also been Tim Crouse—went over to Murdoch's house and said, "You're making a terrible mistake; you can't fire her."

I was at home, and I got a telephone call from Rupert, and Rupert said, "Well, I guess I made a mistake." He was very charming. "I'd like you to stay." And I said, "I'd be happy to stay."

He fired me a couple of times, Murdoch, but he always had to hire me back.

Rupert Murdoch hired a guy from Boston who reported to him how the paper editorially ran. In the middle of the meeting, I was trying to explain to him how writers work and that writers are competitive, and they can be competitive and still be friendly and collegial. I said, "I'm sure you would see that in every great newsroom. I don't think it's all blood."

While I'm in there talking to him, Alex smashes open this screen that I had, comes into my office, and starts saying to me, "You have made the biggest mistake! Jim Ridgeway and I wrote this thing! This should have been on page one! What is your problem?!"—arguing with me, and then stormed out. When the guy wrote his report, he said, "This was *Zen and the Art of Newspaper Editing*."

MICHAEL DALY: I'm not too big on bosses, and I was very big on her. She has the right values. She believes in what she does. She's not playing a power game. She's not dumb. She didn't get there by some kind of mechanization, or by dropping other people's corpses—it wasn't politics. She was loyal to people. She was open to ideas. She didn't have an agenda. She loved a good story. She was curious about the world. She likes people—which is very important to be a great editor.

MARK JACOBSON: She was a total character. The boys loved her. The girls didn't know what to make of her. Marianne had these fantastic stories—she was a big, loud person who was also Italian, and she's playing it up to the hilt. She was tough. She wouldn't take any shit. But she loved her people that she loved.

SONIA JAFFE ROBBINS: She was there in the '70s, in the height of the women's liberation, feminist thing, and I think she didn't want it to look like she was promoting women just because they were women, or just because she was a woman. It was harder to get women hired while she was editor in chief than it was when the men were.

MARIANNE PARTRIDGE: I knew Karen Durbin very well. I edited her; she did a very important piece at the time. It was simply called "A Woman Alone."

When the paper was still in the process of being sold to Murdoch and all the different publications were having their various protests, we had had a meeting at Jack Newfield's house in the morning to decide how we were going to approach this, and Karen comes up to me and goes, "Just. Smile." I plastered a smile on my face. She said, "We're going to live through this."

MICHAEL DALY: There's different ways you can handle oppression. If you look at African Americans, there's John Lewis. There's also the Black Panthers. "Empower" was not her thing, but "if I'm strong, that makes women strong." There was a group in the *Voice*, and it was much more a vibe of "Together, we're strong."

RICHARD GOLDSTEIN: We occasionally indulged in homophobic journalism in the name of the First Amendment or whatever crap rationale we used. We got an article about how gay people are ruining the Village. Marianne decided that we should print this. I was enraged. This is before I was out. I knew about this and was just horrified by it. So, I leaked it to the gay paper.

I was still seeing George Delmerico, but I wasn't out yet.* Neither was he. We both had girlfriends at the time. So, I leaked the article, and it was a big

---

* Delmerico was the art director at the *Voice* from 1976 to 1985.

scandal. The gay paper went wild over it. I admitted leaking it, and Marianne called me and said, "Why did you do this? This is horrible. I could fire you." I said, "Well, I'm gay." I came out to her. She said, "OK." She didn't fire me. She didn't agree with it. She understood it.

DENIS HAMILL: Marianne was open to ideas, especially about the outer boroughs. She wanted real, gritty, New York stories that no one else was doing. I would see a little news brief and story about a kid that burnt to death because he knocked over a candle going to the bathroom at night after ConEd* turned off the lights. I said, "This is a real family that's been destroyed. I'd love to do a story on that family." She said, "Go for it. I want that."

MARIANNE PARTRIDGE: I put a lot of culture on the cover, but I treated it like it was news. So, if Bob Christgau wanted to pan Jackson Browne's latest record *The Pretender*, it was another mistake on Bob's part, but nevertheless it went on the front page.

MARK JACOBSON: The *Village Voice* is an apocalyptic publication: every four or five years they have another apocalypse. Anytime a new owner comes in, even if they hated the last owner, it's the end because of this unfortunate self-congratulatory idea about what it was like to work for the *Village Voice*. And the thing that makes it completely confusing is the idea that you were doing something special? It was actually true.

MICHAEL DALY: That was by far the best the *Voice* was—and not because I had anything to do with it. It was really covering the city. Basically, they were paying kids starvation wages, but you didn't mind it, because that seemed to be the spirit of the place. The *Voice*'s romance was that kind of "Let's put on a show!" It would have lost that for me if it all of a sudden became a corporate endeavor.

DENIS HAMILL: She made it more of a city paper. She relied heavily on Jack's ideas. There was nothing that the *Voice* wouldn't let you do.

JAMES HAMILTON: Mark Jacobson and I did a bunch of stories. Marianne Partridge basically gave us a car and said, "Go."

ALAN WEITZ: Mark Jacobson may be the best writer that paper ever had. He has a sideways-glance view of what he's writing about, like film noir.

---

* Consolidated Edison, the electric company in New York.

Mark Jacobson. Photo © James Hamilton.

MARK JACOBSON, "4000 MILES IN THE NICK OF TIME: A SMALL TRIP ACROSS AMERICA," *VILLAGE VOICE*, JANUARY 2, 1978

First off, Vegas is not a writer's town. What are you supposed to say that hasn't been done to death? That Eddie Fisher shrank another inch? That here's where Jerry van Dyke's been all these years? Or that 50-foot-high pink and purple neon signs shaped like upside-down snowcones look silly in the daytime? Anyone with any sense of modesty knows Hunter Thompson said everything you need to know about Vegas. He said, "What Saturday night would have been like if the Nazis had won the war."

MARK JACOBSON: This was on the cover. It was a travel story, and they played it big. The pieces didn't hold together too well, because it was just a bunch of incidents. But they were fun to write. You knew it wasn't gonna amount to anything—we did the weird things that anybody else wouldn't do. It was the kind of thing *Vice* does now. At that time, nobody was doing it.

So, you get this funny little time when Marianne Partridge was there. It was like a free zone. It was like Shanghai in the '20s and '30s, like Paris in the '20s, this little bubble of OK-ness. And then something monstrous is going to come in, and that was going to be the end of it. It could have gone on forever if it weren't for the internet.

CHAPTER 25

"YOU KNEW THAT THE CITY WAS GOING TO ERUPT"

DENIS HAMILL: The Bronx was burning. Crime was rampant. There was Son of Sam and then the blackout. Seventy-seven was the peak of all that stuff. It was grim.

MARIANNE PARTRIDGE: I was the editor during that.

DENIS HAMILL: The night that the blackout hit in 1977, me and Daly ran right out there. We were in a restaurant called Camperdown Elm.

MICHAEL DALY: It was a bar we called "Bar Wars" because there were a lot of conflicts in there.

DENIS HAMILL: We were in there when the lights went out, and then Daly and I, we're trying to get in touch with Marianne Partridge and Alan Weitz. The radio station 1010 WINS was still broadcasting on some kind of emergency generator, so we could get news from them. We heard that there was looting starting in Bushwick. Daly had a rented car from the *Voice* for some reason for another story, and he said, "Let's go!" I had on a white suit.

MICHAEL DALY: We were good enough to know where to go when the lights went out. We knew to go to Bushwick. We were out during the first couple hours, and no one else was out there. The *Times* was probably still trying to figure out how to get to Bushwick.

DENIS HAMILL: We were there for probably twenty hours straight. There was no air-conditioning; we went back to my apartment, wrote it, then went back again. We kept on going back.

MICHAEL DALY: The way the blackout worked, it was like it was re-hearsed. It was like almost the minute the lights went out, there were two hundred thousand people stealing on Broadway in Bushwick. The fires started, basically, because the stores were dark and people needed to be able to see.

I remember we went into the precinct, and there were all these "Wanted for Murder" posters up. In the white part of the city, it was a Summer of Sam. It was not the Summer of Sam in Bushwick. They weren't worried. They had more shootings than you could imagine. But those three days I don't think there was a single homicide in Bushwick. As one cop said, "It's hard to kill somebody if you got both your hands full."

DENIS HAMILL: There was no law and order that night. Even the moon couldn't shine through the L train. You got just bars of moonlight com-ing down.

MICHAEL DALY: The first thing that went was Pampers. People needed shit, and they were broke. You could see it was descending order, from need to want.

They were stealing cars. Looting. They were tying the bumpers to a grate on a store, and they would speed across the street and plow the car into the store across the street, thereby opening up two stores with one car. They started in the Bronx, but there were people who hit a car dealership, and there was a whole caravan that ended up going through Bushwick of stolen cars with people waving out the windows and cheering.

Some guys came out of a pet store with an aquarium with goldfish in it. The cops started chasing them and they dropped the aquarium. And one of the cops stopped and he took a hubcap that had come off a car, and there was a Johnny pump fire hydrant with water coming out of it. He went and filled the hubcap, and he picked up the goldfish and put them in the water.

Nobody quite knew how the police were going to respond to all this shit. That was still in the era where the worst thing you could do, from the police point of view, was make them run.

Then the next day, if you went up on the roofs of the projects, there were all these TVs. It was like a sale. There was a cop up there, joking, "Well, you're looking for a floor model or a . . . ?"

DENIS HAMILL: Newfield, he came up with the headline "Here Comes the Neighborhood."

Michael Daly on the subway in the late
1970s. Photo © James Hamilton.

MICHAEL DALY AND DENIS HAMILL,
"HERE COMES THE NEIGHBORHOOD,"
VILLAGE VOICE, JULY 25, 1977

A sign behind the accordion gates reads: "COME IN. YOUR CREDIT
IS GOOD WITH US."

Bobby heaves a garbage pail through the plate-glass window. Sixteen
minutes later, he has five color television sets, two air conditioners, and a
rack of wristwatches piled into his truck. Bobby stops to help an elderly
man load a sofa onto the roof of a station wagon and races home. "Plug
them in and see if they work," Bobby's mother says as her son carts in the
booty. Of course, there is no electricity.

DENIS HAMILL: You knew that the city was going to erupt. It was a
crazy, crazy year, '77. The city was already on edge from the budget cuts.
There was rampant poverty. There was a serial killer stalking the streets, and
then the lights go out.

CHAPTER 26

"THE FEUDS BETWEEN SARRIS AND KAEL ARE LEGENDARY"

AMY TAUBIN: When he started Movie Journal, Jonas was the only film writer. He was not only writing about the avant-garde; he was writing about art films and Hollywood films. He pretty soon saw that it was too much, and he wasn't that interested in keeping up with Hollywood film, so then he brought in Andrew Sarris.

JONAS MEKAS: We divided the field. I said, "I will cover all the independents and some of the so-called art films, and you can have all the Hollywoods of the world." And that's how it went from '58 to '77.

AMY TAUBIN: I knew Andrew because it was a very small scene. And later I knew Andrew because I knew Molly better. Molly Haskell, his wife.

MOLLY HASKELL: He was very indebted to Jonas for taking him. That was when Andrew did the review of *Psycho* in 1960. He was saying Hitchcock is a great artist, and that was completely anathema. Nobody in this country thought Hitchcock was an artist.

ANDREW SARRIS, MOVIE JOURNAL, *VILLAGE VOICE*, AUGUST 11, 1960

For many years American and British critics have been mourning the "old" Alfred Hitchcock who used to make neat, unpretentious British thrillers before he was corrupted by Hollywood's garish technical facility. Oh, for the days of "The Thirty-Nine Steps," "The Man Who Knew Too Much" and "The Lady Vanishes!" Meanwhile in Paris the wild young men on Cahiers du Cinema, particularly Claude Chabrol, were proclaiming the gospel that Hitchcock's later American movies stamped him as one of the screen's major artists.

A close inspection of "PSYCHO" indicates not only that the French have been right all along, but that Hitchcock is the most-daring avant-garde film-maker in America today.

ANDREW SARRIS: I felt it was just as important and, in many cases, better than many of the Ingmar Bergman movies. Mainstream critics, if you came up with a film that had a serious subject—the war, or poor people, *The Grapes of Wrath*, or something like that—not that there's anything wrong with *The Grapes of Wrath*. But *The Grapes of Wrath* isn't any greater than other John Ford films that are not about poor people and their problems.

MOLLY HASKELL: I fell in love with him through the writing. I was reading the *Voice* and reading Andrew, and I just completely responded to his writing, his sensibility, his take on American cinema directors. He was the son of Greek immigrants. He grew up in Brooklyn and Queens, he was a nerd, and he had this incredible memory of film. That was the thing he and Pauline Kael had in common.* He was very much a Francophile, which I liked. He was writing about the French movies just brilliantly, and nobody else then was, particularly.

I spent a year in Paris after I graduated. He had written the famous *Psycho* review, and then he went to live in Paris like I did. Our first date was to an afternoon screening of a Claude Chabrol film.

There was something in his writing that was spiritual. There was a certain arrogance and propounding this theory that many people thought was crazy. But there was also a kind of humility in that—he was at the service of cinema. He felt that cinema was something larger than he was. It was a time when people were recognizing film as art, and he was part of that.

---

* Kael was the *New Yorker* film critic.

AMY TAUBIN: The feuds between Sarris and Pauline Kael are legendary, and you either were on the side of Sarris or you are on the side of Kael. I was always on the side of Sarris, and therefore, I had total contempt for the *New Yorker*, something that I often feel today.

The auteur theory comes from the *Cahiers du Cinéma*—which was a French film magazine. The auteur theory, which was called the *politique des auteurs*, really looked at film as revealing something about the moral position of the directors, and that every film by a director would have something to do with this position. If that was the case, they had a position in the auteur theory. If that wasn't, they were simply a hack or director for hire.

MARTIN SCORSESE: What Andrew did, especially for young people, was to make you aware that the American cinema, which you had been told was just a movie factory, had real artistic merit. He led us on a treasure hunt.

ANDREW SARRIS: Well, many people have complained—with some justification—that it wasn't a theory at all. What was new was that I took a great many American action directors, genre directors, much more seriously than they had been taken in the past. That was the big debate I had with Pauline Kael—over that.

AMY TAUBIN: She was a sensationalist. And it was all about the immediate sensation she felt watching the movie. She had a position at the *New Yorker* where she could have transformed moviegoing in New York. She could have written about truly great movies worldwide. Sarris, on the other hand, really picked great films, and picked people who would become great directors.

MOLLY HASKELL: He published a two-part article in *Film Comment* in '62 about the auteur theory, and then Pauline attacked him.

PAULINE KAEL, "CIRCLES AND SQUARES," *FILM COMMENT*, SPRING 1963

The auteur theory is an attempt by adult males to justify staying inside the small range of experience of their boyhood and adolescence—that period when masculinity looked so great and important but art was something talked about by poseurs and phonies and sensitive-feminine types? And is it perhaps also their way of making a comment on our civilization by the suggestion that trash is the true film art? I ask; I do not know.

JAMES WOLCOTT: They were very different critics, and then it became a turf fight. And she never mentioned his name in print again. There was a fight for who's going to be king or queen of New York criticism, and Pauline was the most powerful movie critic then, by far.

MOLLY HASKELL: It's really mean-spirited. She attacked him. She created this portrait of film buffs. I mean, there was some truth in it because there was this whole group of people that would go; that was their lives, they would just go from one venue to another. It was called the Theodore Huff Society. She made fun of this group and implied they were gay because they were all men in the group, and it was ridiculous. Then she had her group, and they were all pretty much all male too. Most film buffs at the time were male. That was just the way it was. But it was very insulting. The thing about Pauline is she cultivated her acolytes. And there was even a name for them, the Paulettes.

J. HOBERMAN: Andy taught at Columbia when I was at Columbia as a graduate student. I never took a course with him because by that time to me he was like a moldy fig. I thought his taste in movies was hopeless. I had learned what I was going to learn from his book; I practically memorized *The American Cinema*. I was doing a work-study thing there. One of my jobs was projecting, and I projected for him.

My big breakout article at the *Voice* was on the Super 8 filmmakers, the punk filmmakers—Beth B, Scott B, Eric Mitchell, and Vivienne Dick. There was a scene at Club 57 on St. Mark's Place that was part of it; a lot of them had bands. Jim Jarmusch was connected with this. Suddenly, these young people began making these Super 8 sound films. I got right on it because it was a new underground, but I felt like I had a real story here. Andy would always tell people, when I was at the *Voice*, "He didn't get the job through me." Because I was writing about this other stuff—he couldn't quite get that this is what I really wanted to do.

We weren't pals. I was not a Paulette, although unbeknownst to me Pauline and the Paulettes set me up for this battle with Sarris because Sarris hated Brian De Palma and Pauline loved Brian De Palma.

Dressed to Kill was screening. I don't know who suggested me; I just know that M Mark said, "Why don't you go look at this movie, and if you like it we'll do an interview with De Palma, and we'll run it." They ran it as, like, this point/counterpoint. "Derivative: Sarris. Dazzling: Hoberman." Andy freaked out because he thought this was, like, this incredible Paulette invasion, and it wasn't. I was not going to be beating the drum for the likes of the *New Yorker* film critic. I was at the *Voice*.

Andy had his own circle of friends and acolytes, and I was glad not to be in that. Pauline made overtures to me to join her. They were all guys. Psychologically, you can see what's going on. They were captivated by her—she's a very forceful writer, a great stylist. She went out and she actively recruited. James Wolcott was, when he was at the *Voice*, the most talented writer who was ever there—he was a dear friend of Pauline Kael. He was like the Paulette in residence there.

JAMES WOLCOTT: I was a totally Pauline person. I just loved her writing. It was so freewheeling. It was just so wisecracking. It was so candid. It was so unafraid. The voice and her writing just jumped off the page. I was reading her before I met her. Pauline called me up. She read something I wrote in the *Voice* and invited me to a movie screening.

LETTERS TO THE EDITOR, *VILLAGE VOICE*, JANUARY 8, 1979

Mr. Wolcott, Meet Mr. Sarris:
Dear Editor:

It is common knowledge around the office that Wolcott works overtime as Pauline Kael's hatchet-man. They have even been seen conspiring together at public screenings. What I object to, however, is Wolcott's referring to me in print as "Andy," a reference that suggests a degree of intimacy between us. For the benefit of all the enemies Wolcott has laboriously acquired with his wart-counting bitching-bees, I wish it to be known that we never speak to each other. Consequently, if he promises to stop refer-ring to me as "Andy," I promise to stop referring to him as "Jimmy."

—Andrew Sarris, University Place

James Wolcott replies: Does this mean I'm off the Christmas list?

JAMES WOLCOTT: Well, I never had a relationship with Andrew. I'm not proud of this, but I was taking little shots at him, and he would take shots at me in his column. And now I look back and I feel like, "Oh god, why did I get involved?" Because I'm friends with Molly Haskell now and I love Molly. At the time when you're doing it, it just seems like a way to keep things lively. Feuding had a certain fun to it.

ANDREW SARRIS: We were so gloriously contentious, everyone bitch-ing at everyone. We all said some stupid things, but film seemed to matter so much.

CHAPTER 27

"HOW DO YOU DEAL WITH HOSTILITY?"

MARK JACOBSON: Do you know who the villain of your book is?

ALAN WEITZ: I come to work one day, and I'm called down to a meeting in the publisher's office, and I'm told that Marianne's gonna be fired, and this guy David Schneiderman is coming in, and "You're gonna stay as managing editor."

I'm thinking, "What? You guys want me to go back upstairs and pretend that I don't know Marianne is going to be fired?" Marianne and I were very close. Marianne comes in, and I can't do it. I said, "Take a walk around the block with me." Marianne's feisty, and she goes into Bill Ryan's office. It must have been a great scene.

I decided to get the hell out of there. I'd been through so many firings and changes of command in my life, just at the *Voice*. I was tired of it.

MARIANNE PARTRIDGE: SoHo was just getting started as the hipster place it is today. But before that, it was a place where artists were able to afford to go and were turning it into an interesting place. We were going to do something on the transition, and it was going to be a big story. Somebody in advertising found out about it. But without knowing what the story was, they had a special advertising section, selling to construction, interior design, to turn these places into hipster, beautiful lofts. The publisher Bill Ryan found out and read it while the copy chief was still there, and tore it up and jumped on it—on the fucking galleys.

JOE CONASON: There was a job opening at the *Village Voice* for a city hall reporter, because Michael Daly had left to go to the *Daily News*. I was twenty-three.

I did my first cover story. Somebody that Jack knew was a welfare worker; he was a union activist in the city union. His name is Martin Rosenblatt. Marty, one day, came to Jack with a story about a loft landlord and how this guy was screwing over his tenants in a building on Franklin Street in Tribeca. Loft tenants really had no protection from landlords whatsoever. The landlord had an office in one of the buildings where these people lived on the first floor, and there was a hole in the ceiling of his office, and they had dropped a microphone into his office and taped him and his son. They would talk and scheme against the tenants and say unbelievable stuff like they were going to blow the building up. Crazy stuff.

They had hours of these tapes. I wrote this story called "The Loft Lord Tapes," and it was all about the worst imaginable landlord, what he was doing, and in his own voice. Marianne loved it, and she put it on the front page. This was my first feature story. I'd been writing Running Scared every week, but I hadn't written a feature yet. I was so excited. I came into the office. The paper's there with my name on the front page, my first feature story. I get in the elevator, and one of the other writers says to me, "Marianne was fired today."

Basically, it was because of my story. The advertising department had a big supplement on loft living, and they had told Marianne, "Do not run that story this week on the front page, because we have the loft supplement." She basically told them to fuck themselves. Murdoch fired her, and the paper went into lockdown. My story was just the trigger. But the real news was that she'd been fired by Rupert Murdoch.*

MARIANNE PARTRIDGE: Murdoch was a gentleman. He was polite. He had beautiful suits. He was smart. He was a newspaperman. If the pressmen walked out, he could get down there and show people how to run the press, I'm sure. We had different points of view, obviously, different politics. The *Voice* was not a good fit for him. Several times I knew what he was getting at, and finally he just said, "Aren't you running *a lot* of stories about homosexuality?" It just wasn't a good fit, and I wasn't a good fit for him either.

---

* The *Voice* had run two loft-related pieces within a month: Richard Goldstein and Rob Brill's "City to Move on Illegal Lofts," on May 1, 1978, and Conason's "The Loft Lord Tapes," on May 25, 1978. Both issues had an advertising section touting a first-ever "Loft Expo," directed at people who wanted to furnish their lofts.

MARK JACOBSON: Not to knock the quality of the newspaper, but when I look back on it in terms of international capitalism, that was the end, that was it. Felker was a local guy; he was at Elaine's every night. He came here because New York was cool, man. It's not just Greenwich Village; the whole "village" *Voice* thing was already over by 1956. It was a newspaper of New York, at least when we were all working there. He was fantastic. And now Rupert Murdoch is the owner.*

ROBERT CHRISTGAU: We threatened to go on strike—at ten o'clock in the morning, the whole fucking staff. Cockburn wrote, "Journalists get up at ten o'clock in the morning, they really care about it." [*Laughs.*] We walked Marianne in with her dog. Marianne was the best editor the *Voice* ever had. People did not give her credit.

MARIANNE PARTRIDGE: People put money up, and I got a lawyer. Then the staff—Alex and Jack—would come with me, different guys, everybody, because people are putting their lives on the line. The whole staff walked out. These were not all rich people. People really had to think about whether they could give up their salary for a week, let alone that they might all be fired. It filled me with a great sense of obligation.

This lawyer of Murdoch's said to me, "Why don't you take this? We're offering you all this money, and you could go down to the Caribbean and have a nice time." I said, "Oh my god, you have no idea what the *Voice* is. You don't realize it's practically a sacred duty to run it because of the people who work there."

A mediator had been brought in, and the mediator asked Murdoch's lawyer, "What are the reasons? Has circulation gone down?" "No," he said. "That's the odd thing, it's gone up quite a bit during this time." "Well, have you lost money?" "No, no, it's gone up." So, the mediator said, "I don't understand, what is the reasoning here?" And they said, "The reasoning is that Mr. Murdoch would like her to go."

RICHARD GOLDSTEIN: We decided that he would have had $45 million worth of typewriters. So, we all went out. The entire staff. We were really insulted by having somebody from the *Times*.

---

* Murdoch bought the paper in 1977.

"VILLAGE VOICE NAMES NEW EDITOR,"
NEW YORK TIMES, MAY 11, 1978

The staff statement denounced the attempt to fire her as "an obscene viola-tion of the principle of editorial independence, which has always animated *The Voice.*"

DAVID SCHNEIDERMAN: When I got my job at the *New York Times*—I was an assistant editor when they founded the op-ed page in 1970—one of my jobs was to find people who were not *New York Times* writers, typical establishment centrist writers. I started calling up people from the *Voice.* I got Newfield to write a piece on Attica. The next thing I did is I asked Jules Feiffer during the '76 Republican convention if he'd do a cartoon. Jules did a cartoon. John Oakes, the ultimate overseer, sees it. He says, "We don't run cartoons with words underneath." I don't think it ran.

By 1978, I'd become the deputy editor of the op-ed page. I ran an article by Roger Morris, who worked for Kissinger but quit over Cambodia, saying in effect that the *Washington Post,* the *New York Times* are in the tank for Henry Kissinger. He named the editor of the *New York Times.* I was actually defended by every-body except Abe Rosenthal, who was the big editor. He was just furious. He thought I was a communist. He leaned over to my boss when it was announced I was leaving. He said, "I guess you're gonna miss your commie, aren't you?"

In 1978, I had a bunch of interviews with the publisher, Bill Ryan. I had an interview with a woman who was really out of place at the *Voice.* I don't know how she got there, she was the executive vice president or something, and she was a wealthy woman. The first thing she says to me is, "How do you deal with hostility?" I said, "Are you being hostile to me, or is there some other aspect to this? I can deal with it. I have a big brother." She said, "No, the staff. The staff is going to go nuts if this happens."

I said, "Well, the *New York Times* thing we can deal with. I've published some of these people in the *Times.* So, there should be some goodwill." I was naive.

MARK JACOBSON: Once the word was out she was getting canned and they were gonna bring in this guy, there was a palace revolution.

DAVID SCHNEIDERMAN: I accept the job. I go out to lunch that day to my favorite little Greek place on Eighth Avenue, and it's a beautiful sunny day. I come back out and it's now cloudy. I said to myself, there must be some omen here.

This is the day when you took messages on little pink slips. On my desk, there were, like, a dozen messages. One from Bill Ryan, and eleven from people at the *Voice*. First I called Bill Ryan, and he said, "Jack Newfield said, 'If you go through with this, the *Voice* is going to be a parking lot.'"

The next person I called was Tim Crouse, who had written *The Boys on the Bus*, which was one of the great books about political campaigns. I didn't know him, but I respected his work a lot. He starts cursing at me, screaming at me on the phone. "You fucking asshole, you piece of shit. You can't come!" Just yelling at me. And then he hangs up.

Then I called Newfield, whom I knew a little bit. He said, "Listen, it's not about you personally. It's just that they promised that she would be here to the end of her contract at the end of the year, so Rupert broke his word." I didn't know about that.

There was this standoff with the staff threatening to blow the place up or walk out. I decided I'm not going to back off. Then they started asking to come to my office at the *Times* to visit me. They came in delegations, ten at a time. [*Laughs.*] The first group was the, quote, "A-Team." It was Newfield, Hentoff, Feiffer.

MARK JACOBSON: It was a big fucking to-do. Alex Cockburn was jumping up and down. Watching Cockburn [*laughs*]—he'd pick up a Murdoch paper, and he'd slap it up and down. It was completely ridiculous, but on the other hand it was fun to watch. So, everybody got their venting out about how the *Voice* was going to this even more horrible person than Felker, but nobody understood exactly what that meant, that now you're going to be part of this massive fucking international consortium, and you were going to get a *New York Times* guy to run the place, "the traditional enemy." After that, it just became a corporate property.

DAVID SCHNEIDERMAN: I noticed something very interesting. I was dealing only with men. This is the progressive *Village Voice*. All white men. This is, like, 1979. Ten guys, with Mark Jacobson and Howard Smith, pile into my office. They're sitting on the floor because there weren't any seats there. I think, "I have to listen to this stuff." I decided I was going to pretend to take notes. So, first, it starts reasonably, with Nat being the philosopher king. Nat starts saying what the problem is about Rupert's promise and all that. I wasn't arguing with them, I just listened.

JOE CONASON: Did he tell you I wore a paper bag over my head? There was a comic book character in the paper called Bagman, who had a bag over his head.

DAVID SCHNEIDERMAN: Then Mark Jacobson said, "Listen, you can be a hero or a schmuck." I said, "OK, what do I do that gets me to be a hero? What do I do that gets me to be a schmuck?"

He said, "If you take the job, you're a schmuck; if you turn it down, you're a hero." I said, "Well, I guess I'm a schmuck because I'm going to do it."

MARK JACOBSON: After that we never got along too well.

DAVID SCHNEIDERMAN: Then another group of ten came, and another group, over two days. The next day, as luck would have it, there was a party for *New York* magazine; it was their twentieth anniversary, and Murdoch owned it. I go to the party, and Rupert is there with his consiglieri, his versions of Michael Cohen. Roy Cohn, actually, was one of his consiglieri. Rupert is saying, "What are you gonna do?" I said, "They're really pissed off that you didn't keep your word, Rupert. Why don't we just have me come at the end of the year when Marianne's contract is up? About six months." So, they floated it, and the staff accepted it.

MARK JACOBSON: Schneiderman decides that he's going to rent an office. He picks an office in the Fred French Building—I think it was like Fifth Avenue and 49th Street—in this gleaming building that looks like it was built by some famous Gilded Age architect. He picks exactly the wrong building to try to make *Village Voice* people think that he's a nice guy, right?

He didn't want a mass scene. Maybe his psychiatrist or his public relations person, his Edward Bernays person, told him, "Don't meet with them together. They'll overwhelm you. Meet with them one on one, and you'll make this bond." That's what he decides to do. It goes on for weeks, right? People are going up, like, "Eh, you're gonna go up and see Schneiderman today?" "Yeah, I got a Tuesday appointment." It was just like going to the dentist.

DAVID SCHNEIDERMAN: Dan Wolf had called me—and I had never met Dan—and he said, "Listen, you're never going to be able to run that place if they believe that Newfield or Cockburn or Hentoff are running it." There was a perception under Marianne, fair or not, that they were really in charge of it. I can't look like I'm in their pocket. I started reaching out to people like Richard Goldstein and others who I didn't know but who didn't have roles in the initial group.

I remember meeting with Karen Durbin. I was blown away by how smart she was. She was saying, "There are no women in any authority. We've always had problems." Ellen Frankfort wrote about that—the *Voice* was always like a men's club.* There just weren't a lot of women in any degree of authority. Marianne was the editor, but the managing editor was a male, the art director was male, all the senior editors virtually were male—except, I think, Erika Munk in theater, and Karen Durbin.

Karen said, "You ought to talk to M Mark. You ought to talk to Laurie Stone." The women were telling me about all these women who were not getting opportunities there. They are telling me who to call, and suddenly it dawned on me: the conversations I'm having with the women are much more creative, energetic. There's no posturing, no bullshit. The guys are coming in, just making sure that I wouldn't fuck with their copy, that I wasn't going to come and bring a *New York Times* attitude.

But in terms of the paper and the vision, the women were just much sharper. Karen or M said, "Ellen Willis doesn't have a role there, she just doesn't write; you should try to meet her and get her to do some stuff. She used to write for the *Voice*." And the other thing I noticed, the paper was totally white, except there was one African American editor, Rudy Langlais.

RICHARD GOLDSTEIN: It didn't matter where you were when you got there—eventually the paper would take you over and change you. This happened to David. The paper altered him, in a good way. He was remarkably adept. I watched him go through all kinds of controversies in the paper.

---

* Frankfort's memoir is *The Voice: Life at the* Village Voice.

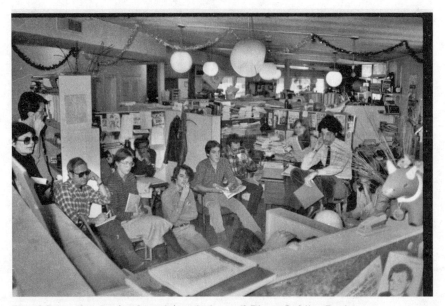

David Schneiderman (on far right) with the staff. Photo © Allen Reuben.

DAVID SCHNEIDERMAN: When I got there, I hired Susan Lyne as my managing editor. I made M the arts editor, Karen the film editor, gave Ellen Willis a column. And Bob Christgau suggested we give Stanley Crouch a column. This is an opportunity rather than a bad thing. This is something that we can rectify. It just didn't make any sense not to have those voices in the paper.

CHAPTER 28

"WE'RE VERY HAPPY TO GIVE THIS TO YOU, BUT PLEASE DON'T PUBLICIZE THIS"

RICHARD GOLDSTEIN: We were the only union shop to form under Murdoch. He came down to the paper after he bought it to address us. He said, "I like the *Voice*. I only wish you would go back in the cupboard." By which he meant the closet. He was Australian. He meant "not be so gay."

Then he also said, "I'm so glad to be in a place where no one has a journalism degree." I shrunk behind my desk.

MARIANNE PARTRIDGE: I thought a small paper like the *Voice* should not have a union. But I also thought a small paper like the *Voice*, owned by Rupert Murdoch, put everybody in the form of being a cog, as opposed to the way it was even under Clay. Under Clay, you could go in and yell and scream. I could understand how they felt—"My god, he hadn't even met Marianne, and he fired her." It was a very independent-minded staff.

RICHARD GOLDSTEIN: Our reaction was, let's form a union to battle him. That's all we can do.

SONIA JAFFE ROBBINS: We decided to show Murdoch that we're serious about this, that "one big happy family" doesn't cut it when we are suddenly part of this other empire. So, we staged a one-day walkout. That was the scariest moment in my life up until that point. This was the first grown-up action I was taking in my life because we could have all gotten fired. And

Members of the *Voice*'s newly formed union picket outside the office, 1977. Left to right: Nat Hentoff, Jules Feiffer, Alexander Cockburn, Karen Durbin, and Joel Oppenheimer. Photo © Sylvia Plachy.

if we didn't get enough people to come out with us, it wouldn't work. But we got almost everybody to walk out. And that was the first step. Then Bill Ryan said, "Oh, OK, I guess you're serious.

RICHARD GOLDSTEIN: We went first to the Newspaper Guild. The Newspaper Guild said, "Great, come on board." And we said, "But we want everybody in the shop to be in one union. We don't want separate unions, and we want to include freelancers." They said, "But why do you care about them?" So, we said, "OK, no." So then we went to a commie union called District 65, and that's who we allowed to organize us.

J. HOBERMAN: I was there when the union got started.* They created this thing, the Bargaining Unit Freelancer. I was the original steward back when they formed BUF. I said, "Look, all the staff writers are front of the book. You got people who are in the paper every single week who are freelance writers. Why aren't they on staff?"

Eventually a lot of us went on staff at the same time in 1982 or '83.

---

* The union formed and joined Local 65 of the Distributive Workers of America in July 1977.

RICHARD GOLDSTEIN: We were probably the only place in the country where freelancers earned vacation. We didn't want anybody scabbing, so we wanted everybody to be in the same boat. Every department in the paper was in the union. Ad takers, art directors, everyone. I was one of the people who worked on that. Jeff Weinstein was the point person.

JACKIE RUDIN: That was intense. Because the union was for the writers, and advertising people got paid differently than the writers, and we also got commissions, and we made plenty of money. They didn't, so they needed a union. And we were warned on our side of the fence that we dare not get involved.

I'm nothing if not a political person. I'd been at the *Voice* for a really long time, and I did not want to lose my job. I was working in playland; who would want to be thrown out? Karen Durbin was one of the most important people in my life. I revered her. And she's asking me, and Jeff Weinstein is asking me, and Richard Goldstein is asking me, and Howard Smith is asking me. There was no way I could say no, so I did it. But things were never the same for me at the *Village Voice* after that. It was thanks to me that the union was able to happen.

LAURIE STONE: The *Voice* made labor history because it included, for the first time, the editors.

BERT POGREBIN: I became the lawyer for the *Voice*. When Murdoch bought *New York* magazine and the *Village Voice*, the *New York* magazine staff quit en masse. And Murdoch quickly replaced them. But at the *Voice*, they immediately decided to go for a union. They were incensed because they had been working at what they felt were low rates and thought the *Voice* was in trouble, and here Murdoch had paid millions.

Murdoch didn't intend to upset what was a moneymaking proposition at that time, which was what the *Voice* was. My counsel to Murdoch was "just stay away and make as few changes as possible." The pitch will be "It's the same *Voice* as before; just the ownership has changed. There's no threat to your journalistic integrity." And he stayed away. The union election had come; Murdoch had not made any changes. It was almost like ninety-five to five.

NAT HENTOFF: I gave him my clearly unwelcome congratulations: "You are the most effective labor organizer I've ever known about."

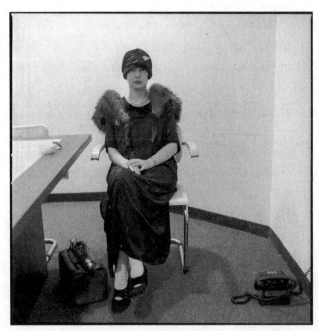

The future *Vogue* fashion writer Lynn Yaeger. Photo © Sylvia Plachy.

J. HOBERMAN: Lynn worked her way up from classifieds through the union, and then was able to become a writer. She is a totally self-made *Voice* person. Of course, now she's at *Vogue*.

LYNN YAEGER: I grew up on Long Island. My dad worked in the city, and he would bring the *Voice* home for me sometimes. It was amazing. Jill Johnston was amazing. I just thought it was an amazing window on another world. I got the job at the *Voice* because I didn't have any money left, and the *Voice* was down the block from the New School, and I thought it would be a thing to do. I was in the classified side with Joe Jesselli for quite a long time.

JOSEPH JESSELLI: It was 1978. I was twenty-one. A newspaper strike had just ended, and they were making money hand over fist. I was hired for the classified department—which had twenty-some-odd people—taking ads over the phone. I worked with Lynn Yaeger for ten years. We were clerks, and that's how we built our friendship. They were making so much money that they had to hire me and Lynn and even another person to deal with corrections and stuff like that. It was union activity that got me involved with other parts of the newspaper.

DAVID SCHNEIDERMAN: Lynn Yaeger is really important for the union. She's become this fucking icon. I found something about Lynn in some big-time magazine, all about her and her look, and I'm thinking, "This is hysterical," because I remember when this was evolving at the *Voice* when she was this kid. She kinda looks the same because she has her little Kewpie doll look, or whatever she calls it.

JEFF WEINSTEIN: Every day, she dressed in '20s clothing. Every single day. She had on '20s flapper drag. I was entranced, and I loved this. She did have the bee-stung lips. It's a little bit more hard-edge, dramatic now, but it was her look. She had the hennaed hair, and she looked terrific. She turned heads, always.

LYNN YAEGER: Oh, honey, in the classifieds I used to sit there in a beaded 1920s gown and a velvet coat. I really had some looks in the classified department. I had white Victorian nightgowns. I got the same reaction I've gotten my whole life—incredulity followed by acceptance.

DAVID SCHNEIDERMAN: She was the customer-complaint person in classified. It was a tough job because people yell at you all day. She was absorbing heat. That's one of the charms of the *Voice*, like the story of Wolcott, who came in as a receptionist. People would come in these godforsaken jobs just because they wanted to get in the front door, and they would somehow get an assignment here.

LYNN YAEGER: Helen Gurley Brown was the editor of *Cosmopolitan*, and she was on a train, and she happened to pick up the *Village Voice*, and she read one of my stories and bought it for *Cosmopolitan*. She called David Schneiderman and said, "Oh, you have amazing writers like Lynn Yaeger." And David goes, "Lynn Yaeger is not a writer. She works in the classified department." But she bought this story for $1,000, which at the time was really a lot.

DAVID SCHNEIDERMAN: Before that, we used to joke that she was Norma Rae of the union.

LYNN YAEGER: The big fights when I got there were that the editorial department acted like the union was for them, and they ignored everybody else. I was into representing all the other people that worked there.

ERIKA MUNK: With the union, it was an obvious necessity, if you're dealing with somebody like Murdoch, to have a position of power as a group. We were all extreme individualists, but as solitary people none of us had any power. That is the argument that finally got people to understand that they might be the next thing to god's gift—in other words, a writer—and still have to join with the people who actually did the work in classified and layout and art. And there were enough lefties, progressive people to carry it, and it worked.

DAVID SCHNEIDERMAN: Lynn stayed tough-minded. She used to be really angry. That's why we called her Norma Rae because she would sit across the table from us during negotiation and shoot daggers through her eyes at the management.

LYNN YAEGER: I liked it because I couldn't get fired and I'm very rebellious, and I liked it because it gave us a way of fighting back. With no union, you have no way of fighting back. You have to do whatever they say, or they fire you. I liked everything about it. I had a "fuck you" attitude at the time.

BERT POGREBIN: During the Murdoch years, the irony was that we never had a strike—though the *Voice* hated Murdoch and ran things against him in the paper that he owned. But they would always vote to ratify whatever agreement.

MAIDA ROSENSTEIN: There was a very strict tradition that we weren't going beyond the expiration of the contract, and that the membership would strike if there wasn't a contract on time. It was a June 30 expiration date.

BERT POGREBIN: That meant ruining the July 4 weekend.

LYNN YAEGER: One time we found out that the managers on their side were going away for the weekend. We thought, "Well, they're obviously going to fold, because they're going away for the weekend."

BERT POGREBIN: They had the "Day of Rage." They would unveil a T-shirt, which had "Wage Rage!" Then they would run through the halls yelling and have a rally outside the building and scream up at the building. But they would all come back at the end of the lunch hour. There was never a strike. One year it was a tough negotiation, and the committee narrowly voted to approve the contract. No less than Nat Hentoff was chastised for being pro-settlement. His people said, "You promised us a strike!"

LYNN YAEGER: It wasn't exactly like the coal miners' union. We were a bit in a dreamworld over how tough we were.

BERT POGREBIN: In the very early days, it was just Bill Ryan, the publisher, literally all by himself. Everybody else was pro-union, anti-Murdoch.

There was no management team. But in the bargaining thereafter, we would have David Schneiderman, and Marty Singerman, who was a Murdoch representative, and so we had more management presence.

DAVID SCHNEIDERMAN: Joe, who was the responsible person, was very tough and used to shoot us daggers, too, but then when we weren't at the bargaining table, he'd pull me over and we would negotiate stuff.

J. HOBERMAN: Joe was more like a union boss. It was a classic thing. They went into the men's room and cut a deal with Schneiderman. Couldn't do that with Lynn.

JOE CONASON: You get the most out of them without a strike. If you strike, the lowest-paid people get hurt. You're out there with a picket sign, but it's actually not a good idea. I got a lot of hot water for that. People were mad at me because I didn't really want to strike. We negotiated very tough union contracts with Murdoch. I negotiated them. Made him *pay.*

DAVID SCHNEIDERMAN: I never quite knew if it was 100 percent anger or part of it was show. I know there was anger because they felt they were underpaid. They bargained successfully to get more money and more benefits.

MAIDA ROSENSTEIN: We were able to negotiate affirmative action language into our contract. All of the diversity, equity, and inclusion efforts that are going on now in cultural institutions and in publishing where everybody's talking about this—the *Voice* was ahead of the curve. You have to give Schneiderman some credit because he actually cared about this issue, and so he was open to doing something.

LYNN YAEGER: We had all kinds of progressive demands. We wanted them to put in a day care center. John Evans, the head of the classified department, said, "This day care center thing is a nightmare because you have to get licensing from the state. How many children are we actually talking about?" "I don't know—like, seven?" He's like, "Well, what if we gave, like, all those parents, like, $5,000 extra?" So, we found some way to solve it. Jeff and I were very good at coming up with unorthodox ways of solving things.

JEFF WEINSTEIN: Lynn was bad cop. I was good cop. At some point people were actually earning real money who had been there a long time, the old white boys. Nat Hentoff, for example, Bob Christgau. I'm not saying it was a ton of money, but if you were doing raises that were based on percentage, it's a regressive raise. The higher-paid people get more money, the lower-paid people get less. In the late '80s, twenty, twenty-five thousand a year, the people who were on the telephones—it wasn't enough for living in New York City.

I had a calculus dream, and I don't know calculus. I did a reverse-percentage raise. You would get higher raises the lower you made, and lower raises the higher you made. Apparently, this had never been done before. They called it the Weinstein Clause.

LYNN YAEGER: It was genius, and we kind of shamed the people who made more money into accepting it.

JEFF WEINSTEIN: The union organizer for the *Voice*, Kitty Krupat, was talking about health coverage. The *Village Voice* had a very unusual health coverage for unmarried couples; they would be covered as spousal coverage. I raised my hand. I said, "Well, if it's unmarried heterosexual couples, why can't unmarried same-sex couples be included?" Kitty said, "Well, no one's ever asked that question before, but there's no reason why not."

MAIDA ROSENSTEIN: Our union, District 65, had a joint employer-union health plan. We had some ability to bargain the domestic partner insurance.

JEFF WEINSTEIN: I went personally to every union member in every department and talked about this benefit and explained it to them, and I got everybody on our side. It was a very divisive contract negotiation because we were ready to strike.

RICHARD GOLDSTEIN: I thought that was so moving that the entire place took this so seriously that they were going to go out on strike.

DAVID SCHNEIDERMAN: The only other company at the time who did that was Lotus. They were the leading software company for writing at the time. No other company in the country gave health insurance to unmarried couples, particularly gay couples, which was unheard of.

JEFF WEINSTEIN: We called it the "spousal equivalent" clause; it became "domestic partnership" later. That was Bert Pogrebin's term—I agreed to it—which was won in the contract for the first time in the United States. There might have been something six months before in a tiny place in Eugene, Oregon. But it was the first time in a big union contract.

DAVID SCHNEIDERMAN: When the union proposed it, we said, "How do we tell Rupert that one?" We felt he was homophobic. I said, "Well, who says we have to tell him? A few years later, after he sold the *Voice* and used our money to buy 20th Century Fox, he put Barry Diller in charge, who is a noted gay executive. We felt, "Maybe we were even wrong about that."

BERT POGREBIN: When I called Murdoch, I said, "This is a ticket to a collective bargaining agreement that I think they're gonna buy because it's, as far as I know, first in corporate America to cover gay relationships." And I explained the upside economically that we were going to make an otherwise very good deal. He said, "Well, if you could put it in a side letter, or not trumpet it."

I said, "Don't you understand? The reason that this is gonna sell is because they will trumpet it." He said, "Well, if that's the only way, then give it to them."

JEFF WEINSTEIN: What Rupert Murdoch's people said is, "We're very happy to give this to you, but please don't publicize this." Well, the moment they said that I went to the union office, and we wrote a press release. The *New York Times* picked it up and I was interviewed, and for a number of years I was interviewed about this because it became the beginning of what ultimately became gay marriage.

LYNN YAEGER: I believe that Jeff is responsible for the gay marriage Supreme Court decision. I wrote to him. I said, "This is because of you."

CHAPTER 29

"YOU SHOULD CHECK OUT THIS YOUNG GUY DONALD TRUMP"

WAYNE BARRETT: When I started, in the '70s, Trump was this golden boy, and he had not had much press, but it had all been very supportive because he was doing the Grand Hyatt, which was his first big project in Manhattan. And the city was down in the dumps, near broke during the '70s, and he looked like the embodiment of a rising city. And he was getting that kind of press, though not much of it.

I worked on him intensely in '78 while the Hyatt was under construction, had not been completed yet. And that's when I first got to know him.

TIMOTHY L. O'BRIEN: He had gotten the idea to report on him from Jack Newfield. He had asked Jack for advice on who would be a good person to write about, who is emblematic of the intersection of real estate money and politics and power in New York. And Jack said, "You should check out this young guy Donald Trump."

TOM ROBBINS: Jack had a canny eye for these operators. Jack's famous book was *The Permanent Government*. He believed that there were all these characters who had nothing to do with getting elected or unelected but who stayed in power in the city, regardless. He spotted Donald Trump right away as a budding member of that tribe.

Wayne Barrett's
groundbreaking cover story
on Donald Trump, the
future reality TV star and
twice-impeached president of
the United States. Cover image
© Village Voice/Street Media.

TIMOTHY L. O'BRIEN: Wayne would always talk about how he felt that
they had parallel lives in New York. They were almost the same age, and
Trump was on the ascent to be a real estate developer at the same time that
Wayne was ascending as an investigative reporter in New York.

Wayne began looking into the family history. He was at one of the city
archives, and he's in a room looking at documents. There's a phone in there,
and the phone rings.

WAYNE BARRETT: I didn't know whether to pick up or not. "Wayne!
It's Donald! I hear you're doing a story on me!" I'd never talked to the guy
in my life. When he found out I lived in the battered Brownsville section of
Brooklyn, he called to say, "I could get you an apartment, you know. That
must be an awfully tough neighborhood." I told him I'd lived there for ten
years and worked as a community organizer, so he shifted to another form of
identification. "So, we do the same thing," he said. "We're both rebuilding
neighborhoods." And again: "We're going to have to really get to know each
other after this article."

ROBIN REISIG: Trump called him up shortly after he had started reporting and invited him to meet. Wayne did and realized it was a mistake: He didn't know what to ask. He had just started reporting. Of course, by the time he finished reporting Trump didn't want to meet with him anymore.

WAYNE BARRETT: I met with Trump several times over the next few months, taping fifteen hours of energetic monologue, riding with him in his limo, and relaxing through expansive interviews on his penthouse couch. One interview was cut short when Ivana insisted that a grumbling Donald go to the opera with her.

I decided at the start that I wanted to profile him by describing his deals— not his lifestyle or his personality. After getting to know him, I realized that his deals are his life. He once told me, "I won't make a deal just to make a profit. It has to have flair."

TIMOTHY L. O'BRIEN: He explored racial discrimination at the Trump properties towards renters of color and whether they were violating earlier court orders to rent in a discriminatory way. It caused the Justice Department to reexamine the settlement agreement they had reached with the Trumps.

DAVID SCHNEIDERMAN: When I got to the *Voice*, my very first day, Newfield says to me, "There's this guy, Wayne Barrett, you gotta meet. He's a freelance reporter. He's really good. He's got a big article on Donald Trump." I had read about Trump in the *New York Times* a couple of times.

Linda Perney, who was the copy chief then, was on the floor. Victor Kovner, our First Amendment lawyer, was there, and Jack, and this tall guy, who introduced himself as Wayne Barrett. I said, "Nice to meet you. So, where's the article?" Sitting next to Linda is this thing piled up this high [*motions about knee-high*] on yellow copy paper—we still had typewriters then. And I said, "Oh, that's it?"

Linda said, "And Wayne wants every word of it published." Linda did it with a little bit of a twinkle in her eye.

It was really good. Parts of it were pretty dense. But it went into all of Trump's deals. This is a guy who would use tax breaks and other government things to build stuff and make a lot of money off of the taxpayer. He was screwing New York. Sounds familiar, right?

It's many thousands of words; I can't run the whole thing. I said, "Why don't we just break it into parts and run a series?"

WAYNE BARRETT, "LIKE FATHER, LIKE SON: ANATOMY OF A YOUNG POWER BROKER," *VILLAGE VOICE*, JANUARY 15, 1979

Real-estate entrepreneurs do their own advertising, and Trump has a way of doubling or shaving every number when it suits him. In interviews, Donald Trump has laid claim to 22,000 units in Brooklyn, Staten Island, Queens, Virginia, Washington, D.C., and New Jersey. But his testimony in federal court put the total figure around 12,000 units actually owned and managed. Whatever the size or exact dollar value, however, there is no question about the racial, economic, and sexual character of the Trump holdings. Tenants are mostly white. People receiving welfare do not live in Trump-owned apartments. Households with substantial male incomes do.

DONALD TRUMP: Early in my career I was naive about how things worked with some reporters. When a guy named Wayne Barrett called me years ago and said he was from the *Village Voice* and wanted to write a story about me, I said sure, without hesitation. I knew the *Village Voice* was not exactly overloaded with Pulitzer Prize winners, nor was it one of America's most respected newspapers, yet I had been written about very little at that point, and I saw this as an opportunity to promote the Grand Hyatt Hotel, the convention center, and several other projects I was working on at the time. I invited Barrett to my office and my apartment and talked with him openly and at great length. I was 100 percent honest with him, which was easy since I had nothing to hide. And he sat there, acting nice as could be, asking questions, and recording everything on tape.

Having the story appear was frustrating enough. But then federal prosecutors started looking into Barrett's allegations about my business practices. They soon deduced this was a noncase and the whole thing was dropped and done with before I, in my naiveté, really got a handle on exactly what was happening.

TOM ROBBINS: Trump was omnivorous in terms of being able to soak up information about the reporters that he was talking to. He thought that he could figure out a way to get you under his thumb. He didn't have to worry about you anymore because he could come back and use that against you. I've known a number of people that he's done that to, to their great embarrassment. The next thing you knew Trump was exposing them on Page Six.*

WAYNE BARRETT: When I didn't nibble on the carrot, he tried the stick, recounting the story of how a lawsuit he filed had broken a reporter whose copy had irritated him.

DAVID SCHNEIDERMAN: Then as we got closer to publishing, Trump had Roy Cohn—who was his lawyer/consigliere and also was Rupert's guy. So, Roy Cohn called Victor Kovner, our lawyer: "Trump is going to sue you guys, and you're going to be bankrupt over this." We don't give a shit.

All these things were new. We hadn't seen Trump played out in any way. The *Times* had run pretty straightforward stuff about his deals. But this is all the classic Donald Trump stuff. He was going to sue us and bankrupt us.

I said, "He's not going to sue us, because he's not going to destroy Murdoch's thing. He likes Murdoch, and Murdoch likes him for the *Post*."

VICTOR KOVNER: There was no suit. That was the first time, but not the last, in which Wayne focused on the Trump–Roy Cohn relationship. Cohn would complain about the *Voice*, but he never sued us, nor did Trump.

WAYNE BARRETT: If you were in your late twenties or your early thirties and you were looking to hitch yourself to a wagon that would pull you forward—if you could sit down with Roy Cohn and be charmed—there was something wrong with you. I had lunch many times with Roy Cohn. Roy Cohn ate with his fingers. I kid you not. He brought a little glass inside of his coat pocket. He would pop little white pills when he thought you weren't looking. He was the most satanic figure I ever met in my life. He was almost reptilian.

---

* Page Six is an infamous gossip column in the *New York Post*.

LETTERS TO THE EDITOR, *VILLAGE VOICE*, FEBRUARY 26, 1979

A Contented Reader
Dear Editor:

I wish to protest the damage to my professional reputation by the failure of *The Voice* to libel me even once in its February 12th issue.

—Roy M. Cohn
East 68th Street

The editor replies: Thank you, Roy, for taking the time to write. Our reporters and editors make every effort to ensure that the material published in *The Voice* is fair and accurate. We are proud of the results and are pleased you are an avid reader.

DAVID SCHNEIDERMAN: Wayne was so good I put him on staff. He wasn't even a staff writer; he was a freelance writer for years.

TIMOTHY L. O'BRIEN: All the work that the rest of us are doing about Trump is built on the shoulders of the work that Wayne Barrett did.

CHAPTER 30

"YOU'RE HIRING ALL THESE STALINIST FEMINISTS"

DAVID SCHNEIDERMAN: After the first two weeks, Newfield comes in and he said, "You're hiring all these Stalinist feminists." I never heard that phrase before: "Stalinist feminists." He said, "Ellen Willis and Karen." I said, "Jack, these are really talented journalists, and you've got to be kidding me."

KAREN DURBIN: It would've been about '75 or '76, and Jack came up to me on the writers' floor when we were still at 11th Street and University. Jack would come up to you and just blurt. He said, without preamble, "You know, women's lib and gay rights have shoved civil rights right off the table." And he said it very angrily. And I said, "Who designed that table?" I was pissed. But he really believed that, you know?

MARY BREASTED: Newfield was just nasty. I don't know if it was chauvinism or if it was just that he was a nasty person. Somebody had quoted me saying that if Jack had his way, he would censor other writers' pieces.

He said, "Do you really think that?"

I said, "Yes, absolutely, I do, Jack. Given the opportunity, you would." He said, "I never knew that you thought that about me." I said, "Jack, once I tried to tell you something I thought about, an issue of the day. You literally turned your back to me. You didn't even know you were doing it."

His jaw dropped. He was that kind of guy. I didn't have power, in his eyes. And as I got to be more important, then he got more resentful, but he paid attention. He always was scheming and into power games. This whole

"Intellectual soul mates"
Karen Durbin (left) and
Ellen Willis. Photo courtesy
of Nona Willis Aronowitz.

thing of 10 Worst Judges, he would do that without much thought, because he just thought it would make a good piece. I thought he was irresponsible and not nice, but whatever.

LAURIE STONE: Is Jack dead? Good.

VIVIAN GORNICK: The whiteboys and the Stalinist feminists! Erika Munk—she was a hot Marxist. Now it all seems amusing, but we were very serious then. Two things were happening at once: There was the feminist writing—which was indeed making war on all these men. And then there was the actuality of day-to-day working relations. In the working relations I did not experience discrimination. But in the world, of course, I did. And I was certainly one of those Stalinist feminists. Off with his head, whoever it is! [*Laughs.*]

KAREN DURBIN: When it continued into the '80s, it became a war. What was so infuriating about it for us—and I include in the "us" gay men at the paper—was we weren't marching into the editor in chief's office saying, "Goddamn it, get rid of Hentoff. He's saying stuff I don't agree with, I think it's bullshit, get him out of here." But they were marching into the editor's office saying, "You print way too much stuff about gay people. It's embarrassing. I can't do my job in Albany anymore with this stuff on the front page of the paper."

J. HOBERMAN: There was a lot of tension between the feminists and the "whiteboys," which is a name that I gave them because I was allied with the feminists and gay men.

STANLEY CROUCH: There was an alliance of the feminists and the homosexuals at the paper. That left the rest of us just kind of out there—not in limbo, but we weren't automatically in that, what they assumed at that point was going to be an important power bloc.

RICHARD GOLDSTEIN: We considered ourselves the Feminist Faggot Coalition.

J. HOBERMAN: I always got along with Jack well enough—even though he was suspicious of me—because I was a guy, and I was straight. And he actually sometimes used to complain about "Oh, the paper's getting too gay." I'm thinking, "Jack, who do you think reads the paper?" There was no response to that.

DAVID SCHNEIDERMAN: As I hired and promoted women, the men would complain. The women would often complain that I was running all this political stuff in the front of the book, and the front of the book needs to have different kinds of writing and voices. A lot of it came down to how much space was available each week to publish other work.

JOE CONASON: Looking back on it, there was a justified resentment of women editors on the staff that the news and investigative department was so male. It was a boys' club. It wasn't really that women were excluded; it was true nonetheless that it was dominated by men in a way nobody would think was acceptable now, or that I haven't thought was acceptable for a really long time.

MARK JACOBSON: It was frustrating in a lot of ways. I go to the ballet! I don't just hang around and go to cockfights—which is the way you were being portrayed—you're like a serial kind of semirapist and probably didn't like Black people, which was completely untrue in my case.

You got to the point where you hit "it's not worth it, don't even talk about it." And that was the obnoxious, elitist thing on our part, from a male point of view: "Just humor these babes."

ERIKA MUNK: Everybody was arguing with everybody, fucking everybody, drinking with people afterward. Also, people were pretty young. I remember Nat being surely the oldest person in the office. He seemed so patriarchal, and I was already forty. I don't think he was anywhere near as sexist as a lot of the other guys.

It was like being a woman in the '50s. Except, of course, there were a bunch of feminist women. Because Ellen's presence—she was so smart and such a good writer—outweighed six of the normal sexist writing guys, you know?

DONNA GAINES: I remember seeing Ellen Willis's byline. It was the first time I ever saw a woman writing that used her name, spelling out "Ellen" instead of "E."

C. CARR: I remember once working with her, she edited a piece, and I was very nervous about it. I came back from the copy department, and I sat down and started to completely rewrite it because I still felt like it wasn't good enough. And Ellen was horrified. She stopped me, and she's like, "No, stop! It's OK!"

AMY TAUBIN: Ellen was really rooted in working-class politics. And she was working class. She sounded working class; she didn't sound like she went to Yale.

ERIKA MUNK: Ellen Willis was the most brilliant person at the *Voice*, bar none, but also a wonderful editor. She would go through the office looking a little Mr. Magoo-ish. She had trouble with her eyes, so people thought she was standoffish.

VIVIAN GORNICK: She was the only person I have ever known who, when she opens her mouth, there are no two agendas; she's always looking for the truth of the situation. The way she looked for it was different from the way I looked for it. I was passionate about women becoming workers, and she was passionate about women becoming sexually alive. More than alive— sexually independent and alive to their own feelings.

MARIA LAURINO: She was fiercely intellectual. Pop culture was completely absent in her experience. Ellen was so outside of pop culture that when Farrah Fawcett-Majors, that big blonde star—everybody was talking about her, and Ellen looked at M and Karen and said, "What's a Farrah Fawcett?"

J. HOBERMAN: Ellen Willis was the brightest person. The paper was full of smart people, but she was really smart. She wrote these theoretical pieces.

These guys were totally arrogant. They really thought the paper belonged to them. They resented the Stalinist feminists. Karen didn't take any shit. M was a strong person.

MARIA LAURINO: I don't think they were happy that they were called the whiteboys, especially because the issue of race and civil rights and racial equality was so important to them, especially someone like Wayne. He spent his life fighting for the people of Ocean Hill–Brownsville. That was a key part of Wayne's life. It was unfortunate on both sides, very defensive. Everybody was fighting for a piece of the cultural pie with the shrinking space in the paper. The whiteboys were Wayne, Joe, Jack, Pete Hamill, Bill Bastone. And then I was the girl with them.

DAVID SCHNEIDERMAN: It wasn't as if the whiteboys would have objected if I ran pieces by women, but they always felt it was coming out of their hide, which is very reminiscent of what we're going through right now in this country in terms of the cultural and diversification changes. In this case, it was women and minorities.

MARK JACOBSON: I mean, you had Jill Johnston, who was writing with no capital letters—how can you take that seriously? That was the opinion of most people that worked there. It didn't fit that tough-guy shit that the *Voice* was mutating towards—all the boys wore leather jackets, and they'd call us the "leather boys." And it was true! It was completely true. Everything that Ellen Willis said was probably true, you know? She was a big pain in the neck at the time, but she was probably right about everything.

CHAPTER 31

"I'M THE GREATEST PIMP SINCE DUKE ELLINGTON"

STANLEY CROUCH: I was playing the drums and I was starting to write for the *Village Voice* through Gary Giddins.

ROBERT CHRISTGAU: I was the music editor. Schneiderman was very shrewd and had very good taste in writers, and he asked me to edit Stanley Crouch.

I'd seen Stanley read poetry at a conference at Oberlin in 1973 or '74, and I thought he was a complete blowhard. Then he shows up via Gary Giddins. This was a Black writer who knew something about jazz, and I used him, and yes, there was an affirmative action aspect even to that, but on the other hand, the guy really knew a lot, and he just needed to be edited.

GARY GIDDINS: Bob was delighted because one thing the *Voice* needed desperately was Black writers, especially in the music section. He did a couple of pieces by Stanley, and they were good. But then Stanley lost his temper about an edit, and that's when Bob said he wasn't going to use him anymore. Then I edited this piece for the first jazz supplement. I could see what Bob's problem was because Stanley was very undisciplined. The ideas were brilliant—but he was so naive on basic things that the piece was single-spaced, with no margins. I said to Bob, "What'd you think of Stanley's piece?" "Well"—he was a little huffy about it—"he writes better for you than he does for me." I said, "I put it through the typewriter!"

Stanley Crouch, the irascible jazz critic and cultural commentator, 1980. Photo © Allen Reuben.

That gave Bob the nerve to sit Stanley down and just say, "This is the way it works here. Nobody gets by without editing." Stanley's stuff got so much better so fast.

CAROLA DIBBELL: These were the days when we all had answering machines. We came back, and there's a message from Stanley Crouch: "What an editor." [*Laughs.*] Then there's another message a little bit later, and that was "What an editor." I don't know how many, but he left that message on our answering machine.

ROBERT CHRISTGAU: He was the best critic of drumming—according to Gary—who ever lived, because he was a drummer himself, not a great drummer, but boy, he could write about drumming.

GARY GIDDINS: He did a piece about Billy Taylor, a very slick pianist. Critics didn't take him all that seriously. But Stanley wrote this lovely piece defending middlebrowism in jazz.

When I started my Charlie Parker book, he had been researching his for years, and he came over here with a backpack. He dropped about sixty or seventy cassette tapes of all the interviews he had done. He said, "I'm going to leave this with you because you need to make sure you get the story right." It was a hundred people who worked and knew Charlie Parker, many of whom were dead, so it was valuable stuff. That was an incredible act of generosity.

PAUL BERMAN: In my era he was the most distinctive, the most brilliant of the *Voice* writers. Alex Cockburn had skillful prose, but fundamentally it was prissy prose. Stanley Crouch was the opposite: he would just sweep all that off the table and lay out a full orchestra of tones. He was a real stylist.

STANLEY CROUCH, "LAUGHIN' LOUIS ARMSTRONG," *VILLAGE VOICE*, AUGUST 14, 1978

One performance, "Laughin' Louie," perfectly expresses the enigma of the great musician. It opens with a trite theme that collapses into a burlesque of sad jokes and buffoonery from both Armstrong and his band members. . . .

Then, out of nowhere, the trumpeter decides to play something from his New Orleans past. First, he sputters some individual notes; then there is a lovely passage, then more laughter before he quiets the band down for "the beautiful part." Armstrong then plays in unaccompanied melody. Its rich tone conveys a chilling pathos and achieves a transcendence in the upper register that summons the cleansing agony of the greatest spirituals. The band drops a chord under him, and it is over. The feeling one is left with is of great mystery.

ROBERT CHRISTGAU: At a certain point they hired a Black editor named Rudy Langlais.

RUDY LANGLAIS: The *Village Voice* published an article that said the *Amsterdam News* was doing the Black community a disservice: there was no real reporting. I wrote to the editor of the *Village Voice*: "You're right, but the *Village Voice*—which lives in a glass house—has no business criticizing the *Amsterdam News*, because for all its claims of its liberal ambitions, the *Village Voice* has no Black editors. It has a very thin group of Black writers, no Puerto Rican writers. I look at the masthead, I see no names that sound Latin."

I got a letter from Margot Hentoff: "We would like to have lunch with you." They took me to lunch, Nat Hentoff, Margot, and Jack Newfield. They said, "There's a job open."

By the time I got back to my office, I had several messages from Marianne Partridge and Alan Weitz, the managing editor. I met Marianne and absolutely fell in love with her. I thought she was the wildest, wackiest, craziest person I've met in journalism. I loved her spirit. Alan Weitz is guitar playing, a little bit high, which I didn't mind at all because I grew up in that world as well.

Marianne offered me the job. I said, "Look, I need to think about this." I had accepted an ABC Sports job. I had just gotten married, and I was about to make a big salary. What they were paying was so much smaller.

I called my hero and mentor, Clayton Riley. Riley wrote for the *Times* Sunday magazine. This was the writing that I most admired in New York journalism. We spent an afternoon talking. He said, "We've been trying to get into the *Village Voice* for years"—and he was in the epicenter of the Black intellectual world of writers on the Upper West Side at that time—and he said, "You would be our way in."

There were a few writers who appeared from time to time. There was Michelle Wallace and Ianthe Thomas. There wasn't a great deal of interest in Black and Latino writers. The world of the *Voice* was a downtown, insular world. People were anxious if they went above 14th Street. They didn't know and socialize with Black and Latino people.

I took a long walk, and I decided that I was going to go to the *Village Voice*. I could never explain it to my wife, why I made that choice. It was a choice between working uptown in a suit and hanging out in jazz clubs downtown, and I chose hanging out in jazz clubs downtown.

I met Stanley on my first or second day at the paper; the only other Black face I saw was his. I went up to him, and I said, "Who are you? Why don't you write feature stories?" He said, "Nobody will assign me any." I said, "I'll assign you a story."

STANLEY CROUCH: He sent me down [to Mississippi] to cover the fifteenth anniversary of the Freedom Summer of 1964, and that was the beginning of me moving into writing more things outside of reviews of jazz.

I wrote a review during that period of James Baldwin's novel *Just Above My Head*, and I was writing some theater criticism, so the range of things that I was covering started to expand.

I had such a freedom to write about so many different things—departments are so closed off in most publications. You can write a theater review sometimes, then write about a painter, like I did about Bob Thompson. Another time I would write about a review of some jazz band, then go out and write something about Jesse Jackson or Louis Farrakhan.

RUDY LANGLAIS: He didn't become a columnist until maybe two years later. By that time, he'd built up a body of work that was garnering him great attention.

STANLEY CROUCH: I was the first Negro who became a staff writer for the *Village Voice*, which made many protestations for years against racism everywhere. About 1979, I was the first. I got my "first" in. Jackie Robinson and everybody got the firsts. You know, the Negros lived by firsts.

RUDY LANGLAIS: People had become very interested in Stanley—he was this contentious voice in the pieces that he wrote. He had taken it on himself to attack certain other Black iconic figures, principally Miles Davis and LeRoi Jones, the playwright.*

LeRoi Jones was a writer I brought to the paper. He wrote some fascinating pieces, including one about having been sentenced to spend weekends in jail after an incident with his wife, an incident which Stanley Crouch happened to witness and which became part of the case against LeRoi Jones. They almost came to blows in a club one night over stories they wrote about each other that I published in the paper.

STANLEY CROUCH: I think LeRoi lost his mind when he became super Black nationalist, antiwhite, and so forth. He has really been a detrimental influence, so much so that if you make any criticism of something done by white people for what are apparently white reasons, most white people seem to think you must be taking the LeRoi Jones line.

He's one of the most tragic figures in the second half of the twentieth century in America because this was a man who had an extraordinary talent.

---

* Later known as Amiri Baraka.

I mean truly, truly exceptional, but he was so overwhelmed by his guilt for having married a Jewish woman and for having had with her two children and for living downtown and for being sexually confused at a certain point in his earlier life, that he maniacally went into a certain kind of Black nationalism and rejected everything. He became a homophobe. He became anti-Semitic.

He was truly a great loss, because after about 1967 or so he wrote a bunch of agitprop garbage over and over and over. He essentially incinerated his talent in order to make himself more understandable to the simpletons that he should have rejected all along.

Periodically he writes these nasty things about me. See, I was going to throttle him one night in a club because we got into a minor argument. Fortunately some people stepped in—fortunately for him because he's a small guy.

AMIRI BARAKA: He's a backwards, asinine person!

STANLEY CROUCH, "THE LONE RANGER'S REVENGE," *VILLAGE VOICE*, JUNE 18, 1979

Saturday morning, I called writer Steve Cannon, who said to me immediately, "You better get down to the court house. 'Roi got busted. He was arguing on the street about the article you wrote on his play ['Comrade, Comrade, Where You Been,' *Voice*, June 11]; his wife started beating the shit out of him, and the police came along and helped her. I guess he didn't like the review." So much for Cannon's humor.

AMIRI BARAKA, "WHAT KIND OF CROUCH IS THAT?" *VILLAGE VOICE*, SEPTEMBER 3, 1979

Stanley obviously has his job because *The Voice* wants a visible Black but they always opt for one who puts the same ideas as the reactionary white petty bourgeois servants of dying capitalism.

PAUL BERMAN: We struck up a friendship. Stanley was a little older than me, and he was more established at the *Voice*. He was a very friendly, voluble person, and a genius conversationalist. He and I both had the same personal ideal for ourselves, which was to be a certain kind of literary intellectual. He liked the fact that I got into fights, too, so we were both not afraid to be out there saying things that were disliked. We were natural comrades in that way.

GARY GIDDINS: When I first met him, unforgettably, he said, "Duke Ellington was the greatest pimp that ever lived, and I'm the greatest pimp since Duke Ellington." By "pimp," he meant a "con." Ellington looked into any reporters' face and could blow smoke in it, and you'd write it down.

CHAPTER 32

"THE OBIES ARE THE ONLY AWARDS WITH INTEGRITY"

MICHAEL FEINGOLD: The theater section was the tail that wagged the dog. The theater section was never thought of as that important by Wolf and Fancher and the guys out front. It was always thought of as, "Well, this is secondary. The arts are in the back of the book. We're really going to be a New York political paper."

GORDON ROGOFF: They'd hired somebody to do a survey about what readers looked at when they first purchased the *Voice*. The result of that is astonishing. Ross Wetzsteon said the first page they turned to was the Jules Feiffer cartoon. And the second was the theater page. The reviews. Not cinema, not anything else. Not the politics or Nat Hentoff. Jules Feiffer. *Us*.

MICHAEL FEINGOLD: I started at the *Voice* in February of '71, as a freelancer. Ross Wetzsteon was the editor I first went to. I had been a grad student at the Yale School of Drama. I was on my uppers looking for work, and the faculty members at Yale made recommendations, and one of them suggested I send clips to the *Voice*. I sent clips and Ross called me. Ross said, "I like your writing, but we have no openings at the moment," since there were six drama critics working regularly at that time, maybe seven. He said, "But look around, find something you can write about."

I had gotten a review copy of the first biography of Bert Williams. Bert Williams was a Black comedian who wore blackface, and having starred in shows with his partner up in Harlem, when his partner died, Ziegfeld hired him to be a comedy star at the Follies. He's probably the first Black Broadway star. That was my first piece in the *Voice*, a book review about a theatrical star from the turn of the last century.

ERIKA MUNK: I started to write in 1976. I became senior editor in '78. Ross wanted to be a general editor of the features, the long stuff, and I handled the reviewers.

It was a pretty big theater section. I had three pages normally. I had four regular reviewers. Michael Feingold was the lead critic.

MICHAEL FEINGOLD: Erika is a major figure. She also used to write letters to the paper complaining about the reviews under the pen name Phyllis Stein. But I didn't tell you that. Erika as an editor was much more directly challenging. She would ask the hard questions up front, and that's useful in a different way.

Every now and then Erika would make a draconian cut. I would come in with a very elaborate first paragraph, and she would glare at me and say, "You've been reading Henry James again." And she was right.

JAMES HANNAHAM: Feingold can also be really bitchy. One of my favorite things he ever wrote, it was like a ten-year assessment of *Cats*. The opening line is something like "*Cats* and AIDS have been with us for ten years, and it looks like neither of them is going away."

ALISA SOLOMON: Ross Wetzsteon always had a cup of perfectly sharpened pencils on his desk, all the same length and all with perfect points. His desk was always super neat, and his writing was really lovely. He wrote an amazing piece about the Polish theater artist Tadeusz Kantor. He wrote one of the earliest profiles of Irene Fornés, and he also wrote about tennis. He was the chairman of the Obies. He loved the Obies.

GORDON ROGOFF: And the Obies was a big, big, big deal, of course. The *Times* barely wanted to report on the Obies. They didn't like to give the results of the Obies because it was another journal, really.

JONATHAN SLAFF: The Obies was Jerry's idea.

JERRY TALLMER: Sometime during that first year, in 1956, a bunch of us were sitting around the office and asked, "Why shouldn't there be some sort of awards for Off-Broadway, to single it out from Broadway, to stick it in the establishment's eye?" The name actually came from Harvey Jacobs, a novelist who was working in the advertising department.

ED FANCHER: It originally started in the Limelight Coffee House, which was owned by Helen Gee.

MICHAEL FEINGOLD: The very first year of the Obies, Jerry had schlepped to an upstairs loft, where a very crazy actress/playwright named Julie Bovasso had discovered the text of Jean Genet's *The Maids*, which had never been done in the US. She did it with herself and two other actresses in this little loft space hidden away somewhere in the South Village, and won an Obie for that performance, for that production. And that was the first Off-Off show to win an Obie.

ROSS WETZSTEON, "FUCK THE CURTAIN," *VILLAGE VOICE*, MAY 21, 1985

1956. Shelley Winters, starring uptown in *Hatful of Rain*, drove her own car down to the Limelight to host the first Obie ceremonies, and was immediately besieged by photographers from the AP, the *Daily News*, and *Movietone News*. Under the klieg lights of Dumont television, and before a crowd of over 200 members of the new Off-Broadway community, the three top acting awards were presented to Julie Bovasso for *The Maids*, Jason Robards for *The Iceman Cometh*, and George Voskovec for *Uncle Vanya*. 1959: The Obies moved to the Village Gate, with over 500 in attendance, including Anne Bancroft, Arthur Laurents, Diana Sands, Lorraine Hansberry, guest judge Kenneth Tynan, and a contingent from Radio Free Europe.

DIANE FISHER: They were in the Village Gate. I interviewed Art D'Lugoff—the Gate was his baby—and one of the things that he said in that interview was, "Asses count." He jammed a zillion people in that space, in the basement there. That's where it always was in those years, because Art was a friend of the *Voice*.

MICHAEL FEINGOLD: They started out very free-form and rowdy. They're still free-form and rowdy, but now they're larger and there's a certain *tone*.

ERIKA MUNK: One person was nominated from a group. The way we dealt with it was to invite the whole bunch. So, if you can imagine having a

radically gay theater, ten or fifteen of them, and then the whole Living Theatre, and all of these people together, having fun, drinking, talking, singing,
giving funny speeches. It was great.

Gradually, it became more part of the *Voice* as a corporation. That community thing would always be there. But all of a sudden, there were people from
advertising. Really? It was a kind of snobbery, but it also was a very legitimate
distinction—to be nineteenth-century about it—between art and commerce.

ALISA SOLOMON: The Obies were usually on Monday night. Everything
would go to bed in the paper on Monday. It was like going to queer prom. I
was always excited to go, and I would get dressed up. There were people who
had gone on to become film stars that presented the Obies, but that's not
ever what excited me.

DIANE FISHER: Just about anybody you can name. De Niro. Dustin
Hoffman, everybody.

C.CARR: As one who covered the margin of the margin—performers
who invited you to look at their cervixes, performers who sat motionless
for seven hours trying not to blink—I always regarded the Obies as terribly
mainstream. I mean, were "my" performers ever going to win the same award
once presented to Meryl Streep? As it turned out, they were. Occasionally.

ALISA SOLOMON: María Irene Fornés, the great playwright—Ross
wrote a beautiful profile of her. Every time she wrote a play, it won an Obie.

ED FANCHER: We always had one professional actor who would come
make a little speech.

MICHAEL FEINGOLD: The year that Groucho Marx was doing a concert
tour, we got him to host the Obies.

JONATHAN SLAFF: It's the only awards with integrity. You can't campaign for it, which sets it apart from every other award.

MICHAEL FEINGOLD: We don't have "bests" anymore. I was very happy
when we got rid of that. It's not about, there are only five actors, and one of
them has to be the best actor. We give a Best New American Play Award
because it's a money award. But that's the only "best" we give.*

We've done crazy things with that. One year there were five plays, all
wildly different, and we could not agree on what should get the best play.

---

* The Obies stopped awarding "best" categories in 1969.

We gave them each two hundred bucks out of the $1,000, and all five play-wrights came up to accept the best play award.

ALISA SOLOMON: We would make up categories if we needed them. Like, somebody would say, "Shouldn't we give a special Obie to Lori Seid, who's been a tech director for all these downtown theaters for all these years?" And somebody else would say, "What a great idea!" There were no announced nominations.

LANFORD WILSON: I was at Dustin Hoffman's table, and he kept trying to leave because he was sure he wasn't going to win. Ulu Grosbard, who I think had guaranteed his presence, practically had to sit on him.

ALISA SOLOMON: The voting meetings can be very contentious. I remember one where Michael Feingold stormed out. We would usually have two guest judges who were from the theater community, and they weren't the ones in the fight. The fights were always among the *Voice* writers.

DAVID SCHNEIDERMAN: Michael seemed to resign in protest from the Obies committee every year over something. But he always seemed to walk out at the very end, when there were no more votes to be had, so he was able to get what he wanted, but then he would protest. Every year I'd sidle up to Michael and say, "What are you going to quit over this year?" He said, "I don't know yet."

JERRY TALLMER: The only big fight we ever had was over Beckett's *Happy Days* in 1962. The judges that year were Walter Kerr, Edward Albee, and myself, and Kerr adamantly refused to vote for it. He was a nice guy, but very stubborn, and insisted on Frank Gilroy's *Who'll Save the Plowboy?* Finally we divided the prize. Kerr stipulated he'd only accept the compromise if we announced that he was abstaining. So the single abstention in the history of the Obies has been Walter Kerr on Samuel Beckett.

DAVID SCHNEIDERMAN: There was a moment at the Obie awards, and I guess it was our twenty-fifth anniversary at the Puck Building. Dustin Hoffman was there, and Al Pacino was there.

Pacino did a play called *The Indian Wants the Bronx.* He got an Obie for it. He said, "Until I got that award, I didn't know if I was any good."

CHAPTER 33

"THEY THOUGHT THE GAYS WERE TAKING OVER THE *VOICE*"

LUCIAN K. TRUSCOTT IV: The *Voice* was about half gay, I think. When I was growing up, I had the same attitudes anybody else had, discriminatory attitudes. But then I started writing for the *Voice*, and I met Michael Smith, Arthur Bell. There were a lot of gay people on the staff and a lot of gay writers. I came to learn what a ridiculous crock of shit being a homophobe was, and it just went away.

RICHARD GOLDSTEIN: Jill Johnston was the first lesbian published in a major newspaper, openly. Arthur Bell was the first out gay journalist to write in a major paper. We hired gay people during the McCarthy era, which was unheard of.

JEFF WEINSTEIN: I was the first out restaurant critic in the world. The *Voice* was the first in all of this stuff in gay and lesbian coverage.

RICHARD GOLDSTEIN: If it weren't for us, we would have taken much longer to have a gay rights bill in New York, because we crusaded on behalf of that bill. We had a march of fifty thousand Hasidim on city hall when the bill passed.

DAVID SCHNEIDERMAN: Some of the gay members of the staff in my first year there said to me, "Why don't we run a gay pride issue on Gay Pride Day?" Which was in June. I said, "OK, let's do the entire issue gay." We called it a "Gay Life" issue, and it was a Peter Hujar photograph on the front.

RICHARD GOLDSTEIN: For years they carried no advertising. People would hold it so the front page didn't show. That was the only time that people ever folded the paper.

There were dozens of other people who were in that issue over the years: Allen Ginsberg; Christopher Isherwood; Armistead Maupin; Bayard Rustin, the civil rights leader who was also gay, the organizer of the March on Washington. We covered trans politics.

SUSAN LYNE: There were a ton of people who were excited that we were taking it as seriously as we were and that we were celebrating it. And there were plenty of old-guard *Voice* readers who thought we had gone off the deep end, and we should stick to landlords and local politics.

RICHARD GOLDSTEIN: Generally, we were "zapped" five or six times a year by various groups. I was having a long and serious affair with the art director, George Delmerico. We would do layouts at his place. He lived down the block, actually. We were together for about two years, but I wasn't out yet—certainly not to my colleagues—and we decided to do a gay issue in 1979.

DAVID SCHNEIDERMAN: Richard comes into my office and says, "I can't work with George on this project." I said, "Why?" He said, "Because he keeps wanting to sleep with me, and I don't wanna sleep with him."

So, all the circuits in my brain are all fucked up right now because I only knew George at the *New York Times* as having a girlfriend. Then I'm thinking, "Oh, I didn't know Richard was gay." Richard had been married. So, all these circuits were like, "Errrrr! This is very interesting." You never quite knew who was straight or gay on any particular day with some of the people there. But it was great because everybody was out. At the *New York Times*, no one could be out.

RICHARD GOLDSTEIN: We commissioned a portfolio of pictures by Peter Hujar, a very well-known photographer, gay. I call Jules Feiffer and I said, "We're doing this special issue to commemorate gay pride; would you please do a cartoon for us?" So, he said, "Sure, but not for syndication, just for you." An envelope arrives with the cartoon. I opened it up. His cartoons ran these panels. It's something like this: "Can't say 'faggot.' Can't say 'lezzie.' Can't say 'homo.'" Goes on, all the epithets. The last panel, it says,

"Guess I'll have to go back to saying 'nigger.'" That was the cartoon that he submitted.

My hair stood up. I was horrified by this, and what should I do? This is Jules. This is one of his greatest hits. We had a Black editor, Rudy Langlais. I went to show him the cartoon. He was enraged, just enraged.

RUDY LANGLAIS: Jules gave me the strip. Usually, it was just pro forma, you just put it through. Because Jules's work was never changed.

"Well, I think I'll go back to saying nigger"—that was a bridge too far. Because increasingly these kinds of terms referring to Black people began to show up with frequency in the paper. There was one writer whose work referred to Blacks in a cool, hipster way as "spades." And all of a sudden "nigger" in this piece and "spade" in that piece. I had decided that I would not hold my tongue about this anymore.

RICHARD GOLDSTEIN: I went to David. I said, "We can't print this." He said, "Oh my god, what are we going to do? What are we going to do? It's First Amendment, blah, blah, blah, it's Jules." He called Andy Young, a friend of his, some very prominent Black figure from the South, and asked him what to do and, and Andy Young said, "Print it, but not in the gay section." So that's what we did. But because I had advocated not printing it, Hentoff and a bunch of other people were up in arms. You know how the *Voice* used to run these letters from writers complaining about other writers? This is another unique part of the *Voice*: writers fought in the letters column.

RUDY LANGLAIS: I said, "I'd like to write a letter of objection and explaining why I object to Jules's strip." Other editors found out that I had written this letter and asked to sign on to it. I think there were thirteen people all told. Hentoff and Newfield were offended by this, so Newfield wrote a piece—or it may have been Hentoff—referring to how "this would never have happened in the golden age of the *Village Voice*." And I wrote a piece. I said, "Yes, let me remind you what the golden age of the *Village Voice* looked like. There were no Blacks here, there are no Puerto Ricans, there are no Cubans." And I began this litany. "None of those people were here. Are you comfortable with that as the golden age?"

Newfield then wrote a piece referring to us as something like "the *Voice* 13" or "the thought police." This raged almost for a whole summer. There wasn't an event you went to where people weren't talking about this inter-necine war at the *Voice* between the old-guard *Voice* and the *Voice* 13.

A DISSENTING VOICE, JUNE 25, 1979

Dear Editor:
As staff members and contributors at the *Voice*, we would like to dissociate ourself from the Jules Feiffer cartoon in this issue which ends with the racial slur "nigger." Whatever its intentions, the cartoon plays into, and not off, a reactionary sensibility. We find it not only offensive but far from funny and not in the least illuminating.

Stanley Crouch
Georgia Christgau
George Delmerico
Karen Durbin
Richard Goldstein
Pablo "Yoruba" Guzman
Lin Harris
Susan Jaffe
Robert Keating
Rudy Langlais
M Mark
Clayton Riley
Sonia Jaffe Robbins
Mimi Seton

NAT HENTOFF, *VILLAGE VOICE*, JULY 2, 1979

There are two factions at *The Voice*. Some of us believe the reader has to be trusted to make up his own mind. Others want to protect you from "polit-ically incorrect" ideas and language.

RICHARD GOLDSTEIN: I was definitely in the center of this, so I responded by saying I was gay during that episode.

Doing battle with your colleagues was part of the paper. We implicitly thought that the only way to get to the truth about anything was to fight it out, that conflict was how you reveal the truth. That's when I came out.

MICHAEL FEINGOLD: I remember when Richard was not yet out. It was uncomfortable to be in the same room with him, because if he knew you were gay he would project such hostility. And then one day I came into the office, and there was Richard, and the black cloud that had been over him had gone, and he was all sunshine. I said, "Aha, he's come out."

RICHARD GOLDSTEIN: I would be talking to one of the straight guys at the *Voice*, and I would feel this wall come down, my face would tighten, and I would immediately feel this anxiety like they were judging me. And sometimes they were, sometimes they weren't. They were deeply uncomfortable. There was graffiti in the bathroom about some of the gay people at the paper. You'd go to take a piss, and there would be like, oh, "So-and-so has big balls."

I wouldn't call it homophobia, because that's an active thing where you try to hurt people—it was more like a deep discomfort. It expressed itself in all kinds of ways, including one of them screaming that they were working for a "faggot newspaper."

DAVID SCHNEIDERMAN: Somebody came into my office, one of the men, and said, "You're running too many gay covers."

Because I needed to see the flow of what was going on, I used to put the covers up on the wall. I didn't want to repeat headlines, or I wanted some variety in terms of what the lead story was each week. I looked up at the wall behind this writer, and I said, "OK, you tell me how many gay covers are there." And there's three over the first, I don't know, five months, four months I was there. But for him it was, like, a dozen. They thought the gays were taking over the *Voice*.

GUY TREBAY: It was not a great place for gay people for quite a long time. In the '70s and '80s, Arthur Bell was the anointed gay guy, and he did all the reporting until he died rather young. Then there began to be other writers—AIDS was probably the catalyst for that. Gay culture didn't have a lot of space. If you wanted to write about music and you were gay, it was gonna have to be disco music.

Was it a deeply, deeply homophobic place? The answer's yes. I don't know where I would lay the blame for this. But it's a bizarre, and obviously super troubling, prejudice to try to promote. Not because AIDS was going to come and decimate a generation, but because if you track civil rights to feminism to gay liberation, there was this tremendous efflorescence of talent and becoming. All these people—and not just in journalism, but all the arts and all spheres were creating—went on to become super important pillars of the creative community.

Everything that is now central to the culture was originating in the kind of marginalized places we were writing about, and that would have included a lot of gay people. I suppose it's always like a real estate issue. But the white guys had tons of real estate. And also, they [the straight white news reporters] had all the psychic real estate. But that hegemony was coming to an end.

1980–1990

"THIS IS THE DARK SECRET THAT THEY NEVER TALK ABOUT"

CHAPTER 34

"ONE AFRICAN AMERICAN STAFFER IN THE EDITORIAL DEPARTMENT—THAT'S UNACCEPTABLE"

CAROL COOPER: Back in the day, I cold-called people. There used to be places like the Bottom Line where everybody would go to see showcases. That's where you met everybody. If your work was any good, they would know who you were. I was doing mostly what was then being called World Beat—live Caribbean, Latin, reggae. There were a bunch of African artists that were just beginning to be signed by independent labels based in New York. David Jackson—who was a freelance musicologist, very, very knowledgeable, Black journalist from the South—he knew Bob Christgau. He says, "You might want to apply for a job in the copy department at the *Village Voice*," because they just got investigated about whether or not they were in compliance with equal opportunity statutes in their hiring practices. They got a failing grade, OK, because they had virtually no Black people working in editorial at that point in time. This is the dark secret that they never talk about, right?

ROBERT CHRISTGAU: David Jackson knew a lot of arts people in Harlem. One of the people was Thulani Davis, who was a fucking genius, and she gets a job in the copy department.

THULANI DAVIS: When I was hired as an editor, I was told point-blank that my job was to get Black writers, Asian American writers, Latino writers. I was in charge of getting all the people of color. That is how this country works. If you write an anthology of literature, they'll call you up and say, "Could you do the Black chapter?" The *Voice* came out of that same culture.

I got to discover reggae and rap. I was the first person to cover either of those things there. I saw Afrika Bambaataa, all those guys. I wrote my first review in rhyme.

The first time I wrote a feature, I wrote about James Brown, and Nat Hentoff went around the building and asked who I was and went and told the editor, "Whoever she is, keep her, she's great." He championed me through my first firing. He helped me get my first book published.

DAVID SCHNEIDERMAN: I promoted her to senior editor, and she's an all-star. She was just a fucking genius. But she would talk to me about the pressure she felt as the only African American senior editor; I guess she, quote, replaced Rudy, because a lot of Black writers would come to her with complaints about not getting published. If you were African American and we didn't publish you, there was understandable reason to believe it was because we were, like, racist shitheads or something—or didn't understand—which wasn't really the case.

I figured this newspaper has a real problem. One African American staffer in the editorial department—that's embarrassing, unacceptable. I went to talk to Kenneth Clark, the great African American sociologist who was a key witness in *Brown v. Board of Education*, overturned segregated schools. He was a great man. He was on the state board of education. He had a consulting firm. I said, "Can you do an affirmative action study? Try to find out what is going on within the staff, why don't we have any African Americans? What am I gonna do to make a difference?"

RICHARD GOLDSTEIN: Even the cleaners were white.*

CAROL COOPER: Rudy, Thulani Davis, me—we all came in at about the same time as a result of this initiative. We worked in editorial, but I was a copy editor, I was a proofreader. Thulani was a proofreader, and then got

---

* With at least one notable exception: Black actor James Earl Jones was a janitor during the *Voice*'s halcyon days.

bumped up to copy, and then got bumped up to editor. Then the second wave came in. After I'd been freelancing for the *Voice* for about two years, then you started getting people like Greg Tate and Lisa Jones and Nelson George.

RUDY LANGLAIS: The first wave was, as Miles Davis would say, a motherfucker.

ROBERT CHRISTGAU: At a certain point Thulani says to me, "There's this writer named Gregory Tate who you should know about."

GREG TATE: Thulani was a good friend of my mother's. I started reading the *Voice* in the mid-'70s because of Stanley Crouch and Gary Giddins for the jazz coverage, because I was a young jazz head. I noticed Thulani getting bylines. She'd been there about a year, and she said, "You should send some of your stuff to the music editor, Robert Christgau. I think he'd like it."

It took me another year before I finally came up with something that was interesting. It was a review of a Nona Hendryx concert at the 9:30 Club in DC. Bob said, "I can't use this, but the more writing like this I get in the paper, the better I like it." He gave me my first assignments. In August of '81, I got my first piece published on Pharoah Sanders, then James Blood Ulmer, and then Bad Brains, and I was off and running. I was told later that I fulfilled Bob's desire to have a Black Lester Bangs.

Even though it was Rudy Langlais who actually started the trend, but in terms of the music staff, Bob definitely brought myself, Barry Michael Cooper, Nelson George, Carol Cooper in at the same time, followed by Lisa Jones, Ben Mapp. And then Doug Simmons came on; dream hampton and Harry Allen followed. Enrique Fernandez—I'm pretty sure Bob brought him in.

He got to defy the illogic of white supremacy in publishing: "We can't find any qualified Black people." Bob just seemed to trip over them anywhere he went.

ROBERT CHRISTGAU: Greg was exactly the completely out-there, fireworks writer I wanted to have. Then there's Barry Michael Cooper. He handed me a piece about the Funkadelic album.

BARRY MICHAEL COOPER: I loved Riffs, the music section. I looked up Bob Christgau's number in the white pages; I called him twelve midnight. And his exact words were, "Who the fuck are you, calling me so late?"

I said, "Listen, please don't hang up, and I apologize for calling you so late. My name is Barry Cooper. I'm a young Black guy from Harlem, I love Riffs. When I was in North Carolina Central University, I used to wake up at seven in the morning, light a joint, and listen to WOKN in Durham, North Carolina, and they would play the whole first side of a Funkadelic album, *Hardcore Jollies*. I know this music inside out." I wrote a piece called "The Gospel According to Parliament" on spec.

He said, "Listen, let me read it. If it is great, I'll run it, and if not, don't ever call me again this fucking late."

I went to meet him on Friday afternoon. He had his blue pencil, and he's rocking back and forth. He's got that kinetic energy. He said, "You know what? This is really good, and I'm going to run it. I can only pay you seventy-five dollars." I said, "I would have done it for free."

During one of the edits, he said, "Are you familiar with a guy by the name of Nelson George? This guy's been sending me spec pieces. What do you think of him?" I said, "You need to get him in here *today*. This dude is a beast."

NELSON GEORGE: I'd been reading the *Voice* since I was in high school, and that became my guide to life. I lived in the far end of Brooklyn. The *Voice* was my gateway to the whole world of New York downtown. I remember running into Bob Christgau at the jazz club the Bottom Line. I sent him a bunch of clips. I actually have the typed rejection letter from Christgau. Then I got more formal rejection letters later. I tried again. He just told me I wasn't ready yet. That's around 1980. Obviously, all you need to do is tell the kid he's not ready. I kept trying.

CAROL COOPER: He's a unique man, and one of the best line editors I have ever had. I got the job as a proofreader for about a year or two before Bob would let me write music for him. Look, one way or another Bob made everybody pay their dues.

GREG TATE: Bob was rough on writers. Just those edit sessions, man. We were all writing by the seat of our pants. Some weeks it was just on, you would just be hittin' it, you were freestyling. Sometimes you got lost in the sauce, man, but you had to turn the piece in, and Bob would just look at whatever gory mess you'd turn in and say [*imitates Christgau*], "This is unpublishable." Then two hours later, between the two of us, you'd figure out how to make it fly.

We just took that writer's-paper thing to the limit. The person that tested him the most was Barry Michael Cooper. Barry was born again, and he would just be telling these Bible stories for a couple of grafs into a review.

The genius of Bob as an editor and M Mark and Kit Rachlis—they all could edit your work without editing you out of it. You maintain your voice, but Bob was going to show you how your voice could also observe a few basic rules of style and grammar too. For me, that was very necessary, because I was making up words, I was using all kinds of slang, Ebonics, broken English, and various poetic flourishes.

You just have to let him be intimidating because you *will* live. He may make you feel like you're the stupidest person that ever sat in front of him. But you will live. Carol Cooper was lobbying for a staff position at one point, and he told her, "You either write your way into this paper or you won't."

LISA JONES: She's somebody who doesn't get her due. She should have been a staff writer.

CAROL COOPER: Look, I've been a minority in mostly white environments almost all my life, so it wasn't any different from what I had already experienced. By the mid- to late '80s, when there were a lot more Black writers getting bylines in mainstream publications, I could be more selective. But for a while, I was pretty much it. If I didn't say it, it didn't get said.

CHAPTER 35
"THEY CALLED IT GRAFFITI"

GREG TATE: The presence of *New York* magazine gave the *Voice* a nemesis class-wise. The *Voice* that we knew? It really begins in the mid-'70s, because it really was able to define the New York it was speaking to and for, that was not being spoken to. *New York* magazine was really the beginning of journalism that was directed at the New York elite. It provided gutter entertainment for the wealthy.

But the *Voice* really got to be the *Voice* of hip cultures erupting in New York neighborhoods back in the '70s and '80s. In terms of the downtown art avant-garde—that was such a great, fertile moment, that moment in which graffiti and SoHo started to cross-contaminate one another.

Richard was a huge defender of graffiti.

RICHARD GOLDSTEIN: I was teaching at City College in '74 maybe, '73. I met this guy named Hugo Martinez. He had organized graffiti writers into a group called United Graffiti Artists. I was fascinated by this. He introduced me to a lot of these guys. They were from Washington Heights. They were maybe twenty, eighteen—teenagers.

I began to notice these things on the trains. The *Times* ran a piece about this guy, Taki 183, who had written his name all over the subway. But these were really paintings—works of art.

I went down to the yards with them. They weren't hoods of any sort. They had ambitions to be artists, and they were Latino—most were. I wrote a series of pieces. One of them, we ran a train along from the front page to the back page. It was so great. The train wrapped around the paper, and we ran a whole centerfold of photos by Henry Chalfant.

They called it graffiti. It's an Italian word. Roman graffiti is famous. But their real word, the real aficionados, was "writing." They didn't like the idea of anything that involved the art world; it's more like a sport to them. Their ambition was to be what they called All City, meaning that the train would move through the entire city, and their name would be seen by everyone in the city. The mural style, or what was called Bronx bubble style, and Wildstyle—that was Latino. The Black style is more calligraphic; it's more vertical. Eventually these things all merged with breakdancing and all of that stuff and became hip-hop.

RICHARD GOLDSTEIN, "THE FIRE DOWN BELOW," *VILLAGE VOICE*, DECEMBER 24, 1980

Unlike the newspaper that has called for their demise, these bands are racially integrated, which gives writers access to the same cross-cultural energy that animates rock 'n' roll. In fact, the graffiti sensibility has a musical equivalent in "rap records"—another rigid, indecipherable form that can sustain great complexity. I'm sure Ali would agree that rap records are also part of the griot tradition.

RICHARD GOLDSTEIN: We were pilloried, oh, just, pilloried! You know, "Utterly irresponsible! It's destroying the subway system!" It was exactly where we wanted to be, let's face it. This was a real middle finger to the bourgeoisie. My first article was in '73, called "This Thing Has Gotten Completely Out of Hand."* But the big article in the *Voice* was called "The Fire Down Below." So, listen, I loved graffiti.

NELSON GEORGE: The *Voice* was early on breakdancing; Sally Banes did a big article on breakdancing.

GREG TATE: I was talking to Fab 5 Freddy about it. That breakdancing piece was major.

---

* In *New York* magazine.

SALLY BANES: In the fall of 1980, I received a call from Martha Cooper, a photographer and visual anthropologist who specializes in children's play, and a working journalist. For several years she had been documenting subway graffiti. She told me that as a staff photographer for the *New York Post*, she had been sent to a police station in Washington Heights the previous winter "to cover a riot." When she got there she found only a few dejected-looking kids who had been arrested for allegedly fighting in the subway when they claimed they were dancing.

SALLY BANES, "PHYSICAL GRAFFITI: BREAKING IS HARD TO DO," *VILLAGE VOICE*, DECEMBER 24, 1980

"We're not fighting. We're dancing!" they claimed. At the precinct station, one kid demonstrated certain moves: a head spin, ass spin, swipe, chin freeze, "the Helicopter," "the Baby."

An officer called in the other members of the crew, one by one. "Do a head spin," he would command as he consulted a clipboard full of notes. "Do 'the Baby.'" As each kid complied, performing on cue as unhesitatingly as a ballet dancer might toss off an enchainement, the cops scratched their heads in bewildered defeat.

DAN BISCHOFF: You know how they put those black pieces of paper in the subways so that you can graffiti that and not get the tiles dirty? Keith Haring used to draw babies or glowing angels on those things, and people from Europe would cut those things out of the wall and take them home. And they're now in museums and places.

RICHARD GOLDSTEIN: I was teaching at School of Visual Arts. When I found out that Haring was a student at SVA, I thought, "Oh, I should meet him." He took me to his studio. He said, "Oh, look, there's a whole pile of these things I do on blueprint paper. Give me twenty-five dollars, and you can have as many as you want here." I bought two for fifty dollars and brought them down to the *Voice*. And Ross Wetzsteon said, "What the fuck is that?" I said, "It's great. Look at it." I just tacked it up on the wall. I didn't think anything of it, and eventually I at least put it in cellophane.

That's how I met Keith Haring. He was very minimally verbal and intensely observant, very casual about the work he was doing. His later work, which is mostly calligraphic, is brilliant. Once he got sick, his work changed and became more ambitious and mysterious.

Basquiat was active. David Wojnarowicz started out as a graffiti writer. He did art on the sex piers.* I had a column called Art Beat where I covered alternative art, graffiti being part of it.

JERRY SALTZ: In the '70s, you had what we called pluralism—there was no money in the art world, but there were a hundred new theories. There was women's liberation, gay liberation, civil rights, and people started showing up from those constituencies, making art that was more hard-core, say, formalist or art historically correct. There was performance, there was pattern and decoration. The entire '70s got covered beautifully. Jennifer Bartlett, Lynda Benglis, who brought down the entire hierarchy of *Artforum*—she caused a complete rupture. She posed completely naked with a gigantic two-headed dildo in her vulva, and it was on a double-page ad in *Artforum*. And the whole art world completely lost its shit. It would seem like nothing now. Then, art and money started sleeping together.

JEFF WEINSTEIN: The moment graffiti hit the galleries, there was the question, Who's taking advantage of this art, and who's making money off of it? The Basquiat question. We wrote a really, really powerful early piece on Basquiat.

SYLVIA PLACHY: Oh, the shoot with Basquiat was great. He was living around the corner from the *Voice*. He had his huge paintings on the wall. I took out my tripod and I put on my Hasselblad. I even had a light—a reflective light. It's nice and subtle. And he came down the stairs, and he was not wearing a shirt. He looked like he was napping or something. He said, "Well, where would you like me to be?" He stood in front of his painting. I said, "It's fine right there." He said, "Do you want me to put on a shirt?" I said, "Oh, no, this is perfect." Having no shirt made all the difference.

---

* The Christopher Street portion of the Hudson Piers in Greenwich Village was a popular cruising spot for gay men in the '70s and '80s before the AIDS epidemic and before the city renovated the piers.

The artist Jean-Michel Basquiat in his loft, 1986. Photo © Sylvia Plachy.

DAN BISCHOFF: Basquiat put SAMOs* all over the Lower East Side to build a name for himself to get the *Voice* to pay attention to him. We had a big Basquiat print hanging right as you went into the office. We had some Keith Haring, Robbie Conal—the artists who were au courant. And all of them had a ragged revolutionary edge.

GREG TATE, "NOBODY LOVES A GENIUS CHILD: FLYBOY IN THE BUTTERMILK," *VILLAGE VOICE*, NOVEMBER 14, 1989

When Basquiat died last year at the age of 27 of a heroin overdose he was the most financially successful Black visual artist in history and,

---

* A tag that he created with Al Diaz, an early graffiti artist in the '70s. It stood for "same old shit," shortened to SAMO (with the copyright symbol). The *Voice* published an article by Philip Faflick in 1978, titled "SAMO© Graffiti: BOOSH-WAH or CIA?"

depending on whether you listened to his admirers or detractors, either a genius, an idiot savant, or an overblown, overpriced fraud. Besides affording an opportunity for reappraisal of Basquiat's heady and eye-popping oeuvre, the exhibition invites another consideration of the Black artist as bicultural refugee, spinning betwixt and between worlds. When the fire starts to burn, where you gonna run to? To a well without water?

GREG TATE: That's where the title *Flyboy in the Buttermilk* comes from.* It was a piece that tried to encompass the racism that he confronted in his life and career, and then why his work was valuable. It's an assessment of him as an artist, but also looking at his alienation and his response to racism that came from within the art world. He felt very much isolated and alienated from the art world. People were saying his stock was going down and "it's the end of Jean-Michel" right before he died.

RICHARD GOLDSTEIN: Jeffrey Deitch kept showing the work. And then these white artists came along, and graffiti merged with skater culture. All these people who were on skateboards painting—they were white now.

PETER SCHJELDAHL: The great part in the '80s is that for a while the heavy-metal academics and the graffiti kids and the rascal painters were all still drinking in the same bar. But that ended soon, where the markets on the one hand and the academic power plays on the other bifurcated the world.

RICHARD GOLDSTEIN: The Latino guys and the Black guys began to split off and became very alienated from the art world. That's when they refused to paint on canvas. I have work that somebody painted on metal. Leo Castelli even showed graffiti for a while, but he was shamed into not showing it.

They were just ordinary Latino kids from the Heights. It's funny because you grow up in a certain milieu, and you see this and you know, instantly, that it belongs. I always thought the city should commission these people. The trains would be terrific, a globally known trademark of New York. But no, they ended up as felons. Giuliani came along.

I called it visual doo-wop. It was New York as the egg cream. I just ate it up.

---

* This is the title of Tate's first anthology.

CHAPTER 36

"THERE'S SOME MUSIC COMING OUT OF THE BRONX CALLED RAP"

BARRY MICHAEL COOPER: I had this conversation with Bob in January of '80. I said, "There's some music coming out of the Bronx called rap music. This is going to be a game changer." He said, "I don't believe that." I said, "I'm telling you, there's a group called Funky 4 + 1—these four guys, a girl who's a rapper, Sha-Rock. They got a record called 'That's the Joint.' This thing is phenomenal." And two days later, he called me to come down to the *Voice.* "You were right. This is something."

VINCE ALETTI: I was at Tower Records. I was a buyer there, but I also started writing occasionally at the *Voice* with Bob. My first real editing job was when Jeff Weinstein took a three-month break, and I filled in for him as the art editor.

God knows how it became me—well, I wrote one of the first pieces for Bob about hip-hop. I reviewed a hip-hop concert that was at what's now Webster Hall.

ROBERT CHRISTGAU: We were covering hip-hop before anybody except for the *Amsterdam News.* Robert Palmer, who had been at the *Times,* was not insensible to how good hip-hop was, but we did more of it. I certainly am not going to be so modest to suggest that some other music editor would have been as quick on it as I was. I was very quick on it.

GREG TATE: Bambaataa used to be the DJ for the *Village Voice* Christmas party for about six or seven years running. Bam really knew how to promote hip-hop as a thing. He knew the value of the press.

Music critics the late Greg Tate (left) and Nelson George. Photo courtesy of Nelson George.

It was such a small world then. Everything happening in New York was happening below 23rd Street to Canal. On Fifth Avenue, it was Peppermint Lounge, Danceteria, and then on down, CBGB's, and then Mudd Club. Everything that mattered in culture was happening in the East Village, about the twenties on down, east and west.

The first hip-hop show I went to was one that Bob asked me to review, a midnight show at the Ritz. I was still living in DC. He wasn't paying for a hotel. I took the Amtrak up and then took the Amtrak back after the show. It was for a group, the Fearless Four doing "Rockin' It," one of the great one-hit wonders of early hip-hop.

CAROL COOPER: In the mid-'80s, the level of hip-hop writing that new Black writers were bringing into the *Voice* was intense. And part of that was because Robert Christgau loved hip-hop. He loved hip-hop more than he ever, ever loved house or any other marginal music. So, the combination of his editorial support, and a bunch of new writers that he was cultivating who were similarly enthusiastic about it, makes hip-hop a natural pivot point. The amount of writing that we did on world music was equally significant.

NELSON GEORGE: In '81, I got my first real job at *Record World*. Sometime in that year, I sold him a piece about Lovebug Starski, an early rapper. Then I sold them another short piece on Grandmaster Flash. That was the beginning of my relationship with the *Voice*.

BARRY MICHAEL COOPER: Greg Tate and Nelson George became a paradigmatic shift, not only at the *Voice* but in writing and journalism, period. I couldn't hold their Gatorade. They were—and still continue to be— two of the greatest writers that came out of the *Village Voice*, and the *Village Voice* is filled with great writers.

Nelson was critical theory, period, all the way down the line, talking about Black bohemians, talking about hip-hop, and Nelson's way of contextualizing things made all the difference. He made you really, really sit down and think about Public Enemy, about Russell Simmons, about hip-hop— and from top to bottom, from the basement to the penthouse, he would give every layer of what his subject matter was.

NELSON GEORGE: I made it my mission to write about R&B artists. That particular branch of Black music was really atrophying. Tate was really interested in jazz and avant-garde jazz. Barry was interested in funk and different kinds of hip-hop, but also keyboard-driven funk. And then I was really interested in mainstream R&B, which I always felt never got any respect. Carol Cooper was also interested in reggae and Latin music.

NELSON GEORGE, "MARVIN GAYE: THE POWER AND THE GLORY," *VILLAGE VOICE*, MAY 8, 1984

In the '60s Marvin bent his voice to the wishes of Motown, but he did so his way, vocally if not musically. He claimed he had three different voices, a falsetto, a gritty gospel shout, and a smooth midrange close to his speaking voice. Depending on the tune's key, tone and intention he was able to accommodate it, becoming a creative slave to the music's will. . . .

On Berry Gordy's "Try It Baby" Marvin's coolly slick delivery reminds us of the Harlem bars I visited with my father as a child. His version of

"Grapevine" is so intense, so pretty, so goddamn black in spirit, it seems to catalogue that world of black male emotions Charles Fuller evokes in his insightful Soldier's Play.

GREG TATE: We're all about the same age. We had it covered from three different sides. We never really tripped over each other.

NELSON GEORGE: It was amazing that Bob could edit all of these different people. He also was editing Stanley Crouch. See, because Stanley Crouch was musicological, elevated, "I'm telling you what the real shit is." And Tate is really in his "Ironman" phase, so he's writing crazy, psychedelic shit. I'm like white bread in there, just trying to get my shit in there.

ROBERT CHRISTGAU: I tell people Nelson used to write on the fucking subway. People would see him sitting there on the subway scribbling in his notebook.

NELSON GEORGE: I had some writing skills, but Bob taught me how to think about making an argument. And not just to write about lyrics, which is one of the things that was wrong with rock criticism, was that it was all about lyrics, and not enough about music. And Black music was about music. If you weren't writing about syncopation or polyrhythms or how bass and drums interact, then you really weren't writing about the music. You were just dancing around.

RICHARD GOLDSTEIN: There's this whole tradition of white liberals writing about Black music that goes back to jazz—Hentoff, Leonard Feather—and they didn't do a bad job, they introduced the music to the public, but the fact is, they weren't Black. The *Voice* really pioneered this school of expressive Black writing—almost coming close to postmodernism.

VERNON REID: The *Voice* had actual Black writers writing about Black art. That was a big deal. That wasn't happening at the *New York Post* and the *Daily News*. The *Village Voice* actually had Black writers writing about Black stuff, writing about Basquiat and writing about Spike Lee and writing about Chris Rock, you know? They were writing about just-emerging, talented people, and that was important.

CHAPTER 37

"GREG WAS A FULLY FORMED GENIUS"

HARRY ALLEN: The one who was the biggest influence on me was Greg "Ironman" Tate. "Yo, Hermeneutics," where Tate just threw down the gauntlet—it was almost like a grand theory of writing about Black music and Black culture. If there's a piece where a writer lifts Thor's hammer [*chuckles*], and the lightning strikes it, that was the piece for me.

GREG TATE, "YO, HERMENEUTICS," *VILLAGE VOICE*, JUNE 1, 1985

Word, word. Word up: Thelonious X. Thrashfunk sez, yo Greg, black people need our own Roland Barthes, man. Black deconstruction in America? I'm way ahead of the brother, or so I think when I tell him about my dream magazine: *I Signify—The Journal of Afro-American Semiotics*. We talking a black Barthesian variation on *Jet*, itself the forerunner of black poststructuralist activity, given its synchronic mythification and diachronic deconstruction.

HARRY ALLEN: He consumed so much culture and was able to write about it in such a rabidly combinatorial way. You'd go through a paragraph, and he'd have all kinds of things mixed together that he saw as equal or related, and things that were high, low, African, European, Asian, Black, white, Latino, just culture, just mixed.

He saw them all as satellites. If you ever see one of those pictures of a satellite field around the Earth, including detritus and active satellites and operational ones, often it's referred to as space junk. It's like a planet, and then a cloud of dots around it. That's the way Greg seemed to see the artistic universe. Around him, it was a cloud of dots of *every* kind, and he saw them all as having a reason for being there.

That was a real revelation, especially because his writing style was so rhythmic and funky and Black. And because he was talking about Black culture as fundamental and not as an aside, it recast the whole universe for me. I don't think that I would have been able to write about hip-hop the way I did had I not had his example first. His example was the one that told me that I could talk about Black culture *as a basis*—I could talk about it from that reference point. I didn't have to write about it objectively. I could write about it extremely subjectively.

GREG TATE: "Ironman" is from high school. I used to hang out with these guys, we had a little poetry troupe, and one day they were sitting around talking, and my friend said, "Goddamn, man, that boy gets my head so hot, it's like a goddamned iron, man." Then they just started calling me Ironman, and then other people picked up on it. Then when I did my first bylines, I brought it in maybe by the third piece. It was also the name of an Eric Dolphy song that I love, the jazz saxophone player. He had a song called "Iron Man" which was named after one of the NASA spaceships.

LISA KENNEDY: When I was watching *The Last Black Man in San Francisco*, I was thinking that you don't often see depictions of what a Black bohemian vibe is. Greg Tate is that in a way that's definitely like Amiri Baraka–land or something. It's really special. It created an incredible space for people to imagine writing whatever the fuck they wanted, in whatever way they wanted to.

BARRY MICHAEL COOPER: Greg was a fully formed genius by the time he got there. I used to read his pieces and have a dictionary next to me and say, "What does this word 'hermeneutics' mean?" He's a painter. It was a literary collage of Black life that made his subject matter greater and deeper and more intense.

JOE LEVY: Everything was done on Atex* then, and whatever you get—whether it's the first draft or second draft, or maybe it's the fifth draft—is really a blueprint for Greg. The piece will come in and, in jazz terms, those would be "the changes." The changes are set now. Greg's gonna come in and improvise. Like, you'll ask him a question, or he'll be sitting over your shoulder reading, and he goes, like, "No, let's do that better."

I don't know what we were editing. I can type, but I can't spell, and it was all done on Atex, so there's no spell-checking. I'm trying to take dictation from Greg Tate, and there's this pause and he's like, "Uhhhhhh, you went to Yale, right?"

"Yeah."

"So why do you spell like Flavor Flav?"

GREG TATE: "Cult-Nats Meet Freaky-Deke" was my big piece combining race theory and poststructuralist theory in one piece. That was the biggest one among the academic cohort.

GREG TATE, "CULT-NATS MEET FREAKY-DEKE," *VILLAGE VOICE*, DECEMBER 9, 1986

This whatchamajiggy here is about how black aestheticians need to develop a coherent criticism to communicate the complexities of our culture. There's no periodical on black cultural phenomena equivalent to the *Village Voice* or *Artforum*, no publication that provides journalism on black visual art, philosophy, politics, economics, media, literature, linguistics, psychology, sexuality, spirituality, and pop culture. Though there are certainly black editors, journalists, and academics capable of producing such a journal, the disintegration of the black cultural nationalist movement and the braindrain of black intellectuals to white institutions have destroyed the vociferous public dialogue that used to exist between them. Consider this my little shot at opening it up again.

---

* A computer-based publishing system used by newspapers in the '70s and '80s prior to email and the internet.

RICHARD GOLDSTEIN: I read him for his style, rather than for the content. But what interested me as a writer was his incredible ability to project himself through rhetoric. It's incredibly imagistic.

DAVID SCHNEIDERMAN: If Greg was in an issue, I would put his aside for a time when I knew I wouldn't be interrupted. You couldn't leave it in the middle of the piece, right? Otherwise, you'd lose it. It was seamless. Sometimes I went back and read it again, 'cause I felt I missed stuff. But honestly, if there's something I didn't understand, I said, "Well, fuck it, it's OK." Because I knew he was coming from a completely different space.

JOE LEVY: The thing that blew my mind was Tate did this piece where he talked about how people were now dancing differently because records were sounding differently. That must have been in '87, when everything in hip-hop was slowing down. It was a really magical mixture of art criticism and sociology and rubber-on-the-pavement reporting. Not only can no one else write that; no one else is *there* for that. There's no one else at any newspaper in the world who's in that space right then at whatever sweatbox party in whatever part of Upper Manhattan or the Bronx or Brooklyn.

What Greg does as a critic, as a writer, opens up a space.

CHAPTER 38

"THE EDITORS AND WRITERS WERE ALWAYS GOING INTO HIS OFFICE AND YELLING AT HIM"

RICHARD GOLDSTEIN: David was the best editor. With David, it wasn't really conventional, but it was ordered. Under David, you had the emergence of the feminists and the queers. My guess is that David reasoned that this was actually a coming thing and was very good for the paper's profile in a commercial sense. He was this great ringmaster. He had to deal with Murdoch's constant complaints about anti-Israeli stuff in the paper. And then he had to grow the paper in advertising, at the same time dealing with this wonderful madhouse.

ROBERT CHRISTGAU: He was a great editor. There were crucial ways in which he changed the paper for the better. Schneiderman really created Pazz & Jop.* The poll was going, but he saw that it had commercial possibilities. He put it on the front page; he made it a big deal. And then when Chuck Eddy's thing came in, I said, "This guy is so good, we've got to publish some comments." And he said, "OK."

CHUCK EDDY: I don't know if you remember the Pazz & Jop polls later. Christgau would take comments from all the different voters every year.

---

* An annual critics' poll of music, created and run by Christgau, which first appeared in 1971. After ceasing, it restarted in earnest in 1974.

238

Christgau had written something in one of the Pazz & Jop essays: "If you're out there writing about music, knight yourself. Let me know you're out there." I started voting in the poll when I was a college student in Missouri. By the third year I voted, I was a second lieutenant in the army, in Germany.

My third year voting in the Pazz & Jop poll, I sent a really long letter—like eleven pages—to Christgau about the state of music criticism. I ended up getting a check in the mail from the *Village Voice*, and I was, like, why am I getting a check? I saw the issue, and he'd printed, like, this huge chunk of the letter I had sent, and it gave him the idea to put comments in. He had never done that.

ROBERT CHRISTGAU: Gradually, it became, in the late '80s through the early aughts, that format. For a long time, it was a supplement, and then they couldn't afford it anymore. It was all Schneiderman who did that.

JEFF WEINSTEIN: He liked creativity. He liked to publish things that hadn't been published before. He wasn't a copycat. He also knew how to spread authority. He wasn't a micromanager in any way. Some managers will leave people alone because they're not interested in what they do. But David read everything in the paper.

DAVID SCHNEIDERMAN: I felt I had to know what was in the paper—in part, because I didn't want to miss anything that belonged on the cover, and I also needed to make judgments about people and their work. Plus, it was fun. I got paid to read the *Village Voice*.

SUSAN LYNE: It was unlike any publication I'd worked for before; even though it was a weekly newspaper, the deadlines were mostly last minute. Alex Cockburn would push his deadline until after midnight on the night we went to press. He'd go out to dinner, he'd have a few drinks, and then finally he would get to the office, and he would bang out his column. He was utterly charming, brilliant writer, very droll, and don't ever cut his copy. Part of the reason that he delivered his columns so late was that he had figured out that the later he delivered it, the fewer changes there were going to be.

MARK JACOBSON: I left early. It was Schneiderman who made me go, man. How can you hire a guy from the *New York Times* to be the editor of the *Village Voice*? It's so counterintuitive! To me, that was a *shanda*, man. It really bugged me. And we didn't get along. We had a couple of fights. I don't think he fired me because I couldn't write well enough for the *Village Voice*. It was a moment of pique; he just fired me. I figured, "You can't fire me, I quit."

It really felt like, "It doesn't make a difference what's happening in the rest of the world; what's happening at the *Voice* is really the most important thing." And it didn't last that long for me.

KIT RACHLIS: I got a call that the music editorship at the *Boston Phoenix* was open. Punk had exploded. This was '77. That arts section was a farm system for the New York arts world. The film editor and critic was David Denby, who would be hired within a year and a half to go to *New York* magazine. All the news staff would slowly be picked up by the *Boston Globe*. There's a person who was the first person to win a Pulitzer who was at the *Voice*. Her name is Teresa Carpenter.

I got promoted to be arts editor of the *Phoenix*, and late in my second year, David Schneiderman walked through the offices and said, "Bob Christgau says I should meet you." About two or three months later, in February or March of '84, he called me and said, "The executive editor position is open, which is essentially second to me, but you would be the person that is responsible for the arts section. Would you consider it?" I said yes.

So, when David interviewed me, he told me this story about how, within the first few weeks he was at the *Voice*, he heard loud shouting going on, which was not unusual. He walked out of his office, and Fred McDarrah, the photo editor, and Howard Smith were having a ferocious fight. Like, "Welcome to the *Voice*." He said, "I walk out of the office, and their fists are raised, and I said, 'Fred! Howard! Come into my office right now!'" And the fight stopped.

Maybe the second week at the *Voice*, I had an enclosed office, and I hear this huge commotion outside my door. I walk out, and Stanley Crouch and the letters editor, Ron Plotkin, are screaming at each other because Stanley is objecting to how Ron Plotkin has edited either a letter complaining about Stanley or Stanley's response to a letter complaining about him. And they're big guys. They are shouting and screaming at each other, and Stanley either is about to cross the line with something homophobic, and Ron I don't think is gonna cross the line with saying something racist, but they are edging closer and closer. Making it worse is the crowd of people around them, not quite egging them on, but they're not doing much to separate them.

I say to myself, "I'm the person with the most authority here, I've got to do something about this." I come in, and I say—remembering what David had said to me—"Ron! Stanley! Into my office right now!" Except my voice goes up two or three octaves. Has no effect.

Suddenly Bob comes tearing around the corner, Christgau, basically starts moving Stanley toward my office. Shuts the door. And Bob says, "Stanley, I don't know what the fuck's going on with you, but you've been an asshole all week." Stanley and Bob were quite close in those days. Stanley looked at him, and Stanley was just steaming. He suddenly stopped and said, "Bob, you're absolutely right. I don't know what's going on with me, but you're right."

So that was my introduction to the *Voice*.

SONIA JAFFE ROBBINS: At some point, David had his office painted this salmon color, and somebody had read recently that this was supposed to be a calming color. So, we wondered, did he get it painted this color so that in his meetings with writers and editors it would have a subtle calming influence? The editors and writers were always going into his office and yelling at him.

DAVID SCHNEIDERMAN: They would come and act out and try to play mind games. They would whine, they would insist, they would stomp their foot a little bit.

GREG TATE: I used to laugh how every week, Joe and Wayne would have Schneiderman cornered in his office, because his office had that big window. You could see them in there—looming over him, screaming. They were mad about whether or not something got on the cover, how much space they had [*chuckles*], but every week they'd be in there screaming on Schneiderman.

Then I found myself in that same position because I'd written a story about a Black nationalist group. They were on trial for terrorism—the New York 8. I was really caught up in the rapture of that moment, so I went in there and I started screaming at him. Everybody could see what was going on, and I'm sure that Bob probably intervened to keep me from being banned from the building and shit.

DAVID SCHNEIDERMAN: There was one time at the end of a staff meeting—Greg Tate, he gets up and stands over my desk, leans over in my face, and says, "When are you going to publish my piece?"

Well, I thought that was rather an attempt to intimidate me. I said, "Fuck him. It's not going to run for a month now." Because I couldn't let people think that that's how you get published.

The most dedicated I was to working out was when I edited the *Voice*. I worked out my frustration in the fucking gym.

KIT RACHLIS: He wore *New York Times* clothes, but he would wear dad jeans on Friday.

DAVID SCHNEIDERMAN: After Bill Ryan said, "I'd like to hire you, but Murdoch has to approve it," I had an interview with Murdoch. It was a Saturday. I decided to dress in a suit and tie just because it's better than being underdressed. Bill Ryan called. "Rupert only had one comment. He said, 'Is he right for the *Voice*, the way he's dressed?'"

CHAPTER 39

"THEY DEMANDED THAT THEY TAKE OUR PULITZER AWAY"

SUSAN LYNE: I was trying to bring in a few people who could write cover stories that would make noise. Andy Kopkind was brought in to cover what was then a still nascent, but incredibly powerful, gay community that was growing in New York City. This was pre-AIDS. Teresa Carpenter did a series of really brilliant murder stories for us.

DAVID SCHNEIDERMAN: They're beautifully written pieces. The best one was called "Murder on a Day Pass," about this guy—he was institutionalized because he was hearing voices and seeing things, and he kept threatening to kill his wife, and they let him out on a day pass, and he went and killed his wife. The second one was the murder of a *Playboy* Playmate—which was turned into a movie.

TERESA CARPENTER, "DEATH OF A PLAYMATE," *VILLAGE VOICE*, NOVEMBER 5, 1980

Paul Snider never lost the appraising eye of a pimp. One night early in 1978 he and a friend dropped into an East Vancouver Dairy Queen and there he first took notice of Dorothy Ruth Hoogstraten filling orders behind the counter. She was very tall with the sweet natural looks of a girl, but she moved like a mature woman. Snider turned to his friend and observed, "That girl could make me a lot of money." He got Dorothy's number from another waitress and called her at home. She was 18. . . .

He offered to take charge of her and that was nice. Her father, a Dutch immigrant, had left the family when she was very young. Dorothy had floated along like a particle in a solution. There had never been enough money to buy nice things. And now Paul bought her clothes. He gave her a topaz ring set in diamonds. She could escape to his place, a posh apartment with skylights, plants, and deep burgundy furniture.

DAVID SCHNEIDERMAN: The one that was controversial was the assassination of Allard Lowenstein, who was this great progressive leader. He was a congressman for a while, and he led the antiwar movement in the late '60s.

SUSAN LYNE: We didn't think it was going to be controversial at the time. But the fact that the man who killed Al felt like he had been hit on by him was something that a lot of people felt should not have been written. And because he had not publicly come out before he was killed, it was definitely something everyone knew. Many gay men then did not come out, and he was certainly among them.

What she was really trying to do was get behind the headlines of some of these murder stories and to tell the larger cultural context.

We put in three of her stories [for the Pulitzer]. It was the *Playboy* one that was actually cited.

The *Washington Post* won for a story. The writer was an African American woman whose piece was then determined to have been made up.* She was a true up-and-coming writer, a beautiful writer who, for whatever combination of reasons, created a fictional character as the lead for her piece. So, the Pulitzer committee took the prize away. Teresa had been the runner-up. All of a sudden, the *Village Voice* was the winner of the Pulitzer Prize. The underdog wins.

DAVID SCHNEIDERMAN: I was shocked we won. It was just fantastic. Then within a week or two, the attacks started coming, and it was driven by the Lowenstein family, because in Teresa's piece, the guy who killed Lowenstein was Dennis Sweeney, and they both knew each other during the

---

* The writer at the *Post* was Janet Cooke.

Mississippi Freedom Summer in '64. They were down there registering Black people in Mississippi to vote. Teresa wrote a long piece about Sweeney—he was really nuts—and Lowenstein, their relationship, and how this killing came to pass.

VICTOR KOVNER: Sweeney was the man who believed that the CIA had taken control of his mind through cavity fillings in his teeth and directed him what to do. I had known him earlier, before he became completely crazy. He was an activist with the movement.

DAVID SCHNEIDERMAN: Lowenstein's family was outraged and started attacking her work publicly. They got a *New York Post* columnist to attack it. They didn't focus on the gay part, but that was the real story. I knew this from Victor Kovner because they told him that. They attacked her over *implying*.

VICTOR KOVNER: Larry Lowenstein was my neighbor.* I recall the family being very upset because he was a revered figure—still is—and he was not out. He was married, he had a couple of children. He was divorced from his wife, and it was not known that he was bisexual or had bisexual relations.

The anger was intense. It was more the sadness of the untimely death of Al, and the fact they felt that that article was not sufficiently respectful of him. There was no basis for a cause of action against the *Voice* and Teresa. That article had been appropriately vetted, says *I*, who vetted it.

TERESA CARPENTER: In my research, I was satisfied that what the story says was true. The reader has got to trust me when he or she is reading the piece. I do not feel compelled to attribute each and every piece of information to its source.

DAVID SCHNEIDERMAN: They demanded that the board of the Pulitzers take our Pulitzer away. Nothing ever is easy with the *Village Voice*, right? We're fighting to keep it, they're fighting to get rid of it, because of these right-wing people. I got so fed up that I decided to write an editorial about it defending the piece and also attacking our attackers. I said, "Shit, let's just run the piece again." We reran it. That went on for about eight months, that whole battle.

---

* Larry was Al's brother.

Then the board of the Pulitzer reaffirmed the award, so we kept it. Politicians would say, "Oh, it's just personal ads, that's all the *Voice* is." They thought the way to dismiss us is by saying that we're not a serious newspaper. That's why winning the Pulitzer was very important. Even though it's a mainstream award, it gave us credibility.

CHAPTER 40

"WE WERE LIKE A KUMQUAT"

BILLY ALTMAN: I started writing for the *Voice* in '76. I've always loved sports, especially baseball and hockey. And in 1981, I approached David Schneiderman about writing about sports.

The very first piece, I went to a Mets game in June of 1981. It was "cushion night." When you go to the ballpark you're sitting on those wooden little seats, right? So, at some point, someone decided that it would be a great promotional item. As it happened, it was not a close game. The Mets were winning in a laugher, by a lot of runs. And fans started throwing the seat cushions onto the field, OK? And at some point, the other team, which I think was the Cubs, left the field, and then the PA announcer, they had to plead with the fans to not throw any more cushions on the field or the Mets are gonna forfeit the game. My headline for the piece was "Let Them Eat Cushion."

It was surprising to people at the *Voice* how much feedback we were getting. The paper realized that people who read the *Voice*—many of them were sports fans. There began to be some talk about having some dedicated page or pages to sports.

RUDY LANGLAIS: I created a sports section called Jockbeat.* My idea was to take writers who were not sportswriters—Jack Newfield, Joe Conason, Margot Hentoff's daughter. And Alex Cockburn loved soccer, so I had him cover the World Cup. I had a writer named Barbara Long who came into my

---

* Jockbeat was an occasional feature during the late '70s. It later became a column as part of the section called The Score.

office one day.* She looked like Kathy Bates with a black patch over her eye and a walking stick. She comes in, this booming voice: "Hey, kid! I want to be your Hemingway. I want to cover bullfighting."

One of the first calls I got was from Ishmael Reed: "I want to be your Norman Mailer. I want to write about boxing for you. There's a big fight coming up in New Orleans. Muhammad Ali is fighting Leon Spinks, and I want to cover that fight." It became one of our most celebrated cover stories.

I then brought in Clayton Riley, who I assigned to cover the New York Yankees. They had a very controversial team: Reggie Jackson and Billy Martin were on that team. I began to develop José Torres, who had been a light heavyweight boxing champion. I assigned Clayton to cover the Triple Crown horse races that year, and he wrote quite famously about that. The sportswriting in the paper was, for my money, quite sensational.

DAVID SCHNEIDERMAN: Truth is, we all loved sports, so we just wanted to see what it'd be like if we had a different way of writing about sports. Ross found Dave Herndon.

DAVE HERNDON: I was doing freelance articles for *Sport*, a monthly sports magazine. The *Voice* was thinking about starting a sports section, so my name surfaced. That gave me a lot of cred—that I was affiliated with a real sports magazine.

The Score was the name of the section, and Jockbeat was a notes column. Jockbeat was sacrosanct. That never got cut. It was lively and attitudinal and funny and a microcosm of the section for the way that it combined actual sports information and insight and analysis with snarky commentary and absurd humor.

ALLEN ST. JOHN: It was also very non-*Voice*-y in a way, because for the most part the *Voice* was all about the big, long narrative. We never used one word when seventeen would do.

DAVE HERNDON: We weren't trying to do what the dailies did. We were very consciously an alternative voice. I just read a cover story that I edited by Nelson George that was about Willie Randolph. Willie Randolph was

---

* Barbara Long regularly wrote about boxing for the *Voice* in the '60s. She reappeared briefly under Rudy Langlais's tenure.

the captain of the Yankees. He had grown up a little bit ahead of Nelson in Brownsville. So Nelson got off this great story, *his* Willie Randolph story. So here we got the captain of the Yankees, who is from Brownsville, and Nelson George grew up right behind him and played Spaldeen with him in the projects. Nobody else but Nelson George could handle that topic. Nelson had also covered the Yankees for the *Amsterdam News*—so he had the long view on these legendary Yankee teams and players and managers.

ALLEN BARRA: I went out to eastern Pennsylvania, where Larry Holmes, the heavyweight champion, lived. He never got any publicity; he never got the credit he deserved. I wrote a story about that: Why is the media ignoring a Black champion like this?

MICHAEL CARUSO: We weren't beholden to the teams. Few people even recognized us. But hey, if we got kicked out of the locker room, we were just as able to do our work and write stories from watching it on TV. We didn't care who we pissed off. So, we could say all the stuff that the Knicks fans were thinking about what a lousy team it was, and how James Dolan sucks.

ALLEN BARRA: We were more sympathetic towards the players than the mainstream press. There was so much with the Mets and Yankees back then: labor issues, racial problems. It was pre-woke race consciousness. Back when the Mets looked like they were building a dynasty and had Darryl Strawberry and Dwight Gooden, there were so many arguments among the players. Then of course there was drugs, we found out. I did a long piece on Darryl Strawberry. I've got maybe two boxes full of nasty letters. I'd thought there wasn't this much racial hatred left in New York.

MICHAEL CARUSO: We could print all the swearwords. And for athletes, that's like half to three-quarters of their vocabulary.

ALLEN ST. JOHN: In the *Wall Street Journal*, you're writing about the Yankees, the first reference would be "Derek Jeter." And the second reference would be the very stilted "Mr. Jeter." If you were writing about Derek Jeter for the *Village Voice*, it would be "Derek Jeter," and then the second reference would be "Mariah Carey–banging motherfucker."

RUDY LANGLAIS: James Wolcott came to me and said, "I'm a big Orioles fan, and the Orioles are going to win the World Series. Can I write about the

Orioles in the World Series?" So, I assigned it to him. And the Orioles took a big lead in the series, and then they blew the series. Now, they blew the series coming up on a weekend, and I had a spot reserved for Jimmy Wolcott's piece of several pages. And come Friday, the first of the deadlines, I couldn't find James Wolcott.

It's coming up on Sunday. Monday is our closing. I've got a two-, three-page hole in the paper. I have spent money on his expenses covering it. It's the first time that the *Voice* has gotten World Series credentials to cover an event.

Finally, I reached him on Sunday afternoon, and he says, "I'm really fucked up. The Orioles lost the World Series, and I can't write."

So, I called the only writer who I knew could possibly help solve this, Robert Ward. Robert Ward was a legendary sportswriter in New York. He had written some big, explosive exposés of Reggie Jackson and the Yankees and Roger Staubach. And he was from Baltimore. Monday, Robert Ward walks in—high on speed, he had been flying since I called him—and he drops on my desk:

O h h h h h h h h h h h h h h h h h h h h h h h h. Shiiiitttttttttttt. Jesus Fucking Shit. Oh Christ. Agh. Arg . . . I can't believe it. The Os have blown the World Series. I just can't stand it. Can't fucking stand it. It's making me wild. They can't have pulled this shit on me. No, it didn't happen. In game two Dave Parker didn't make that throw to the plate. He threw the hail in the stands. Eddie Murray scored. Then the Os went on and swept two in Iron City, and everything is all right. That's what happened, isn't it, Doctor? Yes, I'll have the Valium.

—October 28, 1978

RUDY LANGLAIS: It was absolutely brilliant. I never spoke to James Wolcott again after that.

MICHAEL CARUSO: Nobody even knew the *Voice* had a sports section. Nobody knew *why* the *Voice* had a sports section, and as a result, I could do anything I wanted. We could cover the Mets and the Giants. Or I could do a story about big-wave surfing in Waimea.

DAVE HERNDON: I attended a sales conference with Schneiderman one year. I said, "Yeah, I realize that being the editor of the *Village Voice* sports section is like being the wine editor of *Road & Track*, but here I am."

BILLY ALTMAN: I think it was David's, I'm going to say, *bright idea* to have the sports section all the way in the back of the paper, which meant in the '80s that we followed at least twenty to thirty pages of porno ads. I really wasn't into giving people from the ballpark copies of the whole paper.

DAVE HERNDON: I did an article about the best ultimate frisbee team in town. I was randomly at the beach in Santa Cruz, and there was a frisbee tournament, and the team of two guys that won the freestyle competition were from Washington Square. They had all this crazy street style, and they were extremely talented.

We did one of the first articles about surfing at Rockaway Beach, and taking your golf clubs on the D train to go play a public course in the Bronx. Pro wrestling was starting to gain traction in the '80s, in popular culture. Dan Bischoff wrote a cover story right when wrestling was starting to take off—it just blew up, it flew off the newsstand. I can remember the kicker on this story was "The question about pro wrestling is not whether it's a sport, but is it art?"

JEFF Z. KLEIN: I was there in June 1994, when all this happened in the same week: The Rangers and the Knicks got to game seven of the finals. The Gay Games are going on in New York—ten thousand amateur athletes coming to New York in celebration of queer sports, which was a big deal for us, obviously. The World Cup came to New Jersey, so Ireland was playing Italy in New Jersey, and the whole world's watching. And then O. J. Simpson was in the Bronco chase. All in the same week! We covered all of it.

JEFF Z. KLEIN: Caruso brought in a comedy and parody element, and also great writers like Joyce Carol Oates. He would get guys who would later write for *Seinfeld*—or already were writing for *Seinfeld*—and do these parodies.

MICHAEL CARUSO: I was a real sucker for big-name writers. She wrote on Mike Tyson. She was in her boxing phase at that point. It was a classic *Voice* moment because I published this thing and everybody was congratulating me. The letters editor, Ron Plotkin, he shows me this angry letter: "What does Joyce Carol Oates know about boxing? She's a mousy little woman, and she doesn't know what she's talking about. She couldn't get in the ring herself." He said, "I'm gonna run it. Actually, while I think she has a valid point, this guy has a valid point of view." I was like, "The letter writer is completely misogynistic. I just got this great writer to write for us." He ran it, and she took it very well.

ALLEN ST. JOHN: Bob Costas was a super-huge fan of the section.

BILLY ALTMAN: He was a different kind of sportscaster. He read the *Voice* because we were writing alternative stuff, and he appreciated additional perspectives.

BOB COSTAS: I didn't always agree with it, but I was always interested in it. I don't look like some hipster hanging out on the street corner, even if I was more likely to read the *Village Voice* than my other sportscasting peers.

JEFF Z. KLEIN: Spike Lee was a fan. David Letterman was a fan. We'd have a car-racing story, and all of a sudden, out of the blue, Letterman would contact the guy who wrote it.

DAVE HERNDON: Spike Lee wrote a basketball article. I thought it needed work, and I kicked it back to him. You know, "Bring this up and talk about that and don't do that"—editing. He wasn't having it. So, I'm the guy that spiked a Spike Lee article.

TOM PEYER: Phil Rizzuto was a shortstop for the New York Yankees in the 1950s. He became a broadcaster. As he got older, he was a real spark plug of a personality. Let's say he was an *undisciplined* broadcaster. He would go off on a lot of subjects during the game, sometimes when he probably should be talking about the game.

PAUL LUKAS: He was notorious for these tropes. Like, if someone got under his skin, he called him a "huckleberry." He was famous for leaving the game early to beat the traffic. He would work the first six innings or something, and then his broadcast partner would broadcast the rest of the game, and he'd just leave.

TOM PEYER: Seely got the idea. The first time we talked about it, we were well into a night at a bar. This was all done in bars.

HART SEELY: We were big Yankee fans; the Yankees were terrible. We were watching these games and listening to Phil Rizzuto. I don't remember which of us had the idea, but we started writing down things Phil Rizzuto said and taping the game so we could transcribe them. We sent the stuff to Jeff Z. Klein, who was the sports editor. About a day later, he got back to us. "We're gonna do this every week." He came up with the phrase "O, holy cow."

BOB COSTAS: It was clever, but it was also affectionate—which is I think the way almost everybody felt about Scooter.*

JEFF Z. KLEIN: Everyone loved Phil Rizzuto. Hart's genius was to know this and realize that written down it's like a Zen koan—or maybe a haiku. It's perfect.

HART SEELY: We could hear every now and then his broadcast partner saying, "That was pretty poetic, Phil," and we knew we were getting through to him. We were told that he wasn't sure how to take it because he was a really old guy. But he had gone to various people, and Yogi Berra laughed. So that was the key.

Let me read you one. This is called "My Secret." And it was done on August 19, 1992. This was a game between the Oakland A's and the New York Yankees with a guy pitching in the fifth inning with one out, the bases empty, the Yankees leading.

> *When I'm driving to Yankee Stadium and back*
> *I do it so often*
> *I don't remember passing lights*
> *I don't remember paying tolls*
> *Coming over the bridge*
> *Coming back over the bridge*
> *I remember.*

TOM PEYER: You can't hear that and tell me you don't hear a little Sylvia Plath in there.

BILLY ALTMAN: One year I did a Mets "Consumer Guide," and I graded every player. And I gave like A, B minus, C plus.

---

* A nickname given to Rizzuto by a teammate for his short strides when running to base.

ALLEN BARRA: I was told by an editor of mine at *Sports Illustrated* that the kind of stuff we were doing changed the ways in which they covered sports: a lot looser, a lot less formal, shall we say?

JEFF Z. KLEIN: I went to the *Times* a year after I left the *Voice*, and a couple guys there said to me, "Oh, the *Voice* sports section? I love it." They'd pull out of their drawers little things we'd written.

BILLY ALTMAN: Starting in 1984 I would write a piece about one of the guys on the Mets, and then the paper would come out on Wednesday. Then somehow by Sunday, the *New York Post*, the *Daily News* would have a piece on that player. It happened more than a few times, OK?

JEFF Z. KLEIN: Paul Solotaroff wrote about steroids. And Paul Solotaroff was himself a bodybuilder, so he was very familiar with steroid culture, which at the time was very little known about. He wrote about how people were juicing, their testicles shrink, and they're gonna rage. It was a huge sensation. I remember that *Saturday Night Live* that next weekend did a skit with Schwarzenegger. At the end, they said—they got serious—"Steroids are no joke, they can really mess you up." They broke character. I'm sure it was because of the article.

MICHAEL CARUSO: One of the things that we pioneered was sabermetrics. *Moneyball.* Sabermetrics revolutionized baseball, and then the rest of sports. In the old days, the coaches and scouts would just go with their gut—"He seems like a good player. He seems like he's strong"—but they didn't really apply statistics. Sabermetrics was the real study of how does this batter hit left-handers versus right-handers? How does he hit late in the season versus early in the season? How does he play on natural grass versus Astroturf? We were on it very early, because we were nerds. Allen Barra was a big fan of Bill James.

ALLEN BARRA: I have to confess, I never understood most of what the hell Bill was writing about, but I loved his writing. He was like the Pauline Kael of baseball writers.

DAVE HERNDON: I had a guy that wrote about odds, betting football. This guy was from the Island of Misfit Toys, but he was a super analyst on betting football. We had a statistician who worked for the Elias Sports Bureau. He would do a little box called Stat Man. This was before analytics.

MICHAEL CARUSO: Barra himself developed his own football application, Max Mad, taking some of those same principles and applying them to football. Now it's even been applied to basketball and hockey. Jeff Klein deserves credit for some of that too. He started applying it to hockey.

The *Voice* was a very antijock kind of place. They were not really set up to like their own sports section. We were such a weird animal. We weren't apples *or* oranges. We were like a kumquat.

JEFF Z. KLEIN: We were truly woke, quote/unquote, twenty years before any other sports section. When I got there, I tried to bring in more gay, lesbian, queer writers. Hilton Als was a great young writer, and he approached me and said, "I love these wrestling shows." Not wrestling like the Iron Sheik, but these things where gay men wrestled each other. It was some kind of very small subculture. It was so unsportsy. And yet sportsy. A lot of the queer writers appreciated what we did.

DAVE HERNDON: Richard Goldstein brought me a guy one day who wanted to write about the Mets—a gay man. He wrote this gushy paean to the sex appeal of various Mets. He had this unforgettable line—how "George Foster could bring his big black bat over to my house anytime."

A lot of people—especially in the sports end of it—that are in the newspaper business, they resent being called the Toys and Games department. [*Laughs.*] I didn't care. We were having a blast.

CHAPTER 41
"CERTAIN DEATHS HIT REALLY HARD"

CAROL COOPER: When I met Lester, he was on the wagon. I thought he was the sweetest human being I'd ever met. My impressions of Lester are nowhere near as extreme as those of people who've met him during his wilder days. At the time that he and I met, he was starting to see more Black music, see some hip-hop, and he was starting to expand his purview. So, we'd run into each other sometimes. He was part of the scene. I used to bump into him when he was editing with Bob.

JAMES WOLCOTT: The *Voice* did a piece once on him which was sort of sad; it was about how he was the worst slob in journalism. It was all about how he cleaned himself up. He was sort of unkempt. A lot of it had to do with drug habits. Lester could write a five-thousand-word piece in one night, depending which drugs he was on, and that doesn't lead to good hygiene.

RJ SMITH: I grew up in Detroit and would ride my bike out to the suburbs. My friend would go visit *Creem* magazine, which was in Birmingham. But I was just too afraid to go in and actually introduce myself to Lester Bangs, one of my heroes.

Lester Bangs had just written this famous piece about "fuck New Year's Eve" in the *Voice* about all the terrible things that he'd done in his life and previous New Year's Eves, and how this one was going to be another one. The first time I came to the *Voice* to meet Bob, whoever was at the next cubicle over was saying, "So Bob, what should we do, what's going on for New Year's Eve?" And Bob says, "I don't know. Should we invite Lester over to the office?" "Oh, no! Holy shit, no! I just read his piece, he'll trash the joint!"

The late Lester Bangs in his New York City apartment, 1981. Photo © Christina Patoski.

GREIL MARCUS: I knew Lester as a lonely person, and I never knew him as a party person.

The word "gonzo" was invented by Hunter Thompson to describe his own writing. It was a heroic, self-congratulatory term that meant *Go crazy, say anything, the truth is out there somewhere, make it up if you have to, but get your hands on it and wring its neck.*

Both Lester and Thompson, at his best, in *Fear and Loathing in Las Vegas* and *Fear and Loathing on the Campaign Trail*, were humanists, not crazies. They were classicists, not anarchists. But they weren't afraid of craziness and they weren't afraid of anarchy.

LESTER BANGS: One thing that really fucked me up at *Creem* was that I got caught up in the whole idea that Lester Bangs was this thing, this idea. I call it, like, Hunter Thompsonism. It's when you pay more attention to your image than you do to your work. And that destroys your writing.

I mean, there was a time in my life when I would have got all drunk and everything like that, and I would have been all exhibitionistic and like that, but if I act like that, I might live a long time, but I won't live very long as a good writer. That's just the way it goes.

I know that a lot of people my age—I'm thirty-one—still aren't married, don't have any kids, looks like they may never have any kids. And so, if, as seems to be the trend, the population gets older and older, I guess more and more people, and I include myself in this totally, are going to be old people, you know, in old houses, puttering around with old things. I mean, I can actually see myself twenty years from now puttering around with my beat-up old copies of Velvet Underground and Stooges records.

JAMES WOLCOTT: Certain deaths hit really hard, and Lester's really hit hard in the New York scene. His death is a total tragedy. He did all these drugs, and then when he had gotten off the drugs and he took a milder dose to go to sleep, he never woke up. Some people said it was Darvon. But the thing about Lester is, if you were supposed to take one or two tablets, he never took one or two.

ROBERT CHRISTGAU: He wasn't the bad boy, not in my experience. John Morthland called me, who was Lester's best friend, and he wrote for the *Voice*. He was on phone call duty. He called one person, he called another person, he called another person, he called another person.

We did a big two-page spread about him. I wrote the obituary. People were shocked and dismayed because, really, it was sudden. It was unexpected.

JAMES WOLCOTT: I remember seeing him at CBGB's not long before his death, and he was really nicely dressed, wearing a really nice sweater, all shaved and combed and all that. It was very, very sad.

GREIL MARCUS: At a certain point, a number of us at *Rolling Stone* felt we simply had to meet Lester—who was this person? So I culled some money out of the paper's then bare-bones budget and flew him up from San Diego to San Francisco.

After many hours of listening and talking music, going to the *Rolling Stone* offices, introducing him to people, he went back to La Jolla. We were all thrilled to have met him.

After he died, when I collected and read hundreds of letters he'd written over the years, I found that this visit had been a terrible trauma and disappointment to him, something he never quite got over. He thought we were flying him up to consider hiring him as an editor, and when there was no offer, he felt rejected—when nothing of the sort had ever occurred to any-one. WE JUST WANTED TO MEET HIM.

CAROL COOPER: Lester was very much his own creature, and even when he was saying things that he knew would offend somebody, which he did, quite often, it was always with that rock 'n' roll head. "Well, I'm a rebel, I'm a rocker, and I'm just going to say this the best way I know in order to get the fullness of my attitude towards this idea into the world."

CHAPTER 42

"WE HAD A BOMB SCARE ONCE A MONTH"

DAVID SCHNEIDERMAN: Three weeks in, I get a call from Rupert's lawyer, a guy named Howard Squadron. "Rupert wants you to fire Victor Kovner." I knew this was a no-no. I said, "I'm not going to fire him, and if I do, I'm toast here." He said, "Rupert wants it."

I then decided to call up Murdoch's president. Because there's something about the call that didn't seem right. Rupert never mentioned it to me. Why would he suddenly want me to do this? I told him the story, and he said, "Rupert doesn't give a shit who the lawyer is." It suddenly dawned on me that people in the Murdoch company will invoke his name if they want me to do something. This is a good lesson: not to believe anything unless I heard it directly from Rupert.

MARIANNE PARTRIDGE: When Schneiderman and I met, I said, "One of the things that will happen is Murdoch will try to change your lawyer. And you must fight that. You must not give up Victor under any circumstances, because we've never successfully been sued. If you are told, 'Do not publish this story, it will destroy the paper,' you will have to think twice before you publish a story." The publisher has the libel. The lawyer is critical in a paper like us. Every. Single. Week. *Somebody* was going to threaten to sue the paper. He called later and said, "Funny you said that."

VICTOR KOVNER: In each change of ownership, there were questions as to whether we would continue as counsel. Jack at one point told one of the new owners, *screaming* at the top of his lungs, that if they replaced me, he would resign and go to another paper in the city.

A promotional T-shirt for the advertising
department, circa 1996. Photo © Meg Handler.

DAVID SCHNEIDERMAN: About six months in, I was out in Vermont, my first vacation since I went to the *Voice*. I get a call from Rupert's guy. He's complaining about stuff we'd written about the *New York Post*, because we had been ranting about the *Post* every week, either in the press column or Newfield or Conason.

I pick up the phone. He doesn't even say hello. He says, "David, can you name a single newspaper in the country that is permitted to criticize its owner?" I said, "No. I don't think I can." He said, "Well, why should the *Voice* do that?" I said, "Because the *Voice* is different. If you want this to be the *Village Voice*, you have to let us do what we're doing. What's the big deal?" He said, "Be careful." I always figured I could get fired at any minute.

JAMES WOLCOTT: Everyone at the *Voice* remembers when Alex Cockburn did a column about Rupert. He said something like, "The dizzying prospect of so many new asses to kiss." But Murdoch did not put his foot down on the paper, although there was every good reason to think he might, but he actually didn't. The *Voice* was making money then.

ALEXANDER COCKBURN: He's a very dangerous guy. He's one of the most dangerous people in the world. In England, he controls half of the news media market, and in Australia he is enormously powerful.

JONATHAN Z. LARSEN: We can thank Murdoch for Donald Trump. Because he's helped him more than any other single person, so I consider him a total villain of our day. In terms of the *Village Voice*, he was a pretty damn good publisher for the paper. He left it alone. The Press Clips page was constantly attacking Murdoch, and he permitted it. One thing you can say about Rupert Murdoch, he is a professional publisher.

ED FANCHER: Ed Koch knew Murdoch. Ed Koch said to Dan one day, "I'm going to lunch with Murdoch, who's just bought the *Village Voice*. Do you want to come with me?" So, Dan went. Dan told Murdoch, "If you fool with the *Village Voice*, if you try to influence them in the least bit, you're not gonna have anything. They will walk across the street and rent another office and have a new newspaper within twenty-four hours." He never tried. Murdoch was a businessman. He didn't want a bunch of bohemians walking across the street and starting a new newspaper.

VICTOR KOVNER: I'm sitting in my office one day, and I got a call from Dan Wolf. "We've been sued by some Chinese restaurants, and they are seeking injunctive release." The article was about how you could go to Chinatown, and in a number of restaurants, if you were Chinese and savvy, you could be served dog—which, of course, is a popular food and meat in China but not permitted under New York law. I read the article, which was very funny, satiric, and light, and I thought, "This is ridiculous."

CLARK WHELTON, "DOBERMANS ARE DELICIOUS," *VILLAGE VOICE*, MAY 18, 1972

Besides the scoop-the-poop law, other answers are now being sought to the dog problem in New York. . . .

In search of an answer, I went to Chinatown, where the dog problem is minimal. . . . A local restauranteur, said, "How many chances do we get to eliminate hunger and pollution at the same time?"

CLARK WHELTON: This is 1972. Dan had sent me out to Wisconsin to cover the primary elections out there in Madison.

VICTOR KOVNER: I had to be in court the following morning, because they wanted an order to get the *Voice* to withdraw the papers that were on the newsstands as part of their claim for libel and other torts—damaging their businesses, injurious falsehood.

The judge was an old friend of mine, Samuel Spiegel; he was the assemblyman from the Lower East Side. He used to represent parts of Chinatown.

I begin my First Amendment response. I get maybe a minute into it. He turns, and he says to me and everyone, "This is an outrage!" He had never seen anything so offensive, so baseless, so damaging to these fine businessmen! And he said, "This is so outrageous that the only thing I can do to remedy this situation is to require the lawyer for the *Village Voice* to come with me and these plaintiffs, and go over to Chinatown for lunch, and inspect the kitchens and eat the food, so that he can tell his client that only the finest, lawful food is served in these restaurants."

The courthouse is two blocks from Chinatown. We troop over. We go to three or four different restaurants to taste the food. We walked through the kitchen and are being shown that there's no dog being served. Then we sit down to a couple of delicious meals. That's it.

I called Dan. I said, "The case is over. They've shown me that there's no dog food being served. I told them that it was a satirical piece." Dan laughed, and we set aside a pleasant day's work.

Then, about a week later, Clark came back from vacation. He called me and he said, "Victor, that was not satiric. That was true."

FRANK RUSCITTI: We had a bomb scare once a month probably, because someone didn't like what the *Voice* wrote. It was a big joke to us all. Nobody ever took it seriously. Of course the police did, and we'd all have to leave the office for the morning.

GREG TATE: I wrote the review of Michael Jackson's "Bad," which was a cover story called "I'm White." I got death threats for that one, which they published. First you get the letters, and then you get the bomb threats. Especially on Broadway. That period the building got emptied routinely because of one bomb threat or another. People just mad as fuck.

Nobody would really talk about it in mainstream media—he was not trying to look Black anymore. That was right at the beginning of him starting to go into the bleaching phase, and then even more chiseled—the addiction. It's one of those ahead-of-the curve *Voice* pieces that provoked the wrath of the masses.

GREG TATE, "I'M WHITE! WHAT'S WRONG WITH MICHAEL JACKSON?" *VILLAGE VOICE*, SEPTEMBER 22, 1987

There are other ways to read Michael Jackson's blanched skin and disfigured African features than as signs of black self-hatred become self-mutilation. Waxing fanciful, we can imagine the-boy-who-would-be-white a William Gibson-ish work of science fiction: harbinger of a transracial tomorrow where genetic deconstruction has become the norm and Narcissism wears the face of all human Desire. Musing empathetic, we may put the question, whom does Mikey want to be today? The Pied Piper, Peter Pan, Christopher Reeve, Skeletor, or Miss Diana Ross? Our Howard Hughes? Digging into our black nationalist bag, Jackson emerges a casualty of America's ongoing race war—another Negro gone mad because his mirror reports that his face does not conform to the Nordic ideal.

FRANK RUSCITTI: The letters section was one of the great American spaces for the kooks of the world. It was the early internet. I used to collect the crazy letters. I had three boxes of them. There were plenty of people who called, the tinfoil-hat people. The crazy callers would talk about how they had something akin to a staple that was in their mouth or in their nose, and that was the thing that the government was controlling.

A guy wrote to us that he sent his finger to George Bush, and he wanted us to be the first ones to know it. A guy once cut off pieces of his skin and attached it to a letter and sent it to the *Voice*. That was one of my most memorable pieces of mail.

RJ SMITH: You'd go to work, and Frank would say, "I've talked to this guy, and he doesn't sound like he's doing well today." There was some East Village lunatic, derelict murderer who was clearly not compos mentis, not in his right mind, who the police were looking for. He just wanted to talk to somebody. Pretty soon after that, they found a severed head in a bucket in a Port Authority or Times Square locker.

PAUL BERMAN: A big piece of mine was a Q&A with an American veteran in the Spanish Civil War named William Herrick, where Herrick told me about crimes committed by the American communists in Spain. He had a confession—that his fellow soldiers in the Abraham Lincoln Brigade had killed their own officer, and it was a nasty thing, because the officer was Black.

RJ SMITH: I remember a demonstration outside the *Voice* after he wrote the piece. These people in their eighties—there were still some veterans living in the city, old-school radicals. And they had a picket line outside the *Village Voice* on Broadway. They were chanting "Berman is vermin!"

PAUL BERMAN: They are the Jewish working class of long ago, so they are five feet tall, and very tough guys, except eighty years old. They are real bruisers. They demand that I be fired, and they denounced me as a racist. So, it was quite something. All the *Voice* staffers came down to the sidewalk to see this picket line, because it was the most amazing picket line.

RICHARD GOLDSTEIN: Maybe this is a legend, but somebody called someone "half a motherfucker." And the person was a midget and sued us. We thought hahaha, and we published it. Now, these were all settled. I don't think we ever lost a lawsuit. When you consider the stuff that was in the paper, it's remarkable. It's either a testament to Victor or a testament to the goodwill of people who were insulted. Maybe both.

DAVID SCHNEIDERMAN: Wayne was doing an article on the union at the *New York Post*. It was the mailers' union. Wayne got beat up by them. They really beat him up. This is when Murdoch still owned their paper.

Wayne came and said, "We have to sue the *Post*." I said, "Wayne, it's really hard to sue yourself."

He said, "Oh, I never thought about that. Can we still do it?"

RICHARD GOLDSTEIN: I've told you my Victor Kovner/Harvey Milk story, right? I was reviewing Randy Shilts's biography of Harvey Milk.* I get a call from Victor. It's late at night, I'm at the paper. And he says, "Richard, how do we know that Harvey Milk was gay?" Because part of the libel thing was—did it appear anywhere else in print? I couldn't believe that he did not know that Harvey Milk was gay. So, I said to him, "Victor, I fucked him." [*Laughs.*]

---

* *The Mayor of Castro Street: The Life and Times of Harvey Milk.*

CHAPTER 43
"YOU MUST BE WAYNE BARRETT"

FRANK RUSCITTI: Barrett was relentless with his interns. When someone wanted to work for Barrett, I used to warn them about two things: The first was that Wayne would hire you to work twenty hours and work you sixty. And Wayne will make you cry, because he did.

JOSEPH JESSELLI: Wayne and his volatility—people just feared him.

WILLIAM BASTONE: I think I was maybe intern number four in Wayne's intern history. Maria Laurino was an intern, became a staff writer. Barbara Turk was an intern. I was a little concerned, because I knew that I was definitely in over my head. But what's the worst that could happen?

I'd never been in a courthouse in my life. Almost immediately, he would say, "Go down to the state supreme court and look for this case."

When he interviewed me for the job, he asked me certain questions like, "Do you know who Meade Esposito is?" And I'd say, "Oh, yeah, he's the head of the Brooklyn Democratic Party." So, I knew enough of those things where he was like, "I won't have to explain everything." I was definitely the exception to the rule. I worked in an office with him for fifteen years. Every single intern who came after me, the overwhelming majority of them had absolutely no idea who anyone was. I ended up as the buffer for most of these poor kids.

TOM ROBBINS: Wayne operated out of one small, maybe fifteen-by-ten, windowless office. Bastone was in the office and Conason was in the office, and a half a dozen interns were in the office. It was like a Marx Brothers movie, everybody spilling out the door. There were so many people. I would sometimes camp out. There was a desk that I appropriated right outside where Frankie Bones worked. Frankie Bones was answering the phones at a desk across from him.

FRANK RUSCITTI: I was the intern coordinator. I loved it. The interns—it was like major slave labor, pretty much. There were, at any given point, twenty to thirty unpaid high schoolers and college people just hanging out at the *Voice.* But it was also a good in for a lot of them. My biggest piece of advice to every single intern—and they were always shocked when I said this—was, "You've got to kiss ass." Because even in our wonderful, equal, left-wing environment of social justice and we're-going-to-change-the-world, people still like to have their asses kissed.

There was a cruelty to Wayne with his interns because he was so demanding of them that if they didn't find the exact piece of information, he would tear them a new asshole. On the flip side, Wayne Barrett's interns were the ones who always went on career-wise, and he always got them pages in the *Voice.* At least another half a dozen out there who are now all investigative reporters writing for the *Washington Post,* the *Times.* They all got there in good part due to Wayne Barrett.

JOSEPH JESSELLI: When Julie Lobbia's mother met him, she said, "Oh, you're Wayne Barrett. Why did you make my daughter cry?"* He was so upset about that. He came to me and said, "Do I really?" I said, "Absolutely—you're terrible." Then he thought he could make up with flowers, like a typical man, like, with a woman. But people who are like him, they can't help themselves. They know they're smarter than everyone else.

JOE CONASON: If you were working with him on a story, you better be driving, too, because he was not shy about telling you, "Get your ass in gear. I don't care. You're my friend. I love you, but I'm going to scream at you if you're not done. If it's not the way it should be, I will scream at you, I will stop talking to you."

TOM ROBBINS: I met him at a fundraiser for some publication. Wayne had written a story about his nemesis Al Shanker, who had been the head of the teachers' union, United Federation of Teachers. Shanker had taken

---

* Lobbia wrote the Towers and Tenements column in the 1990s and died very suddenly of ovarian cancer in 2001.

a copy of it and written, "This is New York's leading anti-Semite, Wayne Barrett," and he had put it on the desk of everybody in the state legislature. Wayne just started right in, screaming about this to me. You could tell he was proud, but he was also outraged. This is our first conversation. Zero to sixty.

He almost made me punch him. We had our own battles, that's for sure. I was one of the few people who would tell him to go fuck himself, which he didn't enjoy very much. But we stayed friends till the end, which, with him, was no small feat.

JOE CONASON: We did two parts about Alfonse D'Amato. When he was first running for the US Senate, monstrous person that he was, he had been running Nassau County and the town of Hempstead as his fiefdom, a Republican, incredibly corrupt machine. Wayne went out to D'Amato's house and got chased away by D'Amato's father—may have tried to run him over with a car. Wayne was constantly getting into scrapes because he would confront people.

DAVID SCHNEIDERMAN: Wayne decided he wanted to write a profile of Cardinal O'Connor, who was then at the archdiocese of New York. A bit of a charmer, he was very different from Cardinal Spellman, who was in the '50s and a real rabid anticommunist. Wayne grew up Catholic.

JOSEPH JESSELLI: He was thinking about becoming a priest at one point.

RICHARD GOLDSTEIN: He once wrote that the cardinal of New York was a registered Republican. And cardinals—priests in general—are not supposed to have an affiliation. But O'Connor had an affiliation with the Republicans, and Wayne was ready to report this.

DAVID SCHNEIDERMAN: He interviewed O'Connor many times. They had long conversations. Finally, the piece is ready. He gives it to me on a Friday, and we edit it. And it was really a very different piece for Wayne because it wasn't investigative reporting. He was getting into depth about this man and where he came from, his background—it was really quite fascinating. It was a Monday night when everything came together. We were closing the paper. He comes in; he was almost literally sweating. He was exhausted and enervated.

I said, "What happened?" He said, "O'Connor keeps working me over." He kept calling him back—and not about details, but about Catholicism.

He kept trying to appeal to Wayne's Catholicism, and Wayne was exhausted over it. That's the only time I saw Wayne sweat over a piece. Ever.

RICHARD GOLDSTEIN: He goes home at night, and he gets a call from O'Connor. He says, "Wayne, come home." Of course, he published the story.

DAVID SCHNEIDERMAN: The other time something like that happened was with Mario Cuomo and Andrew. Andrew was his father's consiglieri when Mario became governor. First, we loved Mario. The *Voice* always had these interesting relationships with politicians.

JANIE EISENBERG: Jack was close with Mario Cuomo, and they met over an argument about a judge that Jack wrote about, a guy named John Monteleone. Jack did one of his 10 Worst Judges. Monteleone was one of them, and Cuomo called him up and said, "I think you got something wrong here." And Jack said, "I don't think so." And then they met, and they hit it off, and that was the beginning of a long friendship.

TOM ROBBINS: Jack was a guy who believed in the romantic, big figure in history. One of the things he was good at was bringing attention to people that he would then anoint. He did it with Mario. When he said someone was really worth listening to, people paid attention.

WAYNE BARRETT: Mario would sulk for extended periods of time when I did a really tough piece on him, which I did many of. But as a human being, as a soulful person, I think he is the favorite of mine that I covered. He has much thinner skin than his son does. His son, Andrew, if you write something very critical about him you can't get him off the telephone. He could go on for hours.

DAVID SCHNEIDERMAN: They loved Ed Koch in the '50s and early '60s, when he was close to the *Voice*. Then when he became mayor, Newfield decided he was like the Antichrist, so we started attacking Koch all the time.

Same thing with Mario, not quite as nasty. Mario becomes governor, and Wayne wrote some very tough stuff on him. And one day Wayne finds himself in an elevator with Mario at the World Trade Center, which is where the governor's New York office was. Mario starts berating him about his work and again about Catholicism and abortion. Everybody used to go at Wayne about this stuff.

JOE CONASON: We went after Democrats a lot because they were in power most of the time here.

Wayne Barrett promoting his book *Rudy! An Investigative Biography of Rudy Giuliani*, on the former mayor. Photo © Catherine D. Smith.

ANDREW CUOMO: The first time I heard my father curse was talking to Wayne Barrett. If you were in a position of power, you were guilty unless you could prove yourself innocent. He could be a tad harsh—just a tad.

DAVID SCHNEIDERMAN: They had these incredibly long conversations. Trump thought he could buy Wayne off with an apartment. Andrew thought he could buy him off through charm or thought he could buy him off through Catholicism, and nobody could. Wayne couldn't be bought, which was one of the great things about him.*

WILLIAM BASTONE: We were in the midst of this story about Geraldine Ferraro that did not get published. It was about her husband's organized crime connections. We were chasing down all sorts of stuff dating back to her first congressional campaign: who donated money, who hosted fund-raisers, what wise guys bought tickets to her dinners, who the husband did

---

* In an interview with NPR, Wayne told the story of Trump calling him when Wayne was researching Trump: "He started talking to me about how he had broken this other journalist by suing him and driving him into bankruptcy."

business with. So, we were building this case that there were significant con-nections between her and a bunch of wise guys.

One of the guys—we'd been looking for weeks. His birth name was Dominic Santiago, but he was known as Nicky Sands. Knockabout wise guy from Middle Village who survived what appeared to be a mob rubout, was shot like thirteen times. He was someone who was involved in the forma-tive years of Geraldine Ferraro's political career. There were whispers about whether she might have had a personal relationship with him.

Then one afternoon, Wayne gets an anonymous call. This person says, "Nicky Sands, he's in Beth Israel Hospital. He just had surgery." And hangs up.

We don't know if it's true or not. We walk up to Beth Israel on First Ave-nue. Back then the front desk was this circular desk at which there's a woman receptionist. So, Wayne goes up and says, "Do you know what room?"—I don't know if he uses Dominic Santiago or Nicholas Sands—"is in?" She's looking down and says, like, "No, we don't have anyone by that name there." I circled around the back of the desk and see she has a Post-it note that said, "Nicholas Sands, room 304. Do not give out information." I couldn't believe it was sitting right there.

I waved him over. We just walked into the hospital, into the room, and there in the hospital bed is Nicky Sands. He's lying there in a grog. He's by himself in the bedroom, lying under the blankets. I'm, like, petrified. Now, I'm not scared enough to have actually done this: I had the tape recorder with me, so I had turned the tape recorder on and put it under the hospital bed.

Wayne pulls up a chair and sits down next to him like he's visiting an old friend. And I'm standing on the other side of the bed, freaking the fuck out. I'm, like, twenty-two, twenty-three. And Nicky Sands is in and out. He comes to and he looks at Wayne and he just says, "You must be Wayne Barrett."

CHAPTER 44

"I HAD A SHOOT-OUT WITH NAT HENTOFF ON THE ABORTION ISSUE"

NAT HENTOFF: The *Voice* has been politically correct in many of its aspects since before that term was ever used. The paper used to go to bed on Monday. On Monday nights, the editors would literally cut out passages, sometimes whole paragraphs, of some of the writers that might possibly offend Blacks, lesbians, gays, radicals. And I wrote a couple of columns about that.

The most controversial subject-issue I've ever gotten involved in was when I became prolife. Many liberals are very angry at me because of that. They could understand it, they say, if I came to it from a religious perspective. But I'm still a Jewish atheist, and that really bothers them. And I come to it entirely from the point of view of biology, and what *Roe v. Wade* has led to. So, when I say I'm prolife, I mean prolife across the legal board.

NICK HENTOFF: He basically came to the abortion debate through euthanasia.

JESSICA HENTOFF: He was very libertarian. A lot of times he voted libertarian. He liked to argue. He was an extremist. And in some ways, he was so far left, he was right. And so far right, he was left.

STANLEY CROUCH: He had a very unassuming personality. But I also was fascinated with the fact that he was never not reading. He always had something that he was reading, and whenever I would see him in the Village, he would be walking down the street reading. I used to have this concern. I felt that he would get run over or hit by a car, because he didn't seem to be paying attention to what was going on around him. He was into something.

JEFF SALAMON: He urinated with his hands on his hips, in a Superman- or Wonder Woman–style pose. In all my many years of trying to not make eye contact in men's rooms, I've never seen—or pretended to have never seen—anyone else do that.

STANLEY CROUCH: When I was at the *Voice*, there was a feeling more of tolerating Nat than actually valuing him as a special guy. Because at the time I was there, that's when political correctness, like a blob, had just come up out of the swamp and was swallowing up everything that came in its path.

But Nat Hentoff was like this glacier that would not be consumed.

ALLEN BARRA: I had a shoot-out with Nat Hentoff on the abortion issue. But Nat went out of his way to be really nice to me. He'd say, "Come in here and listen to this," and he'd put headphones on you and make you listen to something you wouldn't ordinarily have listened to.

ERIKA MUNK: Nat had a different kind of charisma, a haimish, patriarchal—if that didn't sound so terrible—charisma. I couldn't bear the fact that this man, whose writing I have loved for so long, who is so great on the First Amendment and so great about jazz, was talking at conservative conventions. We always were friendly, but I just didn't wanna talk to him about freedom of speech anymore because I couldn't bear his sexual politics. We agreed to disagree. A civilized conversation.

NICK HENTOFF: He was as far from a misogynist as can possibly be.

JONATHAN Z. LARSEN: He drove people completely crazy, because he was so well known, and such a strong voice, and we gave him such a presence in the paper, that to be constantly attacking abortion rights was incredibly uncomfortable for a lot of us. I mean, imagine our trying to shut Nat Hentoff up.

NAT HENTOFF: Three editors, all women, stopped speaking to me after my first prolife piece there. In two of the cases I didn't feel much of a loss. The third woman became the editor in chief for a time, and we agreed there were other things we can talk about.

DAVID SCHNEIDERMAN: Karen Durbin came in and was infuriated by a Nat Hentoff column on abortion. I was shocked. "I shouldn't run his column because you don't agree with it?" "Well, you know, we have to stand for our rights."

ALISA SOLOMON: They sent me to Wichita to cover Operation Rescue, which was blocking health clinics where abortions were provided.

I had a funny experience there, because Nat Hentoff was famous for being against abortion. I would go to interview Operation Rescue people. They'd say, "What newspaper you from?" I'd say, "The *Village Voice* in New York." They'd say, "Oh, where Nat Hentoff works," and then they would open their hearts to me. It was hilarious.

LAURIE STONE: People like Mailer and Hentoff, they were just ordinary, old-school, male fuckheads. The kind of people who should never have existed, but since they have existed, we can only celebrate their disappearance.

I went to cover a Right to Life convention in Cherry Hill, New Jersey, for a different publication. I went there undercover; I actually was registered, and I stayed at the hotel. The "right to life" people gave me the press packet, and what's in it? A big piece by Nat Hentoff.

And I thought, "Oh my fucking god, you fuckhead. You absolute scumbag, absolute oppositional piece of shit." And that was that.

CHAPTER 45
LA DOLCE MUSTO

MICHAEL MUSTO: I was obsessed with Arthur Bell. He wrote a column called Bell Tells. He was an openly gay, very vocal activist and entertainment gossip columnist. He didn't really care about nightlife, he didn't like loud clubs, but he did cover cabaret, movies, theater, as well as very serious gay issues. He was a groundbreaker. I adored his column. I hung on every word and just loved the *Village Voice*.

I would freelance occasionally for the *Voice*. In the '80s I did a piece for Karen Durbin, and she loved it. Having the in with Karen Durbin was very important to me, because sadly enough Arthur Bell died in '84. I think he had diabetes; I never got all the details.

RICHARD GOLDSTEIN: I was with him when he was dying. Karen and I got into bed with him at St. Vincent's Hospital. He wanted us to get into bed with him.

Arthur was a deeply political person. One of my models at the paper was Arthur, because though he was a bona fide gossip columnist, he was an activist as well. He was incredibly intrepid and was very courageous, but also very funny at the same time. I named his column Bell Tells. He was a professional.

Arthur's very good friend was Vito Russo, who wrote *The Celluloid Closet*, which is one of the great works of independent scholarship. That's the circle that Arthur moved in. You can see that this crossover between gossip and politics was really uniquely *Village Voice*. This was gossip from the left. Arthur is a very important figure in that shift. That was the tradition of the gay gossip columnist that Michael Musto took over.

MICHAEL MUSTO: I waited a while and wrote Karen a letter: "I'm so sorry about the passing of Arthur, but if you do look for a replacement,

Joey Arias (left) and Michael Musto pose in New York City, 1988. Photo © Catherine McGann/Getty Images.

please consider me," never thinking anything would come of it. Then I got a call to do a sample column. I met with David Schneiderman, who at the time was the publisher-editor. He talked to me about what are the hot clubs right now, and I told him. He also made it clear to me that if I got the job, they were not looking for a replacement who was going to try to be Arthur Bell. The person was free to explore the column and use their own voice in it.

Then Marilyn Savino, she was David Schneiderman's secretary, pulled me aside, and she goes, "I think you got it."

I went with La Dolce Musto. Not just because of Fellini's *La Dolce Vita*, which is about a gossip columnist surrounded by crazy fabulous people. But "La Dolce Gilda," on *Saturday Night Live*, by Tom Schiller, was this brilliant homage to the Fellini film with Gilda Radner.

Even though being openly gay can shut doors, for the most part, it opened doors, because it became my niche, it became my persona. "He's the gay gossip columnist." There were no other openly gay gossip columnists.

In 1985, Liberace was dying of AIDS at this point, and he was promoting Radio City shows that he was doing, where you would never have known the man was sick. He flew in on a big rope, he looked like Big Bird, he entertained. He was hilarious, too. You know what? He almost came out to me, because he started to tell me a joke about a cross-dresser with a penis. He had been told I was openly gay, so that was his little nod to me.

Me running stuff like that made people aware of me, and also the fact that I was writing about edgy people. I loved RuPaul, because she was doing a *Starrbooty* character, which was a Black exploitation homage, like a Pam Grier spoof. She became omnipresent in the scene. Every night I saw RuPaul, and every night it was, "Everybody say love." "This is the front, and this is the back." Randy Barbato and Fenton Bailey were called the Fabulous Pop Tarts. They were like a techno duo, a Pet Shop Boys kind of thing, and they were also party promoters. They were very hot on RuPaul. Now they produce *Drag Race*, which is a phenomenon.

CATHERINE MCGANN: Drag is huge now in a way that I could have never imagined.

MICHAEL MUSTO: I was the only one covering this, pretty much. Now little kids are running around in drag, because they've seen *Drag Race*. I think it's great. It's the world I helped fight for, but there is an aftershock of, "Wait a minute. Where do I fit into this?" In the old days, my column was one of the few venues for drag queens.

Now they're on TV shows, but back then they were not household names. Half the people were like, "Why are you writing about these people? Who cares?" And the other half was, "Thank you for giving a voice to these people."

MICHAEL MUSTO: At this point, I wasn't so galvanized politically about writing about celebrities being gay. It took me a while to really have that lightning bolt, where I just became outraged by the closet.

It was not cool at the time to say Rosie O'Donnell was a lesbian, Ellen was a lesbian. I went there. The tabloids went there, but very few of the mainstream media would go near those topics. Rosie O'Donnell even wanted to come out at one point to *People* magazine, and they turned down the story. Even if you handed it to them. "I'm not being outed! I'm coming out." They were obviously afraid their readers didn't want to hear it. That's how treacherous it was to go on those land mines.

JEFF WEINSTEIN: The first famous name to do outing was this guy Michelangelo Signorile.

MICHAEL MUSTO: Michelangelo Signorile was a great mentor to me. Still is. He was fearless. When Malcolm Forbes died, and the press was writing he was in love with Liz Taylor, which is a lie that Liz Smith—who was closeted herself at the time—had propagated, he just blew it all wide open and said, "He was gay." It became the big outing debate.

RICHARD GOLDSTEIN: I don't believe in outing unless the person is an active homophobe, like Roy Cohn, where there's a hypocrisy in public life. I have gotten into a lot of battles with some gay activists over this.

Michelangelo Signorile is the person who I really did combat with. He believed that it should be done all the time—it wasn't just hypocrites. He thought any famous person who was gay should be outed because they're role models.

Jodie Foster, she was a target of his, and Cindy Carr convinced me that this is not a good thing—that this is authoritarian. We had vehement discussions about this. She influenced me a lot. It's the essence of Cindy. Cindy is one of the most ethical people I've ever met. The only man in the paper who even came close to her was Tom Robbins. I often trusted his reflexes.

When the World Trade Center went down, we discovered that the priest who died was gay. Mychal Judge. The firefighters adored him—he was their priest and he died, being with his men when the tower came down. I thought, "This is very important to say because he's such a hero that we have to say he was gay." I went to see Tom about this, and he didn't want us to do it. He said, "It's terrible. He wouldn't have wanted this. He's a priest."

It was a very tricky decision. So finally I said, "Why don't we try to substantiate the fact that he was gay?" He said, "Well, I could call the fire commissioner." And the fire commissioner said, "Oh, yes, it's true. Everyone knew this. The men knew this."

So, then we felt, "This is probably OK." We did publish a piece identifying him as gay, and we're very clear about how beloved he was. He was a real hero. It's just so important to understand that gay people are in every possible incarnation. They do good things and bad things, you know? They're hairdressers—and priests.

JEFF WEINSTEIN: There were a lot of discussions about outing. I can remember the meeting in which Wayne Barrett, Richard Goldstein, and I were mostly the three speakers about this. The reason for this discussion was about Mayor Ed Koch, who was gay—and Wayne had the evidence.

"Vote for Cuomo, not the homo." You remember that? Well, that was when Koch was running for governor: there were pamphlets saying it. We called it the "Hitler factor." Murder is no good, but if you're going to kill Hitler that might be a way of saying that you could kill somebody. What's the outing factor? If there's somebody in public life who will do harm—especially to the queer community—you have to out that person.

NELSON GEORGE: When Koch finally decided he had to shut down the gay bathhouses, there was a whole lot of pressure from a lot of people in the city. You can't close these gay bathhouses and not deal with Times Square at the same time. Giuliani takes a lot of credit, but closing the bathhouses started under Koch.

RICHARD GOLDSTEIN: There was a famous incident where the *Times* outed a Jewish Nazi—and then the guy killed himself. So that was the precedent. In those circumstances, I might have been amenable to it. With Koch, the only thing you could say is that he didn't deal with AIDS very well; there was a lot of anger from ACT UP about him and AIDS. There were posters accusing him and all of that. So maybe it was justified on those grounds. But it wasn't hypocrisy. He was not antigay in any way.

JEFF WEINSTEIN: Wayne wanted to out anybody; anybody who is newsworthy should be outed.

We were talking about a particular case of Ed Koch. He had this apartment in the West Village which had a kind of stairway to another apartment downstairs, and his boyfriend lived in that. Ultimately Ed did some damage, and ultimately he was outed.

RICHARD GOLDSTEIN: He didn't have that apartment on Fifth Avenue because it was rent controlled—no, it was a fuck pad.* So, the question was, do we print it or not?

DAVID SCHNEIDERMAN: It was a soft outing—it wasn't the purpose of the story, ultimately. It may have been that this guy who was allegedly his paramour—knowing Wayne, it may have been some government contract he got. Wayne wasn't trying to out him. This guy is his paramour; he's also getting these government contracts—that's a story.

---

* Koch famously kept his rent-controlled apartment in the Village during his mayoralty.

MICHAEL MUSTO: I still wasn't convinced right away. I was like, "It's up to them to come out." Then I realized there's nothing wrong with being gay, A. B, we're not making these people gay; we're just saying they are. C, the media, especially the gossip media, goes everywhere invasively about celebrities. They're hypocritical in saying, "Gay is the last taboo that we shouldn't go near." As far as "they can come out in their own time," they still can come out in their own time. I'm a writer in an alternative weekly. The mainstream media is not picking up what I'm writing about these gay celebrities. How does that affect them coming out or not?

Just like there's drag queens on TV, now everyone is gay, gay, gay. I'm proud of my Rosie. I'm proud of my Ellen. We're all friends. We're all aligned. You turn on the TV and it's gay, you know—there's Anderson Cooper. There's Rachel Maddow. Even Boy George wasn't really out. He was bi. George Michael wasn't out until he got busted in the bathroom.

To the credit of those people, they all did end up becoming gay activists. Even when Ellen's talk show started, and she wasn't really being lesbian on the show. Then, slowly, she started being out and talking about Portia.

If I have to be proud about something, I helped push that forward—that gay is not a dirty thing.

MICHAEL MUSTO: Danceteria was a great, multilevel dance club, rock-oriented. Limelight was starting to percolate. There were great clubs like Area. Palladium opened, which was a gigantic megaplex, the ultimate big-budget downtown club. The great thing about these clubs is they catered to bohemia. They wanted the yuppies and the bridge-and-tunnels to pay the admission, but they really cared about the bohemia. At the same time, there was also a percolating East Village scene happening. The Pyramid Club was a Polish beer hall that turned into a drag theater/cabaret space. And the art gallery scene exploded in the East Village. There was so much going on.

CATHERINE McGANN: There were all these storefront galleries, and cool little spaces like 8BC, where bands like They Might Be Giants were playing. That's what I wanted to document.

Michael and I—we just hit it off. If Michael hadn't liked me, I can't imagine that we would have stuck together as a pairing like that for as long as we did—sixteen years is a long time. When I first started, it was literally one column, long and skinny. The picture was barely bigger than a postage stamp.

MICHAEL MUSTO: Cindy Adams, the writer for the *Post*, we're polar opposites, but we appreciate each other on some level. She's Republican, I'm not. She's uptown, I'm downtown. Those are the real glory days of New York society, when it all came together, and those were the best club parties in the '80s. If you went to Area, it wasn't a gay party; it was everything. Now it's Tuesday night, gay party, Wednesday night, bachelorettes. It's very niche. The fun thing about going to a club back then was you would see Keith Haring, Dean Johnson, and Andy Warhol. The downtown people were the stars, and I wanted to convey that in my column. The drag queens and the promoters, the DJs, even the bartenders—I treated them on the same level as the movie stars of the time, which were the Bruce Willises, Julia Roberts.

I never tried to get an interview with Madonna, and the only time we ever were close together was at the Madonna *Sex* book party. I thought it'd be funny to do a parody of the *Sex* book because it was such a hot book. There was the famous hitchhiking scene, and Madonna in high heels with a little handbag, so we re-created it. Catherine McGann was the photographer. We went to New Jersey, and I stood outside. I was freezing my nuts off and tucked a little bit, and I did a whole parody write-up.

CATHERINE MCGANN: Michael and I sometimes went to some flat-out scary places, like the Vault. It was a pretty notorious S&M gay club on the West Side way back when Times Square was still a little scary. As time went on, he would get more and more space. It went from that tiny little column, then they would give him a whole page. At the height of everything going really, really well, we would get a double-page spread every week.

It also changed direction. Michael, as he got more well known, naturally started getting invited to all these celebrity things. The column changed in that it became not just about grubby, grungy underground nightlife that was only downtown—there was a lot more celebrity. Michael could traverse both worlds.

LYNN YAEGER: I used to see him at parties and stuff, and he'd be all dressed up, and I thought, "This is like the coolest person on earth; he would never talk to me."

VINCE ALETTI: Karen asked me if I would edit him. I was reluctant to do it because he seemed like such a character, and I thought I couldn't handle him. And of course, I loved him. He was the most professional writer that I dealt with at the *Voice*. I knew half the time when he was filing for me, he'd been up to, like, three or four in the morning the night before, and yet he was never late with a column.

CATHERINE MCGANN: I remember going to the Tunnel and being around all these very glamorous people. In the beginning, Warhol would be around. Michael got invited to what ended up being Andy Warhol's last New Year's Eve. We sat at his table. Andy had a dinner at a restaurant in Tribeca. I was like, "How did I get here?"

MICHAEL MUSTO: I wrote a cover story in the *Voice* called "Death of Downtown," which is one of my more famous pieces. It was a cover of the *Voice*, and Andy Warhol had died.

MICHAEL MUSTO, "DEATH OF DOWNTOWN," *VILLAGE VOICE*, APRIL 28, 1987

But unquestionably the biggest factor in downtown's demise is the high cost of living in Manhattan, which has forced a lot of bohemia into the boroughs and 'burbs, making for a wicked reversal on the old contempt for bridge-and-tunnel: now they're the cool ones.

CATHERINE MCGANN: Warhol went into the routine gallbladder operation and ended up dying, which was horrible. He died as a complication of the operation. His death was a bizarre fluke.

MICHAEL MUSTO: At the funeral, at St. Patrick's of all places, Grace Jones was in black, everybody was dressed for mourning, and they were all giving ridiculous speeches that they could have been talking about Mother Teresa. It's like, "Who are you talking about up there?" Don't homage them with some bullshit, because that's not homage. If you liked Andy, you understood the full person. He was a manipulator. He was a damaged person, yes, but also brilliant.

The clubs were starting to falter from being overhyped. Everyone was writing about downtown, downtown, downtown. That had to explode. In '87, things started changing, and then the Club Kids started percolating. I ended my "Death of Downtown" with a hopeful: nightlife never *really* ends. It always seems like it's over, and then something else happens.

CHAPTER 46

"I'M GOING TO SELL THE PAPER TO SOMEONE WORSE THAN ME"

DAVID SCHNEIDERMAN: I always figured I'd get fired at any moment, but I also felt that the *Voice* was the *Voice*, and you have to let it be what it's going to be. Rupert would call and ask to have lunch or something maybe once a year, and it was all perfectly OK. He never really complained about anything.

JOE CONASON: We would print stuff about him in the paper all the time. Alex did it. I did it. Jack did it. Criticizing the *New York Post*. Criticizing all the shit that he did. In 1980, he was going to get a loan from something called the Export-Import Bank, a US government agency, for his Australian airline to buy airliners from the US. Big, interest-free, beautiful, fat loan—millions of dollars. And he just happened to endorse Jimmy Carter for president—who was president then—in the New York primary against Ted Kennedy in the *New York Post* around the same time that he goes to the White House. We published this whole story in the *Voice*—this really seamy fucking thing that this guy was up to with his businesses, which was one example among a million with him. He was like a Donald Trump type— selling out basically everything, including his mother.

I wrote a piece about the tax breaks that the *Post* was getting on its building on South Street. And meanwhile they're shilling for Koch all over the place, just sickeningly, trying to help him become governor. I wrote this story, just laying out what happened with the tax board, where they got their taxes reduced for the building and the coincidental policies of the *New York*

Post that were favorable to the mayor. There was a picture of Rupert in a tuxedo.

DAVID SCHNEIDERMAN: The next morning I hear from Howard Rubenstein. Howard was Rupert's big PR guy. Howard says to me, "I had breakfast with Rupert, and he's really mad at you." I said, "Over what?" He said, "That article that you guys ran." I said, "Well, it was perfectly OK." He said, "No. It was the picture of him that he's pissed off about. He had a tuxedo on. He felt you were making fun of him being a fat cat or something."

That was a little small shot across the bow.

The next one was much more serious. I got a call in 1983, and it's from his secretary: "Rupert would like to see you."

I walked into his office. He's telling me about how this *Post* building was the old Hearst building. It was near the East River, and the newsprint would come flooding down in barges, and it would dock there. I said, "We're doing OK so far."

Then he turns to me, and he says, "I want you to fire Joe Conason." He didn't yell at me. We ended up in this half-hour dance about me not firing Conason, him wanting me to fire him, and him telling me, "If you fire him, you'll be a hero."

I said, "Rupert, I'm not going to be a hero. In fact, if I fire someone because you asked me to fire him, my career is over as an editor in this town. If you fire somebody because an owner tells you to do it, you have no credibility with your staff." He kept pushing. He just was very persistent.

He finally said, "If you don't fire him in three months"—I'm thinking, "Oh, this is going to be good"—he pauses. "I'm going to sell the *Voice*." I'm thinking, "This isn't so bad."

Because of the look on my face, which was *not* terror, he then says, "To someone worse than me."

I said to Rupert, "I guess you are going to have to sell it, because I'm not going to fire him."

I didn't tell anybody this at all. Then I got the idea maybe I can find someone to buy it.

That December, we're having a little editorial Christmas party, and Marty Singerman, who was then the publisher, comes in the office and closes my door. He said, "You know that conversation with Rupert in August? It never happened." I said, "Marty, that's like the Mafia. He threatened to sell the *Voice*." He said, "David, don't be a wise ass. It never happened."

Alex Cockburn did a column about Rupert trying to buy what was then known as "The Hitler Diaries" that surfaced in Europe in the mid-'80s, which was almost exculpatory about Hitler knowing about the Holocaust. It was very controversial. The London *Times*, one of Rupert's papers in England, bought it. He got this famous British historian to verify that they're legit. It turned out it was a total fraud. Rupert looked like an asshole. Alex Cockburn writes about this. Being a Brit, he knew how to get to Rupert. He quotes Rupert saying, "Fuck Lord Dacre." Lord Dacre was Hugh Trevor-Roper, who was the historian who okayed it.

I'm at home that night; I get a call from John Evans, who was the new publisher. "We just stopped the presses. We turned the trucks around with the papers in it. Rupert's saying, 'Fuck Lord Dacre.' Rupert doesn't talk like that. It's inaccurate."

We have this standoff. The presses had stopped for an hour. I said, "Listen. What if we just keep the word—the letter *F* and just scratch out the *U-C-K*."

He said, "OK." We do it.

Next day, Marty Singerman, who was Rupert's consigliere, tells me to come to his office. He said, "David, that was very dangerous. Don't ever do that again."

Two months later, Rupert put the paper up for sale. He called me down to his office. He said, "David, I've decided to sell the *Voice*, but don't take it personally. I need the money to buy 20th Century Fox." I said, "You mean the *Voice* is that valuable?" He said, "No." He said, "I need money to put on top of money on top of money."

These are the last words Rupert ever said to me—this was in April of 1985: "Keep the lid on a little while longer." Suddenly it occurred to me that that's all Rupert ever wanted.

JAMES RIDGEWAY: The Australian guy—Cockburn and I had lunch with him once. It was very nice. I never ran into any trouble with him, ever, and

I don't think Cockburn did either. And Cockburn is the kind of guy that made everybody pissed off, sooner or later.

LAURA FLANDERS: In his coverage of the Middle East, Alex raised the curtain on the bias that exists in the media, the cruel, casual, conventional wisdom that permitted a complete double standard around human rights abuses by the Palestinian forces and the human rights abuses by Israel. He simply drew a line in the sand and said it was unacceptable to treat two such different benchmarks, these unevenly matched parties.

DAVID SCHNEIDERMAN: Alex took money from some Palestinian group, allegedly, to go to the Middle East and write about it. It was not a cool thing to do. He never had any intention of making that trip.

ROBERT CHRISTGAU: He wasn't bought. That was what he believed.

DAVID SCHNEIDERMAN: I said, "We live in a glass house. We're always attacking people for ethical things. So, I'm going to suspend you."

When I suspended him, he said, "For my last column, can I write about this incident?" I said, "Sure. You can write about it, but I'll reserve the right to also write about it in the same paper."

KIT RACHLIS: For four months, I served as semieditor with David looking over my shoulder. He shifted a lot of responsibilities to me. I was there from May of '84 to late October of '88, so four and a half years. The last year, Karen Durbin oversaw the arts section, and I was given the responsibility of overseeing much of, but not all of, the non-newsy cover stories. I had taken over Guy Trebay's column. Guy was the least likely *Village Voice* person. Blue Oxford shirts, khaki pants, tortoiseshell glasses, and he would walk into the toughest neighborhoods in New York and write about them. It was just extraordinary; he'd write really beautifully. And his pairing with Sylvia Plachy was really a brilliant, genius pairing.

GUY TREBAY: I did the column for twenty years. I don't know how you can characterize it. It was urban anthropology, maybe. I was just going out and reporting on stuff that the mainstream media hadn't gotten to. I was talking to a friend the other day about having been in the Bronx project houses with Afrika Bambaataa. And ABC No Rio, the Times Square Show, and also a lot of gay culture. There was a lot of emergent culture.

I'm kind of a Bronx nut. I just like the Bronx. I did some really early stuff about crack, which came after I was brought to meet the mother-in-law of Eric B. (of Eric B. & Rakim). She lived in a certain housing project. She was a hardworking woman, and her life was being destroyed—as many people's lives were—by crack all around her. I was really compelled by that, and went back and back and back. I always looked preppy, and people used to say to me, "Oh, you go [to the Bronx]—it's so scary." But as long as I was respectful to people, I was treated respectfully. The city had a greater degree of openness.

I'm not a fan of nostalgia *at all*. But I don't think my memory is falsifying to say it was a very yeasty period. Maybe not to everybody's taste, and there were plenty of problems. But there was a porosity. You could move in and out of worlds.

KIT RACHLIS: I loved editing Guy. He would announce, "I'm off to have sex with Kit!" in that very proper Guy way. I would say, "I read your piece, I've made notes," and we would sit in front of the computer together.

David got promoted to be publisher. Rupert Murdoch still owned it. I was David's choice [for editor in chief]. I got interviewed by Rupert Murdoch. There was a seemingly long interregnum, but Murdoch did not announce the successor to David, and it became clear why—he sold the *Voice* to Stern.

DAVID SCHNEIDERMAN: When Rupert said he was selling it, I didn't really have any say over what would happen, but I tried to monitor and keep track of what was going on. Everybody I spoke to had this vision that the *Voice* should become more mainstream. Anybody who's rich foresees it as something that they could read; that's why they want to own it.

Leonard Stern's name started to surface. I didn't know anything about him, I just knew he was a really rich guy.

JAMES RIDGEWAY: The guy that was unbelievable was the parakeet king that came in and bought it. He moved it down to the parakeet factory, that building that used to be a seed factory.* Every once in a while, you'd see some bird seeds on the floor. I met him only once, and he was a smart-ass. He said,

---

* 36 Cooper Square.

"I like to read a paper I can sit on a toilet and read it all the way through." I thought, "Well, I don't think this is the paper you want to own."

LEONARD STERN: I never read the *Village Voice*. I didn't have much interest at that time in my life in music, certainly not their politics. I was always much more middle road in my politics. I wasn't interested in classifieds. I found the articles often long, boring, and self-involved.

I bought it from Rupert. I read it was for sale and I decided to get the financials. I took a good look at several issues. I came to the conclusion that I could do something with it as a business, so I called Rupert up, had a meeting with him, and we shook hands. Simple as that. I've had several business dealings with him over the years, and I found his word good. I found working with him was a delight. He was brilliant, fast, made decisions, a forward thinker, very, very pleasant.

DAVID SCHNEIDERMAN: I had decided that he was going to be a problem owner because he didn't know anything about the paper. I went to meet with Leonard, and I said to him, "I don't know if I'm going to stay." He said, "Listen, stick around for six months, and if you don't like it, we can have a no-fault divorce."

That's when I was both editor and publisher, but then I felt I had to hire a real editor to run the place day to day. That's when I hired Robert Friedman.

KIT RACHLIS: The first few people he hired to succeed him, in many ways, were versions of himself. Which is to say, straight newspaper guys. "Straight" in both senses of the word. Friedman was very much that. He always used a beautiful pen, a fountain pen. He had a terrific reputation as an investigative-reporter editor.

ROBERT I. FRIEDMAN: I started freelancing for various alternative papers, like the *Real Paper* in Boston. And I wrote a story for the *Real Paper* about the *Village Voice* that was pegged to Rupert Murdoch buying the paper. In the course of doing the reporting for that story, I met a lot of folks at the *Voice*. Then in early '84, I went to work for the *Wall Street Journal*, which was a strange career move for me, because I'd been involved in the alternative press mostly.

But after only a year and a half or so at the *Journal*, I got a call from David Schneiderman asking me if I'd be interested in a job as editor of the *Village Voice*. It came totally out of the blue, but he knew me, and the comfort level with me was pretty high among not just David but people like Jack and Wayne and Nat, so I had the seal of approval.

I was gone by July of '86. So almost a year. It was a pretty tumultuous tenure. I was there right at the midpoint of the *Voice*'s lifespan—it was thirty years after it was founded and it's about thirty years before it died. It was a glorious and chaotic moment at the *Voice*. I sent Joe Conason to the Philippines to cover the fall of Ferdinand Marcos, and I also sent him to Haiti that year to cover the fall of Duvalier, "Baby Doc."* I had sent a reporter to the SALT talks—the nuclear disarmament talks—between the United States and Russia. I had a foreign operation. And I worked in the middle of the big height of the AIDS crisis. We won a Pulitzer Prize that year for Jules Feiffer's cartoons.

DAVID SCHNEIDERMAN: When I got there for the first round of Pulitzers [in '80], I thought, "Gee, we should put in for these." And the guy I wanted to enter was Jules. I figured he's a genius, an American original, and he just deserves a Pulitzer.

Teresa Carpenter won for reporting [in '81]. As a result of that, the next year I was invited to be on one of the juries. The jurors have lunch together. I was sitting next to the editor of the *Chicago Tribune*—he was talking about the entries in the cartoon thing. I said, "I hope you're considering Jules Feiffer," and he went on this rant about how he isn't a cartoonist. And it was just really a stupid, ill-informed comment. I mean, Jules is a friggin' genius. And it made me realize how narrow-minded these old, traditional journalists were.

So finally, Jules won. It was really exciting. I called Jules up and he was really excited. He clearly deserved it. I used to have lunch with Jules because he was like an adult and he's sort of a testy, fun guy. He comes down to the *Voice*, and we had drinks, and Jules kept drinking. And it got to the point where he couldn't find his way out of the building; he had too much to drink. And he was just sitting in my office in this semifunny but lugubrious state about the state of the world. And I said, "Jules, you just won a Pulitzer. You

---

* Jean-Claude Duvalier, the president of Haiti from 1971 to 1986, who was overthrown by a popular uprising.

don't have to be depressed about this." And he's like, "That's right, that's right."

JULES FEIFFER: I remember looking at the work of that year and thinking, "I have not had a very good year." Every once in a while, the Pulitzers would play catch-up with people who had been too far out to get the prize when they should have. I should have gotten it when I was doing these strong cartoons against the war in Vietnam and on civil rights. I was happy to get it under any circumstances, but again, it's things not being what they appear on the surface.

JONATHAN Z. LARSEN: When Jules got one, he apparently got up there and said how much he hated the *Village Voice*.

ROBERT I. FRIEDMAN: Winning a Pulitzer Prize with Jules was great. He got mighty drunk at the lunch and we had a nice little good time.

It was an incredible collection of talents. Thulani Davis was there. Hilton Als was there on the copy desk. Sylvia Plachy and James Hamilton. It was just so much writing talent, so much creativity. And the sparks were flying all the time. It was exciting. And I'm sorry it lasted only eleven months, but it was probably the most fun I've ever had.

It was also a very contentious time at the *Voice* because the splits between Blacks and whites, between men and women, between gays and straights, between front-of-the-book and back-of-the-book were all at their peak. Literally, I had a fight between Fred McDarrah and Stanley Crouch break out in my office in front of me. I had to break that up—a fistfight.

My first memory of the *Voice* was the very first editorial meeting I had Wednesday morning. I've been there maybe two, three days. And Wayne Barrett got up and said, "You're not going to edit our stories, are you? This is a *writer's* newspaper." I had actually taken a red pen to somebody's story in the previous two days.

LEONARD STERN: After I bought them, I called all the staff together and I said, "You guys can write what you want. But there's only one thing." In the years Rupert owned it, they wrote about him ninety-two times. It didn't bother him. But I wasn't going to tolerate that nonsense. I said, "Look, I have no desire to interfere with the editorial, and if we succeed financially, that will mean even more pages of editorial because if you have more advertising, then you have more editorial."

I said, "You want to write about me, that's fine. I want one week's notice. I reserve the right to reply on the page opposite where you write it." So, Jack Newfield raised his hand and says, "Well, what gives you the right to do that?" I looked at him and I said, "Jack, I own the place. I'm giving you the right to write what you want. Don't you think I should have the same rights?" That was the end of the problem, and they never wrote about me.

CHAPTER 47

"THOSE PEOPLE AT THE *VILLAGE VOICE,* THEY'RE ANIMALS"

DAVID SCHNEIDERMAN: Ed Koch was a pal of Dan Wolf. They became friends, and Koch used to hang out at the *Village Voice* office. Jack and Victor Kovner, our lawyer, knew him well.

DAN WOLF: David Garth called me.* He said, "You have an assignment." The year was '77. I was out of the *Voice.* He said, "Can you hang in with Ed on a daily basis? He's gonna go off his rocker if he has to ride around all the time with no one to talk to except his driver"—who was a somewhat off, nice guy, but not anyone that [Koch] could talk to or relax with. So, that's how I came in. It seemed like an interesting thing to do. I had never been political. He's an amusing guy, and he can have a lot of fun, and he can laugh at himself.

MICHAEL SMITH: Clark Whelton became Koch's speechwriter, and Diane Fisher worked for him and I worked for him. I maybe succeeded Diane in that job as assistant press secretary and then as a speechwriter working for Clark. Dan Wolf got me the job as assistant press secretary to Koch when I needed a job. And then I moved over to working for Clark and writing speeches, which he never read, incidentally.

DAVID SCHNEIDERMAN: At some point, during his mayoral campaign, he started playing racial politics, and that was the break with the *Voice.* I got

---

* Garth was a political consultant who pioneered political ads, helping to elect Koch, among others.

there after he was elected, but only about a year into his mayoralty. We were at war with him then.

I used to liken it to a really vicious family feud. It was particularly nasty because of the past, having once been close to him. Koch took it really personally—and we doubled down, because we thought he was a traitor with his racial politics.

A lot of it was about when he was trying to cut costs: he would close hospitals in Harlem, and he'd say shitty things about Black people. He was very, very fucked up racially.

People used to complain we were reflexively anti-Koch. And I'd say, "All the daily newspapers praise him and don't really scrutinize him. So, we're the antidote to the dailies. But if you look at the overall coverage, all we're trying to do is correct what's out there." Jack was obsessed with Koch because of this whole "family" split.

LEONARD STERN: I knew Koch quite well. I liked him and I respected him. I thought he was a great mayor and an honest politician. I met him one night, and he said to me, "Those people at the *Village Voice*, they're animals." I looked at him and said, "I don't know if you know, we're a pet supply business."*

MARIA LAURINO: My husband was a former Koch commissioner. Koch basically told his commissioners they weren't allowed to read the *Village Voice*. So of course, Tony always had a copy of the *Village Voice*.

MARK JACOBSON: Wayne had this love-hate relationship with Koch, and Newfield did, too, because Jack was Wayne's mentor for a long time. It was an oedipal kind of deal until Wayne broke away from Jack.

DENIS HAMILL: He gave up his core beliefs. It wasn't just the capital punishment. There was something endearing about Koch on one level, you know. You kind of liked him personally, but he was just really a wheeler-dealer like everybody else, and nothing got done.

ROBERT I. FRIEDMAN: We broke a huge scandal the year I was there with the New York City Transportation Department. It was a big headache for Ed Koch. Tony Ameruso was the guy; it had to do with parking meters. Wayne was the guy who's behind all that.

---

* Stern owned Hartz Mountain, a pet supply business.

New York mayor Ed Koch. Photo © Bill
Golladay; licensed under the Creative
Commons Attribution-Share Alike 4.0
International license.

MARTIN GOTTLIEB: Everyone was focused on him. And Newfield and
Barrett, Conason, later Bastone, Maria Laurino, and Tom Robbins, were focused on who actually ran the city. But when they dug into the plumbing in
the city, it was all the Democratic machines who were handed over different
departments of the city to fill with hacks, who gave out corrupt contracts, and
in 1986 it all blew up in a host of indictments, an absolutely lurid scandal, when
the borough president of Queens, a guy named Donald Manes, was indicted.

MARK JACOBSON: You remember this thing? Koch was involved. They
wanted to lay the hammer on Koch, because there was this whole big thing
about this parking violations bureau—people were collecting money for the
parking meters, and it was all filtering through these politicians. It was an
enormous scandal. So, Jack and Wayne dug up all this shit about them. And
all the borough presidents—this guy Stanley Friedman of the Bronx, and
Donald Manes was our president of Queens—they were snagged.

Donald Manes was, one night, under a lot of pressure. It's about to come
out, and he's dirty as sin. He's expected to become a senator. It's not gonna
happen. He's going down, you know? And he's talking to his psychiatrist
on the telephone. This is apparently what happened: The doorbell rings to
the psychiatrist's house. He says, "Donny, hold on a second. I'm just gonna
answer the door. I'm gonna be right back." So, he goes over, and by the time
he got back, Manes was lying on the kitchen floor with a knife stuck in his
sternum, and he died! So, this is like a fantastic event, right?

NANCY CARDOZO: Not for him.

MARK JACOBSON: It's pretty graphic—I mean, if you saw it in a movie, it'd be great. So, Wayne and Jack were on this story. They owned it.

WAYNE BARRETT, WILLIAM BASTONE, AND JACK NEWFIELD, *VILLAGE VOICE*, FEBRUARY 4, 1986

Ambitious people often become the thing they hate. History is full of young idealists obsessing about some entrenched evil and then replicating that evil when they come to power. The Ayatollah has become the Shah. George Bush spent the 1970s fighting right-wing extremists and now he wraps himself in extremist icons like William Loeb, Jerry Falwell, and Ferdinand Marcos. And Ed Koch, who first achieved fame by conquering Tammany Hall boss Carmine DeSapio in the early 1960s, has become Carmine DeSapio.

DENIS HAMILL: There were just unbelievable corruption scandals under Koch's watch. You just had to say he's either incompetent or he's part of it, one of the two. He polarized the city. But he was the guy that still would say, "How am I doing?" whenever you saw him. I'd say, "You're not doing too fucking good, Ed," and he would get mad.

CHAPTER 48

"JOE AND I VOWED THAT WE WOULD NEVER GO TO A REVOLUTION THAT DIDN'T HAVE A SWIM-UP BAR"

ROBERT I. FRIEDMAN: The *Voice* had done some great reporting by Joe and Bill Bastone early on in my tenure there about Ferdinand Marcos's real estate holdings in New York.

JOE CONASON: He and Imelda owned the Crown Building at 57th and Fifth. They owned 40 Wall Street, which Trump now owns. They owned Herald Center—which is a big shopping center in Herald Square—through disguised ownership. Bill and I did a big story in 1985 exposing this, and it was a worldwide scoop. It forced him to hold an election finally—he had been a dictator for years—the fact that his hidden real estate holdings were being exposed.

WILLIAM BASTONE: We spent a couple of months basically doing background on Joseph Bernstein and Ralph Bernstein, a pair of brothers who came out of nowhere and suddenly were involved in purchasing buildings that were hundreds of millions of dollars.* We were able to trace purchases

---

* The Bernstein brothers testified to Congress about their role in purchasing real estate on behalf of the Marcoses.

of a series of condominiums in Olympic Tower. We rented a boat—we went out to a town on Long Island called Center Moriches, not as far out as the Hamptons, but waterfront. We found a home out there that was also connected to these guys. It was a classic paper chase, where you examine every deed, every mortgage, every transfer of property.

I had noticed that the notary public on all these separate deals across the city was the same guy. It was like, "How could that possibly be the case that it's just a coincidence?" We ended up finding other people involved in the deals who gave us insight into how it all worked. I was still a young reporter. That was one of the great thrills, seeing that story on the cover of the *Village Voice*.

JOE CONASON: The front-page headline was "Marcos Takes Manhattan." You'd see pictures of Filipino politicians holding a *Voice* in Manila. It was a wire photo, and it would go all over the world, so that was cool.

WILLIAM BASTONE: We got to know a lot of the people who were involved in taking over the night that the government fell. It was early evening in New York. All of our friends and sources in New York had taken control of the embassy on Fifth Avenue. Imelda Marcos had this mansion on 66th or 67th. I'd never seen a residence like this before. It's a gigantic mansion—you could think it was a small museum. I ran up to 67th Street—they had just tried to loot the place on the way out. These wildly valuable paintings clearly had just been removed from the wall because the plates with the name of the painting and whoever painted it were still there. At the front door were twenty boxes they had tried to ship by FedEx out of the country, filled with china.

It was ill-gotten gains on their part. They were rich because they plundered the Philippine treasury. They parked hundreds of millions of dollars that they took out of the country in assets outside of the Philippines, in jurisdictions in which those assets would maintain their value and probably appreciate. Classic money-laundering stuff. They had one of Monet's *Water Lilies* paintings. They had an incredible amount of hard assets, paintings, jewelry, and then real estate in the city.

We got in there moments after they had left, and I had the run of the place. I gathered up documents that we used for stories after the fact. I went all the way up to the top floor. She had converted the top floor into a disco. In the disco, she had these velvet banquettes that lined the sides and all these pillows that had these ridiculous sayings on them like, "You can never be too thin or too rich." There were twenty of them, each one more obscene. I regret to this day that I didn't nick one of the pillows on the way out.

ROBERT I. FRIEDMAN: And then six months later—maybe March of '86—Marcos's regime was coming to an end, and I said, "Why don't you go [to the Philippines] since you know the story?"

JOE CONASON: The night before I left, I went to a party at Wynton Marsalis's house with Crouch, and somebody there told me, "You're going where? Oh, they're going to kill you."

We followed the insurgent candidate around. Her name was Corazon Aquino, and I got to know her and her family. We went out to the countryside on election day and found a place where there were these warlords, and they were threatening everybody and making people vote for Marcos.

We had to get out of there before nightfall or they would have shot us, which their own relatives told us—there was an insurgent faction in their family. James was along taking pictures—the greatest travel companion you can ever have.

JAMES HAMILTON: It was a party, basically. There were lots of photographers from all over the world there. It was a very happy time because everyone was hopeful that this is going to maybe get rid of this horrible dictator. Joe was getting great interviews, and we interviewed Corazon. I was backstage on the grandstand taking pictures of her.

We were staying at the Manila Hotel, maybe the greatest hotel in Manila then. Joe and I vowed that we would never go to a revolution that didn't have a swim-up bar.

JOE CONASON: The paper had money then, so we could pretend that we were with the big boys. We were staying in the same hotel with the people from *Nightline* and CBS News and *Time* magazine.

ROBERT I. FRIEDMAN: The idea that the *Voice* would send a reporter and photographer halfway around the world and cover the story—those days were pretty wild.

JAMES HAMILTON: I have pictures in the palace. They ran a very funny picture—big—of these two New York congressmen sitting on Imelda Marcos's bed, looking at each other and laughing. And then pictures of her

Queens, New York, representative Gary Ackerman and Manhattan state senator Franz Leichter on Imelda Marcos's bed in Malacañang Palace after the overthrow of Ferdinand Marcos. Photo © James Hamilton.

famous closet, with all the shoes and clothes. We were set loose in Malacañang Palace. For the Philippines, it was earth-shaking.

JOE CONASON: Then we came home. People were already starting to get killed, out in the countryside, far away from where we were. Violent shit started to happen when all the American journalists left. The election was still being contested. But actually, the real data from the election—polling places—showed that Aquino had really won.

When I came back to the office after that was over, people started applauding.

JAMES HAMILTON: It was like a party.

JOE CONASON: It was a huge party. Except when they started to kill people. But up until that point, it was just great.

CHAPTER 49
"L'AFFAIRE KAREN FINLEY!"

AMY TAUBIN: I was at the *Voice* already when there was the great war.

ROBERT I. FRIEDMAN: What I will most be remembered for in my brief tenure before flaming out is the publication of Cindy Carr's cover story on Karen Finley. That is my legacy, fortunately or unfortunately. I have no regrets about having done that.

C. CARR: There was some friction between the front of the book and the back of the book. And it really blossomed around my Karen Finley cover story, which appeared in '86.

RICHARD GOLDSTEIN: L'affaire Karen Finley! Oh my god!

C. CARR: I wasn't even a staff writer at that point. It was 1982 when I started there as an assistant art director. I did really want to write, and that started through Richard Goldstein. He was doing that page called Art Beat, which usually was one page with various little stories about the arts. And he said to me, "I need women to write for my page; do you know of anyone?" And I said, "Well, maybe me?"

It was probably around 1984. I went to Richard and said, "There are these two artists who have tied themselves together with an eight-foot rope, and they're living tied together for a year. Shouldn't the *Voice* cover this?" I interviewed Linda Montano and Tehching Hsieh. It took over a page in the paper. That was the beginning of my writing about performance art. And from there I went to Stelarc, who was suspending himself by hooks through his skin. I started covering the East Village clubs. There was this whole performance scene happening in the clubs. I started my column called On Edge. That's how I first encountered everyone from Karen Finley to Lisa

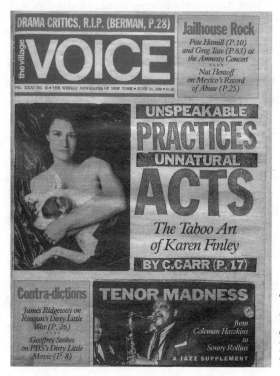

The cover story that caused the "great war." C.Carr's piece on performance artist Karen Finley, 1986. Cover image © Village Voice/Street Media.

Kron, Ethyl Eichelberger. David Cale, who had a great show at the Public Theater—I was the first person to ever write about him. I didn't ever encounter other critics there from the *New York Times* or whatever. No one was out there at two in the morning watching the shows. So, only me.

RICHARD GOLDSTEIN: I still remember her first column where she wrote that these two artists had a loft, and the lede was "Even when they throw down the key to their loft, it is art." She covered the most extreme as well as the most quotidian performance art, and she was deeply sympathetic to them. We discovered Karen Finley.

C.CARR: I had been following her work all through all these clubs from East Village scene and Poetry Project and Danceteria and ABC, and all the places that she would perform, and I thought she was amazing.

The thing that got people when I wrote the piece was that she always used food as a kind of illustration point. There was always sexual content to it. Karen's work is about trying to express these deep emotions that come up sometimes around sexuality or some kind of sexual abuse.

One of her more famous pieces was called *I'm an Ass Man*, where she would take on the male voice and talk about going after some woman because of her ass. There was another piece where she talked about being a little girl being sexually abused by a man, basically jerking off. And illustrating this, she had a pile of ice cream sandwiches on a stool—they were all melted—that she would pick up and squeeze them against her dress at that moment when he's gonna come.

Later, at Lincoln Center, she smeared chocolate on herself, explaining that it's because women are treated like shit. For that piece she was actually naked, covered herself with the chocolate and then put stuff on top of the chocolate. She transformed herself into this object that was like a weird statue. She was doing this work that springs right from the id, which women just don't do—or they didn't. She would dress up in this feminine style and seem like she was being really shy, and all of a sudden this incredible rant would come out of her mouth that you weren't expecting from someone who looked like that.

I actually had Richard Goldstein and Karen Durbin go with me to see a show at Danceteria. I said, "The work is maybe a little challenging for some people. I want you to see what she does before I write it." And they were blown away by her, like I was.

RICHARD GOLDSTEIN: I watched this performance, you know, with the yams. And she was onstage doing this act in which she stuffs yams up in her vagina, and then ejected them.* And while she was doing this, she was incanting this poetry that she wrote, beautiful poetry, an incredibly primal experience. I thought it was absolutely horrifying and brilliant. Guys in that club were so upset that they threw matches at her, lit matches. They couldn't believe what they were seeing. It was very shocking to me, but the art was so clear. It's not about what she was trying to say. It's about how the elements in the work come together. And the notion of somebody baring the most primal parts of their being and commenting on all sorts of trauma in the work. I remember her naked, but I'm not sure she really was. Of course, I saw this

---

* It is not clear that she did this. To quote Christgau, "Goldstein's memory is absolutely the worst."

act and I thought, "She's a great artist. She's a *great* artist. This is about as transgressive as I've ever seen."

C.CARR: She used to do a piece called *Yams up My Grannie's Ass*. To tell you the truth I can't even remember how the yams tied into that. She did use yams, but they were canned yams, and they were soft, and she would be crushing them or pushing them into her body.

I had no idea how this was going to play out, but they put it on the cover, which was a surprise.

AMY TAUBIN: Karen Durbin used to say that "Cindy writes like she just arrived from Mars."

C.CARR, "UNSPEAKABLE PRACTICES, UNNATURAL ACTS: THE TABOO ART OF KAREN FINLEY," *VILLAGE VOICE*, JUNE 24, 1986

A raw quaking id takes the stage, but at first you don't notice since she's wearing an over-the-hill Sunday school dress or a Sandra Dee cocktail party outfit and she's stepping shyly to the mike looking nervous. But then her pupils contract as if she's disappeared inside herself. She's slipped into that personalized primeval ooze now and the floodgates fly open in a loud declamation: "No, Herr Schmidt, I will not shit in your mouth, even if I do get to know you. . . ."

Or, "I go down on that ass with my mouth, my penis still kinda high and hard and I suck suck suck my own cum outta your butt juice with a little bit of yum yum yum yum yum baby liquid shit mixed up with that cum, baby. You can jerk off on my pancakes anytime." She might be stealing the male voice like that. Might be spitting on the stage. Tearing at her taffetas. Smearing food on herself. She might say or do anything up there. Onstage, Karen Finley represents a frightening and rare presence—an unsocialized woman.

C.CARR: I came in to pick up some extra copies, which I always did, especially now because it was on the cover. One of the senior editors who worked with the political writers came up to me and he said, "I just want you to know that I liked the piece, but I can't say so publicly."

Then I went upstairs, and all the front-of-the-book writers, what Karen Durbin used to refer to as the "whiteboys," apparently had gone in to have a meeting with the editor that day. And Nat Hentoff was in on it, and they said, "How can we ever be taken seriously again if you're going to print something like this?" Nat Hentoff's comment was it would have been OK if the writer—namely me—had let the reader know that this artist was insane.

RICHARD GOLDSTEIN: I never have seen them more apoplectic.

AMY TAUBIN: That piece was meant to be incendiary. If it hadn't been the cover, they never would have read it, and they never would have noticed it.

JOE CONASON: You won't find one word written by me about that. I didn't get what—if anything—was valuable about that performance. And I would admit that. I respected Cindy. Cindy thought this was worth writing about, then write about it, fine. I mean, the *Voice* is supposed to be transgressive, right?

WILLIAM BASTONE: Think about how important the front page of the paper was back then. There was no fucking internet—there was real value to being on the cover of the *Village Voice*, and what the paper was telling you was important. All the shit we wrote that landed on the front page of the paper may not have been the most important, popular thing that fucking appeared in the paper. It's the fucking classified ads! Never had more power in my life than the power I wielded because I could get the classified ads early.

BRUCE BARCOTT: The men's room was full of scrawled things about jamming yams up your ass and all sorts of derogatory shit. The message was essentially "This is a bunch of absolute crap."

C. CARR: Suddenly, all these cans of yams were appearing in the office people's desks. It was a little scary for me, actually. Then I started getting all this hate mail. They published an entire page of responses to the Karen Finley piece. I didn't do a reply.

GREG TATE: That was another moment where the *Voice* stepped beyond its own perceived limits politically. It was like, "So you think you're radical; how about this?"

DAVID SCHNEIDERMAN: Pete Hamill became outraged by it. It wasn't anything different from the Stalinist feminists versus the whiteboys—only this time they had Hamill around, who had a lot of stature, so it got out. People wrote about it.

LAURIE STONE: Hamill was more of a star. He was going out with Jackie Kennedy. He was like a celebrity.

SONIA JAFFE ROBBINS: They felt like it was demeaning the entire paper. And we were all arguing, "That's politics. Feminist politics is *also* politics."

MARIA LAURINO: It was hard to watch all of this because my allegiance was to them in so, so many ways. They were friends, they were generous, but they would also frustrate me, because I thought it was ridiculous. It's like, "Cindy Carr is an excellent writer, she wrote a great piece. This is insane." I was negotiating my place and space in the middle of that.

ROBERT I. FRIEDMAN: Pete Hamill wrote a column attacking me for publishing the story. He ended that column with an appeal to readers to send me yams in protest. I got cans of canned yams, and I got actual sweet potato yams. One of them I kept on my desk because somebody had nicely written on the yam, "Friedman, you know what to do with this."

PETE HAMILL, "I YAM WHAT I YAM," *VILLAGE VOICE*, JULY 1, 1986

Last week, after reading the cover story in *The Voice*, I hurried down to the A&P to check out the yams. . . .

I thought the adorable Karen Finley must use very small yams in her performances or have a very large anus. . . .

Carr has given us a brilliant parody of (1) bohemian pretentiousness (2) the emptiness of performance art (3) a certain strain of feminism (4) The *Village Voice* itself.

KAREN FINLEY: Hamill apparently never went to see the performance that he devoted so many words to excoriating, because he imagined that I actually took an uncooked yam and sodomized myself with it onstage. I thought about writing a letter to the *Voice*, but every time I sat down to write,

"I never put a yam in my butt," I'd think, "But what if I had? SO WHAT?" I felt that defending, explaining, clarifying would somehow be giving in to them. In retrospect, I wish I had had a sense of humor about it, that I had used humor to puncture Hamill's posturing. But I had so much invested in being taken seriously. I felt that women were always laughed at or sexualized when somebody wanted to shut them up, and I didn't want to risk that happening to me. I did react to the attacks in one way—they pissed me off so much that I became even more determined to continue doing outrageous work using my body.

FRANK RUSCITTI: Someone from the arts section would come and say, "She didn't shove cans of yams up her ass! They would be cooked yams!" It became, "She shoved yams up her ass," which became, "She shoved cans of yams up her ass." Now, no one believed that she shoved cans of yams up her ass, but the joke just built on itself. So, they played into the Finley thing as long as they could because they knew it infuriated the back of the book.

BRUCE BARCOTT: The *Voice*'s summer picnic, which is hilarious—we went upstate to some park out of the city. It was like throwing cats in a lake. Everybody at the *Voice* was so out of their element. We're all these pasty white people wearing all black. The T-shirt for the event had, *"Village Voice,* Picnic '86." It had a can of yams prominently featured.

MICHAEL GROSSMAN: On the *Voice* softball team that year, the MVP trophy was a can of yams on top of a little pedestal.

C.CARR: I ran into Friedman a few years ago at an art gallery, and he said to me, "I lost my job because of you." And I thought, "What?" I was really shocked.

ROBERT I. FRIEDMAN: I published Pete's column, and I published a photograph of the yam that I got as a result of the column, and a week later I was fired. David Schneiderman called me in to his office and said, "This isn't working out. You're fired." But the story I heard was that Jack and Wayne and Pete went to see Leonard Stern, the owner of the paper, and asked him to get rid of me.

Karen Finley became a national figure. She became the subject of this controversy with the right over her National Endowment of the Arts grant, which was taken away from her. It was a big national issue. I began my *Voice* time with a Pete Hamill cover story about an editor getting fired, and I ended it with a column about me by Pete protesting my judgment. Such is life.

RICHARD GOLDSTEIN: They were very serious journalists. They felt as if their work itself was compromised by this. They're working their butts off, doing really good journalism, exposing villains of all sorts, and then, an artist with the yams comes along and takes the cover. But under the surface of that, this is a deeply primal situation, and they weren't able to assimilate the work at all. It revealed the basis of the most primal fears that men have about women. It's almost Medea-like. It's nightmares, male nightmares about women, but with this brilliant poetry. On the one hand, it was brilliant, and the other, terrifying. This is my interpretation—and I'm sure they felt the same—that this was finally everything art must never be.

I mean, I don't know. They were Bob Dylan fans.

CHAPTER 50

"A CORE OF BLACK WRITERS AND EDITORS BEGAN TO BUILD UP"

KIT RACHLIS: David hired Marty Gottlieb, who was temperamentally very different than Robert Friedman. Robert Friedman was very closed, wrapped into himself, formal. Marty had a wonderful sense of humor. Bit of an unmade bed, and much more open emotionally.

MARTIN GOTTLIEB: I was there from the fall of '86 to the end of '88. On my first day there I was getting a tour around and met somebody who was working at a computer terminal, and I looked over at the terminal. There was a story, and there was the word "bullshit," and it was spelled "bull," space, "shit." And afterwards was a note from the copy desk saying "'bullshit' is one word, as preferred *Voice* style."

MARTIN GOTTLIEB: Something that started to happen at the *Voice* before I was there—there was a core of Black writers and editors, younger people who began to build up.

DAVID SCHNEIDERMAN: Why the *Voice* became such a substantial place for young African American writers was Lisa Jones. She went to Yale, and she started recruiting all these friends from Yale. Through her we got James Hannaham, who came in as an art designer and now is a celebrated novelist. Colson Whitehead came in as M's editorial assistant, started writing for us.*

---

* Whitehead is a two-time Pulitzer Prize–winning novelist.

Hilton Als, Michael Grossman, and C.Carr (foreground, left to right); Michael Caruso (background, in white T-shirt). Photo © Catherine McGann.

LISA JONES: I brought in Lisa Kennedy, Ben Mapp, Gary Dauphin. Hilton Als went to high school with my sister Kellie Jones, so I knew him.

HILTON ALS: There was an ad for the *Voice*, and it said, "Art department assistant: You have to have graphic design skills." I called Lisa Jones, because we had known each other as teenagers. I *really* wanted the job. Then finally, Michael Grossman called, and even though I didn't have any experience doing layouts, it was something that he knew he could teach me.* I enjoyed it, and then I was promoted. When Fred McDarrah left, they promoted me to picture editor. I was the second one in the *Voice*'s history. I was very proud of that. It wasn't just a job; it was a place where you could develop as a being, as a creator.

LISA JONES: Thulani is the link between the post–civil rights kids and the civil rights generation, the Black Arts generation. She hired me to do my first freelance piece. She asked me to do an oral history of Malcolm X from people who knew him who were still living. That's actually how I came to work for Spike Lee, because he saw that piece in the *Voice*.

---

* Grossman was associate art director at the time.

Lisa Jones's *Voice* ID. Jones was instrumental in bringing Black writers to the paper. Photo courtesy of Lisa Jones.

LISA KENNEDY: There was, like, a critical mass of people of color, none of whom were really the same, right? Gary Dauphin and Colson and Beth Coleman. Paul Miller—DJ Spooky. Joe Wood is another person.

GARY DAUPHIN: Joe was another Yalie.

COLSON WHITEHEAD: Joe was on a public-intellectual, Ta-Nehisi Coates, Stanley Crouch type of path. He did a book about Malcolm X.

GARY DAUPHIN: Joe disappeared in the late '90s. Joe liked to bird-watch, and he went up on Mount Rainier, apparently. The story we were able to put together—he didn't really have good equipment, and the snow line was lower than he thought it was going to be. The last person that saw him said Joe didn't really have the appropriate gear on.

LISA JONES: Thulani was instrumental. When I arrived, she was the only Black editor there, and remained so for a long time.

LISA KENNEDY: I'm fairly certain that I'm the first person of color, the first Black person, who was made a manager.

LISA JONES: I started writing my column and then I became a staff writer. Donald Suggs became my editor. I was very interested in culture and style as it tells a story about politics. That was the beat: race and the politics of style. The column was called Skin Trade. I had played around with a bunch of other titles. One was Reckless Eyeballing, which is what Emmett Till was accused of. I didn't write much about hip-hop. I wanted to write

The Howard Beach cover.
Cover image © Village Voice/
Street Media.

about culture. I wrote about hair products. I wrote about the Juneteenth holiday before people—the mainstream—were interested.

MARTIN GOTTLIEB: There was this terrible incident in Howard Beach in Queens, where these three Black kids were in the neighborhood, and they were chased by this gang of kids. They ran over a highway, and one of them was killed by a car. It led to these huge demonstrations around the city. This was an old, hard-core white neighborhood. We tore up the front page.

There was something in those days called the Black Rock Coalition. And one of the people was a guy named Vernon Reid; he was a sensational guitarist, and his band took off, Living Colour, and fortunately he was there. 'Cause if it wasn't for him, it would have been a bunch of white guys writing about a terrible thing that happened to these Black guys.

VERNON REID: I wrote this piece about growing up in Brooklyn. There were neighborhoods that you knew as an African American young person, you knew not to go. Bensonhurst is one, and Howard Beach. You just didn't do it. I was talking about going to Sam Ash out in Brooklyn, and these kids were driving by, and they called me the N-word when I was coming from this music shop.

I actually wound up in a point-counterpoint with Pete Hamill.

These four young African American men approached Bernhard Goetz [the so-called subway vigilante]—this is after the Son of Sam. They didn't have guns themselves, and as soon as they saw the gun, they scattered, and he went after them and shot them. He was seething with rage, and he was looking to act out of that rage. When he shot them, they were fleeing away from him. That's why the kid was paralyzed; he shot him in the back. It had stopped being self-defense.

Pete Hamill was defending Bernhard Goetz, and I was on the other side. Pete was in an "enough is enough" posture, and that Bernhard Goetz had every right to do what he did. I'm not going to say that he was unjustified in his fear. We part company at the point of the trigger pull.

VERNON REID, "FEAR OF THE DARK," *VILLAGE VOICE*, JUNE 30, 1987

For many, many New Yorkers the word black is synonymous with fear and crime and, if I may be so arcane, evil. Many whites, I suspect, see the city almost exactly as it's depicted in the trailer for the movie *The Believers*: a dark landscape of terror dominated by the living embodiment of chaos and destruction and nightmares—a black man. This hysterical nonsense has been passed down from generation to generation with precious little variation since before the dawn of this century and, sadly, is unlikely to change before the dawn of the next one. What's profoundly disturbing about the Goetz verdict is the message that it is reasonable and proper to act on the basis of a perceived threat with deadly force, even if the weapon used is obtained illegally and the person wielding deadly force is untrained in the proper use of firearms. Do I need to add that the mere presence of four black males has also now been legally defined as a perceived threat?

PETE HAMILL, "IT WON'T GO AWAY," *VILLAGE VOICE*, JUNE 30, 1987

And so it ended, with poor Goetz alone in a fierce and frantic crowd, microphones aimed at him like rifles, the shrill voices of strangers piercing the surrounding summer air outside the courthouse. . . . The jury had spoken, declaring Goetz innocent of all charges except possession of an unlicensed gun. But still the man was not free. For the rest of his life, he would be subject to the terrible punishment of celebrity.

VERNON REID: That was an incredibly high-profile thing for someone who was basically a stringer to do. That was probably the height of my journalistic endeavors.

CHAPTER 51
"HIPHOP NATION"

JOE LEVY: The golden age of hip-hop is 1988 in New York City. Like, every time you blinked there was another amazing fucking record. The summer—there's '87 to '88—Eric B. & Rakim, Public Enemy, De La Soul, Stetsasonic, Rob Base & DJ E-Z Rock, Big Daddy Kane, Biz Markie, Roxanne Shanté. Holy fuck. This shit was incredible. Absolutely amazing.

HARRY ALLEN: I met Chuck D my second year at Adelphi in the fall of '82. I had known Chuck about five years when I started writing. I spent some time at Brooklyn College, and I was writing at *The Kingsman*, which was the school paper, maybe '86 going into '87. I wrote this piece for the paper about upcoming hip-hop releases. One of them was Salt-N-Pepa's *Hot, Cool & Vicious*, their debut album. Then I took the text, and I sent it to Greg Tate at the *Village Voice* and didn't hear from him at all.

Then some time later I got a call from Doug Simmons, who was the music editor. My first piece for the *Village Voice* was called "Kickin' Much Base." It was June of '87. It was a review of LL Cool J's album *BAD*.

I remember consciously avoiding writing about Public Enemy. I wanted the world to validate them. I remember seeing them covered in the *Voice* for the first time; it was wild to see people I knew and who were starting to have this cultural effect.

KIT RACHLIS: I met Doug Simmons in a taxicab. He said, "What do you do, man?" I said, "Oh, I'm the music editor of the *Boston Phoenix*." "I have some stuff," he says. "Can I show it to you?" The next week, he came into the office. He was six foot three, six foot four, gangly, midwestern, pretty rawboned.

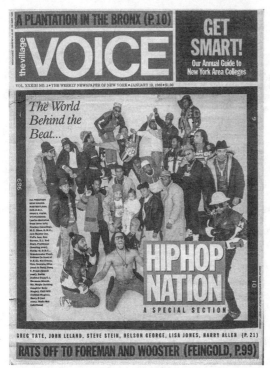

The "Hiphop Nation" cover. Cover image © Village Voice/ Street Media.

DOUG SIMMONS: I read the *Voice* when I was in high school in Omaha, Nebraska. It was sixty cents at the one newsstand in downtown, its four square blocks of bohemia.

I became the music editor in 1985. I had replaced Tom Carson. Hip-hop became the big story. Selwyn Hinds and Dasun Allah, they left the *Voice* and started hip-hop mags. *The Source* didn't exist. *Vibe* didn't exist.

John Leland wrote a very controversial piece. I assigned him to review the Public Enemy album, which he loved. I ran it as the second Riff. Ended up being one of the most iconic records of all time. Nelson George, of all people, got mad that a white guy wrote the review. It was the only time I've ever seen Nelson mad in my life.

NELSON GEORGE: As I remember, it was basically, "They should stay out of politics." I felt like the piece was really some white guy trying to tell Black people to shut up.

JOHN LELAND, "NOISE ANNOYS," *VILLAGE VOICE*, APRIL 21, 1987

When the album's politics announce themselves outright, as in the anti-crack, "Megablast," "Rightstarter (Message to a Black Man)," and "Time-bomb," which throws out lines like, "The one who makes the money is white not black" and "I'm a . . . South African government wrecker," they sound as stale as Prince's "Sign O' the Times," a fifth-anniversary "Message" rehash. The soapboxing is nowhere near as compelling as that migraine tone. . . . Much as I appreciate Public Enemy's textual manipulations, that isn't what I want out of a rap record. I like a good time.

DOUG SIMMONS: I did know I had to put a big name on the record. John Leland, editor of *Spin*, *Newsweek*. He wrote a really fine piece. However, I was blind, and perhaps John was, too, to what an earth-shaking event this record was. It was underplayed.

JOHN LELAND: What was famous about that was Chuck D's reaction to it. Which was fantastic. There was a wonderful searing noise in the first Public Enemy album, *Yo! Bum Rush the Show*. And I wrote about that noise in the review. Doug put the headline on it, "Noise Annoys," which was the name of a Buzzcocks song. When Chuck saw that headline, he was enraged by it. The Buzzcocks reference didn't really mean that much to him. The article wasn't terribly negative. But the headline really set him off. And then it became an inspiration for the title of the Public Enemy song "Bring the Noise."

He went around saying that he wrote "Bring the Noise" about me, and I've been dining out on that forever. The meals get a little cheaper as time goes along.

CHUCK D: I read the headline and got pissed off. [*Laughs.*] Then I read the whole thing. We're full of piss and vinegar and always ready to fight.

HARRY ALLEN: I remember the controversy and Chuck's very negative reaction to Greg Tate's piece in his review of *Nation of Millions*.*

---

* *It Takes a Nation of Millions to Hold Us Back.*

GREG TATE: "The Devil Made 'Em Do It"—that was the big one. It was my review of *Nation of Millions*. That's the one that got me denounced as "the *Village Voice* porch monkey" from the stage.

CHUCK D: I want to apologize for that porch-nigger statement. I was mad. I can take criticism from anybody. I can get criticized all day long in *The Sun*, or *Amsterdam News*, or even on the block. I'm like, all right, I take my licks. But I felt like, damn, at least if I had talked face-to-face with homeboy, I could have explained it, being that he's a brother.

HARRY ALLEN: This is an album that over thirty years later many still regard as the greatest hip-hop album ever made. We thought Tate was the one who was going to knock it out of the park. It seemed like half of the piece was saying, "This is an important album," and the other half was saying, "This Afrocentric or Nation of Islam stuff is garbage."

Tate hadn't spoken about the album on hip-hop's terms. He hadn't talked about the album in a way that someone who, listening to it the first time and just being blown away by what Public Enemy had achieved artistically, would have recognized. Those people were saying this album is an A-plus; he was writing about it as if it were a C. I don't think that his review has aged well, either.

GREG TATE: It was a light critique of the misogyny of a couple of songs. On that album would have been "She Watch Channel Zero?!"—denouncing every Black mom who watched soap operas, but the musical track was killing it. It was a sample of Slayer, so it was like they're taking a hammer to moms sitting around watching soap operas as, like, the end of Black civilization. Then, the last line, I was talking about the antiwoman stuff, and then a friend of mine told me it might have been the result of them suffering from what she called "a LOP"—which is "lack of pussy." Only in the *Voice* could I ever have written that sentence, but that was probably a career maker.

HARRY ALLEN: "Don't Believe the Hype" I'm part of, and that's a record about media and Public Enemy's response to media collectively. Chuck felt that to have a writer to deliver this line and to make this point would be powerful. He asked me to come down to the studio. It took me five or ten minutes.

GREG TATE: It became enshrined in Public Enemy lyrics. In the song, Chuck's got three, four classic lines like, "Writers treat me like Coltrane, insane." All of that's in reference to that piece. Every time they were talking about suckers in the press, they were talking about that review. It was real. *Village Voice* battle scars.

DOUG SIMMONS: I don't know if you remember the *Voice* cover, "Hiphop Nation," which entered the vernacular. I wrote that headline.

GREG TATE: I interviewed Afrika Bambaataa for that.

HARRY ALLEN: The "Hiphop Nation" piece, I knew it was going to be a big issue and I'd be writing a lot for it.

JOHN LELAND: My friend Steve Stein and I did an oral history of break-beat music.

HARRY ALLEN: It wasn't until I saw the color cover, when I saw all those people on it together, that it really hit me how big this was.

This is before there were any hip-hop magazines or anything like that, or *Yo! MTV Raps* or anything like that. You wouldn't have seen anything like this on the cover of any other magazine anywhere. To see it there in big letters—"Hiphop Nation"—it was like almost from another planet. It was our 1619 Project.

GREG TATE: That cover, give or take a couple of people, that was hip-hop. They were all the pioneers. It still seemed very much a New York thing at that point. Because it was the *Voice*, it was still New York talking to New York.

DOUG SIMMONS: There were so many stars in New York. Dorothy Lowe was the photographer—her sensibility really helped. There are a couple people that said, "You got to be careful. Not everyone likes everyone." But it was, like, neutral territory.

I got a fan letter from a copy editor at the *New York Times*. He double-checked my caption on the cover, because there's, like, forty people. Really, it's one of my professional highlights, that caption.

DAVE HERNDON: You know the famous photograph of all these Harlem jazz musicians and writers and the Harlem Renaissance all on a brownstone? It was almost like, "Oh, man. This is kind of like that."

CHAPTER 52

"STANLEY WAS JUST RED-EYED AND READY TO GO"

HILTON ALS: I'll tell you something that happened to me on my first day. Tuesdays were when everybody came in at four because they closed on Monday. I didn't know that. I got to work at ten. I was sitting there by myself, and Stanley walked through, and I said, "Hello," and I went to the bathroom, and he followed me to tell me if I thought I was hired for any other reason than affirmative action, I was mistaken. I went to the bathroom, and I cried. My mother was still alive, and I remember hearing her voice in my head say, "You go back out there, and you do your work."

When I started to write more, I could brush him off much more easily. But when I first started there, I felt very damaged by him. I don't even understand how that could happen in that place.

NELSON GEORGE: We had that writers' room in the front where the freelancers could hang out. You could go in there and you'd see Lisa Jones, you'd see Greg, and shoot the shit. You could spend a whole afternoon talking about music. Stanley would come through there.

We ended up getting along, but at the time, I just thought he thought we were all just nincompoops and didn't know shit, and we were promoting this horrible music. He felt like he was the mayor of Black thought. Stanley was able to cross over to the front of the book more because of that.

He was in his whole Wynton Marsalis phase. Jazz at Lincoln Center is a direct result of Stanley's relationship with Wynton. They had a very particular agenda about what jazz was and what jazz meant. And so, to Stanley, this hip-hop shit was horrible.

Harry *was* hip-hop. His connection to hip-hop was much more visceral, and that really irritated Stanley.

HARRY ALLEN: I called myself—as I still do—the hip-hop activist. It made him focused on me. To have someone like me show up—a fairly well-spoken, college-educated Black guy writing about rap music and saying that it's the greatest thing since sliced bread—it was like more than he could take.

DOUG SIMMONS: I can't even quote it—the language he used about the exploitation of Black pathology. We were encouraging the worst "coonification" of Black culture, and we're actually being oppressive—which, you know, you had to give a thought to because he was a smart man. And plus, he was threatening to punch you while he's making the argument.

He physically threatened me on a few occasions. He said I really deserved to get my ass kicked. He was looming over my desk, and Stanley is an intimidating guy. I'm six foot four, a tall guy.

Stanley was just red-eyed and ready to go. I said, "I do not want to fight you, but if you do fight me, you'll probably kick my ass, but I'm going to hurt you. Generally, when I'm in that situation, I manage to hurt someone really badly by biting them."

It puzzled him. He stepped back. We never came to blows, and we ended up becoming friendly.

ROBERT CHRISTGAU: He was like Lester Bangs in spades. He was this incredibly garrulous, engaging, always brilliant guy, even when he was wrong. I got into a fight with him once. The assistant art director insisted that Stanley do something differently than he had done for some odd reason. Stanley went over there—"You can't tell me to do that, you're just a clerk!" I completely blew my stack. We were standing there, yelling at each other. I could see the fucking veins on his neck. He was a big guy. He had a neck big as your head. [*Laughs.*] At a certain point, he stopped in the middle of it. He said, "Hey, you're really scared, ain't you?" [*Laughter.*]

And I said, "Of course I'm fucking scared! You're twice as big as I am!" And it just ended. [*Laughs.*]

STANLEY CROUCH: I have a Maileresque reaction to the way some people view writers. I want them to know that just because I write doesn't mean that I can't also fight.

GARY GIDDINS: Stanley was having problems. He was doing cocaine. He had a bad temper. But he never let me see it.

STANLEY CROUCH: My temper has gotten out of control so many times over the years. I've always had that thing in me.

MARTIN GOTTLIEB: I remember one story about him being on the subway in the era of boom boxes. Some kid is playing hip-hop at a high decibel level, and he walks right up to him and stares in his face, and says something like, "Our people were not brought here in chains and freed themselves so that you could be making a racket like this!"

DOUG SIMMONS: He hit Ron Plotkin, too. He threatened Guy Trebay, who was the calendar listings editor. Guy claimed that Stanley called him— I believe the word was "faggot." And Guy went to Marty Gottlieb, who was the editor then, and complained. He was warned: "One more incident, violence, and you're out of here."

GUY TREBAY: Yeah, Stanley just went for me one day. I couldn't begin to tell you—would there have had to be a reason? Probably not. I thought he was super cool and really fun. When he was good Stanley, he was great. He was a hoot. He was interested in my interest in elements of African American culture, probably. Maybe not always approving of it, but he knew that I got around the city quite a bit.

I don't really know what his triggers were. But somehow he was set off about me and really physically came at me. I barged into Schneiderman's office, and I'm like, "This can't go on." It was scary because Hilton Als and Donald Suggs pulled him off me. And that says a lot about the *Voice*, because it was right out in the open. They never fired people for that. That's what they should have fired people for. They were making money. They didn't care what you did to each other.

RJ SMITH: I was editing *Voice* Choices. Some weeks you just had more than you could use. Stanley was feeling like, "Why did you cut my thirty words instead of Robert's?" He wants to go outside and talk about it with me. I'm such a fucking idiot, because he would have killed me. I was oblivious.

I'm like, "Well, gosh, I wouldn't want to fight, because I go crazy when I fight, Stanley. I go wild."

Then he talks to me about how he knows how to handle people who go wild, how he got in a men's room stall with a guy who was a martial arts master and beat him up, because if you go in a men's room stall, you can't use your martial arts. And I'm like, "Oh shit. He really means it, he really wants to fight." And I said, "Yeah, let's fight."

Guy, who's been through this before, Guy's like, "Oh shit, oh shit, oh shit."

And it's getting quiet, but Stanley is outgoing and gregarious, and he's smiling and he's having a fucking good time. His life force is being stirred. I say, "Stanley, I love your work. It's just about space, and they wanted a second piece of art in there, so we had to cut something," and he calmed down.

DOUG SIMMONS: Then the Harry thing happened, like, the next week.

HARRY ALLEN: I was making copies of an article about Roxanne Shanté. He came around and he started talking to me. It was that same harangue about how some female artist who had made a record that was particularly graphic, and he had caught his daughter rhyming these lyrics and had been outraged. I might have just said something like, "Well, Stanley, they have a right to make the music that they want to make based on their reality." He said to me, "Yo, man, you want to step outside?"

I remember saying to him, "Stanley, you can go outside if you want. I'm going to stay here and make my copies." Then, with that, he pulled his fist back and punched me in the jaw. He started dragging me towards the utility closet, like he was going to close the door and beat me up in there. I'm struggling against him because I remember once he had said that he used to fight guys and he knocked their kneecaps off. I'm like, "I'm not going out like that." It wasn't a big fight. It was very quick.

GREG TATE: Do you know the movie *A Soldier's Story*, with Denzel Washington? It's got a character in there named Sergeant Waters, who is basically a self-loathing Black man who hates dark-skinned Black folks and particularly southern dark-skinned Black folks. One of the things that Harry said to him was that Stanley reminded him of Sergeant Waters. I think that might have been the straw. That's the point on which Stanley saw red and pimp-slapped Harry.

ROBERT CHRISTGAU: By the way, Stanley is no Uncle Tom. That's bullshit. His mother was a domestic, and he grew up in Watts, and he was tough.

HARRY ALLEN: I got away, he started apologizing, and I was *screaming* at him, "I'm going to get your record collection!" Because I knew that would hurt him. I knew he had a massive record collection, and I knew if I sued him and took it, it would hurt him to his soul.

GREG TATE: He knew where to bring the pain.

STANLEY CROUCH: See, we got in a discussion in which I was saying that one of the reasons that rap music was no good was because it celebrated thuggery and scumbags and violence, and he very adamantly disagreed with me, and so of course I assaulted him. In the interest of talking against the promotion of thuggish behavior, I smacked him.

HARRY ALLEN: I was there yelling at the top of my lungs. At one point, I picked up the phone and started to dial.

RJ SMITH: I'm back in the music cubicle. I heard, like, bang, crash, bang, crash, a couple times. Harry came out, and he called out something like, "Stanley hit me. Call the police." And I said, "Harry, that's a call you're going to have to make yourself."

STANLEY CROUCH: When the police got there, they looked at the cut on his mouth, and they said, "DO YOU KNOW THIS IS NEW YORK CITY?!"

HARRY ALLEN: I called Doug, and Doug was very concerned. He lived nearby, and he came down to the office. He took me to the hospital.

DOUG SIMMONS: Harry was really terrified. I know what he felt like. Harry has a very severe and poised presence. Really dignified but poised. I told him that Stanley's on warning. This will get him fired.

RJ SMITH: I remember showing up to talk to Marty and seeing Stanley and Greg right there by the mailboxes, having this real intense conversation. Greg was shaking his head and was sad as hell, and saying, "This cannot be what happens here." And there was definitely a contingent in the office coming from the anti-yam brigades to protect him.

MARTIN GOTTLIEB: He was revered by certain parts of the office; certainly the front-of-the-book people really were great supporters. There was a petition that he not be fired. There were people who'd come in and tell me how he had basically bullied people for years. But it really didn't matter what anyone said, you know? In this day and age, it's inconceivable that somebody could get away with that and it be considered OK.

He called me, and he said, "I know what you have to do."

CAROL COOPER: I don't want to be an armchair psychologist to tell you why he was so quick to take offense at harmless things or felt that he needed to compete with younger writers, particularly younger Black writers. That stopped once he got a MacArthur Genius award. He felt he had been validated enough.

I think it was George Bernard Shaw who said, "If you tell people the truth, you better make them laugh, otherwise they'll kill you."

Of all the people that Stanley disagreed with, the only one he felt necessary to punch was a younger Black male. There were plenty of white people who he could have punched.

HARRY ALLEN: I don't think it was just that he didn't like rap records; I think it was something deeper.

PAUL BERMAN: I distinguish completely between the intellectual fight and the physical fight. Stanley had some problem going on and was getting physically aggressive with people. He was physically aggressive with me even though he was completely affectionate. It was for the purpose of being obnoxious.

The fights that he got into have reached a degree of notoriety that is unfair to him. People like the idea of a pugilistic writer who's like Hemingway or Mailer, who stabbed his wife; Hemingway, who got in a fistfight with Max Eastman. So that seems like a romantic tradition—like an objectionable but romantic tradition.

DOUG SIMMONS: Stanley walked out of the editor's office. He came in and he sat down in my cubicle, and he started to weep. He bent down, he put his head and face in his hands, and deep sobbing, trembling, weeping, and he said, "I'm so sorry. I don't know why I've done this."

I said, "Stanley, I'm sorry too." Then he gathered himself and he left; he was fired. It was over.

STANLEY CROUCH: I've always said that the best thing that ever happened to me was being hired by the *Voice* and being fired by the *Voice*, not necessarily in that order. After I left the *Village Voice*, that's when my career really took off.

CHAPTER 53

"DO YOU WANNA KNOW ABOUT A REALLY BIG FIGHT THAT HAPPENED IN THE THEATER SECTION?"

ERIKA MUNK: Until the mid-'80s, theater was very important to what would now be called the cultural-political conversation. These wonderful writers—Sam Shepard, Irene Fornés, Adrienne Kennedy—they are still writers who seem ahead because everything has gone so backward. That's why Off-Broadway was exciting.

Broadway was standard establishment thought and form. Tennessee Williams, Arthur Miller, old forms, regular plays with expositions and boring realism, and all of that stuff done for a bourgeois audience. God, I haven't used that word for a bit.

I wrote a lot about the Living Theatre in the *Voice*. Mabou Mines, the Theatre of the Ridiculous, the Performance Group, the Wooster Group, Ontological-Hysteric. The experimental theater in New York was much more connected to the left.

ALISA SOLOMON: I had a friend who was in the Wooster Group, and I remember having my mind blown, not knowing how to frame that stuff, how to talk about it, how to think about it, understand it. And reading the *Voice* was one way that I started to get a sense of how to describe that experience.

LAURIE STONE: We would write about people in the *Voice*, and the *Times* would cover them two years later.

ERIKA MUNK: Do you wanna know about a really big fight that happened in the theater section? The Wooster Group did a play called *Route 1 & 9*. It had a wonderful pornographic film with Willem Dafoe. That was just fabulous. Who would not want to watch Willem Dafoe in a porno movie? He was married to Liz LeCompte.

MICHAEL FEINGOLD: It's really hard to explain Wooster Group pieces. The Wooster Group did a lot of transactions with reality that raised various kinds of hackles. They did a whole series of pieces by Spalding Gray in one of which they have long conversations with his dead mother's psychiatrist. His mother had committed suicide.

LIZ LECOMPTE: Spalding and I recorded his father very closely, so you could hear everything he did, and Ron Vawter, who played Spalding's father, had to lip-synch to the taping so perfectly that people thought he was talking.

It was controversial. A lot of people liked it, but, like, Michael Feingold—he didn't quite say it was obscene, but he made a thing about how you could betray your people, your family, by saying things they might not want to hear. But it was just about Spalding.

MICHAEL FEINGOLD: There was a big question about whether these phone calls were real or fake—I suspected that they were real. I danced around it in the review, producing a lot of commentary on provocation. There were many theaters that did things to provoke, and they found artistic reasons for provocation. One of the challenges of writing about downtown theater is that you really never knew what you were going to walk into. That was exciting and also terrifying.

LIZ LECOMPTE: I love naturalism and realism, but I think of the theater as a three-dimensional canvas where anything can happen, where things can be out of a "natural" order. I want to create an atmosphere that transcends ordinary life. It's a problem that a lot of experimental theater is done by people coming out of Ivy League colleges. All the people who came to me were crazy people.

Money is another problem for experimental theater. Going against the grain and finding something new requires you to commit yourself to things people think are insane.

ERIKA MUNK: *Route 1 & 9* also had a long section in blackface, which was all about a bunch of lower-class Black people ordering fried chicken. It was astonishingly offensive. The New York semi-highbrow cultural world was very white.

MICHAEL FEINGOLD: It was a Pigmeat Markham comedy routine, that telephone routine, done by Kate Valk in blackface. She played it in a sort of tan face, and Willem Defoe played Smithers, the Cockney trader who is the other main character.

HILTON ALS: They called up fried chicken places. I'm telling you, it was *incredible*. They would do it in kind of minstrel voices.

KATE VALK: I swear, I didn't think the Pigmeat Markham was going to be a problem. I really didn't. All the time we spent working on it, I thought it would be so evident because of the context. My feelings are hurt easily. . . . I'm not interested in offending the audience. . . . But it was also a very exciting time. Because of the controversy, houses were packed.

I still don't feel that it's been resolved. Because the blackface gives me a lot of pleasure. It's the most fun I've ever had.

ERIKA MUNK: I decided the way to deal with this incredible event is to have a whole section with different points of view on it. So, I asked Thulani Davis to write about it. I wrote about it, and at least one or maybe two other writers.

THULANI DAVIS, "AVANT-SAVAGE," *VILLAGE VOICE*, JANUARY 13, 1987

There is a callousness lying close to the surface of Route 1 & 9 which makes any confrontation with the work futile and infuriating. It is the kind of callousness that holds that brutality is justified by an artist's grappling for the dangerous edge—not for meaning or truth or anything so naïve. Even on the high of that edge, the creators of Route 1 & 9 and their numerous apologists cannot imagine what it is like to experience their blackface horrors knowing that black people, racism, and alienation are not even the subject at hand, and that blackface is just a device totally divorced from realities as close as Howard Beach.

NELSON GEORGE: No one would have known about them without the *Voice*, quite honestly. Who else was covering the Wooster Group?

GORDON ROGOFF: The role of the drama critic is to be a witness to an event. That was what made the *Voice* better than the *New York Times*, frankly, as a source for understanding what was going on with drama in those years— was that the *New York Times* only had two reviewers at most. The *Voice* had six or seven or eight of us.

ERIKA MUNK: Anyway, Liz was so upset that there was all of this attention paid. I interviewed her. I said, basically, "What on earth were you thinking of?" They decided it wasn't racist; it was just cultural criticism and interesting.

LIZ LECOMPTE: I was shocked. I had no idea putting on Black makeup would make people call us racist. We were in the theater.

KATE VALK: After doing *Route 1 & 9*, everybody's heads were spinning. Because Liz couldn't say, "No, it's not racist." Yes, it is racist. Yes, I'm racist. You're a liar if you say you're not. That's what it was about. And then, to be censored. It just seemed that suddenly the issues were burning. And then, sure enough, right after we opened the piece, Pigmeat Markham dies. It just seemed like a wild coincidence.

CHAPTER 54

"THE *VOICE LITERARY SUPPLEMENT* CROSSED POP CULTURE AND HIGH CULTURE"

M MARK: The *Voice Literary Supplement* happened pretty quickly, in 1980. They said, "It's a go. We're doing it in September," and I had two months. Oh, man, I've never been so scared—I woke up every morning before it was light. I had so many ideas for literary coverage and features, and so many writers I wanted to give space to.

The advertising person, Sally Cohen, was the one who carried the ball. She said, "We don't know how to sell three pages of ads, but we think we could sell a whole publication."

I thought, "Yeah, right."

Then they went to the American Booksellers Association's annual meeting and came back with so many pages of ads pledged. It was shocking to them, it was shocking to me. I believed—but didn't know—that there were other people who were hungry for thinking about and reading and writing about books that weren't in any way mainstream. Outsider fiction. We did a lot of reviews and wrote essays. That's what I really wanted, not just individual book reviews.

JOY PRESS: The *VLS* crossed pop culture and high culture in a way that now seems really obvious, but it was really exciting, and it was aspirational.

Suddenly a pop culture kid could see themselves as fitting into this intellectual and literary world.

PAUL BERMAN: I wrote a piece called "Hark! A Hippie," which was a long, serious essay on Ralph Waldo Emerson and Concord in the 1830s and '40s. I put an immense amount of work into it, basically claiming that we at the *Voice*—and the part of the culture that we represented or expressed—was in the tradition of the Concord transcendentalists of 150 years before us.

TONICE SGRIGNOLI: Paul Berman had really eccentric tastes. He was into anarchism. He would find some little pamphlet, and he would turn it into thousands of words. He would have that freedom.

M MARK: I was full of beans, I gotta say. We felt so free. It felt like a scene from one of those '40s movies where the kids say, "Let's put on a play!" "We can use my dad's barn." "Oh, I'll make the costumes!"

PAUL BERMAN: We thought we were a youth insurgency, and that we were against the *New York Times Book Review*, which just seemed stuffy and hopeless. And we were against the *New York Review of Books*, because it seemed so establishmentarian and respectable and pompous. We were against everybody.

We felt ourselves to be part of the cultural and political insurgency that had come out of the '60s and '70s. We expressed in a way that the other literary papers did not—all the upsurge of new ideas and radical "-isms" that had emerged in the '70s. There was some expression of the various crazy, new, postmodernist ideas that were percolating in some of the universities, and the gay thing, which you could see in our pages and you just couldn't see in the pages of other journals. Our pages were much more likely to have interesting commentaries on Foucault and Derrida.

COLSON WHITEHEAD: We covered a lot of stuff out of Verso and Routledge and a lot of independent presses who were doing theory-based cultural criticism for the first time.

SIMON REYNOLDS: It was just so fucking hip.

PAUL BERMAN: M did a really brilliant job. There was an intellectual excitement around her and a bunch of other people because she was part of a group with Ellen Willis, Karen Durbin, Laurie Stone, Vivian Gornick, and others who represented a lively and thrilling tendency in American feminism. Their feminism was free thinking, undogmatic, culturally oriented, literary, and playful. It radiated energy and creativity.

M MARK: I was in a radical feminist CR [consciousness-raising] group with several people from the *Voice*—like Ellen Willis, Karen Durbin, and Ann Snitow, who was on the fiction board. It was twice a month at various homes. We argued things. It was great. It was kind of a combination of girl talk and serious politics and friendship and laughs.

PAUL BERMAN: She wasn't worried about the orthodoxies and offending a certain opinion which might have been widespread among the readers and might have even been shared by any number of people in the newsroom. The whole mentality was that of free intellectuals and not of party militance.

TONICE SGRIGNOLI: She cultivated an aura of mystery. People didn't even know what M stood for. She lived with Jon Pareles. They had a loft in SoHo, a floor-through, on the second or third floor of a building. She had a very cool aura about her. She had one of the few offices at the *Voice*. It was just three walls or four walls that somebody put a door on. She would hibernate in there behind mountains of books; you couldn't even see her. She hid in plain sight.

JOY PRESS: She and Jim and Cindy all changed their names to initials together: J. Hoberman, C.Carr, and M Mark. It must have been some sort of feminist thing. I'm pretty sure they all did it together.

M MARK: Someone would say, "Did you neutralize the gender in your name so that you wouldn't be discriminated against as a woman?" I'd never thought of it, so I said, "No, but it sounds like a very good idea."

For a while on the masthead, they wanted to list me as my full name, Marsha Mark. But I didn't like it. There was the *Brady Bunch*, but it was also just MAR-sha. It has connotations of puffy sleeves and maybe a little lace—and I'm a tomboy from beginning to end. A friend of mine said, "M Mark—that has a nice ring to it."

JOY PRESS: The *VLS* was unlike anything else that I'd ever seen.

PAUL BERMAN: Contractually, I had to write at least two pieces a month to remain on the health plan, which was onerous for me because my specialty at the *Voice* was long essays that took months to write. If it had been word count, I would have been fine. But it had to be pieces. So, I had to look for short pieces that I could write that wouldn't be too much trouble.

I wrote a book review for M, and she published it. The title of the book was *The Vanderbilts in My Life*. And my review went, in its entirety, "If I had written this book, it would have been a lot shorter"—meaning there are no Vanderbilts in my life.

M was open to that sort of thing. She saw the humor in it, and she had a sense of a playful enjoyment which you don't find a lot in the editors of serious book reviews or literary sections.

JOY PRESS: They had fun with it. They had a summer issue; I think they called it Summer Trash. They got Hilton Als to write a review of Sammy Davis Jr.'s memoir. That was an era when genre fiction was considered embarrassing. Vampire fiction or science fiction—these were not things that educated people were supposed to be interested in.

M MARK: Humor is a big part of what I was aiming for.

M MARK: It began in 1981, and in 1989 it was thought to be successful enough that they pulled it out from the *Voice*. There was what they called "a national edition" that was printed separately, and the production values were slightly higher, so that was pleasing.

JOY PRESS: At one point, I applied for an editorial assistant job there because I couldn't imagine anything better. I met with M, she looked at my resume, and she was like, "You're overqualified. You're going to be really bored." Of course, Colson got that job. But it was OK, because I ended up becoming the editor of the whole thing.

M MARK: Colson I hired right out of college. He was my assistant for a while before he rose to higher things. We hit it off. I was very committed to diversity. For a while my staff was much too white, I thought. I saw I was part of the problem here, I'm not part of the solution. But my one worry about Colson was that maybe he was just too straight. He wore a tie or something.

COLSON WHITEHEAD: I worshipped the *Voice* in high school and college. My older sister, she was a New York hipster who was going to the Ritz and Peppermint Lounge and Palladium, and so she brought me all this great music into the house and a lot of music magazines like *NME* and *Creem* and the *Voice*. So, from junior high, I was reading the *Voice*, mostly the music section. I loved Christgau.

We had our own little corner on the fourth floor next to the art department. M Mark was like, "The third floor is for the simple people."

DAVID SCHNEIDERMAN: She was pretty ferocious about her turf, and the space, and number of pages she wanted, and budget.

The book publishers really liked it. We used to have great annual book parties, and they all came. She would give attention to books that they had trouble getting attention for in the *Times* and even in the *New York Review of Books*.

GARY INDIANA: The *VLS* was a great vehicle, particularly for the writers that were stigmatized as "downtown writers"—Kathy Acker, Lynne Tillman, Dennis Cooper, me. . . . These were writers who were out of the mainstream—the mainstream literary world in the United States is so ghastly anyway. It's a club. At least with *VLS*, people that were not in the club had their own club.

JOY PRESS: You had to take a leap on people. There are people that I took a leap on. Jonathan Lethem did a fantastic essay for me. David Foster Wallace was definitely in Lee Smith's era, although maybe he was writing for *Harper's* at that point already.

LEE SMITH: There were things that infuriated me about it. Once, I was so enraged I was going to write a letter. I wanted to change the tone a bit. There were a number of novelists I'd known for a while starting to publish their books—like David Foster Wallace, Rick Moody, A. M. Homes—who I really believed in, so I wanted to get behind them.

I was much more interested in intellectual attack than celebration. That's a great *Voice* tradition, getting people incensed.

HUGH GARVEY: I wrote this article about how Ethan Hawke had written a novel, and my reporting suggested that he was holding the film rights so he could make a movie based on his own book. So, I had this really mean kicker, something like, "As Divine Brown knows, you can get $50,000 for fellating a movie star. Ethan Hawke seems to have learned that if you're a movie star you can get five times that amount for fellating yourself." Some months later, I was at a party and this publicist says, "Hugh, do you want to meet Ethan Hawke?" Eventually I 'fessed up that I'd written that article. He turned and looked me in the eye and said, "You're Hugh Garvey? Well, fuck you man. Fuck you! Of all the pieces ever written about me, that one affected me most. I was writing in my journal over and over again, 'I'm sucking my own dick, I'm sucking my own dick!'"

CHAPTER 55

"WE WERE FILLED WITH GRIEF"

MICHAEL MUSTO: There was a period after Stonewall, which was 1969, and before AIDS surfaced, which is the early '80s, where it seemed like gay men could run around and romp and have a great time. It was the time of Studio 54, sex everywhere, gay bars and clubs everywhere you turned.

RICHARD GOLDSTEIN: I was never that much into promiscuity. But you could have thousands of partners, because if you went to a bathhouse, you can have three or four at night, and you could go there every night. The scale of it was astonishing. Then there were the piers. The sex became a tribal bonding experience, not an intimacy experience. People went out to the pier at night; there would be eight hundred or nine hundred guys in these derelict piers having sex, with shafts of light coming through the roof with moonlight, and it was very beautiful. I would go there to watch sometimes. It was like a Fellini movie.

JIM FOURATT: We were in an epidemic of STDs in the middle '70s, before AIDS came into the picture. I believe that the New York Police Department made a decision after the Stonewall rebellion—they had to depoliticize the gay community. If you can keep gay men tumescent, they're not going to fight back.

MICHAEL MUSTO: It took AIDS, unfortunately, to light a fire up our ass and start fighting for our lives again, literally.

C. CARR: I remember reading the *Times* that morning in 1981; there was one column about a new gay cancer that was affecting gay men. And I thought, "Gay cancer? Now, what? What will they think of next to blame gay people? Gay cancer?"

336

AIDS activist group ACT UP (AIDS Coalition to Unleash Power) protests at the headquarters of the Food and Drug Administration on October 11, 1988, in Rockville, Maryland. The action, called "Seize Control of the FDA" by the group, shut down the FDA for the day. Photo © Catherine McGann/Getty.

JIM FOURATT: I was running Danceteria, which was a nightclub here. I had been friends with George Harris, who became known as Hibiscus. Hibiscus was a founding member of the Cockettes.* His family was a theater family based around Off-Off-Broadway. One of his sisters came and said, "Jim, George is really sick." I said, "What's the matter with him?" She says, "We don't know. He's in St. Vincent's."

This was when AIDS looked very different. He was grotesque. His nails had grown out—they were all green. He was covered with sores. I remember looking at him and realizing that he was going to die.

MICHAEL MUSTO: They said, "Oh, he's sick, and they don't know what it is, but he's dying. Just go visit him and rub his leg, and he'll know that you're there." And I did. He was gone very quickly. And then it was another one and another one, another one.

---

* A psychedelic theater troupe established in San Francisco in 1969.

ARTHUR BELL, "GEORGE HARRIS (HIBISCUS), 1949–1982," *VILLAGE VOICE*, MAY 18, 1982

Last February, George contracted what he thought was a bad cough. He had his chest x-rayed at St. Vincent's, was told he had pneumonia, and was given an antibiotic and sent home. . . . The doctors at St. Vincent's told Mrs. Harris that pneumonocystis crania pneumonia is a new disease prevalent among homosexuals. The infection can be temporarily suppressed, but in the long range, it's fatal. Like Kaposi's sarcoma, the so-called "gay cancer," this form of pneumonia is believed to be related to the current epidemic of GRID, gay-related immunodeficiency.

MICHAEL MUSTO: They didn't know it was a virus right away. It was total darkness. And eventually, it became clear it was a virus and was affecting a lot of gay men who are dying very grisly deaths at a very young age. Sex became terrifying.

We were filled with grief. There were so many horrible emotions, you can't even begin to imagine—in addition to the rage over the fact that the Bible thumpers were saying, "These are bad people who deserved it." People with AIDS were doubly afflicted: they had this horrible illness, which was extremely terminal at that point, and they were being called sinners who deserved it. Welcome to America.

RICHARD GOLDSTEIN: When Peter Hujar died of AIDS, David Wojnarowicz did a work based on his autopsy.* He drew over the autopsy findings, and it ran in the *Voice* with one of my articles on AIDS, and George Delmerico just left it on his desk, so I took it and framed it, and now it's in the Whitney.

Listen, I can't convey to you the trauma of this. My neurosis saved me more than anything. I couldn't do these things that people were doing. I needed to know the person.

LAURIE STONE: I remember Alex Cockburn saying that he was scared. It was before people really understood how it was transmitted.

C.CARR: In '83, there were activists meeting with the *New York Times* to try to get more coverage of the epidemic. The thing about AIDS in general

---

* Wojnarowicz was a prominent East Village artist who later died of AIDS.

was just the toll it was taking. One of the early deaths was Klaus Nomi.* The obituary that appeared in the *East Village Eye* did not even say the word "AIDS."

JEFF WEINSTEIN: You know how the *Times* is—sluggish. They wouldn't even use the word "gay" in the paper. It was absurd.

RICHARD GOLDSTEIN: If they found out that someone was gay, they would banish them to a distant bureau. They didn't think any gay person could be reliable. Abe Rosenthal—who ran articles about "Why are homosexuals so visible?" back before Stonewall—he was notorious. I'm glad they've become what they've become. But I vividly remember that they called the Stonewall a "homosexual haunt."

The only paper that was really amenable was the *Post*. They hired a guy named Joe Nicholson, who was one of the only out gay journalists at the time to work for a daily. He was a real pioneer, but they allowed that. Whereas the liberal *New York Times* was terrified! Terrified!

I told you the Arthur Bell story about meeting with Iphigene Sulzberger and how she wouldn't use the word "gay" in the paper. And she told Arthur, "Not in my newspaper!" He used to say, "Come on, you can say it! Guh-guh-guh-guh-GAY!" [*Laughs.*]

DAVID SCHNEIDERMAN: Our first stuff was '81 or '82. The *Voice* didn't get it at first. We were right in the middle of it. We couldn't quite figure out how to cover it. Who are the right people to discuss it with? It was a very fraught topic for us.

JEFF WEINSTEIN: John Bernd and Tim Miller, who is one of the NEA Four—they were in a group called Live Boys.** John got sick, and he didn't know what the matter was. But he did a very powerful performance about being ill. They had split up. I covered John's performance for the *Voice*. That was one of the first pieces in the *Voice* about AIDS.

KIT RACHLIS: Richard's first story—there's a paragraph in there that I still have, I can't remember word for word, but he's staring at his breakfast

---

* A German singer based in the East Village.
** The NEA Four were Karen Finley, Holly Hughes, Tim Miller, and John Fleck, whose National Endowment for the Arts grants were removed in 1990.

and he's hearing about this illness. It's spreading through the gay community, and he's terrified; he's staring at his omelette.

RICHARD GOLDSTEIN, "HEARTSICK," *VILLAGE VOICE*, JUNE 28, 1983

The night I sat in Elephant and Castle, table to table with chipper young women and their dapper dates sweating profusely from the knowledge that I was carrying a burden they would never share, may have been the loneliest night of my life. It put me up against the fundamental terror that had kept me straight for so long: the fear of isolation and the certainty of punishment. To be gay meant, for me, to alter the course of ordinary life, risking not just the loss of family and community but the wrath of something I'd struggled to stop calling God. Staring at my omelette of spinach and cheddar cheese, I felt doomed.

DAVID SCHNEIDERMAN: Larry Kramer started going after us, and Richard, particularly. He was just infuriated; we weren't doing enough. To this day, I'm not sure he's right or wrong. We didn't consciously not do stuff. But for Kramer, we didn't raise the alarm bell fast enough. When Leonard Stern bought the paper, Kramer called him up and yelled at Leonard about the *Voice*.

LARRY KRAMER, "1,112 AND COUNTING," *NEW YORK NATIVE*, MARCH 14–27, 1983

The gay press has been useless. . . . (The *New York Times* took a leisurely year and a half between its major pieces, and the *Village Voice* took a year and a half to write anything at all.) How are we going to get the word around that we're dying?

ROBERT I. FRIEDMAN: "This issue sucks, sucks, sucks. There's nothing good in it. I will give you the benefit of the doubt to think that it was mostly stuff that you inherited, but you can do better." He would send me letters like that all the time. He was constantly on my back for not doing more. We did, increasingly, over the period that I was there. I put a condom on the cover of the *Voice*. I think it was the first publication in the United States to ever put a condom on the cover.

MICHAEL GROSSMAN: We did this cover—it was a story that Richard Goldstein wrote called "Condoms Make a Comeback." And it was just a big picture of a hand holding a condom. It was weird to put a condom on the cover. Certain people thought that was crass and we shouldn't be doing it.

ROBERT I. FRIEDMAN: Larry was merciless; he thought Richard was not doing a good job and not doing enough.

LARRY KRAMER, "SECOND-RATE VOICE," *NEW YORK NATIVE*, MARCH 17, 1986

Voice coverage to this day is spotty, second-rate, unimaginative, out-of-date, or stuff we have read earlier elsewhere. In Richard Goldstein, their openly gay senior editor, we have a first-rate example of the Uncle Toms among us—openly gay people who do nothing to help us, when they are in positions where they easily could. I would not like to live with Goldstein's conscience, all these years of being at the *Voice* and not writing or assigning AIDS articles when he should have been. How an openly gay senior editor could sit on his ass for the first twenty-three months of an epidemic that was, and still is, decimating his brothers, defies comprehension. Not that his record has been all that much better since. No, we must not forget the shameful silence of the *Voice*, as we must not forget the shameful silence of the *New York Times* for not writing about the Final Solution when it happened.

RICHARD GOLDSTEIN: I presented a lot of AIDS ideas, and they weren't wanted at first. We were late because there was a reluctance on the part of people to do something that was so negative about sex. It happened to be gay, but I think if it had been a "straight" disease, they would have felt the same.

C.CARR: I interviewed the guy who was in the Silence = Death Collective. They did the posters. They came to the *Voice* to try to do an article about their poster, and the *Voice* just said no.

JIM FOURATT: Most gay men who have been political were terrified about telling the truth about gay men's lives. In the '80s, I was really critical of Richard. Today, when I put into focus his relationship, his coming out, his always being the intellectual about gay life, not having really lived it very much, the way academics do, I have much more compassion for people like Richard.

Richard was afraid of writing about the people like myself who were critiquing the lifestyle, and the promiscuity, and the way it was being dealt with. The use of needles, or the use of amyl nitrate—which was very popular in anonymous sex places—Richard said, "No, that's not important."

Even Larry changed his tune: the person who wrote *Faggots* was suddenly not wanting to talk about lifestyle.

MARK SCHOOFS: Larry's sexual politics and his AIDS politics intersected in a way where he felt that gay men should have less sex and should not engage in the kind of sex that they had in the 1970s and the early 1980s. I'm generalizing, but many men went to the bathhouses or had lots of partners. He felt that that was wrong. And the *Voice* was more like, "People should be able to choose to live their own lives and do so safely through either safe sex or other ways." And this is a debate that is as old as the epidemic, quite frankly, and probably still goes on.

There were times when Larry loved what I wrote; there were times when he was angry at what I wrote. Larry was very strategic about how he would deploy either his charm or his fury, depending upon what he wanted to accomplish.

DAVE HERNDON: Larry Kramer fought with everybody, right? And god bless him.

LISA KENNEDY: AIDS and ACT UP changed how the newspaper covered gay people.

RICHARD GOLDSTEIN: When we finally were covering AIDS, which was much later than I think we should have, we were going to have a column about it. I hired somebody to do it who was HIV positive. I would never have put in somebody who wasn't dealing with the disease. But we were accused of doing precisely that. Then I went to the person, and he said, "I don't want anybody to know." So, we had to take that accusation without revealing the truth. He ended up dying of AIDS. Wonderful guy.

JIM FOURATT: When Nathan Fain became the reporter, he had been diagnosed with AIDS. The paper became very fixated on what Nathan believed would make him well. Anyone who had a different theory, or a different point of view, didn't get any exposure. That was Richard's response—to bring in someone that was a legitimate journalist, who had been diagnosed with AIDS, and make him the go-to person.

LAURIE STONE: I was close friends with Robert Massa. He was also a theater person, and he had AIDS. He had a column called Something Positive.

MARK SCHOOFS: Robert Massa really brought to life what it was like to be a gay man in the maelstrom of the AIDS epidemic—living and, as it turned out, dying. He wrote fearlessly and honestly about his life.

ROBERT MASSA, "SPECIMEN DAYS: A PERSONAL ESSAY," *VILLAGE VOICE*, FEBRUARY 22, 1994

Later, I am alone with my father when he wakes up. We have small talk. Suddenly, he asks if people still get AIDS from transfusions. I'm startled just to hear him say the word. I want to tell him I understand how afraid and alone he feels, but I'm not ready for him to know about me. I tell him to not worry—they screen blood now. He doesn't look convinced but puts his head back and drifts off to sleep. I touch his hand and notice how much our fingers are alike.

LAURIE STONE: There was some memorial observance of Robert in the paper. I wrote a little piece about Robert that was set to music later. It had to do with seeing him when he was dying, going to visit him. He couldn't talk, so he would huff out words a little bit. It was in his brain at that point, it affected his speech and almost his breathing too. He knew that he was dying. He couldn't write, either; we must have used an alphabet that he pointed to and spelled out words.

He said something like, "I don't regret anything," and then he wrote out, "I wish I had written more." I said, "Well, every writer wishes that." Then I asked him, "Why do you think you've inspired so much love?" He wrote back, "I'm not demanding," which was perfect because it was true.

KIT RACHLIS: This was the best part of the *Voice*. The AIDS coverage was where people were truly trying to work out how do you respond emotionally, politically, medically to this horrific and mysterious health crisis?

It was a plague that Reagan was passively, militantly, aggressively ignoring, which was among his worst and cruelest legacies, and the Religious Right—which was, if not at its apogee, close to its apogee and power—was using in the ugliest possible way. And the *Voice* was a citadel against all of that. This is '84 to '88, it's the height of Reagan, and identity politics is dominating liberal left politics/cultural discourse, and there's a lot of reason to feel it's under attack. So, you have ACT UP emerging, Gay Men's Health Crisis, and feminists are feeling under attack. And this is the moment when suddenly, historically, the great liberal Left dominance of the culture from 1932 to 1980, it's clear that that's over.

MARK SCHOOFS: It was right after Robert Massa died I began to write. New York was getting money for HIV prevention, federal dollars, millions of dollars, and they were not spending it. We reported that, and the person who was in charge of that department lost her job.

FRANK RUSCITTI: It was all about finding the cure. So, anytime a new piece came out, it was "Is this the cure? What is being done to find the cure?" Richard, who was instrumental—there was this whole schism between him and the Larry Kramer faction. Kramer was going in one direction as far as cures, and Richard and the *Voice* thought he was totally off base.

RICHARD GOLDSTEIN: We had so many people flogging cures for AIDS at us that we had to develop a standard that this had to be published in a peer-reviewed medical journal or we wouldn't publish it. We had a piece claiming that Jonas Salk had found the cure. The editor at the time wanted to go big with that story. Massa and I teamed up to piss on that story until we reduced it to essentially rubble.

ALISA SOLOMON: The *New York Native*, which was the gay paper, was promoting these weird theories. Like, "AIDS is swine flu, and it has nothing to do with HIV, and you should eat apricots"—I'm making that up—but all this stuff was very questionable.

Richard assigned me to do a story about what happened to the *Native*. A lot of it had to do with its getting crazier and crazier in its discussion of AIDS. There was a vacuum of community AIDS coverage in the city because the *Native* wasn't doing it. So, the *Voice* really filled that hole.

KAREN DURBIN: Nat Hentoff's first reaction to AIDS was not good. He was not at all interested in privacy rights for men with AIDS.

RICHARD GOLDSTEIN: Nat Hentoff had deep emotional problems: he had a persecution complex, and he took positions that made him beleaguered or that made him feel that there was a reason why he was beleaguered. And when AIDS came along, he supported mandatory testing; he advocated firing people. I remember him saying that gay people were "too powerful."

NAT HENTOFF: I almost got socked by a very large homosexual at the *Voice* for that. My reporting had found out, for example, that there were women who had been sleeping with guys who had HIV, and actually more than that, had active AIDS. They didn't know about it. And therefore, they contracted it, and their babies contracted it. There ought to be mandatory notification. First of all, people ought to know they have the disease.

RICHARD GOLDSTEIN: We had thousands of pediatric AIDS cases because of this. I visited wards and saw the babies. It was so traumatic because they looked just like the gay men. The disease creates a look in people and it's a haggard look. I had nightmares after that.

Listen, there were people who wouldn't touch me in the office. I wrote this piece called "Heartsick" about AIDS anxiety, with a Peter Hujar photo illustrating it. I remember one person saying, "Well, I'm sorry, but I have children!" All this stuff adding to my innate anxiety about being gay—which was substantial. Made me very difficult to deal with. I was very harsh to straight guys.

HILTON ALS: The impression that I had was how transformative AIDS was to the paper. It was galvanizing; there was a moving forward in a deep way. I wrote this really critical thing about the art of Gran Fury* and how it reflected white gay men all the time. They had that poster. It was two men kissing. It was *Kissing Doesn't Kill*, something like that. The piece caused a lot of controversy. And you could only do that in the *Voice*—be critical of the thing that you were part of.

LISA JONES: There was more coverage in the *Voice* than there would have been in other New York City papers and written through the perspective of people who had connections to the activist community, writers who were LGBT. But again, just like with the coverage by Black writers, and of Black culture and political issues, it just was always not enough, you know?

I wonder, at the end of the day, what was the disconnect in all this? Was it the money to hire people to cover the beat? Or was it the lack of understanding of the importance of it? But the *Voice* was still instrumental in saying, "This matters."

MICHAEL FEINGOLD: I found myself writing more and more obituaries, and we ran them, and because sometimes the people were important, and sometimes it was just important to remember. And it became finally uncomfortable for me because, well, somebody referred to me as the Alden Whitman of Off-Off-Broadway—the editor of the *Times* obit section at that point.

I got angrier and angrier and swore off writing obituaries for a while unless it was a very important playwright or a figure like Joe Papp. There was a period when it just seemed as though suddenly everybody you knew was suffering from this. Half of Charles Ludlam's company died of AIDS.**

C. CARR: Charles Ludlam—it was just really shocking to the whole scene when somebody like that who has been so important with so much influence, and then they're gone.

AIDS really changed the world for the worse. I wrote the preliminary obituary for Ron Vawter from the Wooster Group. His last solo show was called *Roy Cohn/Jack Smith*, two very opposite gay men who both died of AIDS.

JEFF WEINSTEIN: You know the AIDS Project quilt? I wrote that story. It went on the cover. I did a lot of New York reporting, watching

---

* Gran Fury was an AIDS activist artist collective.
** Joe Papp was a theater producer and director and founder of the Public Theater. Charles Ludlam was a playwright, performer, and director, and founder of the Ridiculous Theatrical Company.

the quilt being pieced together. The previous place was Atlanta. I got the budget to fly to Atlanta with the late photographer Robin Holland. I wrote it as both a political piece and an art piece, as a piece about AIDS, and about gay life.

MICHAEL MUSTO: In 1987, ACT UP was formed. And Michelangelo Signorile, we would hang out in the clubs every night. And this hot guy came up to us and said, "There's something called ACT UP. You should come to the meeting." And he told us about it. And we were like, "He's cute, we should go."

But we should also go because Michelangelo and I were on the phone all day, every day, like, "Reagan won't do anything about this. What are we going to do? People are dying like crazy." It was a combination of grief and terror and utter rage at the fact that it was not being addressed at all by the president. I went to ACT UP, and that did galvanize me.

I started writing about it right away. I had written about AIDS before, in the early '80s. But ACT UP was the beginning of this really organized activism movement spun out of utter rage that Reagan wouldn't mention it.

ALISA SOLOMON: I was one foot in, one foot out of ACT UP. I always identified as an advocacy journalist, which is why I wanted to be at the *Voice*.

MICHAEL MUSTO: In '88, I wrote this whole thing, "ACT UP, Fight Back," about going to DC to scream at the FDA. I wrote a think piece about "Life During Wartime." I wrote about the reality of being a gay man during the height of the AIDS epidemic and the different emotions that come at you. I was actually showering in the dark; I was afraid I would find a lesion or mistake a bruise for a lesion. It was that scary. I talked about screaming at a cabdriver, and then you realize: he didn't do anything, you're yelling at AIDS.

Jeff Weinstein stopped me in the office, and he said, "I like the way your column has become more political."

JEFF WEINSTEIN: He made it really wrong to be antigay in a way that other people didn't do.

MICHAEL MUSTO: I wrote about AIDS's effect on nightlife. I wanted to document the community and how it was still alive; you can't extinguish the whole community.

When AIDS first hit, you were terrified to even shake hands with anybody. On the one hand, clubs had always been a place to hook up, to get sex—this was pre-Grindr, -Tinder, etc. You had to go out. If you started dancing with someone, you might find yourself going home with them. That's how it worked. You might meet a husband or wife there. A lot of people met at nightclubs. Suddenly it was very scary to even think about that.

But on the other hand, clubs have always been an escape hatch. They've always been a little fantasy world. And with AIDS, you really needed that fantasy at night, sometimes. You needed that family, that connection, bonding with other queers. A lot of them were dying. But for that moment, they're all still there. You're clutching on to each other and pretending just for a few hours.

CHAPTER 56

"CHRISTGAU WAS HATED BY BANDS BECAUSE HE WAS SO HONEST"

THE GRADES

An A+ record is an organically conceived masterpiece that repays prolonged listening with new excitement and insight. It is unlikely to be marred by more than one merely ordinary cut.

An A is a great record both of whose sides offer enduring pleasure and surprise. You should own it. . . .

E records are frequently cited as proof that there is no God. . . .

An E– record is an organically conceived masterpiece that repays repeated listening with a sense of horror in the face of the void. It is unlikely to be marred by one listenable cut.

—*Christgau's Record Guide: Rock Albums of the '70s* (1980)

ERIC WEISBARD: The Consumer Guide is one of the great masochistic acts of criticism ever perpetuated.

ROBERT CHRISTGAU: The idea was that there is more "product," let's call it, than there is space and time to write about it. I decided I would call this column where I did these capsule reviews of records the Consumer Guide, and that I would do another thing that hippies weren't supposed to

The "dean of American rock criticism,"
Robert Christgau. Photo © James Hamilton.

do and offer letter grades at a time when pass/fail was at its peak. It was just a way to be contrarian.

ROBERT CHRISTGAU, CONSUMER GUIDE, *VILLAGE VOICE*, 1980

Prince, *Dirty Mind* (Warner Bros., 1980)

After going gold in 1979 as an utterly uncrossedover falsetto love man, he takes care of the songwriting, transmutes the persona, revs up the guitar, muscles into the vocals, leans down hard on a rock-steady, funk-tinged four-four, and conceptualizes—about sex, mostly. Thus, he becomes the first commercially viable artist in a decade to claim the visionary high ground of Lennon and Dylan and Hendrix (and Jim Morrison), whose rebel turf has been ceded to such marginal heroes-by-fiat as Patti Smith and John Rotten-Lydon. Brashly lubricious where the typical love man plays the lead in "He's So Shy," he specializes here in full-fledged fuckbook fantasies—the kid sleeps with his sister and digs it, sleeps with his girlfriend's boyfriend and doesn't, stops a wedding by gamahuching the bride on her way to church. Mick Jagger should fold up his penis and go home. **A**

COLSON WHITEHEAD: He'll pack so much into those five-line reviews. He knew everything. I didn't always agree. I didn't know what he was talking about half the time, but the stuff he liked, he really championed and made me want to buy it.

CHUCK EDDY: I don't know how many people over the years have told me that Christgau is unreadable. I understand that—my ticket into being interested in people writing intelligently about music was figuring out what the hell Christgau was talking about.

ROBERT CHRISTGAU: I didn't want to be a rock critic. My idea was to be a journalist. My ideal was A. J. Liebling. I love sportswriting in general. Some of the sportswriters were great writers. I was a baseball fan; baseball fans love charts and statistics. So, I kept rock 'n' roll statistics. I worked for an encyclopedia company in '64. That taught me compression.

FRANK RUSCITTI: Christgau was hated by bands because he was so honest, and he was so brutal. There's a single out there, I forgot who did it, called "I Killed Christgau."

I don't know why.
You wanna impress Christgau
Ah let that shit die

—*"Kill Yr Idols" (aka "I Killed Christgau with My Big Fuckin' Dick"), Sonic Youth*

CLEM BURKE: A lot of people would take an antagonistic attitude toward Christgau, but I always thought he was pretty right on and honest in his views and very credible.

ROBERT CHRISTGAU, CONSUMER GUIDE, *VILLAGE VOICE,* JANUARY 29, 1979

Lou Reed, *Live: Take No Prisoners* (Arista, 1978)
Partly because your humble servant is attacked by name (along with John Rockwell) on what is essentially a comedy record, a few colleagues have

rushed in with Don Rickles analogies, but that's not fair. Lenny Bruce is the obvious influence. Me, I don't play my greatest comedy albums, not even the real Lenny Bruce ones, as much as I do *Rock n Roll Animal*. I've heard Lou do two very different concerts during his Arista period that I'd love to check out again—Palladium November '76 and Bottom Line May '77. I'm sorry this isn't either. And I thank Lou for pronouncing my name right. **C+**

> *Critics! What does Robert Christgau do in bed?*
> *You know, is he a toefucker?*
>
> —Lou Reed, Live: Take No Prisoners

RJ SMITH: Steve Anderson was his intern and would open his mail at home. Bob had panned the Swans—noise, East Village, dirge-y, Michael Gira, droning, pretentious, whatever. He slammed them in a Consumer Guide. So, Michael Gira jerked off in a baggie, sealed it up, and mailed it to Bob with an angry letter—or witty letter, he would probably think. Bob opens it, reads the letter himself, pulls out a bag of cum, and he hands it to Steve and says, "OK, file this under G."

Wolcott started as a music writer and was writing for Bob. Somewhere along the way, they started sniping at each other through print. At least, Wolcott took shots at Bob, and then Bob started writing about his sex life a lot and problems he and Carola were having, and then Wolcott weighed in on it at least once, and talking about putting up bleachers and having people watch them have sex. That was the classic *Village Voice* arguing with itself in public. It's what we had instead of getting paid well.

GREG TATE: He got really interested in feminism and sex, and he would write these pieces where he would be talking about his own sex life. In one of them he said something like [*laughs*], "I've been fucking the same woman for twenty years, and hopefully I'll be fucking her until she dies." Like, "Not till we die." [*Laughs.*]

DAVID SCHNEIDERMAN: We didn't have the money for everyone to have a computer then. One day, Bob is complaining that at four o'clock, when he wants to do his work, the computers are taken. I said, "Bob, when

I come in in the morning, for hours no one's on these computers." Bob puffs up and says, "I will not change my diurnal urges."

NELSON GEORGE: You'd go to Bob's apartment, and the place is crazy: a warren of records everywhere, and clothes, and you had to duck to get down the narrow hallway. And then he had that little office, which is legendary. There's five records on the turntable playing at any given time, all stacked up. Ornette Coleman, then the sounds of West Africa, then a blues band from England, and then, you know, Olivia Newton-John. And they just come one after another while you're in there trying to edit with him at his little typewriter.

He and his wife were so lovely. When they were trying to have a kid, you could only edit with him during certain times. It was like, "She's ovulating." Bob always gave you a little more information than you wanted.

RJ SMITH: I was to bring my story over to his home. I knock on the door. He buzzes me into the building, comes to the door on the second floor. He's in his underpants with a garbage can, like, right in front of where I'm glad he had a garbage can. And he said, "Put it in the garbage can! Just put it in the garbage can! Quick, quick!"

RJ SMITH: If Bob had never become a writer, never done the Consumer Guide or anything, and was just an editor, he still would be such an influential figure.

GARY GIDDINS: We became great friends, and he's the best editor I've ever worked with. I learned so much about writing from him. Every time I handed in a piece, I walked away knowing something I didn't know before. And he liked working with me because he never had to tell me anything twice.

NELSON GEORGE: He was incredibly blunt, so you're a little scared, but at the same time he was incredibly nurturing once you got past the bluntness.

CAROL COOPER: He was an obsessive line editor. Which meant that at the early stages of working with him, if you were used to the places that left your copy more or less alone, it could be either annoying or humbling, depending on how you felt about it, that he would want you to change almost every other word in something you had already worked on for a week.

COLSON WHITEHEAD: I actually had only one Christgau edit, and it was over the phone. I thought I missed out. But my then girlfriend, Natasha

Stovall, was an interim music editor, so, he did Pazz & Jop in our house in Fort Greene in January of '97. It was like Jesus had come to my apartment. Like, "Oh my god, Christgau's in my house."

JAMES HANNAHAM: My mother was dying of Alzheimer's. It took her a very long time to get through it, and I was panicking. People were offering sympathy without help. Bob took me to lunch, and he gave me the name and number of an eldercare lawyer. He was one of the only people who just did something. It was so small, but it meant so much to me that I feel forever indebted to him for just this one little gesture.

GARY GIDDINS: I remember one guy saying, "You know, people are going to be writing books about Bob." And we all knew what he meant, because Bob is a character. He called himself the dean of rock critics.

I was still writing movie reviews at the *Hollywood Reporter*. And there was a movie called *Looking for Mr. Goodbar*. Remember that? Diane Keaton. It was a pretty bad movie. And Bob walked in—this is when he had this long, straight hair that went down his back—and he walked in very briskly, like, "I'm here—you can start the film!"

And at one point, the Diane Keaton character says something like, "How can you really understand or come to grips with reality?" And Bob said, "Well, for a start, you could stop watching this film!" We all just fell out.

CHAPTER 57

"I GOT THE SENSE I WAS ALMOST BEING HIRED AS AN UNDERTAKER"

MARTIN GOTTLIEB: The political clout of the *Voice* was enormous. It punched way outside its weight class, and the reason was largely because of Jack. He knew the political levers of New York. And when you were to get into a Democratic primary, the *Voice* had an enormous influence on how that primary would go, because people would vote in part on the basis of a *Voice* editorial.

TOM ROBBINS: Jesse Jackson ran for president in '84. He came to New York, and we wrote about "Hymietown," the '84 campaign.* Our attitude about Jackson was that this is a serious guy who, despite his own talent for self-promotion, was actually trying to force the Democratic Party to not just depend upon Black votes, but to include demands that were central to the Black life in the cities. He was saying that years before anybody else was saying it.

MARTIN GOTTLIEB: Jesse Jackson showed up in the office right after the Michigan caucuses that he unexpectedly won. Michael Dukakis agreed to meet with a bunch of us at Republic Airport in Long Island. Al Gore was running as a conservative Democrat that year, and he was supported by Koch. He came, and he gave the best performance of any of them.

---

* In a *Washington Post* interview, Jackson referred to Jews in a derogatory way as "Hymies" and New York City as "Hymietown."

Jack built a lot of that. He had a big role in getting me to the paper. And then I was the editor, and he was basically dictating a major part of the political coverage. He once said to me, "People think I'm the editor of the paper."

I felt I was the editor, and had to speak for everything in the paper, and had to have, hopefully, a collegial but influential role in shaping things. That led to difficulties where I might not have expected there would be.

TOM ROBBINS: Jack had a very close friend, Paul Du Brul, who had written with him for many years in the '60s and the '70s. Paul got very sick, and Jack wanted Paul to write for the paper, and his stories got turned down. And Jack took that to be a great slight to him.

MARTIN GOTTLIEB: And then one day, he left. There were efforts to mediate between us, which Pete Hamill was very helpful at. I look back at it kind of sadly because Jack isn't here to speak for himself.

MARTIN GOTTLIEB: David and I had a disagreement about staffing and budget. He wanted to tighten up the budget and reduce and downsize the staff, not extravagantly, but a bit. And we couldn't agree, and I left.

JONATHAN Z. LARSEN: David Schneiderman approached me about being the editor of the *Voice*. I wrote him this two- or three-page letter. I was not a downtown guy, and so I hadn't paid a hell of a lot of attention. I said, "Wow, this paper does a lot of really good stuff. But here's this and that and the other thing that I don't like about it." My father, Roy E. Larsen, was really the first employee of Time Inc. when it was started in 1922. Henry Luce and Briton Hadden were the two founders, and then my father was the first employee. My father becomes the president of Time Inc.

I got the sense I was almost being hired as an undertaker, because they were all sick of the *Voice*. They thought, "Oh my god, we've got *7 Days*.* We got this huge hit on our hand. Who needs the *Village Voice*?"

LEONARD STERN: I thought there was an enormous opening for much more in-depth coverage of the entertainment markets. I wanted it to be so complete that if there were Off-Off-Broadway productions, they'd all be listed. I did *7 Days* after that.

---

* *7 Days* was a weekly magazine published by Leonard Stern from 1988 to 1990.

DAVID SCHNEIDERMAN: We started it up, and he pulled the plug after two years, which was unfortunate because it just won a National Magazine Award, but we just couldn't make the business work. It was a great editorial product, and Adam was a great editor, Adam Moss. He was, like, this kid at *Esquire*, and he was recommended to me. Adam, that was his first big thing.

JONATHAN Z. LARSEN: They were really beginning to kill the paper off. They wanted somebody to be there while they were doing it. They said, "Look, we're willing to fire a lot of people for you before you even step in. We're going to start withdrawing circulation"—they used to be in the newsstands in Paris and all around Europe, and so that was very costly because the *Voice* was a big heavy paper that costs a lot to ship.

Before I got there, there were, like, four editors in four years; it was just total chaos. None of them had really taken hold and were captive of one part of the paper or another—either the Wayne Barrett, city reporters, or the back-of-the-book sensibility. Even though they might have been there for a year, one of them tried to quit eight times or something. It was chaotic.

Things had really fallen apart. The city editor doing the metropolitan reporting for the paper lived in Philadelphia, and he commuted every day. He would arrive just about in time to go out to lunch. And then he had to leave to take the train to go home, so he'd be there, like, four hours.

And our press critic, Geoffrey Stokes, who had been a wonderful press critic, had decided before I got there to move to Vermont, so he was trying to cover the New York press from Vermont, which meant that every single day we had to pack up all of the daily newspapers and send them air express to Stokes so he could read them as soon as he could possibly get them, because you couldn't buy a lot of these papers up in Vermont. It's even hard to find the *New York Times* up there.

There were editors who would be working from home—almost as if there was a pandemic back then. And they would say, "I'm only interested in editing writers that I want to develop." So, when I got there, I realized on the masthead that you had Ellen Willis and all of these renowned people who supposedly were ready to edit, but when you went to them and said, "I've got a story for you to edit," they said, "No, thank you. I'm already doing something else." "I'm working on a book." "I'm doing a screenplay." "I don't like that writer."

There were these fiefdoms. You had this all-white-male section of the paper, city writers, and then you have the art section, which is multiculti, every sexual persuasion—and they hated each other. You're the editor. You have to embrace both of these camps or at least deal with them, no matter where your sympathies lie, and my sympathies were much more back-of-the-book. I mean, C.Carr—Jesus, was she brilliant. There was some love affair of people walking across the Great Wall of China from one end to the other.* Frankly, I thought a lot of the front-of-the-book stuff about corrupt drywall contractors was really incredibly boring.

So, I had to bring in some editors from the outside. From the beginning, the *Village Voice* was unmediated. It didn't go through layers of editors. The people who wrote beats were passionate about their subject and were allowed to be and were encouraged to be. Whereas in a lot of other papers, you're supposed to be more objective and "let's hear both sides." That was never the *Village Voice* way. The very way that paper was edited was you would sit next to your editor, literally side by side. And every time the editor wanted to change a word, the writer had to approve. It was astonishing. I've never seen it before or since.

But it literally took me, like, two weeks of getting the place organized in terms of covers and future stories and working with the art department to turn it around. Michael Grossman was great. And we had a string of good art directors and really strong covers.

---

* In a piece titled the *Lovers*, performance artists Marina Abramović and Ulay walked from each end of the Great Wall of China and met in the middle. Instead of getting married, they broke up.

CHAPTER 58

"MY GOAL WAS TO MAKE THE *VOICE* LOOK LIKE THE *NEW YORK POST* ON ACID AND RUN BY COMMUNISTS"

ROBERT NEWMAN: Milton Glaser designed the *Voice* for a while. But then George Delmerico was the one who did that great thing with the blue logo and the red strips across the top and bottom and a lot of type: the bold photo, black and white.

MICHAEL GROSSMAN: David Schneiderman was wanting to make a change from George Delmerico. The *Voice* definitely looked like a newspaper, and looked black and white and traditional, and the illustration and photography were contemporary.

I had a connection going back to my *Lampoon* days to the Seattle art mafia. The Seattle people were Wes Anderson; Mark Michaelson; Bob Newman; Kristine Larsen, a photographer; Jeff Christiansen, who was another art director who did special sections for the *Voice*; and Lynda Barry and Matt Groening, pre-*Simpsons*, *Life in Hell* days. I found out about these people. They were looking to come to New York, and I could help.

ROBERT NEWMAN: I grew up in the suburbs outside of Buffalo, New York, in the late '60s. I moved to Seattle in the late '70s. It was like New York but without the challenges involved. And there was all this left-wing, progressive, community, alternative media. I went to work at the *Seattle Sun* as a production person. And then we started *The Rocket* out of the *Sun*.* Wes Anderson—he was in the *Rocket* circle.

There was a whole cultural shift at the *Voice*, where instead of Stan Mack and Mark Stamaty, bless their hearts, it was Peter Bagge and Lynda Barry who were the cultural touchstones. When Fantagraphics moved in, in the early '80s, suddenly there were all these illustrators and cartoonists. We used all these artists, like Kaz and David Sandlin and Scott Menchin. The editor who came after us banned all these artists from the magazine. She called them "East Village artists that can't draw."

There was definitely a split between the New Yorkers and the non–New Yorkers. The non–New Yorkers tended to relate to the *Voice* as a national publication, whereas the New York people always were going on about some local New York shit that I, at the time, could care less about. But as I get further away from it, they really seem to typify the paper the best.

MICHAEL GROSSMAN: When I got to the *Voice*, the front of book looked one way and the back of book looked another. Everybody protected their page or half page or section counts. It was not what I have experienced at any other publication, which is that the job of the creative director and the editor is to conceive of a publication as a whole. There was almost no room for architecture. It was a collection of rooms, and those rooms were defended with weapons.

There were graphic issues. I made all the bylines in the paper the same size. Pete Hamill's column was called Pete Hamill's New York. And so I had "Pete Hamill's" in the same-size type as everybody else's byline, and then "New York" a little bit bigger.

He came back to me with a drawing with "Pete Hamill's" on two different lines, this giant thing.

I said, "That's not fair to everybody else. We can't do that." And he quit; I don't think it was just that. He didn't spend a lot of time there. He acted like a celebrity.

---

* *The Rocket* was an influential music newspaper in Seattle, now defunct.

Iconic *Voice* covers over the years. Cover images ©
Village Voice/Street Media.

One of the signatures on the back of my going-away thing was like,
"Congratulations to the man who chased Pete Hamill away from the *Voice*."

FLORIAN BACHLEDA: Bob's design was a lot more tabloid based.

ROBERT NEWMAN: When I came in, my goal was to make it look like
the *New York Post* on acid and run by communists.

MICHAEL GROSSMAN: The metamorphosis over time—gradually
becoming more of a singular cover that had some graphic impacts on
its own.

ROBERT NEWMAN: There were three New York daily papers: the *Post*,
the *Daily News*, the *Times*—and *New York Newsday*—and the *Voice*. So,
when you go to the newsstand, there would be five papers, all stacked up in a
row. And you go, like, "Fuck."

I wanted them to be much more postery and tabloidy. You had to scream,
because you're in New York. You want to scream.

ROBERT NEWMAN: There's really three legacies—design or visual—at the
Voice, and probably the strongest is the photographs.

When I got to work, I couldn't believe I was sitting at a desk next to Fred
McDarrah. He really was the soul of the *Voice*. He not only had absorbed all
the institutional memory of the place, but he basically felt that he personified
the *Voice*, which he said many times. "I *am* the *Village Voice*!"

Photographers Sylvia Plachy and Fred W. McDarrah. Photo © Allen Reuben.

Oh, he was a scary-ass guy. In the old *Voice* office, the one on Broadway, they once dragged him into the editor's office, which was soundproof, but it had windows all the way across it. So, we're all sitting there, and the editor was yelling at Fred. And Fred was yelling, and they were waving and throwing stuff, but you couldn't hear anything. Fred was the best curser. His favorite phrase was "Fucking fuck!"

JOE LEVY: One of the most amazing things I ever saw in my life was when Ricky Powell brought in his book to show it to Fred. He was a street photographer in New York. A lot of them are Beastie Boys photos taken with a fish-eye lens. And there's this screaming match where Fred is the only one screaming. Ricky's not screaming.

Fred's saying, "What'd you shoot this picture with?" And Ricky pulls out the camera. It's a point-and-shoot.

And it's just Fred McDarrah screaming, "You took that photo with that Mickey Mouse camera! I don't believe it! When you're ready to tell me the truth, you come back here!" And it was the funniest fucking thing you've ever seen.

MICHAEL GROSSMAN: He was really demonstrative, he was cranky, he was jovial, he was cajoling, he was political. He got along with everybody, but in this way where it was often pretty transactional. You could tell when he wanted something. He was working with everybody. So, you know, "Hey, C.! C.Carr! Come-eeer! Come here!"

CATHERINE MCGANN: He would call up the interns first thing in the morning and yell, "Whattaya doing in bed, kid? Get up!" You would do whatever Fred wanted. I was still very much married to my art-school pretensions. I used a wide-angle lens, and I idolized people like Mary Ellen Mark and Diane Arbus and Weegee. And I wanted to somehow find a way to make what I was doing for the paper my artwork, which is pretty tough, because most of the time you have an assignment. Fred was very much like [*claps twice*], "Why isn't the head in the middle?" For a while, he actually banned me from using my wide-angle lens. It forced me to experiment in other ways. And then after a while, he realized my pictures were better.

JAMES HAMILTON: He was photographing Kerouac, Ginsberg, and Dylan. All the characters from that era, from the '50s up until I started working there.

ROBERT NEWMAN: He had a great aesthetic. What we would now call the visual brand of the *Voice* really pretty much owes most of its identity to Fred's photographic aesthetic. It's black-and-white photographs. Very raw. More interested in the content than the form. And much of the form is—it's like punk music. The fact that it doesn't have this veneer of professionalism really doesn't matter.

MICHAEL GROSSMAN: He had this incredible file of every photograph he'd ever taken—which was part of what I had to negotiate at the end of my stay, easing him out. Nominally, he was a *Voice* employee when he had taken them and been paid to go shoot these things, but they were his photographs that he sold elsewhere. The deal was that we could use his photographs without charge. And our budgets were minuscule, and we paid people so badly, that there was an impetus to use Fred's photographs where we could, so that we could have money in the art budget to pay an illustrator or photographer who really was executing on assignment.

SYLVIA PLACHY: The beauty of the *Voice* was that it encouraged everybody to be themselves. And whatever your style is—my style evolved from within. And I'm sure James's also did. His style is more formal.

CATHERINE MCGANN: I loved Sylvia Plachy's work. And at the time, she was doing a series about Queens. They would let her have free rein.

JAMES HAMILTON: Sylvia and I self-edited. We would give a pretty narrow choice. You don't get that freedom anywhere.

MICHAEL GROSSMAN: We tried to crop photos as little as possible to let photographers have a take on things, to choose photographs with them involved in the process. Sylvia was notorious for not showing you her full take. She would show you the photo that she wanted to run. You'd assign a story on the Howard Beach demonstrations, and she'd come back with a picture of a rearview mirror in a car with a silhouette of a bunch of signs, three hundred feet away in the mirror. Sometimes you'd have to say, "This is a really beautiful photograph, Sylvia, and I wouldn't want to edit it or anything, but on the cover, we need something that people are going to be able to read as a demonstration from three or four feet away. Can we look at the other photographs?" And we'd find something that she felt OK about, but it was a negotiation.

ROBERT NEWMAN: Cathy McGann posts on Instagram, and I look at them and I think, "Oh my god, I can't believe the *Voice* ran that stuff." She did Musto's column and would come back with pictures of people naked, having sex in pools. I said, "Cathy, like, do people really do that stuff?" And she said, "Well, when they find out that we're there, they *start* doing it."

CHAPTER 59

"WE WANTED TO DO THINGS THAT WERE MORE GLOBAL"

JONATHAN Z. LARSEN: When I'd been hired, I wrote Schneiderman this letter saying, "The Village doesn't exist anymore as a place. It's a tourist attraction. But as a sensibility, it very much exists. It's all across the country, if not the world. We should be talking to that sensibility—dissident, cynical, downtown sensibility—wherever it exists. It doesn't have to be just downtown New York."

HILTON ALS: That's what was weird about Jonathan: he was trying to make it national. When, for me, it was really about the city.

JONATHAN Z. LARSEN: A lot of that has to do with the energy of Dan Bischoff. I don't know where I found him. He was just so full of energy—it reminded me of the Time-Life News Service at *Time* magazine. He was like a one-man news service, and he would juggle all of these freelancers on the phone. They were in Central America; they were in Europe. They were in Africa. He just ran the whole thing himself—an international desk, if you will.

We did something like eleven cover stories on the Persian Gulf War. Some of them were on things like how we had armed Saddam Hussein leading up to the war because Iraq was fighting Iran, and we sided with Iraq, and we basically created the monster that was Saddam Hussein.

DAN BISCHOFF: As soon as Larsen came, I was made national affairs editor. That was my only title. I came to the *Voice* in '84 or '83, and that was the exact time when publications stopped looking for readers and started looking for advertisers. There was a fundamental change as financialization hit the publishing industry, and it became the communications department of a larger corporation. I always said Murdoch buying the *Voice* is the best thing that ever happened to the *Voice*. All the money that I had to do the things I did came from the fact that Murdoch made the *Voice* incredibly productive, financially successful.

GUY TREBAY: Because Jonathan himself was a moneyed guy, he was not necessarily afraid of using somebody else's money.

DAN BISCHOFF: We wanted to do things that were more global, because the world was becoming global. Jim Ridgeway was in Berlin when the Wall fell. Tiananmen Square happened. These were our people, in a way, in these other countries suffering and being repressed.

GUY TREBAY: Jon Larsen was a fantastic editor for me because he sent Sylvia and me in '89 to the Romanian Revolution. He sent us to Operation Desert Storm.

KIT RACHLIS: Guy's column with Sylvia Plachy's photographs is one of the best things that the *Voice* was publishing.

GUY TREBAY: Sylvia and I went to Budapest. She speaks Hungarian. Our goal was to find László Tőkés, who was the Episcopal bishop in Timișoara, who later turned out to be a corrupt guy but was at the time credited with having triggered the revolution that led to Ceaușescu's fall. I did not produce work that was of any consequence. But we found him. We were stopped by the Securitate and made to get out of the car and empty the car and stand in the freezing cold—by, like, sixteen-year-olds with machine guns in a bad mood.

SYLVIA PLACHY: It was scary. I photographed a guy who was tortured the day before. There were really frightening things going on all around us.

We were going to a famous little town in Transylvania. It was like arriving to a set of an old opera. It was nighttime when we got there, and in Romania they were not allowed to use any lightbulbs bigger than, I don't know, fifteen-watt lightbulbs, so every house looked like it was candlelit. We arrived in this snow-covered village with these little glimmering lights in them.

GUY TREBAY: We got better work out of Desert Storm. We went out into the burning oil fields. We did a story on "Murder Mile," which, looking back, was borderline insane, because our budget was nothing, we had no connection, certainly no cell phones. It was really super foolhardy. Why we were not blown up by a mine, I couldn't tell you.

JOE CONASON: James and I, after the Philippines, put up a map of the world in my office, because we both really wanted to do the same thing again. Somehow. And China turned up not too long after that.

JAMES HAMILTON: Joe and I had been bugging them to cover the student revolution. Then when it looked like it was all going to be over, they said, "OK, you can go."

JOE CONASON: We took a high school girl with us—she was about to go to college—who was fluent in Mandarin to translate.

FRANK RUSCITTI: They got there a little after the fact, three days later or something. The joke in the office was, "This is Joe Conason reporting from the swim-up bar here in Red Square."

JAMES HAMILTON: China was a whole different thing. That was really scary.

JOE CONASON: Martial law was imposed within a few days after we got there. We went out to Beijing University to meet students, because we thought it was students who had gotten killed in Tiananmen. I now know it happened somewhere else and it wasn't mostly students. But people, including the students, thought that students had been killed.

JAMES HAMILTON: A lot of the people in the square that were killed were from the provinces, so nobody will ever get a real head count.

JOE CONASON: They had decorated the whole place with these white paper chrysanthemums—white is the color of mourning in China. They were telling us, "They were going to come and kill us here." They firmly believed that they were going to be murdered by the army. They adopted us, a few of them.

JAMES HAMILTON: They gave us bicycles. That was a big advantage over the journalists who had cars, who could be stopped. We blended in; everyone had bicycles.

JOE CONASON: On the plane, I saw a producer for one of the network news programs. She had one of those metal suitcases filled with hundred-dollar bills. We didn't have a lot of money—we had a couple thousand dollars altogether, and a credit card. You couldn't get into a taxicab and go across town for less than $500.

We rode on bicycles the rest of the time we were there with these students who were taking us around. They showed us everything. The reason James got the pictures of the dead bodies was because they took us to the place which was near in the Forbidden City where they knew that bodies were being kept.

JAMES HAMILTON: We had to go at night. I was basically unzipping body bags and taking flash pictures because there wasn't a light, which was terrifying for everybody because it would give us away.

JOE CONASON: I found it really hard to look while he was doing it. I was zipping up the bags, unzipping. They'd been there for a couple of days. You see the pictures, they're scary as hell. The bodies, it was horrible. These bodies with maggots on them. More than a hundred, in that one place, under this weird sort of tent.

Like an idiot, I chained the bike to a post while we were waiting for him to take the pictures. And then all of a sudden we realized that the people inside the trailer had called the cops. Somehow the students figured out that people had called the police or the army, and they were coming. Everybody's getting on their bikes to get away, and I'm trying to unlock my bike. I was from New York, and I always locked my bike. What an idiot. We escaped in time. We're tearing ass across the Forbidden City, these little alleys.

JAMES HAMILTON: I remember tears streaming down my face. It was a reaction to what I had just seen. All the emotions came out as I was racing away on this bicycle.

I wanted to develop my film. I was nervous about it, and I wanted to at least have negatives ready. There was a Reuters office, and I'd heard that they had a darkroom. So, one night after curfew—curfew was pretty early—I went out walking from the hotel to get to this Reuters office, and a truck full of soldiers came by and basically chased me into the woods. I was scared out of my wits. I lay down and covered myself up with leaves. They were walking all around with guns. I was wearing a white shirt and khakis; it's ridiculous. I was an obvious target at night. I was afraid for my life and didn't make it to the Reuters office. But I escaped because they just gave up and left.

JOE CONASON, "SCENES FROM A FAILED REVOLUTION," *VILLAGE VOICE*, JUNE 20, 1989

In the weeks leading up to the massacre, workers had openly demonstrated their support for the students, and now our friends introduce us to a worker dressed in Mao blue whom they'd just met themselves. He insists upon taking us to a small hospital nearby. He knows where some corpses are being stored. The students and he are convinced that unless we see the gruesome proof, we would never believe what had happened.

JAMES HAMILTON: We sent the raw film canisters through civilians, but they went straight to the *Voice*. They processed them while we were still there in China. They ran on the cover.

MICHAEL GROSSMAN: They were horrifying. Some of them were photographs of death, and really gory. We had a lot of debate about whether to run them, and how to run them, and whether to put one on the cover. The photo that we ended up putting on the cover was not incredibly gory but was clearly a photo of death. There were bodies wrapped in plastic. James had peeled back the plastic shroud around a dead body, and you can see the rope that tied the plastic around this corpse. He could have been strangled.

JOE CONASON: We were there for a few more days. Larsen ordered us to come home. There was a martial law; we couldn't do anything anymore.

This was my genius plan: If we went out the international airport, probably they would take our stuff, the film and the notes and everything. I thought, "Let's not do that. We will instead fly on a domestic plane to Guangzhou and then get on a train to Hong Kong."

We went to Guangzhou. We flew, and then we took a train. We got on the plane. At the domestic airport, there were no other white people there. No guards, nothing. We walked onto the plane. But as we get on the plane, we realize this is, like, a 1952 Soviet-era airplane with no seat belts.

James looks at me and says, "*Now* you've gotten us killed."

CHAPTER 60

"WHEN THE TOMPKINS SQUARE RIOT HIT, IT WAS LIKE SOMEBODY PUT A MATCH TO THE FLAME"

DAN BISCHOFF: The gentrification of the city was starting.

SARAH FERGUSON: It started flipping in the '80s. The city had redlined the East Village, as they did the South Bronx. The city had cut off services in the '70s. Landlords abandoned their buildings or torched them for insurance. It was like Berlin after the war; there were huge swaths of blocks of half-empty buildings. On Eighth Street, half the block was abandoned. It was just empty, rotted out; the junkies had come in and stolen all the pipes. If there had been a fire, sometimes the fire department would punch a hole in the roof to prevent people from squatting there, and also so that if there was a fire that it would just go up; it wouldn't spread.

There was this wholesale abandonment of the area by the city. Then all of a sudden, it started to change. The artists came, the Fun Gallery scene, Gracie Mansion, and it became this new edgy place of art that was very much in protest to the Reagan era.* It was a time of the Reagan bubble with all the yuppie money. The art became radically inflated, and the scene became

---

* Gracie Mansion the art gallery, not the mayor's residence.

pumped up by the media. You could buy a building for $50,000 and then flip it for $100,000.

MICHAEL CARUSO: Everybody hated the yuppies. They were very hateable. They were scrubbed clean, and they wore khakis and were pushing strollers. They didn't belong.

LUCIAN K. TRUSCOTT IV: In the '80s, I had a girlfriend who lived on Waverly in the Village. There was a little sushi joint on her block that was upstairs from a gay cabaret. I remember going in there one night during the week. There were two tables of four Wall Street guys, each table. All of them have their sleeves rolled up. They all looked like fraternity boys, between twenty-five and thirty, and they were just bellowing. We had to leave; we couldn't talk to each other.

That just didn't happen in the '70s.

STAN MACK: Coke was the champagne of drugs—somebody once told me—of people on Wall Street. I remember one woman who worked out a lot saying to me, "Biceps are the new breasts." It was all about power shoulders and making money.

MICHAEL CARUSO: Suddenly, the Christodora happens, this luxury building on Tompkins Square Park. The Christodora was this huge middle finger to the residents.

SARAH FERGUSON: The East Village had been this bohemia. There was really this sense that the neighborhood was its own little cultural island unto itself. People would compare it to Christiania, that little squatter island in Copenhagen. People had less AC back then. On a hot summer night, there were people there all night. There were also homeless people living in the park. The issue about noise had started because there was still the bandshell in the park where bands played. It had great acoustics, actually. The Grateful Dead played there once; Sun Ra, Jimi Hendrix, and Janis Joplin.

At night when the Pyramid let out, the drag queens were going over there and continuing with their shows. They would bring boom boxes, and the neighbors were complaining about noises. Different classes of people were moving into the neighborhood. I wouldn't call it that dangerous; you could get mugged anywhere on the Lower East Side back then.

LENNY KAYE: I'm of mixed feelings. I couldn't take my little daughter to Tompkins Square because the children's playground was littered with glass. I remember going to buy pot on Second Street between Avenue A and Avenue B and asking my friend, the dealer there, "How can you live on this street? Do you carry a gun?"

DAN BISCHOFF: Clubs at that time were like art shows. Basquiat did a big painting behind the bar at the Palladium. My friend and I were downtown at some art event, and a woman came up to me and gave me a pill—looked like a cold tablet, a plastic thing. She said, "Take it home, put it in water." We took it home, and it was an invite to go to Area for opening night. Sarah was part of that scene too. She came in and gave me a story. She was fearless.

SARAH FERGUSON: I was covering all these little factions on the left running around in the East Village and the fight over Tompkins Square Park as this last bastion of protest. It sounds so naive now, but it was this zone of resistance against the marginalizing power of Manhattan.

STAN MACK: I was very involved in that whole scene—the squatters, the homeless, the activists, the anarchists, the revolutionaries, all battling the city—'88 through about '91 or '92. I spent as much time as possible over there.

DAN BISCHOFF: Stan Mack would listen to people and transcribe their dialogue and do a cartoon.

STAN MACK: One of my earliest strips got kinda well known. I did a bird's-eye view of the entire Tompkins Park, where all the different groups hung out. You didn't easily go from turf to turf. It was too dangerous. There were the druggies and the anarchists and the ex–Polish freedom fighters and the chess players, where the feeding trucks showed up to feed the homeless, and so on. That kicked off the series.

Most of the squatters were young. They may have been homeless. Some were addicts. Some were just desperate. There were some young Europeans who were part of it. There was a huge gap between those who were desperate and those who were playing at it.

But there was one old couple, Rex and Rosemary. He was very clearly an alcoholic. The two of them were living in this run-down squat. They were on their own because they were a lot older. I would hang out with them, particularly Rex, who was a big, tough westerner, crude, rough, strong, outspoken, and would confront the crack dealers who were trying to move into some of these squats.

One day, I'm sitting with him. It was the middle of winter. It was quite cold, and he had a little space heater in the middle of his little space. He gave me a place of honor closer to the heater and in the conversation mentioned that he had a daughter who worked for *New York* magazine.

He gave me her name. I called up *New York* magazine and asked for this woman, not believing anything he said. Well, it turned out it was Jeannette Walls, who was writing the Intelligencer column. She said to me, "I won't tell you not to write it, but could you disguise it in some way, just in case, because nobody knows who my father is and mother." I said, "Sure. I don't do gossip." I did fictionalize the magazine. But she told this story later in her memoir, *The Glass Castle*, which was made into a movie.

SARAH FERGUSON: I knew it was going to happen. I was lying on a rock naked, and a snake crawled over me, and I woke up and I said, "There's going to be a riot."

When the Tompkins Square riot hit, it was like somebody put a match to the flame. There was this heat wave in Manhattan, August 6, 1988. I'd gone camping up at Bear Mountain with this boyfriend of mine, and we'd taken the tent on the motorcycle, and I forgot the tent poles. I said, "We have to go back."

We went back on his motorcycle, and I literally rolled down Avenue A, and it had just started, so I was still wearing my shorts and hiking boots, and I went over to Ray's Coffee Shop and got myself a pen and a pad of paper and started taking notes. I just fell right into it.

Things quickly got out of control. There had been posturing between the cops and the protest groups the week before; they had a little mini confrontation in the park. Back then, you could do crazy things. When I first moved to the neighborhood, somebody showed me how to blow up a cop car with a quarter stick of dynamite, just putting it in the tailpipe and lighting a slow fuse. Pre-9/11, it was a different ball game.

DAN BISCHOFF: Guys in those squats were saving up urine, their urine and cat urine—cat urine is better—to throw off the top of the roof when the cops tried to come in. Cops will run away from cat urine. It's a lot better than a gun.

SARAH FERGUSON: The police had said they were going to be back, so they knew there was going to be a big protest on the night of August 6. I don't think anybody knew that the police would arrive in such crazy numbers and cover their badges and just go off on people.

There were four hundred police called in over the course of the night, and they came in on horses and trampled people and pushed people out of the road. I know somebody lost part of their pinky because they got run over by a horse. They indiscriminately charged on the crowd.

It was catching up bystanders, people coming out of restaurants, bars. And they were just pushing everybody out of the park. I was with Dean, my boyfriend, and his ex-girlfriend had showed up—I had this weird love triangle going on.

The police started beating her, and they said, "Get out of the park, you nigger bitch," because she was Black. And Dean said, "Why are you calling her a nigger? There's a Black cop right next to you," and then the police just beat the shit out of them. All this was caught on camera, with my mouth agape, and they had to get rushed to the hospital. They later sued and got $50,000 from the police.

JAMES HAMILTON: A bunch of us were having dinner at Karen Durbin's house, and somebody said, "I think there's going to be something happening at Tompkins Square." I always have my camera with me, so I said, "Well, maybe I'll go check it out." I left and went over.

It became very violent. There were helicopters flying over. There were cops on horseback. It became an insane scene with an overreaction. That's why it's called the Tompkins Square police riot. It's not the "squatters' riot."

There was a picture that caused a bit of a stir, too. It's a bald man; he's got a big gash in his head, blood seeping down, and all these cops are looking at him.

STAN MACK: I have a comic strip, "Class Clash on Avenue B," which looks at all the different players in the protest. There were the Christodora people, who were looking down at these people down in front of the building who were yelling up at them, "Wake up, yuppie scum!" What I loved was the two policemen barricaded in with their shields and helmets, no doubt coming from north of Westchester, and here they are in the middle of this riot. I don't know if they understood what was going on.

SARAH FERGUSON: It was a pretty epic night for me. I had more of a sense of where all the rage and protests had come from than a lot of reporters that were just coming down to the scene and being like, "What is this? Who are these groups?"

MICHAEL CARUSO: That was *our* story. The Tompkins Square Park riot was something we could understand in a way that the *New York Times* didn't. It was basically as if they were sending foreign correspondents down there.

SARAH FERGUSON: The first story had been this really small one about the protest. I got to write a story about the origins of the riot. I parlayed the riot story into a cover story called "Inside the Squatter's Rebellion." That was nominated for a Pulitzer.

SARAH FERGUSON, "OCCUPIED TERRITORIES," *VILLAGE VOICE*, JULY 18, 1989

It's 2 a.m. and I'm huddled in a dark fifth-floor apartment with a dozen squatters, watching across a rubble-strewn lot as a city wrecking crew tears through the top two floors of their former home at 319 East 8th Street. Caught under the high-powered glare of the stadium-style flood-lights, the fire-damaged tenement seems to rise out of the street like a cankerous tooth, casting ominous shadows over the decaying buildings surrounding us.

"It's fucking El Salvador," someone says as an explosion sends one of the 319's brick walls cascading to the ground.

DAN BISCHOFF: She conveyed some of the anger and sense of betrayal that a lot of those people had about New York, the great liberal city.

But when it comes down to property rights, it doesn't make a difference whether you're in New York or Dallas. It's all the same.

CHAPTER 61

DO THE RIGHT THING

NELSON GEORGE: The other thing that should be mentioned is crack. Which fueled a lot of the storytelling.

BARRY MICHAEL COOPER: I was a big fan of the journalism of Gay Talese, Truman Capote, Joan Didion, and I wanted to incorporate the street into that type of New Journalism. I really didn't make my bones until the New Jack City Detroit story.

I went to Detroit for a week. Initially, I was going there to interview Mayor Coleman Young about how Detroit had changed in twenty years. You know, the white flight, the gangs, the drugs, the crack, the violence. And he never gave me an interview.

And then somebody called me. They said, "Listen, you need to be careful, because the cops know that you're here, and you're stepping on their toes. But the real story is not Coleman Young, but his niece Cathy Volsan, who's married to one of the biggest drug dealers in the city."

I found out that was true.

I talked to some kids in Young Boys Incorporated, YBI. They were making almost a billion dollars a year in the Midwest.* It was December 1, 1987. It was a front-page story.

---

* Cooper's original story estimates $400 million a year.

BARRY MICHAEL COOPER, "KIDS KILLING KIDS, NEW JACK CITY EATS ITS YOUNG," *VILLAGE VOICE*, DECEMBER 1, 1987

The people moved like waves of warm water along the sidewalk cafes of Greektown, Woodward's shopping district, and deposited into the concrete cavern of Hart Plaza. Packs of new jacks—all between 13 and 19 years old—covered the area in designer sangfroid and $2000 portable cellular phones, just in case another crew wanted to "step off" into Uzi conflict. They resembled Nam platoons on maneuvers in Elephant Valley. Their classy gear consisted of Gucci and Bill Blass jogging suits, Bally and Diadora gym shoes, shiny gold Rolex watches. Some were so bold they wore diamond encrusted Krugerrands necklaces, hung from telephone-cable-thick gold chains. That's equivalent to Nat Turner fashioning a leather-studded belt out of the same cat-o'-nine-tails used to plow his back. But maybe I'm confusing bravado with ignorance.

BARRY MICHAEL COOPER: Scott Malcomson edited that piece. He was phenomenal. I wanted it to have a novel-like quality.

JOE LEVY: Barry Michael Cooper's Teddy Riley piece for *Rock & Roll Quarterly**—which is the first place anybody outside of the heart of the neighborhood encounters the phrase "new jack swing" or "New Jack City"— that's all Barry Michael Cooper. That piece was amazing.

BARRY MICHAEL COOPER: I heard this rapper, Grandmaster Caz— he had a solo record. He was talking about a guy; he was like, "You a new jack clown." It was a derogatory term initially. It was a put-down, but I liked the way it sounded: "new jack." There was a certain sensibility to it. I wanted to take that and flip it into something else. Near the end of my research for the Detroit story, I started thinking about that term. I started thinking about the music I was hearing in Detroit, which was Teddy Riley and new jack swing—and that's the story that came after the new jack Detroit story.

---

* A music supplement of the *Voice* that ran for six years in the '80s and '90s.

I said, "This whole crack milieu reminds me of F. Scott Fitzgerald and our profound human change in *The Great Gatsby*." That's where I applied it: new jack. New jack swing. New Jack City. It was to give the zeitgeist of the crack era a name. It turned my life around as a writer. Quincy Jones read the story, invited me out to Hollywood. That's where the movie *New Jack City* was produced, and that came out in 1991. It came from that story. It caught people off guard. It actually caught *me* off guard.

NELSON GEORGE: That whole era, either the films were dealing with crack, or Spike Lee was writing about it, or the *Voice* was covering different aspects of it. That's a huge part of having young Black writers there, was they were able to articulate the chaos that it was bringing. And the way it infected the music and the culture.

CAROL COOPER: The first person to ever write about Spike Lee in the paper was me. Spike cold-called me at the *Voice* one day when I was in the copy department and asked me to come and see some things he was working on. I had never heard of him. He just said, "I'm working on some stuff, and I think you should see it." He had just finished *Joe's Bed-Stuy Barbershop: We Cut Heads*. That was his first short, and it was his school project. It was genius. I loved it.

The *Voice* was doing a series of up-and-coming profiles, who to watch that's doing something interesting, and I pitched Spike. I wrote a profile that was very flattering. I had never met a Black filmmaker before. The fact that this guy was young and seriously making films was impressive.

Remember, the only reason I was working at the *Voice* is because they'd already got dinged by a regulatory committee telling them that they weren't Black enough. So, I'm bringing them a story about a young, Black creative person who the *Voice* needed to pay attention to if they wanted to have their finger on the pulse. Chris Blackwell read what I wrote and got in touch with him and ended up funding *She's Gotta Have It*.*

HARRY ALLEN: He was the newest flower in the scene. *She's Gotta Have It*—it was a beautiful fantasy. Watching *She's Gotta Have It*, I wasn't caught up in the story or the conflict or the narrative or the issues as much as I was

---

* Blackwell is founder of Island Records and Island Pictures.

just the feel of the film. It was this movie about this beautiful girl who's got this amazing apartment in a beautifully shot Brooklyn neighborhood. It was what I wanted to be and do.

Then *School Daze*—it was more the politics of it. I had left college a few years before; that whole frat thing was very familiar to me. I had very strong feelings about it, but also to watch a modern film with Black people that's all Black people that's not about crime, but it's about college—that was the thing that most impressed me that I wrote about when I saw it.

LISA JONES: Nelson was instrumental in getting the coverage of Spike.

NELSON GEORGE: Yeah, I met him through a girl. She introduced us because I was still writing at *Billboard*, and he wanted to do music videos after he'd done *Joe's Bed-Stuy Barbershop: We Cut Heads* at NYU. I introduced him to some people, and they didn't give him a job. But he started doing these low-budget videos on his own. He did one with Larry Fishburne actually.

Then I did an article on Russell Simmons for the *Voice*, one of the first big pieces on Russell, in '85. And then I got a phone call: "Hey, this is Spike!" That was the beginning of our relationship. Turned out, I was moving to Brooklyn, and I got a place in Fort Greene. Little did I know I moved literally three blocks from Spike.

I invested a little bit of money I had in *She's Gotta Have It*. The whole Fort Greene thing started happening around him. The whole period from, like, mid-'80s to around 2000, when Fort Greene was like the capital of Black culture, and everyone was there, from Vernon Reid to both Marsalis brothers, new, young jazz guys—they all lived in Fort Greene. I mean, Jesus, everyone lived there. Half the people who worked for *Vibe* lived there—Touré, Kevin Powell, Danyel Smith. Wesley Snipes. Rosie Perez. Roger Guenveur Smith. It was amazing.

Chris Rock knew me through the *Voice*. I met him in Fort Greene. He had this stupid idea for a movie, which turned out to be *CB4*. Chris Rock used to write for the *Voice*. I hooked him up when Joe Levy was doing the music section. Chris really has great taste, and he read the *Voice* every weekend and read all of our stuff, Tate and me and everybody. And he did a couple of music reviews.

Thulani Davis lived two blocks from me on Adelphi. Her husband, who is a musician, Joseph Jarman—he was in this important Black avant-garde group.* But Thulani was collaborating, and she was writing for the *Voice*, and she also was doing the opera while she lived there.** So, Lisa Jones would come and hang out, Tate would hang out at her house. And then Spike would house people in the neighborhood who were in movies he was shooting. So, Halle Berry would be living in Fort Greene, and then she and Wesley Snipes hooked up.

I moved in on the corner of Willoughby and Carlton. Spike's like, "Come around the house." He showed me *She's Gotta Have It*. I watched it in his little, shitty apartment. That was the beginning of a whole era. That was incredible. That all tied together. A lot of the young Black writers in the *Voice* were part of that in some form.

Lisa and Spike got together. Somehow she met Spike after *She's Gotta Have It*.

LISA JONES: I ended up being a production assistant on *She's Gotta Have It*. Eventually I went on to write three books with him about the making of his early films.

NELSON GEORGE: I did the first book that Spike did, which was for *She's Gotta Have It*. Lisa had an avant-garde theater group called Rodeo Caldonia—the most famous person out of it is Lorna Simpson. She's a big visual artist now. There was this whole collective of women. *Interview Magazine* did a piece on them at one point. I had a fundraiser at my house for them. Spike showed up because he had to.

DAVE HERNDON: That was so much a part of the fabric of the paper at that time, Spike's universe. Spike's brother David Lee was a photo intern when I was there.

When *She's Gotta Have It* came out, I went out to watch it in Brooklyn on Flatbush Avenue. I got on the train back into Manhattan, and Joie Lee, Spike's sister, was on the train in the same car I was in—and she was in the movie. So, I walk out of the movie, into the subway car, and there's the same person that I just watched. That's how organically connected everything was in those days.

---

* Art Ensemble of Chicago.
** Davis wrote the libretto for the opera *X, The Life and Times of Malcolm X*.

You'd see Kim Gordon on the subway while the *Voice* is doing Sonic Youth cover stories. There was no membrane between what we were doing at the paper and what was happening in the culture that we covered and the life we lived when we went on the subway and went out on the weekends. It was all one thing. And Spike's cohort was a huge part of that.

LISA JONES: The objective voice? I don't think we believed in that much. We were all about exploring the fallacy of that. Basically, Greg and Vernon were operating the BRC* out of *Voice* offices on Broadway. I was operating my performance group, Rodeo Caldonia High Fidelity Performance Theater, out of my cubicle at the *Voice*. I had costumes and props, like, under my feet in my cubicle. Nobody told me that was wrong.

NELSON GEORGE: David Edelstein did an amazing piece on Spike when *She's Gotta Have It* came out called "Birth of a Salesman," which is one of the most prophetic pieces ever done on him. The trailer for *She's Gotta Have It*, with Spike out here somewhere on Second or Third Avenue selling tube socks, and that idea of Spike as this ultimate salesman—he nailed that.

DAVID EDELSTEIN, "BIRTH OF A SALESMAN," *VILLAGE VOICE*, AUGUST 12, 1989

Lee has conceived the film in a broad, presentational style, with the actors talking right at the audience. (It's like a polyphonic Annie Hall.) . . .

But that's part of the charm—you're not supposed to believe him. As far as I'm concerned, Eddie Murphy has a new kid brother; *She's Gotta Have It* marks the Birth of a Salesman. Attention will be paid.

GREG TATE: Nelson was an investor in *She's Gotta Have It*. I went to the first screening Spike had. He had basically edited, but he hadn't put a lot of the sound and the music in. He was showing a version of the film to raise interest and to raise money. Nelson, he invited a bunch of writers from the *Voice* to see it.

---

* Black Rock Coalition.

What I remember particularly from that screening was a guy, David [Denby], who went on to be a film writer at the *New Yorker*. David said two of the most stupid things about a Spike Lee film anybody's ever said. After that screening, he said, "This film isn't any good, and it will never be."

The other stupid thing he said was when *Do the Right Thing* came out. He was at *New York* magazine, and he said, "This film is irresponsible; it's going to incite riots." That never happened.

NELSON GEORGE: Then Stanley wrote a huge article about how *Do the Right Thing* was irresponsible; it was going to cause a riot.

STANLEY CROUCH, "DO THE RACE THING," *VILLAGE VOICE*, JUNE 20, 1989

In order to bring off his romantic vision of race superseding all, Lee creates a fantasy Bed-Stuy neighborhood. No villains such as drug dealers ever appear to complicate things, nor any middle-class would-be street Negroes like the filmmaker himself. The variety of black people Lee chooses to sentimentalize, capture accurately, or to show admiration for are all lower class. Some even feel animosity for each other. But when the racial call is given, all forms of alienation dissolve and the neighborhood merges into ANGRY BLACK PEOPLE led into a riot by a rail-tailed ne'er-do-well named Mookie, who throws a trash can through the window of a pizzeria owned by an Italian he works for. In the logic of the film, the Italian, Sal, is the real villain because, even though he has had his shop in the neighborhood for 25 years and has watched people grow up and die, he refuses to put the pictures of "some black people" on his wall, which is covered with the images of famous Italian-Americans.

NELSON GEORGE: It became part of the dialogue about the film before it came out. Was this thing irresponsible filmmaking? And the idea that because a Black guy, a delivery boy, throws a garbage can through a window, Black people are going to riot in the theater. How stupid is that? That was a super controversial moment.

Spike was a provocateur. He directed the video for "Fight the Power." Tawana Brawley's in the video. The movie came out during the summer of the Dinkins campaign. Spike directed a video for Dinkins.

SPIKE LEE: It's been reported several places that this film is the retelling of Howard Beach. This is a completely *fictional* thing. We took four things from it: the baseball bat, a Black man gets killed, the pizzeria, and the conflict between Blacks and Italian Americans. I wanted it to be one twenty-four-hour period, the hottest day of the summer. I wanted the film to take place on one block in Bedford-Stuyvesant. So, that's all the stuff I needed to work with. From there I could just go ahead and do what I had to do. Buggin Out's character is a direct reference to the couple days after the Howard Beach incident. Some Black leaders got together and wanted all the Black people in New York City to boycott pizza for a day. It was one of the most ridiculous things I ever heard in my life. That was the whole premise of the film, that in ninety-five degrees, people lose it anyway.

LISA KENNEDY: Spike was important to my development, and to the department. The *Voice* amplified those issues about identity politics, but it was also responding to a culture that was pushing those identities more, too. One of the pieces that Hilton and I worked on was this Spike Lee cover for the Malcolm X movie.

HILTON ALS: It's funny, I wasn't so interested in him, but I liked the way that in the *Voice* you could say that, you know?

GARY DAUPHIN: I interviewed Spike, like, maybe five times at the *Voice*. There was a stretch where every time a film came out, I would interview him. The paper really gave Spike a platform from which to talk about himself and his work in a more expansive, thoughtful way than he probably got at other places.

CHAPTER 62

"THE CENTRAL PARK FIVE CASE WAS A BIG WAKE-UP CALL"

"YOUTHS RAPE AND BEAT CENTRAL PARK JOGGER," *NEW YORK TIMES*, APRIL 21, 1989

A young woman, jogging on her usual nighttime path in Central Park, was raped, severely beaten and left unconscious in an attack by as many as 12 youths, who roamed the park in a vicious rampage Wednesday night, police said. . . .

Five youths were arrested in connection with another attack Wednesday evening, and the police said that they were considered suspects in the assault on the jogger.

WILLIAM BASTONE: It amazes me that no one has written a book about what an unbelievable decade the '80s were in New York. Giuliani. Bad things, like the crack epidemic. The racial killing in Howard Beach. Crown Heights happened a little bit beyond the '80s. John Gotti's rise to power. The municipal corruption scandals.

NELSON GEORGE: There was the Central Park rape case. You had Bush/Reagan, right? Koch, Giuliani, Dinkins. You had crack, hip-hop, Black film, and you had downtown SoHo becoming a new downtown. The '80s is

Central Park Five issue.
Cover image © Village Voice/
Street Media.

a monster decade for the *Voice*. I look back in my datebook and those years were thick with stuff.

LISA JONES: The Central Park Five case was a big wake-up call for Black people of my generation. As the post–civil rights generation, we thought we had dodged racism in a sense. And cases like the Central Park Five and Eleanor Bumpurs and Michael Stewart and Amadou Diallo just brought it back and put it in our laps again and said, "No, this is your inheritance, and you are going to have to continue this fight."

We were all shell-shocked. There was, again, that sense of the *Voice* was doing something, but it was never enough. If you don't have a regular political reporter who's covering the Black community and racial politics, are you really covering it?

JONATHAN Z. LARSEN: That happened shortly after I got there. We did a cover, right off the bat, that was billed as something like "Other Voices." We had probably ten different writers with their different takes on what had happened. Lisa Kennedy had a big part in that package, putting it together.

Nat Hentoff wanted to be one of the writers. I said no. And I said, "Nat, this is really about women, and about Black women and Black kids, and those are the voices we were going to. Nat, we hear from you a couple of times a week on everything"—unfortunately, on abortion—as well as freedom of speech. And he was so pissed off. He never forgave me. He said it was as if I was against freedom of speech. But I didn't want an old white male who we hear from plenty—and he has a whole column! He could write about anything he wants in his column.

LISA KENNEDY: My piece was a pretty emotional first-person piece about how confused I was about the ways in which it was getting parsed at the time. Ellen Willis was my editor. If you're a Black woman, and you're listening to the ways in which people are talking about the jogger, then you're freaked about race and gender and violence. There was no easy entry as an African American woman because of the ways the conversations were getting set up—either it's racism or it's sexism. Reporting turns out to be incredibly important, as opposed to reading media coverage of the reporting, which has its own value. Great reporting is essential in situations like that.

JONATHAN Z. LARSEN: As soon as I got there, I promoted Michael Caruso. I sat down with Michael, figuring out how to cover the Central Park Five. We sent off two people: Rick Hornung nosed around the police department, and Barry Michael Cooper went up to where these kids came from. Barry Michael Cooper's piece turned out to be prescient, because he basically said, look, these kids are not good kids. The defendants in the case were known to be part of gangs that marauded this whole neighborhood. They were innocent, for sure, but let's not make heroes out of them. They were fairly bad dudes, and they had been beating up people at the exact same time the rape was happening. Barry Michael Cooper's piece stood up very well.

BARRY MICHAEL COOPER: I wrote a story called "Cruel & the Gang." I had a friend who lived in a place called Los Tres Unidos on 112th and Madison. One of the kids either lived in there or had a friend in there. People used to complain about some of the kids—Korey Wise* and another kid—coming in and out, starting trouble. Just mischievous stuff. But when

---

* Also known as Kharey Wise.

I asked him, "Do you think they raped?" They said, "Absolutely not." I sat behind Kevin Richardson's mom when he was in court. And the way she broke down and cried when he was on the stand, I said to myself, "Something is not right. I don't know if these kids did this." It was a weird, tragic situation, man.

Those kids, the whole thing about "wilding"—where did the word come from? I said, "I've never heard of a term called 'wilding.'" I've heard of "wiling," somebody "wiling out." This took on a life of its own.

BARRY MICHAEL COOPER, "CRUEL & THE GANG," *VILLAGE VOICE*, MAY 5, 1989

The media has created a name, a handle for the horror that happened in Central Park: "wilding." It is a word that has become a citywide panic button in less than a week, a word used to broad-stroke young, Aframerican males as subhumans who rape, pillage, and throw themselves into an urban bacchanalia invoked by a gold-chained hip-hop god named Tone Loc. The word itself is twisted music for racist ears, the coda for the unfinished symphonies of the Ku Klux Klownsman, hooded and in plainclothes.

BARRY MICHAEL COOPER: This is before everything came out about the wrong DNA. I mean, that horrendous, villainous ad that Trump took out about the death penalty and all that bullshit. It was a bad time, man.

DONALD TRUMP, FULL-PAGE AD, *NEW YORK NEWSDAY, NEW YORK TIMES, NEW YORK DAILY NEWS, NEW YORK POST*, MAY 1, 1989

BRING BACK THE DEATH PENALTY.
BRING BACK OUR POLICE!

Mayor Koch has stated that hate and rancor should be removed from our hearts. I do not think so. I want to hate these muggers and murderers. They should be forced to suffer and when they kill, they should be executed for their crimes.

—*Donald J. Trump*

TOM ROBBINS: He was always a vicious, horrible man. Forget about being president. If you'd asked me, "Who is the worst person in New York?" I would have said "Trump" at any time over the last twenty years. Look what he did with the Central Park Five, running that ad.

BARRY MICHAEL COOPER: They really vilified these kids. They were lower than human life, you know? It continues to haunt New York City to this very day. So, the people's personal hot takes at the *Voice* on the Central Park rape case—it varied. There was no one monolithic train of thought.

NELSON GEORGE: The *Voice* did a ton of coverage—it was different from what was being done in other places. Like, the *Daily News* had that infamous picture of this kid admitting he did this crime, and the police leaked the picture, because there was a concerted effort to get these guys railroaded by officials in New York. I try not to get into racism.

By having so many young Black writers, Barry and people like that, it brings some humanity to coverage that was really still very, "young Black men are criminals and violent animals," which was the take of the *Daily News*. The *Post* was liberal back then. Once the tabloid era came in, they both were heinous about race.

HELEN BENEDICT, *VIRGIN OR VAMP: HOW THE PRESS COVERS SEX CRIMES*, 1992

The story was predominantly covered by men and by whites. . . . The *Village Voice* was exceptional because it intentionally assigned Black writers and women to the story. The jogger stories in the *City Sun*, which has a female editor, and the *Amsterdam News*, both politically weighted weeklies, were written primarily by men.

JONATHAN Z. LARSEN: Rick Hornung stayed on the case. He sat in on these hearings where lawyers were trying to exclude exculpatory information in front of the judge. He was virtually the only reporter who ever showed up at these hearings. They went on for weeks, if not months. Rick wrote this cover for us, which was the first piece of journalism out there that suggested these kids were innocent as charged. That was an amazing piece. Now, it had a huge impact within the *Village Voice* office, because it immediately made Rick Hornung a pariah. The accepted wisdom was that these Black kids were guilty of raping a white woman, right? We're suggesting they're innocent.

One of the people who most dissented was Karen Durbin. The minute she became the editor of the *Voice*, she didn't want to ever have anything to do with Rick Hornung again. He became an outcast at the *Voice*. But that was how heated the battle was in New York, and even within the confines of the *Village Voice*.

BARRY MICHAEL COOPER: That story was overwhelming. Whether other journalists will admit it or not, it was overwhelming. Because the daily news that was coming out of the prosecutor Linda Fairstein's office and Mayor Ed Koch and that idiot, Trump—some people were scared to really dial into it.

LISA KENNEDY: We were able to survive things like George W. and Reagan and AIDS, in part because we were in a place that was that engaged and that copacetic. There was a lot of art going on that we did take solace in but also helped amplify, which is an amazing role to have. So, for all those fights and all that infighting, there was something so alive every day at that newspaper. When things are that bad—that was a space in which I did not feel crazy.

LISA JONES: The *Voice*, it's that two-sided coin. The *Voice* was doing coverage that no one was doing. Could we have had more coverage? Yes. From different perspectives, more women writing about hip-hop? Yes. More younger people closer to the music and culture? Yes. But I'm grateful for what did happen there. It's always important to celebrate what did happen before critiquing what didn't.

At the same time, I appreciate how—this was the late '80s, going into the '90s—they were an incubation pod for Black freelance writers. They were the most important news organization to do that in the '90s. I don't know of another one that could claim such a record—not until the *Times*, in the *2010s*, starts to hire people. So that was like thirty years? We take for granted how much Black artists and artists of color are covered in the mainstream press. You can, any day, turn on the television and see a Black artist on an evening talk show or on the cover of *Entertainment Weekly*. But as late as the '90s, that was not the case.

HILTON ALS: I wanted to be a maker in the world, and I was emboldened by the *Voice* to become that person. Despite people like Stanley Crouch, there was the built-in queerness to it. And then that includes feminism, because of amazing people like Ellen Willis and Karen Durbin. And also Mim Udovitch and Mary Peacock and M Mark and Erika Munk. They were really super-smart women, and they all gave me a chance.

I had come from the *Voice* to *Vibe* and *New York Times* for a little while. Then when I went to the *New Yorker*, and I was writing something, and I was over [my word count], I went to the art department. I said, "Oh, maybe can we cut a few lines off the photograph?" I was so used to the *Voice*—I'd go to the art department and say, "Can you make the picture smaller?" I remember the next day Tina Brown called me and she said, "I want the picture large. I won't say that you don't have balls."

It was such a shock to go into the real world. I was spoiled there because I felt really seen as a writer and as a creator.

COLSON WHITEHEAD: There was more diversity than anyplace I'd been—which was like New York private school and Harvard.

JAMES HANNAHAM: It just felt like New York, like the cab idea of a subway car, the subway car that became an editorial staff.

COLSON WHITEHEAD: They seemed to hire a lot of young people of color, but not promote us. So, you'd never rise above assistant editor. But that meant there are a lot of people in their early twenties who were Black and Asian and were vocal about identity politics and in your face about multiculturalism, and I can't think of another place that was like that in '91, '92. We were like a real bloc, a cultural force—although you would never get really promoted that high, and you'd probably leave before then. You'd get poached by the *Times* or, like, some Condé Nast magazine if you had a certain amount of clout.

LISA KENNEDY: That place did have more writers of color per acre than any other publication. We probably were not very thoughtful about Asian Americans, because I know that there's all these weird blind spots you have as a person of color sometimes.

ANDREW HSIAO: We were kind of busting a move ourselves, right? When I gave a column to Jeff Yang, I remember Jeff and me looking around the whole country, and there were maybe two other Asian American columnists at any newspaper or magazine anywhere. And they were just doing kind of classic opinion column stuff. Whereas Jeff's column was Asian American culture; you can just devote yourself to this topic. We had columns by Enrique Fernandez on Latino culture. In the '90s era, we'd been bitterly criticized by all kinds of people from the left and from the right for being that archipelago of identities—there has to be the abortion column and the AIDS column and the queer column. It was that notion that somehow we were balkanizing ourselves into these discrete identities. I'm not saying there isn't some truth to that. But the multicultural concept was that it's going to be the glorious mosaic; we were going to take Asian American culture so seriously that we could devote an entire column just to that.

This is something very different from today. We saw our projects as a kind of allied multicultural joint project. I felt Greg's success or Colson's success was mine. That's what the *Voice* was doing. It's like centering all of us together, a wave of change.

BARRY MICHAEL COOPER: We changed the way the world looked at Black writers, not only in the '80s, but even now. Because, you know, God bless Rudy Langlais, God bless Bob Christgau, God bless, definitely, Michael Caruso, Scott Malcomson, Doug Simmons. These guys allowed us to really do us, to be ourselves. Because they knew they couldn't tell our stories. Only *we* could tell our stories. And they gave us the room to do it. "Don't edit yourself. Tell. Your. Story."

We at the *Village Voice*, we changed the world. And we will never see a time like that again. Ever. *Ever.*

1990–2000

"THERE WAS SOME SORT OF CULTURAL SHIFT THAT WE DIDN'T UNDERSTAND"

CHAPTER 63

"THE CULTURE THAT WE CHAMPIONED BECAME PART OF THE MAINSTREAM"

NELSON GEORGE: It used to be, the paper gets printed on Wednesday, people would read it on Friday for what they would do on the weekend. And then I'd get phone calls all weekend about articles I'd written. That sense of immediacy, that you were part of a New York City dialogue which the hippest, smartest people were reading—that began dissipating in the '90s, as the paper itself lost its own way.

Where the *Voice* had been the place for young Black writers to start, *Vibe* started siphoning off a lot of the talent that might have gone to the *Voice*. Now they can get real jobs, have a staff job, and not be under the thumb of white editors.

HILTON ALS: It was such a great paper, and then, during that time of great sadness in New York, it was becoming something else. It was becoming less of a raw place, and under Jonathan's leadership it was becoming a straighter magazine.

GARY DAUPHIN: The *New York Times* Style section, and all the concerns that became *New York Times* concerns in the '90s, were field-tested at the *Voice*.

LUCIAN K. TRUSCOTT IV: The way that the *New York Times* came along and started covering art, style, and the back-of-the-paper stuff came right out of the *Voice*. They hired Howard Blum; they hired Mary Breasted.

HOWARD BLUM: They were very censorious of the *Voice*. When I went to see Abe Rosenthal for my interview, he had to make sure you weren't some crazy hippie coming in with a T-shirt from the *Village Voice*, he said. There was real antagonism—probably because of Cockburn and Press Clips.

GARY DAUPHIN: The moment when Guy Trebay left the *Voice* to go to the *Times*, it was really, like, the jig is up.* Which is to say the notion of an alternative space where people did a certain kind of writing moved into the general cultural DNA.

JAMES HANNAHAM: I kind of despised and I still kind of despise the *New York Times*. Their hard-news reporting is fantastic. Their lifestyle pieces make you want to throw your phone at the wall, needling you and pushing all your hatred buttons. It always irritated me that people who were making downtown theater were concerned about the *Times* coming to review. I was like, "If the *Times* comes and likes your downtown performance, you're doing something wrong." They were natural enemies to me.

MICHAEL CARUSO: We were a nonentity to them, too. Although they mined us for stories. So, they read us. But they didn't know us. We didn't hang out in bars with people from the *Times* and the *Daily News*.

RICHARD GOLDSTEIN: The *Times* was our archenemy.

LUCIAN K. TRUSCOTT IV: After I left the *Voice*, I thought about working for the *Times*, so I got to know Abe Rosenthal and I talked to him a few times. I remember getting drunk with him one time, looking at him, and saying, "There's no way I would ever fucking work at the *New York Times*. It wouldn't work out. Me, my attitudes, and the way I am—I could never fit with it." And he said, "No, Lucian, you would never fit in there." I said, "Well, then fuck it. I don't want to work here."

JAMES RIDGEWAY: I could never see how being at the *New York Times* would be great. Once, I was asked to come to the *Times* for a job interview. I talked to them, and they were very polite. And the national editor said, "What do you think we could do to improve ourselves?" And I'd say, "You could take a position and start attacking people." And they said, "Well, I don't think you'd be happy here."

---

* Trebay left to join the *New York Times* in March 2000.

MANOHLA DARGIS: There was some sort of cultural shift that we didn't understand. The *New York Times* covered the Nuyorican Poets Cafe. I read that, and I thought, "Oh, shit. They're doing a story that we do."

MICHAEL CARUSO: If you call the end of the *Voice*'s "glory days" 1990, it was after that, that other places like the *Times* and *New York* magazine started covering the same sorts of political/gender identity issues, it started covering the same kind of music. The culture that we covered and championed became part of the mainstream, so you didn't need the *Voice* anymore.

What we were doing, what we were covering, what we were saying became part of the mainstream. And the *Voice* lost a lot of its cultural importance.

CHAPTER 64

"THE ART WORLD IS SO PECULIAR"

MICHAEL TOMASKY: When you think of the glory days of the *Voice*, I think of the late '60s and into the '70s—the Village of John and Yoko and CBGB's, Allen Ginsberg living over in Alphabet City. And going into the '80s, the art scene with Haring and Basquiat and Schnabel and people like that—that was really the *Voice*'s heyday. And then money and market pressures and gentrification and wealth started to disperse the community of people who read and supported the *Voice*.

JERRY SALTZ: As always, money came and then money went. And when it went, a lot of the '80s art world either collapsed or tastes started turning on a dime, especially when you had artists—quote-unquote barbarians at the gate—that are really good artists. Suddenly there were artists coming from everywhere. All of the YBA, young British artists, would take over. A whole merchant marine of people—they would just show up and say, "I'm a curator; I'm getting a storefront." And we would all go.

On my watch, I always call the 1990s the greatest generation because finally there are more women, and there are more artists of color. Still way short, but much more. There are artists from all over the world finally. And because money had left the art world again, the art world completely was in the hands of anyone who said, like me, that they were an artist, a critic, a curator, a museum person—anything you said you were in the 1990s. You could start an art fair. And that all happened. That was the period I got to cover. Chris Ofili. Damien Hirst. John Currin. Elizabeth Peyton. A Thai artist named Rirkrit Tiravanija. And then the return of money, of course.

JERRY SALTZ: The art world was dancing naked with nobody watching it in the 1970s. And the *Village Voice* was the beautiful watcher, the voyeur, the person, the place that reported that back. Carrie Rickey, Kim Levin—they were women probably for the first time getting a real shot.

ROBERTA SMITH: Until I got outside of the art world, I thought I was a complete fraud. Until I wrote for the *Voice*, I really thought I was the artist's spokesperson, and I wanted the artist to approve of my writing and agree with it. But at the *Voice* I was yanked out of that position almost violently. Writing for the *Voice* was completely exhilarating and the first time I didn't feel fraudulent, and I'd done it for about four years. Someone called me up one night and said, "Hey, I hear Gary Indiana has your job," which turned out to be true. And within a few weeks I was gone from the *Voice*, and my heart was completely broken because in a way I had been taken off a drug, which was writing for the *Voice*.

Finally, one night, John Russell from the *New York Times* called and asked me if I would like to fill in. And that was the beginning of being at the *Times*.

JERRY SALTZ: I actually had never read Roberta in the *Voice*. But I did read Gary Indiana, and man, that stuff was like dynamite—live-wire stuff. You have the '80s, and Peter Schjeldahl and Gary Indiana primarily covering appropriation like Cindy Sherman and Julian Schnabel, Basquiat—that's the early '80s. And then the shift to the late '80s, represented more by the cooler art of Jeff Koons, Richard Prince, coming into his own more.

JEFF WEINSTEIN: I became a staffer as a senior editor in 1980 or '81, to be in charge of the visual art and architecture criticism. Peter Schjeldahl was my chief critic. I was also working with Arlene Raven, Elizabeth Hess. I hired Gary Indiana and stuck with him until he freaked out and left. We did the NEA Four coverage, and we did the Robert Mapplethorpe coverage. I sent Betsy Hess to Cincinnati, where the trial was for Robert Mapplethorpe.

GARY INDIANA: I didn't even believe I could do anything until, quite honestly, I was almost thirty. After I came to New York in 1978, I experienced about three years of chaotic, impoverished, youthful excitement and desperate creative improvisation, followed by a decade of nonstop death of people around me from AIDS—while scrambling for survival the whole time by writing journalism. New York was never the same after the epidemic. In fact, it's been a horribly depressing, punitive city to live in ever since, thanks to the disappearance of so many vital people, and thanks to real estate developers and Wall Street.

Every week I tried to startle people in some way. It was basically an experiment in how many different ways you can carry out an inherently narrow task. I wasn't programmatic about the columns, because most of them were written at eleven o'clock on Sunday night to be turned in on Monday morning. I felt that much of art criticism was very flabby and rote. Why not make it something people would actually enjoy reading?

I was mostly interested in the work coming out of the intersection of the original conceptual art movement—Lawrence Weiner and Joseph Kosuth and so on—and a consciousness about how art functioned, how images functioned in society. I don't like to use jargony language, but there was what one might call a feminist revision of conceptual art going on. People like Jenny Holzer and Barbara Kruger and Sarah Charlesworth, Gretchen Bender, Jennifer Bolande. I was attracted to the kinds of art that I could connect to philosophically. I understood Louise Bourgeois's work right away.

When I had the column, I had a voice that carried quite far. And I was damned if I was going to fucking review art every week without talking about things that were of concern to me.

VINCE ALETTI: My first editing work there was temporarily filling in for Jeff Weinstein as he took a three-month or four-month vacation. I edited Gary Indiana.

GARY INDIANA: I never pilloried an artist unless it was Julian Schnabel. He was a good foil because he was being promoted as a great thing, but actually he's a good artist, he's a good filmmaker. I don't regret it because, you know what, you should only pick on people that are bigger than you are. I always thought, "He can take it." I'm never going to go after somebody that's only had one show in his or her life.

The *Voice* and *Artforum* are probably the only two places I've ever worked where there was absolutely no understanding that the only successful business principle in this country comes from the Mafia: you don't beat up on your own people.

VINCE ALETTI: The first person I wrote about was Dawoud Bey, who was very young, just starting out as a photographer, maybe his first or second gallery show. People are finally coming around to realize that there are all these major Black photographers who've been underrecognized or ignored, but Dawoud is really one of the best. I wrote about Sally Mann very early. She did a book called *Immediate Family* of portraits of her children that was very successful and then very controversial because some of her children were naked in the pictures and some people got very upset.

I was already very friendly with Peter Hujar, the photographer who lived across the street from me and who was never super famous in his lifetime but is now very known. And I was very conscious of him trying to make a living, making pictures all the time but not making money, and how do you put a light on a life and a career together as a photographer? What I did at the beginning was talk to people about why they did what they did, why they took these pictures, and then how they managed to make a life out of it. I wrote about Larry Clark and other people who were more known and successful, and Richard Avedon. But at the beginning I wanted to get to know working photographers and was curious about people starting out.

PETER SCHJELDAHL: I was brought back to the *Voice* from '91 to '98. The most fun I ever had was those years. The *Voice* in the '90s is a real secret treasure.

Because I'm a poet, the poetry kind of withered, and I discovered that there was nothing else I did very well in the world that they paid you for, except art criticism. And also, that I was good at it, and I liked it. With *7 Days*—and then the *Voice*—I had that beautiful weekly rhythm. It's easier to write every week than less frequently. You don't let the power plant cool down, you know? I was able to write about a lot of the new painters: Schnabel, David Salle, and also Cindy Sherman. Eric Fischl, Anselm Kiefer, Sigmar Polke, the Germans.

The '90s were dominated by this surge of deconstruction and poststructuralism and theory and academe, all of whom had absolute contempt for me. You know, belles lettres? And beautiful letters, what's wrong with those? I pushed back against that to some extent. It was exciting.

In the '90s, there had been a recession, and the market crashed in the early '90s. That made it an interesting time. Then there was the appearance of Jeff Koons. My first column on him, my lede sentence: "Jeff Koons makes me sick." And then I said, "My reaction interests me."

It was the *Banality* show. It was carvings and casts of kitsch. Michael Jackson and his monkey. It was a great show, and it was a game-changing show. The fact that I didn't like it is incidental data. I was completely aware of its significance and of its quality, and I affirmed those.

The next day, I was working on West Broadway, and Jeff Koons was across the street. And he ran across. He said, "Peter, 'Jeff Koons makes me sick!' That's so great. That's so great."

It was hyperexpensive to make, and it looked like it was. And that became part of the content. France had a Jeff Koons show at Versailles, and it was perfect, where the first thing you did about being rich was to look rich. It's almost a civic duty.

Koons prophesied this oligarchic moment that we're still in, which I really hate. I really hate the inequality and the rule of money and how price has taken over value. But art is not equipped to change the world; it can be more or less truthful about the world. And Jeff Koons had that value.

And then I got the call from the *New Yorker*.

JERRY SALTZ: When Peter quit, we both racked our brains—who could replace him? Neither of us thought of me. To me, that was a really bigwig position. I completely 100 percent learned on the job. I went to art school, but I have no degrees. I was always in the art world in Chicago, where I'm from. I started an artist-run gallery. I tried to be an artist and then completely failed and had a walking nervous breakdown—which, I did not know then, but everybody has when they're twenty-seven—and stopped making art forever. I was a gigantic loser. Huge. A truck driver, still.

Vince and Roberta basically saved me. In the first year, Roberta said one of the best things she's ever said to me: "If you don't get better, I'm going to kill myself."

The *Voice* is different. That's where I learned the most important lesson, which is, one, you write for the reader—I learned that from Roberta. Two, you really don't have any time to lie.

CHAPTER 65

"INDEPENDENT FILMS WERE COMING INTO THEIR OWN DURING THE '90s"

COLSON WHITEHEAD: The film section was such an advocate for indie film—John Sayles and Spike Lee and David Lynch. That was a real training in production of art, how to talk about art, and having the courage to follow your own weird dream. They took film seriously and taught a lot of people how to watch movies.

LISA KENNEDY: I really did have the best writers in America. I had Jim Hoberman, Manohla Dargis, Amy Taubin, and Georgia Brown, who had come from *7 Days*. They were all very different.

AMY TAUBIN: David Edelstein had terrible writing blocks. For about a year he came in with his—what do you call them? Comfort animals? His was a rabbit.

J. HOBERMAN: We often got lumped together. It's like "intellectual critics interested in obscure things"—this was the rap. The film editor was a referee.

MANOHLA DARGIS: I felt really good when Lisa became the editor. First of all, there was a feminist who was now the film editor. She gave me a range of things to do. I covered a lot of the gay and lesbian experimental film festivals. Later on, Karen Durbin, at her finest, wrote this great piece about her empathy for the Glenn Close character in *Fatal Attraction*. I just thought that was *awesome*, man. There were these really, really great feminists, but it was always a struggle.

ANN POWERS: There was this older generation of women critics. The conversations I had, especially with Amy Taubin, with M Mark, with Cindy Carr—a little bit younger, Donna Minkowitz—were so influential in opening my mind. Amy wrote a piece about *Naked*, by Mike Leigh, and she coined the term "hate-fucking" to talk about this misogynist character. You couldn't do that at another media outlet.

MOLLY HASKELL: Amy and Hoberman were both more interested in independent films. And independent films were coming into their own during that period.

MANOHLA DARGIS: The *Voice* has this long tradition—it's really important—of covering everything seriously. Big movies, little movies, no money, big money, everything.

J. HOBERMAN: I was always promoting Chantal Akerman whenever her movies were showing. Chantal Akerman is this Belgian feminist filmmaker. She made *Jeanne Dielman*, this three-and-a-half-hour movie, basically—a lot of it in real time—of three days in a woman's life. It's more than a landmark; it's an amazing movie. Finally, it got a run at Film Forum. Karen Durbin saw it, and she really liked it, and she recognized that it also was a feminist statement. So, she put it on the cover.

Todd Haynes, I remember reviewing his Super 8 film *Superstar: The Karen Carpenter Story*, and then reviewing *Poison*, the next movie he made. The *Voice* was really behind him. It is sort of shocking that Jim Jarmusch's *Dead Man* got completely ignored by the lamestream press. But these people, Lynch and Jarmusch and Todd Haynes—I mean, it didn't take all that long for them to become names, at least among film circles.

When *Bad Lieutenant* came out, it came out the same week as Coppola's *Dracula*. And Coppola's *Dracula* was supposed to be the big movie, and I just flipped them because that movie is a piece of shit and I loved *Bad Lieutenant*. I went to see this David Mamet show, *Oleanna*; it was playing downtown. And in the intermission there's Abel Ferrara, the director—this is the week that my review of *Bad Lieutenant* came out. He said, "Your check is in the mail."

LISA KENNEDY: We were thoughtful about that '91, '92 boom in Black film: *Boyz n the Hood*, the Hudlin brothers' films. Those were the start of movies that coalesced with what was going on in hip-hop.

NELSON GEORGE: There's a lot of *Voice* columns I wrote during that period, actually, about L.A. The first time John Singleton was written about in the press was probably an article I did in the *Village Voice*. I read the script to *Boyz n the Hood* thanks to Russell Simmons. I wrote a whole thing about L.A. and the gang thing and about this promising young filmmaker. Then you had *Menace II Society*. A lot of the people who were in hip-hop in New York started moving out there, trying to get into films.

It was a very fraught time to be out there. The riot had just happened, Rodney King, and O. J. happened. Luckily I was able to write about a lot of that stuff through the column I did at the *Voice*, Native Son.

Barry was also in Hollywood during that same time. He wrote *New Jack City*, which was a huge hit, and slightly based on his work at the *Voice*.

MICHAEL CARUSO: That was part of that timeline of the *Voice* becoming mainstream.

LISA KENNEDY: Jim taught Manohla. That's sort of how she came to the *Voice*.

MANOHLA DARGIS: I was in graduate school at NYU, getting a master's in cinema studies. The only writing class was taught by Jim Hoberman, who I really didn't know. I knew he wrote for the *Voice*. I took this class, and he really liked me. He ended up quoting me in the *Voice*; I forget why. Then at some point after class, I got a call from Howard Feinstein, who was the film editor at the time. He first asked me if I was "exotic," code for "was I not white?" He thought my name seemed Hawaiian or something. He was like, "Do you know anything about the avant-garde?" I'm like, "Yeah, I've seen some." They offered me a job writing about avant-garde cinema, because nobody at that point really wanted to do it.

They brought me in, and they gave me a column. It was ridiculous. I had never published anything. I had written one newspaper article for my high school paper when I was in seventh grade, and that was it.

So, my first piece was published in the *Voice*, and it was a column. It was called Counter Currents. Immediately after my first column, this group of forty different filmmakers called on the *Voice* to fire me. [*Laughs*.]

AMY TAUBIN: The greatest editor I had—and Manohla Dargis probably says the same thing—was Lisa Kennedy. Because of the way she thinks about writing, she encouraged "What do you think?" Not "I have this certain position; I should support this." Her writing was about very personal stuff.

MANOHLA DARGIS: One of the first pieces that I was really happy with was a think piece on *Thelma and Louise* with Lisa. Lisa really helped me start to become a writer; I was starting to feel confident that I actually had something to say that people wanted to hear. Because that was really hard. Hoberman's shadow was very, very big.

LISA KENNEDY: Amy has a really great feel for American independents and what they can do. She saw things earlier that were rough from young American filmmakers that spoke to her, and she could really tease out.

AMY TAUBIN: Sometime in the '70s, Jonas Mekas, who had left the *Voice* the first time they tried to edit him, had gone to the *SoHo News*, and then the *SoHo News* decided they would edit him, so he left there. And he said to me, "You know about avant-garde film, and you can write, so take over my column." It was the easiest entrance into journalism.

J. HOBERMAN: Amy had a very strong interest in avant-garde, but more than that. She was around during a really fertile period for filmmaking in the '60s. The word "hipster" is so poisoned now, but she always had a sense of what was going on.

AMY TAUBIN: I did a column called Art and Industry. It lasted about five years. I did a lot of interviews with people who were totally unknown, like then producers Ted Hope and James Schamus, people who went on to become major studio figures.

J. HOBERMAN: She liked to defend and help young filmmakers. She was very into the whole Sundance thing. Much more than I was; I hated Sundance. I was more into foreign filmmakers and not as interested in personal relationships with them. Amy did like to do a lot of interviews; she liked to know these filmmakers and champion them.

AMY TAUBIN: Manohla and I both got onto Larry Clark's *Kids*.

I interviewed Harmony Korine, and it was the first time Harmony had ever talked to anyone. Harmony was living in that little apartment over on

Spring Street near Lafayette, and he was living with Chloë Sevigny, and she was eighteen. They were magical, the two of them. And Chloë was smart and knew that she was going to have another kind of life.

AMY TAUBIN: As part of this indie column, I would go to the Independent Feature Market. It was where people showed their films that they had made for absolutely no money. The first year I covered it, I wrote about Richard Linklater's *Slacker*; it was there and not completed. I was probably the first person who wrote about *Go Fish*.* I wrote in my Sundance piece about Todd Haynes's *Poison*. I wrote a huge piece on *My Own Private Idaho*, by Gus Van Sant.

KEVIN SMITH: I was working at this video store for a couple of years, and this guy, Vincent, was the mop boy. One night we just started talking about *Twin Peaks* for some reason. Suddenly we realized that we both liked movies.

One week we read this review in the *Village Voice* about *Slacker*. The review was really good, and the movie just sounded wacked. On my twenty-first birthday we went up to New York to see the movie, and that was the key moment: watching that movie and finding it amusing and different. I thought, "How could someone make a movie like this? There's no plot." And then hearing the audience just go nuts around us. I decided, "That's what I want to do with my life."

The first piece ever written about *Clerks* was by Amy Taubin in the *Village Voice*, and it was after the IFFM (Independent Feature Film Market) in 1993, where it was screened for the first time. She was like, "His style is that he has no style." And I always thought that was really funny, but it's true. It's a conscious effort to not do something wacky.

AMY TAUBIN: It was a guy who had decided to put a world that he knew on film, accurately. And it was fabulous. And it was funny. And it was exciting. So, I thought, "I'll make this column about Kevin Smith."

I called him up, and I said, "This is Amy Taubin. I write for the *Village Voice*." And he said, "You've got to be kidding. Who are you?" And hung up. Really, he thought someone was putting him on.

---

* A groundbreaking lesbian rom-com cowritten by Rose Troche and Guinevere Turner.

I call him back up, and I said, "Kevin, this is the real Amy Taubin. I think your film is wonderful, and I want to interview you because I want to write about you."

He said, "I have the poster with your quote on Richard Linklater's *Slacker* on my wall."

KEVIN SMITH: And she goes, "Well, this is going to be the best interview I've ever done."

AMY TAUBIN: It didn't take much for people to think that I had an eye for this stuff, because *Clerks* was enormously successful. And Kevin went on to be very successful.

AMY TAUBIN, "ART AND INDUSTRY," *VILLAGE VOICE*, OCTOBER 26, 1993

Clerks is the kind of unprepossessing, but enormously talented, first feature that one goes to the market to discover and might easily overlook. Shot in no-budget 16mm black and white, directed, written, and acted with wit and authenticity, it's about a day in the life of a young Asbury Park convenience-store clerk, his friends, lovers, customers, and companion animals. Less glamorous and formally innovative than *Slacker* or *Stranger Than Paradise*, it makes absence of style a virtue in its depiction of blue-collar suburban depression and desire.

AMY TAUBIN: What I learned from Jonas was that the things you care about, you are writing about them for history, and probably most of them will only exist in history because you've written about them. *Clerks* got into Sundance because of my story.

KEVIN SMITH: I will remember that piece on my deathbed.

CHAPTER 66

"I'VE ALWAYS CALLED IT BAJ, BLACK ADVOCACY JOURNALISM"

PETER NOEL: I came to the United States in 1978, and I lived in Harlem a couple of blocks away from the *Amsterdam News*. I started working the day after the Fourth of July. It was the city's biggest Black weekly at the time, and I was just cutting my teeth, trying to do police brutality stories. I was doing feature stories at a small paper in Trinidad, and when I came to this country the issue was police and Black communities.

About three weeks after I started working for the *Amsterdam News*, I picked up a copy of the *Village Voice*. Wayne Barrett was writing about New York City politics. Wayne went into the weeds on issues concerning policy, concerning the city administration, police, and communities, and I said, "Yeah, this is *exactly* what I want to do." I wanted to bring it to the Black press, but I did not want to work for the white press. But the *Amsterdam News* at the time was just interested in "Two people died in a fire today; police suspect arson."

I was covering a case for the *Amsterdam News*. It was a shooting of a Hispanic guy. My story appeared on the front page of the *Amsterdam News*, and Wayne Barrett cited the reporting in this piece, and I call him up. We started talking, we started joking with each other, and he said, "Man, you do some good work, but I think you should come here." I said, "Wayne, I don't think so," but we continued talking, and that gave me a whole level of confidence.

TOM ROBBINS: We did a lot about Sharpton back then. We had a story that every one of us is on the byline. We thought we were providing the

Peter Noel in his cubicle at 36 Cooper Square, 2000. Photo © Georgia
Popplewell.

goods that showed what a fraud Sharpton was, that he would never be able
to raise his head, because we proved that he had been an FBI informant. He
had tried to help the FBI capture Assata Shakur—this famous Black Liberation Army figure, formerly Joanne Chesimard. She's still down in Cuba.
And the fact that he had been hooked up with mobsters and done deals.

In those days, Sharpton had none of the facade that he has now of respect-
ability. He was just this porky guy with a huge peace medallion wandering
around and just looking to get his name in there. He's clearly brilliant, but he
was so twisted, and nothing he said was true, so he just made himself such
an obvious target. We had this enormous story—front-page story—about
Sharpton, which, we thought, "This is really going to be the end of him as a
prime mover." Boy, were we wrong.

MARTIN GOTTLIEB: Joe and Wayne in particular had written about
Sharpton in devastating ways in the past. They found this one guy who was
caught in a city scandal who went to high school with Sharpton and told
these stories about how he rigged—I forget if it was the senior class—it was
some kind of lottery that they had where you got a ticket for one dollar, and
then they called out your number. There's the whole auditorium filled. Sharpton is the head of his class, and he pulls out the ticket. And he says, "And the
winner is. . . . Hey, I won!" And the place goes berserk and chases him off.

JOE CONASON: Sharpton was a crook. Like, seriously, a crook. I don't think he is anymore. He was put up to run for president in 2004 by Roger Stone—you know that, right? A fucking crook, OK?

PETER NOEL: The paper was actually steadily losing Black readership, and they needed somebody to come in. I got the call again from the *Village Voice* because they wanted someone to cover the Central Park trial. Richard Goldstein and I, we instantly hit it off. I said, "Look, I have a particular style." Richard said, "You need to cross that style over to our readership, too—not just Black people reading the *Voice*, liberal whites, too, but they have their own prejudices." I said, "My type of journalism, I've always called it BAJ, Black advocacy journalism. Do not give me an ideological edit. Edit me for different things, structure, but not ideology, not in terms of, like, politics." Richard said, "We have a deal."

Tawana Brawley, the Central Park Five, and all the other police brutality issues—all of those pieces came together.

Bastone and I had two dueling pieces—I did a piece showing Al Sharpton apologized, and he did a piece where he looked into Al Sharpton's mob contacts, that type of thing. So that kind of rivalry went on.

MARIA LAURINO: There was a sense that Peter was too close to Sharpton. And Sharpton had never been a hero to Wayne and Bill Bastone. There was definitely some tension there.

PETER NOEL: I went to the bathroom one day, and I saw on the wall "Peter Noel is Al Sharpton's mouthpiece." "Peter Noel is a stooge." "Al Sharpton's spy." "Peter Noel is a member of the Nation of Islam." This type of thing. This is this great bastion of liberalism—in their bathroom, all of these things were written against me. I wrote back, "Fuck you all." Because if you had gone to the *Village Voice* at the time, it was like graffiti central. They actually cleaned up the graffiti from the bathroom after that.

JOE CONASON: There was friction between Peter and Wayne over that stuff. Sharpton was the representative of the old Brooklyn machine against the guys we liked, who were the insurgent Black politicians, Al Vann and Major Owens, who was very close to Wayne. It sounds weird that you'd favor one side if you're a reporter, but that's the kind of thing we did. We did advocacy reporting, and it wasn't hard to choose the one over the other.

PETER NOEL: Wayne said, "Well, we have to cover the fact that he's doing it, and is he doing it because of his ego? Is he doing it because he's beholden to other people who are using him as a puppet?"

I said, "Well, yes, we may have to say that, but we can't ignore the fact that he's fighting for justice, that a young Black kid was run down in a moped by a police officer, or a young Black man was strangled by some police officer in some kind of choke hold, and we ignore that?" I said, "This is my role here." Wayne wanted me to come to him and clear stories before I did it.

NELSON GEORGE: That's why Sharpton is an interesting character. He was considered a corrupt politician. What was wrong with that coverage, and what's wrong with what's going on in media now, is that they define someone at one point in time, and that's all they're ever gonna be. And amazingly enough, as they get older, people do evolve. People who did shitty stuff—that doesn't mean they didn't do shitty stuff, but they sometimes do good stuff. And sometimes people who did good stuff do shitty stuff.

Peter was able to go and get Black people to talk to him who wouldn't talk to them, and get other stories and other points of view that the *Voice* just wasn't representing. The *Voice* idea was that everyone was corrupt, and so we're looking for the bad thing. Peter was looking for both the corruption and the goodness.

PETER NOEL: Later on, Wayne and I got into a fight over Major Owens, who was a congressman in Brooklyn. He belonged to a certain type of club that Wayne promoted: progressive Black politics. There was also Una Clarke, who was also an up-and-coming politician. She was with the city council, she was from Jamaica, she was fighting people like Major Owens. So, I was writing a piece one day about Una Clarke. Wayne saw the piece on the Atex system and called me and said, "Noel, what is this you're writing about? I told you, you got to come to me." I said, "Listen to me. Major Owens is your nigga; he ain't mine." Wayne looked at me, he smirked a little bit, and we stopped speaking after that for years.

RICHARD GOLDSTEIN: They would hold political endorsement meetings—all men, all white. I had to shoehorn Peter Noel into those meetings. They were furious, especially Wayne. I said, "He writes politics, he's going to be in here."

WILLIAM BASTONE: There could have certainly been a better racial balance [in the news section]. But we would be as guilty of that as just about every other fucking publication at that point in time. I'd say the paper was much better than any other publication around.

PETER NOEL: They were totally resistant, but somehow Larsen said I had to be in there, and they relented. I said, "Look, here's a candidate running in Brooklyn in a district that's really changing. There was a lot of West Indians, but the demographics are changing, and you need to endorse that person who's running in that area." After a while we started endorsing certain people who would never before have gotten that type of endorsement.

RICHARD GOLDSTEIN: We were able to hire and work with people who actually were living the thing they wrote about. Peter Noel was actually at the Slave Theater.* He knew very, very intimately what radical Black politics was like, because he was part of it. Especially the West Indian community—who on earth would cover the West Indian community in New York? Peter knew it intimately—not just because of his identity, but because he knew all these people. I worked for about four months with him on a story about homophobia in the West Indian community. And it was called "Batty Boys in Babylon." Now, who would have imagined that on the front page of a newspaper? What is a batty boy? What is Babylon? Well, you have to know that.

PETER NOEL, "BATTY BOYS IN BABYLON," *VILLAGE VOICE*, JANUARY 12, 1993

Eight years ago in the slums of Trench Town, Jamaica, a would-be murderer named Slickest threw the first stone at Douche, a homosexual who loved to drag in poom-poom shorts and emulate the swagger of a rude batty woman.

"I stoned 'im. I beat 'im with sticks. I'm proud of it," Slickest growls as he recalls the incident to a reporter and friends while browsing in Ethiopian Taste, a record shop on Nostrand Avenue.

The ambush occurred the day Slickest was being initiated into a rudebwoy posse that roamed the alleyways of the island's shanty towns in

---

* Located in Bed-Stuy, it served as a center for Black civil rights activism in the '80s.

search of the much reviled batty bwoys, as homosexuals are known. In these tin-can dungles, it's a mark of manhood to assault or even snuff a batty bwoy in cold blood.

RICHARD GOLDSTEIN: Anyway, the paper sold through the roof because West Indians bought it. It was one of our best sellers. But getting the language of that piece to cross over and be legible—it took us months to do that.

PETER NOEL: It was the fourth-largest-selling issue in the history of the *Village Voice*.

CHAPTER 67

"WAYNE WAS THE FIRST GUY WHO WROTE A BIOGRAPHY OF DONALD TRUMP AND RUDY GIULIANI"

TIMOTHY L. O'BRIEN: I was at Columbia University in the journalism school doing a joint degree with journalism and an MBA. Wayne came to speak to the school about investigative reporting. He was getting started on a book about Trump and asked one of my professors for someone to work with him as a research assistant who had business and political knowledge. I was highly interested, of course, and so I went to work for him.

TOM ROBBINS: Wayne got a deal to write a biography of Trump. That was at the time that Donald had gotten into Atlantic City. It looked like he was really riding high.

DONALD TRUMP: Barrett, whose last book was a major disaster, is still trying to make his name at my expense. He is, I have heard, writing a book about me. The good news for me is that he's never been a writer who could capture or hold anyone's interest.

TIMOTHY L. O'BRIEN: We found out that Trump's birthday party was at the Trump Taj Mahal in one of the main auditoriums. And because they didn't have enough people attending the party, they had thrown the doors open to casino patrons so they could make sure they could fill up the auditorium. So, we thought, "Let's just go, put on coats and ties, and show up and see if we can get in." We walked to the entrance of one of the main auditoriums to the Taj, and I, of course, didn't get recognized.

It wasn't a birthday party by anyone's normal standards. Trump was up on a stage in front of an audience, and Joe Piscopo came out and sang ballads to Trump mimicking Frank Sinatra, and Trump—who was just about to go on an epic and almost fatal slide into bankruptcy—was there presiding over this cult of personality. It wasn't really a birthday party as much as it was a weird, cheap Broadway revue with vaudevillians. That's how he lived every day. Everything about him is the cult of personality.

Wayne, of course, was completely recognized right away by Trump's security. And they said, "You can't go in there."

They began arguing, and I just took a glass of champagne off one of the nearby platters while they were focusing on Wayne. I walked right in and sat down and was there for the whole birthday celebration. Wayne got arrested, and they locked him up in a cell in Atlantic City that night.

WAYNE BARRETT: I'm not there five minutes and they slap the handcuffs on me. Defiant trespass, I was charged with. Not just trespass, man, I was charged with *defiant* trespass. That's a good representation of how Donald felt about me. All the cops down there moonlit for him. At the time he owned 40 percent of the hotel rooms, so the sergeant that arrested me was moonlighting for Donald.

TOM ROBBINS: Wayne writes in his book, "While I stood there handcuffed to a wall, I realized that Trump was probably never going to cooperate with this biographer." I told him it was the best few pages he ever wrote in his life.

DONALD TRUMP: Wayne is a very bad writer.

TIMOTHY L. O'BRIEN: Trump had crashed. He was a has-been by the time the book came out.

JOE CONASON: The fact that Democratic politicians wanted to promote Trump and help Trump and give Trump deals upset Wayne. He just thought this guy was not deserving and he was a con man. Why were all these Democratic politicians giving him whatever he wanted? And it wasn't just Koch; it was also Cuomo and Andrew Stein, who was the borough president at the time. Andrew was very close to Trump. Wayne was on the warpath. He was gonna expose this guy. And he did, repeatedly.

JONATHAN Z. LARSEN: All the criminals coming in and out of Trump Tower, the helicopter pilot who was a drug dealer—oh, he had some incredible stuff—and the Russian mobsters. There is just an amazing amount of stuff in that book. It's a treasure trove.

I didn't even really want to put him on the cover of the *Village Voice*, but it was a deal that Wayne made with Schneiderman, that he would get this sabbatical and then we would excerpt his book when it came out. So, there we were.

WILLIAM BASTONE: How is it even possible that he was the first guy who wrote a biography of Donald Trump *and* Rudy Giuliani? What are the odds?

GARY DAUPHIN: The *Voice* is a place that needs something to be in opposition to. The Clinton years were not a great time for the paper just because there was not a lot to be in opposition to. The paper fared best in periods when there was a really clear enemy. Giuliani was really bracing for the paper's local coverage.

WILLIAM BASTONE: Our interest in Giuliani began mid-'80s—'85, '86—the beginning of the largest municipal corruption scandals in the modern history of New York City. Our first introduction to Giuliani was as the guy who was going to clean up a system that we knew to be corrupt and criminal.

Giuliani was the United States Attorney's head of the Southern District, and he was driving the most serious investigations into New York City government that had taken place in decades. So, we got to know him. We've been writing about this sort of shit for a decade. This was the first time that anybody in a law-enforcement capacity looked at this stuff and thought, "These are crimes. This is racketeering."

For whatever reason, he decided, "I'm going to be the guy who breaks up the five Mafia families in New York, and I'm also going to be the guy who cleans up New York City politics." For us, at the time, that seemed refreshing.

MARIA LAURINO: It was hard to ever say that there was a time when Rudy Giuliani was charming—but in a very, very slim way, before he became completely an insane man, there was this admiration for Giuliani. Giuliani came in to the *Voice* before we did endorsements. We'd have these meetings where you interview the candidates. Rudy married his second cousin. He wanted to marry Donna Hanover, he wanted to get married in the church, so he pretended he didn't know that it was his cousin that he married.

I asked this question about, "How could you not know you married your cousin?" And Wayne went *ballistic* on me. We did not talk for six months, because he was so mad at me that I asked Rudy Giuliani an inappropriate question.

I said, "Well, I don't think it's an inappropriate question. I think it's a question about his moral view of the world. He married his cousin, he lied about it, he's getting an annulment from the church in order to get married to Donna Hanover, so I think it's a legitimate question."

It was an early sign of what Rudy would turn into.

WILLIAM BASTONE: Whatever good feelings the paper had towards him—and Wayne had towards him—didn't last too long into his desire to be the mayor of New York. Anybody who covered Giuliani's first campaign, the one that Dinkins won, and then the second Giuliani campaign—we knew what he was about by then. He was a nasty motherfucker who had a race problem.

And played dirty, frankly. Right before he was elected, I did a cover story and Wayne did the second story about Giuliani. My piece was about how Giuliani used a federal investigator who was attached to the Southern District as his dirt digger—this guy dug up dirt about Dinkins, people who worked for Dinkins, before that Ed Koch—and how he tried to weaponize this stuff for political gain.

MAC BARRETT: Wayne saw Rudy in a very ugly episode, where he was getting ready to run for mayor in '89 and looking to expose Koch's rumored homosexuality to get himself elected. And it was unsuccessful in that, but the effort was ugly in itself. The more he just looked into the man, the more problematic the man became.

WILLIAM BASTONE: Wayne did an accompanying piece about Trump's relationship with Giuliani and how there was an investigation of Trump in the United States Attorney's office that got torpedoed once Trump pledged his backing to help Giuliani get elected. Once his ambitions showed themselves, we had no use for the fucking guy.

MARIA LAURINO: Wayne broke the most incredible stories. He was the one who found the records that showed that Rudy's father had been sent to jail because he worked for the mob. This was Mr. RICO, "I'm gonna prosecute the mob."* Rudy Giuliani's father changed his name, and Wayne got the records. Rudy Giuliani's father—what do you call people, they beat you up if you don't deliver your money?

WILLIAM BASTONE: He had an antipathy towards the Black community that showed itself all the time. He thought it was the greatest thing in the world that he made it a point never to talk about or meet with Al Sharpton. Now, you can say that there are reasons not to do that, and some of those might be legitimate. But he wanted nothing to do with the African American community in the city. Nothing.

The city had emerged from a lot of really bad problems that hung around Dinkins, and he benefited. The crack epidemic, Crown Heights, the murder rate was monstrous—Giuliani was in the right place at the right time.

When he won reelection, it was at a time when there was economic prosperity in the city and in the country. He knew that he had enough control and support in white communities, and that was all he really needed. There was never any outreach to Black communities. Wayne lived in Ocean Hill-Brownsville through the '70s. He lived in Black communities; he had massive numbers of Black friends. And when he saw Giuliani doing this? Giuliani was dead to him.

JONATHAN Z. LARSEN: They hated each other. I had written maybe the first big piece on Giuliani for *Manhattan, inc.* when he was US attorney.** He was an incredibly good US attorney. He really was.

I had stayed in touch with his number-two guy. When I got to the *Voice*, I immediately realized, "Oh my god, Wayne and Giuliani hate each other." So, I dropped all contact with Rudy myself. Because we were attacking him in the *Village Voice* he didn't want to hear from me, and then I went after

---

* The Racketeer Influenced and Corrupt Organizations (RICO) Act of 1970 defines thirty-five offenses that comprise racketeering.
** *Manhattan, inc.* was a monthly magazine covering high-profile New York business figures that published from 1984 to 1990.

Rudy with this Jackie Mason article. We basically prevented him from becoming mayor first time around. Robbie Friedman's piece—that was fabulous. That was the whole schvartzer thing with Dinkins.*

Giuliani said horrible things about Blacks in general. Everybody picked that up, and then *Newsweek*—one of their reporters dug in his notes and found the schvartzer quote, which they had been sitting on and had not published. That whole Jackie Mason thing was so embarrassing for Giuliani, and he didn't lose by much.

MICHAEL TOMASKY: Giuliani was the avatar of Archie Bunker New York.

---

* Mason, a comedian, had called Dinkins a "fancy schvartze with a mustache." *Schvartze* or *schvartzer* is an offensive Yiddish term for a Black servant or employee. Mason was stumping for Giuliani, and the news about Mason's comment helped sink Giuliani's campaign.

CHAPTER 68
"I WAS VERY IGNORANT ABOUT TRANS PEOPLE"

"CROSS-DRESSER KILLED TWO WEEKS AFTER TOWN LEARNED HER TRUE IDENTITY," JANUARY 1, 1994

HUMBOLDT, Neb. (AP)—A woman who posed as a man and dated women was found shot to death with two other people two weeks after residents of this rural area learned her true identity. . . .

Friends said Brandon, 21, had posed for two months as a man named Brandon Teena and had told various stories of having an incomplete sex-change operation or of being a hermaphrodite.

RICHARD GOLDSTEIN: Donna Minkowitz did a lot of work that might be considered transgressive. She was a growing writer, and transgression was our currency.

DONNA MINKOWITZ: I grew up in Brooklyn to a fucked-up, working-class, intellectual Jewish family, and we read the *Voice*. My whole family would read the personal ads aloud to each other.

Richard Goldstein was the czar of all queer content at the *Voice*. That's how he described himself. I wooed him, and it worked. I shared a column with Richard, which we called Body Politics.

Richard called me into his office because there was an AP piece in the *Times* about Brandon's murder, and he was very excited about it. We were excited at what we thought was the story of a woman who lived as a man and dated all these young women who thought she was a man and just successfully did her thing there in rural Nebraska, and then got killed because people couldn't take it.

I saw it as a story of horror. These two young men raped Brandon Teena to punish him for being a trans man, and then when he reported the rape, they came back and looked for him and killed him.

I went out to Nebraska. What surprised me was how naked people's homophobia and transphobia was. From my work in the *Voice*, I had traveled to a lot of parts of the country, writing about antigay things. I don't think I had come across quite as retrograde a social scene in terms of queer and trans stuff as I did in in Lincoln, Nebraska, and then Falls City. It was much worse in Falls City, which was really rural.

In Falls City, I interviewed Lana Tisdel, Brandon's girlfriend, and Lana's mother and sister. Lana and her family told me everybody looked down on their family because her sister dated Black men and they hung out with Black people—they were a white family—and also because they were on welfare. I went to Brandon's high school in Lincoln, and there were all these kids who'd died, but there was no memorial for Brandon, and the school wouldn't talk to me about his death.

DONNA MINKOWITZ: Then the piece came out, and I was shocked to be criticized. I saw my piece as being firmly on Brandon's side. I was startled and probably wounded when trans activists immediately were really critical of the piece. They put up big posters outside the *Voice* saying something like, "*Village Voice* is murdering transsexuals," because then, the trans movement was using the term "transsexual."

The group that protested us was called the Transexual Menace. They had a demonstration in front of the *Voice*. I had never been the subject of a demonstration. In a way, it made me feel important. It was very surreal.

RIKI WILCHINS: There were probably fourteen or sixteen of us, all in black "Transexual Menace" T-shirts right outside the office of the *Voice*, just flyering like crazy. And it was very freeing. It was very exciting. None of us had ever done anything like that. We had purposely made sure to print up a whole bunch of the black "Transexual Menace" T-shirts, with red, dripping,

Rocky Horror lettering on the front, very tongue-in-cheek, and basically said, we're going to block off the building, and anyone who goes in or out of this block gets a flyer.

DONNA MINKOWITZ: I took notes at the demonstration. They didn't know who I was. Then suddenly, someone eventually asked me, "Who are you?" Then they came up to the office to talk to me. Some of the activists were really nice. Leslie Feinberg was not nice and really yelled at me.

LESLIE FEINBERG: This article is a psychosexual, salacious view. It says clearly that Brandon Teena did not identify as a woman and a lesbian, and yet it insists on referring to her as "she" and a lesbian, dwells on the sexual aspects, and even implies that having been raped as a child shaped his identity.

KIMBERLY PEIRCE: I read it, and I fell in love with Brandon. It made me love his vulnerability, his daring, his innocence, the way that he gave pleasure sexually. I was in love with this person who had shaped himself.

DONNA MINKOWITZ: These film companies contacted me to option. I eventually did an option for no money.

KIMBERLY PEIRCE: I was in graduate school at a straight, white, heteronormative environment, living uptown at Columbia University. I want to tell this story of this person who lived and loved as a man. There was no paradigm for that.

At the time that I got interested in Brandon Teena's story, I didn't know trans people, and the lesbians that I knew didn't know trans people. There was not much overlap that I ever saw between trans people and what we would call gay people back then. I knew Brandon was a trans man, and so I was looking for trans people to talk to, both MTF and FTM.* I wanted to understand Brandon on his own terms.

I'm reaching into the dark in a culture that hadn't yet articulated this for itself. And that's important. The culture didn't have a foothold—nor did gay culture have a workout place—for sexual preference, gender identity.

DONNA MINKOWITZ: I use both male and female pronouns for Brandon in the piece. I wanted to honor Brandon's use of the word "he," and I

---

* Male to female and female to male.

also wanted how I use the pronouns to showcase how these different people were fighting over Brandon.

LESLIE FEINBERG: It's not so much how I see Brandon Teena as how Brandon Teena saw himself. I use the pronoun "he" because (a), it's the pronoun Brandon Teena chose, but (b), it's ultimately what he died for.

DONNA MINKOWITZ, "LOVE HURTS," *VILLAGE VOICE*, APRIL 19, 1994

However they classify Brandon, everybody wants her. From photos of the wonder-boychik playing pool, kissing babes, and lifting a straight male neighbor high up in the air to impress party goers at her and Gina's engagement party, Brandon looks to be the handsomest butch item in history—not just good-looking, but arrogant, audacious, cocky—everything they, and I, look for in lovers.

DONNA MINKOWITZ: I was very ignorant about trans people. Many of us in the gay movement were also afraid of the trans movement in some way. We saw it as, "Oh, these people, they really are gay, but they just want to be straight. If they're trans, they get to be heterosexual." It was really ignorant. I didn't know that there were queer trans people or bisexual trans people. I thought that all trans people were straight.

RICHARD GOLDSTEIN: Years later, somebody dredged it up. Suddenly, Donna was persona non grata in queer woke circles. She didn't recognize Brandon Teena was a trans person. The concept barely existed to the extent that it does today. The first thing I told Donna was, "How can you be held to account for something you wrote half a century ago?" People grow and change and evolve.

DONNA MINKOWITZ: It was hard for me to be criticized from a progressive point of view. I was used to being criticized by the right wing, like John Podhoretz. I was used to being criticized by homophobes. After years of being defensive, I realized they were right.

CHAPTER 69

"WE WERE THE BRATS WHO WERE KICKING THEM IN THE SHINS EVERY WEEK"

ANN POWERS: During that time in the mid-'90s when the *New York Press* was ascendant, there was a lot of anxiety and there was a lot of talk among the staff that the *Voice* was going down and things were not going well. I never felt that anyone was anti–the *Voice* until the *New York Press* came along.

TOM ROBBINS: Wretched paper. Wretched. Wretched. Wretched.

JOHN STRAUSBAUGH: Russ Smith saw by the end of the late '80s there was definitely room for another downtown newspaper. In '88 he started the *New York Press*. It would be the alternative to the *Voice*; it would be the anti-*Voice* or the alt-*Voice*. He and I and several others of us at the paper were *huge* fans of the original *Village Voice*—the 1950s, early '60s *Village Voice*, the Dan Wolf–Ed Fancher *Village Voice*. It was a home for all sorts of idiosyncratic, eccentric, brilliant, wacky, very Greenwich Villagey voices. The cliché is that it was a writers' newspaper, but it was. Fancher and Wolf were very hands-off, let writers write what they wanted to write, picked writers that they liked, and then let them go—just get it in on time. It's a great way to run a paper. That's how we ran *New York Press*.

The *Voice* by the late '80s was not that paper at all anymore. Over the '70s and '80s it was into its second or third generation editorially by then, and it had become a knee-jerk, politically correct echo chamber.

When you read the headline on an article, you knew exactly what the article is going to say, and that's a horrible position for a paper to be in. It wasn't everybody. Michael Musto and Ellen Willis were still there, but in general it had become the party organ of New York liberals and lefties. And that's no fun. We said, let's bring some fun back in the weekly newspapers. If nothing else, we were a hell of a lot more fun than the *Village Voice* was at that point.

JAMES HANNAHAM: The spirit of the *Village Voice* was actually sort of ghostly. By the time I got there, the *New York Press* felt more like what the *Village Voice* was intended to be but could not be just in terms of its white male dominance. People started thinking of the *Voice* as a queer paper.

GREG TATE: Fred McDarrah used to lovingly and jokingly refer to it as "our commie, pinko, fag rag." Uptown, when I told folk I wrote for the *Voice*, they said, "Oh, you write for that gay paper." And not as an insult, but just as a matter of fact—they just recognized the paper had a bold, uncompromising sexual identity in a time and place when being gay was equated with being loud, proud, and militant like being Black then was.

SAM SIFTON: I had grown up reading the *Voice*. I grew up on Guy Trebay and Nelson George and Nat Hentoff. The company line was the *New York Press* stood in opposition to the *Voice*. We were going to be cooler than those boomers, and we were going to be scrappier, and we were going to rely on provocative first-person essays.

The alternative press outside of the *Voice*—that whole Association of Alternative Newspapers, all the *Creative Loafing*s of the world, the *City Papers*, and the like—they all imagine themselves standing in opposition to the mainstream newspaper of whatever city they were operating in. It was just different in New York. The *Voice* was sui generis. It was an alternative, yes, particularly in citywide reporting—an alternative to the *Times* and the tabloids, none of which were really doing cultural reporting of the style of the *Voice*.

Russ took a conservative line on things. He was eager to have voices in the paper that weren't what we thought of as the granola-y pabulum of leftie, hippie ideology.

JOHN STRAUSBAUGH: That was the idea right from the start, to be the anti-*Voice*. We were the brats who were kicking them in the shins every week. Clay Felker was the beginning of the end for the *Voice*. It begins taking itself way too seriously.

When the satanist said he wanted to write for us, I said, "Yeah, let's try that." You know? We had Alexander Cockburn as our wacky left, and we had Taki as our wacky right.* People went ballistic when we had Taki and his crew writing in a downtown Manhattan weekly paper. We had these conservatives and right-wingers writing for us. It was a big tent, *huge* tent.

I'd say, "Editorial policies are for editors who don't know how to edit." That's why everything in the *New Yorker* reads like one person wrote it, everything in *The Atlantic* reads like one person wrote it. The way I came to an editorial policy was, "If I like it, I'm running it, fuck you."

SAM SIFTON: That allowed us to be a little bloggy before there were blogs.

JOHN STRAUSBAUGH: I'm sure we were in front of them in some of the arts coverage and cultural coverage. But we were not a *news*paper. We never even tried. I think we had one reporter, and it was a disaster.

SAM SIFTON: You could go to the *Voice* and there would be a great investigation of redlining in the Bronx, or there'd be actual city hall coverage. There's Wayne Barrett writing. That's not what we were about. We were writing about restaurants and bars and music clubs, and publishing essays advocating for heroin use, or running columns written by dominatrixes. That wasn't in the *Voice*.

JOHN STRAUSBAUGH: The paper got really fat for a while—like, mid-'90s was when the paper was at its fattest. I can only speculate that having us doing well in their backyard—our offices a few blocks from their offices—it had to dawn on them eventually that the paid model was not the only model for an alternative weekly, and it was not necessarily the best model for an alternative weekly.

Most alternative weeklies by that point were free. The cover price pays for the distribution. That's basically what it's there for. So, you're paying the truckers—the union truckers in most cases—and you're paying the newsstands to take your thing. If you're distributing it yourself, which we did,

---

* Panagiotis "Taki" Theodoracopulos is a controversial right-wing journalist, originally from Greece, who cofounded the *American Conservative* magazine with Pat Buchanan and Scott McConnell.

and you've got your own boxes on the street, which we did, then you don't need to charge for the paper. On the business end, that works for advertisers because they know if we put a hundred thousand copies out on the street, somewhere around a hundred thousand copies are going to be picked up. Whereas you can't argue that if you're selling it.

We grew and grew and grew and grew until, perceptually, we were on the same level as the *Voice*. Whether it was supported by any other metrics, people perceived us as being the two opposing weekly papers in New York by the mid-'90s. That can't have gone unnoticed.

They pretended we didn't exist for as long as they possibly could. We'd been taking shot after shot after shot at them for six, eight years by then, so we were quite happy when they *finally* started firing back. Anyone who we pissed off with that week's issue—one of the go-to cutting remarks was, "Well, it's no wonder you guys are free, you're nowhere near as good as the *Village Voice*. I'd pay for the *Voice*. I'd never pay for you guys." And we'd always say, "Fine, go read and pay for the *Voice*."

DAVID SCHNEIDERMAN: Leonard Stern's desire was to build a bigger company and make the *Voice* more profitable. The first deal we did was in 1994 for the *LA Weekly*. New Times was bidding for it.* We ended up paying a million dollars less than New Times bid because the people at the *LA Weekly* didn't want to sell to New Times.

Then we started the *OC Weekly*. We got approached by the guys in Minneapolis at *City Pages*. They wanted to sell. They were being squeezed by New Times. Then we got a call from David Brewster saying, "We're going to put the *Seattle Weekly* on the block. Are you interested?" New Times was bidding for that, too. We got it. It infuriated Larkin and Lacey. Then we got approached by the *Cleveland Free Times*, and we bought that. We weren't centralizing anything; we kept all the staff.

Anyway, in 1996, Leonard called me one day. He used to call every day, by the way. Every morning at nine, nine thirty. He said, "I have an idea, but sit down first." I said, "Oh shit." He says, "What do you think if the *Voice*

---

* New Times was a rival alt-weekly newspaper chain founded by Michael Lacey and James Larkin.

goes free?" That was a big deal with the *Voice* because we were the only paid weekly paper.

Circulation had been declining for a long time, not precipitously, but slowly. I tried everything possible to reverse it—we did promotions, we had new art directors—but what was really happening is that the newsstands in New York had been shrinking dramatically because the city had decided that newsstands on the streets were a problem, so they got rid of most of the newsstands. We went from something like twelve hundred newsstands carrying the *Voice* to two hundred. People had to go inside a place to buy it. I knew we were fighting a bit of a losing battle, so I said, "Leonard, I'm OK with it."

LEONARD STERN: The *LA Weekly* was a free newspaper. They were in a much more difficult area to distribute than the *Village Voice* was in Manhattan. I mean, what does L.A. have? Twelve walking blocks? After owning it for a while and understanding how a free newspaper works, I converted the *Village Voice* to free. We took our circulation from, I forget, 75,000 a week to 250,000, in stages. It was enormously successful.

DAVID SCHNEIDERMAN: I knew the staff wouldn't be thrilled, but I didn't realize that the editorial staff would take it as a personal affront.

J. HOBERMAN: There were three things that were always the same price in New York. There was a subway token, a slice of pizza, and the *Village Voice*. I didn't get it. I didn't understand why people wouldn't buy the paper.

AMY TAUBIN: Anything you could pick up for free, people have contempt for. Also, it's the beginning of internet blogging. So as soon as it goes free, it just becomes some blog filled with ancient people.

MICHAEL MUSTO: I was with Lynn when we heard about it, and I was freaking. I just thought, "This is the end." I totally understood why it had to happen. I worried: Is the paper (a) going to be devalued because it's free? And (b) are we still going to get top-drawer advertising at the same rate for a free rag when we already had some, like, "our town" type of publications in boxes? I'm an alarmist. I'm Chicken Little.

JOHN MANCINI: I was on the metro desk at the *New York Post*. The night we heard that the *Village Voice* was going to be free, I was like, "What?" It seemed incredible. Who could think of doing that? That would be insane, giving away a paper. The only things that were given out were shoppers, and there was no journalistic credibility or anything else. So, we said, "Oh my god, they must be in terrible trouble."

CATHERINE MCGANN: In order for them to do that, they would sell these trashy ads at the back of the paper. It put you into a totally different category. Everybody working there was of a certain intellectual caliber, and we're all a bit snobby about our work, and it was very demeaning.

LAURIE STONE: It undermined the idea that this was something of value to pay for, to pay writers now. You don't pay writers now because the culture has determined that intellectual contributions, aesthetic contributions, are something that someone can do on the side, like a hobby. And see what happens to a culture who treats its artists and its intellectuals that way? Not good.

LEONARD STERN: Guess what? They knew nothing about business. They like to hear themselves talk. They thought that my going free would depreciate the value of their writing. But to get four times as much circulation? They were just so wrong; no sense arguing with them. It was my newspaper. It was my risk because if I was wrong, they'd still have their jobs, but a profitable business would turn into a financial disaster. It's a risk I took, and it was amazingly successful. And, as a matter of fact, they came around pretty well within a month. They came around to understanding the strength of free circulation that's targeted: more people were telling them they read their articles.

GREG TATE: I knew at the time that was the smart move to make because they were responding to the threat of *Time Out New York*. It was a competitive move.

MICHAEL MUSTO: When's the last time you saw a newsstand?

DAVID SCHNEIDERMAN: It kept us going at a really high level for many years. We didn't have to worry about circulation anymore because Leonard was willing to put money into it. He spent more on printed copies, but we made it up in advertising. Once the advertisers got over the fact that it was free, it worked.

JUDY MISZNER: That is what enabled them to put the *New York Press* at a distance, because they were gaining traction. The *Voice* hadn't had a lot of competition that was formidable until then. But Russ Smith was smart, and they were putting out some good journalism.

MICHAEL TOMASKY: You could still get away with calling 1990 the very tail end of the era that built the *Voice* into greatness. The community of people, of writers and readers in the Village, in New York, and beyond who made the paper so important and who gave it its electricity—that community still existed, kind of, in 1990. But forces were changing it: rents going crazy, SoHo going from working-class Italian neighborhood to a very hip, artsy neighborhood to a total gentrified chain-store neighborhood—that process was underway. The whole idea of these rent-controlled flops that people could live in for cheap in the Village—that was all really disappearing by 1990.

And William Zeckendorf built Zeckendorf Towers on Union Square in the late '80s, just a couple blocks north of the *Voice*'s office. So, you started to need to be rich to live in the Village, and that just changed it. It dispersed the community of people who supported the *Voice* for the previous fifteen or twenty years, and then by 1995 it was kind of dead.

SAM SIFTON: Fuck the *Voice*. We wanted to kill the *Voice*. We believed, *really* believed, that the *Voice* charging money for its paper was going to be the death of them and the *Voice* would be vanquished by our "information wants to be free" ethos.

And then, of course, the *Voice* went free. It was like getting punched in the face.

JOHN STRAUSBAUGH: We went out and got very drunk that night.

CHAPTER 70

"THINGS GOT A LITTLE WEIRD WHEN KAREN BECAME EDITOR IN CHIEF"

RICHARD GOLDSTEIN: David was my favorite editor. It wasn't only that he was incredibly competent, but that he had an incredible ability to sense when something was going to matter—it didn't matter yet, but it was going to. He authorized a lot of stuff that was ahead of the curve. And he hired Karen Durbin, which was risky at the time.* It's a woman editor. She hadn't been an editor anywhere else.

JONATHAN Z. LARSEN: Durbin was the arts editor when I got there. She had some physical ailments, and she was off seeing stomach doctors. But she would come in incredibly late, go out for lunch, spend a few hours in the office, and leave early. She wasn't into the job at all, as far as I could tell. She stopped talking to Andrew Sarris because she didn't like the way he ate his food. So, Sarris stopped writing. It was just incredible. The arts editor would not speak to our world-famous film critic. I said to David, "Karen is brilliant. She's a wonderful writer, she's a great raconteur. But from my vantage point, watching her for those overlapping months, I saw very little interest in editing, and I think you can do better."

---

* Karen Durbin was hired as editor in chief on April 5, 1994.

COLSON WHITEHEAD: At the time, Lisa Kennedy was a big cultural force. When they were trying to figure out who would replace Jonathan Larsen, there was a whole big, like, "Let's get Lisa Kennedy in there." Everyone was really disappointed when she didn't get the top job.

DAVID SCHNEIDERMAN: I had a bunch of long conversations with her. I just didn't think that she was ready.

TRICIA ROMANO: In its entire history, there wasn't a single Black editor in chief.

DAVID SCHNEIDERMAN: It's a failure.

RICHARD GOLDSTEIN: I actually gave David a long proposal. The proposal said that we should focus on immigrant and emergent communities in the city, and we should cover them just the way we covered Off-Broadway, or any new field, and that we could add this coverage to our political coverage, our feminist coverage, our Black coverage, our gay coverage. I got this idea from working with Peter Noel, because West Indian life had never really been covered.

I don't think this is the reason, but Wayne had a meeting with David and told him that if I became the editor of the paper, it would be a gay paper.

C.CARR: Things got a little weird when Karen became editor in chief. That put her in a different position: then she's a management person. There was a negative attitude toward her that I never understood. I wrote about the NEA culture wars stuff for *Mirabella*, and I wrote a big feature about Aileen Wuornos, a serial killer. It wasn't fluff.

DONNA MINKOWITZ: Ann Powers approached me because she had the idea that we should lobby for a woman and a feminist to be the editor in chief, so we did. Anyway, we were so excited.

I make an appointment with Karen Durbin. She smokes in my face at this meeting, and she announces something that was a surprise to me—that I hadn't quite made my BUF total: the number of articles you were supposed to have within a six-month period to keep your health insurance.* She tells me she's going to give it to me out of the goodness of her heart. I started

---

* BUF: bargaining unit freelancer.

crying; she's smoking in my face. Anyway, it was clear that she wasn't going to make me a staff writer.

RICHARD GOLDSTEIN: One of her ideas was to make the paper friendly to women. It didn't really work. Most of our readership remained male. We had a female art director, and David was behind that.

AUDREY SHACHNOW: I was in Texas designing the *Houston Press*. I happened to win a lot of awards that year. And Karen Durbin saw my work in the awards books and called me and said, "Hey, do you want to come back to New York?" They flew me in, and we hit it off. They hired me because they were also wanting to change the size of the paper. We reduced it two inches in height. It was a money-saving device. It also meant for the editors less words, because they had less real estate, and you can only reduce the type so much.

Whenever a new editor comes in, they always want to freshen it up. An editor travels with their own art director or design director. She wanted it to be lively and bright and fun and graphically well designed. It always had a look, the *Voice*. Very plain—headline in the big sans serif bold type, and copy, lots of copy on every page. There was no breathing room; every inch of space was taken up with copy.

I just made it look more contemporary, changed the fonts, changed some typefaces. I was introducing a little bit of a rest for the eye. I liked to use pull quotes and drop caps and make it easier to read through, rather than that dense sort of *New Yorker* look, page after page of text.

JAMES HANNAHAM: Karen Durbin, I loved. Her word of the day was "fun"—to make the left seem fun. I liked that idea. I still like that idea. Maybe I felt—feel—there's a way to do it where it doesn't look goofy.

AUDREY SHACHNOW: The ampersand. It was her and my favorite thing. They complained about that, did they? The design won a lot of awards, from SPD, Society of Publication Designers, and Art Directors Club.

JOE LEVY: The place was afeared of Karen. I always think of that scene in *Wayne's World* where the Rob Lowe character goes to visit Garth in his basement, and he says, "Garth, I have some ideas for the show." And Garth is tinkering with some remote-controlled hand, and he brings a hammer down on the hand, and he just says into the camera, "We fear change."

The *Voice* was like that: we just feared change. Karen should have been something that the art editors welcomed. She came out of that tradition.

She was a *Voice* product, and the fear was that she'd been working at a glossy magazine, and she would want sidebars, and that was before people were really afraid of sidebars. Nobody talked about "entry points on the page."

AMY TAUBIN: The front of the book felt that Karen was bringing her frivolity downtown and that she was going to make this into a kind of woman's magazine. Now, I didn't support what Karen was doing either, because I didn't see this as being women's frivolity. I saw it as a middlebrowing of the *Voice*.

FRANK RUSCITTI: When Karen Durbin became editor in chief, her first cover was some actor. The front of the book went apeshit, because there was not one news story on the front cover.

KAREN DURBIN: If I get a legitimate chance to run Robert Redford on the cover—and I think this was—I'm going to jump at it.

C.CARR: That was really hard to see her being attacked like that—I didn't think it was right. She always felt that it was because she was a woman that they were attacking her.

RICHARD GOLDSTEIN: When Karen was hired, Wayne came in a dress. Her first day on the job, or second day, he appeared in a dress. He was running around the office giggling, and he came into my office giggling, and I said, "Just get out, please." He claimed it was like an homage to her. She must have thought it was funny.

KAREN DURBIN: I've got no quarrel with Wayne as long as he comes to work in drag at least every other day. Just kidding. I'm going to pay for that.

WAYNE BARRETT: I'm going to be on the mascara beat!

AUDREY SHACHNOW: You had some good old boys there who seemed so very liberal, in their whole demeanor and their whole idea of themselves, who were really the most uptight, sexist guys you'd ever meet. But it was quite a contradiction: to work at the *Voice*, be at the *Voice*, dealing with these guys as a woman, and what the world thought about them, and then the way they really behaved toward women was—the more liberal they appeared in their articles, the less liberal they were.

Fred McDarrah saw me interacting with my son. One time Fred said to me, "If only you could talk to everyone the way you talk to your son." Like, in a motherly way, very "sweetheart," singsongy and sweet.

WILLIAM BASTONE: She was one of the finest editors of the *Voice* that I ever worked with. She probably should have been the editor years earlier.

LYNN YAEGER: She certainly understood, at least in terms of the arts, what the mission of the paper was supposed to be.

KAREN DURBIN: There has to be a joy in it and not just rage. It has to proceed out of genuine love for the world. The *Voice* should reflect the whole lives of the people who put it out. And the reality of those people is that they work hard, they play with exuberance, they wear clothes that give them pleasure. They buy books and records and all that stuff. They live in the material world.

CHAPTER 71

"HAMMER, DRANO, A PILLOW"

CATHERINE MCGANN: I see the '90s as an equivalent to *The Great Gatsby*. There was tons of money and drink tickets and velvet ropes and nightclubs, and the Club Kids came along. It went from being this burnt-out, grubby '80s East Villagey show to tons of money and drugs. You name it—it was like anything goes. Anything. That was very decadent and fabulous to be witness to.

The clubs got bigger and bigger. You started out at these little clubs, and at the end of it I remember going to Club USA or Palladium, these enormous, enormous places that were just crazy. It was very much a "before" and "after" line. I always peg it to Warhol dying. Warhol died in 1987; the next year, 1988, is when Michael Alig and the Club Kids came on the scene.

MICHAEL MUSTO: He had a whole following of people: all these kids with names like Junkie Jonathan, Oliver Twisted, Sebastian Junior, Jenny Talia. I liked a lot of them, and some of them were just attention-seeking, hedonistic, manipulative, and trying to be famous.

MICHAEL ALIG: I remember when that "Death of Downtown" article came out by Michael Musto. We were all just floored. Warhol was going to be our ticket out of there. We were all going to become Warhol Superstars and move into the Factory and re-create the whole thing. I was furious at Michael Musto for writing that article because he was ruining it for all the new kids. So, me and some friends—Michael Tronn and Julie Jewels—met with Rudolf Piper. We asked for one tiny room at Tunnel. The rule to get in was you had to dress up, and if you did that, you could come inside this

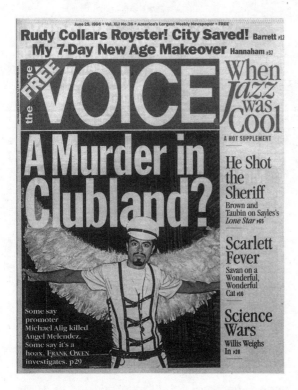

The Club Kid murder cover story by Frank Owen. Cover image © Village Voice/Street Media.

room and drink for free. The first night, we had about six or seven people who dressed up. I guess we were making fun of the Warhol Superstars. We changed our names like they did, and we dressed up in outrageously crazy outfits in order to be a satire of them—only we ended up becoming what we were satirizing.

MICHAEL MUSTO: I started making fun of them from the beginning, but I also admired whatever was interesting about them. I did like the fact that it was a family situation for young queers to come together. They can be part of some kind of family, even if it became the Manson family.

CATHERINE MCGANN: In the beginning, there was a lot of resentment from the old-guard nightclub people—"Who are these young kids coming in?" They really walked in, and they really took over.

MICHAEL MUSTO: Michael Alig was on the cover of *New York* magazine with two other Club Kids.

CATHERINE MCGANN: Some people were more outrageous than others. Alig was more clownish. He would go with this almost clowny, white makeup face and exaggerated lips. At the time, Michael and I would some-times roll our eyes and, think, "Is it Halloween every night?"

FRANK OWEN: Alig invented his own subculture. It was heavily based on the New Romantics from London, so it was not new to me. He ripped off Leigh Bowery—the lightbulbs taped to the side of the head. I thought it was silly.

I came to America when I was writing about hip-hop and house music. I left in November '87. I did a few early things for the *Village Voice*, doing music criticism. Then I decided I wanted to get into investigative journalism. So, who the fuck is gonna employ a music critic as an investigative journal-ist? It's not going to happen except for the *Village Voice*. I pitched it to Doug: I would write about New York nightlife, but I would do it as investigative re-porting. I would basically explore the seamy underbelly of New York night-life because I knew already what was going on. It was pretty obvious that stuff was going to implode.

The first cover story I did for the *Voice* was about after-hours clubs. Then I did a cover story on Peter Gatien. This was before the DEA got involved. Then I did a cover story about Special K, and the person I bought K off in the beginning of the story was Angel Melendez.*

CATHERINE MCGANN: With the whole crazy Club Kid murder story, Mi-chael Musto is the one who broke that. That is New York legend.

MICHAEL ALIG: 1996 was right when everything fell apart. My heroin use was already out of control. I'm surprised that I was even alive. Just a month before, I'd overdosed twice. In the hospital, almost dead, not having any memory of my name or anything. Strangely enough, I saw it as taking this art project to its extreme. I was thinking, "How far can we take it?"

MICHAEL MUSTO: Once he started peeing into punch bowls and push-ing drugs into people's mouth and things like that, it was like, "This isn't cute." Michael called me. He sounded like a mess. He said he was fired from Limelight. He was out of his apartment.

---

* Peter Gatien was the owner of the Limelight nightclub. Special K is ketamine, a tranquilizer.

This is in '96. Michael and his roommate Robert Riggs, who was also known as Freeze, who was another club person, got into a tussle with Angel Melendez, a drug dealer and a person on the scene. One of them got into a tussle with him. The other one helped finish him off. Hammer, Drano, a pillow—all sorts of things were allegedly used, and the body was chopped up and thrown into the Hudson River in a box. Two weeks later I did my blind item.

MICHAEL MUSTO, LA DOLCE MUSTO, "NIGHT CLUBBING," *VILLAGE VOICE*, APRIL 30, 1996

Mr. Mess was fighting with Mr. Dealer about money Mr. Dealer was owed. It escalated to the point where Mr. Dealer was choking Mr. Mess, just at the moment when Mr. Mess #2 happened to walk in. Mr. Mess #2, a quick thinker, promptly hit Mr. Dealer over the head with a hammer. Not happy with that, he and Mr. Mess decided to finish Mr. Dealer off by shooting him up with Drano—a trick even the twisted twosome in *Diabolique* didn't come up with.

MICHAEL MUSTO: He was alternately telling people he did it and then telling people he didn't do it. He now says he never did the Drano thing.

MICHAEL ALIG: I remember it like it was a dream. I remember it the same way I remember a lot of those mornings of the after-hours parties. When I look back, it is very hard for me to delineate what is reality and what is a hallucination.

FRANK OWEN: The person I first heard it from was actually Michael Musto, right? At first I didn't believe it.

MICHAEL MUSTO: I'm standing by the elevator next to him. "What do you think of the Michael Alig thing?" He goes, "What?" I said, "Michael and Freeze, people think that he killed Angel."

FRANK OWEN: I was like, "No fucking way did Michael dismember his friggin' roommate. This is one of Michael's sick pranks." My first job when I came to New York, I was the VIP doorman at the World, a club on the East Side run by Steve Lewis. That's where I met Michael Alig. When I first met

Michael, Michael was like a powder puff, right? He was this silly little kid running around with his mum's underwear on his head. He was the last person you would think of as a murderer.

CATHERINE MCGANN: The idea that he was going around bragging about it is what really tipped the scales for me. It's really an addiction story. I have a lot of sympathy for addiction, but the notion that one was going around bragging about this? That smacks of something else, right? You could make the argument, "Is he begging to be caught?"

FRANK OWEN, "A MURDER IN CLUBLAND?" *VILLAGE VOICE*, JUNE 25, 1996

In the press, Alig continues to pass off the incident as a rumor, invented by a Limelight drag queen, that he played along with until it got out of hand. But several insiders buy the scenario that Michael Musto broke as a blind item in his column two months ago: Alig got into a row with Angel over money he had stolen from Angel, the fight escalated, and Angel started strangling Alig—at which point Freeze, a friend of Alig's, repeatedly hit Angel over the head with a hammer. Though gravely injured, Angel was still alive. So Freeze, Alig, and an unidentified third person decided to finish off the job by injecting the moaning victim with Drano. "Angel did not go quietly into the night," says one source. "According to Michael, the apartment was covered in blood."

FRANK OWEN: When I started doing the story, I don't think people really believed that Michael actually did it. It seemed like one of those things Michael would kind of do just to get publicity, just another one of Michael's sick jokes.

The thing that really convinced me was when Johnny Melendez, Angel's brother, came to town and contacted me. I interviewed Johnny, and he brought in the whole family from Colombia. They hadn't heard from him for weeks, you know? And they were totally devastated. There was a look of grief on their faces. They knew something bad had happened, because Angel was close to his family, even though he was gay; he was still close to his brother

Johnny. At that point, I thought, "There's no freakin' way that Angel would put his whole family through this just for the sake of one of Michael Alig's sick jokes."

Cops didn't do shit. They pretty much gave up on the case.

MICHAEL MUSTO: There was a feeling of, well, it's two white guys who killed a Hispanic drug dealer. There's not really going to be a lot of justice on this, and this might be one of the reasons it took a while for this to be resolved. The murder of Angel Melendez obviously fed right into the idea that "Oh, nightlife people are bad people, and we need to crack down on this." There's a lot of homophobia involved, absolutely.

FRANK OWEN: It was also the fact that Michael Alig was a notorious liar. No, they didn't take it seriously at all. That's when the DEA got involved, not long after, investigating the Limelight.

You only had to walk around and see, like, fifteen-, sixteen-year-old kids passed out on the floor on Special K. It was basically that whole peace, love, and unity vibe of the early rave scene had degenerated into exactly the exact opposite. It's like the Summer of Love. The Summer of Love is 1967, but by the time 1968 comes around, it's all crystal meth and rape and bad vibes. You could see that at the Limelight. It was getting a lot darker.

The DEA wanted to use Michael Alig as a confidential informant against Gatien, right? Peter Gatien was no saint by any fucking means. Gatien knew damn well what was going on at that club. That's when the DEA got involved, they knew that Michael had killed Angel, but they didn't give a fuck, right? Because he was valuable to them as a witness against Peter Gatien.

There was a huge gap between when the "Who Killed Angel?" story came out and when Angel's torso washed up in Staten Island. In that year, Michael was scheduled to be the key witness against Gatien in the trial. So, Michael thought he got away with it. It was only when the body washed up that they no longer could use him.

But even after the body washed up, and they were arrested, the DEA were still visiting him in jail, and taking him on day trips and giving him heroin, just to pump him for more information.

They completely overcharged Gatien with the RICO statute—racketeering, which is supposed to go after big-time mobsters and big-time heads of cartels. So they were basically trying to put this guy away for life.

He didn't deserve that. So, it was a bit of a crusade for me to expose just how crooked the investigation was.*

CATHERINE MCGANN: Michael Musto was over the whole Club Kid thing. *Before* that conviction. We had been doing that for years. It started in '88—so by '97, '98, we weren't really a part of that anymore. By then, Michael was quite a bit more focused on celebrity.

MICHAEL MUSTO: Giuliani, who is still a blight on our society, came around in the '90s as mayor of New York and decided to crack down on the nightlife in order to cater to tourists and co-op owners. Well, guess what: tourists and co-op owners would love the nightlife. Why wouldn't they? Not to mention the fact that nightlife pumps so much money into the city's economy. Provides jobs, provides creativity, sets trends. Why are we demonizing nightlife?

TRICIA ROMANO: Giuliani started enforcing the Cabaret Law, a racist holdover from Prohibition which required venues to get a license for more than three people to dance. Before 1967, performers like Thelonious Monk, Charlie Parker, and Billie Holiday couldn't work in New York for periods of time because they had a criminal record. That part of the law was amended, but by the time I was in New York in the late '90s, clubs had to install expensive sprinkler systems, flameproof wall hangings, and have two exits. This was expensive for small venues that just wanted to have a DJ in the corner spinning music with maybe a few dozen people dancing.

Then there were financially damaging surprise raids—most places couldn't lose a weekend's worth of business. I spent a lot of time in my column, Fly Life, in the early 2000s covering these raids, often done under the shield of the Cabaret Law.

MICHAEL MUSTO: Nightlife springs back from oppression. The more he pushed down, the more we were struggling to keep going. It became a time when there were raids and you were constantly looking behind your back. When that all cleared, there was just a lot of boring bottle-service lounges.

---

* Gatien was not convicted of the RICO charges, but he was convicted of tax fraud and evasion and deported to Canada.

CHAPTER 72

"IT'S LIKE HERDING OCELOTS WHO ARE ALSO ATTACKING YOU"

TED KELLER: I don't know who stabbed who first. I became very good friends with Jeff Weinstein. He literally took me under his wing, took me out to restaurants, told me how to order food, told me how to ask the right questions about food, took me to Century 21 and bought me my first New York coat, from Italy, cashmere, which I owned for twenty years until it finally disintegrated. When I was working on all these little mock-ups of new sections, Karen wandered by and said, "Oh, by the way, don't tell Jeff about this because we're moving his reviews to the back of the book instead of being up front." When what was actually happening was she was going to fire Jeff and replace him with Robert Sietsema.*

RICHARD GOLDSTEIN: It was money, but she had to choose who to let go. Ultimately she had to decide how to save all of this money that David required us to save. It was horrible.

JONATHAN Z. LARSEN: I left, I wrote David a long letter, and I said, "You want things from me that I'm not sure I'm capable of giving you." And of course, they were all the things that he got Karen Durbin to do, which is to shrink the paper, fire a lot of people, eliminate the literary section. Cut out national reporting, cut out international reporting. Of course she eliminated the sports section.

JEFF Z. KLEIN: They restored it about two to three years later.

---

* The food critic who wrote about "cheap eats" in smaller restaurants around the city.

ALLEN ST. JOHN: She said, "I am the *Village Voice*. If I get it, then it should be in the *Voice*. And if I don't get it, it shouldn't." She did not get the sports section. So, she basically came up with this idea of some weird front-of-the-book section. She was basically gonna use the resources and the space from the sports section to do this front-of-the-book section that was going to be so great.

We had a big meeting about this. It was like the trope of a movie of somebody getting to go to their own funeral. At a certain point Karen starts talking about this new section, and about how it's going to be this oppor-tunity to be really on the news and have short things and longer things and have things that were funny and have things that are controversial and have a lot of different voices, to which Bob Christgau just waited till she was done and said, "Yeah, that sounds great. In fact, it sounds exactly like the sports section you just killed."

JEFF WEINSTEIN: The staff walked out for the three of us, Jeff Z. Klein, the sports editor, and Stan Mack.

FRANK OWEN: That Michael Alig cover story, "Who Killed Angel?"—the lawyers did not want to run that at all. The lawyers were like, "No fucking way. You're basically accusing this guy of, like, murdering somebody—and you're doing it based on what, half a dozen off-the-record sources? No way is this gonna happen." I had to get one of the sources to go on the record.

But that was still not good enough for the lawyers, right? And it was Karen Durbin who overruled them—and this was literally just as it was about to go into print—and ran with the story. I really, really liked her. I thought she was a great editor in chief.

C.CARR: This is so silly, but she initiated this thing that they had done at *Mirabella*, where there was some restaurant that made sandwiches—it would bring them in and people could buy them, so they wouldn't have to leave the office for lunch—and she decided to bring that into the *Voice*. And people were making fun of it. Like [*audibly scoffs*], "How can she do such a thing? Like bring sandwiches in here?" Like, what's wrong with *sandwiches*?

PETER NOEL: I had written a piece called "Crooklyn Dodger." At that time, we were experimenting with different styles of journalism—gangsta rap, different things, and I incorporated all that into a big feature piece. She could not understand any of those things at all. She hated it. She said, "This is gangster talk, why in the world would we use this type of language in the paper?" I said, "It's because you're sitting behind this desk and that you don't understand how the city has changed."

There was a cover story I was writing about Giuliani trying to stop the West Indian Carnival. She did not understand why West Indians were so important, and everybody else told her, "Yes, this is part of the city," so she reluctantly agreed to put it on the cover. We got into this heated argument. She said, "I don't think you're doing this paper any good." I quit that day.

DAVID SCHNEIDERMAN: I made the change because Karen lost the staff. She didn't make enough of a transition into being a boss. I just felt, "OK, this is not working out."

JAMES HANNAHAM: It was never a job that anyone had for long. It's worse than herding cats. It's like herding—I don't know—ocelots who are also attacking you.

DAVID SCHNEIDERMAN: At the *Times*, they would stab you in the back. At the *Voice*, they'd stab you in the chest. Everything at the *Times* is like subterfuge; you never know where people are coming from. It was very Kremlin-esque. At the *Voice*, you knew everybody's agenda.

C. CARR: It was very uncomfortable for her. She was being attacked by people on the staff in a way that I never saw any other editor attacked and treated. It was appalling the way she was treated there, a lot of arguing in staff meetings, but also a lot of talk behind her back: "She's so awful. We have to get her out of here." The staff started having meetings—and sometimes I wasn't invited because people knew I was her friend—about what to do about Karen.

She was fired while I was in Indiana. Because when I came back, there was Don Forst.

CHAPTER 73
"WICKED DON FORST"

DAVID SCHNEIDERMAN: I really always felt the *Voice* was a newspaper, not a magazine. It was hard to find somebody who was a newspaper editor who understood that mentality. Usually, I got candidates who were magazine people.

And then out of the blue, Don Forst contacted me. I never thought of Don. But he had been editor of *New York Newsday*, and it was an incredibly good newspaper.* By the time I hired him, he was probably seventy or so.** But he sure didn't look like it or act like it. He was a legendary editor. So, I had a drink with Don. I thought he was a really smart, cool guy.

DOUG SIMMONS: Schneiderman called me and said, "I'm going to give a name to you, and when I ask you what you think about it just let me know. What if Don Forst were to come over as editor?" I blurted out right away, "You're kidding! I can't believe it! It'd be like having Larry Bird join the team." A supernova.

JOY PRESS: Don Forst was brought in to discipline the children. It was felt that it had become out of control. If they fired someone, everyone would change their name in honor of that person, as a protest. The feeling was that Karen couldn't control the staff. And so, Don was the daddy, Don was the iron fist. He just didn't give any of those people or any of those things any air. And Don newsified it.

DON FORST: I'd heard the [*Voice* newsroom] was a tough room to manage. To me, that's not necessarily a bad thing, if people are passionate about what they do. But some of the writers were living too much in the past, with

---

* *Newsday* serves the Long Island area, and in 1985 it launched *New York Newsday*.
** He was sixty-four.

stories that were self-indulgent and too long. I'm not interested in writers' psyches and problems. I came in looking for shorter, more timely stories that have some kind of news peg.

JOHN MANCINI: Don had been a polarizing figure at the Long Island *Newsday*. He was a notoriously early riser and early shower-upper in the office, and I was the first editor in in the morning. So, by the time I got in there at eight, he had been there for two hours already. He was there to plot, to strategize, to find out how he can make somebody's life miserable that day; at the same time it seemed like he was nice to them. [*Laughs.*]

He was a man of his age, plus four stars on that. Meaning: sexist, could be misogynistic, kind of reveled in being the bad boy who could go right to the edge and not get caught. "Never sued successfully," he would say. But both men and women loved him despite ourselves because of his rebellious nature and poking an eye at authority. He made it seem like we were on a pirate ship trying to plunder the world of New York newspapering. He kept a copy of *The Prince*, Machiavelli, on his desk.

DOUG SIMMONS: We all heard the stories. When he was hired, I had close, close friends, dear friends, call up: "What's going on? Call David, tell him to stop." I said, "It looks like it's a done deal." "No, that's *crazy!*" I heard people say, "He uses the N-word," which Don swore to me he never did. I asked him. It was important to me. "He called people fags, he's homophobic, he's sexist. It's insane that you would bring him in!" Oh man, people were stunned and horrified at his arrival.

ROBERT I. FRIEDMAN: When I left the *Village Voice*, I got a job at *New York Newsday* working for Don Forst. And there was never a day that went by when he wouldn't see me and say, "Oh, it's the commie, pinko, faggot *Village Voice* editor." That was his favorite line. Who knew that one day he would become the editor of that "commie, pinko, faggot" rag?

DON FORST: Why did I take this? Because it was insane. Yeah, this is a very exciting place. It's got heterosexuals, homosexuals, lesbians, carnivores, vegetarians, Stalinists, Trotskyites. There is one group that was immediately on my side. The rest of the people are waiting to see if I'm the devil.

J. HOBERMAN: I couldn't stand Forst. I thought that he was ruining the *Voice*. Like firing Jules—that was the first thing he did. Schneiderman wanted it, but Forst had to do it. That was a getting-to-know-you moment. It was a financial thing, and they felt that Jules was taking advantage of them because Jules was syndicating his own work. This guy was synonymous with the *Village Voice*. I mean, if he wants to pick up some extra money after years and years and years of getting peanuts from them, let him do it. But that was Forst, and he fired a bunch of other people too.

JULES FEIFFER: The first eight years, I did not get paid. I ended up, by the time they fired me, making $75,000 a year, which was a sizable chunk of money. Don Forst fired me. He said he could hire three reporters for what he paid me, and I was in an outrage and state of shock. I'd already won a Pulitzer Prize, and basically what other honors the paper had gotten were mostly mine, so I could not believe that they weren't at least offering me a settlement. But they offered me nothing.

LAURIE STONE: They were being fucky to some people I really cared about. Some editors were asked to do their columns for free, in essence. Anyway, the *New York Press* called me, and I gave an interview on the record about some things I thought weren't so great at the *Voice*, and it was seen as a betrayal. I was called into the office. And Don and Doug said, "You're fired." That was it.

JAMES RIDGEWAY: Don Forst had a sick little thing of hiring regular newspaper people and thinking that they could fit in. It didn't work, you know? They're not the same kind of people.

DOUG SIMMONS: There's some folks that he brought with a sensibility that just wasn't right—some editors from *New York Newsday* who were looking for jobs, people he loved. They all needed jobs.

Finally, I suggested to him, I said, "A perfect hire, Don: We should go after Tom Robbins of the *Daily News*. He's a labor reporter." Don's eyes lit up.

TOM ROBBINS: I knew him originally when he was the editor at *New York Newsday*. And then he had washed up on the shores of the *Daily News* because he was desperate for a job. Don was not a guy who worked a lot with copy. He was a big-picture guy, right? He liked front pages and headlines and splash, so these guys were making Don do the stuff he just wasn't comfortable doing.

Wayne called and said, "Forst wants to know if you're interested in this." And I was like, "Yeah, you're damn straight I'm interested." I wanted to go someplace that would just let me write again and do the stories I wanted to do. I knew that was the *Village Voice*. Even though I was giving up about five hundred thousand readers to do it.

The first big story I wrote when I came back was about corruption in the newspaper industry and mob influence in the newspaper industry in New York. It was my favorite story: "The Hoodlums the News Won't Report On," or something like that.

We had the state police coming right through our newsroom, removing boxes, because there was this huge scandal going on—not just in our newsroom, but in the *New York Post* and in the *Times* and in every newspaper in the city. The Newspaper and Mail Deliverers Union, the truckers, was this mob-run operation. I was trying to do the story that nobody had the courage to write.

Doug LaChance, who had been the head of the union and was the number-one gangster, who I had met during the strike, was delighted to be interviewed. He was only too happy to while away the afternoon and the evening telling stories. And it was a story that nobody else in New York would have ever run. It was really rich.

TOM ROBBINS, "THE NEWSPAPER RACKET," *VILLAGE VOICE*, MARCH 6, 2001

He is a big man, six feet two, with wary brown eyes set in a long face capped by steel-gray hair. He is a garrulous talker with a roguish charm that he turns on union members and employers alike. His conversation is a flow of anecdotes about publishers, politicians, and gangsters, interspersed with quotes from Tin Pan Alley tunes, comments about stories in the day's papers, and a well-practiced, self-deprecating humor.

"After I win the Nobel Prize and am made a Knight of Malta, the first sentence in my obituary will still be 'convicted labor racketeer,'" he is fond of saying.

DOUG SIMMONS: Within a week or so I fell absolutely in love with the guy. Partly because Don reached out to me in the sweetest and most brotherly, fraternal way, saying, "I want you to be my managing editor. I want you to be a partner. I want you to tell me if I ever do anything that upsets you." He often did do things that upset me.

And this is another reason why I fell in love with him: he really loved the *Voice*. He would have loved any paper he's the editor in chief of. Don Forst is an editor in chief. Don Forst *is* the boss. Don Forst is the commander. He is the lion in summer.

Don, he came in and he laid down some rules: No first person, which people broke all the time. Single-topic covers. More surprises on the covers! There were too many words! Bigger pictures, *bigger* pictures! And empowering the art department.

TED KELLER: I remember everything about Don Forst, for all my life. Everything, everything, everything. The first two weeks were terrible. 'Cause he kept shoving all these horrible, horrible ideas down my throat. And about a month in, he said to Leonard, "You know, this guy has better ideas than I ever will. So, I'm just gonna let him do his thing."

DON FORST: You gotta grab the reader by the throat. He's on the train. It's hot. He's trying to hit on his secretary; she's not giving him the time of day. His wife is mad at him. His kid needs braces; he doesn't have the money. The guy next to him stinks. It's crowded. You want him to read your story? You better make it interesting.

ALISA SOLOMON: And Gonnerman, reportedly, bless her soul, said something like, "Well, I'm writing for the women at home."*

AMY TAUBIN: He must have felt terrible that he was forced to take a job at the *Village Voice*. That was always my take on him: "I'm a newspaperman. This isn't really a newspaper." And so, he was going to make it a newspaper.

JOHN MANCINI: No greater newsman that I've ever worked with. He knew the heart of the story. I use it to this day, in terms of what is the center of the story? What's the most important thing here? What's the emotional

---

* Award-winning writer Jennifer Gonnerman is now a *New Yorker* staff writer and has been a finalist for the Pulitzer Prize.

center of this? What's the intellectual center of this? What's the policy center of this?

DENIS HAMILL: Kevin Convey worked for Forst in Boston. He said, "There was a robbery at a bodega and the guy got killed. The guy was trying to shoplift a can of corn." I came back and I wrote the story. And gave it to Forst, and he looked up and he said, "The story is terrific, but how much was this can of corn? Go back and find out how much that can of corn cost," because he loved details. "That's how much his life was worth."

JAMES HANNAHAM: He struck me as almost a parody of a newspaperman. He had, like, some dopey rubric about how to write pieces. He was like, "Go to the people. Just go to the people, James." Who *are* you?

C.CARR: Don was so different from any other *Voice* editor. I remember going in to meet him the first day I got back. I knew he had never read the *Voice* before he became editor, so I thought, "Oh, I'll give him a couple short pieces so he can see the kind of thing I do." And he said, "Nah, I don't care."

TOM ROBBINS: It was clear to me, even when I went back to the *Voice*, that he was a misfit.

There was a series of demonstrations against one of the World Trade Organizations in the city, sometime in the aughts, and there were all those nutty anarcho-groups that would go around dressed in black and try to engage the cops. And there was a lot of talk about how those folks were going to create chaos and havoc in the city.

Don gave a front-page story to a guy who's a friend of mine who had very good police sources. It was a completely anti-demonstrator, pro-police story, and I would hear about it for years later from people. And Don didn't get it. Don's attitude was, "Hey, you mix it up a little bit. What's the big deal?"

ALISA SOLOMON: It was an ongoing joke with us that he always wanted me to get an establishment or conservative comment way high up in the story. It's not that my stories weren't properly balanced or fair. They just demonstrated something, and he didn't like what they were showing.

We did that birthday—a seventieth or something? I wrote something like, "I did my best, but I couldn't get somebody to quote who wouldn't wish you a happy birthday."

MICHAEL DALY: He had a sense of mischief, which is important.

WILLIAM BASTONE: He liked the weirdness. He enjoyed the fact that he was working in this environment that had a lot of weird people in it. He was kind of an odd guy himself.

JOHN MANCINI: He really was a bohemian in that way. He was not a libertarian. He would always say, "I have no politics," and that he believed in monarchy rather than democracy. But one of the jobs he took was culture editor of the *New York Times*. And he always made sure people knew that was the title.

MICHAEL FEINGOLD: He used to take me out to dinner at one of his political hangout places and tell me old stories about how he was the editor who had first allowed the word "cunnilingus" to appear in the *Times* in a play review: Michael McClure, *The Beard*. He told the story several times with great satisfaction.

DENIS HAMILL: When he brought me to Boston to write a column, he said, "Listen, the Harvard journalism school, they want to meet you." There was some function, and we sat down and had dinner, and it was the weirdest thing of all. The people started naming their alma maters going around the table. And it was Harvard and Yale and Princeton, and it got to me, and I said, "Staten Island Community College."

Everybody started to laugh, and they said, "No really? Where'd you go?" "Staten Island Community College."

And Forst absolutely loved that. He was banging the table, laughing. He knew exactly that we were going in and throwing a hand grenade into a Yankee bastion. He loved to do that kind of shit.

MICHAEL FEINGOLD: They called to tell me that I had won the Nathan Award.* It was during the era of wicked Don Forst. I immediately called Ross Wetzsteon, and he said, "Oh, that's wonderful news, I've got to tell Don immediately." Two minutes later, Don phoned me and said, "That thing Ross was telling you about, forget that. That didn't happen." He did that just to be wicked because that's what he was like. I was very fond of him even though he was wicked.

---

* The George Jean Nathan Award for Dramatic Criticism.

JUDY MISZNER: He used to tell the story about how, when *New York Newsday* went, he felt like his heart was ripped out. When he got this job at the *Voice*, he felt like he had a heart replacement. He never thought at that point in his career and his age that he would be leading the *Village Voice*.

MICHAEL FEINGOLD: On the other hand, he was *in place* because the *Voice* is really a collection of out-of-place people, people for whom there is no other place. That's your family.

CHAPTER 74

"YOU SHOULD GO DO SOMETHING BIG"

MARK SCHOOFS: I had not intended to be a journalist; I was a philosophy major. And as I was graduating from college, the AIDS epidemic entered my consciousness. I'm a gay man. At that time there were no drugs to treat it.

I ended up getting a job for which I was *completely* unqualified: to run a gay and lesbian newsweekly in Chicago, a city I had never stepped foot in. I became the editor of one of the largest gay and lesbian newsweeklies in the entire United States. We won the city's most prestigious journalism award four times in my two years. No gay paper had ever won this award. It's called the Peter Lisagor Award.

I ended up bouncing around. I went to Romania in 1990 right after Ceaușescu fell. I taught journalism to Romanian students and freelanced for a bunch of newspapers, came back, didn't know what to do with my life, thought about starting a gay newspaper in New York City. Richard Goldstein somehow heard about me—I have no idea how to this day—and asked me if I would join the *Voice*, covering HIV.

JAMES HANNAHAM: Mark Schoofs was my roommate for a while. He was, and probably still is, a workaholic. The sort of person who relaxes by, like, running twenty miles. Just restless and determined.

Part of the reason he started writing about AIDS is because his partner, Mike, died of AIDS toward the beginning of AIDS. He was at a protest where he threw Mike's ashes over the White House lawn. That's in the film *How to Survive a Plague.*

MARK SCHOOFS: I dealt with the pain of HIV by blocking it out. Until I saw the movie, I had very, very vague recollections of that day. My first actual

Voice piece was first person because I had lost my partner, which is a critical element I left out, and I was really grappling with that. I wove my own experience in with the experience of other people who were in what was then called sero-discordant relationships: one person is positive, and one person who's not.

My big breakthrough for the *Voice* was a cover story called "Why There Is No AIDS Vaccine." That took me a long time to report and write, months and months, and I really became an expert on the science of AIDS vaccines. That's when I shared an apartment with James. If you walked into the room, the entire floor was covered with piles, notes from scientific studies about that aspect of the immune system or that particular HIV vaccine or whatever. Literally, you couldn't move because there was so much reporting material. That is how I worked. I was obsessed with the AIDS epidemic. That changed the trajectory of my reporting in my career. They really loved the HIV vaccine piece. They gave it great play on the cover. And Karen was excited about it. Richard was very excited about it.

MARK SCHOOFS: And then they brought in Don Forst, who was this grizzled, crusty old guy. I had written this ridiculously detailed story about the risks of contracting HIV through fellatio. I thought, "Oh, he probably won't like what I'm writing." It didn't faze me that much.

RICHARD GOLDSTEIN: The first thing he did was move a piece on whether oral sex is safe off the front page, or into the corner of the front page.

MARK SCHOOFS: Two things happened. First, he and Richard clashed, and that built up over a long period of time. But Don, for whatever reason—and I still, to this day, consider it pretty surprising—he singled me out and said, basically, "You should go do something big." I don't know why he did that.

I ended up doing this seven- or eight-part series on genetics. After that, I had gone to the world AIDS conference; I realized I wanted to do something on AIDS in Africa. I thought, "This is a massive story."

I prepared a proposal, which first I ran by Richard, and then we gave it to Don. Don said, "I'll think about it." I thought, "OK, he'll get back to me in a couple of days." He, later that day, came by and said, "Do it."

RICHARD GOLDSTEIN: It was Don's idea to send him to Africa, not mine. He had a very complex personality. He could be rather noble at times, and this was a great decision. It cost a fortune.

JUDY MISZNER: Don had to get all his budgets approved through me. He wanted $19,000. I thought about it. That was a lot of money. We never gave any one person $19,000. We weren't set up that way. I had a finite budget, so I made Don take it out of someplace else. I told him, "You give me two pages a week back." We negotiated it.

MARK SCHOOFS: I made one short trip to Africa in December 1998. They were meeting in Senegal; it was basically a "women and AIDS and Africa" group, and they hosted some annual meeting. I went there to get sources, and it proved to be really great. Then I really went over to Africa—it must have been the beginning of 1999—and came back in the fall.

I found a place to be my home base in Zimbabwe, where I rented this back room that was the old servants' quarters. I went to ten or twelve different countries, and when I would go to another country I would pack up for that, but I would always go back to Zimbabwe.

Women and HIV was a gigantic issue in Africa. Women are more likely to contract HIV, there's more women with HIV than men, and all of the social dynamics that would render women more vulnerable to contracting HIV—that was a theme. The search for a vaccine, which turned out to be super interesting because there were these women in Nairobi who appeared to be resistant to HIV and were being studied very intensely, and that was feeding into concepts for an HIV vaccine.

DOUG SIMMONS: AIDS in Africa as a concept: Mark put that in the conversation. Prior to that story, AIDS was a gay tale in San Francisco, in New York, in New Orleans; it was an urban tale of gay men. Mark brought in this story, the heterosexual transmission of AIDS. He rode with truck drivers, and they would stop in rest stops in South Africa, and there would be prostitutes and the truck drivers. It was transmitted, but then the drivers went home and slept with their wives. Then it just became the epidemic. The crisis that at the time was unseen.

It was Richard Goldstein as the editor. It was a perfect pairing.

RICHARD GOLDSTEIN: I had done one of the first pieces on AIDS in the Black community. I interviewed David Dinkins—he was one of the few politicians willing to talk about it. It was a big secret that Black people were getting AIDS because of drug use and bisexuality, down-lowness. I did this big feature, "On AIDS and Race." I knew already that this was a big part of the story. Pediatric AIDS was already happening at Jacobi Hospital. And they were all Black, all the babies.

MARK SCHOOFS: The vast majority of my interviews, very deliberately, were with Africans. They ranged from sex workers in the slums of Nairobi to very, very prominent scientists and government officials. I really wanted to make sure that I was foregrounding all of my reporting on an African perspective, not a Western perspective.

I had gone to Cameroon to report on the origins of the virus itself. There was a world-class virologist who was Cameroonian who had been studying the genetics of the virus and what that tells us about where it came from. There was a strong belief, subsequently proved true, that the origin of the virus was likely in nonhuman primates in that region of Africa—central to west-central Africa.

Right after that, I went to Nigeria—Lagos—which is the most difficult city I've ever reported from. Nigeria is the most populous country in Africa, and Lagos is the megacity of Africa. It's a very watery city. There's lots of bridges and peninsulas and islands. The traffic jams are epic. People cram into these tiny, tiny minibuses that are meant to hold eight or twelve people, but there'll be twenty in them. They'll get stuck for hours, because the traffic will not move. I got around by getting on people's little motorbikes. These kids would be on the equivalent of a moped—and you'd pay them a few naira. They would weave through traffic in a way a taxi never could.

It's one of the world's largest oil producers, but the electricity barely worked. If you had an hour of electricity a day, it was amazing, and that hour would not be one solid hour; it would be broken up into two- or three-minute segments.

I would go to hospitals, or even very, very, very wealthy homes, and they would have fifty-gallon drums filled with water that would be delivered to them because they didn't have piped water. Surgeons would wash their hands by dipping a small bucket into this thing and washing their hands in that water. Omololu Falobi, a wonderful Nigerian journalist—he had chosen a hotel for me; my budget was super, super low, so it's way, way, way out of town. It was a lovely hotel; it was very clean.

I had a fever. And the fever got worse. Cameroon is part of the malaria belt. Most Westerners have no immunity to malaria because we don't have malaria in the United States anymore. There are so, so, so many mosquitoes that you're almost certain to get malaria. I was taking prophylaxis, but the prophylaxis that was available then was very bad. I believe that I contracted malaria in Cameroon. I was staying in a monastery. I'm a very tall person, and my mosquito net did not completely cover me. I'm more than six feet, three inches. I was also going deep into the rain forest. Once, I was in the rain forest, and I'd worn short sleeves. I never did that again.

DOUG SIMMONS: He fell gravely ill. We were really worried.

MARK SCHOOFS: Omololu brought me to a doctor in Lagos, and the doctor diagnosed me with malaria. And furthermore, diagnosed it as drug resistant. Quinine is a terrible, terrible medicine; it gives you all sorts of side effects. I stayed in this hospital for twenty-four, forty-eight hours, very worried about whether they were giving me clean needles. The nurse very sternly said to me, "Don't worry. We're going to use a clean needle!"

RICHARD GOLDSTEIN: At some point I said to him, "You have to come home, you can't keep doing this. Your health is involved, and you have malaria, for god's sake."

MARK SCHOOFS: Don called me and wanted to bring me home. I didn't want to go home. I was on this very hard-to-get Nigerian visa.

I spent one day recovering, and then I started working half days, still being malarial, having fevers. I was writing about Fela Kuti and his brother.* Fela had died, but his brother had been the health minister. Fela denied that AIDS existed, but his brother held a press conference to say that Fela had died of AIDS and to talk with his fans, who were these very poor—what we would call gangs. They were called "area boys." They were poor people, often into petty crime, who lived in the slums and margins of this huge, teeming, unbelievable city who didn't know anybody who died of AIDS, but they did know Fela, and they didn't believe he had died of AIDS.

Next, I was going to this unbelievable slum, which I wish I were like Borges or Gabriel García Márquez, because I would write about it in that way. It was a slum that was entirely built on the water because there was no more land left. It was amazing. But I was doing all of this while having malaria.

---

* Fela Kuti was a Nigerian musician and activist who pioneered Afrobeat.

I didn't wanna leave. I knew that I had a story to tell. I talked with Don on the phone, and I said, "Listen, I'm getting better. I have drugs, I've talked with Western doctors"—that he would recognize as being authorities—"and they say I'm on the right treatment." And he relented, thank god.

I began to write the first piece, which was based in Zimbabwe, and it was about all the orphans. The second piece was about Africans banding together to care for their own. And then the third piece was Fela. But I was beginning to send drafts to Richard.

JUDY MISZNER: It was then we debated on space, 'cause Don wanted more space to run it. We haggled a lot; he convinced me that it was important. He was really relentless about getting the extra space for this because they were really long-form pieces every week.

MARK SCHOOFS: I came back to New York, and I was taking a cab. I left the laptop in the car because I was on my cell phone. That would have been the disaster to end all the disasters, except that when I was in Africa, I was *maniacal* about backing everything up, because I was convinced that I was going to be robbed or lose something. Not only that, I made backups of the hard drive.

We were beginning to start to publish. Suddenly they began coming out like rapid fire. Then it became a little bit of a race.

MARK SCHOOFS, "AIDS: THE AGONY OF AFRICA," *VILLAGE VOICE*, OCTOBER 18, 2005

Penhalonga, Zimbabwe—They didn't call Arthur Chinaka out of the classroom. The principal and Arthur's uncle Simon waited until the day's exams were done before breaking the news: Arthur's father, his body wracked with pneumonia, had finally died of AIDS. They were worried that Arthur would panic, but at 17 years old, he didn't. He still had two days of tests, so while his father lay in the morgue, Arthur finished his exams. That happened in 1990. Then in 1992, Arthur's uncle Edward died of AIDS. In 1994, his uncle Richard died of AIDS. In 1996, his uncle Alex died of AIDS. All of them are buried on the homestead where they grew up and where their parents and Arthur still live, a collection of thatch-roofed huts in the mountains near Mutare, by Zimbabwe's border with Mozambique. But HIV hasn't finished with this family. In April, a fourth uncle lay coughing in his hut, and the virus had blinded Arthur's aunt Eunice, leaving her so thin and weak she couldn't walk without help. By September both were dead.

DOUG SIMMONS: Don said, "This could be it. This could be the one," because he really wanted to win the Pulitzer for Leonard Stern. He referred to Leonard as "my liege."

Winning a Pulitzer, it turns out, you need an exceptional piece of work, and you also need to know how to play the ropes.

MARK SCHOOFS: I wrote the nomination letter.

DOUG SIMMONS: Mark, at Don's suggestion, he called up Gene Roberts at the *Philadelphia Inquirer*—I think he's one of the hotshots on the Pulitzer panel that year—just to chat him up.

MARK SCHOOFS: He had retired at that point, he was a very famous editor, won a bazillion Pulitzers. But I showed him my letter. And in this very courtly, kind way, this man who I literally never met read my letter and said, "What you have to understand is that the purpose of this letter is to explain to the judges why this is the best piece of journalism *ever* published. And your letter just doesn't hit that *tone*." Basically, "You need to turn up the volume—a lot!"

In those days, it was a leaky sieve. People found out beforehand, so I knew that I was a finalist. Don, of course, knew because Don knew all the other editors who were on the panels. It was so incestuous. Getting to the finals, I was over the moon. I was up against the *Washington Post*. There was no way I was gonna win. I held a big celebration dinner that I had made the finals. My parents were there. I chose a really, really nice restaurant, and the people who had read all my drafts, we got together, and I was so excited.

You have to understand, I have seen so much death. I've seen so much sickness in very, very poor conditions, people who should not have been dying. There were drugs available, they should not have been dying, and yet they were dying. And then you're gonna be a finalist for some highfalutin prize—it felt very discordant.

DOUG SIMMONS: Then Don, a day before the news was out, he came into the office and shut the door. He said, "It happened."

RICHARD GOLDSTEIN: We won the Pulitzer over all of these hotshot foreign correspondents. The first openly gay man to win a Pulitzer, I believe. An independent operator, working for the *Voice*, openly gay, wins a Pulitzer in foreign correspondence.

MARK SCHOOFS: Before it was all announced, I knew that this thing had been decided and that at some point I was going to hear. I was at my desk reporting; the phone rings. I can see from the little screen that the extension is Don's extension. I pick up the phone, and Don, in that low, gravelly voice he had, says only two words. "You won."

I didn't believe it.

I called my partner and let him know. Then I just had to get out of the office. I went to Tompkins Square Park, which is a short walk away and is one of my favorite parks in the city. I just sat on a bench. It's springtime, and I was there in the East Village, which felt like the right place to be—the center of AIDS activism—and let it wash over me.

CHAPTER 75
"WHAT'S CRAIGSLIST?"

LEONARD STERN: One of my sons had a new au pair working in his house, helping with the kids. She had just moved to New York. I said to my son, "Where did you find this young lady?" "Oh, on Craigslist in San Francisco." So, I said, "What's Craigslist?

CRAIG NEWMARK: In 1994 I was at Charles Schwab basically evangelizing the internet. I started a little CC [email] list of cool events. It grew by word of mouth, and more people wanted to be on the thing. Over time people started to say, "Hey, can we put this job on there?" Or "Can you post this thing I want to sell?"

And I said, "Hey, how about apartments?" This is the first half of 1995. In the middle of 1995, I had about 240 names on the CC list, and the email tool I was using started breaking.

So, I had to use a list server and give the thing a name. By now, people were already calling it Craigslist. I was going to call it SF Events. But people who were smarter than me said, "Hey, we already call it Craigslist. Let's keep it personal and quirky and just call it Craigslist."

In December 1998 I started making a real company of things.

LEONARD STERN: I started to understand, I went on and I looked at Craigslist, and I said, "This is the future."

The *Village Voice* was heavily dependent on classifieds. We ran millions of lines a year. It was hugely profitable because we got much higher page rates than we got for the front-of-the-book ads. So, I asked our financial people, what would our profit and loss look like if one day we lost 70 or 80 percent of our classifieds? They called me back in less than an hour and said, "Very easy. We go from a very profitable newspaper to a substantial loss."

JUDY MISZNER: It was pretty clear when you removed elements of the classified what it did to the business. The classified business is what sustained the *Voice* and all newspapers.

LEONARD STERN: I thought about it some more—like, for an hour—and I was going to the airport. I had a telephone in my car. I was on my way to Europe. I picked up the phone and I spoke to David, and I made the decision to sell it. I did not want to take the risk. So, after owning it for fourteen years, I decided that the future looks too risky, and the probability was that I was going to be looking at a long-term demise of print newspapers.

DAVID SCHNEIDERMAN: Leonard always said he's going to own it forever. His kids will have it. Then out of nowhere, he calls me. It was somewhere in the summer of 1999. He said, "Did you see those numbers?" I knew the classified numbers, but I was still thinking, "Well, we'll figure out how to beat this." He said, "I have to sell."

I was the optimist. Stupid me. Leonard was able to see around corners in terms of the economy like no one else I have ever known. He called the 1987 recession six months before it happened. I was stunned, but Leonard was a force of nature. I didn't have any great arguments against what he was seeing there. The numbers are the numbers.

LEONARD STERN: I hired an investment banker who was an expert in the publishing business. I said, "Sell it." It took them a month or two, and it was over. New Times were trying to buy it. I thought those people were terrible people from what I had heard, not based on firsthand knowledge. They had just a terrible reputation. And David didn't want to have staff put up with people like that. So, I said, "OK, we won't sell it to them." We turned out to be right on that one.

DAVID SCHNEIDERMAN: He said, "You can't say publicly why I'm selling it because I won't get a good price." I wasn't allowed to say, "I'm selling it because Leonard decided that the classifieds were going to fall off the earth."

This group came in—Weiss, Peck and Greer—and two other banks: Goldman Sachs fund and a Canadian bank. They seemed to be nice guys. I felt they were going to be the most reasonable, plus they had the money to do it. Then Leonard called up, he said, "The New Times guys want to come in and offer us." I said, "Leonard, I beg you not to do that. They'll destroy this place. They're going to fire everybody." I completely freaked. They came in with an offer that was $10 million more than what the Weiss, Peck and Greer guys wanted. I said, "Leonard, it's your money, but I just think it'd be a terrible legacy for you to sell to these guys," so he took the lower offer. He sold us to Weiss, Peck and Greer, so I'm relieved.

If the New Times guys bought it, I wasn't going to stick around. I always felt that part of my role was to try to protect the paper's independence from any owner. I felt that from the time I was editor. I thought I had dodged a bullet, and thought these guys were going to be good. They said they'll probably keep it for five years.

Probably a week or maybe not more than two, I get a call from one of the bankers who knew I had steered it to them for less money. They were aware that I didn't want the New Times guys. "The New Times banker just called." I said, "So what?" "He wants to get together and talk about merging." I said, "Wait a fucking second, we just closed this deal." He said, "We have to listen. We represent money of investors." I said, "Shit."

We're having dinner with Jim Larkin and Mike Lacey. That was, for me, an incredibly uncomfortable dinner. We exchanged financials with New Times. Lacey just ripped into the *Voice* and said it's overstaffed, and everybody's lazy.

I said, "What the fuck are you talking about?"

"This is what we do in Phoenix. Why do you have all these theater critics?"

I said, "Do you have any fucking idea what theater in New York is like compared to Phoenix?" I was insulted. We got into this huge argument. I said, "You've got to be joking. You'd say that you can do it on one theater critic in Phoenix, so we can do one theater critic in New York? You're fucking nuts."

Nick DeCarlo, who was my CFO, would come up with all these arguments for why we shouldn't buy them. They were losing money in a bunch of their papers. They hated me because I had bought these other papers that they wanted, and they knew exactly how I had done it and they just were infuriated. Plus, I wasn't an owner, and they were furious that I was having a say. They didn't even think I should be at the table.

I fought it for five years.

2000–2023

"WISH YOU WERE HERE"

CHAPTER 76

"I'M FROM THE INTERNET, AND THE INTERNET IS COMING!"

ANIL DASH: I moved to Manhattan summer '97—I was twenty-one years old—and I saw the banner in Cooper Square. And I was like, "That's where the art is!" It was a very Pollyanna-ish view. I went through a couple of gigs, and I was hustling. At that time, you worked in "computers"; it wasn't even the internet yet. Three years later, 2000, was when I had gotten laid off from the dot-com boom going bust the first time the bubble burst. I had been in the music business, and I'd seen Napster and been like, "Oh, this business is done."

Then I saw a job listing in early 2001 for the *Village Voice*. My best friend growing up, his mom's boyfriend was the op-ed editor for a local newspaper, the *Harrisburg Patriot News*. He was my view of the media world. That how I found out what the *Village Voice* was. I was a big Prince fan, and he had a song, "All the Critics Love U in New York." Later on, I would realize it was basically about Christgau and Nelson George.

AKASH GOYAL: I grew up with relatively conservative Indian parents on Long Island, and it was one of those classic situations where it was unsaid that I would likely become a doctor. I'm the son of a doctor.

I started seeing bands play in the city. I would always do it in secret. I would read who was coming to town in the *Voice*. I discovered media studies and communication towards the end of my years in college. I moved back in with my parents in Long Island. I remember seeing a classified ad for a part-time editorial assistant at the *Long Island Voice*. I faxed my resume from my parents' house, and within, like, five minutes I got a call. I threw on this really cheesy sharkskin suit. Ward Harkavy walked in, he was the editor in chief, and he grabbed the knot of my tie, and he goes, "Welcome aboard. Lose the tie."*

Two months in, somebody was flipping through the *New York Post*, and there was an article about a merger that happened. It was like, "Nothing is expected to change, except for the folding of the *Long Island Voice*." That's when I wound up in the digital team at the *Voice*. This was in February or March of 2000. It was part production, part copyediting. It was basically taking the contents of the paper and making sure that they get put up online correctly.

ANIL DASH: I got the gig beginning of July 2001. I could talk well for a guy who programmed computers. That was the superpower. I remember the first time I saw Musto, the first time I saw Christgau. Those were still rock stars to me. I was supposed to work on the classifieds. At that time, overwhelmingly, the real estate listings are what paid the bills. It was some personals and the real estate listings. My third day there, Craigslist launched in New York. I knew. I was like, "Oh my god."

It hadn't been in New York; it had been in San Francisco. I knew all about it from friends in the industry there. That was how they found all their apartments.

I didn't know anything about protocol, and I'm just talking to somebody: "Hey, what are we doing about Craigslist?" My boss who'd hired me, he'd run the digital stuff for a long time. I didn't realize I was antagonizing my boss on my second day of work. They were like, "Who's Craig? What are you talking about?" because it wasn't a big deal here yet. I was like, "Oh my god, we're screwed!"

AKASH GOYAL: He was definitely sounding the alarm bells. It was this pompous response: "Everyone's got a price. We'll just buy him [Craig Newmark] out." I remember being like, "You people have *no clue* what you're up against if you're being warned that your industry is potentially going to be

---

* The *Long Island Voice* was a paper started with Andrea Stern as publisher and John Mancini as editor in chief. It printed from April 1997 to January 2000. Ward Harkavy later joined the staff at the *Voice*.

disrupted and you might be decimated as a business and your approach is, 'Oh, whatever, we'll just buy him out.'"

By Craig making that free in the first place, that was a "fuck you" to the establishment.

DAVID SCHNEIDERMAN: In the mid-'90s, Fujitsu showed me technology where they took *Village Voice* classified ads and they put them online and showed you how they become searchable. It blew my mind. I remember saying, "Find me a two-bedroom with a fireplace in Chelsea." Six ads come up. Whoa. That was amazingly efficient and terrific. I said, "Let's do this. Let's create this technology."

It looked great. Then Fujitsu decided that they didn't want to be in that business, so that went away. We kept looking for partners. At one point, Knight Ridder approached us, and they were developing a series of websites based in cities, and they wanted to partner with us. I remember being so fucking arrogant. "OK. We have something they want. What are they gonna do for me?"

JAMES HANNAHAM: 1995 was when the World Wide Web started cooking. It seemed as if, for a while, there was only one story. And that story was "This is on the internet now!" There was no opinion. There was no nothing for a really long time. It was just like, "Here it is! On the Web!"

Then around that same time, I heard a statistic that chilled me to the bone. One dollar a word was a good rate in 1953. Pay for freelance writers has been going steadily down as inflation goes up. I was like, "Well, I don't see this changing. Maybe I should jump off this ship before it sinks."

JUDY MISZNER: We started to realize that we needed an online strategy for content. We need to start to look at our website as something separate and apart from the newspaper. One is cannibalizing the other—that was the biggest issue. If we started to put everything online for free, the listings, etc., then you're losing a lot of revenue from the classifieds. But if we didn't put them online, people aren't gonna get a response.

ELIZABETH SPIERS: There weren't that many publications that were really online at the time. Even the *Observer* would put the paper online once a week. *New York* magazine had a website, but it was owned by a separate company.

ANIL DASH: I had a personal blog, but I was writing about tech. I was just a nerd writing about nerd shit, but it would get picked up. Nobody had a blog then. This is so early. *Gawker* had not yet launched. And *HuffPo* had not yet launched. I'd been blogging from '99. It's just a hobby, whatever. Also, there was *no* audience. There was no Google News. There was no way to find this stuff. There's no social media. So how would you know? I couldn't tell people, "The whole world is about to change, and it's these weird, janky-looking websites like Craigslist." I felt like Chicken Little. I'd be like, "This is where it's all going. Whether it is culture or arts or 'this is where I want to get an apartment' or classified ads, personal ads, or dating— it's all going here." A couple months after that, Match.com launched, and I couldn't explain to people, "I'm from the internet, and the internet is coming." Because it sounds crazy, right?

DAVID SCHNEIDERMAN: The minute Craigslist came to the city, literally within a few weeks, our ads—it was slow. Then it stopped growing, and it never grew again.

JUDY MISZNER: Like, overnight, a switch flipped.

ANIL DASH: I don't think anybody would anticipate how quickly it shifted. I was the only person in the office using Google. I'd been there three months. I had immediately stumbled into every fraught business thing that was happening, just like a bull in a china shop.

And then 9/11 happens.

CHAPTER 77

"STOP THE PRESSES!"

ANIL DASH: I had been there three months. I'd been up till two or three in the morning, working on something on the website, and crashed. My alarm went off at nine o'clock. And I turn on the TV, which is so funny—I would *never* turn on the TV first thing in the morning—but I did then. The first plane had hit, not the second. I was just like, "Oh, this is like some accident, some dumbass doesn't know how to fly a plane." I was having breakfast. The second plane hit, and I immediately got a bunch of AOL Instant Messenger—AIM—messages from people. That was this really jarring moment.

We had alerts and email for when there would be a problem with the computer servers. And what it was, it was the spike in traffic: there were so many people rushing to the website within ten minutes the site started to fall over.

ALISA SOLOMON: I was called for jury duty that week. It was Tuesday. I must have left around eight thirty in the morning, maybe a little earlier than that. I took the A train to Chambers Street. When I got out at Chambers Street, I saw a bunch of people standing on the sidewalk, gaping up at the World Trade Center. There was a giant hole and one of them aflame.

There was a guy on the corner taking pictures with a digital camera, and those were not that common yet. I don't know what came over me, but I said, "I'm a journalist, can I have your pictures? Can I have your phone number?"

As we were standing there watching, the second plane came and hit it. People were freaking out. And then, suddenly, I thought, "I'm going to be late to jury duty." Of course, it was clear there was no jury duty that day.

I stood in line for the pay phone in the court building. I had a flip cell phone, but there was no service. The first person I called was Don Forst.

"You won't believe what I just saw. You want me to talk to people and try to write something?" He said, "Well, we've already gone to the plant, so we'll cover it next week."

I said, "I have the phone number of a guy who has pictures." He said, "Get up here."

I walked up. All the subways were closed, so it took me a while to walk up. I started talking to people, listening to them waiting for phones on line. I didn't do formal interviewing, but I talked to people. I took some notes. I got up to the office after however long it takes to walk from down there up to Cooper Square, probably forty minutes.

JUDY MISZNER: We happened to have a board meeting. It was at some office on Lexington Avenue in the 40s. I was commuting on the train; they had said a plane hit the World Trade Center. It was bizarre—I got out of Penn Station, and I just immediately got into a cab. I'm looking behind me, and you could see the flames. My husband was in the South Tower, so I'm trying to get ahold of him, and we did connect, and he said—this is before it hit—"Everything's OK. I'm gonna evacuate anyway." We see the other plane.

David Schneiderman and I decided to walk down to the office. We're seeing the people coming up, and they were covered in ashes. At this point the other tower had collapsed. I wasn't freaking out because I had spoken to my husband.

R.C. BAKER: I had started in '99 being the print overseer. By that time we were printing at *Newsday*. That's when we changed from negatives to PDFs. So, 9/11, I had my stick with all the pages on it. It's eight o'clock in the morning, and I'm waiting on the train at Penn Station, and a guy gets on the train and says, "We got to get out of here. They're attacking the city; they've already bombed the city!" I just figure, you know, "nut," and I drink my coffee. It wasn't until we came up in Queens and I looked back that I saw the towers burning.

Our original cover was a pair of gloved hands climbing a chain-link fence because we were doing a thing about the DC protests because everybody was protesting Bush.

TED KELLER: It was this World Trade Organization protest. We closed at, like, three o'clock in the morning for some reason, because Forst was into it. I go home, and I crash. I'm dead asleep. I live in the West Village. I hear this bang over my head at, like, eight thirty in the morning. That was when the plane was going by. I didn't know what it was. Don Forst called me and said, "Get the fuck in here."

R.C. BAKER: The towers are going down. I had a flip phone. I called my wife, and I called Don, and I said, "Don, our cover? It doesn't seem quite right." He said, "No, no, we're fine." Fifteen minutes later, the phone rings.

JUDY MISZNER: The office was pretty empty. Alisa was down there. She had sent some pictures to Don, and they were amazing. We get down to the office and we get inside, and there's my husband in Don's office. He pulled out a bottle of scotch and he gave him a drink when he came in.

ALISA SOLOMON: I walked into Don's office, and he took a look at me, and said, "Sit down." He opened his desk drawer and poured me some scotch. He said, "Drink this," which I did. I don't think I ever drank scotch in the morning before in my life. And then he sat me down at the terminal just across from his office. He said, "Just start writing down what you saw," and I sat there and wrote.

I remember Julie Lobbia walked through. She was getting her stuff and going to the hospital. I sat down and wrote a thousand words, fifteen hundred—literally what I saw. Meanwhile, they called the guy and got the pictures.

ALISA SOLOMON, "THE BASTARDS!: TERRORISTS BRING WAR TO OUR SHORES," *VILLAGE VOICE*, SEPTEMBER 11, 2001

A real war has come to these shores now, bringing massive violence into America for the first time. The terrible human casualties of today's attacks haven't even begun to be counted yet. Some of the intangible ones to come are obvious—the First Amendment, for starters. The altered city skyline is only the most visible manifestation of the size of the change.

JUDY MISZNER: He said, "I never thought in my life I'd say, "Stop the press." They were not going to wait too long for us to replace it. We had a very short period of time—and within an hour, get them an image, a headline.

ALISA SOLOMON: Don did something that was actually really generous to me—he came out of his office and used the phone where I was sitting to call the plant and literally say, "Stop the presses." He did that on purpose. An uncharacteristically menschy thing for him to do.

R.C. BAKER: He did do that for her benefit because they weren't running yet. I wrote a piece about what it's like being on press. I said, "No one says, 'Stop the presses,' because it's too loud. If you need to stop the press, you just put your thumb down and then they stop." He was telling her, "This is a hugely important story that you're working on."

They got the photo from that guy; I think they gave him two hundred bucks. I don't think there's credit for that photo of the plane hitting the tower in that issue.

I'm out there printing it. I walk in, and they're screaming at me, because they always waited for me to come before they would start the presses. It was a literal shouting match.

ANIL DASH: It was so intense. Like, everybody was working 24/7, every single journalist. On the tech side—all we did was just keep the website running. Because all of a sudden, everybody went to the internet, like, "What's local news in New York doing?" It wasn't easy to just have a website up and running back then. There was nothing on the *New York Times* yet. And I don't think there was anything on CNN, or maybe they just had their first headline. Deeply intertwined with my memory of the day is people wanting to find out what's going on. Over the course of the morning, we had to take everything else off the site. There was one plain web page. It had no styles—it was whatever the default font was in your web browser, pure plain text: "Here's the facts that we know."

AKASH GOYAL: It was a scramble for several days. I remember having to show my ID to get below the police barricade at 14th Street just to even get into the office. A lot of people who were family members of people that were missing were sending photos of their family members and dropping off photos of their family members to the *Voice*, being like, "Can you help me find my husband?" Or "Can you help me find my brother?" We started making photo galleries and putting up these pictures.

JESUS DIAZ: And then Forst uses something that he wanted to use on a cover for years and years and years.

R.C. BAKER: Don, being Don, came up with a very *Daily News/New York Newsday* headline: "THE BASTARDS!"

JUDY MISZNER: He loved those tabloid headlines.

TED KELLER: It's the worst part of Don. He was enjoying it. He always wanted to use the word "bastards" on the cover, on any cover. He didn't care who the bastards were, and it was this weird, apolitical thing. It was like, "Pearl Harbor, the bastards who attacked us!" That's what it was. And I was like, "Fuck you." It was one of those close-to-breaking points between him and me. It was a lousy cover.

R.C. BAKER: It's getting into early evening. I'm on the platform at Long Island, waiting for the LIRR. On the other side, trains were pulling in, and people were pouring off the trains. On my side, there was me and two other people because no one was going into the city. I've got thirty copies of the issue in my messenger bag, and this guy comes up to me and just doesn't say hello or anything. He says, "Did you see what those bastards did?!"

It was horrible, but I couldn't help but laugh. I said to him, "Mister, you need this." I handed him a copy. And there it is, "THE BASTARDS!" across the cover of the *Village Voice*. So, Don's instincts may have been right.

JUDY MISZNER: The next one was an interesting one. We were all pretty blown away when we saw what Ted wanted to do for it. Ted Keller had that postcard over the old towers, and it was: "Wish You Were Here."

R.C. BAKER: It's a masterpiece. One of Ted's things was, "This is the only thing on the cover, nothing else." And all it said was, "After the Fall."

TED KELLER: I remember going back that day from the offices to my apartment and being totally lost. Because at least in those days, you could look from 10th Street, look straight down through the Washington Square arch, and see the World Trade Center on the left and look to the Empire State building perfectly on your right. I always had a sense of where I was in this big, messy city.

I think Don knew that he had blown it. He was very subdued about the cover, and the joy that he had gotten out of doing "THE BASTARDS!"

thing was replaced by something that I rarely saw out of him, a lost feeling. The magnitude of it came to him well after it should have. And he didn't have any ideas. He didn't know what to do.

Nobody cared until the day after 9/11 about the World Trade Center. Nobody cared because we always thought it was going to be there. They are our mountains, they're our geography. They weren't buildings. They were our North and South Poles, at least for those of us who lived in the lower half of Manhattan. When the towers themselves were lost, all that stuff gained immensely more emotional resonance.

I was looking for something that expressed the loss we felt. It was based on a little picture that had appeared in the *Village Voice*, by somebody who was then a staff photographer, Kristine Larsen. It's the classic minimalism-maximalism. Someone raised their hand in front of the skyline of New York, with the World Trade Center in the background as if they had it in the palm of their hand. I'd never seen a romantic view of the World Trade Center before.

I sat down and drew it out in very simple form. I walked back with a sticky, and I put it on Don's desk. Don looked at it. He sighed this long sigh. "Go do it."

The cover of the issue two weeks after 9/11. Cover image © Village Voice/ Street Media.

CHAPTER 78

"YOU ARE CHOOSING THE WINNERS!"

MICHAEL MUSTO: My column had always been doing a tightwire act of funny-serious, serious-funny. I would mix some crazy party and then go into an ACT UP protest. I had no problem reintroducing things that some people might think are trivial. I knew that some people turned to my column for a giggle or for information about what was going on and for entertainment, so that was my role.

ANIL DASH: Google News launched because of 9/11. They got so many headline searches for news that they created Google News in October 2001 to respond to demand.

I get so mad about this. It was made by software engineers who could not understand the thumb they were putting on a scale, that what they chose to put into Google News would shape the news ecosystem. I would shout up and down about it, *"You* are choosing the winners!" And they would deny, deny, deny. The same way Facebook still does today that they choose the winners of what information services and which misinformation gets shared. All that started then—nineteen years ago!—was a coder making an algorithm that chooses what information people could see but denying that that was an editorial choice. The die was cast then.

AKASH GOYAL: There was a mass migration to digital media. If you're trying to figure out which hospital somebody is in, TV is not going to do that for you. So digital was the only medium where that could potentially come to fruition. We were getting news out that was on a hyperlocal level compared to what most traditional news orgs were doing. It sped up the news cycle.

ANIL DASH: I don't think we could understand how big a shift that was, the idea of abundance of information and content. We had been so constrained by physical constraints—"I am going to hold a CD or DVD, a newspaper"—that predicting the change, you sound like a crazy person. If you say to a person in 1995 what the media world is gonna look like in 2005, let alone in 2015, it sounds like science fiction, right?

AKASH GOYAL: Blogs obviously had this interactivity, which was a thing that made it new. People needed to talk to each other after 9/11, and digital allows you to do that in a way that one-way media don't. Everybody as a society was feeling this need for connection and the need for understanding. Here's a medium that allows you to connect. You want to hear about what happens the moment it happens, not in the next morning's paper.

GARY DAUPHIN: If you want a fight that happened in the '90s, which the *Voice* totally lost, it's this fight for digital content. The *Voice* was a place that was based on a really powerful relationship between the reader and the community. One of the big conceits about Black writing is that the relationship between the writer, the subject, and the audience—it's all one community. Giving up the subscription and going free just married the paper to the worst possible digital model. What the *Voice* should have done is paywall subscriptions—narrow transactional relationships between people—and really sell what it had, which is community. The *Voice* is an invisible, emotional community.

JAMES HANNAHAM: Freelancers were like the canary in the coal mine with the economy. And then the work vanished. I had been talking to *Spin* about going on contract. Then 9/11 happened, and it was like, "We have no more advertising!"

ANIL DASH: Real estate classifieds dropped, like, 70, 80 percent, that fall, September, October. Like immediately. And that was my job. I remember being in a big-deal publisher meeting, and I'm looking around, and they're like, "Well, the attacks, but it'll come back when people move back into the city and do whatever." And I was like, "I don't think so."

This was the wildest thing: you'd call the number, and it went to the *Cleveland Free Times*, and they would fax the order back to New York, and somebody would type it in. I was like, "*This is madness!*" Like, you should just go to the website and type in, "I have an apartment on the Lower East Side, does anybody want to be my roommate?" I was like, "Guys, we're gonna get our asses kicked."

CRAIG NEWMARK: It's largely publishers who have missed the boat. Sometimes it's easier to say something like that instead of taking responsibility.

DAVID SCHNEIDERMAN: The classifieds of the *Voice* were half of our revenue. The question is, do you bastardize that? It was a zero-sum game. The only thing Leonard Stern could've done is, "OK, let's set up a version of Craigslist, and whatever happens to the *Voice* happens." Now, in retrospect, maybe somebody should have done that.

Newmark did destroy newspapers. There's no two ways about it.

CHAPTER 79

"WE HAVE TO UTILIZE THE WEB TO STAY RELEVANT"

ANIL DASH: Nick Denton showed me the prototype of *Gawker*. I knew him from the blogging world. I introduced him to Liz Spiers, the first editor of *Gawker*.

ELIZABETH SPIERS: When I met him, Nick was a serial entrepreneur who had been a journalist in the '90s for the *Financial Times* and *The Economist*. Nick started Gizmodo in August of 2002, thinking that it might be good marketing for the software company that he wanted to do. And nobody really commercialized blogs at that point. There weren't ads on blogs; that wasn't a thing. So, when he approached me about writing *Gawker*, I agreed to do it, thinking that it would be a ten-hour-a-week project, and it just very quickly took over my life. We launched *Gawker* in December of '03.

Nick might have tried to recruit Michael Musto to contribute to *Gawker*. But I know he liked Musto's columns and the way he approached it.

ANIL DASH: We went to KGB Bar on Fourth. He had one of those clunky old laptops. He's like, "Here's this thing." They had the gadget site at first, Gizmodo, and then they did *Gawker*. He was like, "We're updating gossip here six times a day." I was like, "This is wild."

I worked up my courage, like, a week or two later, and I went down to Musto—and I was like, "Hey, this guy who I know from San Francisco, he showed me this thing. You should take a look at it. They update it all the time." He's like, "OK."

He wasn't dismissive. He was polite about it. But it's like, "I do my thing once a week. Why would I care if they're updating six times a day?" He'd never heard of a blog—this was not a word people used at that point. I couldn't make the case. It was exactly the same thing as Craigslist.

DAVID SCHNEIDERMAN: It was really hard getting people in the newsroom to buy into it, but the younger people did. Nat Hentoff was still writing on a typewriter. Nat refused to give up his friggin' typewriter. We were in different eras. They saw it as a threat.

MICHAEL MUSTO: *Gawker* was a huge influence, and they were exciting. They had brass balls, they had nerve to write whatever they wanted. It was like *Spy* magazine in a new form where they had items all day long. They wrote about me a lot. And they were actually very nice to me, usually. Some people felt that I was the original *Gawker*.

But all that energy was taking away from the *Voice*, and it was very savvy of the *Voice* to realize we have to jump on this bandwagon, we have to utilize the web as a tool to stay relevant, because, again, why wait till Wednesday to get a lot of this information? There was also the matter of, "The writers should get paid extra if they have to also blog."

ELIZABETH SPIERS: Writers, especially people who're getting paid to write for print, viewed it as a cannibalization of their job. They didn't want to write online and not get paid the same rates that they're getting paid for print. And that was a legitimate concern.

It took Nick a long time to even acknowledge that *Gawker* could be a real business. And also, there was just no competition. I didn't understand why media companies weren't adding blogs, even then.

ALLEN BARRA: So much of what the *Voice* sportswriters were doing prefigured blogs.

WILL LEITCH: The idea of *Deadspin* was to have it be an alt-weekly for the world of sports, because there wasn't one. A lot of the *Village Voice*'s power came as a response and in a way to react to the weaknesses of newspapers. That's what *Deadspin* did with the world of sportswriting that is now infused throughout sports all across the board.

When *Deadspin* got really, really popular really fast, ESPN had a little blog section, and you started to see all of these publications start to have little blog things, and the *Village Voice* was a part of that.

ALLEN ST. JOHN: I was writing for the *Village Voice* and the *Wall Street Journal* at the same time, both writing about sports. And the strange thing was, I was writing almost the same thing. What the *Wall Street Journal* wanted and what the *Voice* wanted—this would have been early 2002, 2003 maybe—they were looking for the smart preview piece, the smart analysis piece, and they're assuming that people have gotten their news elsewhere.

MICHAEL MUSTO: It increasingly became like a survival of the fittest. Perez Hilton had evolved as the big gossip site, and it was strictly internet. He was plugged into all the young talent, and he was posting a lot of sometimes racy things; he was getting tons of traffic. It became clear that this was taking a lot of the energy out of the alternative weekly.

AKASH GOYAL: We actually approached Musto quite a bit about turning his column into a blog. Eventually, we succeeded.

ANIL DASH: By late '02, early '03, you just saw the media world going there. I was, like, the tools are all out there; you can just get them. But who's gonna write it? Because they were this network of all the different alt-weeklies, there was no single strategy.

AKASH GOYAL: When it comes to writing about topical news and writing about breaking news and writing about, like, politics, there is this shelf life to it. You could be having your point of view in the conversation faster than waiting for it to go to the presses.

Jim Ridgeway used to give us early breaking news; we'd put up digital-only articles.

ANIL DASH: Trent Lott—do you remember when he had to resign because he praised Strom Thurmond and segregation? In blogs, this was a huge deal because the people who caught it were bloggers. They were like, "This has been underreported, and he's endorsing white supremacy"—and that was back when people still resigned for that. "The bloggers have called it out, how come none of these papers have called it out?"

AKASH GOYAL: When Kara Walsh took over, then we did get more serious about the tech side of things.* We brought on three developers who wrote code.

---

* Walsh was the VP of *Village Voice* Online.

AKASH GOYAL: We made Village Voice Radio right around the time that podcasting was becoming a thing. We were ahead in spirit, but behind in logistics, if that makes any sense.

CHUCK EDDY: There was one point where they called me in and they said, "Chuck, we have a predicament. We need to hire a porn reviewer. We figured you would know somebody." And I was, like, why would they think I would know somebody? And then I'm like, "Actually, I do." Nick Catucci was hired as the porn writer. It wouldn't be hard to go back and look at Nick's columns and see what ads are on those pages. I assume those columns all appeared around the time that the *Voice* had activated its website.

AKASH GOYAL: When he started doing it, every porn studio in America and probably even overseas started sending boxes and boxes and boxes of porn. He had nowhere to put it. We started putting all these boxes on shelves inside the radio studio.

ANIL DASH: I shared one of the cubicles with Robin Byrd for a year, who would do the weird cable access topless show. She had a show on Village Voice Radio.

AKASH GOYAL: It was kind of like a skunk-works operation. It never felt like, "I'm working in a professional digital company."

MICHAEL MUSTO: They had me doing a gay porno review column. They wanted me to have a pseudonym. So, I used Waldo Lydecker, who's a pervy, old, closet queen in the movie *Laura*, played by Clifton Webb. That didn't last very long, but it was extra money. I enjoyed watching the porno movies and reviewing them as if they were arthouse films.

ANIL DASH: Nick clearly got the internet.* Like, he would be at those *Gawker* events. He was in that world.

MICHAEL MUSTO: All they wanted was for me to literally read the column out loud. It was the easiest podcast. I'm like, "I'm getting an extra $250 just to read my stupid column?" The podcast went on for a while, but I thought, "This is doomed."

ANIL DASH: Nobody listened to it. It was zero. I was like, "I don't know why we're doing all this." The only place you can know it exists is we had a little thing on the homepage: "Village Voice Radio. Tune in now," and there

---

* In 2004, Nick Catucci became the online managing editor.

was a little promo box. I was like, "This is at least forward-looking." But the implementation of it was so bad. If they'd have done the exact same thing two years later, they could be Joe Rogan or something.

MICHAEL MUSTO: The *Voice* was ahead of the game in the chart of the clicks online.

ANIL DASH: Everybody until that point in history had this article of faith that "I'm gonna write this story and a million people are gonna read it."

We had a thing where if you were inside the office, it would show you how much traffic your story got. It'd be like, "Three hundred people read this online"—which was a lot in those days on the internet.

The first time we turned the switch on I was like, "They're gonna beat us up in the hallway!" We got, like, ten emails in an hour from people being like, "What. The fuck. Is that?" And the first ones are, "Don't worry, that's not public. That's just us." They're like, "No! Nobody should see this!"

It was *everybody*. There were writers: "I don't want my editor to see this." There were editors: "I can't let my writers see what the other writers are doing." Because this person makes more money than this person, but that person is generating ten times as many views as this person. It was a shit show in five minutes. It was so bad. It was as if we had published everybody's salaries.

AKASH GOYAL: We won the National Press Foundation award. We went to this gala in DC, and Dan Rather was the master of ceremonies. In the year 2000, they gave it to WashingtonPost.com; 2001 was VillageVoice.com. Next year was MSNBC.com. Then it was the *New York Times*, then it was CNN, then *National Geographic*, then Bloomberg. It was insane that we won that award. We felt accomplished but also out of our league at the same time.

ANIL DASH: I got canned. It was February or March of '03. I just re-member being so crestfallen, because I was like, "This is the best job I'm ever gonna get." It was a total surprise.

The website was a total afterthought. I was the first person hired specifi-cally for building website features. By the time I left, it was a core part of the business.

After I got fired, I ended up working for my friends who'd built the tools for the blogs that we used at the *Voice* but also that were used by *Gawker* and *Huffington Post*. That's what I did for the next seven years. It was like we were the arms dealers to the rise of social media.

In 2005, after Katrina, there was an editorial retreat in New Orleans. They had all the editors from all the papers. They asked me to come speak. I'd said on my blog, "I tried to get them to do this, but I got fired, and I couldn't do it."

I got an email. It might've been Forst that emailed me. Nobody ever has a moment where your boss's boss's boss sends you an email out of the blue and says, "I wish we'd listened to you."

CHAPTER 80

"SLUT BOY"

RICHARD GOLDSTEIN: I've worked for every editor. Ten, at least. Finally ending with the nightmare of Don Forst. We were fire and ice. He had a lot of anxiety about gay people. It doesn't mean he didn't get along with all of them, but he definitely didn't get along with me. It was the assertiveness that pushed his buttons.

AMY TAUBIN: I knew from the moment Forst got there that there would be war between him and Richard.

DOUG SIMMONS: He couldn't stand Richard. Don admired Richard's talent, put him on the cover all the time. Richard was executive editor. He just didn't like him. And every once in a while he would get up and leave and say, "I'm gonna pull Richard's tail."

RICHARD GOLDSTEIN: He called me "Slut Boy." That was his name for me. They forced me to sit in on sessions where there would be, like, three or four guys from management, and they would be cackling over the whore ads. The meeting was designed so that we would read the lead ads aloud and laugh and cackle. Lesbians he referred to as "toads." He would call people and say, "Get your pretty little ass in here." He would comment on women's breasts. But I was really the main target, and I took it, up to the point where I thought, "I gotta do something about this."

I went to see a lawyer, and the lawyer said, "You should file this because you actually can really protect yourself by doing this." So, then I went to the paper's lawyer—and she told me that "your sexuality is one of the few areas where you're protected. Your boss can insult you up the wazoo, but if they attack your sexuality, you have grounds." The people who threatened to sue him at *Newsday* were a group of women who had been harassed this way. But they decided that he was very good at hiring women, so they didn't sue him.

DENIS HAMILL: He would say inappropriate things, probably, but he wouldn't *do* inappropriate things. If somebody does good work he wouldn't care if it was male, female, gay, straight. He used to call me up and say, "Fucking Michael Musto this week is so fucking great. I read this guy. I didn't even know this world existed." He'd loved him, you know?

MICHAEL MUSTO: He was very supportive to me, paternal, comforting. Let me do what I wanted. He wasn't homophobic with me. That doesn't mean he wasn't homophobic with other people. I did hear different innuendos in the office about inappropriate things he said about women and their body parts. It was very old-school newsroom. He hadn't caught up.

CHUCK EDDY: He liked me. He liked my legs. I remember wearing shorts and him actually catcalling my legs at one point. But he called me a mensch.

AMY TAUBIN: He liked to talk dirty in front of big staff meetings. One on one. He liked to make people uncomfortable by doing that. He wanted to put all these feminists in their place, and he wanted to make it clear that he could fire them. I could be wrong, but I thought he did this pretty much with every woman there. Daring you to say, "Go wash your mouth out with soap."

Don Forst was a lech. He would corner me in the hall. And he was a careful lech. He would get physically, uncomfortably close. And he wanted to talk about, basically, sex. It would be sex in movies. "Who do you go to movies with?" He told me, "Your editor wants you out of here, and I could keep that from happening." It was all about power.

JOHN MANCINI: He famously wanted the dance editor Elizabeth Zimmer to do a story about backsides of the NBA, and she refused. That was early on because he was trying to show he was gonna bring mischief to the scene. A certain dance critic might have said, "Yeah, well, that's a great idea."

JOY PRESS: I had heard whispers; I did not encounter it personally. He was extremely, actually gentleman-like. After one of my issues would come out, he'd give me a bottle of scotch. Or he'd say, "Take your husband out for a nice dinner on me." When I was pregnant, he gave me a book of taxi vouchers. So, he was very paternal to me. During the Monica Lewinsky scandal, I remember sitting in a room, brainstorming or chatting with

Doug and Don, and I remember Don saying how outrageous it was that Clinton had done this. "Sure, I might want to sleep with my assistant, but I'm not gonna do it."

That's one of the things that we are talking about now that was inconceivable to talk about then, because it was the water that we were bathing in. Everybody talked to women that way.

DONNA MINKOWITZ: When I was very new at the *Voice*, there was a gay male film editor. He would make comments about my breasts all the time in front of other people. It made me really uncomfortable, but I didn't think I could do anything about it because he was a gay man. There wasn't this concept that gay men might also sexually harass women. I said nothing to anybody.

DAVID SCHNEIDERMAN: When the #MeToo thing started happening, I said to my wife—I'm sorry to admit this—I said, "I don't think when I was at the *Voice* that was going on." That's how out of it I was.

We figured Alex Cockburn was sleeping with a lot of people. That was a given. Actually, anytime an attractive female intern showed up, there was an assumption that Alex was going to sleep with her. Now, in retrospect, you'd never let that happen in this era. Ross was supposed to have slept with half the staff in the old days. I figured Joe Conason was having relationships on and off. He was a young guy who was single.

It never dawned on me that any of it would be, quote, a problem. And no one even brought it up that way. That shows you what that era was like.

RICHARD GOLDSTEIN: Now, this is an important thing. But because of the ethic today about people sleeping with their secretaries, or people they have power over and all that—the bohemian ethic is that anyone can sleep with anyone, but if the person you want to sleep with says no, that's it. And you cannot punish the person; you cannot penalize the person in any way for turning you down.

RICHARD GOLDSTEIN: He agreed to leave me alone, and so it stopped at that point, but he tried his very best to get me to leave. He would call me in and say, "There's a job at the *Times*, they need somebody on the culture desk, and I can give you a recommendation if you want to go up there. Very good salary." And I'd say, "No, I'm very happy here." He did everything he could to frustrate me as much as possible. If I wrote for another publication, he would say I couldn't do it. Nobody in the *Voice* was ever stopped from writing anywhere they wanted. He didn't want me on television.

I was finally fired, but only when the paper was about to be sold. It looked like they were doing this now because they were firing other people and there couldn't be any objection. And then they tried to reduce my severance.

DON FORST: I had two executive editors, and I only needed one.

RICHARD GOLDSTEIN: That's when I sued them. I was ahead of my time suing them for sexual harassment because of endless derogatory comments about my body and my sexuality.

JUDY MISZNER: He felt he was wrongly let go. But we had pressures, and we had to make decisions around who we could keep, who we couldn't.

RICHARD GOLDSTEIN: It was settled. And part of the suit was that I should sign a gag order. I said, "This is the *Village Voice*. You can't do that." I don't know who may have signed those orders, but I didn't. There was no admission of liability in my lawsuit.

JUDY MISZNER: In my eight years there, I had never witnessed or heard him say anything derogatory about a woman, about being gay. Never. Never, never once. In the eight years I was there, Richard never walked into my office. I never got a complaint from Wayne or Tom. I never got a grievance. There is no way I would have tolerated anything of that nature at all. I'm not discounting it, and I'm not saying it didn't exist.

JOHN MANCINI: Richard was a man in full; he didn't need validation from Don. And what Don thought was playful, Richard took offense at, quite rightly.

He's lucky he was charming to some of us, right? Because if he wasn't, he would have been gone a long time ago. I think about the #MeToo era all the time. Where would you even start with Don? He was, in so many ways, a great person and, in so many ways, trapped in the times. He was born in 1935. So, think about that.

CHAPTER 81

"THEY HAD COMPLETE CONTEMPT FOR THE PAPER"

JAMES RIDGEWAY: I hate those assholes who ruined it and wrecked it. Yeah, those fucking pricks. First of all, there were the two of them. . . . What was the bad one? Lacey. Larkin was the business guy, and Lacey was the master asshole of the whole crowd. Well, they were—what do you call libertarian-politic-type people? Or they didn't have any politics, and they were just into money. But they had nothing to do with journalism; they were just pricks.

DAVID SCHNEIDERMAN: The Weiss, Peck and Greer guys left. I thought, "Maybe I can try to make the best of this and see if these guys at New Times will be reasonable." We talked, and they said a bunch of nice words. I remember writing this email to the staff saying, "I think this can work out." I didn't want them to run to the exits. I figured if they're going to get fired, at least get severance versus quitting over this thing. I could tell the minute the deal closed it was going to suck.

I remember being in a meeting with five of their, quote, executives in New York, and they just thought they knew everything and we didn't know anything about the internet. I'm saying, "You guys got to be joking." The *Voice* had a great site; we had won awards.

After the deal was signed, they poured in from all over, these schmucks from New Times, and they had tons of corporate people. I remember sitting in a meeting in my conference room, and I was suddenly inconsequential. I was like a potted plant.

I don't know if I'll ever forgive Mark Jacobson for this. So, Mark Jacobson writes the story for *New York* magazine which was about how these guys are really interesting, and maybe they'll do something good. And he was critical of the *Voice*—he didn't think it was very good. Mark was one of these people, who I actually liked a lot, who always felt the *Voice* used to be great at some point—usually when he was there. He gave them too much credit.

MARK JACOBSON: To just say that the guy was another dick wouldn't have made a very good story. There was a chance he'd be all right. I mean, it wasn't big, but who knows? Things might happen.

I like to write about people I like. I rarely write about somebody I don't like or I can't find something good about. So, I probably was fucking up in that regard when I was writing about him.

Lacey wanted me to show him around, see what New York was really all about. So, one night we went up to the KGB and above the KGB, which is like this famous literary bar. We went on the top floor. This guy Denis Woychuk, who owns KGB and the theater downstairs—he has this fantastic lair upstairs, these fancy, famous guitars. Lacey goes up there, and he's like, "I saw Bruce play!" He's like one of those guys. "This is really coooool!"

I didn't really realize that he was as cutthroat as he was.

MICHAEL LACEY: Look, a lot of people think I'm a prick. But at least I'm a prick you can understand. I don't sneak up on you. You can see me coming from a long way away. Like the Russian winter.

JUDY MISZNER: When I met them, all of my worst fears came true. They were both really crude, unprofessional, old-boys'-club bullies. Here I was, a woman in a leadership role at their flagship paper. They had one woman in the editorial group. I wanted to wash my hands every time I shook them.

At the beginning, they wanted information, and they were very complimentary of what we've accomplished. But then as the deal got solidified more, the truer colors came out. One of the guys wanted to sit in on one of our sales team meetings. The sale wasn't done yet. And this guy just took over the meeting and tried every way to be very demeaning and demoralizing to me. It was horrible. I almost quit. But I felt I still had work to do in transitioning and that it would be better for everyone there if I stayed. It was one of the worst days of my professional career.

DAVID SCHNEIDERMAN: The editors weren't necessarily assholes the way Larkin and Lacey were. Some of them were actually pretty good editors. The corporate mentality and the sales mentality was pretty sick and fucked up. If that company still existed, they would have dozens of sexual harassment lawsuits. Dozens.

It was Skip Berger who had that famous quote.* When they were looking to buy the *Seattle Weekly*, he said, "You guys are just about booze and testosterone." They liked that. They felt that was a badge of honor.

TOM ROBBINS: Lacey and Larkin showed up, and they didn't want to talk to anybody. I remember going upstairs and meeting individually with Lacey. He was there for, like, a week, and they hadn't introduced themselves to people. I said to Larkin, "Why don't you guys call a meeting and introduce yourselves?" So that was the dumbest idea I ever had, because then Lacey actually does call the meeting.

J. HOBERMAN: The whole staff is there. It was in the big conference room. Lacey, I don't remember if he puts his boot up on the table or if I'm remembering it like that. He's letting people go on. People had a lot of problems with Don. Some people, myself included, thought, "Who knows, maybe things will get better." He listened. He was good-natured. People were either being friendly or cautious or saying nothing.

TOM ROBBINS: Lacey sits down and puts his goddamn cowboy boots up on the table and says, "Get ready to say goodbye to your friends"—and so pisses off Syd Schanberg, one of the greatest reporters of our time, that Syd literally got up, walked out, and never came back.** Lacey just made a fool of himself. He sounded like a buffoon. Syd told me later, "I just realized there was no point—I was never gonna write for this guy."

But you'd think a guy sitting in the same room with Sydney Schanberg and Nat Hentoff would have some sense of the fact that these are some of the giants of journalism. And he couldn't give less than a shit. He made that clear by putting those big cowboy boots up on the table, just the worst single display.

J. HOBERMAN: They had complete contempt for the paper.

---

* Berger is a former longtime editor in chief of the *Seattle Weekly*.

** Sydney Schanberg is best known for his coverage of the war in Cambodia, which won a Pulitzer. The movie *The Killing Fields* was based on a book of his reporting.

MICHAEL MUSTO: I was nervous. Mike Lacey mentioned me in the meeting as being important, and so I thought, "OK, I'm safe." But I didn't like what New Times was doing in terms of obviously chopping heads, chopping all the marquee names one by one.

BILL JENSEN: They weren't fans of criticism in newspapers. They very much had such a hard-nosed approach when it comes to reporting; they never wanted to see any kind of story that didn't have any reporting in it. But criticism was such an important part of the *Village Voice*—just reading a book or listening to a record and then writing about it.

That was the biggest fundamental difference between what that culture was versus the *Village Voice* culture. Not to say that the *Village Voice* wasn't doing reporting, but there were a lot of think-piece cover stories that the *Voice* was doing that just were not really what the New Times did. So, when they came in, they came in with a wrecking-ball mentality of "You're not going to do what you've been doing for forty years. You're going to do it *this* way now."

That's really where the rubber started hitting the road.

DOUG SIMMONS: Christine Brennan would say, "I can't wait to start reading a newspaper that doesn't have the word 'meta' in it." [*Laughs.*]

JOE LEVY: They hated the paper the way that people who are from outside of New York hate New York. And that isn't *necessarily* homophobic or racist. It just always happens to rub up against homophobia and racism. Just always *happens* to be at the same table. Sometimes eating off the same plate.

AKASH GOYAL: They came in with a little bit more of a corporate feel. Like the CIO—he came in and he wore suits. I used to walk around in my socks.

It was a leaderless team at that point. Kara was let go. I gave my resignation. Michael Cohen was the new publisher. I put in my two weeks' notice, and I don't remember being talked to by anyone during that two-week period. I remember being asked to come meet with him, the conversation going something along the lines of, "What is it that you want? Do you want a better title? Is it money? Like, everyone's got a price." I remember that phrase, "Everyone's got a price."

After a few weeks of my leaving, somebody else resigned, and then somebody *else* resigned. Somebody reached out to me, being like, "We're losing a lot of people. You got to help us." I was like, "Sorry, not my problem."

VINCE ALETTI: I did leave in 2005, and really, within the month after I left, every other arts editor had been fired. One person was left. All my friends at the paper had left or been fired. When Richard was fired, for me that was the last straw. And that's when I started planning to figure out how to get out, even though I really did get along with Don Forst. He liked me a lot. I brought in Jerry Saltz. He was a big Jerry Saltz fan.

JERRY SALTZ: I'd had two interviews at *New York* magazine. I said no twice. And then two of my best friends said essentially the same thing: "Are you insane? Go! That's a real job, you idiot. The *Voice* is going to fold." I had no idea it was going to be good. And I got the job. Very lucky.

Art criticism began to die at the *Voice* for a simple reason. Because of money, they broke the job up so there was more than one voice. They broke the credibility of having an art critic.

DAVID SCHNEIDERMAN: These guys had no intention of letting me do anything. It was very painful to watch because I felt, on one level, that maybe I failed because this happened. On the other level, I didn't have control over the final decision; it was the bankers.

It was like watching a car crash. I had this idea, which turned out to be totally fallacious, that they would leave me alone to develop online stuff, and that's how I would keep my hands in.

Wayne called me in desperation once—it was the worst phone conversation I had with him. He said, "You gotta do something." I said, "Wayne, I can't. I have no power. They got me in this little world here."

JUDY MISZNER: They wanted to have the *Voice*, the crown jewel. They wanted bragging rights on it, but they did everything they could to destroy it.

CHAPTER 82

"THE INMATES WERE RUNNING THE INSTITUTION"

TOM ROBBINS: Don had illusions that he could hang on to his job. They treated Don shabbily, but at the same time, he was making an absurd amount of money, like four hundred grand or something—a very nice number to not do heavy lifting.

I don't shed any tears about the fact that they said, "Oh, we can do better than this"—which they could, much as I loved him. I had no idea that these guys were going to be as grotesquely unsuited to the job as they proved to be from day one.

TRICIA ROMANO: The next year or two was chaos. We had something like six editors in chief. First, after Don left, Doug was made interim editor in chief. That didn't last very long. There was a controversial story that ran that was found to be partially made up, but that was just an excuse.

TOM ROBBINS: That was the only time I ever felt sorry for Doug Simmons. Because that was where Lacey wrote it on the napkin: "Old hack Ward Harkavy will now take over. Simmons is out." I was sitting right next to Lacey, and he wrote this thing on a napkin, and he says, "Yeah, put it up online." They put it up. Doug and I never really hit it off, but I felt so bad for him. Such a terrible way to treat somebody after all that.

DOUG SIMMONS: I was gone in ten minutes. I knew that it was gonna come.

TOM ROBBINS: I stood at the bar arguing with Lacey about Jim Ridgeway. Ridgeway, the guy who discovered Ralph Nader, who's written a phenomenal number of books, who had broken every story. And he was like, "Some people don't know when to leave," referring to Jim's age. He just tortured Ridgeway.

JAMES RIDGEWAY: Somewhere, I had met the lawyer for Murdoch in New York. And when I got fired, somebody said, "You got to get that woman." She was really great. And man, did she fuck those guys over. That woman got me a whole lot of stuff. And then I put her on to Nat Hentoff and everybody else I knew, and she helped a whole lot of people. I thought it was really funny that Murdoch's lawyer was screwing off Lacey. I thought it really served him right, you know?

ERIK WEMPLE: They closed on the *Voice* in November 2005. Then it was the spring of 2006 when they started in earnest, interviewing people for the *Voice* job. I had already been working as the editor of the *Washington City Paper* for a few years. Alt-weeklies were still solvent. David Carr—he was my career guru, which he was to just about everybody—he goes, "You're not interested in that *Voice* job, are you?"* I said, "No, not really. Why would I move? DC is fun right now. And there's a lot to report on." But then he planted the seeds, and I couldn't really get the notion out of my head.

I did send them an application for this job. I got a call from Andy Van De Voorde. I met with them in Scottsdale, and we had dinner at a Thai place—they're very much a meal-oriented group of decision-makers. Van De Voorde called, said I was a real serious finalist. I flew out there *again*. Lacey just tells me, "The job is yours. You're doing this." It was *incredible*. My daughter was just weeks old; I was really concerned about if we really wanted to make this move, but these people are *forceful*.

It was very clear—they loved the brand. They were *pumped*. They were also really excited about overturning the way that it looked and felt. They were excited about putting their template on it. They wanted to, and they eventually did install some of their chain's film critics either to the supplement or to replace the *Voice*'s own proprietary critics.

With each passing day, it became more and more clear that I was being hired into a managing editorship. They had Andy Van De Voorde, who

---

* Carr was the late, infamous *New York Times* media critic.

managed the personnel. He recruited people directly, found good reporters, and hired them onto various papers. I remember one day they told me, "Oh, we've hired your arts editor."

That's Joy Press. [*Laughs.*] Joy, for sure, she was excellent. She was introduced to me as my first hire. And if that had been the long and short of it, I was still like, "OK, I'll deal with that." But it got worse.

I came to find out they had targeted several positions or people for layoffs. I remember telling them, "Look, I will deal with your need to cut the budget, but I need some say in it." And I remember getting the distinct message back that there was *no way* that would happen. Even though I was then the titular top editor of the *Village Voice*, they would not show me a document. What pushed me over the edge was this. They said, "We will meet in New York in a week or so"—in a hotel room or some meeting room—"and we will have all the top people from the company and you. And we will show you the budget." I said, "You know what? That sounds not like a meeting; that sounds like a beatdown."

This goose was already basically cooked. It was as if they were hiring an implementer.

TOM ROBBINS: He came, he had one meeting, and then never came back. There was nobody in charge; the inmates were running the institution.

CHAPTER 83

"DONALD TRUMP SAID YES!"

TOM ROBBINS: Blum showed up. They hired Blum because there was an item in the paper about how there had been no editor. It was one of the women who worked as an assistant in the events listings—Angela Ashman. Angela had taken a course that Blum taught at Columbia, and she recommended him, and they talked to him. And they hired him. They were embarrassed that they hadn't hired anybody.

DAVID BLUM: Angela actually showed me an ad that was in the paper. It said, "Looking for an editor in chief," a big, like, half-page ad. I sent a resume and clips. After about three weeks, I got an email from Mike Lacey. For whatever reason, we connected. I had sent him an article that I had written about the Signature Theatre Company, which is a little Off-Broadway theater company, for *New York* magazine. He thought that was, like, the definitional kind of story that the *Voice* should run. I wasn't going to disagree. I remember talking about it as something that could be kind of a guerrilla version of *New York* magazine for a type of person that was aspirational, but in a slightly different way. I didn't think the *Voice* thought enough about who was reading it.

He called me up the next day and said, "You know what, I cancelled all my other meetings. Fuck it, you've got the job." I was shocked. And he sent a bottle of wine over to my apartment, made a reasonably generous offer. It included a year of severance if I were to get fired. That was the best part of it, as it turned out.

TOM ROBBINS: He was pretty miserable. The stories that I did for him are the only stories I ever did for the *Voice* that when I look back, I really cringe at the way he redid the ledes and the headlines and whatnot. He was such an off note.

J. HOBERMAN: We used to beat up on Blum all the time at his ludicrous editorial meetings. Just used to insult him all the time.

MICHAEL MUSTO: I thought he was cool. And he assigned me to do Sarah Silverman, which was a cover. Maybe it was a little uptown for the *Voice*, but so was Jonathan Larsen.

DAVID BLUM: I thought we were doing some stories that mattered and got attention. Angela Ashman did a hilarious story about Constantine Maroulis, which actually was my absolute favorite cover line: "This is Constantine Maroulis. He wishes you knew that." Kristen Lombardi, I gave her the idea to do the story about the 9/11 first responders and the deaths that occurred.* I was reading about it in the *New York Times*, a small story. This could be a great investigative piece, and she did it, and she won whatever that award was for the alt-weeklies for best investigative piece.

I made some bad decisions. Probably a little precipitous to cut the sex columns. Rachel Kramer Bussel never forgave me, I don't think.** I created a different sex column that I called Married, Not Dead. It was written by a forty-year-old woman who is adjusting her sex life to being older. I discovered something on the first day, which I should have thought of, which was nobody wants to read about people over the age of about twenty-six or twenty-eight having sex. And *Gawker*, of course, was a constant, soft drumbeat throughout my tenure. They made fun of me for hiring people from the Columbia Journalism School.

ELIZABETH THOMPSON: He brought in Mara Altman, which people were horrified by and suspicious of, because she was this young woman— which in hindsight seems unfair. There was a lot of whispering and jealousy.

DAVID BLUM: I thought the *Gawker* stuff was good for the paper. It meant that people were talking about it.

JOY PRESS: When Dave started, he came and introduced himself, and he was like, "Oh, I know a lot about books, so if you need help assigning books." In all the years that I had been a book editor, nobody had ever done

---

* Maroulis was a finalist in *American Idol*. Lombardi was a staff writer.
** Bussel wrote a sex column called Lusty Lady.

anything like that, right? This dude, literally the first thing he ever says to me is this thing about how he can tell me what books to assign.

Dave Blum had worked at *Spy*. And *Spy* used to make fun of Donald Trump all the time. Famously, about tiny hands. A book was coming out that was something to do with *Spy*. He just thought it would be really clever to get Donald Trump to review a book about *Spy*.

I literally heard Dave coming down the hallway, and he comes running into my office. And he's like, "You're not gonna believe it! You're not gonna believe it! He said yes! He said yes! Donald Trump said yes!"

Guess what? Donald Trump never wrote the review.

CHAPTER 84

"THEY LOVE FIRING PEOPLE"

MICHAEL LACEY: You don't get rid of good people just to save money. They're too hard to find.

DAVID BLUM: They love firing people. Christine Brennan actually once said to me, she started reminiscing, "I remember the first person I fired," and she was saying it like, "My first Christmas. . . ."*

One of the first things they told me about was how the union contract allowed you to fire "for taste." Everybody was fired for taste. That was such latitude. This was a union-negotiated thing. It meant that if you were fired for taste, as opposed to anything else, they had to double the severance.

MAIDA ROSENSTEIN: If you were a writer, it was a month for every year of service. It was a very nice exit packet. That "taste clause," which had worked well for so many years when there was a real relationship—so that this was a way that people imagined could be a graceful exit for people without, like, blood fights—that fell apart.

ADAMMA INCE: There was nothing in that contract that management could not get around. There was always a loophole. The contract was basically just to keep the staff quiet. What New Times came in and did with a contract in hand: they wiped us out.

ROB HARVILLA: I was working in the East Bay, at the *East Bay Express*. Obviously, it's like, "We're gonna be letting Chuck Eddy go, and you would be replacing him." I started at the *Voice* in April of 2006.

---

* Brennan was an executive with New Times; she served as executive managing editor of Village Voice Media.

CHUCK EDDY: I remember Andy Van De Voorde taking me out for lunch and asking me a lot of micromanaging questions about how I ran the music section. I was shell-shocked. A part of me that was like, "Well, no one else is gonna be able to do this job." It was a blur. I remember crying.

ROB HARVILLA: Ward Harkavy was the interim editor. My first *Village Voice* staff meeting, the very first thing that happened was the reading of a petition protesting Chuck Eddy's firing. I remember sitting there quietly and trying to respect the terrible absurdity of this situation.

ELIZABETH THOMPSON: Everybody was ready to hate him. He ended up being this amazing editor who's gone on to do great things, but everyone was primed to be against him.

ROB HARVILLA: Christgau wrote a cover story while I was there where he went to a concert every night for a month. I came in April, and they fired Christgau in August. In the end, I only worked with Christgau for a few months. I can pretty much picture his phone number, like, the digits, and dialing the number and saying, "Hey, they want to meet with you with a union rep." And Bob turning to his wife, saying, "Carola, they're firing me." That's one of the top two shittiest moments of my life, certainly in my career, that phone call.

JESUS DIAZ: New Times had some fuckface who was just really cold and didn't care who you were—Andy Van De Voorde. We were arguing that Bob still had value, he's the "dean of rock criticism." So, this fuckface was saying, "His writing's not as good as it was."

And he asked Rob Harvilla what he thought. Now mind you, we didn't know who the fuck Harvilla was. He was asked, "Would you fire Bob Christgau?" He said, "No, I would not." Because of that, Rob had gained immediate respect. That was the greatest thing I ever saw. That took balls.

ROB HARVILLA: It doesn't feel like all that tremendous an act of defiance in retrospect. I hope it stood for something. I was designed to be in that meeting as this silent approver.

ROB HARVILLA: I was very worried about Pazz & Jop from the beginning. The previous year over one thousand people had voted. Pazz & Jop was a *Village Voice* property but was undeniably a Bob Christgau production. It was synonymous with him more than even the *Voice*. I feared immediately that many hundreds of people are going to not vote now that Bob Christgau is not involved. And late that year, *Idolator*, which was then the pretty nascent Gawker Media music blog, announced that they were running their own Pazz & Jop poll, Jackin' Pop, that pretty explicitly was designed to take over, based on the fact that the *Voice* had lost institutional respect.*

DAVID BLUM: The Pazz & Jop poll was taking place, and Rob Harvilla wrote this fantastic essay. I said, "Yes, let's do it. Let's put it in." He's editing it, we're closing. And suddenly, I get this email from that guy Vanderveer, or something like that, who said, "We don't really want that Harvilla essay. Bill Jensen has written something."

BILL JENSEN: Lacey likes to fight. Lacey calls me up: "Go write something." I was in the office, and I had a bunch of little Knob Creek bottles. I started drinking and just started fucking typing. I don't really remember all of it. I remember my last line. "Dewey defeats Truman, motherfuckers!" This was something that was never, *ever* meant to see the light of day, you know?

Lacey showed that to Harvilla and said, like, "Well, we're running this if you don't respond." Then somebody leaked it.

DAVID BLUM: I said, "Thank you, but no. We're going to print the Rob Harvilla." Right after I told them that, our staff had its weekly staff meeting. I shared the news, and I actually got the only sustained applause that I ever received at the *Village Voice*. That really meant a lot to me, honestly. I got a call from Wayne Barrett afterwards. He said, "You got balls." Having Wayne Barrett say you had balls also meant a lot to me.

I got a call that afternoon from Lacey's assistant asking me if I could get on the next flight to L.A. so that I could drive down to some place between L.A. and San Diego, some hotel, and meet them for breakfast, and it was going to be Lacey and that woman. Christine. Ugh.

I flew out the next day to L.A.; I drove down to wherever. I spent the night. I was told to come to breakfast at nine. I get down there at nine. I see the three of them sitting there, and they have finished eating their breakfast.

* Jackin' Pop was co-curated by Michaelangelo Matos, who is, full disclosure, a close friend of the author's and helped edit this book, and Maura Johnston, who succeeded Harvilla as the *Village Voice*'s music editor from 2011 to 2012.

They excised me from the breakfast part of the breakfast meeting, but I insisted on ordering something because I was starving, which seemed to be not on the menu. I knew that I was being called on the carpet for having taken this position.

I was trying to hire a managing editor, which took me a very long time to do. On my second day of employment, I said to Lacey, "Look, if it doesn't work out, we'll just get somebody else." And Lacey said, "No, if it doesn't work out, I'll get somebody else for *your* job." I knew I wasn't gonna be leaving the place voluntarily.

ADAMMA INCE: We were talking about story ideas, and Wayne Barrett was like, "What happened to all the people of color here?"

I was the only Black person in the room. At that time, New Times had gotten rid of virtually every single Black person in edit, except me.

And then David Blum said, "Well, you know, Black people don't really graduate from high school, so it's hard to get any Black people at the paper."

I'd let Wayne and Tom and all those people argue with him until he said that, and then I was like, "You gotta be kidding me."

DAVID BLUM: If that was interpreted in any sort of racial context that would have been incorrect. The thing that I said that became most inflammatory, which I most regret is—but to be clear, what I regret is saying it to a large group of people where it had the ability to be misunderstood—I acknowledged that this was not easy to do, or maybe even used the word "hard." I had been working very diligently and had added multiple, diverse members of the staff. Then there was a bit of pushback of, "What do you mean by 'hard'?"

It can be interpreted multiple ways. And one of them is that you're suggesting that there aren't enough people of color in the mix of who could be hired. I was frustrated that every time there was somebody that I wanted to hire, the *Washington Post* had already hired them. This was not something that I took idly.

ADAMMA INCE: I was just like, "What about all the Black people that were here when I first got here and up until New Times took over?" And then I specifically said, "What about Greg Tate?" And then he says, "Greg Tate is Black?"

And he was like, "Well, why are you so angry? Why are you raging?" I was like, "Oh, we're gonna go down the angry Black woman road?" So, I was like, "I'm gonna go have a cigarette."

I smoked my cigarette, I went to Mihlee in HR. I told her what happened. She called the New Times guy, the asshole.

I'm going back to my office, and Blum comes out of his office. He calls me in, and he's like, you know, "I'm not racist. I'm really not racist." And he gives me a hug.

DAVID BLUM: I had met with Adamma the next day, apologized for having said anything that could cause her pain. And she accepted, very graciously.

Michael Cohen gave me essentially the same advice that Mihlee did, which was you should not answer questions like that in a group.* You should just say, "That's an important question. I want to think about it. Let's meet tomorrow."

But the minute Lacey heard about it, that was it, boom. I realized that to some extent I was just another victim in the thing. I was there six months and got a year of severance. So, most of the money I made from Village Voice Media was for work I did not have to actually do. It was a sad day for me.

On the Monday of the week that I was fired, which took place on Friday, I had a long-scheduled lunch with Wayne to talk about stories. At one point, he says to me, "Dave, you know, so Bill Jensen's in town. He's staying at the Chelsea Hotel. Why is he here?" And I said, "He's here just for the week." Because that was what I'd been told.

And Wayne said, "But he's at the Chelsea. Nobody stays at the Chelsea if they're here for a week. They only stay at the Chelsea if they're here for a month. He's not here for a week. He is not here for the reason he told you. You should watch your back." I thought, "I am getting absolute solid gold investigative thinking from Wayne Barrett," absolutely incredible. And sure enough . . .

BILL JENSEN: I walk into the building, and this is swirling. I was already there for web business. After Erik Wemple did his thing and decided not to take the job, I started talking to them. I had been rebuilding the *Boston Phoenix*

---

* Cohen was the publisher of the *Voice* at that time.

website, and they offered me the job of running all of the digital on the editorial side for all of the Village Voice Media papers. I moved to Phoenix.*

I go in and I have a meeting with the editorial staff, and I say, "This is what's happening. Believe me, I don't want this. I just moved to Phoenix. It's not gonna be me. We just got to get these papers out." That might have been the spring arts issue—it was a thick issue.

I had already said to Lacey, I said, "Listen, the way this place is, you should just go and get one of your guys in here." I said, "Tony Ortega or Rick from Phoenix," both newspaper guys. Both had broken stories. He wanted Tony, so I knew Tony was coming.

I was like, "All right, I've got one issue where I'm going to be editor in chief of the *Village Voice*. I want to knock it out of the park." It was Ultragrrrl.** It was a great-looking cover. And the story was great.

I remember, during that time, working a lot with Brian Parks. Two issues before that, the paper had printed a page twice and missed another page of the story. I didn't want a mess-up, so I was there until, like, three o'clock in the morning on pub night. No editor had ever done that before with Brian. I remember Brian giving me a really nice bottle of whiskey afterwards. That was my one week as editor of the *Village Voice*.

And then Tony came in. I was walking around the city with Tony. At one point, we walked past a building, and he's like, "This is where I bought my first Walkman!" He was so excited, and he, like, screamed in the city, kind of like a Mary Tyler Moore moment: "I love this city!"

I was like, "All right, this is good." I finally was able to get out of Dodge.

ROB HARVILLA: I had an idea of what New Times didn't like about the *Voice* as it currently existed. And I had an idea of what New Times wanted the *Voice* to be. They wanted to take the *Voice* name and then just fundamentally and completely transform the *Voice* into this different thing staffed by entirely different people.

LYNN YAEGER: We thought that we were like the holy grail—like, this is what they always wanted. This was the star. I always liken it to a Louis

---

* Phoenix is where New Times, Inc., is headquartered.

** Full disclosure: he's referring to a cover story about an early "influencer," Sarah Lewittin, that was written by the author of this book.

Vuitton bag. All your life, you wanted the bag, and then you got the bag. And then, like, a month later, you're like, "Why did I want this bag? Like, it was stupid. It was overpriced. Nobody cares if I have it."

They were obsessed with having it. And then, when they had it, they were like, "Who cares?"

JOY PRESS: I remember meeting with Mike Lacey and him complaining about Hoberman: "He needs to stop writing about these obscure movies that no one can pronounce the filmmaker's name." I said to him, "This is New York. So those movies that Jim is writing about, there's a line around the block for people to see those movies. This is why the *Voice* is important. Anybody can write about a blockbuster movie." He didn't care. New Yorkers don't want some fucking generic shit. They want to read about Wong Kar-wai, or whoever it was that he couldn't pronounce. It was so insane to me. I started interviewing. I was out of there.

JESUS DIAZ: They were really gunning after our health care. That was the one thing that we would never, never give up on. And it was a very young negotiating team. We unified as a whole shop. We were smaller in number, right? But we got meaner. That was a wonderful negotiation for me because it looked like we were going to get crushed, but the staff got it together. We never gave up on our health care.

TRICIA ROMANO: During the seven years that New Times ran the paper, it was death by a thousand cuts, as they slowly fired everyone.

MAIDA ROSENSTEIN: I negotiated several contracts with the *Voice*, really, till the very end. They got rid of all the stalwarts of the union, like Hoberman, Lynn Yaeger. It was just so awful.

DAVID BLUM: I thought Lynn was honestly a national treasure, and the *Voice* should not let her go. Lacey wanted her out from the beginning. She was a union leader. That didn't help. He just didn't like her. Everybody that was fired after I left were people who Lacey and Larkin wanted me to fire while I was there. I refused.

MICHAEL MUSTO: When Lynn left, I lost my comrade in arms. She was at *Vogue* already; she never looked back.

LYNN YAEGER: Well, I can tell you exactly what happened. I was wearing a gigantic velvet skirt that puffed out and a little sweater with reindeers on it because it was, like, December 24 or 28 or something. And I was just going into the office for a minute.

And I walk in, and Tom Robbins says to me, "There's going to be layoffs today." And I said, "Well, that's a shame. Who?" He said, "You." And I said, "No. No way." But it was true. It was me, Hentoff, and maybe a couple other people.

I was very shocked. Tony had me in his office, and it was like he was reading off a script. I said, "How can you lay me off? I'm the best one."

J. HOBERMAN: It was heartbreaking. For some reason, I got along with Ortega. I was this straight white guy; I could talk to him. He was very ashamed when he had to fire me. He actually told me, "It's not my idea." It was a shock, but it was not a surprise. I had been such a loudmouth—in a good sense. I was the chief steward. I was arguing with them and with him at the table; that was my job. I was very glad to do it because it alleviated some of the misery of just being there and seeing what was going on. It was so awful to go in there. These empty cubicles, just terrible. They killed it. Their stupidity was a part of it, but it was like a willful stupidity.

MICHAEL MUSTO: It was depressing to see. I hate the word "iconic," but some people who created their beat—like Christgau, Hoberman—these really accomplished writers axed obviously because New Times didn't want to pay the old-school salary.

ELIZABETH THOMPSON: Thirteen years later, we're seeing this played out on steroids. It was so sad to see it happening to the *Voice*.

I remember being in the office, and hearing Tony just screaming at someone on the phone—like, just like, "God, no! I'm not!" Really back and forth. I'm like, "Jesus Christ! Who is he talking to?" And then he was like, "Nat! Listen to me! Nat!"—screaming. And I was like, "Oh my god. He's talking to Nat Hentoff!"

ED FANCHER: I ran into him one day in the supermarket, and he came over to me and he said, "Ed, do you know what happened to me?" I said "No, Nat." He said, "I just got fired after fifty years."

NICK HENTOFF: He didn't let open-heart surgery or a severe illness that he had interfere with his columns. From '58 on, he never left the *Voice* until he was fired by Michael Lacey—he was the one who told Tony to fire him.

He was the longest-serving writer there. He was probably one of their most expensive employees in terms of benefits and salary, and so I think he made an economic decision.

Mike Lacey on some level was jealous of the gravitas that my father had over his career in journalism, as opposed to what Lacey was able to accomplish, outside of the monetary benefits of running an advertising juggernaut, particularly an advertising juggernaut that focused on the [alleged] trafficking of young girls through Backpage, where they really made a lot of their money. But I knew a lot of people who worked at the *Phoenix New Times* when Mike Lacey was hands-on editor there, and I wasn't very impressed with him. He reminds me of having a low, base character, and like Donald Trump, people don't matter very much to them.

TOM ROBBINS: I left in the beginning of '11. I was acting as a shop steward. But I had been through this repeatedly, where they would notify me to say, "Oh, we're going to lay somebody off," and we would have an argument about it. But I would sit there to make sure that they didn't at least shortchange somebody to what they're entitled to. And then one day it was Wayne. And I was like, "At this point, he's the franchise. You can't be serious."

He was pretty stunned. It was funny—Wayne had so many times threatened to quit. He'd had so many great blowups. One time, sitting in Don's office, he had dragged me into it, and Wayne pounds the table and says, "I'm out of here! What's my severance?" And Don took this little piece of paper and wrote something on it and slipped it over to him, and it was like a European zero with a hash mark, a slice across it. "Here's your severance. Nothing." And Wayne of course never understood, because he was a lousy union guy, that severance comes when they lay you off, not when you quit.

JESUS DIAZ: I remember him saying, "Diaz, I thought this was going to be the place where I was going to retire."

TOM ROBBINS: Wayne was the last straw. Wayne had brought me there in '85, and he brought me back in 2000. So, I said, "I'm going to leave with the guy who brought me to the dance."

CHAPTER 85

"IF THE NATIONAL ORGANIZATION OF WOMEN CALLS, JUST FUCKING HANG UP ON THEM"

MICHAEL MUSTO: The crash of 2008—that devastated the media because anyone that was hanging on was pushed off a cliff.

ELIZABETH THOMPSON: It was the end of people being paid living salaries or six-figure salaries to write columns in New York City.

BRIAN PARKS: That was also the start of the whole financial crisis. All of a sudden it became cut, cut, cut, cut, cut, cut. It was a grim time for everybody.

Tony would do battles with them [Lacey et al.]. He wasn't afraid of them; he was also willing to fight back against some of their more awful edicts.

DAVID BLUM: The *Voice* never recovered from going free. I was actually proposing to Lacey that we should start charging. Those urine-soaked boxes were the most disgusting distribution model I've ever seen in my entire life. Lacey was not willing.

JUDY MISZNER: They saw that there was a real opportunity in the adult business.

AKASH GOYAL: It was just amazing to see later, when everything went to shit, you had the New Times guys building Backpage, which was purely a rip-off of Craigslist. Their solution was to basically take the same thing, clone it, but then allow ads from [alleged] sex traffickers and people that shouldn't be putting ads up anywhere.

JAMES LARKIN: We started to feel it in San Francisco in about '98, '99, and we decided we'd better do something about it, so in 2004 we launched Backpage.com, which was the descendant of the back page of our newspapers.

ROBERT SIETSEMA: It turned out that New Times was built upon an empire of porn. The sex ads took a sinister turn when they took the back page and put it online. It had been a mixture of things before, and, yes, it had porn. And you could actually make a case for the *Voice* being buoyed up by massage parlors filled with exploited immigrant Asian women. It took us a while to realize what those really meant. And that may have undermined the credibility of the *Voice* in the long run, but then New Times took it and ran with it and turned it into something even more horrible.

JAMES LARKIN: The model that we tinkered with started in Greenwich Village going back to 1955 of the *Village Voice*, OK? They started classifieds with adult ads, with stripper ads, all kinds in the back of the book, totally legal, always have been legal; it's not a Johnny-come-lately business. So, all through the '70s, '80s, and '90s, all of our papers carried adult.

ED FANCHER: We had massage ads and model ads, and the head of the classified department came up to me one day, and she said, "We have these massage ads, and the men who come in to place these ads look like a bunch of Italian gangsters to me."

I figured if they were prostitute ads, I didn't want them. But they probably were. I mean, you couldn't separate them. I didn't want to just kick them out tomorrow because I didn't want to start an issue of freedom of the press, somebody saying, "He's censoring these ads," so I thought it was easier just to phase them out over thirteen weeks, which worked fine. And then they would build up.

MARTIN GOTTLIEB: If there was one issue that united the front of the book, the back of the book, and the business offices of the *Voice*, it was the sex ads. Everyone said, "This is a matter of free speech. The *Voice* will allow anyone to say or advertise what they want." They made a ton of money on it. And if you were Nat Hentoff, First Amendment free-speech purist, that was free speech; if you're a feminist, if a woman wants to advertise whatever services she wants to, that's her business. She's allowed to make her money the way she wants. There's no problem.

LISA BIRNBACH: There was a lot of noise about all the sex notices and escorts. And it made me sad that when you'd say the name of the paper in a mixed community, that's what people started thinking about, was, "Oh, I saw the ad for triples and for orgies." I'd say, "Yeah, but it's much more. We do some very important journalism, investigations." But it was hard to get people to really pay attention.

JAMES RIDGEWAY: It was constantly attacked and made fun of by the *New York Times* and other mainstream papers, and they thought it was a commie paper, or they thought it was a sex paper. And it was a little of all of it, you know? I always remember those trannies who would come in to place ads, and they were, like, incredible, knockout women. They would be great. I wish they would hire them, and we can hang around with them, the *Paris Is Burning* crowd.

FRANK RUSCITTI: The ads were *unbelievably graphic*—a picture of a woman, spread, laying on her stomach, with a little star over her anus. That graphic. John Evans, who was a publisher at one point, he would try and get them to leave. The idea was to try and clean up those pages, so he did something like quadruple their rates. And that didn't change a thing. They still came in.

You knew what those ads were for. Gay ads with a guy and a dick in his face. It was always a star over the dick. And it was, like, "male masseuse."

I do remember conflict between the women writers and the women editors and those ads. Nobody liked it. Voices were raised about it. But the fact that they took in so much money superseded everything else.

DAVID SCHNEIDERMAN: We took pictures away. It made the *Voice* look tawdry, the photos. Leonard called up one day, and he said, "Look at all these ads in the *New York Press* with pictures. They're taking all this business away from us." We only had a column of these ads at that point. He said, "You got to open up the spigot."

DAVID SCHNEIDERMAN: New Times got done in by their arrogance. If they had just said, "Listen, we think it's legitimate business, but we understand there are problems; we're going to work extra hard to keep the stuff out." The [alleged] sex trafficking stuff, which is the problem—they made some motions toward it, then said they'd cooperate with the police, but the reality is, based on the charges against them, they encouraged it while saying they were discouraging it.

Once they bought the *Voice*, they had debt, too, and they were desperate to work off the debt, and as the ad sales were declining, they needed revenue, so they just opened up the spigots on Backpage.

BRIAN PARKS: There was an internet law that says, if you're just like the poster board of something, you're not liable for the content on it, if people are just, "Here—we are a big chalkboard, you can write whatever you want, but it's your content, you're responsible for it." That was the theory.* From what I understand, New Times started to have too much of an active role. They then became responsible for the behavior of their advertisers. That's what got them into legal trouble.

MICHAEL LACEY (VIA INTERNAL EMAIL): Backpage is part of the solution. Eliminating adult advertising will in no way eliminate or even reduce the incidence of prostitution in this country. . . . For the very first time, the oldest profession in the world has transparency, record keeping and safeguards.**

TOM ROBBINS: Nobody was under any illusions as to what they were making the money on, and they were telling us, "Oh yeah, they make a lot of money on Backpage." So that drove our argument in some of the union negotiations.

---

* Parks is referring to Section 230 of the Communications Decency Act of 1996, which states, "No provider or user of an interactive computer service shall be treated as the publisher or speaker of any information provided by another information content provider."

** This email is part of the government's case against Backpage. The federal government alleges that Backpage's founders and named employees "engaged in criminal acts while operating Backpage including conspiracy, facilitating prostitution, and money laundering." The original charges brought by Kamala Harris, the attorney general of California in 2016, included "pimping," but those charges were dismissed. A judge ruled a mistrial at the end of 2021. Central to the case is that Backpage's employees were aware of the nature of the ads and moderated ads for obviously illegal activity, which might be considered "acting as a publisher."

ELIZABETH THOMPSON: I remember being really upset when I was an editor there later, and we had to have a big staff meeting basically about the outcry over these ads in the back of the *Voice* that were essentially [allegedly] sex trafficking. They tried to lump in the sex ads in the back with the "sex work is work" argument.

BILL JENSEN: I was there towards the tail end, when they tried to pick a fight with Ashton Kutcher. That was pretty misguided.

R.C. BAKER: We had a cover of him looking like a moron because he'd been attacking Backpage. And so, we wrote this story saying, "Get your facts straight, guy." I just thought, "That seems kind of desperate."

ELIZABETH THOMPSON: Tony Ortega, in front of the entire staff, said, "If the National Organization of Women calls any of you directly, just fucking hang up on them." It was astounding to hear an editor in chief saying that as this rallying cry.

TOM ROBBINS: When Lacey and Larkin left the *Voice*, and they decided to go with Backpage and to spin off the *Voice* and the other publications, I said, "Well, that tells you everything. These guys came in the door saying, 'We care about really good, quality journalism.'" And instead, what they really cared about was the money.

BRIAN PARKS: We were relieved. When they were using the edit to defend the business practices, it was just embarrassing. It was like, "Thank god I don't have to worry about Backpage anymore."

DAVID SCHNEIDERMAN: When Craigslist got out of that business, they shut it down.

JUDY MISZNER: And then they have that Carl Ferrer.* You know his story, right? He was their classified guy. He went to jail. Smarmy. He created Backpage for them. In 2018, Carl Ferrer was convicted in federal court of

---

* Ferrer was the CEO of Backpage. The case also names other employees—Scott Spear, John "Jed" Brunst, Dan Hyer, Andrew Padilla, and Joye Vaught—for conspiracy to commit money laundering, conspiracy to facilitate prostitution, concealment of money laundering, and forfeiture, pleading not guilty. Dan Hyer, the sales and marketing director, pled guilty to conspiring to facilitate prostitution. Lacey and Larkin et al. invoked a First Amendment defense, and Spear, Brunst, Padilla, and Vaught have pled not guilty. Attempts were made to contact Larkin, Lacey, Van De Voorde, Ortega, and others through various channels. There was no response, or the opportunity was declined. On

pornography, etc. He pled guilty to prostitution, money laundering. Then he decided to cooperate with the Feds, which is probably what led them [the federal government] to take down Larkin and Lacey.

DAVID SCHNEIDERMAN: He was indicted, but he flipped. He's going to testify. Some other people are indicted. Plus, Backpage [allegedly] set up a shell company in Holland.

BRIAN PARKS: You'd think they would have taken the hint like Craig at Craigslist did at some point and said, "Let's not mess with that."

TOM ROBBINS: So now they're sitting there indicted, god bless 'em. They're facing criminal charges, the two of them. They couldn't stop. Just horrendous.

DAVID BLUM: You rarely get the opportunity in life to see the guy that fired you wearing prison garb and being hauled off in handcuffs. That was a happy day.

MARK JACOBSON: Lacey seemed like he was playing this role of a barbarian at the gate—that's what he wanted to be. Then the decision to go with the massage ads and jettison the *Village Voice*—I don't understand how you make that decision. You have to be pretty cutthroat, right?

He's in jail, so I guess he made the wrong choice.* [*Shouts into recorder*] "Hey, Mike! Maybe you should have done that one different!" Nobody is gonna put the editor of the *Village Voice* in jail. I mean, the First Amendment's gonna save his ass, right?

DAVID SCHNEIDERMAN: Did you ever see the picture of Lacey and Larkin in orange jumpsuits? I remember looking at it, saying, "You know, it's not enough."

July 31, 2023, James Larkin died by suicide from a gunshot wound to the head, a week before the new trial was set to begin.
* The trial began in August 2023. Lacey was found guilty of one count of international concealment of money laundering; Spear and Brunst were convicted of a conspiracy to violate the Travel Act by facilitating prostitution, as well as dozens of money laundering violations. Each face up to twenty years in prison. Padilla and Vaught were acquitted of all charges.

CHAPTER 86

"IT WASN'T MY *VILLAGE VOICE* ANYMORE"

ELIZABETH THOMPSON: Tony was completely obsessed with Scientology. Running Scared became completely about Scientology. He's in the *Going Clear* documentary.

BILL JENSEN: He became like Captain Ahab. The Scientology stuff makes sense in L.A., not in New York. Lacey finally had enough of that.

R.C. BAKER: Then they brought in Will Bourne. Will Bourne was a great, *great* editor.

JESUS DIAZ: Will Bourne was hired by New Times. And Jessica Lustig was his number two. They wanted them to fire Feingold, Musto, and Robert Sietsema. And they refused. But the way they refused was just wonderful. They called a staff meeting. Will told us they wanted these firings, even though he was hired with the promise that he wouldn't be laying off anybody. Will and Jessica, they walked out without management knowing that they had walked out.

Will is no Rockefeller. He had a family to take care of. I know that he struggled later on. It was hard to find a newspaper to edit, and there were fewer of them around.

MICHAEL MUSTO: The great thing about internet gossip is that by the time Christine called me in in 2013 to lay me off, I already knew, because *Gawker* had a piece about it. But *Gawker* had already approached me to do a weekly column, and so did Out.com.

When Christine did call me in, she was dressed in black like it was a funeral. She was charmless. She didn't say, "Thank you for your time at the paper. Thank you for promoting us tirelessly." Those are all the things that

Don Forst had said to me through the years. I was doing everything to keep the job and had a pretty healthy run. My column ran from '84 to 2013.

JESUS DIAZ: Then they sold to Peter Barbey, and that was a great day.* We were being bought by a guy with a lot of money, and he accepted the union.

R.C. BAKER: When Peter Barbey bought the paper, I had said to him, "Well, if you're looking for a really good editor, and you want to bring back the old *Voice*, there's a guy who meets both criteria."

JESUS DIAZ: He hired Will Bourne, and that was an exciting thing.

JOE LEVY: From the outside, what it certainly looked like was that the New Times wanted to destroy the *Village Voice* and Peter Barbey wanted to publish the *Village Voice*. Peter ran bookstores in Arizona, where among the publications they sold was the *Voice*, and he noticed how incredibly passionate people's attachment to the paper in Arizona was. He had an attachment to it himself.

Now, I don't think he bought it with a clear plan of what to do with it, but part of what it seemed like his plan of what to do with it was to let it be the *Village Voice*. He brought Will Bourne back. He brought Lucian Truscott back into the fold. I was there for three or four months. I had to fill some gaps.

JESUS DIAZ: People were noticing the paper. Their returns were fewer and fewer. We increased the print run. People were picking up the paper, you know?

We soon realized that we were dealing with Fredo. For about five months, Will built a really young, talented editorial group. But two things went against Will. One was this idea by this publisher who sold Peter on the idea that we should do a fashion magazine. I know that Will and her were definitely not on the same page.

And Fredo—Barbey—the guy would just come in, like, on a Monday. He wanted to have a meeting with Will. A Monday! We had a paper to get out. Will was writing all the headlines, but this guy was just going in there and wasting his fucking time. Every Monday like clockwork, you know?

---

* Barbey is a billionaire, the owner of Reading Eagle Company, and an heir to the VF Corporation, which owns Lee jeans and the North Face, among other major brands. He bought the paper in 2015.

Supposedly, Will told Peter to get the fuck out of his office. And that was the end of him. From there, it was over. This last gasp of the *Voice* and the comeback or whatever you want to call it.

R.C. BAKER: Peter Barbey came and killed all adult ads. The Backpage scandal was so bad, he didn't want anything to do with it. And to be honest with you, it seems like killing those ads went a long way to destroying the revenue stream into the paper.

MICHAEL MUSTO: When Pete Barbey bought it, I thought, "This is like a miracle. This is the pot of gold." This is a man with a lot of money. He actually cared about the paper. And I thought he would run it for a long time. I didn't think he could work a *total* miracle and make the paper urgently needed again. But I thought he would make it something of quality that could last.

I was surprised when Peter made it web only. I think he was probably just tired of losing that much money.

At that point, it wasn't my *Village Voice* anymore. It felt like living after the apocalypse, like a bomb is dropped and you're living in the rubble. Everybody was doing their best to survive. But it wasn't the fun, exhilarating place that it had been.

They had my La Dolce Musto column in the last issue.* I feel like I was really there 'til the end.

---

* He's referring to the last print edition in 2018 under Barbey's ownership before it was revived by Calle in 2020.

CHAPTER 87

"WAYNE COULDN'T BELIEVE THAT TRUMP WAS WINNING"

WAYNE BARRETT, "TIME FOR SOMETHING NEW," *VILLAGE VOICE*, JANUARY 4, 2011

There is also no other job where you get paid to tell the truth. Other professionals do sometimes tell the truth, but it's ancillary to what they do, not the purpose of their job. I was asked years ago to address the elementary school that my son attended and tell them what a reporter did, and I went to the auditorium in a trench coat with the collar up and a notebook in my pocket, baring it to announce that "we are detectives for the people."

TOM ROBBINS: Wayne just got to work. He started writing all these pieces for the *Daily Beast* and the *Daily News* and whoever else would run him. He did some very good stuff when he was flat on his back, ailing from this lung thing he had.* Wayne appreciated the fact that Trump could be a serious player, given his willingness to play the race card, which was clear from his debut speech that he was gonna go after illegal immigrants and Mexicans. As long as you're going to outwardly play the race card in the Republican primary, you can actually command a lot. And Wayne understood

---

* Barrett was a nonsmoker who died of interstitial lung disease and lung cancer.

that. He was surprised as the rest of us the way that Trump just mowed down the rest of the opposition and that nobody could stand up to him.

WILLIAM BASTONE: He knew that Trump was appealing to something that was going to have traction with people and that wasn't just a passing thing. I said, "Wayne, don't you think people see through this and they understand that he's really just a con man and a huckster and a racist?" The stuff goes back, at that point, almost thirty years with his father and avoiding renting apartments to Black families in Brooklyn.

And he was like, "No, that's gonna be a plus for him, for the people that he's going to end up attracting." I was like, "You're crazy, Wayne. You're crazy."

There was talk that he may have used racially charged or racist remarks when he was doing *The Apprentice*. And I said, "So Wayne, if it ever came out that Trump used those words or used the N-word?" And Wayne said, "That would be good for him." He was totally right. And then nine months later, he's talking about shooting people on Fifth Avenue. Trump understood that "there's really nothing I can do [wrong] because these people hate the people I hate, and we're all gonna be together."

TOM ROBBINS: When I was at the *Observer*, I had a column in there called Wise Guys. And at that point, Trump was talking about running for president. This is 1987; that was thirty years before he actually ran, almost. He was focused on this from the very beginning. And none of us took him seriously.

So many people went back after Trump became a leading candidate for the presidency to find copies of that book, and at that point it hadn't been reissued.* Wayne had a box of them in the basement, and all these reporters kept making this trip to see Wayne in Windsor Terrace, and he was giving them copies of the book until his wife, Fran, said, "Wayne, these books are selling for $500 on eBay! What are you giving them away for?"

---

* Barrett wrote a book titled *Trump: The Deals and the Downfall* (HarperCollins, 1992). It was rereleased by Regan Arts in 2016 as *Trump: The Greatest Show on Earth: The Deals, the Downfall, the Reinvention.*

He didn't care. But Judith Regan, god bless her, she was smart enough to realize that there was some money to be made here. She gave Wayne a nice piece of change to write a new introduction and reissue the book.

TIMOTHY L. O'BRIEN: It's now an important historical document because Trump became president. It is a much more important book than anyone could have thought of at the time.

TOM ROBBINS: As someone who worked with the tabloid press for a long time, the people who invented Trump were all those tabloid gossip reporters who dined out from all of his items over the years and who reported them right up until the time he ran for president. This is one of the great unrecognized crimes of the press. We in the tabloid press created Trump; it wasn't Wayne. Wayne was going after him.

JONATHAN Z. LARSEN: This is the media's Frankenstein's monster. Trump would call, using a fake name, saying, "I'm the PR guy for Donald Trump. I really shouldn't be telling you this, but he's about to get divorced, and he's got three women he's looking at. There's Marla Maples. There's so-and-so." Very often the people that he was speaking to recognized his voice. They loved it. It was free copy.

Barrett really did have some incredibly good information on Trump, how he built Trump Tower. The head of the concrete union was mobbed up. There was this crazy woman who bought the apartment just underneath Donald Trump's because she was sleeping with the concrete guy, and she wanted to install a pool. It's astonishing, the stuff he got. It's a national treasure now that we have Wayne Barrett's reporting. As soon as Trump became president, everybody was picking through all of Wayne's files.

WILLIAM BASTONE: Wayne knew it was gonna happen. He figured it out. Maybe he wasn't 100 percent certain, but everyone was shocked. Especially for New York reporters who had covered him and spoken to him and followed his career—for us, he was this clown/con man who existed to be in Page Six. And somehow our country sat there and went, "Oh, yeah, he'd be better doing that job than Hillary Clinton"? You might have sensed it, but when it happened? It still was a shock.

TOM ROBBINS: I sat with Wayne on election night. Right up until the time the actual votes came back, Wayne couldn't believe that Trump was winning. He'd been ill for over a year or two; he didn't move around a whole lot, but that night he was really upbeat when we got there. He said, "Got the exit polls and she's going to win in a walk and we're going to win the Senate." He was so optimistic, and then he just got quieter as the evening went on. Just stopped talking. It really took the wind out of his sails.

But god bless. He had the biggest year of his life in 2016. Literally every reporter in America who wanted to do a story about Donald Trump made his way to Wayne's house in Windsor Terrace. He got a lot more acclaim in the last year than he'd ever gotten in his life, so that was nice for him to get.

TIMOTHY L. O'BRIEN: Wayne died the night before the inauguration.

MAC BARRETT: The funeral, it was in Brownsville, a big, beautiful church there that was meaningful to him.* It was really overwhelming. Some five hundred people were there. It felt like every journalist and many pols in New York were there, and it was surreal, really. Chuck Schumer spoke. The governor spoke. All of his family.

MIKE BLOOMBERG (VIA PRESS STATEMENT): Wayne Barrett was a tenacious reporter in the tradition of the old muckrakers who could sniff out corruption and special interest politics a mile away. No elected official always saw eye-to-eye with Wayne, including me. But I always respected his deep sense of moral purpose and encyclopedic knowledge of city politics, accumulated through a lifetime of tireless research. I had the chance to break bread with him on occasion, and behind the scathing pen he wielded was a good guy with a big heart who loved New York City. His death is a major loss for New York journalism, but students of our city's history will be reading his work for decades to come.

MAC BARRETT: The governor talked about Mario being on the phone with my dad and his memories of overhearing those conversations and the swearwords involved.

ANDREW CUOMO: As a public official who was subjected to Wayne's scrutiny many times, I can attest that his intellect, tenacity, and knowledge were second to none. He did his job without malice and with an absolute dedication to the facts. Wayne was a truth finder and a truth teller regardless

---

* Our Lady of the Presentation Roman Catholic Church on St. Mark's Avenue.

of whether it was convenient, popular, or easy. Wayne was never afraid to speak truth to power, and those who listened were the better for it.

TOM ROBBINS: Roger Stone, he's one of the guys who really invented Trump as a political figure. He was the *only* person that spoke of Wayne Barrett with vitriol. It was because Wayne actually understood what kind of scams that Trump was up to and could never put up with it.

ROGER STONE (VIA TWITTER): Wayne Barrett was a piece of human excrement posing as a human being. Rot in hell, you prick.

MAC BARRETT: Schumer tweeted something about how if there's anything wrong with heaven, we'll find out about it.

CHARLES SCHUMER: He was a great investigator. He helped uncover in my race against Senator D'Amato that he had missed a whole lot of votes, which helped me win. He had complete integrity. He never gave up. In this day and age, we need more Wayne Barretts, and it's hard to accept he's gone.

WILLIAM BASTONE: Wayne was there first. The longest. He was in such a sweet spot in terms of these monsters that have almost destroyed the country. Wayne would have been the go-to guy about all of this. But it was not to be.

WAYNE BARRETT: My greatest journalistic prize was when D'Amato called me a "viper" in his memoir. I want it on my tombstone.

CHAPTER 88
"THE *VOICE* CAN BRING TO BEAR A HISTORY"

MICHAEL CARUSO: I actually had a meeting with Peter Barbey. I talked to him for one cup of coffee about going back to the *Voice* at one point. I said, "Here's what you need to do." I put out a pretty radical plan. I said, "Look, Manhattan is dead as far as the *Voice* goes. It's covered well by the *Times* and *New York* magazine. You got to move the offices to Brooklyn. And you've got to hire a whole crew of young reporters, and you got to start covering Brooklyn and some of the other boroughs, but especially Brooklyn, and make that the new cool base of the *Voice*." The way I put it was, "You got to make it the *Village Vice*." *Vice* had really captured something interesting, and then they became too big for their britches.

Greg Tate is fantastic. Nat Hentoff is great. Michael Feingold. And it's no problem having them be part of the mix, but you want to find the new version of those people. The *Voice* should have been all over AOC if the *Voice* was around in any real sense.* And not only that, but who else works with AOC? Who's coming up in her office who's gonna run for something next year?

MICHAEL MUSTO: What was the *Voice* an alternative to at that point? There already were a million cable channels. There were streaming channels. There was liberal media. There were drag queen TV shows. The mainstream has subsumed the underground. It's everywhere. You don't have to wait till Wednesday and pick some paper out of a box to read about the gay nightlife. It's all over the social networks. You go on Facebook, there's a million queers

---

* AOC: US Representative Alexandria Ocasio-Cortez, from New York.

you can talk to about all kinds of things that you had to leave the house to do in the old days.

JOE LEVY: What could the *Voice* do? It's New York City, for fuck's sake. Well, the fucking subway system is crumbling. The fucking governor is stealing money from the city. The mayor is selling the fucking city to a billionaire from Seattle, the richest man on the *fucking* planet is getting a billion-dollar tax break to devour Queens and Manhattan!

What could the *Village Voice* do? Gee, I don't know. Be fucking Jane Jacobs for 2018? Because nobody's doing that. Nobody! And it's absolutely fucking insane to not have the paper do that local coverage at this particular time and place.

You look at the growing pains of every digital publication, digital brand, that's supposed to have supplanted any print publication in prominence or importance. They're scaling back. They're unionizing. They're shutting down their shops *because* they're unionizing.

So, what could the *Voice* do? Be a shining example for these people? Including the troubles of the *Voice* being a shining example, because all the shit comes home to roost. The crazy robber-baron world in which we live, in which no one, not *Vice* or BuzzFeed, no one except Google and Facebook and Amazon, will make any money. We're in some fucking crazy repeat Gilded Age.

So, what can the *Voice* do? Bring to bear a history. There's very little doubt in my mind that the *Village Voice* could do good and important work on a local level. Not just in city politics, but in the arts, and particularly in the world of identity politics, which was something that the *Voice* specialized in, as well as in what is coming to be an important issue, which is a growing awareness of the persecution and rights of sex workers.

So, without the *Voice*, there is one *less* advocate for the rights of sex workers, or the rights of immigrants. One *less* outlet hearing those voices. One *less* place to be noticed as an aspiring playwright, musician, choreographer. I don't know who did theater coverage better than the *Voice* did.

The *Voice* is a place that took things seriously—small things, developing things, emerging things—that other places didn't. That's what it always did.

AFTERWORD

The *Village Voice* still exists. You probably wouldn't know it unless you are a media fanatic based in New York, but it does. The nation's first alternative newspaper comes out semi-regularly in print, instead of weekly, and lives mostly online. Entrepreneur Brian Calle bought it in 2020, two years after it had gone out of print, after billionaire Peter Barbey had shut it down.

I first came to the paper as an intern in 1997. I was a student at the University of Washington in Seattle and working at the university newspaper, *The Daily*, which I later learned was a training ground for future *Voice* contributors, like acclaimed NPR music critic Ann Powers and future Pulitzer-winning photographer Samantha Appleton. Appleton had gotten an internship at the *Voice*, which planted the idea in my head, so I submitted a resume. Frank Ruscitti, the longtime *Voice* intern coordinator, plucked it out of the pile and paired me with Frank Owen, a nightlife reporter who had proven the case of the Club Kid murder of Angel Melendez. As I was a feature writer who focused on nightlife, it was a perfect match.

By day I walked to the *Voice* and worked on stories with Frank; by night I went clubbing, saw the greatest drag performers on the planet (Mistress Formika, Jackie Beat, Justin Bond, and the World Famous *BOB*), and went dancing to techno and drum 'n' bass.

Frank and I worked on a story about female DJs together. Frank was from England and was a clubber like me. In the grand tradition of the *Voice*, we covered the world we were part of.

I went back to Seattle, but after a few years I came back to the *Voice* via the fact-checking department. Soon I had a column, Club Crawl. I covered every corner of the New York underground, including the decades-old, outdated, racist Cabaret Law, which was used to shut down small bars and lounges that had dancing without a license.

In 2000, I was given the opportunity to write a longer, more in-depth column, called Fly Life, which also covered the nightlife scene. I wrote about neofeminist burlesque and the underbelly of clubland. I won an award for a feature about sobriety in nightlife—but my time was coming to an end. I was ultimately laid off for "matters of taste" by the New Times regime, their handy, one-size-fits-all method of being able to fire many of their union staffers based on the rule that Maida Rosenstein had warned the union about.

After the twin, untimely deaths of Nat Hentoff and Wayne Barrett in early 2017, former *Voice* writer Michael Tomasky had the idea to hold a reunion; he didn't know he would also be hosting a funeral for the print edition, which was killed that week. Hundreds of *Voice* employees from all departments gathered for several hours at a space near the *Voice*'s Cooper Square offices, where the names of those who died were read from the stage. The last living founder, Ed Fancher, was still with us, was then ninety-five years old, made a brief speech, and Jonas Mekas, the *Voice*'s first film critic, then ninety-four years old, was there too. It was a momentous occasion and far too short. It was then that I thought, "We must capture these voices before they are gone forever," and embarked on this book.

The next year, the *Voice* closed for good. Or so we thought. Calle's resurrection is still very *Village Voice*-y, and like other once-grand brands—*Spin*, *Vibe*, *Rolling Stone*—if you don't look at it too closely, it somewhat resembles its old self, the one that had the city in its grip. In one issue, there was a great-looking cover, an art review of Nan Goldin, and even a column by Michael Musto, still dishing the goods as if he'd never left.

But it's missing the revolutionary feeling that everything is being done for the first time, or that it's the only place where one can write in first person, take sides, be experimental. The *Voice* is also missing its mirror, New York, in its role as the center of the political and cultural universe. The internet has dispersed the culture. The *Voice*—its voice, its content—is nowhere and everywhere.

As Dan Wolf, the founding editor in chief, wrote in the *Voice*'s first anthology, "We concluded that there is a 'secret' group in America that is somehow vaguely uneasy about life in Peoria. They found us. We have found some of them."

ACKNOWLEDGMENTS

A wise person once said, "If writing a book were easy, everyone would do it." And it's true—I have been able to complete this book only because of the generosity of my friends around the world.

The day before I was due to sign the contract for this book, my boyfriend, Skyler Atkinson, died in a motorcycle accident. I should have been in a celebratory mood; instead, I was thrown into the depths of shock and grief. It is only due to the patience of the publisher and my editor, the generosity of acquaintances and strangers, and the support of my closest friends that I was able to begin the book. It is also because of them that I was able to finish it.

Many thanks to the hundreds of people who supported a GoFundMe and my Patreon, which helped me through the first year; as a freelance writer, every dollar was helpful and appreciated. And all my gratitude to Bo Gilliland and Aaron Mindel, who kept me sane and safe by offering financial assistance in those first weeks.

I am forever indebted to Joe Conason, who has served as my henchman and gamely wrote endless letters of recommendation for grants and residencies; to Nelson George for his astute advice and encouragement; to Lucian Truscott and Tracey and Ruby for putting me up in Montauk and who took me to interview Jules Feiffer on Shelter Island; to Adrienne Day and Prateek Sarkar and Carla Spartos, who offered their homes for weeks and months at a time while I came to research and interview in New York City; to Joe Levy and Susanne Rehnstrom, who let me watch their cats, Bo and Kit, in their East Village apartment; to Jason Sellards, who opened his NOLA home to me while I began to write; to Jack Hazard and Caroline Bozier and Ellen and Alison for showing me the city; to Whitney Pastorek, who let a perfect stranger stay with her in Nashville; to Ethan Schoonover and Bea, who hosted me at the world's most exclusive residency in Concrete, Washington, for a week where I worked out the nuts and bolts of Jill Johnston's chapter; to Andy Brooks for his home and comfort in London; to Alana Petraske for her kindness; to Georgette Mojer-Petraske for taking me in in the south of France to heal; to Christina Wheeler, for always being there; to Lois Pierris for our trip to Mexico, where I met my Chico kitty. Much love to the Atkinson family—Luckie, AnnMarie, Emily, Travis, and Rienne—and to Skyler's friends Tom and Caitlin, who opened their arms to me.

Thanks to my Jersey Italian families, the DelSordos—Irma, Denise, Uncle Dennis, Jeanie, Cousin Lisa, et al.—and the Romanos and Linfante. Many thanks to Aunt Patti for the TikToks, cat videos, and long calls of no-BS advice (P.S., it's *SAUCE*, not gravy). And thanks to Phil Elberg for the support.

Residencies at MacDowell, Millay, and UCross enabled me to write large sections of the book, unblocking the hardest puzzles of the manuscript. Love to my Millay posse (Bobby, Spencer, Mokha, Jo, Rose, Shayan), my Ucross peeps (Darrel, Nathalie, Kelli, Jennifer, Michelle, Sharon, Ricardo, Abbey, and Tracey Kikut), my MacDowell fellows (Isabel, Ndinda, Greg, Zack, Sojourner, Pamela, Mairead, Arvin, Samhita, Furen, Andrea, Bailey, Emma, Kelly, Jeanne, Mary Beth, Sara, Simón, JJJJJerome), and all the other great artists and writers I met at these sacred places. I thank you for sharing your processes and your art and your support. And many thanks to Kit, the Chico cat whisperer, who made it possible for me to attend these residencies for long stretches of time.

Grants from the Whiting Foundation, Artist Trust, 4Culture, MacDowell, and the City of Seattle enabled me to pay for transcription and research assistance. I'm grateful to the University of Washington's School of Communications' Christine Harold for connecting me with a student, Abigail Taylor, who worked as an intern.

Over the years, I used a variety of transcription services that still needed a lot of work. Many thanks to the skills of Mary Phillips-Sandy, who donated so much of her time, and others who took up a transcript or two to help out. And thanks to Matt Haber, who gave me work and championed the project. Much gratitude to Jonathan Sposato and Bruce Barcott for their support.

Thanks to Gillian McCain and Lizzy Goodman, who generously shared their oral history processes with me; to Porochista Khakpour, who helped this newbie navigate the early first-book waters; and to Caryn Ganz, who talked me down off several ledges.

And to my gang of gals across the country: Sally, Sara, Mari, Baby Zap, Ang, Carey, Susan Char, Morgan, Jeanine, Susan K, McGrath, Kristal Monkey, Jeanne Fury, Melissa, Leahbutt, Sia, Spartois, A-day, Toof, Lange, Squishy, Carly, and Pepperpot. As they say on *The Golden Girls*: "Thank you for being a friend—you're a pal and a confidante." May we all be able to hang out on a lanai together in our old age.

Thanks to the boys: Pollywog, Matt Corwine, Bo, Tyler, and Adam. To Dan Savage for his early advice, and to Erica Barnett for our media bitch sessions.

I am in awe of my illustrious agent, Betsy Lerner, and how her merciless scythe helped get this book down to a publishable length. And I'm grateful to my editor, Colleen Lawrie, for her patience (so, so much patience!) and keen edits, and to PublicAffairs for believing in the importance of a book about the *Village Voice*.

I am forever in debt to my *Village Voice* family who helped out during the editing process: Jessica Bellucci-Colucci for being an early reader; Camille Dodero for her pointed fact-checking and transcription work; Lenora Todaro for her editing help; and R.C. Baker for his ample assistance with archives and research. Many thanks to *Voice* photographers Sylvia Plachy, James Hamilton, Allen Reuben, Meg Handler, the McDarrah estate, Catherine D. Smith, and Catherine McGann for granting permission to use their photos in the book. And thanks to Abby Nolan for the feminist photo.

And I'm especially grateful to Michaelangelo Matos for his shared enthusiasm, blunt advice, and crisp editing, who told me, repeatedly, "YOU CAN DO IT," when I truly believed it was impossible. This is *all your fault*!

If I have forgotten anyone, I apologize. Along with Richard Goldstein, I have the absolute *worst* memory.

I am forever in debt to the hundreds of people in this book who told me their stories, including Richard Goldstein, David Schneiderman, Robert Christgau, Lucian Truscott, and Susan Brownmiller, and the many others who gave hours of their time in early stages of the reporting and helped set me on the right path.

And many thanks to Greg Tate, who died before he could read the book that he encouraged me to undertake. Ever a generous soul, he gave several suggestions for the title, including the one we landed on: *The Freaks Came Out to Write*, a perfect Tate-ism, a play on words from the Whodini song "The Freaks Came Out at Night," and a nod to the alt part of the culture at the *Voice*. The world is poorer without Greg in it.

And, finally, I am eternally grateful for Ed Fancher—for his time, for his sense of adventure, and for founding the greatest newspaper that ever existed.

BIBLIOGRAPHY

Introduction

Warhol, Andy, and Pat Hackett. *POPism: The Warhol Sixties*. San Diego, CA: Harcourt, 2006.

Wolf, Daniel, and Edwin Fancher. *The Village Voice Reader: A Mixed Bag from the Greenwich Village Newspaper*. New York: Doubleday, 1962.

Chapter 1: "We wanted a certain kind of newspaper"

Lennon, J. Michael. "An Excerpt from Mailer's Last Interview: The *Village Voice*." Project Mailer. *Mailer Review* 8 (September 2014). https://projectmailer.net/pm/The _Mailer_Review/Volume_8,_2014/An_Excerpt_from_Mailer%E2%80%99s_Last _Interview:_The_Village_Voice.

Persoff, Ethan, John Wilcock, and Scott Marshall. "John Wilcock, New York Years, 1954–1971." Ethan Persoff and Scott Marshall, 2021. www.ep.tc/john-wilcock/.

Tallmer, Jerry. "Birth of a Voice, Chapter 4: The Best Job in the City." *AM New York*, February 27, 2014. www.amny.com/news/birth-of-a-voice-chapter-4-the-best-job-in -the-city/.

"Village Voice Co-Founder Reflects on His Life in Publishing and His Years at the New School." *New School News*, March 21, 2019. https://blogs.newschool.edu /news/2019/03/village-voice-co-founder-reflects-on-his-life-in-publishing-and-his -years-at-the-new-school/.

Wilcock, John. *Manhattan Memories*. Lulu.com, 2010.

Wolf, Daniel. Interview by Roma Connable, 1993. Oral History Archives at Columbia University, New York. https://doi.org/10.7916/d8-nstb-aw98.

Chapter 2: "We were amazed with how many writers walked into the *Voice*"

Hentoff, Nat. *Speaking Freely: A Memoir*. New York: Knopf, 1997.

Johnston, Jill. "Biography." JillJohnston.com, accessed May 1, 2023. https://jill johnston.com.

———. *Marmalade Me*. New York: E. P. Dutton, 1971.

Lewis, David L. *The Pleasures of Being Out of Step: Nat Hentoff's Life in Journalism, Jazz and the First Amendment*. New York: CUNY Journalism Press, 2013.

Nichols, Mary Perot. Interview by Roma Connable, December 14, 1993. Oral History Archives at Columbia University, New York. https://doi.org/10.7916/d8-60fc-8c39.

Tallmer, Jerry. "Birth of a Voice, Chapter 2: Lunch and the 4 Voices." *AM New York*, February 13, 2014. www.amny.com/news/birth-of-a-voice-chapter-2-lunch-and-the -4-voices/.

Chapter 3: Quickly: A Column for Slow Readers

Hooker, Zachary. "John Wilcock: Interview 101." *Bidoun* no. 18 (June 2009). www
.bidoun.org/articles/john-wilcock.

Lennon. "An Excerpt from Mailer's Last Interview."

Mailer, Norman. *Advertisements for Myself.* London: Penguin Books, 2018.

Persoff, Wilcock, and Marshall. "John Wilcock, New York Years, 1954–1971."

Tallmer. "Birth of a Voice, Chapter 4."

———. "Birth of a Voice: John Wilcock, Writer, Mailman." *AM New York*, February
2015. www.amny.com/news/birth-of-a-voice-john-wilcock-writer-mailman/.

Wilcock. *Manhattan Memories.*

Wolf, Daniel. Interview by Roma Connable.

Chapter 5: "The *Voice* was her weapon"

Koch, Edward I. Interview by Ed Edwin, 1976. Oral History Archives at Columbia
University, New York. www.columbia.edu/cu/lweb/digital/collections/nny/koche
/introduction.html.

Nichols, Mary Perot. Interview by Roma Connable.

Paletta, Anthony. "Story of Cities #32: Jane Jacobs v Robert Moses, Battle of New York's
Urban Titans." *The Guardian*, April 28, 2016. www.theguardian.com/cities/2016
/apr/28/story-cities-32-new-york-jane-jacobs-robert-moses.

Chapter 6: "Just the fact that it was the '60s helped the *Voice*"

Hooker. "John Wilcock: Interview 101."

Newfield, Jack. *Somebody's Gotta Tell It.* New York: St. Martin's Press, 2002.

Chapter 7: "Jack Newfield really wrote about the things that he believed in"

Gross, Terry. "Jack Newfield, Looking for the Man in the RFK Myth." Fresh Air Ar-
chive: Interviews with Terry Gross. NPR, 1997. https://freshairarchive.org/segments
/jack-newfield-looking-man-rfk-myth.

Newfield. *Somebody's Gotta Tell It.*

Chapter 8: "What he was doing was very important for cinema and for the arts"

Warhol and Hackett. *POPism.*

Chapter 9: "Is this obscene?"

Hentoff, Nat. "The Crucifixion of a True Believer." Gadfly Online, January 12, 2012. http://
gadflyonline.com/home/index.php/lenny-bruce-the-crucifixion-of-a-true-believer/.

———. *Speaking Freely.*

Lewis. *The Pleasures of Being Out of Step.*

Chapter 10: "I call him the first rock critic"

Christgau, Robert. *Going into the City: Portrait of a Critic as a Young Man.* New York:
Dey St., 2015.

lostfootagefilms. "Robert Christgau: Rock n' Roll Animal (1999) Part 1 of 4." Video,
YouTube, posted 2011. www.youtube.com/watch?v=OTCZq_n- 5qA.

Rath, Arun. "Robert Christgau Reviews His Own Life." NPR, March 1, 2015. www
    .npr.org/2015/03/01/388695420/robert-christgau-reviews-his-own-life.

Chapter 12: "I was shocked by what I saw there"

Newfield. *Somebody's Gotta Tell It.*

Chapter 13: "I sure hope those people get their rights"

Davis, Kate, and David Heilbroner. "Stonewall Uprising." *American Experience.* PBS, April
    26, 2011. www.pbs.org/wgbh/americanexperience/films/stonewall/#cast_and_crew.

Chapter 14: Running Scared

Stout, David. "Mary Perot Nichols, 69, Who Led WNYC, Dies." *New York Times*, May
    22, 1996. www.nytimes.com/1996/05/22/nyregion/mary-perot-nichols-69-who-led
    -wnyc-dies.html.

Chapter 15: "Carter buying the paper didn't seem like a big deal"

Newfield. *Somebody's Gotta Tell It.*
Wilcock. *Manhattan Memories.*

Chapter 16: "Holy Mother Ireland. It's the women's liberation movement"

Gross, Terry. "Ellen Willis, Feminist and Writer." NPR, November 10, 2006. www.npr
    .org/templates/story/story.php?storyId=6467648.
Wolcott, James. *Lucking Out: My Life Getting Down and Semi-Dirty in Seventies New
    York.* New York: Doubleday, 2011.

Chapter 17: "She was a woman talking from inside her mind"

2929artifacts. "Vito Russo's Our Time: Episode 6—Writers." Interview by Marcia
    Pally. Video, YouTube, 1983. Posted August 17, 2010. www.youtube.com/watch?v
    =bbb9jfunymw&t=577s.
Dinsmore, Christine. "Radical Reflections." *New York Blade*, April 24, 1998. www
    .christinedinsmore.com/documents/ny_blade_johnston_profile.pdf.
"Episode 6: Jill Johnston." Produced by Eric Marcus. *Making Gay History.* Studs
    Terkel Radio Archive (podcast). December 10, 2020. https://radiopublic.com
    /making-gay-history-lgbtq-oral-hi-GqRA95/s1!3d65c.
Friedan, Betty. *Life So Far.* New York: Simon and Schuster, 2006.
Johnston, Jill. "Jill Johnston on Palin: Little More Than a Smokescreen." *HuffPost*, No-
    vember 4, 2008. www.huffpost.com/entry/jill-johnston-on-palin-li_b_131930.
———. "Judson & Johnston, Together Again, I: Dance Quote Unquote—the
    Spirit of the '60s." *The Dance Insider & Paris Arts Voyager* (blog), November 19,
    2018. http://danceinsiderblog.wordpress.com/2018/11/19/judson-johnston-together
    -again-dance-quote-unquote-the-spirit-of-the-sixties/.
———. *Lesbian Nation.* New York: Simon and Schuster, 1973.
———. *Marmalade Me.*
———. "Was Lesbian Separatism Inevitable." *Gay & Lesbian Review*, January 2006.
    https://glreview.org/article/article-121/.
Mailer, Norman. *The Prisoner of Sex.* London: Weidenfeld and Nicolson, 1971.

Chapter 18: "Clay Felker was a celebrity fucker"

Frankfort, Ellen. *The Voice*. New York: William Morrow, 1976.
Newfield. *Somebody's Gotta Tell It*.

Chapter 19: "I was a little bit intimidated by Karen Durbin"

Frankfort. *The Voice*.
Lewis. *The Pleasures of Being Out of Step*.
Newfield. *Somebody's Gotta Tell It*.
Willis, Ellen. "Lust Horizons." *Village Voice*. October 18, 2005. https://www.village voice.com/lust-horizons/.

Chapter 20: "We're against gentrification, and we're for fist-fucking"

Frankfort. *The Voice*.
Monaco, James. *Media Culture: Television, Radio, Records, Books, Magazines, Newspapers, Movies*. New York: Dell Publishing Company, 1978.
Newfield. *Somebody's Gotta Tell It*.
Nichols, Mary Perot. Interview by Roma Connable.

Chapter 21: "The music section was suddenly in flower"

DeRogatis, Jim. "Lester Bangs: Last Interview." *Perfect Sound Forever*, September 1999. www.furious.com/perfect/lesterbangs.html.
Marcus, Greil. "'A Humanist, Not a Crazy' (Interview Re: Lester Bangs, 05/18)." May 18, 2018. https://greilmarcus.net/2018/05/18/a-humanist-not-a-crazy-interview-re-lester-bangs-05–18/.

Chapter 22: "A sitting state supreme court justice read the decision and cried"

Newfield. *Somebody's Gotta Tell It*.

Chapter 23: "We started writing what they call the New Journalism"

Bernstein, Dennis. "An Interview with Laura Flanders on Alexander Cockburn." CounterPunch, July 31, 2012. www.counterpunch.org/2012/07/31/an-interview-with-laura-flanders-on-alexander-cockburn/.
Moore, Michael. "Michael Moore Remembers Jim Ridgeway." *Rumble with Michael Moore Podcast*, February 21, 2021. www.youtube.com/watch?v=bETs7-8IKcs.

Chapter 24: "The *Village Voice* is an apocalyptic publication"

CUNY TV. "Eldridge & Co.—Wayne Barrett." Video, YouTube, August 17, 2015. www.youtube.com/watch?v=pU6-Ndn85wY.
Frankfort. *The Voice*.
Monaco. *Media Culture*.
Newfield. *Somebody's Gotta Tell It*.

Chapter 26: "The feuds between Sarris and Kael are legendary"

Gross, Terry. "*Fresh Air* Remembers Film Critic Andrew Sarris." *Fresh Air*, NPR, June 21, 2012. www.npr.org/transcripts/155504428.

Powell, Michael. "A Survivor of Film Criticism's Heroic Age." *New York Times*, July 9, 2009. www.nytimes.com/2009/07/12/movies/12powe.html?pagewanted=all.

Chapter 27: "How do you deal with hostility?"

"Village Voice Names New Editor." *New York Times*, May 11, 1978. www.nytimes.com/1978/05/11/archives/village-voice-names-new-editor-staff-vows-a-strike-over-move.html.

Chapter 28: "We're very happy to give this to you, but please don't publicize this"

Hentoff, Nat. "When Rupert Murdoch Was My Boss." *Village Voice*. August 3, 2011.

Chapter 29: "You should check out this young guy Donald Trump"

Barrett, Wayne. *Trump: The Deals and the Downfall*. New York: HarperCollins, 1992.

González, Juan. "A Classic State Capitalist: How Donald Trump Profited from Public Subsidies and Political Favors." Truthout, June 30, 2016. https://truthout.org/video/a-classic-state-capitalist-how-donald-trump-profited-from-public-subsidies-and-political-favors/.

Shephard, Alex, and Theodore Ross. "There's No Check on Trump Except Reality: A Q&A with Wayne Barrett." *New Republic*, December 1, 2016. https://newrepublic.com/article/139094/theres-no-check-trump-except-reality-qa-wayne-barrett.

Trump, Donald, and Charles Leerhsen. *Trump: Surviving at the Top*. New York: Random House, 1990.

Chapter 30: "You're hiring all these Stalinist feminists"

Lewis. *The Pleasures of Being Out of Step*.

Chapter 31: "I'm the greatest pimp since Duke Ellington"

Boynton, Robert S. "Stanley Crouch: The Professor of Connection." *New Yorker*. October 29, 1995. https://www.newyorker.com/magazine/1995/11/06/the-professor-of-connection.

HistoryMakers. "Video Oral History Interview with Stanley Crouch, May 21, 2001, and March 3, 2002." The HistoryMakers African American Video Oral History Collection, Chicago.

Iverson, Ethan. "Interview with Stanley Crouch." DO THE M@TH, April 8, 2016. https://ethaniverson.com/interviews/interview-with-stanley-crouch/.

Swain, Susan, and C-SPAN. "In Depth with Stanley Crouch." C-SPAN, October 5, 2003. www.c-span.org/video/?178466-1/depth-stanley-crouch.

Chapter 32: "The Obies are the only awards with integrity"

"'Fuck the Curtain': An Oral History of Off-Broadway." *Village Voice*, May 20, 2019. www.villagevoice.com/2019/05/20/fuck-the-curtain-an-oral-history-of-off-broadway/.

"Ghosts of Obies Past." *Village Voice*, May 31, 1994. www.villagevoice.com/2019/05/17/ghosts-of-obies-past/.

Chapter 34: "One African American staffer in the editorial department—that's unacceptable"

Davis, Thulani. "On the Sacred Bard of the 1960s Chicago Jazz Scene." Literary Hub, December 11, 2019. https://lithub.com/on-the-sacred-bard-of-the-1960s-chicago -jazz-scene/.

O'Neill, Luke. "Generations of *Village Voice* Writers Reflect on the Paper Leaving the Honor Boxes." *Esquire*, August 23, 2017. www.esquire.com/news-politics/a57165 /village-voice-oral-history/.

Chapter 35: "They called it graffiti"

Jabbour, Alan, James N. Hardin, and American Folklife Center. *Folklife Annual 1986: A Publication of the American Folklife Center at the Library of Congress*. Washington, DC: Library of Congress, 1987.

Chapter 39: "They demanded that they take our Pulitzer away"

Montgomery, Paul L. "'Deception Denied by Reporter for *Voice*.'" *New York Times*, May 11, 1981. https://www.nytimes.com/1981/05/11/nyregion/deception-denied -by-reporter-for-voice.html.

Chapter 41: "Certain deaths hit really hard"

Coupe, Stuart. "Lester Bangs Interview." Creep Show, February 10, 2003. Archived at Wayback Machine. https://web.archive.org/web/20030210051527/http://www .thecreepshow.net/mag/lester.htm.

DeRogatis. "Lester Bangs: Last Interview."

Marcus. "'A Humanist, Not a Crazy.'"

Chapter 42: "We had a bomb scare once a month"

Goodman, Amy. "Alexander Cockburn Speaks Out on Rupert Murdoch, the Israel-Palestine Conflict, and the Politics of Anti-Semitism." Democracy Now!, November 25, 2003. www.democracynow.org/2003/11/25/alexander_cockburn_speaks _out_on_rupert.

Chapter 43: "You must be Wayne Barrett"

Rutenberg, Jim. "A Muckraker Who Was Eulogized Even by His Targets." *New York Times*, January 30, 2017.

Chapter 44: "I had a shoot-out with Nat Hentoff on the abortion issue"

Hentoff. *Speaking Freely*.

Lamb, Brian. "Speaking Freely, a *Booknotes* Interview with Nat Hentoff." *Booknotes*, C-SPAN, September 16, 1997. www.c-span.org/video/?91396-1/speaking-freely.

Lewis. *The Pleasures of Being Out of Step*.

Chapter 46: "I'm going to sell the paper to someone worse than me"

Bernstein. "An Interview with Laura Flanders on Alexander Cockburn."

Ruttenberg, Jay. "This Is Not a Fashion Critic: An Interview with Guy Trebay." Fashion Projects, January 16, 2013. https://www.fashionprojects.org/blog/4553.

Chapter 49: "L'affaire Karen Finley!"

Finley, Karen. *A Different Kind of Intimacy: The Collected Writings of Karen Finley*. New York: Thunder's Mouth Press, 2000.

Chapter 51: "Hiphop Nation"

Barrow, Jerry L. "The Secret History of Public Enemy's 'Yo! Bum Rush the Show.'" OkayPlayer.com, 2016. https://www.okayplayer.com/originals/secret-history-public -enemy-yo-bum-rush-the-show.html.

Christgau, Robert, and Greg Tate. "Chuck D All Over the Map: An Interview by Robert Christgau and Greg Tate." *Village Voice*. October 22, 1991.

Chapter 52: "Stanley was just red-eyed and ready to go"

Boynton, Robert S. "Stanley Crouch: The Professor of Connection." *New Yorker*, October 30, 1995. www.newyorker.com/magazine/1995/11/06/the-professor-of -connection.

HistoryMakers. "Video Oral History Interview with Stanley Crouch."

Chapter 53: "Do you wanna know about a really big fight that happened in the theater section?"

Als, Hilton. "Making Theater: An Interview with Elizabeth LeCompte." *Paris Review*, March 30, 2017. www.theparisreview.org/blog/2017/03/30/making-theater -an-interview-with-elizabeth-lecompte/.

Savran, David. *The Wooster Group, 1975–1985: Breaking the Rules*. Ann Arbor, MI: UMI Research Press, 1986.

Zinoman, Jason. "It Was Familial, Incestuous, Dysfunctional: The Wooster Group: An Oral History." *Time Out New York*, January 24, 2005.

Chapter 54: "The *Voice Literary Supplement* crossed pop culture and high culture"

Press, Joy. "A Short Oral History of the *VLS*." *Village Voice*, October 1, 2001.

Chapter 55: "We were filled with grief"

Lewis. *The Pleasures of Being Out of Step*.

Chapter 56: "Christgau was hated by bands because he was so honest"

Christgau, Robert. *Christgau's Record Guide: The '80s*. New York: Da Capo Press, 1994.
———. *Christgau's Record Guide: Rock Albums of the Seventies*. New Haven, CT: Ticknor and Fields, 1981.
———. "Consumer Guide." *Village Voice*, January 29, 1979.
lostfootagefilms. "Robert Christgau: Rock n' Roll Animal (1999) Part 1 of 4."

Chapter 61: *Do the Right Thing*

Glicksman, Marlaine. "Interview: Spike Lee." *Film Comment*, July 1989. www.filmcom ment.com/article/interview-spike-lee/.

Chapter 64: "The art world is so peculiar"

Barron, Michael. "Interview with Gary Indiana." *White Review*, April 2016. www
.thewhitereview.org/feature/interview-with-gary-indiana/.

Haslett, Tobi. "The Art of Fiction No. 250." *Paris Review*, 2021. www.theparisreview
.org/interviews/7852/the-art-of-fiction-no-250-gary-indiana.

Pemberton, Nathan Taylor. "Gary Indiana Coughs up Some 'Hairballs of Insight'
from His Vile Days as Art Critic." *Interview Magazine*, March 20, 2019. https://
www.interviewmagazine.com/culture/gary-indiana-tells-painter-sam-mckinniss
-about-his-vile-days.

Vera List Center. "Roberta Smith, Criticism: A Life Sentence, Part One, November 5th,
2009." Video, Vimeo, February 22, 2010. https://vimeo.com/9651694.

Chapter 65: "Independent films were coming into their own during the '90s"

Duritz, Clinton, and Kevin Smith. "A Conversation with Writer and Director Kevin
Smith." *Film History* 8, no. 2 (1996): 237–248. www.jstor.org/stable/3815337.

Longworth, Karina. "Kevin Smith: 'I Am So, Like, Sick of Movies and Shit': On
the Road with the Cult Filmmaker Turned Podcaster Turned DIY Warrior." *LA
Weekly*, April 14, 2011. Archived at Wayback Machine. https://web.archive.org
/web/20110414112547/https://www.laweekly.com/content/printVersion/1240966/.

Tenreyro, Tatiana. "The Improbable True Story of How 'Clerks' Was Made." Vice,
October 21, 2019. www.vice.com/en/article/zmj8g9/an-oral-history-of-clerks
-25th-anniversary.

Chapter 67: "Wayne was the first guy who wrote a biography of Donald Trump and Rudy Giuliani"

Campbell, Jon. "How a Young Donald Trump Forced His Way from Avenue Z to
Manhattan." *Village Voice*, https://www.villagevoice.com/how-a-young-donald
-trump-forced-his-way-from-avenue-z-to-manhattan/.

CUNY TV. "Eldridge & Co.—Wayne Barrett."

Trump and Leerhsen. *Trump: Surviving at the Top.*

Chapter 68: "I was very ignorant about trans people"

Dry, Jude. "As 'Boys Don't Cry' Joins National Film Registry, Kimberly Peirce Ad-
dresses Its Complicated History." IndieWire, December 12, 2019. www.indiewire
.com/2019/12/kimberly-peirce-interview-boys-dont-cry-transgender-1202196536/.

Minkowitz, Donna. "How I Broke, and Botched, the Brandon Teena Story." *Village
Voice*, June 20, 2018. www.villagevoice.com/2018/06/20/how-i-broke-and-botched
-the-brandon-teena-story/.

Pedram, Arno, and Isoke Samuel. "Is It Too Late Now to Say Sorry?" *The Bias* (transcript), December 2020. http://podcasts.nycitynewsservice.com/hindsight-transcript/.

Tysver, Robynn. "Cross-Dresser Killed Two Weeks After Town Learned Her True
Identity." AP News, January 1, 1994. https://apnews.com/article/6d811e00773d
86e37fe99d58b7b5b4ad.

Chapter 70: "Things got a little weird when Karen became editor in chief"

Friedman, Roger D., and Pat Wechsler. "Intelligencer," *New York* magazine, September 19, 1994. https://books.google.com/books?id=KuMCAAAAMBAJ&pg=PA13&dq=karen+durbin&hl=en&sa=X&ved=2ahUKEwjBn5nU5f7vAhUHrJ4KHVS0BZ8Q6AEwBXoECAcQAg#v=onepage&q=karen%20durbin&f=false.

Friend, Tad. "The Last of the Red-Hot Lefties," *New York* magazine, April 25, 1994. https://books.google.com/books?id=9cMCAAAAMBAJ&pg=PA48&lpg=PA48&dq=rick+hertzberg+karen+durbin&source=bl&ots=mMERXL8boC&sig=ACfU3U0aoUGFrQRMqcOLHdWNmeNM7Pjyow&hl=en&sa=X&ved=2ahUKEwiy36rF2_7vAhXXtp4KHbEyC1AQ6AEwDXoECBIQAw#v=onepage&q=rick%20hertzberg%20karen%20durbin&f=true

Glaberson, William. "AT WORK WITH: Karen Durbin; In the Out Crowd and Loving It," *New York Times*, December 7, 1994. https://www.nytimes.com/1994/12/07/garden/at-work-with-karen-durbin-in-the-out-crowd-and-loving-it.html

Chapter 71: "Hammer, Drano, a pillow"

Bollen, Christopher. "Michael Alig." *Interview Magazine*, March 24, 2010. www.interviewmagazine.com/culture/michael-alig.

Chapter 73: "Wicked Don Forst"

Bumiller, Elisabeth. "New Editor Changes the Cadence of the *Village Voice*." *New York Times*, February 13, 1997. www.nytimes.com/1997/02/13/nyregion/new-editor-changes-the-cadence-of-the-village-voice.html.

Sutherland, Scott. "Comforting the Afflicted, Afflicting the Comfortable." *Vermont Quarterly*, April 2000. https://www.uvm.edu/vtquarterly/VQSPRING00/village.html.

Chapter 75: "What's Craigslist?"

"Craigslist/On the Record: Craig Newmark," SFGate, August 15, 2004. www.sfgate.com/business/ontherecord/article/CRAIGSLIST-On-the-record-Craig-Newmark-2733312.php.

Chapter 78: "You are choosing the winners!"

Ingram, Mathew. "Craigslist Isn't Killing Newspapers." April 21, 2007. https://www.socialmediatoday.com/news/craigslist-isnt-killing-newspapers/500020/. From I Want Media, "Media Interviews. Craig Newmark: Craigslist Isn't a Media Menace." April 20, 2007. http://www.iwantmedia.com/people/people66.html.

Chapter 80: "Slut Boy"

Barron, James. "*Village Voice* Reduces Staff and Evidently Morale, Too." *New York Times*, August 9, 2004. www.nytimes.com/2004/08/09/nyregion/village-voice-reduces-staff-and-evidently-morale-too.html.

Chapter 81: "They had complete contempt for the paper"

Jacobson, Mark. "Can New Owner Michael Lacey Make the *Village Voice* Relevant Again?" *New York*, November 3, 2005. https://nymag.com/nymetro/news/media/features/14987/.

Chapter 84: "They love firing people"

Jacobson. "Can New Owner Michael Lacey Make the *Village Voice* Relevant Again?"

Chapter 85: "If the National Organization of Women calls, just fucking hang up on them"

Demko, Paul. "The Sex-Trafficking Case Testing the Limits of the First Amendment." *Politico*, July 29, 2018. www.politico.com/magazine/story/2018/07/29/first-amendment-limits-backpage-escort-ads–219034/.

ReasonTV. "The Rise and Fall of Backpage." Video, YouTube, June 26, 2019. www.youtube.com/watch?v=DPchvgMsjl8.

Chapter 87: "Wayne couldn't believe that Trump was winning"

Goodman, Amy. "How Donald Trump Threatened an Investigative Reporter, Attempting to Bribe Him with a Free Apartment." Democracy Now!, July 5, 2016. www.democracynow.org/2016/7/5/how_donald_trump_threatened_an_investigative.

Rutenberg. "A Muckraker Who Was Eulogized Even by His Targets."

INDEX

firing Victor Kovner, 260

negotiating union contracts with, 184

the sale of the *Voice*, 286–288

Schneiderman's interview, 242

staff criticism of, 284–285

threatening to sell the *Voice*, 285–286

unionization of the *Voice*, 178–180

music

Black journalists, 219–220

bringing in Black writers, 33, 221–223

the Consumer Guide, 349–354

expanding rock coverage, 130–132

Greg Tate's contributions, 221

jazz, 33, 54–55, 62, 198–200, 221–223

Lester Bangs, 139–140, 256–259

New Jack City story, 377

Patti Smith performances, 135–136

Pazz & Jop polls, 238–239, 238(fn)

putting culture on the cover, 159

rap, 220, 225, 230–233, 377

rock critics, 58–64, 126–127, 131–132

Tate's influence and writing style, 234–237

World Beat, 219

musicians, 133–135

Musto, Michael, 276(fig.), 426

ACT UP, 347

AIDS crisis, 337–338

Arthur Bell's death, 275–276

Barbey buying the *Voice*, 521

Blum's editorship, 502

changes in the club scene, 437

Club Kids murder story, 437–443

declining relevance of the *Voice*, 527–528

digital media, 485, 487

Don Forst's homophobic attitude, 490

Gawker, 484

gay porn reviews, 486

making the *Voice* free, 429–430

New Times layoffs, 510–511, 519–520

Nader, Ralph, 146–147

Naked (film), 404

Nathan Award (George Jean Nathan Award for Dramatic Criticism), 453

Nation of Millions (Public Enemy), 316–319

National Press Foundation award, 487

NEA Four, 339, 339(fn), 399, 433

Neel, Alice, 50

New Jack City (film), 376–378, 405

New Journalism, 31–32, 148

New Times news chain, 428, 428(fn), 464–465, 493, 496, 504, 504(fn), 505, 508–516, 519–520, 530, 541

New York magazine, 114, 116, 153(fn), 180, 373, 494

New York Native newspaper, 340–341, 345

New York Post, 35, 191(fn), 226, 245, 261, 265, 284, 361, 387–388, 429–430, 470

New York Press, 425–428, 430–431, 449, 515

New York Radical Feminists, 99

New York Radical Women group, 98

New York Times, 4, 15, 87, 173–174, 186, 329, 338–341, 384, 395–396, 399, 453, 502, 515

New Yorker magazine, 127, 165(fn), 402, 427

Newfield, Jack, 2, 146, 292

Bobby Kennedy, 41–45

corruption among judges, 145

Dan Wolf's hirees, 35

hiring on at the *Voice*, 35

hiring "Stalinist feminists," 193–194

investigative journalism, 3

lead poisoning articles, 45

machismo attitude, 98

Mary Nichols's investigation of Scotto, 88–89

Murdoch firing Marianne Partridge, 174

New Journalism, 32

New York blackout of 1977, 162–163

Richard Goldstein's first articles, 58

Tricia Romano began her eight-year career at the *Village Voice* as an intern. As a contributing writer she wrote features and award-winning cover stories about culture and music. Her reported column, Fly Life, gave a glimpse into the underbelly of New York nightlife. She has been a staff writer at the *Seattle Times* and served as the editor in chief of the *Stranger*, Seattle's alternative newsweekly. A fellow at MacDowell, Ucross, and Millay artist residencies, her work has been published in the *New York Times*, *Rolling Stone*, the *Daily Beast*, *Men's Journal*, *Elle*, *Alta Journal*, and the *Los Angeles Times*, among others. She lives in Seattle, Washington. This is her first book.

PublicAffairs is a publishing house founded in 1997. It is a tribute to the standards, values, and flair of three persons who have served as mentors to countless reporters, writers, editors, and book people of all kinds, including me.

I. F. STONE, proprietor of *I. F. Stone's Weekly*, combined a commitment to the First Amendment with entrepreneurial zeal and reporting skill and became one of the great independent journalists in American history. At the age of eighty, Izzy published *The Trial of Socrates*, which was a national bestseller. He wrote the book after he taught himself ancient Greek.

BENJAMIN C. BRADLEE was for nearly thirty years the charismatic editorial leader of *The Washington Post*. It was Ben who gave the *Post* the range and courage to pursue such historic issues as Watergate. He supported his reporters with a tenacity that made them fearless and it is no accident that so many became authors of influential, best-selling books.

ROBERT L. BERNSTEIN, the chief executive of Random House for more than a quarter century, guided one of the nation's premier publishing houses. Bob was personally responsible for many books of political dissent and argument that challenged tyranny around the globe. He is also the founder and longtime chair of Human Rights Watch, one of the most respected human rights organizations in the world.

·   ·   ·

For fifty years, the banner of Public Affairs Press was carried by its owner Morris B. Schnapper, who published Gandhi, Nasser, Toynbee, Truman, and about 1,500 other authors. In 1983, Schnapper was described by *The Washington Post* as "a redoubtable gadfly." His legacy will endure in the books to come.

Peter Osnos, *Founder*